Learning with the Lights Off

Learning with the Lights Off

Educational Film in the United States

EDITED BY DEVIN ORGERON, MARSHA ORGERON, AND DAN STREIBLE

OXFORD
UNIVERSITY PRESS

OXFORD
UNIVERSITY PRESS

Oxford University Press, Inc., publishes works that further
Oxford University's objective of excellence
in research, scholarship, and education.

Oxford   New York
Auckland   Cape Town   Dar es Salaam   Hong Kong   Karachi
Kuala Lumpur   Madrid   Melbourne   Mexico City   Nairobi
New Delhi   Shanghai   Taipei   Toronto

With offices in
Argentina   Austria   Brazil   Chile   Czech Republic   France   Greece
Guatemala   Hungary   Italy   Japan Poland   Portugal   Singapore
South Korea   Switzerland   Thailand   Turkey   Ukraine   Vietnam

Copyright © 2012 by Oxford University Press, Inc.

Published by Oxford University Press, Inc.
198 Madison Avenue, New York, New York 10016

www.oup.com

Oxford is a registered trademark of Oxford University Press

Learning with the lights off : educational film in the United States / edited by Devin Orgeron, Marsha Orgeron,
and Dan Streible.
     p.   cm.
Includes bibliographical references and index.
ISBN 978-0-19-538384-3 (hardcover : alk. paper)—ISBN 978-0-19-538383-6 (pbk. : alk. paper)
1. Educational films—United States—History and criticism. 2. Motion pictures in education—United States.
I. Orgeron, Devin. II. Orgeron, Marsha. III. Streible, Dan. IV. Title.
LB1044.L43   2011
371.33'523—dc22   2011005141

1 3 5 7 9 8 6 4 2

Printed in the United States of America
on acid-free paper

We dedicate this book to Ro-Revus

TABLE OF CONTENTS

FOREWORD

At a Fourth of July picnic in 2006, I found myself sitting across the table from Oscar-winning cinematographer Haskell Wexler. He had been recently selected by the International Cinematographer's Guild as one of the ten most influential cameramen in history and had a star on Hollywood's Walk of Fame. He also directed one of my favorite feature films concerning the tumultuous 1968 Chicago political protests, *Medium Cool* (1969). Wexler was eighty years old, physically spry, and mentally sharp. He extended his hand and we introduced ourselves.

Although he didn't know it, we had one thing in common: the place where we both began our careers in film. So I asked him, "Do you remember working with Johnny Walker at Encyclopaedia Britannica Films in Wilmette?"

His eyes lit up. "How do you know about Johnny?"

"I worked at EBF from 1965 to 1980 and he told me you started there and worked with him."

"Johnny taught me how to thread a camera," Wexler said with tears glistening in his eyes. "Those were great days. My friends in features can't believe it when I tell them about the freedom we had making those 16mm movies. Sometimes I wonder if I dreamed it or was it really part of my life?"

It wasn't a dream but most physical traces are now gone. When I was in my twenties I started as a writer/director for Encyclopaedia Britannica Films (EBF), fifteen years after Wexler had moved on. While Wexler came to EBF after serving in the Merchant Marines during World War II, I was fresh from three and a half years in the U.S. Air Force during the Cold War.

Prior to the Air Force, Northwestern University's Jack Ellis introduced me to film, diverting me from my first love, radio broadcasting. After I graduated from Northwestern in 1960, Ellis encouraged me to study film in France and I was fortunate to win a Fulbright Scholarship for a year overseas. While in Paris I ran into Milan Herzog, head of film production at EBF. Herzog was shooting an ambitious series of 120 short classroom films—French lessons called *Je Parle Français*.

When I returned home from Paris, my local draft board welcomed me with an invitation to report for a physical. Rather than enter the Army, I enlisted in the Air Force's officer training program. The closest I got to making a film in the Air Force was testing aerial photography equipment in upstate New York. We flew low over dairy farms, annoying the cows as we snapped our photos. After completing my military obligation, I reconnected with Herzog who hired me to work for EBF in Wilmette, Illinois.

The timing was fortunate for me. The Soviets launched Sputnik in October 1957 and now had men and even a dog orbiting the earth. The country worried that we were falling behind the USSR and if we doubted it, all we had to do was look to the night sky. Money for educational films was part of the race to bring American students to an academic level above their Soviet counterparts. The Cold War had come to the classroom. Congress's Elementary and Secondary School Act of 1965, Title II, authorized millions for library resources and Title III allocated even more for audiovisual aids. Nothing spurred government spending like fear.

There had been educational films since movies were invented. The largest surge in production came after the Japanese bombed Pearl Harbor in 1941. We knew that training films could be used as part of our rapid mobilization for war. They worked then as effective supplementary tools for teachers, so why not bring them into the classrooms of the Cold War era? During the fifteen years I worked for EBF, government subsidies drove 16mm educational film production to record numbers. The classroom use of sound motion pictures represented the greatest advance in education in the twentieth century. Films covered the arts, social studies, sciences, and humanities. There were complete filmed courses in chemistry, physics, and foreign languages. Films were designed for the primary grades all the way through college.

But the films being made hardly resembled Hollywood movies. To begin with, the typical budget for films like my twenty-minute 16mm productions ran from $15,000 to $20,000. At the same time, an average Hollywood movie cost millions of dollars. In 1989, when I produced *Honey, I Shrunk the Kids* for Walt Disney Pictures, our production budget was $24 million, a thousand times the budget for my most ambitious educational film a decade earlier at EBF. Because of large feature film budgets, many production decisions at Disney were corporate issues. A day of extra shooting or a change in the cast needed Disney management's approval. The bosses back at Burbank, at what we called "the mouse house," viewed each day's filming and sent comments to us. If they felt we lacked a good take, they would order that we reshoot the scene.

At EBF, once a project was approved, I was pretty much on my own, so long as I didn't go over budget. My bosses at EBF didn't screen "dailies" as all

Hollywood studios do for feature films. They didn't see anything until I previewed the edited film at a management screening. Afterward, they sometimes made suggestions for minor changes, but it was too late to make major corrections. Most of their comments concerned words in the narration. So although lacking a big budget, the nontheatrical creative team had a lot of freedom that feature filmmakers envied. As Haskell Wexler said, it was hard to believe it wasn't just a dream. Sadly, the 16mm film industry suddenly died in the early 1980s. I moved on to feature films and got a job overseeing visual effects at George Lucas's Industrial Light and Magic.

Some of my early films for Encyclopaedia Britannica were photographed using a 16mm Bolex, a small spring-wound Swiss camera. For more serious work, we used battery-powered cameras. The German Arriflex-S model was preferred for scenes in which sound was not recorded. I shot several wildlife films using the dependable Arriflex. Then there was the French Éclair NPR, a quiet camera that, when not mounted on a tripod, fit comfortably on the shoulder. This was the choice of documentary crews, useful when sound was simultaneously recorded. The Éclair permitted filmmakers to follow unrehearsed events as the action unfolded. In 1973, I made a twenty-seven-minute film called *The Newspaper Story*. Four crews simultaneously filmed a day in the life of the *Los Angeles Times*. Working from a rough outline, we filmed and recorded the sounds and images of events as they occurred. Our crews chased after reporters, sat in during editorial meetings, followed a sports writer to a basketball game, and watched as workers set the big presses rolling. Without the Éclair I don't know how we could have done it. We didn't know it at the time but this film turned out to be the last comprehensive documentary of a big city newspaper before the ubiquitous use of computers, cell phones, and digital photography revolutionized the process. Reporters used typewriters and photographers shot photos on film that had to be chemically developed and printed on paper.

In 2009, producer Peter Jones wanted a few scenes from my 1973 film for his ambitious, two-hour PBS documentary, *Inventing LA: The Chandlers and Their Times*. Scenes from thirty-six years ago were clearly from an era gone by. Jones contacted EBF but the video they offered was of such poor quality he couldn't use it. Fortunately, I still had a good 16mm print of the film from which we made a clean digital transfer. Jones only used a few scenes from my documentary but was grateful to have them.

In Hollywood, during the 1960s, the most popular camera was the 35mm Mitchell. It was a wonderfully precise instrument but it took a crew of technicians to tend to it. Just lifting the camera from its case onto a heavy tripod was a job for two strong camera assistants. So it is not surprising that 16mm nontheatrical films were the first to be truly mobile. Partly because of the equipment used, theatrical and nontheatrical films became separate disciplines in the same lively art. Just as the impressionist painters of the mid- to late nineteenth century were able to take their newly invented paint tubes outside the studios and paint "en plein air," thus creating a new look for paintings, so did 16mm filmmakers have a freedom that was not available for Hollywood films with their massive 35mm equipment. Nontheatrical filmmakers were not better artists, nor did they make better films, but their 16mm "disadvantage" occasionally resulted in stunning work never seen in feature films.

Sadly, their work rarely got attention outside the darkened classroom or school assembly hall. Now, the essays collected for this book present a comprehensive guide to educational film, from the early visions of what the future held at the dawn of the twentieth century to a review of 16mm film collections that survive in the twenty-first.

I was fortunate to be part of the golden age of 16mm films. In fifteen years, I wrote and directed more than fifty films, then moved on to features just as the 16mm industry was crumbling behind me. In the early 1980s, classroom projectors and pull-down movie screens yielded to seventeen-inch TV monitors. Sixteen-millimeter film gave way to VHS videotape and cable connections. Entire 16mm film libraries were given away or tossed out. Maintenance of the Los Angeles Unified School District's large 16mm collection was defunded, leaving no librarians to protect it. Films were "borrowed" from the shelves never to return or were discarded before the library's doors were closed forever.

As videotape began replacing film in schools, many production companies, including EBF, made quick transfers of their 16mm film library to U-matic ¾-inch videocassettes. Although we now regard this as an archaic and abandoned video format, U-matic tapes became the masters for the VHS tapes they hoped to sell to schools. The quality was terrible; the end result looked nothing like the bright and clear 16mm image we were accustomed to seeing. One cinematographer I knew became physically ill when he saw what had become of the pictures he worked so hard to master on film. Some companies saved storage costs by discarding their 16mm originals once video transfers were made. Later, when these same companies wanted to upgrade to DVD, they had only inferior tape "masters" to work from.

To get decent digital quality one must go back to the film negative or print. Some rights holders and companies have lost track of the 16mm versions of works they own. The old filmmakers like me, people who should be advocates for their films, are dying off. It is also costly to convert films to the more accessible (for now) digital formats. Not only are my own films in jeopardy but thousands of films, many better than mine, should be restored, transferred to digital media, and made available again. But that costs money, in a quantity that neither the private sector nor nonprofit archives are spending. People spend more time watching moving images than they ever have, yet a whole era of filmmaking is in danger of being lost.

Since there appears to be little immediate profit to be made from salvaging 16mm films, few entrepreneurs are stepping forward to make digital transfers.

Having seen many films from that era, I know there are thousands worth preserving. The question is, who knows and cares about them? People under thirty years of age have likely never seen a 16mm film projected in a classroom. As pointed out in this book's introduction, there are active 16mm print collectors such as Rick Prelinger, Skip Elsheimer (A/V Geeks), Geoff Alexander (Academic Film Archive of North America), Jay Schwartz (Secret Cinema), and dozens of others. The splendid work these collectors are doing is our last chance to see these films before another generation passes and more are lost.

Old prints are fading and we need an earnest effort to salvage what we can. *Learning with the Lights Off* is part of that effort. This is a book that takes these films seriously and helps to keep them alive. I didn't know about most of the things discussed in this book but I should have. Sadly, these films are rarely discussed or taught in school, even university film classes. Were I to teach a course in the history of film or our modern culture, along with the great technical developments in film over the past 100 years, I would certainly include a unit on this frequently overlooked period in film history, a time when 16mm films took off on their own and offered lessons to everyone, even their big brothers in feature film. But learning about this time isn't as easy as it is to study mainstream feature films. The literature is inadequate and limited. That's why this book is so helpful; perhaps essential.

Film lovers interested in these movies must become researchers, collectors, critics, and archeologists. Information in this book can help you track films down. Although below the radar to most, there are many treasures to be discovered. It is a large and varied library, ripe for rewarding study. I am delighted with what editors Devin Orgeron, Marsha Orgeron, and Dan Streible have assembled in the pages of this book. It is my hope that it will inspire further interest in preserving 16mm films for future generations.

Thomas G. Smith
May 18, 2011
Glendale, CA
16mm filmmaker, 1965 to 1980

ACKNOWLEDGMENTS

Our editor at Oxford University Press, Shannon McLachlan, was delightful to work with. Her good cheer, creative ideas, and collegiality made our jobs as writers and editors a pleasure. Editorial assistant Brendan O'Neill always promptly answered our queries and handily facilitated much of the detail work.

The amazing Skip Elsheimer, a.k.a. the "A/V Geek," played a monumental role in making many of the films discussed in this volume accessible by sharing his own copies of films with researchers and uploading them (and others) to the Internet Archive (IA). Skip created the Vintage Educational Film section at IA, which will be a valuable resource for researchers in this area for many years to come. His generosity with his ideas, time, and resources is truly unparalleled.

We also thank the research assistants who did important legwork for this book. Barrett Brown at North Carolina State University (NCSU) made many trips to the library, lugging massive, musty tomes for lengthy sessions at the scanners. Paul Fileri and Debashree Mukherjee at New York University (NYU) did likewise and gave valuable feedback. The interlibrary loan services at NCSU and NYU were kept busy retrieving hundreds of articles and books. This book could not have been written without the support of their crucial library services.

For their behind-the-scenes contributions, we owe gratitude to Les Waffen at the National Archives and Records Administration, Katie Trainor and Kitty Cleary at the Museum of Modern Art, Jonah Volk, Geoff Alexander, and David Shepard.

Finally, we acknowledge our superb cast of contributors for their keen ideas, in-depth research, and true patience. We feel fortunate to have worked with such a capable and inspired group of scholars.

Devin Orgeron
Marsha Orgeron
Dan Streible

ABOUT THE COMPANION WEBSITE

http://www.oup.com/us/learningwiththelightsoff

Oxford has created an easy-to-navigate companion website for *Learning with the Lights Off*. Many of the films discussed in this collection are scarce in their original distribution format. Wherever possible, we have located and digitized these works, allowing readers the opportunity to view the material being discussed in each chapter. Our hope is that this practice will serve as a model for how to increase accessibility to nontheatrical moving images. Though filmographies for individual chapters in this book include URLs for online videos, the information on the companion website should be considered the most reliable.

Learning with the Lights Off

INTRODUCTION

DEVIN ORGERON, MARSHA ORGERON, AND DAN STREIBLE

For those whose conscious lives intersected with the first three-quarters of the twentieth century, the following scenario will likely be familiar: After entering a room at a designated time and listening to an introduction, the lights are switched off. In the darkened room a 16mm projector whirrs, triggering a beam of light leading to a screen at the front of the room. The moving images—usually running ten to thirty minutes—instruct the audience on what to do in the event of a nuclear emergency or the most efficient way to sell products door-to-door; explain the lifecycle of bees or the safe handling of machinery; illustrate a surgical method or the way wheat is grown and harvested by American farmers; train soldiers on how to avoid venereal diseases; teach teenagers how to be good citizens; or present a lesson on the art of Leonardo da Vinci or a play by William Shakespeare. The screening is followed by questions from the audience, a written assignment, or a group discussion.

Millions of people around the world have been instructed by way of film. They have gathered in classrooms, auditoriums, places of worship, museums, libraries, fraternal lodges, union halls, and living rooms; at workplaces, convention halls, fairs, meeting rooms, seminars—even in movie theaters. They have watched films selected from a massive corpus of work, often referred to as *educational, instructional, informational, practical, useful, pedagogical, nontheatrical,* or *nonfiction.* These films targeted audiences of all ages and levels of sophistication, but they were often designed for viewers of a specific age, educational level, field of study, profession, region, gender, religion, or race. An astounding range of organizations and individuals produced these films, including the major Hollywood studios, independent companies formed for nontheatrical film purposes, museums, government agencies, philanthropic foundations, professional societies and associations, universities, corporations, unions, religious organizations, teachers, and even students.

Although plentiful, widely screened, and remembered (fondly or otherwise) by the millions who saw them, these films constitute a neglected aspect of film studies and film history. This is at least partly, as Elizabeth Ellsworth has observed, because film scholars have historically tended to operate "from the long-standing

Figure I.1. The image of rapt children with eyes glued to the screen peppers the literature about educational films. From Ben D. Wood and Frank N. Freeman's book *Motion Pictures in the Classroom* (1929), 38.

assumption that education films subordinate aesthetic expression and formal innovation to such an extent that they become insignificant as *film* practice," resulting in a collective refusal to "come to terms with the cultural and educational importance of a film practice that plays an important role in one of the central institutions of socialization, the schools."[1] Although referring specifically to classroom films, Ellsworth points to a longstanding bias that has elevated the theatrical motion picture over the nontheatrical film as worthy of study: "As long as debates about auteurs, aesthetics, popularity, and filmic enunciation dominated media studies, the highly formulaic, seemingly banal styles and structures of educational media, and the institutional nature of their use and exhibition, ensured their marginalization."[2] This mistaken preconception, coupled with the breadth of educational film practice, combined to make serious consideration of educational films a seemingly impractical and unworthy venture.

Theatrical cinema has long dominated film studies. The allure of fictional narratives, an influential wave of auteur-based criticism that emphasized aesthetic

---

[1] Elizabeth Ellsworth, "I Pledge Allegiance: The Politics of Reading and Using Educational Films," *Curriculum Inquiry* 21 (Spring 1991): 42.

[2] Elizabeth Ellsworth and Mariamne Whatley, *The Ideology of Images in Educational Media: Hidden Curriculums in the Classroom* (New York: Teachers College Press, 1990), 2.

expression, and an international film history canon allowed film studies to align itself with other disciplines. Though the justification was often hard-won, cinema became an academically justifiable object of study in part through a process of exclusion. This largely practical bias, however, has shifted in notable ways. As scholars tend increasingly to the myriad ways in which our contemporary lives are mediated (social-networking interfaces, cell phones, video games, and so forth), our historical relationship to moving images, never as monolithic as might once have been presumed, has begun to undergo reevaluation. Far from being unanalyzable or unworthy objects of study, nontheatrical films, and especially educational films, tell us a great deal about the shape (and shaping) of the cinematic century. This volume, therefore, emerges at a critical moment. These materials, their histories underexplored and their futures uncertain, are now opened up to the critical scrutiny they deserve.

One reason the scholarship on educational film has been slow to materialize might have to do with the vastness of the primary, historical literature associated with it. Some of the strongest works on educational films are, in fact, themselves historical writings, including an enormous body of how-to literature. The conception of "educational film" precipitated a nearly century-long debate in publications representing fields as varied as sociology, school administration, mental health, literary studies, the sciences, childhood education, government, industry, and psychology. There were myriad journals publishing essays in these fields and thousands of books similarly tuned in to the idea of motion pictures as an educational medium. References to these appear throughout this anthology.

There are, however, important scholarly precedents that paved the way for *Learning with the Lights Off.* Anthony Slide's *Before Video: A History of the Non-Theatrical Film* (1992) has been a valuable resource for scholars beginning to explore this area.[3] Slide dedicates a significant portion of his book to films with educational intentions. Using a rich group of primary sources, Slide provides a historical overview of nontheatrical film and considers the educational function

---

[3] Anthony Slide, *Before Video: A History of the Non-Theatrical Film* (Westport, CT: Greenwood Press, 1992). Authors other than Slide have explored the subject of educational film, though they have not approached the subject with the aim of studying this kind of filmmaking as a whole. Most scholarly publications have focused on a type of educational film as part of a larger argument about a different or broader topic of study. Following the social studies model, many of these studies often rely on scientific data sets or utilize educational films to make larger claims about communications theory. Those working in the field of education—especially in the sociology of education—have also produced notable scholarship on the subject of educational media, although their interests often lie in more pragmatic explications of a given film's (or type of film's) pedagogical effectiveness or ideological orientation. A few of these works are worth noting here, and many others are cited throughout the reader. Jack Ellis's "Film for Education: Consideration of Form," published in the *Journal of the Society of Cinematologists* in their 1964–1965 issue,

of many commercial productions. Although *Before Video* is largely a reference book, each chapter includes tantalizing allusions to areas that deserve comprehensive study. In fact, many essays in *Learning with the Lights Off* provide in-depth coverage of subjects Slide briefly references, including Jamison Handy, medical films, the Teaching Film Custodians, Henry Ford, and Electrical Research Products, Inc. (ERPI).[4] This volume, then, owes a significant debt to Slide's research.

Geoff Alexander's *Academic Films for the Classroom: A History* (2010) is also a valuable resource and a first-rate reference book, especially for those interested in the major individuals and companies involved with what he refers to as "academic film."[5] Focused on key figures from the industry as it took shape in the mid-century through its pinnacle in the 1970s, Alexander is especially skilled at biographical detail (having established relationships with many of these people) and insightful corporate profiles. Alexander is also invested in his particular definition of the "academic" film as its own unique category, distinct from non-classroom films that served educational functions and from films deemed "un-serious." Alexander's commitment to this point of view is important insofar as it indicates the longevity of these debates over what educational film is or is not (what it should or should not do) which have been, as we will explore in the historical chapter that follows this introduction, with the genre since its inception. With regard to educational technology—including film—L. Paul Saettler's

---

offered a pioneering though brief look at the phenomenon of the educational film and educational television. Ken Smith's *Mental Hygiene: Classroom Films 1945–1970* (New York: Blast Books, 1999) is a mass market book consisting primarily of summaries, only peripherally useful for the scholar of educational film but an enjoyable introductory foray into the world of mid-century films of the social guidance variety. Robert Eberwein's *Sex Ed: Film, Video, and the Framework of Desire* (New Brunswick, NJ: Rutgers University Press, 1999), one of the only recent books focused entirely on educational film, considers the history of just one of the many genres of "ed film." Heather Hendershot's *Shaking the World for Jesus* (Chicago: University of Chicago, 2004) devotes a chapter to the science classroom films of the Moody Institute. Readers may want to consult Elizabeth Wiatr, "Between Word, Image, and the Machine: Visual Education and Films of Industrial Practice," *Historical Journal of Film, Radio and Television* 22 (2002): 333–51, for a useful historical approach to the subject of early twentieth century film education in relationship to emerging theories about visual culture, as well as Charles Acland's recent work—especially "Curtains, Carts and the Mobile Screen," *Screen* 50 (Spring 2009): 148–66. John Mercer's *The Informational Film*, first published in 1977, is an especially interesting book focused on the technical and psychological study of the "informational" film. It includes a syllabus for a course that Mercer taught on this subject at Iowa State University the same year of the book's publication. At the time, the university housed the American Archives of the Factual Film, which now resides at the Library of Congress. John Mercer, *The Informational Film* (Champaign, IL: Stipes, 1981).

[4] Slide, *Before Video*, 3; 11–13; 22, and 63; 45; 95–96; 89–92.

[5] Geoff Alexander, *Academic Films for the Classroom: A History* (Jefferson, NC: McFarland, 2010).

The Evolution of American Educational Technology, first published in 1990, is an authoritative reference for the history of the many education organizations, journals, projects, producers, and media discussed here. His book has been updated as recently as 2005, but Saettler's work began in the 1960s. McGraw-Hill published his book *A History of Instructional Technology* in 1968, a portion of which the National Education Association circulated as *The Technical Development of the New Media* as early as 1961.[6]

Scholarly interest in educational film is on the rise. The recent surge in interest is partly attributable to the biannual Orphan Film Symposium. Beginning in 1999, Dan Streible and his colleagues at the University of South Carolina assembled scholars and archivists to screen and study neglected films. The 2006 symposium in particular was themed "Science, Industry, and Education." Half of the authors in *Learning with the Lights Off* presented at that gathering, and most of the others have attended at least one "Orphans." Educational motion pictures are part of the nontheatrical film tradition, which has also become a newly invigorated area of study. In 2008, for example, the Society for Cinema and Media Studies announced a Scholarly Interest Group for Nontheatrical Film and Media. Educational films are now finding their way back into the academy and the classroom. The feature film still reigns, but nontheatrical motion pictures have made significant inroads into media studies, particularly as the study of documentary has expanded to include neglected genres of nontheatrical nonfiction, including films of the educational variety.

Themed anthologies and journal issues have begun to build a foundational literature for the study of nontheatrical film, some dedicating a significant portion of their pages to educational films. Vinzenz Hediger and Patrick Vonderau's anthology *Films that Work: Industrial Film and the Productivity of Media* (University of Amsterdam Press, 2009) covers a variety of nontheatrical categories, mostly historical accounts from Europe. The forthcoming anthology *Useful Cinema* (Duke University Press), edited by Charles Acland and Haidee Wasson, does likewise, with a North American focus. A 2007 nontheatrical issue of *Film History* (19, no. 4, editors Anke Mebold, Martina Roepke, and Dan Streible) includes amateur productions as well as educational and industrial ones. The fall 2009 "Orphans No More" special issue of the *Journal of Popular Film and Television*, edited by Elizabeth Heffelfinger and Heide Solbrig, frames educational movies within "ephemeral films and American culture."

---

[6] L. Paul Saettler, *The Evolution of American Educational Technology* (Englewood, CO: Libraries Unlimited, 1990; 2nd ed., Greenwich, CT: Information Age Publishing, 2004; 3rd ed., Mahwah, NJ: L. Erlbaum Associates, 2005); Paul Saettler and National Institute of Education, *An Assessment of the Current Status of Educational Technology* (Syracuse, NY: ERIC Clearinghouse on Information Resources, 1979). See also Larry Cuban, *Teachers and Teaching: The Classroom Use of Technology since 1920* (New York: Teachers College Press, 1986).

Nontheatrical films, however, have historically suffered from limited access and archival scarcity. Circulating primarily as 16mm prints, their sponsoring institutions often deemed them expendable when their use-value waned, and especially once video prevailed as an "easier" means of production and distribution.[7] Without the visionary efforts of a small group of collectors, archivists, curators, and institutions, many more of these works would likely have disappeared into landfills. Thousands, of course, are indeed lost, but many thousands more survive. And some now circulate again, occasionally in their original film format or more frequently along digital channels, affording a degree of access that has the potential to exceed their original circulation.

Beyond some of the films themselves, what has been lost is a sense of the significant role these films played in American and world history, cinematic and otherwise. This volume seeks to redress this obscurity through essays that explore these questions: How was film envisioned as an explicitly educational medium? How and when did films function as conduits of information? Who made educational films and for what purposes? What was their function in the eyes of producers, distributors, exhibitors, commentators, and spectators? The prevailing conception of the motion picture's entertainment—or even documentary—role has overshadowed the medium's longstanding and at times hotly debated pedagogical function. As this collection reminds us, the conceptualization of film as a conduit of knowledge and a shaper of human behavior, as an instrument of ideas and ideology, can be traced back to cinema's earliest years.

What Was an Educational Film?

"What kind of pictures do you prefer?" a questionnaire asked Chicago schoolchildren in 1919. One wrote, "I like educational pictures best, especially those with Charlie Chaplin."[8] The child's amusingly loose use of the term *educational* in relation to moving pictures warrants consideration, as it begs a question that recurs throughout this collection of essays: What is an educational film?

As the Visual Education Division of Los Angeles schools observed in 1929, "it is significant that the cinema was first used for educational rather than theatrical

---

[7] For more on the history of 16mm films in libraries see Elena Rossi-Snook, "Persistence of Vision: Public Library 16mm Collections in America," *The Moving Image* 5 (Spring 2005): 1–27.

[8] Estella L. Moulton, "Our School Children and the Movies," *Visual Education* 1 (June 1920): 25–26. While the young informant who deemed Chaplin films educational also said he found Chaplin's *Shoulder Arms* (1918) entertaining, such designations are blurry. At its blurriest, the term "educational" connoted its opposite. The Hollywood producer-distributor called Educational Pictures dealt in low-budget short comedies throughout the 1920s and 1930s, having quickly abandoned its educational mission in the teens.

purposes."[9] Indeed, cinema's roots in the work of such scientific investigators, lecturers, and visual experimenters as Eadweard Muybridge and Ètienne-Jules Marey
would indicate that this capacity to educate was part of the original impetus for
the medium. There was, however, a battle waged over film's most ideal, useful, and
valuable (both socially and economically) functions, which led to many of the
cross-purposes that might have befuddled the child-respondent above. Much of
this battle revolved specifically around classroom film use, not only because this
was perceived as the most risky and also potentially beneficial forum for educational film but also because it emerged as the largest and therefore most important
market for nontheatrical film producers. The historical overview we provide in
chapter 1 therefore pays special attention to the literature about classroom educational film use in accordance with the historically disproportionate volume of
debate and attention it received.

Schools were, of course, just one segment of a much larger market that included businesses, churches, societies, and other nontheatrical exhibitors of this
kind of film. We have opted to use the term *educational* because we believe it to
be a useful umbrella under which to collect scholarship on films that were used
to teach, inform, instruct, or persuade viewers in a variety of ways and contexts.
So while we consider the reason and nature of a film's production as part of this
definition, it is not the sole factor in deeming a film "educational," since the context of exhibition and use is equally important.[10] While classroom films (whether
produced for or used within the classroom) are the most familiar kind of educational film, this collection presents historical thinking on a range of films that
functioned educationally. Though the majority of the films discussed here were
intended to serve pedagogical functions, we sought a term inclusive enough to
allow for other, perhaps unexpectedly educational, film materials.

There is a historical rationale behind our choice in words as well. The term
educational has long been used in relation to films, both of the theatrical and
nontheatrical variety, and the quest for a definition of educational film is an old
concern. In his 1910 catalog of educational films, George Kleine (an influential
producer-distributor in commercial motion pictures) took a stab at the concept:
"The word 'educational' is here used in a wide sense and does not indicate that
these films are intended for school or college use exclusively. They are are intended

---

[9] *Visual Aids in Education* (Los Angeles: Visual Education Division, Los Angeles City
School District, 1929), 19.

[10] John Mercer is similarly interested in context, suggesting that films should be organized
"according to the kind of learning they produce, not according to their content." Mercer argues
that informational films (which he distinguishes, for example, from skill films) "stimulate learning
of facts, processes, verbal development, concepts, principles, and so on." See Mercer, *Informational
Film*, 1, 3. While Mercer's categorical demarcations are valuable, our intention here is to explore
the array of educational purposes film has served more generally.

rather for the education of the adult as well as the youth, for the exhibition before miscellaneous audiences, as well as for more restricted use."[11] Andrew Phillip Hollis (director of visual education at the University of North Dakota), writing in 1926, asked, "What is meant by the term Educational Film? It is not strange that so new a product suffers some confusion in nomenclature." Noting several abuses of the term and the potential problems with the implications of "classroom film," "text film," and "propaganda film," Hollis continued:

> In practice, things are named from their dominant purpose or use. It is obvious that nearly every theatrical motion picture will convey information of some sort about life and customs, but we do not, therefore, call a Mae Murray film educational. Those films should be included in the term "Educational," that are predominantly educational. "Nanook of the North," a theatrical film, is nevertheless one of the best of the educationals; most scenics and industrials might be permitted to bear the label. These can properly be called "general educationals."[12]

In 1940, behavioral psychologist G. L. Freeman astutely observed that "the question is not so much which motion pictures are educational as how to make motion pictures educate."[13]

These authors, from significantly different backgrounds, arrive at a conclusion, which points to our conceptualization of the term: films used for educational purposes are justifiably deemed educational. Restricting the definition by exclusion of, say, industrial, training, or sponsored films, ignores the way these productions were historically conceived and used. Educational films were understood as having the potential to teach ideas, facts, and skills, as well as morals and social behaviors, in a wide array of contexts, inside and outside of the classroom. In this way, *Learning with the Lights Off* is entering a long-standing, rather thorny definitional debate—one nearly as old as the cinema itself. The book's individual authors come at the debate from a variety of angles, but the

---

[11] George Kleine, *Catalogue of Educational Motion Pictures* (New York: Kleine, 1910), 1.

[12] A. P. Hollis, *Motion Pictures for Instruction* (New York: Century, 1926), 3, 4. Shortly after publishing this book, Hollis became affiliated with a commercial venture called the National School of Visual Education, based in Chicago. The company's ads offered to train people for jobs in electrical work—using only the 16mm films mailed to their home, along with a tabletop projector loaned at no charge (*New McClure's*, Dec. 1928, 13). See also A. P. Hollis, "The Effectiveness of the Film and Demonstration in Teaching Cooking," in Frank N. Freeman, *Visual Education: A Comparative Study of Motion Pictures and Other Methods of Instruction* (Chicago: University of Chicago, 1924).

[13] G.L. Freeman, "The Motion Picture and Informal Education," *Journal of Educational Sociology* 13 (Jan. 1940): 258.

term *educational* adequately encapsulates the range of social, industrial, pedagogical, and spectatorial practices they explore.

This collection of essays, then, addresses the breadth of the motion picture's educational guises over the course of the twentieth century. It focuses on American educational *films* (as opposed to videos) from the silent era through the 1980s, when film prints, film strips, and film projectors began rapidly disappearing from the classroom, the library, the club meeting, and the convention hall. The focus on American film stems from our desire not to spread the focus of the collection so thinly that we fail to do justice to what is already an impossibly large subject. Though the essays collected here defy any suggestion that "American educational films" are a unified category, we hope that readers will come away from *Learning with the Lights Off* with an understanding of the United States' particular—albeit diverse—pedagogical uses of one of the twentieth century's most significant technologies.

Collecting and Projecting in the Twenty-First Century

Learning with the Lights Off is situated at the precipice of a global shift in the function and format of learning. The essays gathered in this collection examine, in roughly chronological order, a century's worth of material that challenged and changed the way people received, disseminated, and thought about information and the transmission of knowledge. The questions raised during the heyday of educational film are raised again today, in the era of Wikipedia, Google Earth, "smart phones," game systems, Skype video, web-based file sharing, and Internet delivery of television and movies. Our relationship to information, we are learning once again, is anything but stable and, though we are only occasionally aware of it, it is often dictated by parties—corporate, political, religious, academic, professional—whose motives are only visible in retrospect.

In this spirit, *Learning with the Lights Off* is both an Internet-age project and a film preservation beneficiary. Most of the educational works discussed in this volume were shot on motion-picture film between 1910 and 1980. However, the contributors and editors have collaborated with collectors, libraries, and archives to make many of these films available online at the Internet Archive. This nonprofit library of digital media includes a moving image section. Within that (under Cultural and Academic Films), a Vintage Educational Films collection indexes some of the works featured in *Learning with the Lights Off.* We also direct readers to such films that were already online, often due to the efforts of those who cared enough to oversee the triple media migration of film to video to digital to web.

Learning with the Lights Off therefore facilitates close readings of the films discussed throughout its pages. To help readers see the movies under discussion throughout the book, each essay has a filmography of works analyzed (with a

"Related Films" section for those only briefly referenced). Following the format of Rick Prelinger's *The Field Guide to Sponsored Films*, published by the National Film Preservation Foundation in 2006, each entry lists where to access viewing copies and indicates whether these are original 16mm prints or copies in video formats. Commercially available DVDs appear alongside library and archive holdings, and URLs are included for entries that can be found online. For added convenience, we have also created a companion website that includes links to all of the films discussed in this book that are available on the internet. There are, of course, thousands of educational film titles that go unmentioned in the pages that follow. We encourage readers to use WorldCat.org, a global database that searches the media holdings of thousands of libraries, to seek out additional educational films, and to consult Elena Rossi-Snook's guide to educational film collections at the end of this volume.

We are committed to access. However, we also encourage the screening of educational films in their native formats whenever possible. The sensory experience of being in a room with the lights off and a projector running is an important part of understanding these underappreciated films. As with all other forms of cinema, most of the works do not survive, but a healthy sample does. Collectors, screening venues, and archives still project 16mm prints. Among those who continue the tradition are contributors to this book—Skip Elsheimer, Rick Prelinger, Elena Rossi-Snook, and Gregory Waller. There are numerous other individuals who serve, often avocationally, as curators, programmers, collectors, projectionists, media archaeologists, and exhibitors of films in the digital age: Geoff Alexander (Academic Film Archive of North America), Jay Schwartz (Secret Cinema), Nancy Watrous and Michelle Puetz (Chicago Film Archives), Jeanne Liotta (Firefly Cinema), Stephen Parr (Oddball Film and Video), Craig Baldwin (Other Cinema), Liz Keim and Marina McDougall (the Exploratorium), Greg Pierce (Orgone Archive), Andrew Lampert (Anthology Film Archives), Caroline Frick (Texas Archive of the Moving Image), Valarie Schwan and Karen Collins (People of the Pavement), Dennis Nyback, Tim Caldwell, Ken Smith, Giles Rosbury, Bradley Eros, Brian Frye, Melissa Dollman, Amy Sloper, Dwight Swanson, Joanna Poses, Melinda Stone, Jenni Olson, Luke Savisky, Allen Ruppersberg, Stephen Slappe, Jonathan Quinn, J. Fred MacDonald, Adam Sargis, Heather McAdams, Andrea Grover, and (before becoming codirector of the Telluride Film Festival) Gary Meyer.

Additional local and regional organizations supporting public screenings of educational films include Northeast Historic Film (Bucksport, Maine), Pacific Film Archive (Berkeley), Aurora Picture Show (Houston), Basement Films (Albuquerque), Pleasure Dome (Toronto), Minnesota Film Arts (Minneapolis), and Chicago Filmmakers.

The perpetuation of the American educational film in public consciousness has taken on two registers: appreciative/aesthetic and comic/ironic. The former began in the genre's own heyday. Outside of awards and festivals sponsored by the industry itself, the particular genius of Marcia and Amos Vogel's Cinema 16 film society is notable. Beginning in New York in 1947, Cinema 16 regularly programmed "straight" educational films in programs alongside experimental and documentary work. Continuing until 1963, the society's curated programs drew large audiences and critical attention to these films. (Amos Vogel continued such programming in his University of Pennsylvania classrooms until he retired in 1991.) Starting in the early 1970s, avant-garde cineastes at Anthology Film Archives and the Collective for Living Cinema (an artists' group) occasionally added educational works to their New York screenings. Geoff Alexander's curatorship of the Academic Film Archive of North America collection takes a respectful approach to the cinematic skills of the best educational filmmakers of the postwar generation. To a large degree, the contributors to *Learning with the Lights Off* have devoted their research to these films because they understand the works to be significant and interesting in their own right.

However, the majority of educational film presentation in the past thirty years has been in comic or satirical contexts. Large television audiences have been exposed to the campiest and most dated examples of social guidance and educational films. Archivist Richard Scheckman brought educational film clips to *Late Night with David Letterman* in the 1980s. In those same years, *Night Flight,* an overnight program on cable's USA Network, regularly included segments (produced by Stuart Samuels, Stuart S. Shapiro, and Cynthia Friedland) that exploited the baby boomer generation's knowing response to such films. Another fringe, ingenious application of educational kitsch on television was Paul Reubens's comic use of films such as *Lunchroom Manners* (1960) in *The Pee-wee Herman Show* (1981, HBO) and *Pee-wee's Playhouse* (CBS, 1986–1991).

Beginning in 1991, two television series extended familiarity with campy, mid-century educational films, reaching audiences that included viewers too young to have experienced 16mm film in the classroom. *Mystery Science Theater 3000,* which maintains a fan-based presence on the web, began showing entire educational shorts, accompanied by its characters' sarcastic verbal riffing at "bad" movies. *Alphabet Antics* (1951), *The Home Economics Story* (1951), *The Chicken of Tomorrow* (1948), *What to Do on a Date* (1950), *Uncle Jim's Dairy Farm* (1963), and others introduced a new generation to Coronet-level production values and to the name Jam Handy. Also starting in 1991, *The Simpsons* TV series introduced running cameos of the character Troy McClure. Voiced by Phil Hartman, his tag line began, "Hi, I'm Troy McClure. You may remember me from such educational films as. . . ." The brilliant satirical titles in his mock filmography include *Here Comes the Metric System, Two Minus Three Equals Negative Fun, Lead Paint: Delicious but Deadly*, and *Meat and You: Partners in Freedom.*

Such satirical and ironic references to the "classical" educational film work best when they deftly expose the style, content, ideology, audiences, and social functions of the originals. In a way, this comic insight into what these now-historical films reveal about American culture is not so distant from the aim of the essays in this book. *Learning with the Lights Off* offers a critical examination of how these thousands of long-neglected short-running movies were part of the cultural fabric of a nation.

1

A HISTORY OF LEARNING WITH THE LIGHTS OFF

DEVIN ORGERON, MARSHA ORGERON, AND DAN STREIBLE

> Although the picture falls within the unhappy category known as
> "educational films," it is nevertheless entertainment in a full sense.
>
> —Frank S. Nugent, *New York Times*

In his review of *The Human Adventure* (1935), a documentary about archeological
sites explored by the University of Chicago's Oriental Institute, Frank Nugent humorously alludes to a dilemma that has always plagued this volume's object of
study.[1] An "unhappy category" indeed, the educational film, regardless of how one
defines it, has been subject to debate from the start. This chapter provides a selective account of its history in the United States gleaned from the substantial—
indeed, at times overwhelming—print materials associated with this industry. The
tremendous size and scope of this literature begins to suggest its relevance, both to
that larger and better known American film industry and to our culture more
broadly. Debates over film's educational use inside as well as outside of the classroom have been with the medium since its inception.

In a superb 1988 essay about early efforts to market home projection systems for
nontheatrical use, scholar Ben Singer observes that discussions of potential classroom applications for motion pictures appeared in *Moving Picture World* and *The
Show World* in 1907, the first year of publication for both trade journals. Throughout the Progressive Era, a nationwide explosion of press dealt with the subject of
moving pictures in the classroom.[2] Magazine accounts began appearing about broad
instructional applications of moving pictures. In 1908, journalist John Meader
reported that "several of the larger cities' educational and philanthropic institutions
have adopted the moving-picture plan of instruction and entertainment," adding
that "regular manufacturers ... are now beginning to realize the possibilities offered

---

[1] Frank Nugent, review of *The Human Adventure*. *New York Times,* Oct. 30, 1935.

[2] Ben Singer, "Home Cinema and the Edison Home Projecting Kinetoscope," *Film History* 2
(Winter 1988): 51.

in the educational field, and nearly all the most progressive [movie] houses are now exerting a certain portion of their efforts in this direction."[3] Meader's observation demonstrates that the idea of educational film was being used both to conceptualize as well as to market films in the early twentieth century.

A leading trade journal, the *Moving Picture World* characterized its own "endeavor to crystallize the wave of sentiment that is abroad in favor of the educational value of the picture" in its January 1911 debut of the column "In the Educational Field." Detailing progress in the implementation of educational possibilities, *Moving Picture World* also revealed less noble motivations behind some educational film programming. It reported that troubles with "the local clergy and the press" in Buffalo, New York, were threatening to lead to theater licenses being revoked, which in turn compelled local theaters to decide to devote "a whole day for the benefit of the tuberculosis exhibition" in order to avoid "incurring further unfavorable comment from the pulpit and the press."[4] In 1926, movie journalist Terry Ramsaye noted a similar motivation: "*Educational* pictures were born of a necessity in complying with Sunday show legislation in New York City in 1908, when so-called lecturers were added to the film shows to give them pretext of a defense as institutions of instruction."[5] These examples explain some endorsements of the medium's educational capacities. However, they do not negate film's educational potential or its use.

There was always something schizophrenic about the demands and expectations placed upon the educational mode, in large part because it needed to be differentiated from frivolous and morally suspect entertainment movies. In 1920, psychologist L. L. Thurstone (perhaps humorously) put it, "If a film that purports to be educational is too entertaining we had better look it over again to see if it is really educational." Writing in *Visual Education,* he suggested that "a film may be of the very highest educational value as a teaching tool, even if it is extremely boring and uninteresting to the casual onlooker." "Its entertaining features are secondary but desirable," he concluded.[6]

Finding the "just right" temperature at which to pitch the educational film would never quite be resolved, as the widely divergent tones of educational films made throughout the twentieth century attest. In 1923, educational reformer May Ayres Burgess proclaimed that any element of amusement in classroom films rendered them "unpedagogical": "The classroom film does not need to be funny; it does not need to be clever; it does not need to tell a

[3] John Meader, "The Story of the Picture That Moves," *The Bohemian* (Sept. 1908): 363. Brackets ours.

[4] "In the Educational Field," *Moving Picture World* (Jan. 21, 1911): 128, 129.

[5] Terry Ramsaye, "Movie Jargon," *American Speech* 1 (Apr. 1926): 360.

[6] L. L. Thurstone, "What Is an Educational Motion Picture?" *Visual Education* 1 (Apr. 1920): 25.

story."[7] Many of her contemporaries disagreed, however, averring a balance needed to be struck between elements of information and engagement. Still, school films needed to distinguish themselves from the pablum being peddled to the masses. And some advocates embraced making informational films entertaining as well. Writing in 1926 about health films, such as those made to prevent tuberculosis, diphtheria, and rickets, Thomas C. Edwards of the National Health Council explained that many people will not take the time and energy to read but "will sit through several reels of films and carry away certain important facts, through a natural interest in action portrayed in graphic form and mixed with entertainment."[8] Narrative strategies might, in other words, help the medicine go down.

A decade later it would be necessary to warn teachers against using films *as* entertainment. Education professor M. R. Brunstetter claimed that "many untrained teachers" used film as an educational pacifier, a mistake "probably carried over from film theater-going habits."[9] Motion pictures might have special communicational abilities, but they required a skilled teacher to make them effective. It was also incumbent upon the manufacturers and distributors to make film's educational possibilities known to conventional exhibitors as well as to those overseeing alternative exhibition circuits. By 1910, the Essanay Company categorized its releases as Comedy, Dramatic, Western Drama, Industrial, and Educational, featuring such short educational releases as *Aviation at Los Angeles* and *The Ostrich and the Lady.* The *Edison Kinetogram* categorized certain films as educational starting in 1910 with *United States Life Saving Drills.*[10] In 1913, the Edison company also began providing educational films for its Home Projecting Kinetoscope, which used an idiosyncratic 22mm film.[11]

Developments on the educational film front escalated throughout the teens, despite both definitional and tactical barriers, in large part due to the Progressive Era's faith in educational reform and the betterment of society, which was perfectly matched with the educational capabilities of the motion picture. In 1911, *Moving Picture World* reported introductions of moving pictures into schools in Rochester, Cleveland, Chicago, and the public library in Madison,

---

[7] May Ayres Burgess, "Motion Pictures in the Public Schools," *Elementary School Journal* 23 (May 1923): 681.

[8] Thomas C. Edwards, "Health Pictures and Their Value," *Annals of the American Academy of Political and Social Science* 128 (Nov. 1926): 134. This issue was a symposium on motion pictures, with Arthur Edwin Krows, Terry Ramsaye, and Charlotte Perkins Gilman, among others, publishing pieces. Reprinted as *The Motion Picture in Its Economic and Social Aspects,* The Literature of Cinema series (New York: Arno Press, 1970).

[9] M. R. Brunstetter, *How to Use Educational Sound Film* (Chicago: University of Chicago Press, 1937), 12.

[10] *Essanay Guide,* Apr. 15–30, 1910; and *Edison Kinetogram,* June 1, 1910, 9; both available at the Margaret Herrick Library of the Academy of Motion Picture Arts and Sciences, Los Angeles.

[11] Singer, "Home Cinema," 51, 60–66.

Wisconsin; similar plans were underway for New York, San Francisco, Oakland, Pittsburgh, Milwaukee, Minneapolis, Baltimore, and Washington, DC.[12] In 1919, the board of education in Evanston, Illinois, created a "bureau of visual education," in order to facilitate more efficient and effective classroom use of educational motion pictures.[13] But even as schools and libraries were beginning to utilize film educationally, debates raged over the appropriateness of bringing film into a scholarly setting. What was the point of incurring such expense? More important, how might motion pictures negatively impact America's youth in the institutions where their intellectual growth was supposedly assured?

The answers to these questions lay partly in countering the medium's reputation as frivolous and harmful by promoting its educational properties. Advocates went to great lengths to achieve this. Film could conquer time and space, revealing that which could not be readily seen (and, later, heard) in most classrooms. Footage of wheat harvesting in Kansas, meatpacking in Chicago, or salmon migration in Alaska could be replayed to students in a classroom in Peoria, Atlanta, or the Bronx. In 1912, Frederick Talbot discussed the way that microcinematography captured parasites attacking blood corpuscles: "The film was shown lately before a gathering of medical men, and created widespread interest, as it introduced them to a phase in the life of the parasite which hitherto had been beyond their comprehension."[14] Surely these special abilities and applications could sway even the most doubtful of the cinema's critics.

If, indeed, film's ability to amuse was "its least important appeal," as one museum director contended, then it was up to an array of pontificators, researchers, and advocates to convince the public and the specialists that its educational abilities might be harnessed.[15] Still, the medium's ability to entertain in an educational context could be an asset. As movie critic Winifred Aydelotte put it, "To this day, I have never forgotten one detail of those old flickers. And I *have* forgotten practically everything that the thin, bony structure of learning in the little red schoolhouse hoped I would remember."[16] Children watching a film about Napoleon, Aydelotte continued, "are on the screen with Napoleon and his soldiers," experiencing a simulation of reality so that "children live the events pictured on the screen and they become part of their own experience."[17] (See fig.1.1.) If

---

[12] "In the Educational Field," *Moving Picture World*, Jan. 21, 1911, 129.

[13] W. Arthur Justice, "Visual Instruction in the Public Schools of Evanston, Ill.," *Visual Education* 1 (Jan. 1920): 12. Evanston schools had been using films since Nov. 1918.

[14] Frederick A. Talbot, *Moving Pictures: How They Are Made and Worked* (1912; reprint, Philadelphia: Lippincott, 1914), 167.

[15] George W. Stevens, "The Muse of Motion Photography in Museums," *Metropolitan Museum of Art Bulletin* 11 (Sept. 1916): 204.

[16] Winifred Aydelotte, "The Little Red Schoolhouse Becomes a Theater," *Motion Picture Herald* (Mar. 1934): 35.

[17] Ibid., 88.

Figure 1.1. The Hollywood-oriented *Motion Picture Herald* provided this illustration for Winifred Aydelotte's "The Little Red Schoolhouse Becomes a Theater," March 1934, 35.

movies could be more engaging than books or teachers, then they could enhance students' educational experiences. Some applications, of course, such as educating Talbot's medical men about parasites, were to have no entertainment aspect to them, but would logically maintain a dry informational tone.

By the 1940s, pundits only occasionally questioned the "supposedly educational ends" of much educational film use, except perhaps when they were not used as *educational* films. The unhappy result of informal and unpurposeful use in schools, churches, or clubs, claimed G. L. Freeman in 1940, was that "very little of this well-intentioned effort meets with the standards of 'education' as carried by other and better understood media of communication or the standards of 'entertainment' demanded by the commercial theater." The growing pains of the educational film industry included the ongoing problem potential exhibitors had with sorting through "this mass of unanalyzed, unclassified, and unassimilated material" being produced by "business houses, service organizations, and various propaganda groups." On the other hand, educational films were often handicapped by the inability to "command the lively attention and critical respect that is accorded entertainment features," not only in the classroom but in many other "more informal types of education."[18]

Where the first decades of educational film use most often found commentators urging educational filmmakers to avoid being too entertaining lest the patina of frivolity denigrate their product, by the 1940s most advocates realized that "engaging films" (the vagueness of the term hints at the problem itself) were potentially more educational by virtue of the attention given them by spectators. As a study of the Santa Barbara, California, schools from 1941 reported, "There is no reason why education cannot be entertaining, or why entertainment cannot be educational. . . . Schools can utilize the local movie theater as a community resource without contaminating the school or sterilizing the theater." Still, the same study concludes that "the greatest development of curriculum thinking came when teachers began to shift their thinking from methodological to educational purposes in the use of motion pictures, and when they began to make use of motion pictures for specific purposes in the unit, not merely as novelties and 'interest-getters.'"[19]

This notion of using film's entertainment capacities for—but not in lieu of—educational purposes is echoed throughout the 1940s, at least partly reflecting the perceived effectiveness of engaging filmmaking methods used

---

[18] G. L. Freeman, "The Motion Picture and Informal Education," *Journal of Educational Sociology* 13 (Jan. 1940): 257–58.

[19] Reginald Bell, Leo Cain, and Lillian Lamoreaux, *Motion Pictures in a Modern Curriculum: A Report on the Use of Films in the Santa Barbara Schools* (Washington, DC: American Council on Education, 1941), 169, 176.

upon military personnel in wartime training films. Charles F. Hoban Jr., an influential figure in the field, observed this, writing that "in developing films for . . . important educational purposes, the Army applied to educational films the dramatic techniques hitherto used only in entertainment films."[20] The U.S. Navy alone produced 1,100 training films (mostly two-reel) in just three-and-a-half years and claimed to have distributed more than 10,000 different training films during the war.[21] This concentrated use gave administrators and teachers some significant argumentative leverage in the postwar period in terms of convincing school boards to spend more on classroom film than in the prewar period. Still, teachers were advised that it was most appropriate to treat films the same way as they did textbooks, maps, and charts: "Dispel the idea that films are a 'treat' or that you are putting on a 'show.'"[22]

Perhaps the most compelling argument about the debate was made by F. Dean McClusky in 1947. The professor of education compared the division of films into "those which entertain" and "those which educate" to similar categories of literature. Such divisions failed to sustain themselves, he argued, as "many novels and plays which were written in the first instance to entertain are used in schools for highly desirable educational purposes."[23] Therefore, McClusky contended, films were what one made of them, emphasizing the role played by exhibitors and exhibition contexts.

For Good or Bad: Harnessing the Influence of Motion Pictures

The Motion Pictures relate to and directly bear upon and control to an unbelievable extent, the trend of the mind and the education and morals of every man, woman and child in the community.
—*Chicago Motion Picture Commission, 1919*

We have, it is true, a struggling subdivision of what we call "educational" pictures, failing to see that all pictures are educational, for good or bad.
—*Charlotte Perkins Gilman, 1925*

---

[20] Quoted in Gloria Waldron, *The Information Film* (New York: Columbia University Press, 1949), 12. For an important study of film use during the war see Carl Hovland, Arthur Lumsdaine, and Fred Sheffield, *Experiments on Mass Communication* (Princeton, NJ: Princeton University Press, 1949).

[21] Orville Goldner, "The Story of Navy Training Films," *Business Screen* 6 (May 15, 1945): 29, 83.

[22] Norma Barts, "Techniques of Using Film in Classroom Teaching," *Educational Screen* (May 1946): 270.

[23] F. Dean McClusky, "The Nature of the Educational Film," *Hollywood Quarterly* 2 (July 1947): 372.

The influence of motion pictures on citizens—especially the young, foreign-born, lower-class, or uneducated—was a concern for Progressive-Era America. That concern continued through the 1920s, as the visual education movement flourished alongside a booming Hollywood. Professor of education Edwin A. Lee summed up the overall perception in 1923: "The motion picture is the single most potent educational factor in our present-day civilization. A student body of over fifty millions attends some performance every week of the year."[24]

An array of theories and rhetorical tropes began circulating in the early twentieth century regarding the powers of the moving image, especially over children. Some argued that the motion picture possessed hypnotic powers; others argued that moviegoers—especially children—were getting daily theatrical doses of harmful and corrupting ideas; others claimed that going to the movies at night resulted in eyestrain and, more generally, in children being less able to learn at school the next day.[25]

What cinema historian Miriam Hansen has called "the myth of universal language" existed in rhetoric about cinema from its inception. "The universal-language metaphor," she writes, "was soon adapted by industrial publicists and advertisers." By 1915, the likes of Edwin S. Porter, D. W. Griffith, and writer Jack London—not to mention the studio Universal Pictures—were invoking the concept. By 1920, the press commonly used it as a truism. The educational sector was equally quick to speak of moving pictures as universal in their capacity to reach and to instruct virtually anyone, even the illiterate. Francis Holley, head of the largest international educational film distributorship, used the cliché verbatim in a 1921 interview with *American Magazine:* "The motion picture is a universal language."[26]

---

[24] Edwin A. Lee, "The Motion Picture as a Factor in Public Education," *Elementary School Journal* 24 (Nov. 1923): 185. The preceding epigraphs are from Chicago *Motion Picture Commission Report* (Sept. 1920), quoted in Estella L. Moulton, "Our School Children and the Movies," *Visual Education* 1 (June 1920): 24; and Charlotte Perkins Gilman, "Mind-Stretching: The Mental Area Can Be Made Coterminous with the Universe," *Century Magazine* 111 (Dec. 1925): 219, reprinted in *Red Velvet Seat*, ed. Antonia Lant (New York: Verso, 2006), 287.

[25] See, for examples of such arguments: George Elliott Howard, "Social Psychology of the Spectator," *American Journal of Sociology* 18 (July 1912): 40; Florence Butler Blanchard, "The Woman's Club: Its Attitude toward Visual Education," *Visual Education* 1 (Sept.–Oct. 1920): 17; reported by Ernest Dench, *Motion Picture Education* (Cincinnati: Standard Publishing, 1917), 13, 15.

[26] Miriam Hansen, *Babel and Babylon: Spectatorship and American Silent Film* (Cambridge, MA: Harvard University Press, 1991), 77. Edwin S. Porter quoted in "Portrayal in Lieu of Spoken Word," *Moving Picture World*, Aug. 13, 1915, 1328; Jack London, "The Message of Motion Pictures," *Paramount Magazine,* Feb. 1915, reprinted in *Authors on Film*, ed. Harry Geduld (Bloomington:

With the great influence of motion pictures presumed, advocates were embracing motion pictures as a tool for wide-ranging purposes, including classroom use, public health management, and instruction on citizenship. As social psychologist Arland Weeks argued in "The Mind of the Citizen" (1915):

> The instant response of millions to the moving picture creates a
> suspicion that the propaganda of reform has quite too fully relied upon
> a relatively unpopular method—that of printed or spoken arguments.
> The same forces of perception and emotion which now so often go to
> waste in attention given to distressingly weak subject-matter at the
> cheap-show place might, if applied to social ends, work in brief time
> advancement which otherwise would require centuries. . . . Control
> images, and civilization may be made to approximate any ideal.[27]

This was certainly an idea picked up by many government and public advocacy organizations. In 1936, Jean Pinney of the American Social Hygiene Association wrote that "social hygiene is a subject which naturally lends itself to interpretation through the motion picture," applicable to both lay and professional audiences. Noting that the spread of knowledge was the only way to stop the spread of disease, Pinney emphasized the need for engaging material and a reliable nontheatrical circuit, especially given the "difficulties of making any educational film for commercial distribution" if the information is "scientifically accurate" and comes up against a conservative censorship board.[28] Although the National Board of Review had no purview over educational films (though they tried to promote film as a teaching tool by providing information on educational films), local censor boards might reject a film depicting, say, details about how syphilis was transmitted, whether it was explicitly educational or merely posing in educational garb.[29]

Theatrical interests, however, often felt encroached upon by nontheatrical exhibitors offering free shows. In fact, some distributors refused to rent films to

---

Indiana University Press, 1972), 106–7. The many educational-sector invocations of the "universal language" rhetoric include Moulton, "Our School Children and the Movies"; and earlier, "Growing Use of Commercial Motion Pictures," *Iron Age*, Apr. 10, 1913, 886. Francis Holley is quoted in Aaron Hardy Ulm, "Once Blind, He Now Helps Others to See," *American Magazine* 92 (Oct. 1921): 55.

[27] Arland Weeks, "The Mind of the Citizen," *American Journal of Sociology* 21 (Nov. 1915): 391.

[28] Jean B. Pinney, "The Motion Picture and Social-Hygiene Education," *Journal of Educational Sociology* (Nov. 1936): 158, 162–64.

[29] Wilton A. Barrett, "The National Board of Review of Motion Pictures—How It Works," *Journal of Educational Sociology* 10 (Nov. 1936): 178. See Eric Schaefer's essay in this volume for discussion of the relationship between hygiene and exploitation films, and Skip Elsheimer's essay, which includes a discussion of educational films and venereal disease.

schools or churches due to pressure from their theatrical customers. In other cases "school people or church people have frankly started opposition theaters of their own with the avowed intention of running the commercial exhibitors out of business."[30] *Educational Screen*'s catalog, *1000 and One*, critiqued this short-sighted "boycott" strategy in 1924, pointing out that theatrical prints that might be repurposed for nontheatrical use were, instead, being shelved due to pressure from commercial exhibitors.[31]

Concerns about the movies' influence upon children in particular were most famously spurred in the early 1930s by the Payne Fund Studies, in which a group of prominent social scientists sought to assess what effects movies had on the behavior and attitudes of young audiences. As educational researcher Charles Hoban Jr. observed in 1942, the Payne Fund Studies ultimately "demonstrated that motion pictures are a powerful medium of education," whether—as Charlotte Perkins Gilman suggested twenty years prior—for good or bad. Furthermore, Hoban noted that films were commonly used to influence thought well beyond the classroom, including "the education of the farm population in newer agricultural practices, in sales campaigns, in the development of general good will toward a product or an industry, in vocational training, in technical research, in analysis of sports performance, and in many other vocational and avocational situations."[32] Film's influence, recognized in these prewar years, would be most strategically directed in the 1940s.

World War II played the greatest part in the "at long last" recognition of the motion picture's value as a tool of teaching and persuasion. Films not only helped train millions of soldiers but also did important work on the home front. As documentary advocate Mary Losey put it in her 1943 call to arms, "Films can help win the war, if we use them intelligently." Losey urged "schools, libraries, Y's, churches, motion picture councils, forums, civilian defense councils, service clubs, social agencies, trade unions, women's clubs" to disseminate films that would shore up support for the war effort.[33] By war's end, a clear consensus existed: Motion pictures were not just influential, they also could be effectively used for specific instructional purposes, which was itself a significant victory in a long-fought battle.

Toward a "Visual" Education: The Long Justification Period

In the very first issue of *Visual Education*, a survey of students and teachers in Evanston, Illinois, produced the following commentary on motion picture use in the classroom:

---

[30] Burgess, "Motion Pictures in the Public Schools," 679.

[31] "Foreword," *1000 and One* (Chicago: Educational Screen, 1924), 8.

[32] Charles F. Hoban Jr., *Focus on Learning: Motion Pictures in the School* (Washington, DC: American Council on Education, 1942), 9.

[33] Mary Losey, *Films for the Community in Wartime* (New York: National Board of Review, 1943), 9.

FIFTH-GRADE TEACHER: "Pictures are almost the only means many children have of gaining knowledge of the topography of a country. Few of our pupils have had the opportunity to travel, and moving pictures stimulate their interest in a subject and induce them to do more research work."

FIRST-GRADE TEACHER: "Moving pictures have brought to us things we need in our work in the way of illustrative material which it would be impossible for us all to go and see. For instance, today we had a song about geese building their nests by a reedy lake and if it hadn't been for our last movie we wouldn't have had so easy a time understanding what a reedy lake was."

STUDENT: "I think the movies have helped us a great deal. Our knowledge of the manufacture of things we see in the home is much larger. We can remember how things were made if we see them made. We can't remember so well if we read about it."

STUDENT: "Before I saw the movies here at Lincolnwood I knew almost nothing of the outside world."[34]

As these testimonies suggest, motion pictures of many stripes seemed to bring the world and its workings into the classroom, transcending time and space in a fashion that was impossible to tackle so efficiently and effectively with any other medium. Such enthusiasm was not hard to find; nor were critiques of using film in educational contexts, especially the classroom. Proponents and critics of educational motion pictures took to the printed page on a quest to justify their respective visions and anxieties. Advocates, detractors, and middle-grounders duked it out for decades over whether or not film had the ability to properly, efficiently, economically, and effectively uplift and inform the masses. Throughout much of the twentieth century, independent researchers as well as those supported by such institutions as the Carnegie Corporation, the Rockefeller Foundation, the Alfred P. Sloan Foundation, the Fund for Adult Education, or the Film Council of America, conducted hundreds of studies that sought to determine the medium's educational capabilities and liabilities.

In 1955, F. Dean McClusky, a leading figure in audiovisual education, looked back to the conceptualization of visual education "as an antidote" to "book learning." School museums, a phenomenon of the early 1900s, sought to "bring the world to the child," he said, by showing all manner of visual material. In addition to displaying physical objects, these museums incorporated photographs, slides, maps and charts, stereoscopes and 3D stereographs, magic lanterns, stereopticons, and other means of visualizing knowledge. By the early 1920s, motion picture holdings were included in this pedagogical arsenal. The

---

[34] All quotations from W. Arthur Justice, "Visual Instruction in the Public Schools of Evanston, Ill.," *Visual Education* 1 (Jan. 1920): 18–19.

visual education movement gave these films (and filmstrips) an inordinate amount of attention.[35]

Advocates of film's educational uses made claims for implementations that went well beyond obvious classroom potentialities. In the teens, John Randolph Bray's animated military-training films revolutionized the expedited teaching of such difficult subjects as map reading, dealing with indirect fire, and the effective use of artillery horses in a fashion that, one author (naively) claimed, "shuts off all arguments regarding both the relative and absolute merits of the motion picture method of teaching."[36] Teaching "Americanism," patriotism, and good citizenship to adult immigrants was, many argued, necessary to national security—and ideally suited to the cinematic medium. In the 1920s, the U.S. government, with the aid of Hollywood studios, developed plans to show "patriotic and educational films in the steerage of trans-Atlantic steamers so that the potential citizen may know something of our customs, our ideals and our backgrounds before reaching our shores."[37] William F. Russell, dean of education at the University of Iowa, argued in 1920 that "we need to have available for the unrestricted use of every city and state, every Council of Defense and Americanization committee, every patriotic meeting and class in citizenship, a series of films especially designed to supply this need."[38] Reformers claimed that films were ideal for teaching prisoners "right conduct" and the fact that "obedience to law brings comfort and happiness and disobedience to the law the contrary."[39]

Trade periodicals dealing with visual education proliferated in the 1920s. *Reel and Slide* was the first in 1918, changing its title to *Moving Picture Age* the following year, followed by a host of others such as *Educational Film Magazine, Visual Education, The Screen, The News Letter* (supported by the Payne Fund), and *Educational Screen*. These journals often had ties to the visual education organizations forming in these same years, such as the National Academy of Visual Instruction (*Moving Picture Age/Educational Screen*), the Visual Instruction Association of America, the Society for Visual Education (publishers of *Visual Education*), the

---

[35] F. Dean McClusky, "A-V 1905–1955," *Educational Screen* 34 (Apr. 1955): 160–61. "Bring the World to the Child" was the slogan of the School Museum of St. Louis, which opened in 1905. It is considered the first such museum in the United States.

[36] Charles Frederick Carter, "Speeding Military Training Films," *Educational Film Magazine* (Jan. 1919): 15.

[37] Sidney R. Kent, "The Motion Picture of To-Morrow," *Annals of the American Academy of Political and Social Sciences* 128 (Nov. 1926): 31. Kent, an executive at Famous Players–Lasky, notes that these films were supplied at no charge by the American government in conjunction with the Motion Picture Producers and Distributors of America, the Hollywood trade association formed in 1922.

[38] William F. Russell, "New Films for Teaching Americanism," *Visual Education* 1 (Apr. 1920): 16.

[39] William Horton Foster, "Why They Need the Motion Picture Most of All," *Visual Education* 2 (Mar. 1921): 24.

Table 1. Audiovisual Education Organizations and Periodicals

Organizations in the Visual Education Movement
- National Academy for Visual Instruction (1919, folded first year)
- American Educational Motion Picture Association (1919, folded first year)
- Society for Visual Education (1920–present)
- National Academy of Visual Instruction (1920–1932)*
- Visual Instruction Association of America (1922–1932)*
- National Education Association Dept. of Visual Instruction (NEA DVI) (1923–1946)

*Merged with NEA DVI in 1932; NEA Dept. of Audio-Visual Instruction (1947–1971) became Association of Educational Communications and Technology (1971–present).

Periodicals
- *Educational Film Magazine* (1919–1922)
- *The Screen* (1920–1922, "for business, school and church")
- *Reel and Slide* (1918–1919)
    changed title to *Moving Picture Age* (1920–1922, National Academy of Visual Instruction)
    changed title to *The Educational Screen* (1922–1956)
        absorbed *Visual Education* (1920–1925, Society for Visual Education)
        absorbed *Visual Instruction News* (1927–1932, University of Kansas)
            merged with *Audio-visual Guide** (1947–1956)
            to form *Educational Screen and Audio-visual Guide* (1956–1971)
            AV Guide: The Learning Media Magazine (1971–1973)

**Audio-visual Guide* (1947–56) was the ultimate title of a set of periodicals published by Educational & Recreational Guides, Inc.:
    Group Discussion Guide (1936–1941), which included joint issues with
        Photoplay Studies (1935–1940)
        Photoplay and Radio Studies (1940–1941)
        Photoplay, Radio and Newspaper Studies (1941)
    becoming *Film and Radio Discussion Guide* (1942–1945)
        and *Film and Radio Guide* (1945–1947)

- *International Review of Educational Cinematography* (1929–1934, International Educational Cinematographic Institute, League of Nations)
- *The News Letter* (1935–1971, Edgar Dale, Bureau of Educational Research, Ohio State University)
- *Audio-Visual Communication Review* (1953–1963, NEA Dept. of Audio-Visual Instruction)
    AV Communication Review (1964–1977)
    Educational Communication and Technology (1978–1988)
        merged with *Journal of Instructional Development* (1977–1988)
    Educational Technology Research and Development (1988–present)
- *Audio-Visual Instruction* (1956–1978, NEA, Dept. of Audio-Visual Instruction)
- *[Bertha] Landers Film Reviews* (1956–1989)
- *Business Screen* (1938–1977) continued as
    Business and Home TV Screen (1978–1979)
    Back Stage Magazine Supplement/Business Screen (1979–1980)
    Business Screen (1980–1982)
    Computer Pictures (1983–1995)

(continued)

Table 1. (*continued*)

- *EFLA Bulletin* (1945–1967, Educational Film Library Association)
  merged with *The Filmlist* and *Film Review Digest*
  became *Sightlines* (1967–1993)
      EFLA Bulletin (1977–1987; published between issues of *Sightlines*)
      became *AFVA Bulletin* (1988–1993, American Film and Video Association)
- *EFLA Evaluations* (1979–1987)
  became *AFVA Evaluations* (1988–1993)
- *The Film Counselor* (1947–1953, Film Council of America)
- *Film Forum Review* (1946–1949, Institute of Adult Education, Teachers College)
- *Film News* (1940–1958, American Film Center)
  Film/AV News (1958)
  Film News (1960–1981)
  Film and Video News (1984)
- *Film World: The Basic Magazine of the 16mm Industry* (1945–1951)
  Film World and AV World News Magazines (1951–1960)
  Film World and AV News Magazines (1960–1966)
- *See and Hear: Journal on Audio-Visual Learning* (1945–1953)
  combined with *Business Screen* in 1954
- *Southern Film News* (1947–1950, Southern Educational Film Production Service)
- *Teaching Tools* (1953–1960)
- *TechTrends* (1985–present, Association of Educational Communications and Technology)
- *Educational Broadcasting Review* (1967–1973, National Association of Educational Broadcasters)
  Public Telecommunications Review (1973–1980)

Bureau of Educational Research at Ohio State University (*The News Letter*), and the National Education Association's Department of Visual Instruction (which became the Department of Audio-Visual Instruction in 1946 and later the Association of Educational Communications and Technology).[40] See Table 1.

Catalogs of available educational pictures also began around 1920, serving as guidebooks for those programming nontheatrical venues. *Moving Image Age* compiled one of the first: *1001 Films: Suggestions for the Compilation of Film Programs for Americanization, Boy Scouts, Churches, Clubs [etc.]* (Chicago, 1920). When *Educational Screen* took over the publication as *1000 and One: The Blue Book of Non-Theatrical Films* in 1926, the annual catalog became an indispensable

---

[40] The Department of Visual Instruction was formed as a response to the (Charles H.) "Judd Report" of 1923, cosponsored by the Motion Picture Producers and Distributors of America and the National Education Association. See F. Dean McClusky, "Public Schools," in *Sixty Years of 16mm Film, 1923–1983: A Symposium* (Evanston, IL: Film Council of America, 1954), 46–59.

guide for users and providers of 16mm educational films, soon listing thousands of available titles. For decades regular users knew it simply as the *Blue Book*.[41]

A. P. Hollis's *Motion Pictures for Instruction* (1926) attempted this in book form, describing roughly 1,500 educational films, providing context, and presenting research findings to guide use of the material. When H. W. Wilson Company, known for its book indexes, published its first *Educational Film Catalog* (1936–1945; continued as *Educational Film Guide* through 1962), it included "a selected list of 1175 nontheatrical films, classified, annotated, and graded."[42] Manufacturers of projectors issued their own (less selective) listings, such as *Directory of Film Sources: Where To Buy, Rent and Borrow 16mm Films* (Victor Animatograph, Davenport, Iowa, 1929) and *Free Films for Schools, Clubs, CCC Camps, and Other Non-theatrical Users* (DeVry, Chicago, 1939, continued as *Free Films Source Directory*).

In 1942, the American Council of Education (ACE) and its Committee on Motion Pictures in Education published *Selected Educational Motion Pictures: An Encyclopedia,* which elevated the quality of such resources. The council put its imprimatur on five hundred 16mm films deemed the best by a panel that included teachers who had tested them in their classrooms as well as the students they taught.[43] The encyclopedia aimed to provide a better guide than previously existed by testing and designating pedagogically useful movies. Rare at the time were tomes like William H. Hartley's *Selected Films for American History and Problems* (Teachers College, 1940), which provided in-depth description and evaluation of works for a single discipline.

New organizations and publications appeared over the course of the 1930s and 40s, notably the Educational Film Library Association, which formed in 1943 and published bulletins from 1945 to 1993. Other periodicals entered the fray, most importantly the monthly *Business Screen* (1938–1976), which also published resources such as *The Index of Training Films* (1946) and *Sports, Physical Education and Recreation Film Guide* (1947). (See Table 2 for information on finding educational film and video titles.)

---

[41] The catalog changed titles as follows: *1001 Films: Suggestions for the Compilation of Film Programs for Americanization, Boy Scouts, Churches, Clubs* [etc.] (1920); *1000 and One: The Blue Book of Non-Theatrical films* (1926–1948); *Blue Book of 16mm Films* (1949–1953); *Blue Book of Audio-Visual Materials: Films, Filmstrips, Slides, Recordings* (1954); and *Blue Book of Audio-Visual Materials* (1955–1964).

[42] Dorothy E. Cook and Eva Cotter Rahbek-Smith, *Educational Film Catalog* (New York: H. W. Wilson, 1936), v. The book excluded films available only on flammable nitrate stock. *Motion Pictures for Instruction* had a precursor in A. P. Hollis and R. A. Corbett, *Free Slides, Films, Charts, and Photographs for Schools, Clubs and Extension Workers* (Fargo: North Dakota Agricultural College, 1919).

[43] *Selected Educational Motion Pictures: A Descriptive Encyclopedia* (Washington, DC: American Council on Education, 1942).

Table 2. Finding Educational Film and Video Titles
When the first two major guides—*Educational Film Catalog/Guide* (H. W. Wilson, 1936–1962) and *Educational Screen's* annual *Blue Book* (1926–1964)—ceased publication, two other entities led the field for the rest of the century.
A longtime publisher of authoritative bibliographic volumes, R. R. Bowker issued several filmographic resources, beginning with the *North American Film and Video Directory* (1976). Its *Educational Film Locator* (1978) went through four editions, the last entitled *Educational Film and Video Locator of the Consortium of College and University Media Centers* [CCUMC] and *R. R. Bowker* (1990). The CCUMC also issued a CD-ROM, *Precision One MediaSource* (Brodart Co., 1995), with similar listings of educational film and video titles. Other CD-ROM resources include *Bowker's Complete Video Directory on Disc* (1999, covering "educational, instructional, and documentary films") and *Bowker's Audio & Video Database* (2000).
The other major English-language publisher of educational media locators is the National Information Center for Educational Media (NICEM). Glenn McMurry assembled its first *Index to 16mm Educational Films* (McGraw-Hill, 1967), which ran nearly a thousand pages. The University of Southern California (USC) created the center in 1967, an outgrowth of nine years of research into automated cataloging systems. Director of the USC Film Distribution Division, McMurry used educational film catalog entries as the basis for a computer database that grew to 20,000 titles by the time NICEM began. Bowker and others published subsequent editions of the NICEM *Index to 16mm Educational Films* until 1984, when USC sold the database to a commercial firm, Access Innovations. With the ability to sort records and print computer-generated lists, in 1969 NICEM and Bowker published separate indexes to 16mm film, 35mm filmstrips, and 8mm film cartridges, as well as educational audiotapes and even overhead transparencies. The NICEM *Index to Educational Videotapes* appeared in print six times (1971–1985) before the *Film and Video Finder* (1987–1997) combined the two formats. The regularly updated content next appeared in 1989 as *A-V Online*, with CD-ROM and online access. As of 2011, NICEM reports that it indexes nearly a half-million nonprint items. However, access to the *Film and Video Finder Online* (nicem.com) is by paid subscription only. All of these indexes provide titles, dates, producers, running times, subject categories, and abstracts for each entry, as well as directories of production and distribution companies.
Many other educational motion picture catalogs were circulated throughout the twentieth century, peaking in the 1970s. Researchers will find printed catalogs from the major university film distribution hubs and extension services (Indiana University, Penn State, University of Wisconsin, New York University, USC, et al.) and smaller institutions. A few idiosyncratic books, such as Salvatore J. Parlato's *Superfilms: An International Guide to Award-Winning Educational Films* (Scarecrow, 1976), provide focused perspectives. The series of *Footage* sourcebooks are also valuable aids: Richard Prelinger and Celeste R. Hoffnar, *Footage 89: North American Film and Video Sources* (Prelinger Associates, 1989); Richard Prelinger, Cyndy Turnage, and Peter Kors, *Footage 91: North American Film and Video Sources* (Prelinger Associates, 1991); and *Footage: The Worldwide Moving Image Sourcebook* (Second Line Search, 1997).

The long justification period for educational film use, however, first escalated in the 1920s, when visual education was being pitched as essential to the modernization of America. Indeed, the modernization of education was intimately tied to national improvement, innovation, and health. Several arguments came into focus in the 1920s and recur throughout the following decades regarding film's educational prowess. Many argued that film would uplift the medium and industry as a whole, elevating patrons' expectations and forcing producers to enrich the content of movies across the board. Early advocacy writings often focused on the efficacy of the eye as a perceptive organ in an effort to prove the motion picture's superiority. As the first issue of *Visual Education* explained, "It is a matter of common experience that we learn more rapidly and retain longer when our learning is based upon first-hand contacts with materials and processes. . . . The eye, through which knowledge comes to us, is second to no other one of the senses."[44] Not only, this argument went, does the motion picture present material in a more learnable way but it also conveys information more economically, staying with the spectator for a longer period of time.

Retention went alongside the belief that motion picture images were more convincing and "real" than other visual aids or teaching methods. With microscopic cinematography, students could witness a world inaccessible to the unassisted eye; events could also be compressed from days to minutes onscreen. As one self-taught medical film producer, Dr. Joseph Franklin Montague, explained, he could depict the dissection of a human body in just over an hour on film, though the process of dissection itself takes "months of careful work." Students who might otherwise be crammed into a medical theater, trying to catch a glimpse of a "malodorous cadaver," could instead appreciate the whole process—and even repeat aspects that might have been difficult to understand—"from the seat of a comfortable chair in the lecture hall."[45]

In addition to this capacity for capturing distant happenings and compressing time, Director of the Lincoln School of Teachers College at Columbia University Otis Caldwell argued in 1922 that film was stimulating to its spectators, increasing interest and inspiring additional reading on virtually any subject it depicted, a sentiment echoed throughout the advocacy literature.[46] Although teacher guidance was needed to ensure that film was not making students passive about the learning process, it was widely agreed that film could encourage active learning and foster enthusiastic audience reactions. Film's economy—its alleged ability to teach not only more effectively but also more quickly—also reverberated in the literature. "If a truthful and characteristic motion picture film were available," wrote Harvard professor of physiography Wallace W. Atwood in 1920, "it would teach more in a few minutes than any other illustrative material."[47]

---

[44] "Why the Society for Visual Education?" *Visual Education* 1 (Jan. 1920): 7.

[45] Joseph Franklin Montague, "What Motion Pictures Can Do for Medical Education," *Annals of the American Academy of Political and Social Science* 128 (Nov. 1926): 140.

[46] Otis W. Caldwell, "The Need of Experimental Investigation of Visual Instruction," *Visual Education* 1 (Jan. 1920): 11.

[47] Wallace W. Atwood, "First Steps in the Study of Geography," *Visual Education* 1 (Jan. 1920): 23. In 1920, Atwood left Harvard to become president of Clark University. In 1932, the newly formed International Film Foundation announced Atwood as its president. The foundation was to be an independent "centralized producing and distributing organization for educational films." However, it was never heard from again after releasing, in conjunction with Fox Film Corp., *The Cry of the World* (1932). Editor Louis de Rochemont compiled excerpts from Fox Movietone newsreels into a themeless chronology of world events, and Fox donated the nontheatrical rights to the foundation. "Most of the personnel of I. F. F., including President Atwood," *Time* reported, "were previously connected with the visual education department of Fox

Although this efficiency claim would later be refuted by respected educational researchers, it was one of the assets touted by early advocates and especially by those who sought to convince school administrators of film's fiscal worth.

Pontificating about the amazing nature of film as an educational tool was one thing, but pundits figured out quickly that this would not suffice to persuade the doubtful to implement educational film usage, especially from a financial point of view. Scientific methods would be required to effect the mass modernization of educational methods through film use, hence the beginning of a series of experiments—some more methodologically sound than others—that were regularly reported starting in the early 1920s.[48] In 1919, one author could easily complain that "the exponent of motion pictures has little evidence upon which to base his claims, for experimental data on this subject are practically non-existent"; within a decade, there would be a plethora of data sets with which to make claims either for or against film's educational capacities.[49] Considering motion pictures alongside photographs, lantern slides, museums, stereoscopes, maps, graphs, and excursions, researchers tried to ascertain how film compared with other pedagogical methods.

While some studies, such as *Motion Pictures in History Teaching* (1928), which reported on the effectiveness of the pioneering Yale Chronicles of America Photoplays, found significant gains (around 20 percent) for students instructed by film, some of the highest-profile studies to come out about instructional motion picture use did not wholeheartedly endorse the widespread use of film.[50] In 1924, University of Chicago educational psychologist Frank Freeman compiled thirteen studies of visual versus nonvisual methods of education. The resulting publication did not simply affirm the moving image's inherent superiority as a teaching medium. Rather, the studies in the volume

---

which, after spending $300,000 on educational films in the last two years, has ceased to function." "New Group to Issue Its First Films Soon," *New York Times*, Apr. 26, 1932; "The New Pictures," *Time*, May 16, 1932. (The 1932 International Film Foundation was unrelated to the long-lived organization of the same name created by documentary filmmaker Julien Bryan in 1945.)

[48] For a thorough accounting of significant educational film research from the teens through the 1950s, see Charles F. Hoban Jr. and Edward B. Van Ormer, *Instructional Film Research 1918–1950* (1951; reprint, New York: Arno Press, 1970), especially chap. 2, "Major Film Research Programs in the United States."

[49] John V. Lacy's early study, "The Relative Value of Motion Pictures as an Educational Agency," first appeared in *Teachers' College Record* in November 1919 and is reprinted in *Visual Education* 1 (June 1920): 33+. An interesting precedent is David Sumstine's "Educational Research and Statistics: A Comparative Study of Visual Instruction in the High School," *School and Society* (Feb. 23, 1918): 235–38.

[50] Daniel C. Knowlton and J. Warren Tilton, *Motion Pictures in History Teaching* (New Haven, CT: Yale University Press, 1929), 87. The study also found appreciable gains in memory retention and in class participation among the experimental (film) group.

Figure 1.2. Rockville Fair, [Maryland] 1928. (National Photo Company Collection, Library of Congress.) This prizewinning exhibit from a school fair in Rockville, Maryland, illustrates the impact of the visual education movement of the 1920s. "The Motion Picture Educates While It Entertains," reads a placard at the top-center of the bulletin board; beneath it is the inscription, "Preserving Historical Motion Pictures for Posterity," illustrated with newsreel images. "The Motion Picture Makes Scenes from All Lands Familiar," reads another (right), hanging above stills from *Chang* (1927, filmed in Siam). Some images are from science films, but most are stills from Hollywood features from 1916 to 1928: *The Ten Commandments, The King of Kings, Moana, The Big Parade, The Mystic, The Amateur Gentleman, Les Miserables, Bardelys the Magnificent, Ben-Hur*, and *The Blue Boy*; there is also one of soprano Anna Case recording for the Vitaphone in 1926. The screen device (right) is probably an opaque projector.

provide mixed and even unfavorable results in terms of film's efficacy not only in the classroom but also in other instructional contexts: "The results of the experiments reported in this monograph give color to the opinion that mere presentation by motion pictures is not of itself of any advantage." Freeman's conclusions are tempering in nature, trying to bring scientific observation to bear on a subject that was causing palpable excitement in the educational community. Taking a step back from the rush to educate with the eyes, Freeman reports on the significant expense of visual education as well as on the tendency of proponents of film use to hyperbolize the medium's pedagogical potential: "We are told that it will in whole or in part displace the teacher or the textbook, that it will speed up education tenfold, that it will make education absorbingly interesting and thoroughly permanent." Indeed, these claims were repeated ad infinitum in the literature of the period.

Educational psychologist H. Y. McClusky's study of the content of educational motion pictures, reported in Freeman's compendium, concludes that given the "difficulties and the expense attendant upon the production, distribution, and projection of educational motion pictures that their contents should be limited to subject matter which cannot as well be presented in any other way." Not only, Freeman concludes, are there advantages to using still pictures in certain instructional situations ("it permits analysis" and "provides the opportunity for a more active study attitude on the part of the pupil"), but there are certain circumstances (such as teaching science) in which films are notably inferior to other methods, such as demonstration by the teacher. Freeman also concludes that films do not necessarily stimulate student interest more than other teaching techniques, tackling one of the prevailing claims to the medium's superiority.[51]

In a two-year study sponsored by Eastman Kodak, Frank Freeman teamed with Ben Wood, director of Columbia University's Bureau of Educational Research, to assess "the value of motion pictures as supplementary aids in regular classroom instruction." The study grew out of George Eastman's 1926 announcement that a Kodak survey of teaching films concluded that not enough films for classroom use had been produced; that the expense of classroom film use was prohibitive; and that the value of film as a teaching aid had not yet been adequately established for school authorities to make the expenditures needed for effective motion picture use in the classroom. Eastman Kodak agreed not to rent or sell films or projection equipment to schools during the period of the experiment but it provided the films and funding for the project. Clearly, this seriously limited the scope of the study even as it enabled it to transpire under more controlled conditions than Freeman's earlier experiments.

Working with directors of visual education in twelve cities, Freeman and Wood used experimental and control groups of teachers to carry out the ambitious investigation, which involved "nearly 11,000 children in more than three hundred Geography and General Science classes, taught by nearly two hundred teachers, in grades four to nine . . . in twelve cities." Unlike Freeman's previous study, in this experiment all of the films were intentionally made for classroom utilization. These productions constituted a collection known as Eastman Teaching Films (or, later, Eastman Classroom Films), which soon became widely adopted. The films made minimal use of intertitles, avoided

---

[51] Frank N. Freeman, ed., *Visual Education: A Comparative Study of Motion Pictures and Other Methods of Instruction* (Chicago: University of Chicago Press, 1924), 63; 3–4; 64; 76. The studies were conducted in fourth-to-eighth-grade schools involving 649 children in Illinois (Evanston, Urbana, Oak Park, Joliet, and Chicago), as well as in Detroit and Cleveland (ibid., 88).

storytelling, and abstained from "pedagogical tasks which can be better accomplished by other media of instruction." Not unlike Freeman's earlier study, this one concluded that teaching films should never be conceived of as a substitute for teachers. This time around, Freeman's study did not deliver the same mixed results as the prior study, leading the authors to conclude that "the demonstrated contributions amply justify the extensive use of films of this type in our schools." Students taught by film were found to excel in "questions of fact," and also demonstrated "superiority" in "explanatory and conceptual test items."[52]

Though these studies are far from whole-hearted endorsements, most were more concerned about film's potential detrimental effects on its spectators. Writing in the *International Journal of Ethics* in 1923, Joseph Roy Geiger expressed an oft-repeated concern about film's imposition of passivity on its spectator, which discouraged creativity and self-expression; he also noted other common concerns of the time regarding eyestrain and the time moviegoing might take away from healthier outdoor activities.[53]

In the 1930s, studies sought to grapple with sound film usage and the ongoing need to improve implementation. The American Council on Education published a series of studies in the late 1930s, which evolved out of earlier support from the Payne Fund, to assess the status of film in the classroom. The Educational Motion Picture Project involved major educational film commentators Edgar Dale, Frank Freeman, and Charles Hoban Jr. Noting the difficulties still impeding educational film use, the ACE called for a single agency to provide information to "schools and universities, producers and distributors, administrators and teachers," an unheeded call that would be made by many others through the 1950s.[54]

In the 1940s, experiments "to see if classes taught with films did better than those taught with the usual methods" were largely a thing of the past. According to Dale, "Fifty such experiments (of varying scientific exactitude) offered the almost unanimous conclusion that films conveyed information in ten to twenty percent less time than usually required by other methods."[55] In the war and postwar eras, "effective use" would be the mantra of advocates, administrators, and teachers, in both school and other educational contexts, including the military (see fig. 1.3). Extensive film use in all of the branches of the military made film's educational capacities seem virtually irrefutable. The U.S. Navy's "six reasons for using instructional films as training aids" summed up the justifications of

---

[52] Ben D. Wood and Frank N. Freeman, *Motion Pictures in the Classroom* (Boston: Houghton Mifflin, 1929), xviii, 210, 4, 36, 228.

[53] Joseph Roy Geiger, "The Effects of the Motion Picture on the Mind and Morals of the Young," *International Journal of Ethics* 34 (Oct. 1923): 72–73.

[54] *The Motion Picture in Education: Its Status and Its Needs* (Washington, DC: American Council on Education, 1937), 4.

[55] Edgar Dale, "The Real Film Problem," *The News Letter* 10 (Dec. 1944): 1.

The chart has been used successfully with many groups of Navy instructors. It has resulted in better understanding of the three phases of using instructional materials: PREPARATION, PRESENTATION, and FOLLOW-UP. Actually, its lesson is not limited to training films, but has application to all situations in which instructional materials are used. Good teachers recognize that, to increase the effectiveness of instructional materials, it is necessary to "Plan Your Instructional Hour Wisely."

Figure 1.3. Lessons learned during World War II filtered into civilian culture. Teachers were taught optimal usage of audiovisual materials. In the first panel, a uniformed navy officer previews "Points to Look For" during a film. Second (bottom), a projector screens *United States Navy Training Film 13650*. Last comes a summarization chart, discussion, and test. W. H. Durr, "Promoting Better Film Utilization," *See and Hear* (December 1945): 32.

prior decades, only now they were assumptions: "(1) to learn more, (2) to remember longer, (3) to increase interest, (4) to make training uniform, (5) to build morale, and (6) to save time."[56] So invested was the military in training films that the U.S. Navy produced the meta-film *Film Tactics* (1945), an instructional film to teach naval officers how to present films effectively in the training of sailors. (*Film Tactics* begins from the point-of-view of a trainee who falls asleep during a screening; we then see his dream-self standing inside his own head, looking out through his own eye sockets, watching himself watch the classroom film!)

Though much of the wartime and postwar rhetoric remained the same— "we must revolt from the authoritarian, rote, thoughtless drill, textbook-worshipping methods"—the fact of film's role in any educational scenario no longer seemed disputable; rather, it had become almost entirely uncontroversial.[57] Justification was, at long last, a thing of the past. This is not to say that criticisms of using movies—those entertainment-heavy tools that induced passivity—disappeared altogether. Rather, these critiques were now reduced to intermittent squawks from the sidelines, overwhelmed by the widespread sentiment that films had revolutionized the production of knowledge not only for school children but for all spectators, fostering critical thinking, curiosity, and efficient training in unparalleled ways. As Charles Hoban Jr. put it in 1941, "There is no longer any question whether motion pictures should be used in school. . . . The more fundamental question is how they should be used to obtain the best results."[58]

Helping Teachers Teach

> The essence of good teaching is the vivid and unmistakable presentation of ideas; if cameras can be so manipulated as to help teachers in the hard climb up the laborious steep, may God speed the operators in their enterprise, endowing them with wisdom to know that no easy substitute can be contrived for all the hard work, giving them skill to cheer us all along the difficult road.
> —*C. H. Ward, high school English teacher, inaugural edition of* Visual Education, *1920*

The great refrain on film's educational use was that it should not and would not replace the human role in facilitating knowledge. "A motion picture may supplement the sermon," wrote Edward M. McConoughey in 1916, "but can never take

---

[56] George H. Fern and Eldon Robbins, *Teaching with Films* (Milwaukee: Bruce Publishing, 1946), 5.

[57] Edgar Dale, "The Real Film Problem," *The News Letter* 10 (Dec. 1944): 1.

[58] Hoban, *Focus on Learning*, 21.

its place."[59] Freeman's 1924 omnibus repeated this sentiment: "The superiority of the [live] demonstration over the film seems to indicate that there is a distinct advantage in the actual personal presence of the instructor." Freeman takes pains to reaffirm the value of teachers as the primary conduits of information, cautioning that long classroom films are problematic because "they take over the rightful function of the teacher," whereas shorter films allow teachers to utilize the media to fit their own lessons.[60]

The need to defend the teacher emerged at least in part due to predictions about the motion picture's potential to dramatically reorder the world of education. The age of mechanization generated concerns about people being replaced by machines, and anxieties about projectors taking over the classroom were expressed publicly. Thomas Edison's prediction that moving pictures would replace books was repeated and refuted for more than thirty years across the body of academic and popular literature.[61] By the 1940s, the sentiment most often echoed was that proper and effective film use was even more demanding for teachers than other more rudimentary visual aids and that films could never threaten the primacy of books in an educational setting, which was quite a reversal from the dominant thinking in the first decades of the twentieth century.[62]

Teachers clearly needed, however, to be taught how to use films. Don Carlos Ellis and Laura Thornborough's *Motion Pictures in Education: A Practical Handbook for Users of Visual Aids* (1923) was an early response to that need.[63] Many complained that teachers showed films but did not actually teach with them. While it may seem obvious to us now, it was commonplace for teachers to be advised that they should see films before they showed them in their classes, an act that was difficult in a school system utilizing a film rental system that made previewing films all but impossible (see fig. 1.4). For this reason, advocates in the early 1920s strongly advised that schools or school systems appoint a director of visual instruction who could arrange advance screenings or provide detailed information

---

[59] McConoughey, *Motion Pictures in Religious and Educational Work with Practical Suggestions for Their Use* (New York: Federal Council of the Churches of Christ in America, 1916), 14.

[60] Freeman, *Visual Education*, 50, 80.

[61] See, for example, Ward, "Fact of 1925," 35–36; George H. Fern and Eldon Robbins, *Teaching with Films* (Milwaukee: Bruce Publishing, 1946); Nelson L. Greene, "Motion Pictures in the Classroom," *Annals of the American Academy of Political Social Science* 128 (Nov. 1926): 122. Even radical behavioral psychologist B. F. Skinner (although he did not write about film or video per se) maintained that human teachers would always need to guide the use of "teaching machines." *The Technology of Teaching* (New York: Appleton-Century-Crofts, 1968).

[62] See, for example, Gerald McDonald, *Educational Motion Pictures and Libraries* (Chicago: American Library Association, 1942), 12.

[63] Don Carlos Ellis and Laura Thornborough, *Motion Pictures in Education: A Practical Handbook for Users of Visual Aids* (New York: Thomas Y. Crowell, 1923).

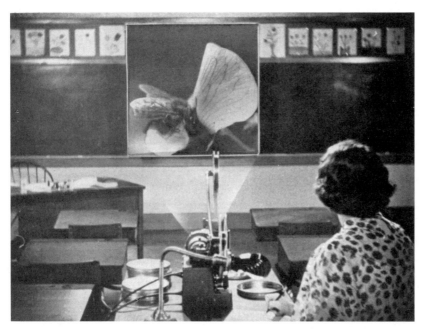

Figure 1.4. By the 1930s, proponents of visual education urged teachers to preview films, both to gauge their effectiveness and to plan for their integration in lessons. M. R. Brunstetter, *How to Use the Educational Sound Film* (University of Chicago Press, 1937), 13.

to teachers, a position that would be standard in urban school districts by the 1950s. Furthermore, they advised teachers to use pictures in a fashion that subordinated the medium to the curricula and textbooks. Teachers were also counseled to edit out less relevant material from commercially made films, tailoring reels to fit their individual classroom plans.[64] Some school districts were able to work with "jobbers" who were "willing to cut and combine one or two reels into one to suit our needs, thus frequently making one very good reel out of two doubtful ones," real do-it-yourself work in an era of uncertain film dependability.[65]

Other ways that educators were trained included free summer institutes, such as that sponsored by DeVry Corp., the Chicago manufacturer of projectors. Its 1925 schedule listed sessions on using the portable projector in industry, projecting in places of worship, demonstrations on projector operation, teaching lessons, merchandising, and the International Harvester Company's use of motion pictures.[66] By the early 1920s it was commonplace for "teachers' leaflets" to be included with film purchases, and later years would witness differently pitched

---

[64] Hollis, *Motion Pictures for Instruction*, 16ff.

[65] Clarence E. Howell, "First Experiences with Portable Motion-Picture Projectors," *Elementary School Journal* 27 (Oct. 1926): 107.

[66] Hollis, *Motion Pictures for Instruction,* 237–39.

study guides for students as well. These provided, according to A. P. Hollis, "additional facts concerning the topics in the reels, and suggestions for teaching" and became increasingly sophisticated—with discussion questions, activities, and contextualizing information—in the decades to come.[67]

Teacher training for handling film prints became a serious enterprise. Pennsylvania and New Jersey required a laboratory course in motion picture instruction for teacher certification by the late 1930s, at which point around one hundred teacher-training institutions offered similar courses.[68] The first annual conference on Motion Pictures and Education was held in 1935 at the University of Illinois, with 150 in attendance. The ACE's Educational Motion Picture Project developed conferences and courses on the subject, producing a handbook, Edgar Dale and Lloyd Ramseyer's *Teaching with Motion Pictures* (1937).[69] The book began life as a mimeographed manuscript, circulated among and critiqued by experts in visual education. Among other things, it provided administrators with ammunition to take to their school boards when arguing for funds.

As Dale and Ramseyer observed, teaching with film was no easy task. Not only was it important for teachers to screen and understand films in advance of using them, but implementation was key to the lesson's effectiveness. Teachers were faced with numerous decisions: for example, if a film should precede or follow a lesson, if it should be stopped for discussion or played through, or how many times it should be screened.[70] Since a consideration of such issues had to be repeated with each film a teacher wanted to use, it became clear that teachers were in need of guidance regardless of their level of experience. Furthermore, because films are such dense, material-rich texts, it was especially important— Dale and Ramseyer argued—for teachers to have a strategy for approaching selective aspects of any film they showed based upon intimate knowledge of both the film and their audience's capabilities.

To meet these informational needs, organizations published a proliferation of catalogs in the middle part of the century, including the H. W. Wilson *Educational Film Guides*, the *Blue Book* series, and the longstanding *Educators Guide to Free Films*, which first appeared in 1941 (and is still in publication as of 2011!).[71]

---

[67] Ibid., 10.

[68] *The Motion Picture in Education*, 3. According to Paul Saettler, in 1914, the Educational Motion Pictures Bureau "was the first producing company to issue teaching syllabi with their educational films." Saettler, *Evolution of American Educational Technology*, 97.

[69] *The News Letter* 1 (Nov. 1935): 2, 11.

[70] Edgar Dale and Lloyd Ramseyer, *Teaching with Motion Pictures* (Washington, DC: American Council on Education, 1937), 41.

[71] *Educators Guide to Free Films* (Randolph, WI: Educators Progress Service, 1941–present). A professor of education at the University of Wisconsin, John Guy Fowlkes, began publishing *Educators Index of Free Materials* in 1937.

Additionally, thousands of directories and catalogs were issued by agencies of the federal and state governments, as well as nonprofit organizations, such as *U.S. Government Films for Public Educational Use* (1955–1964); *Library of Motion Pictures: Films Available for Schools, Clubs, Industry, Free from Your State Savings Bonds Office* (1968); and *National Directory of Safety Films* (National Safety Council, 1943, 1973).[72]

As noted earlier, the events of World War II brought not only respectability to the educational motion picture but also a testing ground for efficacy. After the war the lessons learned by military instructors were passed along to school teachers. There was a new emphasis on teacher involvement in screenings, especially providing engaging introductions, appropriate stops during screenings, and rigorous discussions. Concerns about ballooning classroom sizes bolstered the call to perfect motion picture use in the classroom.[73]

Perhaps the greatest help on the educational film front came in the form of financial assistance. National legislation—most importantly the National Defense of Education Act of 1958 and the Elementary and Secondary Education Act of 1965—provided federal dollars to support equipment and 16mm print purchases (among other things) for American classrooms. In turn, these acts stimulated production and the proliferation of new film-producing organizations, which could better anticipate sales volume because of increased school purchasing power. The late 1950s and 60s saw a burst in educational filmmaking activity, with scholarly consultants almost always credited onscreen as a testament to producer attempts at making high-quality, appropriate films on an array of specialized subjects, all aimed at facilitating classroom use. Even the social guidance film *Dating Do's and Don'ts* (Coronet, 1949, a camp classic since at least the 1970s), begins by citing its consultant, Dr. Reuben Hill, "Research Professor of Family Life, University of North Carolina."

---

[72] In the 1970s complaints still circulated about the faulty nature of educational film reference works. J. Williams Youngs Jr. claimed that the numerous indexes of educational films were relatively useless lists. He referred to works such as Westinghouse's *Learning Directory* ("a comprehensive guide to instructional materials in all media," 1970–1973), *Index to 16mm Educational Films* (1967–1980), and *Index of Educational Videotapes* (1971–1982). The diligent teacher would, he explained, have to search out reviews in sources like *Media and Methods*, journal of the American Society of Educators, 1969–2006, *Film Review Digest*, or *Landers Film Reviews*. J. William Youngs Jr., "Educational Films and the Historian," *History Teacher* 8 (Aug. 1975): 589. Other such postwar resources included the Institute of Inter-American Affairs' *Catalog of Educational Films* (1949) and the U.S. National Commission for UNESCO Panel on Educational Films report, *United States Educational, Scientific and Cultural Motion Pictures Suitable and Available for Use Abroad* (1950).

[73] For more on this see Robert Wagner, "Design in the Educational Film," *Educational Research Bulletin* 33 (Sept. 15, 1954): 141–48.

Fig. 32. The follow-up discussion after the showing of the film provides an opportunity to clinch key points and correct misconceptions.

Figure 1.5. Pedagogical books and essays sought to teach the teacher how best to use motion pictures in the classroom. Photograph from George H. Fern and Eldon Robbins's *Teaching with Films* (Bruce Publishing, 1946), 96.

Producing "Practical Films"

> We are using slides and motion pictures extensively in our school work. We are awaiting very anxiously the coming of actual text-book work in this line. Why are school folks so slow in recognizing this wonderful opportunity for using the most susceptible of the five senses?
> —*A. J. Stoddard, school superintendent, Beatrice, Nebraska, 1920*[74]

By the 1910s, rather than accepting theatrical leftovers, advocates were calling for higher quality classroom films. A lack of viable productions threatened to stymie film education. Early on, some bragged of the proliferating availability—though not necessarily the elevated quality—of educational films, as *Moving Picture World* did in 1911 when it noted the recent publication of a catalog with "upward of perhaps three thousand different subjects . . . prepared solely for the mental uplift and betterment of society" covering "history, geography, botany, travel, entomology and ethnology," not to mention "the latest advances made in the fields of surgery, pathology, biology, and bacteriology . . . zoology, ornithology, geology, microscopy, aeronautics, mineralogy, metallurgy, and the science of naval and military warfare."[75]

---

[74] "What School Superintendents Think," *Visual Education* 1 (Sept.–Oct. 1920): 20.

[75] "The Educational Field," *Moving Picture World*, Jan. 21, 1911, 129. The author is likely referring to Kleine's *Catalogue of Educational Motion Pictures* (1910).

From such plenitude one might infer that all the film education movement needed was willing exhibitors and a captive audience. Quantity might be one thing, but quality or suitability was another. Many producers were repackaging their theatrical films and rebranding them as "educational." Major feature production companies, wrote A. P. Hollis, "who alone have the technical equipment and capital necessary for quality film production have shown no inclination to produce purely educational films."[76] Writing from the perspective of the church in 1916, Edward M. McConoughey propounded that:

> Too much stress cannot be laid upon the importance of first-class films. It is a mistake to show in churches films that have already been discarded by photo-play houses. For everybody will recognize the pictures except the few who refuse to go to see the "movies." Too many religious organizations use films, scratched and torn, because they are cheap, or use photographs worn indistinct and those in which the story suddenly jumps, because whole sections of the wornout film have been cut out.[77]

By the early 1920s, some companies were catering "to the church screen and producing adequate material of the highest grade."[78] But for many fledgling educational film exhibitors, repurposed theatrical films were the most affordable entrees into nontheatrical film use. In 1916, General Film Co. (where Katherine Carter, an ex-schoolteacher, headed the educational division before leaving in 1914 to start her own educational film business[79]), Universal, Edison, Paramount, Pathé, Kleine, Gaumont, Éclair, Hepworth American, and Mutual Film all boasted what McConoughey called "so-called educational films" in their catalogs.[80]

Following Eastman Kodak's introduction of 16mm safety film in 1923, the range of film topics, as well as the companies producing and distributing them, expanded significantly, but not to the point of solving problems of quality and scarcity. A school, for example, could invest valuable resources in outfitting themselves with the proper equipment "only to find endless difficulty in securing material worth projecting," a *Visual Education* editorial ran, because "the chief thing obtainable from commercial companies' lists of 'educationals' is fond hope and keen disappointment."[81] In 1920, *Visual Education* reported

---

[76] Hollis, *Motion Pictures for Instruction*, 220.

[77] McConoughey, *Motion Pictures in Religious and Educational Work*, 14.

[78] William S. Mitchell, "How to Use Motion Pictures in the Pulpit," *Visual Education* 2 (Oct. 1921): 5.

[79] "The Picture in Education," *Moving Picture World*, Apr. 11, 1914, 200.

[80] McConoughey, *Motion Pictures in Religious and Educational Work*, 37.

[81] Nelson Greene, "Editorial," *Visual Education* 1 (Apr. 1920): 5.

that it had "numerous inquiries from schools having projectors which are forced to stand idle for lack of usable materials," a truly unforgivable situation given the significant expense involved. Furthermore, they warned the users of their "Film Field" exchange guide about the "present chaotic and discouraging situation" of procuring films for educational purposes:

> Constant disappointment must be expected. Often the nearest exchange will not have a print in stock; or the film will be out and unavailable on the date it is needed; or the film will be worn and in bad condition; or the price will be hopelessly high; or the shipment will go astray; or slight attention will be paid to your communication; etc., etc.[82]

Clearly one impediment to film supply was the limited profitability of producing nontheatrical films, which would never be able to achieve anything like theatrical grosses. As May Ayres Burgess observed in 1923, an educational film producer could spend thousands of dollars on a series of films about a specific subject that would then realistically be marketable for one grade level in one subject area, a serious fiscal deterrent for any business. Furthermore, making certain kinds of educational films might involve weeks of difficult photography ("to show a toad shedding his skin depends . . . on the ability of the producer to secure the co-operation of the toad") to yield images that may last only seconds on the screen.[83] Because some films—like health education pictures—carried with them the expectation that they would be available at no charge for the "public good," production had to be subsidized by a philanthropic or governmental agency willing to foot the bill. Writing in 1926, Andrew Phillip Hollis observed that "attempts made by educators or those interested in the educational film to produce classroom films for serious study purposes have practically all ended in financial loss, or at best in profits too modest to break any comparison with theatrical producers."[84] However, Hollis also optimistically contended that the "vast non-theatrical market" could be "40 times the size of the theatrical market when it gets the projectors."[85] For the time being, however, an individual educational film was highly unlikely to yield significant profit.

Given these difficulties it is not surprising that sponsored films—productions subsidized by a company, agency, institution, or organization—had a place in visual education. As the 1924 edition of *1000 and One* justified their inclusion

---

[82] "The Film Field," *Visual Education* 1 (Sept.–Oct. 1920): 49.

[83] Burgess, "Motion Pictures in the Public Schools," 677, 681.

[84] Hollis, *Motion Pictures for Instruction*, 222.

[85] Ibid., 231.

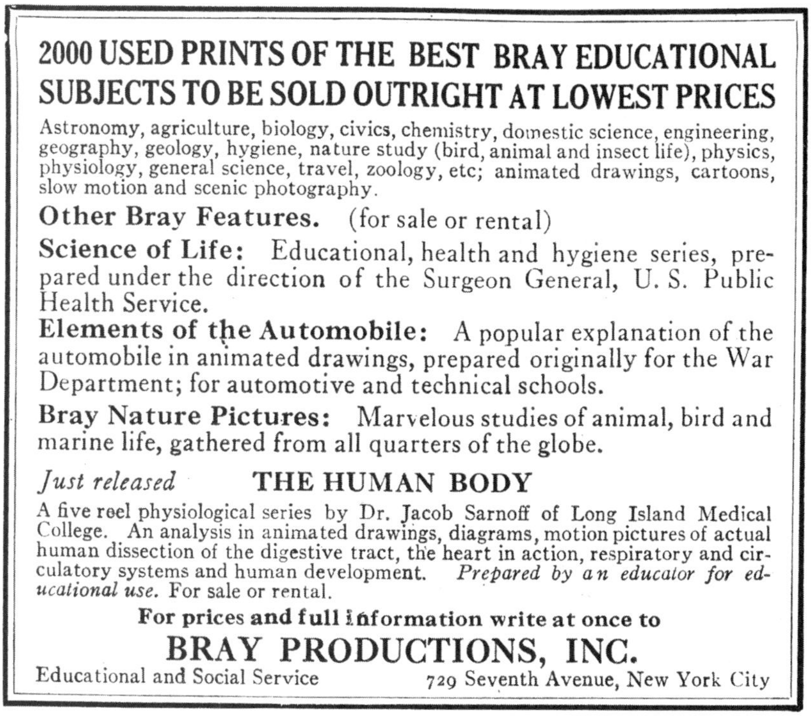

2000 USED PRINTS OF THE BEST BRAY EDUCATIONAL SUBJECTS TO BE SOLD OUTRIGHT AT LOWEST PRICES

Astronomy, agriculture, biology, civics, chemistry, domestic science, engineering, geography, geology, hygiene, nature study (bird, animal and insect life), physics, physiology, general science, travel, zoology, etc; animated drawings, cartoons, slow motion and scenic photography.

Other Bray Features. (for sale or rental)

Science of Life: Educational, health and hygiene series, prepared under the direction of the Surgeon General, U. S. Public Health Service.

Elements of the Automobile: A popular explanation of the automobile in animated drawings, prepared originally for the War Department; for automotive and technical schools.

Bray Nature Pictures: Marvelous studies of animal, bird and marine life, gathered from all quarters of the globe.

Just released **THE HUMAN BODY**

A five reel physiological series by Dr. Jacob Sarnoff of Long Island Medical College. An analysis in animated drawings, diagrams, motion pictures of actual human dissection of the digestive tract, the heart in action, respiratory and circulatory systems and human development. *Prepared by an educator for educational use.* For sale or rental.

For prices and full information write at once to

BRAY PRODUCTIONS, INC.

Educational and Social Service   729 Seventh Avenue, New York City

Figure 1.6. This Bray Company advertisement sells "used prints" while renting out newer ones. Note the boast that *The Human Body* (1925) was *"Prepared by an educator for educational use,"* a marketing tactic that spoke to critiques that educational film producers were not properly preparing films in consultation with professional advisers. *1000 and One*, 4th ed. (June 1926), 6.

within their pages, industrial films "have considerable educational value . . . [and] . . . being 'free' films, they frequently enable a school or community with modest resources to complete a program of film showing which would be impossible if rental had to be paid on all the reels shown."[86] In 1936, *Educational Film Catalog* included "some films made for advertising purposes . . . when the votes of our collaborators indicated they were useful for classroom work. Those preferring not to use such films will be able to recognize them by the producer's name."[87] Although these might be less than stellar arguments from an ideological perspective, they point out the ways that educators sought to fill the significant gaps created by a lack of material. Some pundits argued that any commercial interest should be kept out of the classroom. Administrators reported not using industrial films because "there was too much advertising matter and propaganda in

---

[86] "Foreword," *1000 and One: The Blue Book of Non-Theatrical Films for 1924* (Chicago: Educational Screen, 1924).

[87] Dorothy E. Cook and Eva Cotter Rahbek-Smith, *Educational Film Catalogue* (New York: H. W. Wilson, 1936), vi.

them."[88] However, industrial and sponsored films (made as public relations films) found their way into the classroom regularly throughout the better part of the twentieth century. As Nelson Greene, editor of the *Educational Screen*, argued in 1926, if industrial films abandoned overt direct advertising of their products, the films could "be made truly educational by proper handling by the teacher."[89] In its 1951–1952 directory, *Film World* noted 1,084 sponsors, with almost 70 percent from industry and the rest divided among educational, government, religious, medical, and social science sectors.[90]

Some corporations were establishing themselves as industrial film leaders, making quality films in consultation with educators for specific pedagogical applications. Yale University, the Harvard Film Service, and the University of Chicago were producing films (historical, psychological, scientific, and so on) in the late 1920s and 30s. In 1927, Western Electric was at the forefront of synchronous-sound motion picture technology, forming Electrical Research Products, Inc. (ERPI), a commercial concern with ties to the University of Chicago. ERPI would go on to produce short 35mm sound films until 16mm sound-on-film projectors were introduced in 1934, resulting in the final victory of 16mm over 35mm for nontheatrical use.[91] The teaching films made for Eastman's grand experiment of 1926–28 were the basis for Eastman Teaching Films, Inc., a Kodak subsidiary set up in 1928 to produce more titles and to sell prints to schools. New production continued into the mid-1930s, resulting in a collection of more than two hundred 16mm silent films. Print sales continued until 1943, when the newly formed Encyclopaedia Britannica Films acquired the Eastman Teaching Films library. Through the 1950s, Britannica added to and updated the original silent films. (See Table 3.) Hollywood concerns began considering the educational film market seriously in the 1930s in addition to marketing "theatrical productions which have educational significance."[92] As Craig Kridel's chapter in this anthology observes, the reediting of feature Hollywood films into shorter films for classroom use was just one way Hollywood entered the educational film enterprise.

Though the temptations to enter educational film production in the postwar era were greater than in earlier decades, it could still be said in 1947 that "the

---

[88] Cline M. Koon and Allen W. Noble, *National Visual Education Directory: A List by States of 8,806 School Systems, including an Inventory of Audio-Visual Equipment* (Washington, DC: American Council on Education, 1936), 10.

[89] Nelson L. Greene, "Motion Pictures in the Classroom," *Annals of the American Academy of Political and Social Science* 128 (Nov. 1926): 125.

[90] Leo Beebe, "Industry," in *Sixty Years of 16mm Film*, 93.

[91] Slide, *Before Video*, 89.

[92] *Motion Picture in Education*, 2.

Table 3. Encyclopaedia Britannica Films, Inc.

Among the many producers of classroom films, Encyclopaedia Britannica Films (EBF) was perhaps the most successful, launching its products at the beginning of the boom period for educational reels. Hundreds of schools and libraries used the company's productions, which numbered up to a thousand titles.

The film corporation's relationship to the redoubtable printed *Encyclopædia Britannica* obviously allowed it instant name recognition and authority. The encyclopedia, first published in Edinburgh in 1768, was acquired and published by American firms from 1901. In 1928, the Sears Roebuck company bought the publishing brand, selling it to advertising executive, philanthropist, and University of Chicago vice president William Benton in 1943. He maintained ownership until his death in 1973; thereafter a foundation bearing his name, run by his son Charles, managed the company until 1996.

Upon buying Encyclopaedia Britannica, Inc., Benton simultaneously created its film production/distribution subsidiary. Although unable to persuade the University of Chicago to be a full partner, he provided the financing that made it part owner. To launch Encyclopaedia Britannica Films at full strength, Benton acquired two of the most influential entities in the educational film business. From Western Electric, he bought Erpi Classroom Films, Inc., which included production facilities and a large library of films. Benton also convinced George Eastman's company to donate the Eastman Teaching Films collection to the university. Thus EBF began with a foundation of more than 500 titles. In an industry known for marginal economic status, Benton made the motion picture operation into a viable, large-scale business. He bought out the University of Chicago's share in 1952.

However, EBF was not simply built to exploit these assets. Its productions established a reputation for quality, both technical and educational. The company's success was also attributable in part to a large sales and support team that visited schools frequently.

In 1966, near the height of the boom in educational film, the company became Encyclopaedia Britannica Educational Corporation (EBEC), producing and marketing other audiovisual media for schools—filmstrips, supporting texts, and eventually video and web-based media.

Financier Jacob Safra bought the ailing corporation in 1996, creating Encyclopaedia Britannica Holding S.A. Copies of most of the original Britannica films continue to be sold on video. The stock footage company Getty Images licenses access to video clips from the library of EBF material, with more than 300 titles on-hand in complete form. Safra's holding company, however, has the original film elements in deep storage, with no known plans to access or preserve them. Meanwhile, many libraries and archives have prints available, and some of the early EB productions are now in the public domain.

Sources: "Britannica Films," *Time,* Apr. 24, 1944; "Help on Celluloid," *Time,* Apr. 29, 1957; "History of Encyclopædia Britannica," Jan. 2010, http://corporate.britannica.com. Also, Kenneth Kaye, "40th Anniversary of Encyclopædia Britannica Films and Its Predecessor Companies, 1928–1968," unpublished ms. (1968), provided by Charles Benton, who commissioned this study while president of EBEC.

production of educational films is expensive and to date has not proven generally profitable."[93] Still, the postwar era saw film production rise to almost 1,000 nontheatrical films each year, with the 1948 *Educational Film Guide* listing almost 3,800 16mm educational films, most of them produced in Chicago (see Table 4),

---

[93] Floyde E. Brooker, "Motion Pictures as an Aid to Education," *Annals of the American Academy of Political and Social Science* 254 (Nov. 1947): 105.

Table 4. Chicago: Epicenter of Educational Film

While Hollywood was in the process of becoming the motion picture capital of the country, the American educational film industry's undisputed center was emerging in the Midwest: Chicago, Illinois. The University of Chicago was partly to credit for this development, with a roster of faculty and alumni who took center stage in the educational film movement over the decades. Numerous educational film studies as well as motion picture productions came out of the University of Chicago, and its press was one of the key publishers of books on the subject.

Chicago was home to publishers of *Visual Education*, *Educational Screen*, and *Business Screen*, three of the most prominent publications in the nontheatrical field, as well as the industry bible *1001 and One: The Blue Book of Non-Theatrical Films*. Major educational film producers Electrical Research Products, Inc. (ERPI) and Encyclopaedia Britannica Films had direct ties to the University of Chicago. Coronet, producer-distributor of social guidance films par excellence, was headquartered in the city. Charles Benton's company Films, Inc. became the largest nontheatrical 16mm film distributor in the country. And at nearby Northwestern University, G. L. Freeman headed up the University College Motion Picture Project for adult education.

The producer of the first educational film catalog in 1910, George Kleine, was based in the Windy City, as were the Society for Visual Education, Educational Film Library Association, American Library Association, University Broadcasting Council, National School of Visual Education, and Film Council of America (in nearby Evanston). Projector manufacturers DeVry, Ampro, Victor Animatograph, and Bell & Howell were also Chicago-based.

In 1917, the city's school system became the first in the United States to create its own educational film library.

New York, Detroit, or Los Angeles.[94] As the market grew, producers could afford more frequent use of color and sound, elements that audiences had grown accustomed to in theatrical contexts. Businesses like General Electric and Bell Telephone utilized more training films in the postwar period, and producers like Coronet, Encyclopaedia Britannica Films, Vocational Guidance Films, Centron, and McGraw-Hill Films flourished, filling niche markets. (See fig. 1.7.) The number of 16mm film libraries in the United States grew from 897 in 1949 to 3,660 ten years later.[95]

Despite the appearance of a booming industry, in the early 1950s many complained that the anticipated postwar boom in school purchasing power had "failed to materialize." More firms were making educational films, supplying a marketplace with limited demand. Demand was limited because when a school or library purchased a print, it was typically projected until it wore out or until time proved its content irrelevant or inaccurate.[96] The U.S. State Department did open up new markets in a Cold War boom of international

---

[94] Waldron, *Information Film*, 16.

[95] Seerley Reid of the U.S. Office of Education issued government bulletins reporting on the growing number of libraries, from *A Directory of 897 16mm Film Libraries* (1949) to *A Directory of 3,660 16mm Film Libraries* (Washington, DC: GPO, 1959).

[96] See, for example, Ned L. Reglein, "The Plight of Educational Film," *Hollywood Quarterly* 4 (Spring 1950): 309–10. Reglein also provides a useful overview of the costs of production and distribution.

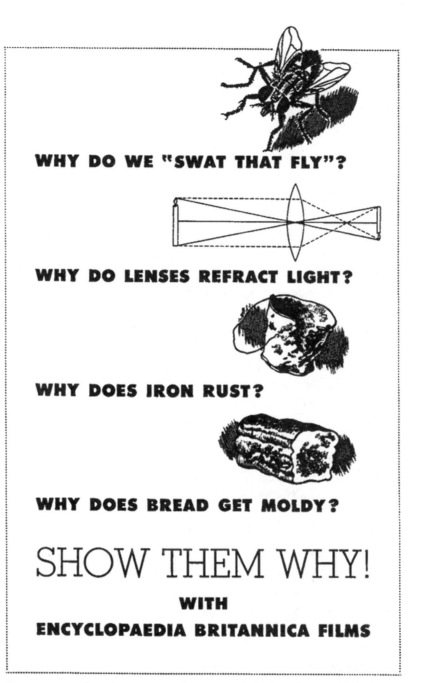

Figure 1.7. Encyclopaedia Britannica Films, Inc. was the leading educational film producer-distributor in the postwar era. *Business Screen* 6 (May 15, 1945): 84.

"good will" propaganda, sending positive stories of American industry and society all over the "developed" and "undeveloped" world. From the State
Department's efforts emerged the U.S. Information Agency (USIA, 1953–
1999), whose Motion Picture Service division produced and distributed thousands of nonfiction films to "educate" nations around the world throughout
the Cold War.

American government agencies of all stripes had been producing and continued to produce films for training and public education, beginning with the
Department of Agriculture (see fig. 1.8), military, and Bureau of Mines in the
1910s, later continuing with the Office of Indian Affairs, Tennessee Valley Authority, Federal Public Housing Authority, Weather Bureau, and Central Intelligence Agency. In fact, virtually every agency of size produced informational
films, some in-house, others contracted to commercial companies. Although
Hollywood studios and newsreel services had such government contracts, more
often the work-for-hire went to nontheatrical producers.[97]

In 1957, nontheatrical producers chartered two professional organizations,
both still in operation. Headquartered in Washington, DC, the Committee
(later Council) on International Non-Theatrical Events (CINE) began as a
group jurying hundreds of films from a variety of categories (such as industrial,
educational, religious, documentary, and student), designating which would
represent the United States at international festivals. Early on, CINE partnered
with the National Education Association to showcase festival winners in Washington, DC. Since the early 1960s, the nonprofit group has promoted such films
with its CINE Eagle awards.

The Industry Film Producers Association (IFPA) began in Los Angeles as a
trade organization and grew into the largest such group. With its Cold War origin, IFPA's first iteration had closer ties to the military-industrial complex than
it did to the education sector. It gave awards to films in the categories of indoctrination[!], training, public relations, and sales promotion—not education.
Tellingly, four of the first five IFPA awards went to aerospace manufacturer
North American Aviation, Inc. and its subsidiaries, which were making films
with the Defense Department. The 1958 awardees included *F-100 Spin Indoctrination*, a training film for fighter pilots; and *Sodium Reactor Experiment
Fabrication,* a report on the nation's first nuclear power plant (made for the U.S.
Atomic Energy Commission).[98] Filmmakers with defense contracts obviously

---

[97] Mercer, *The Informational Film*, 30. An early federal publication was *Motion Pictures of the
U.S. Department of Agriculture: A List of Films and Their Uses* (Washington, DC: GPO, 1920).

[98] "Industry Film Producers Cite First Film Awards," *Business Screen*, Production Review
Annual (1958): 72. In 1959, the IFPA award became known as the CINDY (Cinema in Industry). The
association has had several name (and identity) changes, becoming the Information Film Producers

Courtesy of Educational Screen

Figure 1.8. The U.S. Department of Agriculture Motion Picture Studio with its staff and cameras. From A. P. Hollis, *Motion Pictures for Instruction* (Century Co., 1926), 52.

had much bigger budgets than those without, often using high-end 35mm equipment. The USIA, even in its first year of operation, had tens of millions of dollars with which to commission its 16mm documentaries.[99]

The fifties also saw new fantasies of an emerging television market, which producers hoped would finally bring the educational film industry into a state of

---

of America, and eventually the International Association of Audio Visual Communicators (IAAVC). See also the CINDY Awards website, www.cindys.com and the CINE Awards site, www.cine.org.

The other 1958 awards went to: Autonetics, a division of NAA making missile guidance systems, for *Brains: Who Needs Them with RECOMP?*, promoting a computer made for the Air Force; Ramo-Wooldridge Corporation (later TRW), an aerospace company working on missile systems, for its "indoctrination" film *Security Is Your Responsibility*; and Rocketdyne, a division of NAA making rocket engines, for *Road to the Stars,* a full-length PR piece about space exploration. Curiously—and symptomatic of the Sputnik panic in the United States—*Road to the Stars* was also the English title of an acclaimed Soviet documentary on the same topic, then in American theatrical release). Both *Road* movies were screened in educational contexts for several years (though apparently not together). The Air Force and USIA acquired prints of the Soviet version. *Doroga k zvezdam* (1957, Leningrad Popular Science Film Studio, 52 min., a.k.a. *Russian Rocket to the Moon* in 16mm distribution), directed by Pavel Klushantsev, includes art and set design greatly resembling parts of *2001: A Space Odyssey* (1968). Artkino distributed an English-language version in the United States. "Man in Moon: U.S. or Russ?" *Los Angeles Times,* February 16, 1958; "Two Soviet Imports Open at the Cameo," *New York Times,* June 5, 1958.

[99] "U.S. Urged to End Film Propaganda," *New York Times,* May 15, 1954.

assured profitability. In the late 1940s, costs to produce an educational film ranged from $5,000 to $30,000 per ten-minute reel. Films were sold by the producer to a dealer, who would then sell to other dealers or film libraries, with prices ranging anywhere from $19.50 to $50 to purchase a one-reel film, or $1.25 to $6.00 a reel for rental. Selling 200 prints of a one-reel film targeted at an adult audience would have been considered "a good sale" at this juncture, generating $7,000 to $10,000 in revenue.[100] And though the television market did help to extend the shelf lives of some educational films, television companies also got involved with production and distribution, with CBS buying Bailey Films and Film Associates in 1969, and NBC creating NBC Educational Enterprises in 1970.

In 1969, more than 14,000 educational films were produced in the United States, most in color and almost all shot on 16mm film.[101] In 1975, that number was down by two-thirds, with 4,000 to 4,500 works produced—although still represented by almost 1,000 distributors. This decline in production was a result of (1) a significant shrinkage in federal support, (2) the ongoing challenges of efficient and centralized distribution, and (3) a stubborn lack of clear channels of communication between teachers, administrators, distributors, and producers. As filmmaker Vincent Tortora and educational media consultant Peter Schillaci observed, teachers, departments, and even school systems were regularly demanding previews of all films prior to adoption, resulting in thousands of preview films circulating the country with little way for distributors to accurately keep track of them, leading to a dismal "preview to purchase ratio" of between ten and twenty to one.[102]

The 1960s and 70s also witnessed significant stylistic and pedagogic changes in educational films. There were now many types of films to choose from in terms of presentational style. Certain kinds of films became de rigueur—such as the open-ended or "trigger" film, intended not to be didactic but rather to let spectators hash things out for themselves. Such films allowed for a reassertion of the teacher's or group leader's role, since leading an effective discussion after such a film was as much if not more important than the film itself. Though new video formats displaced educational film prints, in 1977 more than 15,000 nontheatrical films were made, many of them of the informational variety.[103]

---

[100] Waldron, *Information Film*, 56, 87–89.

[101] Thomas Hope, *AV-USA 1969* (Rochester, NY: Hope Reports, 1970), 16, 14. Tom Hope was a former Kodak sales representative who worked with 16mm clients. From the 1960s through the 1990s he issued field reports, market research, and statistical assessments of the nation's nontheatrical AV users. During World War II, Hope helped train servicemen in the production of military training films. Hope conversation with Dan Streible, July 23, 2003.

[102] Vincent Tortora and Peter Schillaci, "The Educational Film Industry," *Previews* (Oct. 1975): 10–11.

[103] Mercer, *Informational Film*, iii.

Exhibition

Even in their earliest iterations commercial movie houses were not entirely devoid of educational content. However, they proved to have a complex relationship to films that deviated from entertainment and went beyond the reporting function of actualities and, by the teens, of newsreels. Local theaters could, on occasion, be talked into showing edifying programs. A "photo-play house" in Pawtucket, Rhode Island, for example, "situated among the mills and in the immigrant quarter of the city" in the 1910s, offered "a civic and patriotic program" one evening each week.[104] More programmatically, in 1920 the Motion Picture Theater Owners of America pledged to offer free educational film matinees to high-schoolers. Programs lasted one hour per day (longer on Saturday mornings), and theaters received gratis print loans from the Bureau of Commercial Economics (BCE), a nonprofit venture launched in 1914. One iteration was noted in the *New York Times*, when the so-called American Educational and Industrial Theater opened at the Savoy movie house in New York in 1921, running only such fare from noon to 1 p.m. daily.[105]

Some theaters showed films as part of particular campaigns, such as New York state's diphtheria immunization crusade, which found *New Ways for Old* (1926), a one-reel film sponsored by Metropolitan Life Insurance, circulating in commercial movie theaters in conjunction with radio, church, and newspaper contributions.[106] Novelty presentations were sometimes deployed, as when the state health department commissioned a cartoon, *A Two-Family Stork* (1926), about prenatal care. Reportedly, when the film was shown "in a store window of a Hudson River city," visits to the local maternity clinic doubled or tripled. The film (and many like it) also circulated for several years on small "automatic movie" machines.[107] However, for theatrical shows, arrangements were negotiated on a case-by-case basis. Theater owners relied on a steady stream of entertainment-seeking customers and were displeased by unmarketable feature films or competition from nontheatrical exhibitors.

---

[104] McConoughey, *Motion Pictures in Religious and Educational Work*, 21, 24. McConoughey discusses similar arrangements in Orange, New Jersey, and Hartford, Connecticut.

[105] "First Educational 'Movie' Theater to Open Monday," *New York Tribune,* April 16, 1921. The Bureau of Commercial Economics initiative is not well documented, but evidence appears in unexpected sources, viz., Testimony of W. L. Clark, To Amend Section 27 of the Merchant Marine Act of 1920, Hearings before the Committee on the Merchant Marine and Fisheries, U.S. Congress, House, 67th Cong., 1st sess., October 28, 1921, 140–41. See also, Testimony of Francis Holley, Hearings on Internal-Revenue Revision, House Committee on Ways, U.S. Congress, July 29, 1921, 311–14.

[106] Thomas C. Edwards, "Health Pictures and Their Value," *Annals of the American Academy of Political and Social Science* 128 (Nov. 1926): 135. Edwards reports 90% of parents who brought their children in for immunization credited seeing the film for their action.

[107] Ibid., 136.

It was therefore in nontheatrical venues that the educational film took hold. The teens saw educational film exhibition increasing significantly. In 1915, for example, the San Francisco World's Fair showed more than sixty films classified as "industrial, religious, educational, and governmental."[108] However, the Bureau of Commercial Economics was responsible for a large-scale push to show educative industrial films worldwide, with its impact continuing through the 1920s. As Sean Savage's research has shown, this nongovernmental organization quietly reached millions of people. The original implementation of its altruistic mission was idiosyncratic, the vision of a single philanthropist who had no ties to the educational system or the movie industry. Francis Holley, an engineer who had become blind for several years, devoted his life to visual education when he regained his eyesight.

The bureau collected prints of sponsored films donated by manufacturers, government agencies, newsreel services, trade associations, civic groups, churches, and schools. Most were nonfiction films documenting manufacturing processes. If Holley judged a work to have "educative" value and no overt advertising, the bureau distributed it. He testified to Congress that the BCE had amassed 55 million feet of film, reaching an audience of 34 million in 1920. (Two months later, Holley boasted to *American Magazine* that his audience was 60 million.) The bureau used a fleet of "projection trucks" to bring free open-air screenings to spaces rural and urban, in dozens of nations. In the United States, it also loaned prints to universities, extension services, American Legion halls, military posts, and many other public institutions.[109]

A year after the launch of the Bureau of Commercial Economics, a psychologist holding great optimism for the future of film's classroom applications asked if "a projector in every grammar and high school" was "practical," acknowledging that film producers, school boards, state departments, and the bureau of education would have to band together in order to create a functional educational film circuit.[110]

As with any new technology, cost confronted film advocates. In 1916, the Toledo Museum of Art reported that installing a 35mm projection setup cost

---

[108] Godfrey M. Elliott, "The Genesis of the Educational Film," in *Film and Education*, ed. Godfrey M. Elliott (New York: Philosophical Library, 1948), 13.

[109] Sean Savage, "The Eye Beholds: Silent Era Industrial Films and the Bureau of Commercial Economics," master's thesis, New York University, 2006; and "Unraveling the *Madison News Reel:* An Unlikely Convergence of Collage, Industrial, and Local Film," *The Moving Image* 8, no. 2 (2008): 61–77. See also Francis Holley, "Industrial Education and the Uses of the Cinematograph in Public Instruction," *Proceedings of the Second Pan American Scientific Congress,* vol. 5 (Washington, DC: GPO, 1916), 160–65; and Ulm, "Once Blind," 55.

[110] Lawrence Augustus Averill, "Educational Possibilities of the Motion Picture," *Educational Review* (Nov. 1915): 396–97.

around $300.[111] In 1921, *Visual Education* reported 9,000 nontheatrical projectors in use, most of them "standard size" (35mm), despite the fact that their implementation was more expensive than small-gauge outfits. Of the many "substandard" formats marketed in the era of silent film apart from 16mm, only a few made headway among educational users. These were generally products of the French company Pathé and were mostly adopted in Europe. The 28mm system that Pathé unveiled in 1911 had success in Europe and Canada, but in the United States only a few institutions purchased its Pathéscope prints and projectors. (The 1924 edition of *1000 and One* notes its exclusion of 28mm films because "it requires a special projector" and would therefore be "useless to the great majority of our readers.")[112] The so-called Pathé Rural, a 17.5mm format, briefly became France's "standard for pedagogical screenings" and nontheatrical presentations in remote areas. The 9.5mm amateur format created in 1922 (Pathé-Baby) enjoyed global popularity for a few decades, but it too had little presence in America.[113]

Although 16mm remained the dominant nontheatrical exhibition format, by the 1960s, suppliers of educational audiovisual materials supplemented 16mm film sales with the still cheaper and more portable 8mm film (and Super 8mm from 1965 on). Some school libraries (like many private collectors) opted to acquire reduction prints of theatrical films, especially as teaching about cinema itself emerged within the academy. Schools with limited budgets could acquire 8mm prints, for example, of silent-era features and shorts, ranging from Robert Flaherty's *Nanook of the North* (1922), Sergei Eisenstein's *Ten Days that Shook the World* (1928), and the whole three hours of D. W. Griffith's *Intolerance* (1916) to Keystone comedies, recut newsreels, and Encyclopaedia Britannica documentaries. By the early 1970s, one could purchase 8mm and Super 8mm prints of movies and television series with soundtracks, including the likes of TV news coverage of Apollo missions, *The Godfather I* and *II* (1972/1974), or Warren Beatty's *Reds* (1981).[114]

---

[111] George W. Stevens, "The Muse of Motion Photography in Museums," *Metropolitan Museum of Art Bulletin* 11 (Sept. 1916): 204.

[112] "Foreword," *1000 and One*. See Anke Mebold and Charles Tepperman, "Resurrecting the Lost History of 28mm Film in North America," *Film History* 15, no. 2 (2003): 137–51. For historical information on small-gauge film formats, see Alan Kattelle's authoritative *Home Movies: A History of the American Industry, 1897–1979* (Nashua, NH: Transition, 2000).

[113] Christel Taillibert, "Pathé Rural," trans. Martyn Stevens, *Cinerdistan*, Oct. 13, 2009, www.cinerdistan.co.uk/path%C3%A9_rural.htm; Alexandra Schneider, "Travel with Pathé Baby: The Small-Gauge Film Collection as Historical Archive," *Film History* 19, no. 4 (2007): 353–60.

[114] See Ernest Callenbach, "The State of 8," *Film Quarterly* 19 (Summer 1966): 36–39. Blackhawk Films, based in Davenport, Iowa, was the most consequential distributor, beginning its rentals and sales in 1947. See also *8mm Sound Film and Education; Proceedings of a Conference Held at Teachers College on November 8, 9, and 10, 1961*, ed. Louis Forsdale (New York: Columbia University, 1962).

In the late 1960s, a vogue for using 8mm film loops peaked. A 1968 UNESCO report said that "the cartridge loop projector has made a significant impact upon educationists concerned with audio-visual media." The format was designed specifically for small-group or individual instruction. These short teaching films (running no more than four minutes) were mounted in cartridges and played on special machines. Allowing a student or teacher to play the film easily, immediately, and repeatedly (without turning the lights off), loops offered tailored learning experiences. Users could pause to view a single image. Thousands of machines were in use in the United States, with nearly forty production houses offering an estimated five thousand titles.[115]

As some early observers would smartly point out, setting up a projection system at a school was typically less costly than setting up a classroom science laboratory; once films were considered a need (as labs already were) they would not face the same psychological funding obstacles.[116] However, there was also a need to establish practices for print labeling since it was difficult for the layperson to ascertain whether film was inflammable or not, leading some to call for a law requiring manufacturers to mark nontheatrical film product "non-inflammable for *educational use*."[117] Calls for portable projectors capable of showing non-inflammable film ratcheted up in the teens and became commonplace by the early 1920s, when Eastman Kodak's 16mm safety stock and projectors addressed the worst of these logistical problems. The complexity of conceiving of an alternative to 35mm stemmed largely from the reduced availability of titles printed on other film gauges and the diminished image size when a smaller projector was used in auditorium settings. To be fully useful, argued the director of visual instruction for the state of New Jersey, projection equipment had to be portable, simple to operate, and sturdy. It had to run on the available electrical source, provide good visibility, and be able to freeze on an image.[118] By the 1940s, it was a given that educational films

---

[115] Geoffrey Bell, *8mm Film for Adult Audiences*, Reports and Papers on Mass Communication, no. 54 (Paris: UNESCO, 1968). Many professional articles about 8mm film appeared in education and science journals. Examples include Robert T. Kreima, "The 8mm Film in Education," *Educational Media International* 2, no. 1 (1968): 4–6; Joan R. Forsdale, "The 8mm Film Loop: What Does Research Suggest about the Value of the Short Accessible Film?" *Media and Methods* 6 (Nov. 1969): 56–58; and A. H. Crocker, "8mm Film in Education," *Educational Media International* 13, no. 3 (1976): 22–24.

[116] Nelson L. Greene, "Motion Pictures in the Classroom," *Annals of the American Academy of Political and Social Science* 128 (Nov. 1926): 126.

[117] R. F. Egner, "'Why' Change Motion Picture Standards," *Visual Education* 2, no. 5 (May 1921): 11–12.

[118] Clarence E. Howell, "First Experiences with Portable Motion-Picture Projectors," *Elementary School Journal* 27 (Oct. 1926): 101. The ability to freeze on a single frame for study purposes was available to instructors using the so-called analytic projector, which many manufacturers sold.

EQUIPMENT RECOMMENDED FOR MOTION PICTURE ACTIVITIES

1 Classroom projector (portable)	$200.00 to $300.00
1 Bench rewind	5.00 to 10.00
1 Mending block or clamp	5.00 to 10.00
Razor blades, scissors, and Eastman film cement, oil can, and projector oil	
1 Extra lamp	3.50 to 8.50
1 Extra reel	.50
1 Metal container with cover for scrap film	
1 Roller screen (4 x 5) for classroom	15.00 up
1 Darkened room	

If films are used for entertainment purposes in an assembly room or auditorium, the following are essential:

1 Semi-portable or professional projector and accessories	$300 to $1000
1 Fire-proof booth equipped according to fire code	
1 Metal stand or work table (built-in)	
1 Extra metal film container or humidor	
1 Chemical fire extinguisher	
Necessary tools such as pliers, screw drivers	

Figure 1.9. An indication of the cost of showing films in schools. *Visual Aids in Education* (Los Angeles City School District, 1929), 22.

were distributed on 16mm, projected by smaller machines, and served many functions.[119]

Auditoriums equipped with fireproof booths proved the most common arrangement prior to the 1920s, although semi-mobile booths—erected, for example, on piano casters to facilitate limited movement—were an acceptable alternative.[120] In the schools of Evanston, Illinois, students were trained to run the 35mm prints (see fig. 1.10), which were scheduled by grade and projected at scheduled times throughout the day and across the district. But in other states, such as Massachusetts, all projectionists were required to be licensed, forcing teachers to go through the licensing process and limiting their use of student labor at screenings.[121]

---

[119] See, for example, Gerald McDonald, *Educational Motion Pictures and Libraries* (Chicago: American Library Association, 1942), 7.

[120] W. Arthur Justice, "Visual Instruction in the Public Schools of Evanston, IL," *Visual Education* 1 (Jan. 1920): 14.

[121] Clarence E. Howell, "First Experiences with Portable Motion-Picture Projectors," *Elementary School Journal* 27 (Oct. 1926): 103.

STUDENT OPERATORS AND TYPICAL BOOTH

A MOTION PICTURE CLASS IN AN EVANSTON SCHOOL

Figure 1.10. As *Visual Education* illustrated in its inaugural issue (January 1920), students could help with the projection of 35mm film by working in a fireproof booth, such as this auditorium-style setup in a public school in Evanston, Illinois.

Just how many nontheatrical exhibitors there were at various historical moments is difficult to gauge. In 1921, *Visual Education* predicted that "within five years, at the present rate of growth, the educational use of the film will exceed that of the theatrical field in the quantity of film in circulation and within ten or more years to come it will surpass it by a large percentage."[122] One estimate for

---

[122] Egner, "'Why' Change Motion Picture Standards," 12

1924 claims that there were 15,000 motion picture projectors employed in non-theatrical exhibition.[123]

Mobile exhibition played an important role in film's educational applications, especially for rural communities where more permanent forms of exhibition were not feasible. For example, beginning in 1917 and continuing into the early 1920s, the North Carolina Department of Education implemented a plan "for bringing visual instruction to rural communities." The Department of Public Instruction selected moving pictures with "entertainment and educational value" and sent them to rural communities via twenty portable operating units that consisted of "a motion picture projector, a Delco light plant, and other necessary equipment, all mounted on a ¾-ton truck" (see fig. 1.11). Reportedly, attendance at these events was consistently impressive. The programs blended "purely educational subjects" with other films, like "simply good, wholesome comedies" selected from the state's collection of eight hundred motion pictures—and the success of the enterprise was gauged by the "live discussions [that] crop out in that wholly spontaneous way" at each event. They were reaching "people who never saw the movies," and were willing to "walk eight or ten miles to attend these meetings."[124]

In 1945, Edgar Dale looked to the future, asking, "Will the motion picture theater become an anachronism, to be replaced by television and 16-mm. non-theatrical film showings in churches, schools, unions, granges, and homes?"[125] Although Dale's imagined future did not come true (at least not yet), after World War II nontheatrical film exhibition escalated across the country at all educational levels.

The National Educational Television (NET) network was founded in 1952 with significant financial support from the Ford Foundation to provide educational broadcasts in an otherwise commercial medium. Stations all over the

---

[123] Hollis, *Motion Pictures for Instruction*, vii. Hollis reports (221) manufacturer claims that 30,000 projectors "have been sold to schools, churches and business firms."

[124] Fred A. Olds, "How North Carolina Uses Motion Pictures in Its System of Community Service," *Visual Education* 1 (Sept.–Oct. 1920): 21–24. For an examination of a federal project to bring educational films to rural North Carolina in this same period, see Jennifer Zwarich, "The Bureaucratic Activist: Federal Filmmakers and Social Change in the U.S. Department of Agriculture's Tick Eradication Campaign," *The Moving Image* 9, no. 1 (Spring 2009): 19–53. See also two essays in *Journal of Popular Film and Television* 37 (Fall 2009): Allyson Nadia Field, "John Henry Goes to Carnegie Hall: Motion Picture Production at Southern Black Agricultural and Industrial Institutes (1909–1913)," 106–15; and Noah Zweig, "Foregrounding Public Cinema and Rural Audiences: The USDA Motion Picture Service as Cinematic Modernism, 1908–1938," 116–25. Both are part of the special-themed issue "Orphans No More: Ephemeral Films and American Culture," ed. Elizabeth Heffelfinger and Heide Solbrig.

[125] Edgar Dale, "What's Ahead for Hollywood?" *The News Letter* 11 (Nov. 1945): 1.

INTERIOR VIEW OF ONE OF NORTH CAROLINA'S
"MOVIE TRUCKS"

Figure 1.11. One of twenty mobile projection units operated by the state of North Carolina to show motion pictures in rural communities. In *Visual Education* (September–October 1920): 22.

country joined the network during the 1950s. As a mid-1960s commentator observed, programming was often "desultorily inadequate," especially live broadcasts, which often came across as amateurish and technically inadequate in comparison to their polished film equivalents.[126] This was also, however fleetingly, a new outlet for educational films.

---

[126] Lewis Herman, *Educational Films: Writing, Directing, and Producing for Classroom, Television, and Industry* (New York: Crown, 1965), 310.

Writing for the launch of the Education Film Library Association's journal in 1967, James Limbacher noted CBS's announcement of its Electronic Video Recording (EVR) system, which "aroused considerable interest among educational and library circles," with some insiders "predicting that if it works, EVR might supplant both 16mm and 8mm projection in the classroom."[127] But this was a false dawn. Even three years later, Jack Gould of the *New York Times* could report, "The blue-sky ballyhoo over home video cartridges of many different types and different applications is getting somewhat out of hand." The EVR, he noted, did not have its first commercial sale until late 1970. The following year CBS ceased development of the technology.[128]

However, the fact that an EVR player plugged into a television monitor indicated the future for educational media and signaled the impending death of widespread educational *film* use. At the end of the expansion period for educational films, in the late 1960s, it was estimated that more than half of A-V spending by schools—over half a billion dollars—went to nontheatrical films and equipment.[129] These dollars not only went to 16mm, but also to 8mm, Super 8mm, and a variety of other forms, novel and short-lived. By the late seventies, schools and libraries were purchasing commercial releases on Laser-Disc and other optical videodisc systems, which made a modest impact for a decade.[130] Not until the eighties did VHS videotapes earn the lion's share of the market for movie sales.

The New Modern: Television, Video, Computers, and the Death of Educational Films

> I find television very educational. The minute somebody turns it on, I go into the library and read a good book.
> —*Groucho Marx*

Writing in 1946, audiovisual experts Francis Noel and Elizabeth Noel (both of whom served terms as chief of California's Division of Audio-Visual Education) made a prediction:

---

[127] James Limbacher, "The World of Film . . . 1977," *Sightlines* 1 (Sept.–Oct. 1967): 15.

[128] Jack Gould, "The Great Day Isn't Exactly at Hand," *New York Times*, November 15, 1970; David Fischer, "The Quest for Home Video: EVR," *Terra Media,* August 26, 2004, www.terramedia.co.uk/media/video/evr.htm. Although an EVR player output a video signal, the images and sound were actually recorded on 17.5mm film (not magnetic or digital videotape) transported in a round cassette.

[129] Thomas Hope, *AV-USA 1969* (Rochester, NY: Hope Reports, 1970), 9.

[130] For excellent overviews see Lois McLean, "Videodiscs in Education," Dec. 1985, *ERIC Digests,* www.ericdigests.org/pre-924/discs.htm; and Tom Howe, "RCA SelectaVision VideoDisc FAQs," *CED Magic* website (2009), www.cedmagic.com/home/cedfaq.html#header.

New devices will make possible low-cost color and three dimension projection. The stereoscope, modernized, will again return, taking a prominent place in classroom instruction. Vectographs [3-D photographs] will come into general use especially in the visualization of mathematical concepts. . . . A sound motion picture projector will be manufactured especially for classroom needs. These will be probably followed later by small individual desk projectors for use by individual students.[131]

Forecasts such as this were a veritable trope in visual education literature, especially in the postwar era when so many technological capabilities were emerging. Although the Noels may not have gotten all of the details of future educational film use correct, they were spot-on about some, and their mention of "individual desk projectors" can certainly be imagined, albeit a bit more interactively, in the context of "computer assisted instruction," as it was being called in the 1960s. Along with the advent of video technologies, such modernization helped to extinguish the era of educational film use.

The emergence of television, video, and computers were all viewed with mixed excitement and skepticism by those with a stake in the educational film industry. In 1961, the head of the FCC famously disparaged commercial TV as a "vast wasteland," and the social science "effects" literature at that time generally reported the negative impact of watching television. Yet educators and policymakers maintained hope in educational television.[132] These technologies opened up new markets and an exploding technological industry that inundated educators with promises of a brighter future for "smart classrooms" and smarter students. While on the one hand billed as the new "modern," promising to revolutionize, simplify, or economize educational media use, they also threatened established modes of production, distribution, exhibition, as well as pedagogy.

The first sustained discussions about television's potential impact on educational film surfaced in the 1940s. Writing in 1948, A. W. Vandermeer opined that "the pessimist can reasonably predict that television may accomplish what 150 years of textbooks and 25 years of movies have failed to do, namely to relegate the average teacher to the status of a combination monitor and record clerk." The teacher replacement debate reared its head once again in Vandermeer's equation, as it did in many of the considerations of television's potential

---

[131] Francis Wright Noel and Elizabeth Goudy Noel, "Looking Ahead Twenty-Five Years in Audio-Visual Education," *Educational Screen* (Feb. 1946): 68.

[132] Godwin C. Chu and Wilbur Schramm, *Learning from Television: What the Research Says* (Washington, DC: National Association of Educational Broadcasters, 1968), reported a consensus that television could be an effective learning tool when correctly deployed; cited in Saettler, *Evolution*, 429.

classroom use. However, the more important insight has to do with the idea of dissemination without the constrictions of motion picture projection equipment, which had become more convenient, certainly, but still presented many challenges that seemed possible to eradicate with a new technology like television. Once its significant "mechanical limitations are overcome," wrote Vandermeer, television "can bring the brilliant scholarship of the genius and the matchless technique of the master-teacher to even the most isolated schoolroom."[133] Concerns about image size, color, and technical difficulties aside, television seemed even at this early stage to promise yet another modern revolution in educational moving image dissemination.

By the end of 1953, an estimated 26.5 million television sets were being used in the United States, offering an unprecedented market for educational film for the general public, particularly of the "travel, safety, and sports" variety.[134] Most TV stations aired freely available sponsored nonfiction films as filler programming. The National Association of Manufacturers series *Industry on Parade* (1950–1960), for example, appeared in fifteen-minute episodes on nearly every station in operation. Accordingly, the 1950s saw a shift away from educational motion pictures on film to the potential uses of public broadcasting, as well as closed-circuit instructional or educational television, especially for schools, adult education, and the military. As film historian Jack Ellis put it in the mid-1960s, "Television is a marvelous electronic means of distributing and exhibiting the moving image accompanied by sound. . . . Much of what educational television transmits *is* educational film, with the images and sounds transported on a 16mm cellulose acetate strip and the kind of edited assemblage possible only in film."[135]

As early as 1951, a study of instructional television for naval air reservists concluded that "TV and TV recordings [16mm kinescopes] were found to be superior to local instructors and about equal in effectiveness." Experiments in the public schools of Philadelphia and Washington, DC, indicated both significant advantages to instructional television, as well as student and parent enthusiasm about the medium.[136] The professional literature of the 1950s documents a notable realignment of interests in and curiosity about "ITV"

---

[133] A. W. Vandermeer, "From Textbook to Movie to Television," *Elementary School Journal* 48 (Jan. 1948): 276.

[134] Leo Beebe, "Industry," in *Sixty Years of 16mm Film*, 97.

[135] Jack Ellis, "Film for Education: Considerations of Form," *Journal of the Society of Cinematologists* 4 (1964–65): 31.

[136] William Allen, "Audio-Visual Materials," *Review of Educational Research* 26 (Apr. 1956): 128–29. Allen cites the study by psychological researchers Robert Rock, James Duva, and John Murray, *The Effectiveness of Television Instruction in Training Naval Air Reservists, Instructional TV Research Reports* (Port Washington, NY: U.S. Naval Special Devices Center, 1951).

(instructional television) and distance education. With the allure of "the new modern," educational film had certainly lost its glimmering associations with the future.

However, 16mm educational film production continued in great volume for another two decades. Broadcast television arrived in the 1950s, but classroom-friendly video formats did not displace 16mm screenings until the 1980s. Thus, it is important to keep in mind the distinction between televised content (however delivered—broadcast, cable, satellite, microwave relay), which was viewed on a TV set, and content provided as a video recording (tape, disc, computer file) played back at a particular site. Videotape, available to professional producers from 1956 on, did not penetrate the classroom market until the diffusion of "home video" cassette formats, particularly Betamax (introduced in 1975) and VHS (in 1976).[137] As late as 1982, a scholarly book on educational media could still limit discussion of videotape to schools recording lectures for off-campus students.[138] But the diffusion was otherwise rapid. In 1985, an early issue of *Tech-Trends* reported, "VCRs Silently Take Over the Classroom," and the *Index to Educational Videotapes* listed 60,000 titles for sale. In 1988, the Consortium of University Film Centers, founded in 1971, signaled video's new dominance by changing its name to the Consortium of College and University Media Centers.[139]

Part of the push to bring television into the educational arena had to do with what many commentators anticipated would be an impending educational crisis—a steep increase in students and a shortage of teachers in the baby boom era. Their ongoing pontification often found its imagined corrective in the promise of new technology. Closed-circuit television instruction might, some argued, replace certain aspects of person-to-person instruction, reinvigorating age-old teacher replacement debates and anxieties, now tuned to the latest technology. In 1950, there was only one educational television station; in 1957, there

---

[137] The ¾-inch U-matic videotape, successfully marketed after 1970, was adopted by many schools teaching media production. Television news and industrial producers used the format, but distributors of educational content seldom sold titles on ¾-inch videotape. Patricia Ann Brock, *Educational Technology in the Classroom* (Englewood Cliffs, NJ: Educational Technology, 1994), 163.

[138] Leslie Wagner, *The Economics of Educational Media* (New York: St. Martin's Press, 1982), 28, mentions Colorado's SURGE program (State University Resources from Graduate Education), which launched in 1967. Students earned master's-level course credit by watching video replays of lectures recorded a day or two previously (presumably on professional one-inch videotape) and delivered to a viewing site by courier.

[139] William L. Reider, "VCRs Silently Take Over the Classroom," *TechTrends* (Nov.–Dec. 1985): 14–18; *Index to Educational Videotapes,* 6th ed. (Albuquerque, NM: NICEM, 1985); Consortium of College and University Media Centers site, www.ccumc.org.

were twenty-seven.[140] These stations could show previously produced educational films or new programming made for television (whether live or recorded on film or, after 1956, videotape).

Videotape offered producers and exhibitors yet another way to envision distribution and viewing. As educational film stalwart Charles Hoban Jr. itemized the new technologies of instruction in 1975, educators now had many choices beyond the educational film, including "instructional television, the audio cassette, the three-sided box for individualized instruction, computerized instruction, gaming and simulation, etc., etc."[141] Film was just one of a myriad of media and mediated options for the classroom or any other public interface with educational technology.

Many of the old debates about film use would be retooled for these new technologies, especially regarding the lack of availability of "appropriate material" on video, television, and computer. Furthermore, as Richard Hooper wrote in his 1969 critique of educational A-V aids, "A Diagnosis of Failure,"

> most educational hardware is not custom-built for education, but a
> (lucrative) spin-off from the consumer industry. . . . The task of
> locating materials from catalogs and brochures is formidable. . . .
> Film clips, still pictures, discs and tapes, lie in their millions across
> the country, unknown, often uncataloged, and mostly unused. Once
> located, the problems of retrieval and evaluation are, despite the
> growth of videotape, audiotape, and film libraries, vast. The
> evaluations of educational films, distributed regularly by the
> Educational Film Library Association, are intensely subjective,
> based on the previews of three adults and no members of the target
> audience.[142]

In what could be confused with discourse about the current state of educational films residing in archives, Hooper's complaints about using educational media in the 1960s remind us of the challenges faced by current scholarly researchers, both in terms of finding educational film materials and in seeing or utilizing the

---

[140] F. A. Ficken, "The Use of Films and Television in Mathematics Education," *American Mathematical Monthly* 65 (June–July 1958): 393. Ficken also discusses concerns about television replacing teachers, 402.

[141] Charles F. Hoban [Jr.], "The State of the Art of Films in Instruction: A Second Look," *Audiovisual Instruction* (Apr. 1975): 30. Note that Hoban's "gaming and simulation" refers to role-playing and board games then extant, even if it seems a prescient allusion to the digital simulations and computer/video games of twenty-first-century education.

[142] Richard Hooper, "A Diagnosis of failure," *AV Communication Review* 17 (Fall 1969): 254, 267.

materials once found. The films—which, as Hooper suggests, were never easy to account for—are, in many cases, still out there. Decades of neglect, however, have buried them deeper within institutional or private collections. Researchers, librarians, and archivists must be diligent about locating such films. As technology changes and media migrations occur, we find ourselves removed from original formats but with greater access to content, as the Internet Archive amply demonstrates.

In *The Evolution of American Educational Technology,* L. Paul Saettler observes that the rush to the next new technology has always been a part of America's educational landscape, formal or otherwise, often resulting in bouts of enthusiasm and investment that factionalize educators as well as those observing from the outside. Advocates and detractors with various economic, political, and institutional allegiances have, from the moment film began to be used in educational contexts, squared off over the latest technological and ideological shifts. The result is a dense, rich, and largely neglected history, one that tells us a great deal about two institutions—education and cinema—that helped define the contours of the last and present centuries.

2 THE CINEMA OF THE FUTURE: VISIONS OF THE MEDIUM AS MODERN EDUCATOR, 1895–1910

OLIVER GAYCKEN

Before the Supreme Court defined cinema primarily as "harmless entertainment," a variety of commentators, including inventors, journalists, and businessmen, characterized it as a medium destined to educate.[1] Indeed, many of the pioneers of cinema foresaw educational applications for the emerging medium. The traveling lecturer and photographic inventor Eadweard Muybridge envisioned his chronophotographic images as aids for students of the fine arts.[2] The French physiologist Etienne-Jules Marey, although largely indifferent to the cinema's synthesis of motion, worked within a tradition that saw certain applications of cinematic technology, such as high-speed cinematography, as prostheses for limited human senses allowing for the investigation of the hitherto invisible. Marey's assistant, Georges Demeny, used his expertise with the moving image to invent what he called the chronophonoscope, a device to help the deaf learn to

Support for the completion of this essay was provided by a study leave from Temple University and a visiting researcher position in Department II at the Max Planck Institute for the History of Science during 2008 and 2009. I would also like to thank David Cantor for inviting me to present a version of material at the Works-in-Progress Seminar, National Institute of Health History Office, Bethesda, Maryland, where I received particularly helpful feedback from Mike Sappol. Thanks are due as well to Christine Blättlinger and Janina Wellman for the invitation to the workshop "Was There a 'Cinematographic Turn' in the (Life) Sciences around 1900?" at the Zentrum für Literatur-und Kulturwissenschaft, Berlin, Germany, where I presented a version of this material and benefited from many insightful comments. Finally, I am indebted to the editors of this volume for their helpful suggestions that resulted in substantial improvements.

[1] For the story of how Hollywood cinema came to be defined as "harmless entertainment," see Lee Grieveson, *Policing Cinema: Movies and Censorship in Early Twentieth-Century America* (Berkeley: University of California Press, 2004); and Richard Maltby, *Harmless Entertainment: Hollywood and the Ideology of Consensus* (Metuchen, NJ: Scarecrow Press, 1983).

[2] See Phillip Prodger, ed., *Time Stands Still: Muybridge and the Instantaneous Photography Movement* (New York: Oxford University Press, 2003). For more on how the traveling lecturer prefigured and participated in early cinema culture, especially the culture of instructive amusement, see Charles Musser in collaboration with Carol Nelson, *High-Class Moving Pictures: Lyman H. Howe and the Forgotten Era of Traveling Exhibition, 1880–1920* (Princeton, NJ: Princeton University Press, 1991).

speak.[3] One of the leading figures of the French film industry, Charles Pathé, proclaimed, "the cinema is the newspaper, the school, and the theater of tomorrow."[4] The Anglo-American producer Charles Urban (discussed below) created a large collection of educational films, as did Pathé's chief rival Léon Gaumont.[5] In the early 1910s, Thomas Edison made headlines by declaring that films would soon become a widespread and indispensable aid in the classroom, a prediction that on occasion he amplified into the more exciting and alarming notion that films would soon replace textbooks.[6]

---

[3] For an account of Marey and Demeny's motion picture work, see Marta Braun, *Picturing Time: The Work of Etienne-Jules Marey (1830–1904)* (Chicago: University of Chicago Press, 1992). While this article focuses primarily on educational ideas as promulgated by nonscientists, professional scientists also had visions of cinema as an educative force that both overlapped with the territory outlined in this essay (in the work of Jean Comandon, for example) and constituted a separate tradition, as in the case of Marey. An informative overview of the early history of research science and cinema can be found in Virgilio Tosi, *Cinema before Cinema: The Origins of Scientific Cinematography*, trans. Sergio Angelini (London: British Universities Film and Video Council, 2005). See also Thierry Lefebvre, "Scientific Films: Europe," and Scott Curtis, "Scientific Films: USA," in *Encyclopedia of Early Cinema*, ed. Richard Abel (New York: Routledge, 2005), 568–72; *The Educated Eye: Visual Pedagogy in the Life Sciences*, ed. Nancy Anderson and Michael R. Dietrich (Lebanon, NH: University Press of New England, 2012); and my "'The Swarming of Life': Moving Pictures, Education, and Views through the Microscope," *Science in Context* 24, no. 3 (September 2011). For other accounts of scientists whose research led them to use cinematic technology, see Jimena Canales, "Photogenic Venus: The Cinematographic Turn and Its Alternatives in Nineteenth-Century France," *Isis* 93, no. 4 (2002): 585–613; Hannah Landecker, "Microcinematography and the History of Science and Film," *Isis* 97, no. 1 (2006): 121–32; and Charlotte Bigg, "Evident Atoms: Visuality in Jean Perrin's Brownian Motion Research," *Studies in History and Philosophy of Science* 39, no. 3 (2008): 312–22.

[4] Charles Pathé, quoted in Georges Sadoul, *Histoire du cinéma mondial des origines à nos jours*, 6th ed. (Paris: Flammarion, 1949), 49. Sadoul does not date this quotation, nor does he provide a source; however, the period that he is discussing is 1903–1909. Sadoul points out that François Dussaud, a professor, inventor, and sometime Pathé collaborator, actually authored the sentence, but Sadoul maintains that the sentiments were expressed on behalf of Pathé. Thierry Lefebvre quotes this sentence as well, and provides the following citation: François Valleiry, "Une [*sic*] interview de M. Dussaud," *Phono-Ciné-Gazette*, June 15, 1906, 225–26. See Lefebvre, "Film scientifique et grand public. Une rencontre différée," in *E. J. Marey: Actes du colloque du centenaire*, ed. Dominique de Font-Réaulx, Thierry Lefebvre, and Laurent Mannoni (Paris: Arcadia, 2006), 159–67.

[5] For an account of Gaumont's encyclopedia project, see Frédéric Delmeulle, "Contribution à l'histoire du cinema documentaire en France: Le cas de L'Encyclopédie Gaumont (1909–1929)" (PhD diss., Université de Paris III, 1999).

[6] Edison's pronouncements appeared in Frederick James Smith, "The Evolution of the Motion Picture," *New York Dramatic Mirror*, July 9, 1913, 24; and F. P. Hulette, "An Interview with Thomas A. Edison," *Moving Picture World*, July 22, 1911, 104. For a bevy of citations in this vein, see Ben Singer, "Early Home Cinema and the Edison Home Projecting Kinetoscope," *Film History* 2, no. 1 (1988): 51–54 and 60–61.

More than scattered epiphenomena, these pronouncements about cinema's future were remarkably persistent and widespread. This essay outlines the contours of educational cinema and its major developments by focusing on both the arguments advanced on its behalf as well as examples of films that were considered educational before 1910.[7] Two related and frequently commingled formulations of the cinema's relation to education held sway in this period. Many commentators saw the cinema as already, and perhaps inherently, educational because of the medium's technological features, in particular its ability to recreate motion and to archive events. This type of argument was particularly prominent before 1900, cinema's novelty period, when the cinematographic apparatus and its capture of motion were considered instructive in and of themselves, in the tradition of other optical "philosophical toys" and mechanical marvels. At the same time, appeals for a cinema that would be more explicitly educational at some point in the near future envisioned a pedagogical repertoire of films and screening situations distinct from the emerging culture of commercial cinema.

In one of the earliest histories of cinema, Thomas Edison's assistant W. K. L. Dickson and Dickson's coauthor and sister Antonia made the following claims for the new medium: "The advantages to students and historians will be immeasurable. Instead of dry and misleading accounts, tinged with the exaggerations of the chroniclers' minds, our archives will be enriched by the vitalized pictures of great national scenes, instinct with all the glowing personalities which characterized them."[8] An initial distinguishing characteristic of this passage is its use of the future tense (advantages "will be immeasurable"). Although occurring in a book entitled *History of the Kinetograph, Kinetoscope, and Kinetophonograph*, here history gives way to futurology, and the forecast calls for an educational cinema.[9]

This passage grounds its imagined future in a certain understanding of cinematic properties, which it invokes in two comparisons. First, the passage

---

[7] For a similar perspective, see Luke McKernan, "Education," in *The Encyclopedia of Early Cinema*, ed. Richard Abel (New York: Routledge, 2005), 214–15. McKernan, "'Something More Than a Mere Picture Show': Charles Urban and the Early Non-Fiction Film in Great Britain and America, 1897–1925" (PhD diss., University of London, 2003), contains an excellent discussion of early educational cinema.

[8] W. K. L. Dickson and Antonia Dickson, *History of the Kinetograph, Kinetoscope and Kinetophonograph* (New York: Albert Bunn, 1895), 51–52; facsimile ed. (New York: Museum of Modern Art, 2000).

[9] To be fair, the Dicksons have a capacious conception of the cinema's future that encompasses just about everything: "What is the future of the kinetograph? Ask rather, from what conceivable phase of the future it can be debarred. In the promotion of business interests, in the advancement of science, in the revelation of unguessed worlds, in its educational and re-creative powers, and in its ability to immortalize our fleeting but beloved associations, the kinetograph stands foremost among the creations of modern inventive genius" (Dickson and Dickson, *History*, 52).

draws a distinction between the questionable veracity of the textual ("misleading accounts," "exaggerations") and the cinema's inherent truthfulness. Since the "chroniclers' minds" are the source of "exaggerations," what recommends cinema in this regard is precisely its mindlessness. In other words, the suggestion here is that cinema possesses a technological accuracy that is free from the distortions of subjectivity, which builds on a discourse established over the second half of the nineteenth century that linked the photographic image to objectivity.[10]

The second comparison draws a distinction between the "dryness" of traditional chronicles and the cinema's experiential intensity, which it signals with such phrases as "vitalized pictures" and "glowing personalities." The notion that the cinema could provide accounts that glow with vitality represents a widespread strand of reaction to the first screenings of motion pictures that celebrated the medium's sensory immediacy. Certain names for the cinema during the first decade, such as "living pictures" or "animated photography," indicate further this conception of a vivifying technology.

This understanding of cinema was easily allied with the advocacy of sensory experience in education. Implicit in the Dicksons' contrast of the dryness of textual records and the intense, image-based experience of the cinema is a preexisting discourse about the value of the senses in education. A prominent articulation of this discourse was the notion of the object lesson, which came from the theories of Johann Heinrich Pestalozzi, a Swiss educator and educational reformer. Influenced by his reading of Jean-Jacques Rousseau's treatise *Émile: or, On Education* (1762), Pestalozzi believed in the primacy of sensation, which led him to emphasize the importance of studying actual objects as an initial step in learning. He reversed the traditional importance accorded to the teacher's lecture, arguing that direct, concrete perception should precede verbal description. Only after an initial encounter with the object was the student encouraged to name it and identify its characteristics.[11] In the United States, Pestalozzi's ideas began to find a small audience by the 1820s, and they were popularized in the 1860s by Edward Sheldon's object-lesson plan (the "Oswego plan") and Francis W. Parker's "Quincy methods." The latter included such natural history lessons as taking field trips and planting seeds (leading some parents to complain that Parker had turned schools into "mud-pie factories").[12] Some schools created "object lesson

---

[10] See Lorraine Daston and Peter Galison, *Objectivity* (New York: Zone Books, 2007).

[11] *Anschauung,* a kind of immediate perceptual truth/insight, was an important term for Pestalozzi and represented the goal of his method. On *Anschauung,* see Henning Schmidgen, "Pictures, Preparations, and Living Processes: The Production of Immediate Visual Perception (*Anschauung*) in Late-Nineteenth-Century Physiology," *Journal for the History of Biology* 37 (2004): 477–513.

[12] My account of Pestalozzi's educational philosophy and its dissemination in the United States is indebted to L. Paul Saettler, *The Evolution of American Educational Technology* (Englewood, CO: Libraries Unlimited, 1990), 36–41; "mud-pie factories" on 40.

boxes," repositories of everyday objects such as plants and mineral specimens with which students could interact directly.

These specific examples formed part of the wider Progressive education movement in America, sometimes called the "new education," which rose to prominence during the last quarter of the nineteenth century. A central tenet that recurred across the various strands of this loosely woven movement was an emphasis on learning by doing. Although cinema frequently was understood as a medium that promoted passivity, the rhetoric of reformers consistently described motion pictures as close analogues for certain forms of activity, especially traveling and nature study.[13] The Dickson passage renders this advantage in terms of how the cinema can provide students with an enriched sense of key historical moments that is similar to having been there and thus constitutes a form of virtual witnessing.[14] Furthermore, the cinema's qualities as an educational medium versus traditional approaches of book-based learning, rote drills, and memorization frequently were distilled into an opposition between the moving image's vivid immediacy and the textbook's "dryness." Cinema, in other words, provided an alternative to the perceived aridity of traditional learning. Few advocates for educational cinema had a background in educational theory, but the frequency of the dry versus vivid comparison indicates that these ideas had become part of the turn-of-the-century vernacular.[15]

---

[13] See Singer, "Early Home Cinema," 53, where he cites Anthony M. Platt, *The Child Savers: The Invention of Delinquency*, 2nd ed. (Chicago: University of Chicago Press, 1977). On the alliance between early cinema and travel, see Jennifer Peterson, *Education in the School of Dreams: Travelogues and Early Nonfiction Film* (Durham, NC: Duke University Press, forthcoming). On the introduction of nature study into North American public schools, see Sally Gregory Kohlstedt, "Nature, Not Books: Scientists and the Origins of the Nature-Study Movement in the 1890s," *Isis* 96, no. 3 (2005): 324–52. Elizabeth Wiatr, "Between Word, Image, and the Machine: Visual Education and Films of Industrial Process," *Historical Journal of Film, Radio, and Television* 22, no. 3 (2002): 334, notes the importance of thinking about film as a "vicarious" experience for visual educators of the 1920s.

[14] For the classic account of virtual witnessing, see Steven Shapin and Simon Schaffer, *Leviathan and the Air Pump: Hobbes, Boyle, and the Experimental Life* (Princeton, NJ: Princeton University Press, 1985); for an extension of the concept of virtual witnessing to the question of science content in Hollywood films (which thus addresses the matter of their educational value) see David Kirby, "Science Consultants, Fictional Films, and Scientific Practice," *Social Studies of Science* 33, no. 2 (April 2003): 231–68.

[15] Consider, for example, Herbert Spencer, who writes that child-centered and self-directed learning methods lead to a "vividness and permanency of impression which the usual methods can never produce. Any piece of knowledge which the pupil has himself acquired, any problem which he has himself solved, becomes by virtue of the conquest much more thoroughly his than it could else be" (Herbert Spencer, *Education: Intellectual, Moral and Physical* [New York: D. Appleton, 1896], 155; cited in Platt, *The Child Savers*, 58). The "vividness and permanency of impression" that "learning by doing" imparted carried over from the domain of educational theory into the work of promoting cinema as an educational force.

Overall, this educational philosophy represented an attempt to organize the curriculum according to what its proponents saw as the natural laws of human development. Although novel in many respects, Progressive educational reform also built on well-established ideas, such as the ancient hierarchy of the senses that placed vision above hearing, touch, taste, and smell. Since vision was seen, so to speak, as more intuitive than other means of instruction, it presented an invaluable and primary resource for educators, and the cinema's obvious visual appeals allowed it to fit neatly into arguments for "education by the eye." Visual learning via the cinema thus updated a venerable form of instruction by linking its tenets to a modern technology.[16]

The Dicksons employed rhetorical devices that typified the arguments for cinema as an educational medium in the decades to follow, providing a primer of the basic ideas that persistently would link cinema and education. These arguments found support in many films from the first decade of U.S. cinema history, a period during which nonfictional titles constituted the majority of films produced.[17] The most prevalent genres of early nonfiction—the actuality, the travel film, the popular science film, and the industrial film—were concerned primarily with providing information: about current events, travel to foreign places, scientific advances, or what a manufacturing process looked like.[18] In this sense, many of these films can be characterized as educational. In other words, the cinema of attractions and its proclivity for spectacular display and direct viewer engagement is frequently also a cinema of epistemophilia.[19]

In 1904 the Westinghouse Electric & Manufacturing Company commissioned American Mutoscope and Biograph to produce a series of films chronicling manufacturing activities at three of its factories. Photographed

---

[16] As Jennifer Peterson points out in this volume, the concept of "efficiency" was also often employed to characterize the linkage of cinema to education.

[17] Story films became predominant around 1903 or 1904. See Charles Musser, "The Transition to Story Films, 1903–1904," chap. 11 in *The Emergence of Cinema: The American Screen to 1907* (Berkeley: University of California Press, 1990), 337–69.

[18] Often early nonfiction films are referred to as "actualities," which is an imprecise term. See Frank Kessler, "*Actualités*," in *Encyclopedia of Early Cinema*, 5–6, for a helpful disambiguation.

[19] See Tom Gunning, "The Cinema of Attractions: Early Film, Its Spectator, and the Avant-Garde," in Thomas Elsaesser, ed., *Early Cinema: Space, Frame, Narrative* (London: British Film Institute, 1990), 56–62. For an account of how the aesthetic of attractions was linked to other epistemic practices, see also Gunning, "In Your Face: Physiognomy, Photography, and the Gnostic Mission of Early Film," *Modernism/modernity* 4, no. 1 (1997): 1–29; reprinted with corrections in *The Mind of Modernism: Medicine, Psychology, and the Cultural Arts in Europe and America, 1880–1940*, ed. Mark S. Micale (Stanford, CA: Stanford University Press, 2004), 141–71.

by G. W. "Billy" Bitzer (who would go on to work as D. W. Griffith's cinematographer), these films (known as the "Westinghouse Works" series) were exhibited at the company's pavilion on the grounds of the Louisiana Purchase Exhibition, commonly referred to as the St. Louis World's Fair. Collectively, they supply an example of how the cinema functioned as a source of knowledge.[20]

Writing about the Westinghouse films, journalist John Brisben Walker noted, "[The kinetoscope] is a wonderful instrument that does not seem to have been fully appreciated from its educational point of view. . . . It was fortunate, then, that two men [John Patterson and George Westinghouse], each so noted in his own work, should have given the schools these object-lessons in the use of the biograph which we find at the Louisiana Purchase Exposition."[21] Since the great expositions of the late nineteenth and early twentieth centuries were thought of as gigantic object-lessons, the presence of the term "object-lesson" in a description of these films is unsurprising.[22] Walker's use of the term is interesting, however, since he praises the *use* of the films. This distinction indicates something exemplary about how the films were deployed (see fig. 2.1).

---

[20] Twenty-one of these films are available at www.memory.loc.gov/ammem/papr/west. The website notes that twenty-nine Westinghouse Works films were listed in the American Mutoscope and Biograph catalog. The Westinghouse films are just a few of many sponsored films made by American Mutoscope and Biograph, which also produced films for the U.S. Post Office Department, Department of the Interior, and Navy; see Musser, *Emergence of Cinema*, 359–60. Other films, such as the Edison motion pictures made about or around President McKinley's assassination in 1901 and *Electrocuting an Elephant* (1903), serve equally well to illustrate the issues of educational cinema during this period. The McKinley films are available on the "American Memory" section of the Library of Congress website; the page is entitled "The Last Days of a President: Films of McKinley and the Pan-American Exposition, 1901," http://memory.loc.gov/ammem/papr/mckhome.html. This collection of Edison titles includes films of McKinley's inauguration, films of the Pan-American Exposition, which McKinley visited and where he was assassinated, and films of his funeral. It also includes the remarkable and curious *Execution of Czolgosz, with Panorama of Auburn Prison*, which combines actuality footage with a reenactment of the first official execution by electrocution in U.S. history.

[21] John Brisben Walker, "World Instruction in Pictures: How Westinghouse and Patterson Use the Biograph," *The Cosmopolitan* (Sept. 1904): 529. I was led to this source by Sarah Gooch, "Casting a Guide Box: Object Lessons, World Expositions, and the Westinghouse Films," paper presented at the Film and History Conference, Dallas, Texas, Nov. 2006. I am also indebted to her for sharing her seminar paper on the Westinghouse films with me.

[22] Tom Gunning notes, "the term 'object lesson' became the buzz word which justified the World Exposition as an educational experience" ("The World as Object Lesson: Cinema Audiences, Visual Culture, and the St. Louis World's Fair, 1904," *Film History* 6, no. 4 [1994]: 425). See also Emmanuelle Toulet, "Cinema and the Universal Exposition, Paris 1900," *Persistence of Vision 9* (1991): 10–36. Toulet writes that the exhibition "was intended as a gigantic national 'school'" (31).

Figure 2.1.   Film as object lesson; video still from *Testing a Rotary* (1904).

The Westinghouse Works series demonstrates how the educational content of films during this period depended to a large degree on layers of contextual information.[23] Most likely the films would have been supplemented either by a lecturer, whose commentary performed alongside the films would have aided in interpreting the images, or a musical accompaniment, which would have supplied similar, albeit less overt, guidance.[24] The screening venue itself provided a frame for the experience. The films were projected in the company's 326-seat

[23] Viewing the films today, whether as part of an avant-garde compilation or as downloaded files from the Library of Congress website on a computer screen, is vastly different from what a visitor to the World's Fair would have experienced. For an example of these films' affinities with the preoccupations of the avant-garde, see the inclusion of *Westinghouse Works, Panorama View Street Car Motor Room,* on the DVD set curated by Bruce Posner and David Shepard, *Unseen Cinema: Early American Avant-Garde Film 1893–1941,* disc one ("The Mechanized Eye"); available at www.unseen-cinema.com.

[24] I have not been able to locate any specific evidence of either a lecturer or music in the Westinghouse pavilion at the World's Fair; however, as Musser notes, Biograph's sponsored films were "made for lecture formats rather than amusement" (Musser, *Emergence,* 360). A newspaper account of a preview of the Westinghouse Works films in Pittsburgh's Carnegie Hall mentions, "Walter E. Hall rendered some pleasing organ selections during the evening" (*Pittsburgh Post,* May 12, 1904; cited at http://lcweb2.loc.gov/papr/west/westabot.html).

pavilion, whose elaborate electrical lighting, itself a Westinghouse product, supported the portrayal of the Westinghouse companies as providing state-of-the-art modern technologies.[25] The pavilion was located in Machinery Hall, a vast building that also contained the generators that powered the World's Fair itself. This frame of the machinery at the heart of the World's Fair also resonated with the films' content, reinforcing their depiction of the march of progress and American technological modernity. These motion pictures were part of a constellation of mutually reinforcing messages whereby the films, the Westinghouse auditorium, the Machinery Hall, and the World's Fair each contributed to an overarching object-lesson.[26]

Although certainly about industrial processes, the Westinghouse Works films are different from most industrial films, which typically follow the transformation of raw material into a finished product. In fact, their appeal is spread across various modes of early nonfiction, demonstrating a general tendency toward generic crossover in this period. As records of daily activities in factories, the films function as actualities; because of their emphasis on technology, they function as popular science films; and *Girls Taking Time Checks* evokes the "factory gate" genre.[27] Most prominently, however, the Westinghouse films were organized according to the conventions of the travelogue, with the series providing a virtual visit to the works, a tour behind closed doors (see fig. 2.2). As Walker wrote: "They give the inside of a great factory in which more than eleven thousand men are employed. In such an establishment it is not possible to admit

---

[25] As the Library of Congress notes to the films mention, a bank of newly developed Cooper Hewitt mercury vapor lamps illuminated the interior scenes. Cooper Hewitt was itself a Westinghouse company, so the use of these lamps constitutes another instance of an element of the film, in this case the light that makes the scenes visible, forming part of the overarching celebration of the company's advanced technologies.

[26] This observation introduces a larger point that this essay's emphasis on cinema history only hints at, which is how the history of cinema as an educator is inseparable from other media histories. Indeed, as Tom Gunning has pointed out, the role of film at the St. Louis World's Fair was minor and parasitic; see Gunning, "World as Object Lesson," 423.

[27] Another film that Walker mentions that does not seem to have survived also belongs to the genre of early cinema that has come to be called the "factory gate" film. Walker describes this film as follows, "But the Westinghouse exhibit has in reserve for you an even more remarkable scene. A single film holds no fewer than four thousand portraits of men and women, undoubtedly the largest picture as to numbers ever produced. These four thousand were gathered behind the doors of one section of the factory, and when the biograph was in position the doors opened. The scene for a few moments resembles that of a hive of bees swarming. Then, as the crowd which had been jammed against the door separates, the workingmen come more slowly." For an appreciation of the factory gate genre, see Tom Gunning, "Pictures of Crowd Splendor: The Mitchell and Kenyon Factory Gate Films," in *The Lost World of Mitchell & Kenyon: Edwardian Britain on Film*, ed. Vanessa Toulmin, Simon Popple, and Patrick Russell (London: British Film Institute, 2004), 49–58.

Figure 2.2. Film as virtual voyage; video still from *Panorama Exterior Westinghouse Works* (1904).

visitors. . . . Yet the whole world has a curiosity regarding these great establishments of which we hear so much in the newspapers. The Westinghouse biograph pictures gratify this curiosity in a way that is even more attractive than would be a trip through the factory."[28] Although the Library of Congress website arranges the films alphabetically and by subject, it is not difficult to rearrange the titles to produce a likely narrative that begins with the opening "panorama" approaching the works by train; continues with the women taking their time checks; proceeds to many other views of working; and concludes with the most spectacular films, the panoramas of the interiors. The half-minute close-up *Steam Whistle* could have served as punctuation—either as a conclusion to the "day in the life" structure, a beginning, a marker of a shift change, or some combination of these possibilities.

While extraordinarily rich visually, like most of early cinema, these films are not models of didactic clarity. They have no intertitles, and the only contextual information a contemporary viewer receives comes from an opening title, which was not part of the original print. Although contextual information can supply a considerable amount of information not inherent in the images and thus lead to a better understanding of how these films function as an educative experience,

---

[28] Walker, "World Instruction in Pictures," 531.

these images also contain ambiguous moments that pose problems for educational use of the films. Walker described a moment in *Welding the Big Ring* in the following way:

> As the crucial moment arrives, four welders seize their hammers. The ring is lifted by a crane out of the furnace. The four heavy hammers jump forward to do the work of welding. They strike with an energy that shows there is not a moment to lose before the iron grows cool. Blows descend, sparks fly. One man is struck on the thigh, through accident, by his neighbor's hammer, and limps off apparently with a broken leg; but notwithstanding his suffering, knowing that the extra hammer is needed, he braces up, steps back and helps finish the work.

Reviewing this moment (forty seconds from the end), it is difficult to reconcile Walker's account with the screen image. The description magnifies and distorts the moment, changing the location of the blow (the hammer appears to strike a glancing blow to the man's foot, although it is difficult to tell with certainty), and its severity—the man steps away briefly, with only a barely perceptible limp, and does not appear to be in the kind of pain a broken leg would involve. Of course, it is possible that the injury is more serious than it looks and that the injured man downplayed the extent to which he was injured, perhaps in part because of the unusual situation in which the workers found themselves—illuminated by extremely bright lights, and having been told, one imagines, that they should perform their tasks as if the camera and lights were not there.

Resolving this discrepancy is less important than understanding its relevance to the concept of cinema as an educational medium. Proponents of visual education tended to understand cinema as reproducing the thing or the experience itself. But the moving image's density of information, so consistently singled out for praise with words like "vivid," also harbored ambiguity. The Westinghouse films contain other examples of film's ability to record the unexpected, where something excessive or unwanted intrudes into the shot. In *Panorama View Street Car Motor Room*, debris suddenly falls down from the space above the top of the frame, momentarily halting the progress of the crane's forward movement; in *Girls Taking Time Checks* one of the girls drops her check (see fig. 2.3), causing a disruption in the orderly procession.[29] In these moments, a countercurrent to cinema's ability to provide an obviously superior visual record becomes particularly evident.

---

[29] The falling debris occurs at around 1m/frame 1800.

Figure 2.3.   Film as recorder of the contingent; video still from *Girls Taking Time Checks* (1904). (Library of Congress.)

This tendency to record instances of contingency could distract from the orderly processes demanded by pedagogy.[30] As Elizabeth Wiatr has noted, *Panorama View Street Car Motor Room* does not deliver "a comprehensive visualization leading to knowledge" but instead provides a view that proceeds in "a fragmentary, impoverished manner that works against the viewer's comprehension."[31] Here the obverse of cinema's capacity to educate becomes visible, namely its capacity to distract by its attention to surface phenomena. Much of educational cinema's development involved devising methods to harness cinema's dazzling profusion of detail toward the goals of education while remaining cautiously open to the visual pleasures that formed the basis of its appeal.

From 1903 to 1905, audiences began to display a preference for story films, and this development affected the understanding of cinema's future as an educator. The arguments for cinema as a generally educative medium persisted, but

---

[30] A notable exception from this period is Boleslas Matuszewski, whose anecdote about how one of his films of the Russian emperor helped to resolve a political fracas (because the film captured the emperor's salute that allegedly had not been proffered) demonstrates the importance of "a whole anecdotal side of History that until now has escaped the imagination of narrators" (Matuszewski, "A New Source of History," trans. Laura U. Marks and Diane Koszarski, *Film History* 7, no. 3 [1995]: 322–24).

[31] Wiatr, "Between Word, Image, and the Machine," 340–41.

as it became clearer that cinema's primary function would be as popular entertainment, a different vision of the future of cinema as an educational medium began to emerge. Charles Urban, whose promotion of cinema as an educational medium was unrivaled in its zeal and persistence, had already been an innovator in introducing popular science films into commercial venues in 1903 with "The Unseen World," a series of microcinematographic films made in collaboration with F. Martin Duncan.[32] As other producers turned overwhelmingly to story films, Urban redoubled his commitment to cinema's nonfiction/educative mission by presciently adopting the strategy of promoting nonfiction cinema as a separate sphere.

In 1907 Urban published an extended expression of his thoughts about the cinema's educational mission in a pamphlet entitled *The Cinematograph in Science, Education, and Matters of State*. He envisioned a future for the motion picture free from its enslavement to the interests of the entertainment industry. "The entertainer," the producer argued, "has hitherto monopolised the Cinematograph for exhibition purposes, but movement in more serious directions has become imperative, and the object of this pamphlet is to prove that the Cinematograph must be recognised as a National Instrument by the Boards of Agriculture, Education, and Trade, by the War Council, Admiralty, Medical Associations, and every Institution of Training, Teaching, Demonstration, and Research."[33] Invoking familiar arguments, Urban claimed that film was a uniquely efficient educator. "A series of living pictures imparts more knowledge, in a far more interesting and effective manner, in five minutes, than does an oral lesson of an hour's duration." He went on to claim that films do "the work of text books without their dryness."[34] The subjects he saw as suited for the cinematograph included geography, cultivation and production, history (both through reenactments and as recordings of current events), industrial knowledge, and demonstrations of trades and industries.[35] Even when he discussed the cinematograph's importance

---

[32] For more on "The Unseen World," see Timothy Boon, *Films of Fact: A History of Science in Documentary Films and Television* (New York: Wallflower Press, 2008), 7–32; and McKernan, "'Something More,'" 69–76.

[33] Charles Urban, *The Cinematograph in Science, Education, and Matters of State* (London: Charles Urban Trading Company, 1907), 7. Portions of this text were reprinted in a series of articles that appeared in the *Moving Picture World*: Charles Urban, "The Cinematograph in Science and Education," Aug. 10, 17, and 24, 1907. See also Thierry Lefebvre, "Charles Urban et le film d'éducation: Brèves réflexions sur quelques documents des Archives Will Day," *1895*, "The Will Day Historical Collection of Cinematography and Moving Picture Equipment," *numéro hors-série* (Oct. 1997): 129–35.

[34] Urban, *Cinematograph*, 15, 10.

[35] Urban's call in this area soon found an echo in the United States: "The moving picture machine offers a partial solution of the problem of imparting individual instruction in the trades.

in matters of state—by which he primarily meant military applications such as recording artillery tests, aerial cinematography of maneuvers, or film as a means of recruiting military personnel—the primary application was educational.

More than half of the pamphlet was devoted to the scientific uses of the cinematograph, including a long discussion of using film to record surgical procedures. Urban quoted from a 1903 lecture delivered at the International Congress of Medicine in Madrid by Dr. Eugène-Louis Doyen, whose discussion of moving pictures and surgery advanced a number of arguments about the cinema's unique properties: the cinema allowed for better sightlines than those afforded by a crowded surgical theater; the cinema was able to preserve the skills of the finest surgeons for posterity, which was especially useful in the case of rare operations; and the cinema could serve as a teaching tool for practitioners, allowing them to critique their own procedures after the fact.[36] The pamphlet concluded with a consideration of what Urban considered his company's achievements in the realms of bacteriological science, horticulture and agriculture, industry and commerce, physics, anthropology (for the preservation of threatened civilizations), zoology, and botany (especially time-lapse films of plant growth).

In 1908 Urban began his collaboration with Frank Percy Smith, who at the time was employed as a clerk at the British Board of Education. Smith worked at the Urban company for over a decade and went on to become one of the most celebrated popular science filmmakers of his generation, primarily through his work on the "Secrets of Nature" series in the 1920s and 1930s.[37] Two of the best-known films Smith made while at Urban dealt with the housefly, *The Acrobatic Fly* and *The Fly Pest,* and together these films encapsulate the delights and ambiguities of the educational cinema around 1910. *The Acrobatic Fly* arose out of an investigation of fly physiology and a desire to illustrate the fly's tremendous strength, which the film accomplished to remarkable effect with images that evoked other iconographic traditions, such as the flea circus (see fig. 2.4).[38] These unusual images of the fly prompted curiosity about the

---

Next to actually doing the thing, or seeing a skilled workman do it, is the seeing it done in a series of moving pictures" (*Scientific American Supplement* 68 [1909]: 79; cited in Rudolph Matas, "The Cinematograph as an Aid to Medical Education and Research," *Southern Medical Journal* 5, no. 8 [Sept. 1912]: 524).

[36] For more on Doyen's vision of cinema as an educational force in medical science, see Thierry Lefebvre, *Le Chair et le celluloïd: le cinéma chirugical du docteur Doyen* (Brionne: Jean Doyen, 2004).

[37] See my "Secrets of Nature," in *Encyclopedia of the Documentary Film*, vol. 3, ed. Ian Aitken (New York: Routledge, 2005): 1195–97.

[38] *The Acrobatic Fly* is a 1910 reissue that includes elements from the two earlier films, *The Balancing Blue-Bottle* and *Blue-Bottle Flies Feeding* (both 1909).

Figure 2.4. Demonstrating the marvels of fly physiology; video still from *The Acrobatic Fly* (Percy Smith, 1910). (Nederlands Filmmuseum.)

methods employed to achieve the effects.[39] Smith, in order to answer these questions and to defend himself from accusations of animal cruelty, pointed out that the flies had been restrained with nothing more than a silken thread and that their "juggling" was in fact their attempt to walk on the objects they had been given. The film's educational qualities were merged with its entertaining aspects, participating in a tradition of instructive amusement that uses wonder to instill curiosity.[40] To borrow Smith's gustatory metaphor to describe the cinema's educational mission, *The Acrobatic Fly* demonstrated how to mix "the powder of instruction in the jam of entertainment."[41]

While *The Acrobatic Fly* celebrated the wondrous and amusing possibilities of the magnified world, Smith also made *The Fly Pest* (1910), which contained a different

---

[39] In an interesting twist on the notion of education, the film led to the frequent suggestion that the flies had been "educated." For a later instance of "educated insects," probably influenced by Smith's films, see Yuri Tsivian, "The Case of the Bioscope Beetle: Starewicz's Answer to Genetics," *Discourse: Journal for Theoretical Studies in Media and Culture* 17 (Spring 1995): 119–25.

[40] On this tradition, see Lorraine Daston and Catherine Park, *Wonders and the Order of Nature, 1150–1750* (New York: Zone Books, 1998).

[41] "Experiences of Mr. Percy Smith. His Scientific Work on Behalf of Kinemacolor and Kineto, Ltd.," *Kinematograph and Lantern Weekly* (Mar. 30, 1911): 74. For more on this dynamic and on how the educational rhetoric surrounding early cinema was carried forward in the 1910s, see Amanda Keeler, "Sugar-Coat the Educational Pill: Using Film and Radio for Education, 1907–1930" (PhD diss., Indiana University, 2011).

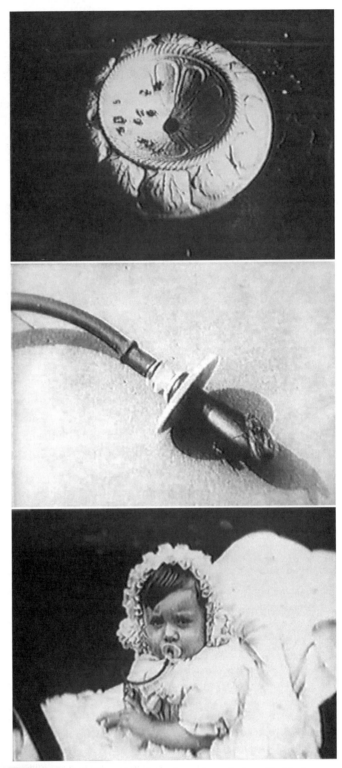

Figure 2.5. The fly as agent of disease; video stills from *The Fly Pest* (Percy Smith, 1910). (Nederlands Filmmuseum.)

approach to the insect.[42] The first section of the film described the fly's life cycle, and a second section demonstrated how the fly could spread disease, concluding with a three-shot montage that illustrated how a baby might contract tuberculosis thanks to a housefly (see fig. 2.5).[43] This stigmatization of the fly as an unsanitary little menace indicates a modern hygienic discourse quite different from the juggling-fly films' aesthetic of astonishment.[44]

These changes resonated with the shift in the American cinema landscape at the turn of the 1910s, as an increasingly prominent chorus of voices called for the transformation of cinema. Reformers envisioned the cinema as a place where the medium's "impressionable" audiences—usually understood as children, immigrants, and women—could learn about useful things like science, history, and civics, instead of learning the lessons of cheap melodrama, which had earned the nickelodeon the epithet "the school of crime."[45] This reaction was part of what has been called the "Arnoldian response" to the "problem of cheap amusements," where instead of repression, cinema reformers worked to transform the medium from within.[46] *The Fly Pest* thus heralded a different approach in two senses. It both contained a "reformed" view of the housefly, and it was itself a form of inoculation against the "filthy" mass of films that constituted the average nickelodeon screening.[47] This difference is also manifest at the level of film style, with *The Fly Pest* making

---

[42] This film was made at the behest of American anti-fly crusaders; see Edward Hatch Jr., "The House Fly as Carrier of Disease," *Annals of the American Academy of Political and Social Science* 37, no. 2 (1911): 168–79.

[43] The same film is preserved as *De Vliegen: Wetenschappelyke Film* at the Nederlands Filmmuseum. Other fly films from this era that contain similar material are *The House Fly* (Edison, 1912) and *Le plus dangereux des insects, la mouche* [The Most Dangerous of Insects, the Fly] (Pathé, 1913). The latter may be the source of images in *The Fly*, a Pathégram title from the 1920s, which I was able to see in the private collection of Jay Schwartz. This film combines a sequence where a fly juggles objects within an overarching hygiene lesson that presents the fly as a disease vector.

[44] See Naomi Rogers, "Germs with Legs: Flies, Disease, and the New Public Health," *Bulletin of the History of Medicine* 63, no. 4 (1989): 599–617.

[45] As Lee Grieveson notes, this epithet for the nickelodeon first appeared in the Women's Christian Temperance Union journal, *Union Signal*, in 1906; see Grieveson, *Policing Cinema*, 265.

[46] See William Uricchio and Roberta E. Pearson, *Reframing Culture: The Case of the Vitagraph Quality Films* (Princeton, NJ: Princeton University Press, 1993), 21–24. Uricchio and Pearson refer here to Matthew Arnold's influential *Culture and Anarchy* (1869), which "proposed a means of combating moral infection through culture." This position was often translated into attempts "to forge a cultural consensus that would incorporate rather than repress disruptive forces such as workers and immigrants by extending a vision of sweetness and light across the boundaries of race, gender, ethnicity, and class."

[47] My thanks to Scott Curtis for suggesting the idea of regarding *The Fly Pest* as an inoculation. For a similar attitude toward visual materials, see H. K. Kleinschmidt, "Educational Prophylaxis of Venereal Diseases," *Social Hygiene* 5, no. 1 (1919): 27–40.

extensive use of intertitles and thus anchoring its visual appeals in a layer of verbal authority.

As widespread and successful as *The Fly Pest* was as a means of public health education, it contained aspects that were somewhat at odds with the film's hygienic message. Appeals to the horrific and the wondrous lurked behind its soberly informative dimension, which became evident in stories about how the film faced threats of censorship, as in the following letter from an exhibitor to distributor George Kleine:

> We gave a special showing of *The Fly Pest* recently to the members of the Board of Health, School Officials, Police officials, representatives of women's clubs and public officials generally. It was given with the understanding that possibly part of the film would be withdrawn from general showing because of its disagreeable features but as we expected practically every one of the officials who attended personally asked us to show every bit of the film.[48]

A clipping from a Portland, Oregon, newspaper about a screening organized for local doctors at the Arcade theater put it succinctly: "'The Fly Pest' is the most educational as well as most revolting motion picture film that has ever been exhibited anywhere."[49] These reactions, which acknowledged the possibility of objectionable content while insisting on the overall necessity of such images, indicated how the film's Progressive ethos could challenge certain aspects of genteel society in the name of scientific advancements.[50]

Both fly films featured prominently in George Kleine's *Catalogue of Educational Motion Picture Films* (1910). The catalog was an outgrowth of the uplift movement, and its stated goal was to collect and order all the films produced during the first fifteen years of cinema history that could be considered educational. In the introductory material, Kleine invoked familiar arguments about visual education, dubbing the catalog "An Educational System by Visualization." He commented:

---

[48] Frank Altman to George Kleine, May 30, 1910. Altman was the manager of the Theatre Voyons in Lowell, Massachusetts. At least one screening of the film in Indianapolis was stopped by the police; see J. N. Hurty, Secretary, Indiana State Board of Health, to the H. Lieber Co., Apr. 25, 1910; both letters in "The Fly Pest" folder, "Historical File," box 26, George Kleine Collection, Manuscripts Division, Library of Congress (hereafter "Kleine Collection").

[49] "Menace of Flies Is Told by Film," clipping in "The Fly Pest" folder, Kleine Collection.

[50] For a description of how German cinema reformers had a similar position that melded conservative and progressive elements, see Scott Curtis, "The Taste of a Nation: Training the Senses and Sensibility of Cinema Audiences in Imperial Germany," *Film History* 6, no. 4 (1994): 445–69. See also Jennifer Peterson, "The Five-Cent University: Early Educational Films and the Drive to 'Uplift' the Cinema," chapter 3 in *Education in the School of Dreams*.

Progressive educators will welcome this opportunity to instruct their classes in any of the above subjects by means of first-class motion pictures. Education thus imparted is never likely to be forgotten, and pupils who are slow in memorizing text-book instruction absorb the same knowledge very readily and rapidly when conveyed by moving pictures, which teach as no words do.[51]

The catalog's collection of more than one thousand films was assembled into a quasi-systematic order, constituting what Kleine envisioned as "a library of motion pictures to which the educator will turn for illustrations as freely as to a library of books."[52] In its conception, the catalog resembled the archival ambitions of a number of Kleine's precursors while pointing ahead to future calls for the institutionalization of educational cinema, notably in Vachel Lindsay's *The Art of the Moving Picture* (1915).[53]

The catalog was remarkable not only for its considerable size but also for how it formed a hinge between two eras: an earlier era that was characterized by a broad conception of education and included a prominent role for entertainment, and a later era that was typified by a more focused conception of education and harbored more concern about the deployment of visual pleasure. Kleine's vacillating opening remarks attested to this transitional moment. He wrote that, "in a sense, all subjects are educational," but then immediately qualified that assertion by allowing the need to restrict the domain of the educational film to "a reasonable area."[54] As Kleine's catalog indicates, by 1910 the transition from a model of educational film as a competitor for the mantle of Cinema to one that envisioned educational cinema as a particular application for a specific audience was well underway, although incomplete.[55]

The uplift campaign in the trade press, for instance, which became widespread in the early 1910s, tended to call on the notion of educational film as a component of the overall transformation of cinema. In 1911, the *Moving Picture*

---

[51] [George Kleine], *Catalogue of Educational Motion Picture Films* (Chicago: Bentley, Murray & Co., 1910), 3.

[52] Kleine, *Catalogue*, 6.

[53] For a careful and revelatory reading of Lindsay's work, see Peter Decherney, "Vachel Lindsay and the Universal Film Museum," chapter 1 in *Hollywood and the Culture Elite: How the Movies Became American* (New York: Columbia University Press, 2005), 13–40. See also Haidee Wasson, *Museum Movies: The Museum of Modern Art and the Birth of Art Cinema* (Berkeley: University of California Press, 2005).

[54] Kleine, *Catalogue*, 3.

[55] For more detailed accounts of the popular science films by Charles Urban and Percy Smith, as well as George Kleine's educational film catalogue, see my *Devices of Curiosity: Early Cinema and Popular Science* (Oxford University Press, forthcoming).

World inaugurated a regular column entitled "In the Educational Field" (later "Education and Science" and "The Moving Picture Educator"), which was a part of its "endeavor to crystallize the wave of sentiment that is abroad in favor of the educational value of the picture."[56] The trade journals *Motography* and *The Nickelodeon* also ran occasional articles advocating for an educational cinema. Frederick A. Talbot, a popularizer of science and technology, wrote *Moving Pictures: How They Are Made and Worked* in 1912, which included a chapter entitled "Motion-Photography as an Educational Force." Talbot's rhetoric indicates the persistence of certain tropes related to cinema's educative efficacy: "Indeed, there is not the slightest doubt that a thousand pictures will impress themselves upon the schoolboy's mind, and impart to him more definite knowledge of their subject in one minute than hours of hammering with the aid of text-book and blackboard."[57] Similarly, Leonard Donaldson's *The Cinematograph and Natural Science: The Achievements and Possibilities of Cinematography as an Aid to Scientific Research* (1912) began with a chapter entitled "The Cinematograph as an Educator—Motion Pictures in the Schools."[58]

As these examples demonstrate, the flowering of interest in cinema as an educational medium around 1910 continued debates from the first fifteen years of cinema history. And these debates about the consanguinity of cinema and education, in turn, partook of discussions about the status of vision in education that were prominent in the second half of the nineteenth century. The visions of cinema as a modern educator in the United States participated in a Progressive ethos of optimism about the confluence of technological developments and human perfectibility. In this context cinema appeared as an ideal ally in the struggle against ignorance. The prominence of educational rhetoric during the cinema's first two decades can prompt us to reevaluate familiar films from the vantage point of their educative function.[59] It can also prompt us to seek out the films, many of which are now barely known, in which the prophets of cinema's educational mission placed their faith.

---

[56] "In the Educational Field," *Moving Picture World*, Jan. 21, 1911, 128.

[57] Frederick A. Talbot, *Moving Pictures: How They Are Made and Worked* (Philadelphia: J. B. Lippincott, 1912), 314; reprinted in 1970 by Arno Press as part of the "Literature of Cinema" series. Talbot's book *Practical Cinematography and Its Applications* (1913) includes the chapter "The Preparation of Educational Films." Both books are available at archive.org.

[58] Leonard Donaldson, *The Cinematograph and Natural Science: The Achievements and Possibilities of Cinematography as an Aid to Scientific Research* (London: Ganes, 1912).

[59] For example, D. W. Griffith's films *The Drunkard's Revelation* and *The Country Doctor* (both 1909) are, in addition to being landmarks in the development of cinematic storytelling, a temperance film and a film about diphtheria.

Filmography

The Acrobatic Fly (1910) 2 min., 35mm

PRODUCTION: Charles Urban Company/Kineto. DIRECTOR/
PHOTOGRAPHY: Percy Smith. EDITOR: Charles Urban.
ACCESS: BFIfilms YouTube channel, www.youtube.com/
watch?v=8hlocZhNcoM.

The Fly Pest (1910) 6 min., 35mm

PRODUCTION: Charles Urban Company. DIRECTOR/
CINEMATOGRAPHER: Percy Smith. SPONSOR: American
Civic Association /New York Merchants' Association. ACCESS:
BFI; Nederlands Filmmuseum.

Films of the Westinghouse Works (1904) 35mm

PRODUCTION: American Mutoscope and Biograph Company.
CAMERA: G. W. Bitzer. ACCESS: Library of Congress, 21 items
online at http://lcweb2.loc.gov/papr/west.
Runtimes based on projection speeds between 14 and 16fps; total
runtime = 54:47.

Assembling a Generator (3:18)
Assembling and Testing Turbines (2:42)
Casting a Guide Box (5:36)
Coil Winding Machines (2:09)
Coil Winding Section E (2:25)
Girls Taking Time Checks (2:44)
Girls Winding Armatures (1:55)
Panorama Exterior Westinghouse Works (5:36)
Panorama of Machine Co. Aisle (3:22)
Panorama View Street Car Motor Room (2:35)
Panoramic View Aisle B (2:19)
Steam Hammer (3:29)
Steam Whistle (0:38)
Taping Coils (2:22)
Tapping a Furnace (5:12)
Testing Large Turbines (3:32)
Testing a Rotary (2:49)
Welding the Big Ring (6:12)
Westinghouse Air Brake Co. Westinghouse Co. Works (3:19)
Westinghouse Air Brake Co. Westinghouse Co. Works (Casting Scene)
(3:06)
Westinghouse Air Brake Co. Westinghouse Co. Works (Moulding Scene)
(3:32)

Related Films

***Electrocuting an Elephant* (1903) 1 min., 35mm**
PRODUCTION: Edison Manufacturing Company. CAMERA:
Jacob Blair Smith or Edwin S. Porter. FILMING DATE: Jan. 4, 1903,
Luna Park, Coney Island. ACCESS: Library of Congress; DVD set
Edison: The Invention of the Movies (Kino).

Films of McKinley and the Pan-American Exposition (1901)
PRODUCTION: Edison Manufacturing Company. ACCESS:
Library of Congress, http://memory.loc.gov/ammem/papr/
mckhome.html.

Total run time: 1h6m25sec.

Arrival of McKinley's Funeral Train at Canton, Ohio (0:41)

Circular Panorama of Electric Tower (1:26)

Esquimaux Game of Snap-the-Whip (0:26)

Esquimaux Leap-Frog (0:48)

Esquimaux Village (0:51)

Execution of Czolgosz, with Panorama of Auburn Prison (3:24)

Funeral Leaving the President's House and Church at Canton, Ohio
(3:07)

Horse Parade at the Pan-American Exposition (2:26)

Japanese Village (2:40)

The Martyred Presidents (1:04)

McKinley's Funeral Entering Westlawn Cemetery, Canton [Ohio]
(3:11)

The Mob outside the Temple of Music at the Pan-American Exposition
(1:13)

Opening, Pan-American Exposition (1:48)

Pan-American Exposition by Night (0:51)

Panorama of Esplanade by Night (0:59)

Panoramic View of Electric Tower from a Balloon (1:20)

Panoramic View of the President's House at Canton, Ohio (1:24)

President McKinley and Escort Going to the Capitol (2:02)

President McKinley Reviewing the Troops at the Pan-American Exposition (1:28)

President McKinley Taking the Oath (0:44)

President McKinley's Funeral Cortege at Buffalo, N.Y. (6:54)

President McKinley's Funeral Cortege at Washington, D.C. (6:14)

President McKinley's Speech at the Pan-American Exposition (1:17)

President Roosevelt at the Canton Station (1:31)

Sham Battle at the Pan-American Exposition (4:59)

Spanish Dancers at the Pan-American Exposition (1:18)

Taking President McKinley's Body from Train at Canton, Ohio (0:59)

A Trip around the Pan-American Exposition (11:20)

3 COMMUNICATING DISEASE: TUBERCULOSIS, NARRATIVE, AND SOCIAL ORDER IN THOMAS EDISON'S RED CROSS SEAL FILMS

MIRIAM POSNER

When surgeon John F. Urie worked with Chicago's Hull House in 1912, he faced an uphill battle. Urie attempted to instruct working-class families on how to prevent the spread of tuberculosis (TB). But time and again, he complained, when visiting health workers gave tenement-dwelling families careful instructions on how to avoid contagion, the families' "parrot-like" compliance masked a stubborn refusal to adopt necessary behavioral changes. Once the health workers were out the door, tenement families went back to sharing drinking cups with infected people, disposing of sputum improperly, and failing to dust with the alacrity Urie recommended. While "patients had a glib familiarity with . . . what conduct of life they should adopt," Urie fumed, "it is only occasionally that any real effort to follow prescribed rules was observed."[1]

In fact, laypeople were often dubious of health workers' claims about how TB germs were spread. Although scientists generally accepted the germ theory of disease by the 1880s, many laypeople remained unconvinced at the time Urie was writing. The skepticism was partly due to the serious challenges the theory presented to domestic and civic values. The simple act of drinking from a common communion cup, for example, was now fraught with danger, as were everyday activities such as kissing or handling food. These challenges, combined with germs' invisibility to the naked eye, meant that the families Urie visited regarded the surgeon's warnings with skepticism. Many preferred to believe, as people had for centuries, that environment or heredity was to blame for TB.[2]

Contagion, the idea that illness could be transmitted through contact, was not just a new way of thinking about disease. It was a new way of seeing the world. Germ theory created sometimes unwelcome relationships between people

---

[1] John F. Urie, "Family Contagion in the Tuberculosis Problem," *Journal of the Outdoor Life* 9, no. 2 (1912): 97–101.

[2] See Nancy Tomes, *The Gospel of Germs* (Cambridge, MA: Harvard University Press, 1998).

of different races and classes. Moreover, according to the theory, even well-intentioned and seemingly innocuous gestures were viewed with suspicion. Contagion, write Alison Bashford and Claire Hooker, inspires anxiety and prompts a need for control: it "implies absorption, invasion, vulnerability, the breaking of a boundary imagined as secure, in which the other becomes part of the self."[3]

Urie advocated the enforced segregation of TB patients, but less strident public-health campaigners looked for more subtle ways to convince people of the danger of germ contagion. This essay describes one such method of persuasion: a series of six films that the National Association for the Study and Prevention of Tuberculosis (NASPT) made in collaboration with the Edison Company: *The Red Cross Seal* (1910), *The Awakening of John Bond* (1911), *Hope: A Red Cross Seal Story* (1912), *The Price of Human Lives* (1913), *The Temple of Moloch* (1914), and *The Lone Game* (1915). Edison released a film each winter to coincide with the anti-TB organization's annual Christmas Seal campaign.

These films did not simply offer instruction; they also provided narratives. The people Urie lectured may have been weary of outright preaching, but narrative is not just a sugarcoating for a didactic message. In these one-reel silent films, narrative performs the crucial work of making germ theory comprehensible, intelligible, and acceptable. The films instruct audiences in the importance of narrative and of contagion at critical points in the histories of both systems, helping us to appreciate the changes they entailed. Indeed, the films reveal unexpected similarities. They show how a disease can function remarkably like a story: by knitting diverse people and places into reciprocal, if unequal, relationships.[4]

Tuberculosis and the NASPT

An ancient disease, TB thrived in the cramped working conditions and living quarters of factory floors and tenement buildings. For this reason, in the late nineteenth and early twentieth centuries, TB was widely understood as a disease of the poor. Until the advent of streptomycin in 1943, no cure for TB existed. So

---

[3] Alison Bashford and Claire Hooker, "Introduction: Contagion, Modernity, and Postmodernity," in *Contagion: Historical and Cultural Studies,* ed. Bashford and Hooker (New York: Routledge, 2001), 4.

[4] Martin S. Pernick first described the Red Cross Seal series in "The Ethics of Preventative Medicine: Thomas Edison's Tuberculosis Films: Mass Media and Health Propaganda," *Hastings Center Report* 8 (June 1978): 21–27. Pernick also discusses *The Temple of Moloch*, along with other contemporary health films, in "More Than Illustrations: Early Twentieth-Century Health Films as Contributors to the Histories of Medicine and of Motion Pictures," in *Medicine's Moving Pictures: Medicine, Health, and Bodies in American Film and Television,* ed. Leslie J. Reagan, Nancy Tomes, and Paula A. Treichler (Rochester, NY: University of Rochester Press, 2007), 19–35.

physicians in the early twentieth century emphasized prevention for the unin-
fected and sanatorium treatment, healthful eating, and bed rest for the infected.

Germ theory and the Progressive Era's enthusiasm for social change spawned
a network of voluntary organizations dedicated to educating Americans about
hygiene. The NASPT, which endures today as the American Lung Association,
began as a number of small, local anti-TB leagues. The first of these, the Pennsylvania Society for the Prevention of Tuberculosis, emerged in 1892, and in 1904
the local organizations united under the national association.[5]

The annual Christmas Seal campaign was an important source of income
for the NASPT. Schoolchildren, clubwomen, fraternal organizations, and
civic-minded volunteers all peddled the stamps, which each year featured a different illustration. Purchasers could affix the one-cent seals to packages and letters.
Confusingly, the seals carried the name and emblem of the Red Cross until 1920.
The Red Cross was responsible for the stamps from 1907 to 1909, but beginning in
1910 the NASPT was the chief administrator and beneficiary of the campaigns.[6]

As motion pictures became more widely exhibited in the first decade of the
twentieth century, the NASPT came to see the medium as an ideal way of disseminating information efficiently to large audiences. Films ensured that audience members were exposed to NASPT-sanctioned messages. In addition, a film
screening could attract enthusiasm that a lecture could not match. Cinema's storytelling power, moreover, offered a way to entwine the new science of germ
theory with captivating narratives that could bring the message home.

Tuberculosis and the American Film Industry

The NASPT's interest in sponsoring films coincided with the young movie industry's interest in benevolent organizations. Concerned about a growing censorship
movement, film producers and exhibitors in the 1910s were determined to raise
the social prestige of motion pictures. Turning to progressive organizations for
storylines and moral messages, filmmakers converted harsh social realities like
poverty, usury, and crime into sober-minded but popular films that addressed
both lower- and upper-class audiences.[7] From this perspective, producing films

---

[5] S. Adolphus Knopf, *A History of the National Tuberculosis Association* (New York: National
Tuberculosis Association, 1922), 18.

[6] See *Transactions of the National Association for the Study and Prevention of Tuberculosis* 8
(1912): 31; hereafter cited as *Transactions*.

[7] For more on these Progressive-Era social problem films, see Kay Sloan, *The Loud Silents:
Origins of the Social Problem Film* (Chicago: University of Illinois Press, 1988); and Kevin
Brownlow, *Behind the Mask of Innocence: Sex, Violence, Crime: Films of Social Conscience in the
Silent Era* (New York: Knopf, 1990).

for the Christmas Seal campaign made good business sense. And because the films entered general release, producer-distributors like Edison earned rental returns as well as social credibility.

If it seems strange that educational films about TB entered wide release, this is because the designation "educational" had yet to describe a separate route for film production and distribution. Audiences of the 1910s were accustomed to watching theatrical pictures about topics that we might expect to encounter in the classroom or in the newspaper. Social-problem films shared a billing with actualities (nonfiction films), scientific films, and fictional dramas and comedies.[8]

Films in the 1910s were distinct in other important ways as well. The Christmas Seal films fall within the period film historians call the "transitional era." These years, from approximately 1907 to 1915, witnessed enormous industrial and stylistic changes for cinema. Filmmakers introduced an arsenal of techniques that ushered cinema from short, vaudeville-like vignettes toward the immersive, heavily narrative medium associated with film's classical era. From this experimental period, a distinct style emerged: a unified, cause-and-effect-based plotline that relied on conventionalized editing to create a coherent sense of space, time, and character.[9] The TB films, produced while these changes were underway, at times reveal glimpses of an earlier stylistic mode: theatrically tinged acting, for example, and the frequent presence of coincidence. Such glimpses, noticeably archaic amid the newer logics of narrative and contagion, suggest the gravity of the transformations underway in ideas about film and disease. We might see in these moments of stylistic friction a reflection of the tension between old and new ideas about storytelling and disease.[10]

---

[8] Kay Sloan and Lee Grieveson, among others, have described how theatrical films came to be regarded primarily as vehicles of entertainment, rather than edification or social change. Sloan argues that feature-length films edged out shorter, more didactic one-reel films after World War I, while Grieveson argues that the prospect of censorship gradually encouraged filmmakers and audiences to cast film as a harmless diversion. See Sloan, *Loud Silents*; and Lee Grieveson, *Policing Cinema: Movies and Censorship in Early-Twentieth-Century America* (Berkeley: University of California Press, 2004).

[9] Charlie Keil dates the transitional period in his book title, *Early American Cinema in Transition: Story, Style, and Filmmaking, 1907–1913* (Madison: University of Wisconsin Press, 2001). The years between 1907 and 1917 are offered in Robert Pearson's "Transitional Cinema," in *The Oxford History of World Cinema,* ed. Geoffrey Nowell-Smith (New York: Oxford University Press, 1996), 23–42. Kristin Thompson favors the years 1909–1915; see David Bordwell, Janet Staiger, and Kristin Thompson, *The Classical Hollywood Cinema: Film Style and Mode of Production to 1960* (New York: Columbia University Press, 1985), 246–64.

[10] Pernick, "More Than Illustrations," makes a similar point about contemporary films' medical point of view, noting that while films of this era "emphasized aspects of the new etiology, they also retained many older causal concepts as well" (23).

The Red Cross Seal Films: Fitting Germ Theory into and against
Familiar Narratives

Four of the six Edison Red Cross Seal films are known to be extant: *The Awakening of John Bond*, *Hope*, *The Temple of Moloch,* and *The Lone Game*.[11] In these works, TB forges links between social groups, new chains of cause and effect, and novel understandings of the relationship between individual bodies and the body politic.

Hope: A Red Cross Seal Story (1912)

Hope gives audiences practical suggestions on battling TB, but it also performs more subtle work by easing audiences into a world that includes an invisible population of bacteria. In making this transition, *Hope* calls on the techniques of theatrical melodrama to address the discomfiting novelty of germ contagion. It's useful to compare the film's plot with the structure Tzvetan Todorov defines as an "ideal narrative." In this schema, a story begins by depicting a stable situation, which is disrupted by a force of some kind. This force is overcome and equilibrium is reestablished, but the second equilibrium is never identical to the first. In *Hope*, the disruptive power is the TB bacillus, and it is the NASPT that intervenes to restore order. True to narrative form, however, the final equilibrium is different from that of the story's opening. The world of the film's close is a subtly reconfigured place that accommodates both the TB bacillus and the organization necessary to keep it in check.[12]

The opening shot establishes our first equilibrium: it shows a busy, prosperous-looking bank office, presided over by a handsome young bank president, John, and his older unnamed clerk. The arrival of a letter soliciting donations for the NASPT is the first development that interrupts the business's efficient flow. John's smug reply, however, restores the office to order. "This is a country town," his response letter reads. "We don't have consumption here and therefore don't need a sanatorium."[13]

---

[11] The fate of the other films may be related to this incident: "Two of the [NASPT's copies of the Edison] reels are now worn out and cannot be replaced because of the destruction of the negatives by the recent disastrous fire at the Edison plant." "Report of the Executive Officer," *Transactions* 11 (1915); 31.

[12] Todorov, *Introduction to Poetics*, trans. Richard Howard (Minneapolis: University of Minnesota Press, 1981), 38.

[13] As Jennifer Horne points out, situating *Hope* in a country town allowed the NASPT to bring attention to TB's presence in the countryside as well as to provide a film suitable for rural venues. Horne, commentary track, *Hope: A Red Cross Seal Story*, disc 1, *Treasures III: Social Issues in American Film*, DVD (National Film Preservation Foundation, 2007).

The next shot introduces us to the disruptive force that will provide our story's tension: a cough. The bank clerk relaxes in his family parlor with his daughter Edith, a pretty young woman. The room's handsome furnishings and prominent hearth bespeak domestic warmth. The entrance of the bank president, Edith's intended, completes the neat circle of home, work, and family. Only Edith's slight cough—the visible manifestation of the bacillus—interrupts the scene's tranquility. But in the economical vocabulary of narrative filmmaking, in which a cough is never just a cough, we are encouraged to recognize the beginning of a chain of disorder.

In the next scene, Edith visits the family doctor. His diagnosis—TB, of course—is met with a somewhat incongruously outsized reaction from Edith. In contrast to the relatively naturalistic acting of the previous scenes, Edith's gestures here suggest the more stylized techniques of theatrical melodrama. Wringing her hands, clutching at her chest, and gazing skyward, Edith (played by Gertrude McCoy; see fig. 3.1) asserts a kinship with the heroines of another mode.

The combination of melodramatic acting with a more verisimilar style is not unusual in films of this period.[14] Conjoining these conventions with TB, however, sets up an interesting tension that demonstrates just how drastic a narrative solution is required. Melodrama's hallmark is the recognizability of its players. "The universe," writes Peter Brooks, "must always show itself as inhabited by cosmic ethical forces ready to say their name and reveal their operation at the correct gesture or word."[15] A mustachioed villain, for example, might represent the presence of evil in the world, while a white-costumed heroine often stands in for goodness. In the altered narrative schema of germ theory, however, evil may be a near-invisible bacterium. Tuberculosis, cosmic villain though it may be, does not "say its name" in the conventional sense. Rather, as Edith's cough indicates, TB instrumentalizes the very body of the heroine. Edith recognizes this fact when she flees her home for a city sanatorium. By invading the body of the heroine, a traditional melodramatic manifestation of goodness, TB has compromised dramatic convention. Clearly, a new kind of solution is called for in this TB melodrama.

In a sequence that uses science and religion to address the problem of a compromised heroine, two pamphlets from the NASPT offer just such a solution. The first pamphlet, clinically titled *How to Avoid Consumption (Tuberculosis)*, presents the NASPT's emblem, the double-barred cross of Lorraine, on an

---

[14] See Roberta E. Pearson, *Eloquent Gestures: The Transformation of Performance Style in the Griffith Biograph Films* (Berkeley: University of California Press, 1992).

[15] Peter Brooks, *The Melodramatic Imagination* (New Haven, CT: Yale University Press, 1976), 40.

Figure 3.1. Edith reacts to her diagnosis. Frame from *Hope: A Red Cross Seal Story* (1912).

antiseptic field of white. The second pamphlet's illustration depicts the cross of Lorraine in a halo of light, floating above outstretched hands. Titled *Hope,* the pamphlet offers a quotation from Matthew 4:16: "The people which sat in darkness saw a great light, and to them which sat in the region and shadow of death, light is sprung up." Religion has joined forces with science to provide a solution to meet the needs of the most skeptical audience members. The NASPT presents itself as a new kind of hero, sanctioned by no less an authority than Jesus Christ—as well as by Robert Koch, who first isolated the TB bacillus. Coming on the heels of Edith's crisis, the shots of the brochures address both body and soul, establishing a new, narratively satisfying solution.[16]

The town's response to Edith's problem, a rousing parade in support of a local sanatorium, both resolves the film's conflict and presents a model for the audience. The quintessential expression of town pride, civic values, and orderly enthusiasm, the parade allows the community to acknowledge the presence of TB contamination and the NASPT while simultaneously upholding the traditional values of family and community that Edith's cough had earlier seemed to threaten.

The film's closing scene reaffirms the NASPT's new place in the social order. In footage inset in a picture frame, Edith (now restored to health) and John

---

[16] For more on "tuberculosis religion," see Tomes, *Gospel of Germs,* 113–34.

present a vision of harmonious domesticity—a reminder of what the TB bacillus has put at stake. The NASPT's brochure, nudging us to remember how this vision has been achieved, replaces the couple in the picture frame, enshrining itself in the domestic sphere. Finally, Santa Claus nods at us from a Red Cross Seal, his direct address appealing to the audience to remember its own place in this new order.

Hope thrust audiences of 1912 into an altered world, but not a totally unfamiliar one. By playing the havoc-inducing TB bacillus against the bonds of family and community, and by testing and then reaffirming the heroine's virtue, *Hope* both acknowledges the disruptive potential of germ theory and offers a satisfying means of restoring order. Audiences must look to a new authority—the NASPT—to reorder this new world. But they need not fear, *Hope* reassures them, that the new world will not recognize the old values of family and community.

The Temple of Moloch (1914)

The Temple of Moloch is instructive in more ways than one. For middle- and upper-class audiences, it demonstrated the importance of charity and labor standards. For lower-class audiences, it offered lessons in hygiene. But it also performed less explicit work: contagion acted as a uniting narrative device, showing that bacteria could bind together people from seemingly dissimilar backgrounds.

One way to understand how *Moloch* accomplished this is to compare it with a common transitional-era method of ensuring narrative cohesion, in which a particular object—a dropped watch, for example, or a lost umbrella— becomes a device that unites characters and situations.[17] Here, however, the shared object, the TB bacillus, happens to be invisible. As in *Hope*, the audience had to rely on telling gestures, like coughs or dangerous dust, in order to understand where the germ had traveled. By making the germ the shared object of the film's plot, *Moloch* accomplished a number of things: it made the narrative more easily intelligible, it encouraged audience members to search out the germ in otherwise innocuous scenes, and it tied together characters of diverse backgrounds.

The film's title derives from a cult condemned in the Bible for sacrificing children to fire (and also from *Cabiria*, a very popular film distributed earlier in 1914, which featured the temple prominently). The temple in the Edison film is a factory, and the film immediately sets up a contrast between the factory owner's elegant home and the squalor of the factory floor. The opening scene shows a family, the Pratts, breakfasting in their cheerful upper-class

---

[17] See Keil, *Early American Cinema*, 57–58.

dining room. Mr. Harrison Pratt, off to work, kisses his family and leaves through a rear door.

Pratt's departure through the rear of the shot is matched in the next shot by an entrance. Hunched and coughing, a worker struggles to bring an anvil through the factory door. The film's editing has connected Pratt to his laborer, picking out a bond that Pratt himself cannot recognize. Dr. Jordan, an anti-TB advocate who comes to the factory to advocate for sick workers, demonstrates his concern for the coughing laborer, shielding him from Pratt even as the industrialist orders him off the floor.

A cut delivers us to a tenement household, and we learn that the fired laborer is Eric Swanson. In this series of scenes, the film posits a relationship between the three disparate locales. As the film will show us, it is TB that unites these settings and their inhabitants. The laborer, who has contracted TB through unsafe working conditions, will in turn deliver TB to the Pratt family. The physical gestures that define characters' relationships to each other—Pratt's affectionate kiss, Swanson's acceptance of food from his wife—also describe routes of TB transmission. At the Swanson home, Dr. Jordan enters and performs an instructional pantomime: Avoid sputum, do not allow anyone to drink from your glass, open the window for fresh air, and keep the baby away from dust. The doctor recommends removing the Swanson baby to a preventorium, but Mrs. Swanson refuses. Moreover, as soon as the doctor exits, the Swanson family returns to its previous unhygienic habits.

Their actions recall John F. Urie's complaint about working-class people's "parrot-like" propensity to claim adherence to rules of hygiene while privately behaving otherwise. *Moloch* addresses this intractability, not by providing photographic evidence of alien-looking germs but by showing the routes—home, work, family—by which the germs can travel. The bacillus is a novel idea, *Moloch* acknowledges, but it moves in narratively discernible ways.

Alas, it is not long before the circle of contagion encloses the Pratt family. Eloise, daughter of the factory owner, takes an interest in benevolent work (and in Dr. Jordan), visiting homes and selling Christmas Seals. All would seem to be well but for the slight cough of Alfred, Eloise's younger brother. As in *Hope*, the cough foreshadows calamity: Eloise and Alfred become ill with TB. We learn later that the Pratts' sickness comes from none other than Mr. Swanson's daughter, whom the Pratts had employed as a nurse. Although the families were reluctant to recognize their connection to one another, TB makes this recognition unavoidable.

The film achieves its climax by drawing its main players together. Eric Swanson, now mourning the loss of his baby, receives the news of Eloise's infection as poetic justice. Confronting the Pratts at their home (fig. 3.2), Swanson rails against the injustice his family has suffered at the hands of Pratt. His tirade chastens Pratt, who vows to clean up his factory and help stop tuberculosis. Swanson's

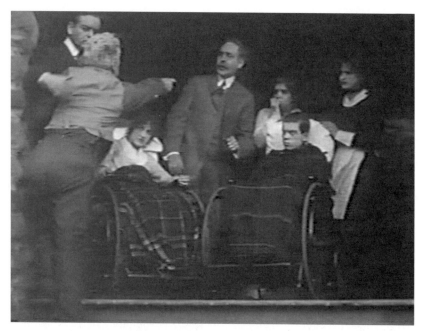

Figure 3.2. Swanson confronts the Pratt family. Frame from *The Temple of Moloch* (1914).

fit of temper hints at a hidden aspect of the film's seemingly benign message. Lurking beneath its invocation of mutual responsibility is the NASPT's perception of the threat embodied by socially marginalized groups.

The Temple of Moloch ends, like *Hope*, with the new equilibrium of a marriage: Eloise Pratt, now recovered, marries Dr. Jordan. In the film's final sequence, the two stand before a Christmas tree as they receive a check from her father for anti-TB work. The couple's embrace, which fades into an image of the 1914 Christmas Seal, suggests a reassuring return to the fold of upper-class domesticity (and, as in *Hope*, an integration of the NASPT's priorities with family life).

Moving Picture World praised *The Temple of Moloch*'s ability to speak simultaneously to two worlds, writing that the film succeeded in "quickening what is best in the universal heart, awakening recognition of our mutual relations."[18] For middle- and upper-class audiences, the film held out the specter of TB as a kind of biological avenger. To fight TB was to safeguard the future for middle-class American families. For lower-class audiences, *Moloch* offered a detailed lesson in domestic hygiene, as well as the prospect of dead children as punishment for lapsed vigilance. The TB bacillus was far from neutral. It was energetically committed to "our mutual relations": to the ties that bind society (however unwillingly) together.

---

[18] *Moving Picture World*, Nov. 14, 1914, 936.

The Lone Game (1915)

The final Edison Red Cross Seal film, *The Lone Game,* demonstrates the impressive versatility of the TB bacillus. Not only can the bacterium provide narrative tension, but it can also grow in importance by borrowing qualities from its historical milieu—in this case, the increasing likelihood of war. Loosely based on the 1915 book *T.B.: Playing the Lone Game: Consumption,* by Thomas Crawford Galbreath, the film urges TB sufferers variously to seek cures close to home, to fight the disease tirelessly, and to get medical attention without delay.[19] In linking the fight against TB with the presumed American qualities of perseverance, patience, and courage, the film encourages TB sufferers to see themselves as soldiers in an epic battle.

The film interweaves three characters' struggles with the disease: Phil Proctor out West; Dean Anderson out West (but in better circumstances); and Grace Proctor, Phil's sister, in an Eastern sanatorium. The film's not-entirely-successful linking of cause, effect, time, and location highlights a quandary that faced filmmakers during the transitional era: how to logically connect the diverse settings and characters demanded by increasingly complex narratives. Formalized editing and composition rules would eventually solve this problem. *The Lone Game,* however, calls upon two additional devices to assist in narrative coherence: the TB bacillus unites the characters thematically, while a series of coincidences advances the plot. Such narrative coincidences were in fact falling out of fashion in favor of plots motivated by psychology or character traits.[20] In *The Lone Game,* such coincidences set up an interesting tension between the presumably impartial logic of germ contagion and this fictional world's insistence on providing its characters with edifying object lessons. The two objectives would seem to be at odds, but their interplay makes a curious kind of sense in this transitional era: the world of *The Lone Game* can accommodate both the dispassion of germ theory and the moralizing guidance of a universe that "says its name."

Grace Proctor, a pretty but penniless young woman, is hit by a streetcar on her way to a job interview. Her rescuer is Dean Anderson, a wealthy young man whom, it soon emerges, her brother Phil had tutored. As Grace tells Phil's story, a series of flashbacks depicts his growing illness, his initial misdiagnosis, and his decision to go out West to seek a cure.

Later, Dean is himself diagnosed with TB. His doctor advises the wealthy young man to go West. Dean looks stricken, but his father offers a bracing pep talk: "My boy, that means that your fight starts to-day.... Will power, patience and back-bone are your weapons to conquer the lone game." In this pronouncement,

---

[19] Thomas Crawford Galbreath, *T. B.: Playing the Lone Game Consumption* (New York: Journal of the Outdoor Life Publishing, 1915).

[20] See, for example, Bordwell, Staiger, and Thompson, *Classical Hollywood Cinema,* 13.

Dean's father echoes Thomas Galbreath, who exhorted his readers to wage war on their disease: "Getting well of tuberculosis is not a romantic diversion. . . . It is a *fight*." Linking TB with a battle allowed TB crusaders to give the disease a new set of associations. They could encourage compliance with instructions for confinement and hygiene by appealing to a sense of duty. They could combat growing fears of contagion by encouraging a view of sufferers as crusaders in a noble fight. And by associating TB with plucky American determination, TB crusaders could later associate their work with the other fight in which America would soon be engaged: World War I. Galbreath is more explicit about this connection: "Even before [World War I] began, another slaughter, overwhelming and unnecessary, was going on," a slaughter caused by "the T. B. germs."[21]

As both fate and contagion would have it, Grace, too, is stricken with TB. Her story demonstrates the importance of seeking help early and of placing one's health in the hands of experts. Urged by a friend to seek immediate attention for a cough, Grace receives not only a correct diagnosis but also a complimentary stay in an Eastern sanatorium. The NASPT wanted urban audiences to follow Grace's example, since refusal to seek treatment was a common source of social workers' ire. In fact, however, TB sufferers had reason to fear official involvement in their cases. By 1908, eighty-five cities required doctors to register TB cases with the state; patients feared losing life-insurance policies and other discrimination.[22] Grace, however, suffers no such hesitation, and is rewarded with a full recovery.

In Phil's story, the audience was instructed in the danger that awaited the penniless consumptive out West. Heading west was common among TB sufferers desperate to find a cure. Lured by rumors of salubrious air and ample accommodation, "lungers" arrived in Colorado, New Mexico, and Arizona to find towns overrun with fellow-sufferers.[23] Phil, turned away from a sanatorium, suffers "the tortures of a living death." His death scene is the site of another of the film's coincidences, as Dean happens upon the dying Phil (fig. 3.3) and finds a letter addressed to Grace.

Phil's death and their shared disease give Dean and Grace (now cured) a new sense of mission, culminating in Grace's vocal performance at the annual Christmas concert for Red Cross Seals. Here, the camera sits in the audience, merging the onscreen concertgoers with the audience in the theater. As in *Hope*'s climactic parade, *The Lone Game* models community boosterism, implicitly comparing the movie audience with the civic-minded onscreen donors who dig

---

[21] Galbreath, *T.B.*, 23, 73.

[22] Sheila M. Rothman, *Living in the Shadow of Death: Tuberculosis and the Social Experience of Illness in American History* (New York: Basic Books, 1994), 189.

[23] Ibid., 214–17.

Figure 3.3. A coincidence: Dean happens upon the dying Phil. Frame from *The Lone Game* (1915).

deep for Red Cross Seals. Just as *The Temple of Moloch* concludes with a sizable donation, *The Lone Game* helpfully displays a $500 check. It was not simply hygiene that these films sought to make gospel, but philanthropy as well.

The penultimate shot of the film, Dean and Grace's embrace before his parents, promises the renewal of family and the neat conclusion to a difficult struggle. It is noteworthy that the film endorses the coupling of two consumptives. Well into the 1910s, physicians debated whether tuberculosis was hereditary, and whether consumptives had a responsibility not to marry. Yet Dean and Grace have emerged from TB unscathed; indeed, the crucible of disease has made them stronger. As war would strengthen and unite a nation, TB would forge sturdier Americans. Dean and Grace are not weak-lunged disease carriers but battle-hardened patriots.

Crossing the Country with Film and Camera

"Backed up by the publicity of the National Association," boasted the NASPT in 1912, "and reinforced by the work of hundreds of Anti-tuberculosis Associations and Red Cross Seal agents, these films have attracted more attention than even the most sanguine of their promoters had thought possible."[24] The films

---

[24] Phillip P. Jacobs, "Tuberculosis in Motion Pictures," *Journal of the Outdoor Life* 9 (1912): 302.

were indeed a success, bolstered by the local associations' determination to place the films in theaters and deliver them to a receptive audience. Proceeds from 1912's *Hope*, the NASPT declared, have "never been equaled in the history of the Edison [filmmaking] activities."[25] In addition to theatrical release, Edison made its TB films available to educational campaigners (for a fee).[26]

Thus it was that TB films appeared in movie theaters and lecture halls across the country, from Newport, Rhode Island, to Lima, Ohio, to Oakland, California.[27] The *Washington Post* reported that 5,000 people attended a program at the Red Cross headquarters that interspersed *The Red Cross Seal* and *The Awakening of John Bond* with lectures on water filtration and mental hygiene. Cedar Falls, Iowa, schools organized a "Health Week" featuring *The Lone Game* and *The Price of Human Lives*. A 1913 program brought the films to parks across New York City's Lower East Side. Frequently, volunteers sold Red Cross Seals before and after screenings. Often, theatergoers were provided with an educational lecture or exhibit to accompany the films.[28]

It was not unusual for NASPT officials to take the shows on the road, as two Maryland campaigners did in 1916. Armed with prints of *The Price of Human Lives* and *The Lone Game*, the officials visited every county in Maryland, staying on the road from May through October. In each town, the officials set up their show either in theaters or in the open air, stopping to conduct a brief survey of "the poorer sections in which the car stops, especially the sections devoted to the negro population." A similar traveling show in New Jersey likewise demonstrated an interest in surveying as well as educating the populace. A photographer preceded the show, documenting unhygienic local conditions and mounting the photographs as part of an educational display.[29]

This tendency to combine film screenings with investigation or education points to film's ability to monitor behavior even as it purports to model it. Indeed, the mobile film screenings suggest a later development: the TB

---

[25] Homer Folks, "Address of the President," *Transactions* 9 (1913): 24.

[26] "'Movies' on Fake Cures," *Journal of the Outdoor Life* 10 (1913): 369.

[27] "Another Health Film," *Newport* (Rhode Island) *News*, Nov. 10, 1911; "Public Health Picture Films," *Lima* (Ohio) *Daily News*, Dec. 21, 1913; "Pictures Used in Fight against White Plague," *Oakland* (California) *Tribune*, Dec. 19, 1911.

[28] "Health Exhibit Opens," *Washington Post*, Sept. 17, 1912; "Health Week," *Waterloo* (Iowa) *Evening Courier and Reporter*, Nov. 9, 1916; "Health Picture Shows This Week," *New York Times*, June 30, 1913. I am indebted to Scott Simmon for this last reference.

[29] "Tuberculosis Crusade Is On," *Frederick* (Maryland) *Post*, May 16, 1916; Millar Knowlton, "The New Jersey Tuberculosis Exhibit," *Transactions* 8 (1912): 213. Traveling motion-picture shows were part of an older tradition, dating to film's earliest years, in which roving exhibitors set up shows in small-town venues. See Charles Musser and Carol Nelson, *High-Class Moving Pictures: Lyman H. Howe and the Forgotten Era of Traveling Film Exhibition, 1880–1920* (Princeton, NJ: Princeton University Press, 1991).

association's chest X-ray campaigns. Beginning in the 1930s, the association sent vans equipped with X-ray machines into working-class neighborhoods, where residents were encouraged to screen themselves for tuberculosis. In these mass campaigns, the lens was trained directly on the kinds of communities scrutinized by the traveling TB shows.[30]

The extent and determination of the exhibition campaign suggest a kind of missionary zeal on the part of NASPT officials. It is not hard to see why. Film was understood to have a uniquely intoxicating effect, particularly on untutored recent immigrants. The medium's influence could be detrimental, or, as the NASPT claimed, it could be enlightening. Motion pictures seemed to have the potential to enter viewers' psyches and exercise unprecedented influence. The anti-TB crusade, lacking a vaccine or cure, needed just such a tool. Indeed, screenings of the Red Cross Seal films could bear an uncanny resemblance to mass inoculations. A day-long 1912 program, for example, repeated an hour's worth of TB films to wave after wave of Los Angeles schoolchildren.[31]

For its part, the Edison Company reaped praise for its affiliation with anti-TB work. The *Moving Picture World* wrote that Edison's Red Cross Seal films, along with Urban-Eclipse's *The Fly Pest* (1910) and Pathé's *Boil Your Water* (1911), "forced the recognition of the motion picture . . . as the greatest educational agency since the discovery of the art of printing."[32] In fact, the films stimulated such excitement that the NASPT complained in 1912 that it now acted as a clearinghouse for other benevolent organizations interested in filmmaking.[33]

The NASPT worked with Edison until 1915, but the organization continued to make films with Plimpton Epic Pictures, a company led by Edison's former studio head, Horace Plimpton, who had left Edison's company that same year. Film remained an important part of the NASPT's education campaign, as it did in the campaigns of many modern-minded reform organizations. The NASPT also produced a feature-length film, *The White Terror* (1915), in collaboration with Universal, and *The Invisible Enemy* (1916) with the independent E.K.O. Film Company (run by scenarist and actress Emma K. Oswald). The Wisconsin Anti-Tuberculosis Association also issued a four-reel film called *The Power of the Penny* (1915).[34]

---

[30] See Alton L. Blakeslee, *And the Spark Became a Flame: The Beginnings of Mass Chest X-Ray* (New York: Queensboro Tuberculosis and Health Association, 1954); and Catherine Caulfield, *Multiple Exposures: Chronicles of the Radiation Age* (Chicago: University of Chicago Press, 1990), 144–45. For a consideration of the context and ethical dimensions of Progressive-Era public health filmmaking, see Pernick, "More Than Illustrations."

[31] "Picture Show as Educator," *Los Angeles Times*, June 16, 1912.

[32] Review of *The Awakening of John Bond*, *Moving Picture World*, Nov. 18, 1911, 535.

[33] Livingston Farrand, "Report of the Executive Secretary," *Transactions* 8 (1912): 31.

[34] "The Power of the Penny," *Journal of the Outdoor Life* 13 (1916): 84; review of *The Great Truth*, *Moving Picture World*, Dec. 2, 1916, 1325; Farrand, "Report," 29–31.

The Red Cross Seal films demonstrated that educational filmmaking could have popular appeal. Blending instruction with narrative, the films testify to the belief that the momentum of a story is powerful enough to send a weighty lesson home. Arriving as they did at critical points for both germ theory and cinematic narrative, the films also prompt us to think through some of the unexpected links between narration and contagion. Contagion, like narrative, lines up players and situations in an orderly series of events, transmitting both plot points and disease from one episode to the next. Narrative, like disease, winds its way deep into the body, evoking strong (and, the NASPT hoped, behavior-altering) feelings. Both systems require people to search out clues that give meaning to seemingly random assemblies of people and things. The United States of the 1910s was more urban, more saturated with media, and more industrialized than ever before. Perhaps in this setting narrative and contagion answered similar needs. Both systems make logical sense out of what might otherwise seem a crowded, arbitrary, and disorderly world.

Filmography

The Awakening of John Bond (**1911**) **1 reel (919 ft.); 35mm**
PRODUCTION: Edison Manufacturing Co. DIRECTOR: Charles J. Brabin. STORY: Bannister Merwin. CAST: Bigelow Cooper (John Bond), Miriam Nesbitt (Grace Bond), Mary Fuller (Nellie O'Brien), Harold Shaw (George O'Brien), Philip Tannura (the younger O'Brien), Kathleen Coughlin (the younger O'Brien), Joseph M. Levering (treasurer of the Tuberculosis Committee). NOTE: A landlord learns the importance of maintaining healthy living quarters when his wife contracts TB. ACCESS: 35mm viewing copy (with German intertitles), British Film Institute/National Film and Television Archive, Yale University Film Study Center.

Hope: A Red Cross Seal Story (**1912**) **1 reel (1,000 ft.); 35mm**
PRODUCER: Thomas A. Edison, Inc. DIRECTOR: Charles J. Brabin. CAST: George Lessey (John Harvey), William West, Gertrude McCoy (Edith), Charles Ogle. ACCESS: The National Film Preservation Foundation's DVD set *Treasures III: Social Issues in American Film, 1900–1934* (Image Entertainment, 2007), with musical score by Marty Marks and audio commentary by Jennifer Horne. Also, 35mm viewing prints at the Museum of Modern Art and the Academy Film Archive; 35mm archival print and VHS viewing copy, University of Michigan Historical Health Film Library.

The Lone Game (**1915**) 1 reel (1,000 ft.); **35mm**
DIRECTOR: Edward C. Taylor. WRITER: Mary Rider. CAST:
Bessie Learn (Grace Proctor), Robert Walker (Dean Anderson),
Wilfred Young (Phil Proctor). ACCESS: DVD set *Edison: The
Invention of the Movies* (Kino, 2005) reproduces the Museum of
Modern Art 35mm viewing print; musical score by Ben Model.

The Price of Human Lives (**1913**) 1 reel (1,000 ft.); **35mm**
WRITER: Epes Winthrop Sargent. NOTE: The manufacturers of a
fake cure for tuberculosis change their ways when the reform-minded
fiancée of one of the partners discovers their work. ACCESS: No
copies known to exist.

The Red Cross Seal (**1910**) 1 reel (1,000 ft.); **35mm**
PRODUCTION: Edison Manufacturing Co. NOTE: A wealthy
young man saves the object of his affection by purchasing her tenement building. ACCESS: No copies known to survive.

The Temple of Moloch (**1914**) 1 reel (1,000 ft.); **35mm**
PRODUCER: Thomas A. Edison, Inc. DIRECTOR: Langdon West.
WRITERS: James Oppenheim, Mary Rider Mechtold. CAST:
Warren Cook (Harrison Pratt), Nellie Grant (Mrs. Pratt), Bessie Learn
(Eloise, their daughter), Yale Boss (Alfred, their son), Harold Vosburgh
(Dr. Jordan), Carlton King (Eric Swanson, a former employee of
Harrison Pratt), Mathilde Baring (Mrs. Swanson), the Swanson baby.
ACCESS: 35mm print at the Museum of Modern Art, New York (not
available for viewing). 16mm print at the Cineteca del Friuli, Gemona
(Italy). 35mm print and VHS viewing copy, University of Michigan
Historical Health Film Library. Nontheatrical distribution by Black-
hawk Films; copy at www.archive.org/details/temple_of_moloch. RT:
13:19, including historical introduction text by Anthony Slide.

4 VISUALIZING INDUSTRIAL CITIZENSHIP

LEE GRIEVESON

Visual instruction flourished in the United States in the immediate post–World War I years, buttressed in part by the temporary revision of the social and political function of cinema and its place in the liberal public sphere that operated during the war.[1] The proponents of visual instruction drew on a loosely configured mixture of pedagogical and psychological theory to argue that visual material and concrete imagery were closer to lived experience than the abstractions of language. Visualization provided richer and more useful pedagogical experiences for students, many argued. Informed by this perspective, instructors integrated museum materials, still images, and moving pictures into the classroom. The validation of the pedagogical potential of moving pictures became central to the postwar explosion of discourse about visual instruction. Motion pictures were prized for their ability to represent movement, mimicking phenomenological experience in a way that was distinct from still images and objects. Film reels could bring visualized experience from across the world into the classroom and other educational forums, such as churches, community centers, and civic clubs.[2]

Moreover, moving pictures and other visual materials "spoke" to those populations of immigrants whose English-language skills were unformed, the very

My thanks to Lora Brill, Peter Kramer, Devin Orgeron, Marsha Orgeron, and Dan Streible for help in writing this essay. Research for this essay was facilitated by the Arts and Humanities Research Council. This is for my friend Haidee Wasson.

[1] Lee Grieveson, *Policing Cinema: Movies and Censorship in Turn of the Century America* (Berkeley: University of California Press, 2004), 208–12.

[2] See, for example, J. J. Weber, *Comparative Effectiveness of Some Visual Aids in Seventh Grade Instruction* (Chicago: Educational Screen, 1922); Frank Freeman, ed., *Visual Instruction: A Comparative Study of Motion Pictures and Other Methods of Instruction* (Chicago: University of Chicago Press, 1924); U. S. Department of the Interior, Bureau of Education, *Visual Education Departments in Educational Institutions* (Washington, DC: GPO, 1924); W. H. Johnson, *Fundamentals in Visual Instruction* (Chicago: Educational Screen, 1927); Anna Verona Dorris, *Visual Instruction in the Public Schools* (Boston: Ginn, 1928); F. Dean McClusky, *Visual Instruction: Its Value and Its Needs: A Report* (New York: Mancall, 1932); and Charles F. Hoban, Charles F. Hoban Jr., and Samuel B. Zisman, *Visualizing the Curriculum* (New York: Cordon, 1937).

groups who were frequently singled out as most in need of education as socialization into the ways of America. The new technology of what some called "pedagogical cinematography" could, it was hoped, transform curricula, experiences, and institutions.[3] In doing so it would underpin a more efficient and productive educational system that would sustain a social and democratic order seemingly rendered fragile by the widening class divisions and the influx of immigrants needed to sustain the growth of large-scale industrial capitalism. The necessity to create a "social and civic consciousness" among "aliens" who, as one scholarly study put it, "were hostile, or at best indifferent, to American traditions, institutions, and practices" became more pressing in the immediate postwar period.[4] Discourse on the meaning of citizenship and national identity proliferated in the early 1920s. The visual instruction movement dovetailed in intriguing ways with these anxieties about the formation and management of citizenship. Cinema might be refashioned, many hoped, to promote "social health" and the production of a liberal civility.[5]

To these ends, a flurry of civic, governmental, and commercial organizations emerged from 1919 onward to proselytize for the importance of visual instruction; to produce and distribute educational films; to test the efficacy of educational films; and to participate in a reordering of pedagogical practices for a mass population. The following discussion maps the intellectual and political contexts that shaped this era's sense of the social function of a pedagogical cinema. I trace this development through liberal ideas about pedagogy and postwar America's intensified anxieties about the sustenance of liberal democratic order and the place of mass media in the shaping of consciousness and conduct. I focus thereafter on films made by the Ford Motor Company during this period. The Ford company became a significant producer of films in the teens and twenties. In these films, the company sought to utilize cinema as part of its expansive strategies to educate immigrant working-class populations in new modes of "productive" conduct and the new configuration of political economy mandated by monopoly capitalism. The films were initially distributed free of charge to commercial movie theaters and nontheatrical venues, such as schools and factories. They became among the most widely

---

[3] The National Alliance of Pedagogical Cinematography was founded in New York in 1921 by Alfred H. Saunders, founder-editor of *Moving Picture World* and *Motion Picture News*. "New Organization for Classroom Films," *Educational Film Magazine,* May 1921: 1.

[4] J. G. de Roulhac Hamilton and Edgar W. Knight, *The Making of Citizens* (Chicago: A. C. McClurg, 1922), 11, 6. Hamilton and Knight's study had been commissioned by the War Department in 1920, and published as *Education for Citizenship* (Washington, DC: GPO, 1921).

[5] Hamilton and Knight, *Making of Citizens,* 30.

seen films of the silent era.[6] This "Fordist" cinema was a significant example of the broader impetus to imagine motion pictures as a pedagogical form to shape the attitudes and conduct of working-class populations.

The Political Economy of Visual Education

Visual instruction can initially be positioned in a longer history of the political economy of education in the United States and other liberal regimes. Liberal political philosophy had long declared the importance of education in developing the cognitive and moral qualities seen as necessary for citizenship in a democratic polity. Philosophers like John Locke, John Stuart Mill, and Jean-Jacques Rousseau positioned education as central to the production of liberal subjects, from what Locke designated as the "wax" of the child, and thus to the establishment and maintenance of economic and political order.[7] The liberal ideals of self-government and individualism dovetailed with the developing economic principles of laissez-faire capitalism. Integral to the formation of the United States as a democratic, republican polity was the belief that "civic" education was crucial for the effective formation and governance of what Rousseau called "social man."[8]

In the nineteenth century, the political threat of an expanding working class required liberal regimes to educate members of this class for their roles as citizens. The state thus created more administrative functions to enhance security and to underpin the formation of a liberal political economy.[9] The invention of a public school system in the mid-nineteenth century in the United States, and its proliferation in the latter parts of the century as urban and immigrant populations expanded, is the most visible result of the construction of education as a

---

[6] *Ford Times*, for example, claimed that the Ford films were, by 1917, shown in 3,000 theaters a week to between four and five million people. The nontheatrical trade journal *Reel and Slide* wrote in 1918 of the innovative system of distribution of the films via Ford dealers, claiming the films reached 6,000 exhibitors a week and thus an audience of five to six million. In 1920, the company was claiming a minimum of 4,000 theaters and a coverage of one-seventh of the weekly motion picture audience in the United States. By 1924, *Ford News* asserted that the films had been seen by sixty million people worldwide. *Ford Times*, Feb. 1917: 302; *Reel and Slide*, Mar. 1, 1918: 31; "Factory Facts from Ford," Accession 951, box 11, Research Center, Henry Ford Museum (hereafter RCHFM); *Ford News*, Oct. 1, 1924, 1.

[7] John Locke, *Some Thoughts Concerning Education* (London: A. and J. Churchill, 1693); Jean-Jacques Rousseau, *Emile: Or, On Education*, 1762, trans. Allan Bloom (New York: Basic Books, 1979); John Stuart Mill, *Considerations on Representative Government* (London: Parker, Son, and Bourn, 1861).

[8] See Rush Welter, *Popular Education and Democratic Thought in America* (New York: Columbia University Press, 1962).

[9] Jürgen Habermas, *The Structural Transformation of the Public Sphere*, trans. Thomas Burger (Cambridge, MA: MIT Press, 1989), 129–40.

process of socialization into "correct," or what was frequently called "good," citizenship.[10] Making productive citizens became the central goal of a reconfigured education system, precariously balanced between liberal ideals of individual attainment and of the common good. The liberal educational philosopher John Dewey expressed this ambivalence most clearly: "When the school introduces and trains each child of society into membership within such a little community, saturating him with the spirit of service, and providing him with the instruments of effective self-direction, we shall have the deepest and best guarantee of a larger society which is worthy, lovely, and harmonious."[11] Likewise, in his 1916 book *Democracy and Education: An Introduction to the Philosophy of Education*, Dewey argued for the import of education in "enlisting of the person's own participating disposition in getting the result desired, and thereby of developing within him an intrinsic and persisting direction in the right way."[12] This unstable balance of "enlisting," of individual "ownership," and of "the right way" to live— of the principles of individuality, cultural inclusiveness, and civic solidarity— subtended ideas and practices of education through the early decades of the twentieth century.

The public education system was commonly understood as a practice of "civic education," which differed from what can be called "philosophic education" because, as William Galston puts it, the "purpose [of civic education] is not the pursuit and acquisition of truth, but rather the formation of individuals who can effectively conduct their lives within, and support, the political community."[13] Civic education would produce a curriculum saturated with the values of liberal political economy and increasingly focused on the production of "useful knowledge" for the workers who would sustain a new industrial economy.[14] The "Progressive education" of the early twentieth century focused on a child-centered experiential pedagogy that mandated paying more attention to the autonomy of the child and deemphasized book and rote learning. This transformation of pedagogical practices was connected to broad changes in the conception of childhood attendant upon shifts in demography and class structure in the late

---

[10] On the history of the public school see, for example, Lawrence Arthur Cremin, *The Transformation of the School: Progressivism in American Education, 1876–1957* (New York: Knopf, 1961).

[11] John Dewey, *School and Society* (1915; reprint, Chicago: University of Chicago Press, 1971), 29.

[12] John Dewey, *Democracy and Education: An Introduction to the Philosophy of Education* (1916; reprint, New York: Macmillan, 1950), 32.

[13] William Galston, "Civic Education in the Liberal State," in *Liberalism and Moral Life,* ed. Nancy L. Rosenblum (Cambridge, MA: Harvard University Press, 1989), 90.

[14] William J. Reese, *History, Education, and the Schools* (London: Palgrave, 2007), in particular 79–94.

nineteenth century.[15] It was connected also to the construction of liberal person-hood and the sustenance of a liberal political economy.

Visual instruction would be a subset of this Progressive education, one aspect of a broader shift in pedagogic practices that sought to bring experience into schools and so make them more productive for a liberal political rationality. It emerged as a subject of discourse and as a practice at a critical moment in the imagination of the socialization of diverse populations. The influx of southern and eastern European immigrants; the migration of African Americans north-ward and of farmers to the cities; innovations in finance, production, communi-cations, and retail that thrust individuals into a national marketplace; labor, women's suffrage, and African Americans' civil rights agitation—these and other events in the early twentieth century combined to seemingly threaten the foun-dations of American citizenship and civic solidarity. After World War I, these imagined threats to social and political order would be intensified, as a wave of nationalism shifted the agenda away from cultural pluralism to coercive efforts to stamp out communism, anarchism, and other movements for social equality. The "Red Scare" of 1919 spawned conditions favorable to the passage of the Emergency Quota Act in 1921 and the Immigration Act of 1924, which radically reduced immigrant movement to the United States. The Emergency Quota Act limited the annual number of immigrants who could be admitted from any country to 3 percent of the number of persons from that country living in the United States in 1910, according to the U.S. Census. The Immigration Act of 1924 cut that number to 2 percent according to the 1890 U.S. Census. This latter law specifically targeted southern and eastern Europeans, who began emigrating in large numbers in the 1890s; it also prohibited the immigration of East Asians and Asian Indians.[16]

The use of moving pictures as part of socialization practices and as part of the construction of what we might call a "liberal civility" emerged, as I have noted, most clearly from 1918 and accelerated in the early 1920s as a series of organiza-tions began to make, distribute, and exhibit films. During the same period, other groups emerged to proselytize for visual instruction and the integration of films into educational spaces and practices. The parameters of this effort were indeed broad, informing production, distribution, and exhibition from a plethora of gov-ernment organizations that included municipal, state, and federal governments; major corporations; and social reform groups. Together, these endeavors marked an attempt to utilize cinema as a pedagogical strategy for molding conduct. It is toward an examination of one aspect of this development that I now turn.

---

[15] William J. Reese, "The Origins of Progressive Education," *History of Education Quarterly* 41 (Spring 2001): 1–24.

[16] Edward George Hartman, *The Movement to Americanize the Immigrant* (New York: Columbia University Press, 1948), 216–66.

Civics and Citizenship in Fordist Film

In 1914 the Ford Motor Company established a Motion Picture Department to produce educational films and to distribute them widely, initially free of charge via Ford dealers, to movie theaters and other public spaces, including factories, schools, and prisons.[17] Accounts suggest the company spent the significant figure of $600,000 annually on film production, in a period when the average budget for commercial feature films was around $50,000.[18] "In taking these steps" of developing educational films, the *Ford News* observed, "the Ford film department believes that the long-neglected and dormant educational value of the motion pictures sacrificed in the desire for money grabbing, will be taken advantage of to carry out its fundamental purpose of true usefulness."[19] Moving pictures were regarded at the company as a pedagogic medium distinct from commercial cinema, capable of shaping new modalities of conduct by articulating particular ideas about selfhood and citizenship, industry and "progress," as well as social and political order. The films articulated perspectives on conduct and citizenship consistent with the company's investment in shaping the conduct of working-class and immigrant populations to function in the revised economic configuration of monopoly capitalism exemplified by Ford. These perspectives were seen by diverse audiences, as the films mobilized the Fordist agenda beyond the factory walls to myriad sites within the public sphere.

Ford invested in motion pictures as an educational force at the same time as it developed the innovative assembly-line process that transformed industrial practices, marking a revolution in production processes. The division of labor into separate and increasingly routinized and mechanized tasks on the assembly line enabled the direct control of the movement and pace of workers and so dramatically increased productivity and the extraction of surplus value from laboring

---

[17] On the circulation of the films, see *Ford Times*, July 1916: 534–40; *Ford Times*, Feb. 1917: 302; *Reel and Slide*, Mar. 1, 1918: 31; and "Factory Facts from Ford," accession 951, box 11, RCHFM. In a letter to Henry Ford, Irving R. Bacon, the official photographer and painter at Ford, claimed a high point of 7,000 "contacts" before the company started charging for the films in 1918. Bacon to Ford, Feb. 11, 1921, accession 1, box 172, folder 19, RCHFM.

[18] David Lewis, *The Public Image of Henry Ford: An American Folk Hero and His Company* (Detroit: Wayne State University, 1976), 115. Lewis claims that by 1918 Ford was "the largest motion picture distributor on earth." While this may be an exaggeration, it is clear that the figure of $600,000 annually represents a very significant investment in cinema. For example, Hollywood film producer William Fox wrote in 1919 that three Tom Mix feature films averaged $42,000 to produce. See Lillian Wurtzel Semenov and Carla Winter, eds., *William Fox, Sol M. Wurtzel, and the Early Fox Film Corporation* (Jefferson, NC: McFarland, 2001), 101.

[19] *Ford News*, Feb. 1, 1922: 6.

bodies.[20] The mass assembly line was accompanied by a significant rise in worker wages, to five dollars a day, which was tied directly to efforts to make the workforce more productive and to quell the tide of worker resistance and radicalism manifested in a higher turnover of staff and an "epidemic of strikes" in the 1910s.[21] Higher wages contributed to an emergent culture of consumption. Transformations in factory production practices were accompanied by a whole set of educational practices at the company that sought to socialize workers in various ways. Language learning for immigrant workers was connected to ideals of civility, morality, and Americanization. Classes on, for example, table etiquette, budgeting, and how government worked in the United States were common.[22] Samuel Marquis, head of what was called the "Sociological Department" at Ford, stated that the curriculum sought to "make the men more efficient in our work in the shop, but also to prepare them for better citizenship. The first thing we teach them to say is, 'I am a good American,' and then we try to get them to live up to the statement."[23] Or, in Henry Ford's formulation: "These men of many nations, must be taught American ways, the English language, and the right way to live."[24] The import of education as moral training and guidance in the right way to live was central to the company's goals, which were expansive and frequently articulated as the shaping of a new citizenry. "We want to make men in this factory as well as automobiles," Henry Ford was quoted as saying, and this goal to "make" citizens infused activities to pedagogically shape a new workforce, as well as to steer workers away from both working-class and immigrant community traditions and from associated strike action and radical political upheaval.[25]

Most notable in relation to these goals was Ford's Sociological Department, which was set up in 1914 to administer the five-dollar working day. To be eligible for this new wage, the worker needed to demonstrate his (or less often her) fitness in "coming up to certain standards of cleanliness and citizenship," in particular

---

[20] David A. Hounshell, *From the American System to Mass Production, 1800–1932* (Baltimore: Johns Hopkins University Press, 1984), 217–62; Harry Braverman, *Labor and Monopoly Capital: The Degradation of Work in the Twentieth Century,* (New York: Monthly Review Press, 1998), 127–62.

[21] *Iron Age,* Apr. 1913, cited in David Montgomery, *The Fall of the House of Labor: The Workplace, the State, and American Labor Activism, 1865–1925* (Cambridge, UK: Cambridge University Press, 1987), 240. Between October 1912 and October 1914, Ford had to hire 54,000 workers to maintain an average workforce of 13,000. This marked an annual turnover of workers of 416%.

[22] Stephen Meyer III, *The Five Dollar Day: Labor, Management and Social Control in the Ford Motor Company, 1908–1921* (Albany: State University of New York, 1981), 156–62.

[23] Steven Watts, *The People's Tycoon: Henry Ford and the American Century* (New York: Knopf, 2005), 217.

[24] Ibid., 215.

[25] J. Abell, "The Making of Men, Motor Cars, and Profits," *Iron Age* 95 (Jan. 7, 1915): 33–41.

that s/he did not drink alcohol or have boarders at home, and that s/he regularly deposited money in a savings account, maintained a clean "well conducted home," and had a good moral character.[26] The elaboration of standards of domesticity as "civility" was central to the creation of class distinctions.[27] The management of conduct was tied to various forms of productivity, correlating versions of civility and citizenship with economic practices of production and consumption at the company. Technologies of production, "sociology," and education as subject construction were combined, with moving pictures as a potential pivot. Just "as we adapt the machinery in the shop to turning out the kind of automobile we have in mind," Marquis explained in 1916, "so we have constructed our educational system with a view to producing the human product in mind."[28] Together, these varied practices of investigation and education were designed to ensure productivity, to preclude and manage industrial unrest, to create ideological ties between capital and labor, to maximize worker commitment to the increasingly deskilled jobs central to mass production, to obviate the need for state intervention into the economy and worker welfare, and to enable an expanded consumer economy that would support increased production. Writing in the early 1930s, Antonio Gramsci would call these combined practices "Fordist," the classic example of the production of hegemony.[29]

In 1921, amid the upsurge of interest in visual instruction, the company established a new film series, the "Ford Educational Library."[30] Central to this effort were titles grouped under the category "Civics and Citizenship of the United States." In the nontheatrical trade publication *Moving Picture Age*, Ford claimed

---

[26] Henry Ford, *My Life and Work*, in collaboration with Samuel Crowther (Garden City, NY: Doubleday, Page, 1922), 128. Women were eligible for the wage if they were the head of a household and had an immediate blood relation dependent upon them, but they could not work at Ford if they were married. See Oliver Zunz, *Making America Corporate, 1870–1920* (Chicago: University of Chicago Press, 1990), 138–44.

[27] On this process more generally see Stuart M. Blumin, *The Emergence of the Middle Class: Social Experience in the American City, 1760–1900* (Cambridge, UK: Cambridge University Press, 1989); and Mary P. Ryan, *Cradle of the Middle Class: The Family in Oneida County, New York, 1790–1865* (Cambridge, UK: Cambridge University Press, 1981).

[28] Samuel Marquis, "The Ford Idea in Education," *Addresses and Proceedings of National Education Association* 64 (1916): 915.

[29] Antonio Gramsci, "Fordism and Americanism," in *The Gramsci Reader: Selected Writings, 1916–1935,* ed. David Forgacs (New York: New York University Press, 2000).

[30] The initial production of films from 1914 was grouped into a newsreel-like series entitled the "Ford Animated Weekly." A new series was produced from 1916 until 1921, the "Ford Educational Weekly." The Ford films, making up 1,500,000 feet of motion pictures, were donated to the National Archives in 1963. See National Archives publication no. 70–6, Mayfield Bray, *Guide to the Ford Film Collection in the National Archives* (1970); also available at the Internet Archive, www.archive.org/details/guidetofordfilmcoobrayrich, although its listing of individual film titles is far from complete.

the aim of this new series was to "establish the foundation for a reference library of motion pictures to be used by schools."[31] Likewise, the *Ford Times* a year later claimed the "films will be made to correlate with the textbook."[32] In this way the films initiated an expansion of the company's educational goals and their connection to the flourishing visual instruction movement, taking the principles of Fordist education as initiated in the factories to the schools and so reaching populations that would go on to populate factories at Ford and elsewhere. A catalog for the Ford Educational Library described it as "organized visual instruction."[33] The goal was to sell the films to universities, schools, and churches for permanent libraries. Universities in particular were encouraged to buy them and assemble such libraries, which might be disseminated regionally.[34] Selected Ford films were shown at the National Education Association meeting in 1922, amid debates about visual instruction that led the NEA to establish a committee to survey the field.[35] The NEA established a Department of Visual Instruction in July 1923.

The eleventh volume of the Ford Educational Library's "Civics and Citizenship" series was entitled *Democracy in Education* (ca. 1919).[36] A slightly expanded edition of the film was exhibited at the 1922 NEA meeting. Typical in some respects of picture production at Ford and of the company's economic and ideological investment in motion pictures, education, and history, this one-reel elliptical film traces "a sturdy race of resourceful, independent, clear-thinking men, who rebelled at tyranny," from the signing of the Declaration of Independence (a draft of which is shown on screen) to World War I. "In 1916," an intertitle states, "many who thought that the crowded conditions and manifold temptations of city life had completely destroyed those ideals so firmly established by our forefathers."

---

[31] *Moving Picture Age*, Feb. 1921: 30.

[32] *Ford News*, Jan. 1, 1922: 1.

[33] "The Ford Educational Library," 1922, accession 951, box 14, RCHFM.

[34] *Ford News*, Jan. 1, 1922: 1, and Feb. 1, 1922: 3. Costs were five cents per foot to buy and fifty cents a day per reel to rent.

[35] *Ford News*, Mar. 1, 1922: 5. The committee was financially supported by the Motion Pictures Producers and Distributors of America, after its president Will Hays had appeared at the NEA summer meeting in 1922. The MPPDA was seeking ways to turn a profit from the emerging educational market, but also to ensure this did not impinge on the profits of theatrical motion pictures. The committee also suited their public relations goals to deflect critical regulatory attention away from commercial cinema.

[36] The National Archives research catalog lists two film prints of *Democracy in Education* in the Ford Collection. Item FC-190a is dated ca. 1919 and runs five minutes; item FC-486 has a 1922 copyright notice printed on the film, which runs six-and-a-quarter minutes. Clearly the film was produced in 1919, and repackaged as part of the Ford Educational Library in 1922. Ford films were regularly altered and rereleased for the Library series. The 1922 version has additional titles and footage, as follows: (1) an intertitle and shot, after the shot of draft of the Declaration of Independence: "—and established a democracy in which life, liberty and the pursuit of happiness are guaranteed to all," followed by a shot of a crowd of smiling children walking toward the

"Liberty took up arms," reads a subsequent title card, "turning the tide and making the world safe for Democracy." This abbreviated political history connects the autonomous, independent self—the liberal self of what has been called "possessive individualism," enshrined and made practical in the Declaration and Constitution—to political independence, global assertion, and a liberty or democracy imagined principally as security. The title makes clear that democracy is secured by education, mainly in the form of the school, but also, implicitly, in the form of the pedagogic film. Between shots of schoolrooms, titles tell us "public school must make Democracy safe for the world," and "school training must result in the development of those qualities which are essential both to the happiness of the individual and to the strength and vitality of the nation." The "exercise of the fundamentals of democracy in the schools," a guide to the film in a 1926 book on visual instruction observed, "lays the foundation for a free and independent nation."[37]

Democracy in Education thus offers a civics lesson in the import attached to education for the individual and the community in liberal theory. The film draws explicitly on John Dewey's 1916 book *Democracy and Education*, a connection suggested also in the short document Ford produced to accompany the film when it was reissued as part of the Ford Educational Library. It is education, the film states, that makes people happy and secures the vitality of the nation. Schools and cinema must, the film goes on, in a way that directly mirrors Dewey's language, teach "methods which will result in SELF-DIRECTION . . . SELF-APPRAISAL . . . [and] SELF-CONTROL." These "methods" of being produce

---

camera; (2) two additional shots after the intertitle: "In 1916, there were many who thought that the crowded conditions and manifold temptations of city life," showing a city street and then a tenement building with washing hanging out to dry; (3) after intertitle ending "had completely destroyed those ideals so firmly established by our forefathers. But at the challenge of autocracy—" a shot of a ship slowly sinking; (4) after the title card reading "SELF-CONTROL—the ability to conduct one's own business with the respect for the rights of others," an additional title appears: "CO-OPERATION—the ability to work with and through other people in the achievement of social purposes." This is followed by a shot of people building a wooden trailer. (5) In the concluding sequence, the benefits of education include government and science, but the 1922 version adds the intertitle "Art," followed by a shot of a statue. Ford also produced a booklet— *Ford Educational Library, Civics and Citizenship of the U.S.: Democracy in Education* (Feb. 25, 1922)—guiding teachers in how to describe and explain the film for students and this follows exactly the 1922 version. The digital movie files available via NARA's online catalog (archives.gov) are identical to those hosted by the Internet Archive (archive.org). My thanks to Dan Streible for guidance here.

[37] Detroit Public Schools, *Course of Study in Visual Education* (1926): 65. *Ford News* commented: "The importance of school training to the individual's happiness and success and to the nation is shown." Feb. 1, 1921: 4.

selfhood, understood as self-possession and self-discipline, and not as collectivity, like, for example, in the unions that were banned at Ford. This conception of "the rights and duties of a citizen," as the film's teaching guide framed it, is crucial, as the film's history and civics lesson works to update the liberal capitalist citizenship that was historically allied to ideals of autonomy for the new machine or mass assembly age that necessitated revisions to the liberal political technology of individualism.[38] In doing so, the film connects to the broader educational goals of the company to create what Michael Buroway has called an "industrial citizenship" that worked to offer a muted version of classical liberal conceptions of self-determination that befitted the truncated form integral to mass-assembly industrial practices.[39] It is education, then, both in the Ford film and in the company, that functions as a pivot between the liberal ideals of self-determination and the necessity of "self-control" and that is thus productive of social, economic, and political order. The concluding sequence's shot of the U.S. Capitol, illustrating "the genius of government," underscores the connections running from the shaping of selfhood, nation, and political order.

Democracy in Education's account of the pedagogic formation of political and economic order was shaped by its immediate political and economic context. The depression of 1920–21 had many questioning the vitality of large-scale industrial capitalism. Union activity and the ideological challenge of newly formed Soviet Russia raised further questions about a Fordist economic and political order. The Ford Motor Company banned union membership and clamped down violently on attempts to unionize its workforce.[40] At the same time, the company made overtly anti-Soviet and anti-union propaganda, utilizing film in the project to educate the public about the "evils" of other economic and political systems. In a short 1919 animated film entitled *Uncle Sam and the Bolsheviki-I.W.W. Rat* (fig. 4.1), for example, an American farmer stands behind grain bags with the words "American Institutions" on them and beats a rat bearing on its back the words "Bolsheviki (IWW)."[41]

The intertwined goals of the Ford films as exemplified by *Democracy in Education* underpinned other films produced by the company. Together, the Ford productions told brief lessons about American political and economic

---

[38] *Civics and Citizenship of the U.S.: Democracy in Education.* The Ford publication erroneously refers to Dewey's book as *Democracy in America.*

[39] Michael Buroway, *Manufacturing Consent: Changes in the Labor Process under Monopoly Capitalism* (Chicago: University of Chicago Press, 1979), 113.

[40] Stephen Norwood, "Ford's Brass Knuckles: Harry Bennett, the Cult of Muscularity, and Anti-Labor Terror, 1920–1945," *Labor History* 37, no. 3 (1996): 365–91.

[41] The Industrial Workers of the World had attempted to unionize auto workers at Ford as early as 1913. See Meyer, *Five Dollar Day*, 91–92. See Scott Simmon's note on this film in the book for the DVD set *Treasures III: Social Issues in American Film, 1900–1934* (San Francisco: National Film Preservation Foundation, 2007), 93–94.

Figure 4.1. *Uncle Sam and the Bolsheviki-I.W.W. Rat* (1919), animated by Ford Motor Co.

history that spoke both to the corporate conception of the "correct" interrelationship between state policy, the economy, and society and to the project of "Americanization."

In *The Road to Happiness* (1924), for example, we are told a story about the modernization of a rural economy by the combined forces of automobility and government in building new roads. Indeed, the film was made in conjunction with the Bureau of Public Roads of the U.S. Department of Agriculture and thus, in its making, exemplified the conception of liberal political economy that mixed laissez-faire economic policies with activist state intervention.[42] In the film, a young farmer is instructed by his bad-tempered father to deliver eggs to market, but he misses the connecting train because the roads are bad. His eggs are destroyed along the way. The father blames the boy for being lazy. Later, at school the boy is invited to enter a competition to write an essay about his local community. He writes about the need for good roads, which will enable the easy transportation of rural goods. In this way the film cleverly combines education with the necessity of improving roads to enable better commerce and to make rural spaces more accessible. *The Road to Happiness* makes a case for a modernization

---

[42] Thomas K. McCraw, "American Capitalism," in *Creating Modern Capitalism: How Entrepreneurs, Companies, and Countries Triumphed in Three Industrial Revolutions,* ed. McCraw (Cambridge, MA: Harvard University Press, 1997), 317.

of rural communities through road traffic, a policy important to the federal and state governments in this period, as they developed new governmental practices to facilitate automobility to enable the smoother flow of commerce.[43] This project would be important to the development of a national market, in particular by incorporating the rural hinterland within industrial capitalism. Commercial automobile manufacturers were of course invested in the project to develop a national market, as the movie makes clear. The road to happiness, then, is created by the collaboration of commerce and state, the development of a new technological space that enables market expansion, the incorporation of rural America into a consumer economy, and the consolidation of large corporations.[44]

Ford made other films about American monuments and history. *The Story of Old Glory* (1916) documented the history of the American flag. *Where the Spirit That Won Was Born* (1918) showed the historic sights of Philadelphia. *Washington, D.C.* (1918) likewise pictured the nation's capital, showing off government buildings (the Treasury; State, Army, and Navy departments; Patent Office; and the White House). The Ford Educational Library's history series *Landmarks of the American Revolution* (1920) showed the historic sites associated with the revolutionary war. *Presidents of the United States* (ca. 1917) was a text-heavy account of major issues facing each president since Madison, connected in particular to aspects of economic history. For example, the entry for John Quincy Adams (president from 1825 to 1829) runs: "Tariff and the means of communication were the great questions of the day. Protection of America's 'infant industries' was secured through the tax on certain imports and the Erie Canal opened up the Northwest Territory to a more rapid development." Again, Ford proposed a political economy as exemplified by the protectionist tariff question that was predicated on the codependence of economy and state intervention.

American history, monuments, and geography were widely regarded in this period as subjects of critical importance for the pedagogic project of "Americanizing" diverse populations. The articulation of public memory as commemorative

---

[43] Most notable here was the creation of the Bureau of Public Roads in 1918, as well as the passage of the 1916 Federal-Aid Road Act and the 1921 Federal-Aid Highway Act, both of which supplied money to states building new roads. See Peter J. Ling, *America and the Automobile: Technology, Reform, and Social Change* (Manchester, UK: Manchester University Press, 1990), 37–63. Stan Luger has argued that this support for highway construction dovetailed with a dismantling of urban rail transportation, a project to which major automobile manufacturers were also fully committed. Stan Luger, *Corporate Power, American Democracy, and the Automobile Industry* (Cambridge, UK: Cambridge University Press, 2000), 12.

[44] I draw here from Chris Otter, "Making Liberal Objects: British Techno-Social Relations, 1800–1900," *Cultural Studies* 21, no. 4 (2007): 570–90.

and patriotic activity became increasingly tied to representation, informing the establishment of public festivals, celebrations, pageants, and museum exhibitions.[45] The early twentieth century witnessed also the establishment of genealogical societies like the Sons and Daughters of the American Revolution, historical preservation societies, and a "living history" movement that informed the establishment of museum villages, including the Greenfield Village Museum established by Henry Ford in 1929.[46] The formation of a public—and visual—historical consciousness informed other pedagogic motion picture projects within the visual instruction movement, perhaps most notably the series produced by Yale University Press between 1923 and 1925, the "Yale Chronicles of America Photoplays."[47] In a pamphlet produced to advertise the series on American history, the connections between history and the formation of a liberal civility among diverse populations were made clear: the films, the press asserted, constituted a "powerful instrument for the stimulation of patriotism and good citizenship among native Americans and foreign born citizens alike."[48]

Likewise, in an advertisement for the Ford Educational Library in the non-theatrical trade journal *Moving Picture Age* (January 1920), the Ford films were pictured being projected to an audience of schoolchildren (see fig. 4.2). A female teacher shows students images from a film displaying a typical domestic interior, with the father reading a newspaper as (presumably) his wife and child sit around the fire. Off to one side are images from another film, seemingly a political scene that, given the company's investment in American history and the film *Democracy in Education*, is most likely a representation of the signing of the Declaration of Independence. In this, the advertisement connects political history and a particular articulation of domesticity as central to what it defines as the "teacher's new task," that being the project of "Americanizing" the "children of foreign-born

---

[45] John Bodnar, *Remaking America: Public Memory, Commemoration, and Patriotism in the Twentieth Century* (Princeton, NJ: Princeton University Press, 1992).

[46] Michael Wallace, "Visiting the Past: History Museums in the United States," in *Presenting the Past: Essays on History and the Public,* ed. Susan Porter Benson, Stephen Brier, and Roy Rosenzweig (Philadelphia: Temple University Press, 1986), 137–61.

[47] On the Yale films, see Ian Tyrrell, *Historians in Public: The Practice of American History, 1890–1970* (Chicago: University of Chicago Press, 2005), 75–88; and Roberta E. Pearson, "A White Man's Country: Yale's *Chronicles of America*," in *Memory and Popular Film,* ed. Paul Grainge (Manchester, UK: Manchester University Press, 2003), 23–41.

[48] *The Chronicles of America Photoplays* (New Haven, CT: Yale University Press, n.d.), 10, cited in Pearson, "White Man's Country," 27. Likewise, historian Dixon Ryan Fox argued that the films gave immigrants "roots with which to draw moral and intellectual nourishment from America's past." Dixon Ryan Fox, "Patriotism on the Screen: The Use of the 'Chronicles of America Motion Pictures' in Americanization," *Ohio History Teachers Journal* 34 (May 1924): 457–58, cited in Tyrrell, *Historians in Public,* 81.

"Americanization"
—the Teacher's New Task

Figure 4.2. Ad in *Moving Picture Age* (January 7, 1920).

parents." Americanization, like citizenship, was connected both to a political form of belonging and to the articulation of class standards of civility, a logic that had also underpinned the investigations of Ford's Sociological Department and the shaping of worker attitudes and conduct.

Conclusion

Visual instruction in "civics" in the immediate post–World War I period partic-ipated in a broader governmental project to shape the conduct of diverse popula-tions, becoming part of a liberal political rationality that was tested by the transformations of modernity. Most critical here were the related issues of large-scale population movements, massive shifts in the economic order, and atten-dant transformations in political management. The Ford films are an important example of an attempt to utilize cinema as part of a pedagogic project. They work in particular to visually articulate principles of political economy and to shape historical consciousness. In this way, Ford hoped that the films would par-ticipate in the invention and shaping of tradition as the production of historical memory about America's founding and its structure of liberal governance as one way of shaping the conduct of working-class and immigrant populations.

Yet for all the promise of visual instruction, the presiding mode of discourse in the later 1920s and early 1930s was frequently one of puzzlement at the failure of visual forms to transform pedagogy. Although moving pictures were integrated into education in various ways, proponents often ruefully acknowledged that the wholesale transformation of education was not realized. Certainly, there were practical reasons for this. The invention of 16mm motion-picture film in 1923 had reduced the costs of prints and projectors, but these were still not inconsiderable expenses for cash-strapped school districts, even more so after the introduction of sound. The utopian dreams of moving pictures as central to a new regime of visual instruction could never quite counteract the persistent anxieties about the psychic and social effects of cinema. Ongoing investigations into those effects, such as the Payne Fund Studies (1929–1932), consistently argued that movies had deleterious social and psychic effects.[49] It was this perspective that dominated public discussion of commercial cinema and impacted policy decisions, including Hollywood's establishment of the Motion Picture Production Code of 1930.

One of the offshoots of the social science investigations of the motion picture would be the sustained study of cinema, the initiation of instruction about visual media that would also frequently be shaped by some of the issues around the pedagogical formation of conduct that subtended the establishment of visual instruction. Early formations of film studies at universities in the 1930s frequently elaborated a mode of study that would teach viewers how to escape the mimetic effects of cinema and to ethically shape a liberal selfhood from the practice of movie viewing.[50] Visual instruction segued here into instruction utilizing visual "texts" for the formation of ethical subjectivities—a task taken on by a discipline that would come a generation later to be called "Film Studies."

Filmography

Democracy in Education (ca. 1919) 5 min., 35mm; rev. ed. (1922) 6 min.
PRODUCTION-DISTRIBUTION: Ford Motor Co., Ford Motion Picture Laboratories. Film no. 11 in Ford Educational Library's Civics and Citizenship of the United States series. ACCESS: NARA (film, video, and online); Internet Archive, www.archive.org/details/democracy_in_education_ca_1919, and democracy_in_education_1922.

The Road to Happiness (1924) 3 reels (23 min. survive), 35mm
PRODUCTION: Ford Motor Co., Ford Motion Picture Laboratories, in cooperation with Bureau of Public Roads, U.S. Department of Agriculture, as well as the Highway Education Board and National Automobile Chamber of Commerce. CAST: Frank and Annie

---

[49] Garth Jowett, Ian C. Jarvie, and Kathryn H. Fuller, *Children and the Movies: Media Influence and the Payne Fund Controversy* (Cambridge, UK: Cambridge University Press, 1996).

[50] Lee Grieveson, "Cinema Studies and the Conduct of Conduct," in *Inventing Film Studies,* ed. Grieveson and Haidee Wasson (Durham, NC: Duke University Press, 2008), 3–37.

Matthews (a farm couple), Louise Renker (teacher), Milton Delaney Hall and James R. Allison (members of Board of Supervisors), Charles Fenton Russell, Thomas H. MacDonald (as himself, chief of Bureau of Public Roads), President Calvin Coolidge. Published with booklet *The Road to Happiness: A Highway Motion Picture.* ACCESS: NARA. Also, DVD (Historic Fairfax City, 1985; 30 min., narration by George A. Hamill) and online via the Federal Highway Administration's Eisenhower Interstate Highway System website, www.fhwa.dot.gov/interstate/videogallery.htm.

Uncle Sam and the Bolsheviki-I.W.W. Rat (ca. 1919) 40 sec., 35mm
PRODUCTION: Ford Motor Co. ACCESS: NARA; DVD, *Treasures III: Social Issues in American Film, 1900–1934* (National Film Preservation Foundation, 2007); www.filmpreservation.org/dvds-and-books/clips/uncle-sam-and-the-bolsheviki-i-w-w-rat-ca-1919.

Related Ford Educational Library films at the National Archives

Landmarks of the American Revolution (1920). History series; theatrical distribution by Federated Film Exchanges of America.

Presidents of the United States (ca. 1917). Ford Education Weekly no. 49; rev. ed. *The Presidents of the United States and Their Times* (1921). 856 ft. (approx. 13 min.)

The Story of Old Glory (1916). Ford Education Weekly no. 49.

Washington, D.C. (1918).

Where the Spirit that Won was Born (1919). 2 reels. Ford Education Weekly no. 137. Goldwyn Distribution Co.

5 FILM EDUCATION IN THE NATURAL HISTORY MUSEUM: CINEMA LIGHTS UP THE GALLERY IN THE 1920S

ALISON GRIFFITHS

In the mid-1920s the American Museum of Natural History (AMNH), located in New York City on Manhattan's Upper West Side, was "the chief source of visual aids for the city," supervising a small army of delivery men to bring lantern slides and motion pictures to elementary, middle, and high schools.[1] No charge was made for these slides and films (not even for delivery), and the AMNH received a pittance from the city's board of education to fund this enterprise. The history of cinema's relationship to the AMNH began far earlier, though, and can be traced to 1908, when the AMNH first exhibited film to visitors. Within a few years, cinema was a major part of the museum's visual educational services, consisting of exhibitions to school groups, public programs, and internal screenings to staff. The AMNH also sponsored filmmaking expeditions, including a 1912 Department of Anthropology trip to the American Southwest during which museum artist Howard McCormick made films of the Hopis.[2]

Given that the public museum has been largely overlooked as an institution of film sponsorship, production, and exhibition in film studies, my goal here is

My thanks to Barbara Mathé, head of the Special Collections Department at the American Museum of Natural History, for her unstinting support in accessing the archive. Thanks also to William Boddy, my research assistant Ece Ergen, and the collection editors for suggestions and editorial advice.

The Special Collections Department of the AMNH Research Library includes archival material relating to the history and operation of the museum, which is housed in the Central Archive. Documents from the Central Archive are cited below as CA-AMNH.

[1] "Education Through Schools, Colleges, and Universities," *AMNH Annual Report* [hereafter *AR*] 57 (1925): 13.

[2] For a discussion of this expedition, see chap. 7 of my book *Wondrous Difference: Cinema, Anthropology, and Turn-of-the-Century Visual Culture* (New York: Columbia University Press, 2002), 283–311.

Figure 5.1. Slide and film delivery cars outside the AMNH, waiting to take the latest shipment to New York City's public schools, ca. 1926. (Courtesy Department of Library Services, AMNH.)

to examine the complex and competing interests of this branch of educational film activity during the period from the late teens through the early 1930s.[3] The history of the role of film in the gallery at the AMNH illuminates an experience of cinema distinct from that of the auditorium model of film viewing, where films were shown at the museum either as separate events in the auditorium with no lecturer present or were integrated into public lectures. One unexplored area of the AMNH's involvement with film concerns its role in promoting a program of visual education for New York City schoolchildren, both within the museum as part of its own public film programs and through the circulation of films to extramural screenings in public schools. How, for example, did the lantern slide and motion picture lending policies of the Department of Education at the AMNH contribute to a nascent idea of media literacy in the United States in the 1920s and 30s? How did the AMNH's role as a supplier of free lantern slides and films to New York City schoolchildren make it possible for visual aids to be integrated into the curriculum and used in teacher training?

---

[3] For a history of the emergence of film use at the AMNH, see chapter six of *Wondrous Difference*, 255–82. For more on the role of film in the gallery at the AMNH, see my essay "Film and Interactive Media in the Museum Gallery: From 'Roto-Radio' to Immersive Video," in *Shivers Down Your Spine: Cinema, Museums, and the Immersive View* (New York: Columbia University Press, 2008), 232–82.

This chapter investigates what the AMNH's commitment to visual education might tell us about the status of motion pictures within public education at the time, and what cinema's adoption in the classroom reveals about its place within the AMNH. Of course, the museum's involvement in cinema was not simply that of an educational film distributor. Tens of thousands of students visited the museum each year (as they continue to do), many to watch films (today, IMAX) as a part of their field trips. The museum also offered frequent lectures illustrated with lantern slides and films for its members, the general public, and schoolchildren. The AMNH was, therefore, a hub for initiatives in visual education in the late 1920s. In 1927, for example, the museum was used as a venue for a teacher development program organized by the City College of New York's dean of education, who taught a thirty-week course, "Visual Aids to Instruction."[4]

The mid- to late 1920s were exciting, if occasionally frustrating, times for advocates of film for nontheatrical purposes. Among the issues facing the AMNH were: (1) how to meet the public's appetite for film (audiences increasingly expected illustrated lectures for members, the general public, and children); (2) how to acquire suitable film content for these events; (3) how to distribute lantern slides and films to New York City's public schools; and (4) how to use the AMNH as a showcase for the technology of motion pictures itself, including the latest in color processes. (An example of the latter role is a lecture that was jointly organized by the American Association for the Advancement of Science, the education departments of the museum, and New York City in 1928, during which the head of Eastman Kodak's research lab demonstrated the new Kodacolor process, the first 16mm color film stock.)[5]

Other issues under debate included the AMNH's decidedly mixed experience with film in the gallery. These included the viewer-activated Dramagraph, or "automatic projector," which allowed visitors to press a button to watch a film in a freestanding box, a sort of precursor to today's multimedia interactive exhibits where visitors watch videos and sometimes interact with computer programs. A Dramagraph was installed in the Southwest Indian Hall in 1927 and another beside the Virginia Deer Group in the Hall of North American Mammals. Despite liberating film from the AMNH's auditorium (built in 1900 at the museum), screening room, and classroom, the gallery-based automatic projector was both unreliable (it lasted no longer than a month before breaking) and difficult to

---

[4] Letters from Dean Pam Klapper to George Sherwood, Apr. 27 and July 7, 1927, in file 1267f (1927), box 1267, CA-AMNH.

[5] The lecture, demonstrating the "possibilities of reproducing accurate color pictures for school room instruction and private use" was delivered by C. E. K. Mees of the Eastman Kodak Company. Press Bulletin, November 10, 1928, CA-AMNH.

maintain due to the challenge of locating suitable museum-owned footage to use in it.[6]

The AMNH also became an informal lobbyist for visual education in the nation's largest school system, which was confronting budget shortfalls and sprawling bureaucracy. For example, in 1927, museum director George Sherwood, in his essay "Visual Education Aids by Film," complained that it seemed "astounding that in constructing new schools" the New York City (NYC) Department of Education "should make provision for projection booths and then fail to provide projection apparatus for the booth."[7] The museum's service to the public school system was largely charity work, since the subsidy they received from the Board of Education (a meager sum of $3,750 in 1926) came nowhere near the 1926 operating costs of approximately $23,000.[8] These issues tell us a great deal about the hurdles facing advocates of visual education in the 1920s. From the mundane but essential task of keeping NYC motion-picture projection permits up to date, to the laborious but crucial job of apologizing to angry members turned away from sold-out screenings, the film activities of the AMNH provide a fascinating case study into the diverse and contested ways in which film became embedded in the museum, from visually documenting official expeditions to illustrating exhibits in the gallery. But this case study also reveals a great deal about film's role in the public sphere more generally. For example, we can find echoes of several of the issues facing the AMNH and other nontheatrical exhibition sites, such as clubs and churches. Given the AMNH's unwieldy organizational structure, nontheatrical film exhibition was especially challenging for the museum, at a time when the maturing Hollywood system of production, distribution, and exhibition made nontheatrical exhibition increasingly marginal.

From Lantern Slide to Motion Picture Library, 1869-1930

Classroom instruction in history, geography and science, more than ever before is being supplemented by the use of slides and motion pictures.
—AMNH *Annual Report,* 1925

Soon after its inception in 1869, under its founder and first superintendent Albert S. Bickmore, the AMNH began a lantern slide collection for use both in

---

[6] Letter from George Sherwood to James L. Clark, June 21, 1927, box 1237, CA-AMNH. According to the minutes from a luncheon of trustees and the Educational Committee, October 5, 1927, plans were also afoot to install Automatic Projectors at the opening of the Fish Hall and the Komodo Lizard Group. For more on the rise and fall of Automatic Projectors at the AMNH, see Griffiths, *Shivers Down Your Spine,* 243–50.

[7] Letter from Sherwood to Raymond L. Ditmars, New York Zoological Society, July 7, 1927, in file 1927 A-F, box 1290.1A, CA-AMNH.

[8] "Rapidly Expanding School Service," *AR* 58 (1926): 18.

its public programs and on loan to New York City public schools. With the inauguration of the Department of Education at the AMNH in 1880, the museum launched an aggressive program of slide acquisition. Following the introduction of improved camera technology in 1888, the museum ensured that all its expeditions were equipped with up-to-date cameras. The earliest lecture series for members' children was in spring 1904, when six lectures were given: "Ants, Bees, and Wasps"; "Sea Beach at Ebb Tide"; "How to Study Reptiles"; "Some Common Rocks and What They Mean"; "The American Indians and How They Live"; and "The Home Life of the Birds."[9] In 1906, Bickmore turned over responsibility for visual education to George H. Sherwood, who became director of the Department of Public Instruction, which oversaw "all the work connected with the public schools and the lecture system . . . as well as the general photographic work and the custody of all negatives, photographs, electros, and slides belonging to the museum."[10] By 1911 the AMNH was regularly using motion pictures in lectures. It soon accumulated prints of appropriate commercial films, including *Paul J. Rainey's African Hunt* (1912; donated by Rainey); films of African wildlife by Martin and Osa Johnson; footage shot in the Antarctic during the Shackleton Expedition (1914–1917); and in-house films of the ceremonial life and material culture of Native American tribes. The museum's education curator Grace Fisher Ramsey offers clues about the early rationale for film use at the AMNH. In her 1938 book on museum education, Ramsey wrote: "It soon became evident that the explorer must not alone be a specialist in his line but an expert camera man as well, for the films brought back to the museum were considered an important part of his collection in that they gave a clear and comprehensive picture of life and conditions in remote corners of the globe" (see fig. 5.2).[11]

By the end of the 1930s, the library at the AMNH contained more than 750,000 feet of film, some of it acquired as a direct result of fellow curators taking heed of Ramsey's recommendation. Despite Sherwood's ambition for the AMNH film collection to become "the finest library of natural history films," he tempered his enthusiasm by referencing the "difficulties of caring for so much film, much of which is in infrequent circulation," and argued that the "film library should be increased cautiously and that out-of-date-material should be scrapped."[12] The problem of storing flammable 35mm nitrate film stock became so acute that the museum later disposed of a significant number of films. For

---

[9] Grace Fisher Ramsey, *Educational Work in Museums of the United States* (New York: H. W. Wilson, 1938), 123–24.

[10] "Rapidly Expanding," 16.

[11] Ramsey, *Educational Work*, 182.

[12] Department of Public Education, Minutes of the Meeting of the Trustees Committee on Education, December 14, 1928, 2, file 1237.3 (1928–1929), CA-AMNH.

Figure 5.2. Lantern slide library at the American Museum of Natural History in the mid-1920s. (Courtesy Department of Library Services, AMNH.)

example, despite acquiring the copyright to photographer Edward S. Curtis's 1914 film *In the Land of the Head Hunters* in 1924, the AMNH did not keep the 35mm print and probably destroyed it during the 1950s or 60s when much of the older, flammable film stock was purged from the collection.

The AMNH first circulated its lantern slide collection in 1915, when a financial arrangement was drawn up with the New York City Board of Education, which made it possible for approximately 20,000 slides to be made available to the city's schoolteachers for classroom use. The AMNH staff were proud of this initiative, noting somewhat smugly in 1924 that it "would not have required the powers of a soothsayer to foretell how valuable this new line of Museum cooperation would prove to teachers and pupils in the city schools." The success of the program was measured by the exponential growth it enjoyed in its first quinquennium, from nearly 12,000 slides lent to 51 institutions in 1915, to more than 80,000 slides lent to 164 schools in 1920. Colored lantern slides, in huge demand, were delivered free to hundreds of schools, where they "vitalize[d] the study, not only of natural-history topics, but of geographical, economical and historical subjects as well."[13] The AMNH identified four reasons for this expansion. The first was the growth in the number of schools equipped to project stereopticon lantern slides, due to the new stress on "visual instruction methods in teaching"; second, there was a greater

---

[13] "The Museum and School Service," *AR* 58 (1926): 99.

availability of slides made possible by the multiplication of lecture sets and the arrangement of slides into 170 different groups; third, there was increasing integration of slides into curricular themes; and the final factor was the promotion of the visual education movement by the NYC Board of Education, under the tutelage of the director of Public Education and Visual Instruction, Ernest L. Crandall.[14]

However, similar success could not be celebrated regarding the museum's use of motion pictures in public schools, which, the same *Annual Report* complained, "still remains small because of the limited size of our motion picture library, and because so few of the school buildings, comparatively, are equipped for the use of motion pictures." Visual instruction via motion pictures had therefore developed slowly "because of the great cost of production in relation to the demand for its use, and on account of the great expense to the schools of projection equipment, booth, etc." Initially, only a small number of schools could take advantage of the opportunity to request films; however, as word spread among the principals that "free films, useful in geography, history, nature study and biology could be secured from [the] museum, they made a great effort to have their schools equipped with standard projection apparatus in a booth which would satisfy all requirements of the fire laws."[15]

By 1922, the AMNH was devoting considerable resources to lantern slide production, allocating the fourth floor of its building to the storage of "files of our negatives and photographs, photographic dark rooms, preparation rooms, studios and laboratories." The motion picture library was housed in the museum's attic, a bizarre choice for the flammable films. The museum employed a delivery crew of four messengers and four automobiles to distribute the slides, films, and nature collections to New York City schools.[16] The museum also adjusted its program of lectures in 1921, including courses where only motion pictures would be shown and experimenting with the format (the suggestion to show only films apparently came from the teachers). Parallel with growing slide circulation, attendance at museum lectures doubled in 1921, from 75,000 to 150,000 children.[17] Over the years, slide collections were assembled that complemented films and that could address key curricular themes. By 1924, the museum had at its disposal 95,618 feet of motion picture film; 309 reels were lent and used in 316 screenings with a total of 115,849 pupils in attendance.[18]

---

[14] "Public Education in the Museum and in the Schools," *AR* 56 (1924): 133.

[15] Ramsey, *Educational Work,* 183.

[16] The messenger service at the AMNH was severely stretched due to a shortage of vehicles and messengers. The years 1922 through 1925 saw a reduction in the number of natural history specimens delivered to schools, a result one assumes of the increased demand for slides and motion picture shipments to the five boroughs; *AR* 57 (1925): 80.

[17] *AR* 54 (1922): 41.

[18] "Public Education," 133; "World Photographic Life Records," *AR* 56 (1924): 15.

The mid- to late 1920s were years of exponential growth in moving picture activity at the AMNH, both in terms of supplying films for school use and acquiring films for internal screenings. Film work at the museum can be broken down into four types of activities, starting with acquisitions, consisting mostly of films donated to the museum by production companies and individuals. For example, in 1917, 254 colored lantern slides and 1,830 feet of 35 mm film of American naturalist and essayist John Burroughs were donated by photographer Albert Houghton Pratt; and in 1923, Martin Johnson donated a copy of his extremely popular adventure animal safari film released that year, *Trailing African Wild Animals*. Other notable acquisitions included: an anonymous 1925 gift of two sets of *Chronicles of America*, a forty-seven-reel series distributed by Yale University Press; eight reels of *The True North*, a 1925 record of Captain Jack Robertson's trip across Alaska and Siberia; two prints of *Nanook of the North* (1922) from Pathé; footage shot in the Nile region by George D. Pratt; and films of Arthur Vernay and John Faunthorpe hunting animal specimens in India (1922–1923).[19]

The second museum film activity involved borrowing prints. For example, in 1918, the State Conservation Commission, General Electric, and Prizma (producers of color film) all loaned films to the AMNH, and we see significant growth between 1922, when 76 reels of film (63 screenings) were borrowed, and 1924, when that number increased to 309 reels (316 screenings). Organizations credited in AMNH's *Annual Report* with lending films in 1922 included the New York State Conservation Commission, the U.S. Navy Recruiting Bureau, the Roosevelt Memorial Association, and the New York City Board of Water Supply. The AMNH also rented films from 12 exchanges in 1922 (rising to 91 by 1926).[20] The number of pupils watching films at the AMNH in 1922 totaled 18,286, growing more than sixfold in just two years.[21]

The third activity was coproduction. At times the AMNH would be asked to "furnish suggestions and illustrative material for motion picture films of a popular educational character," such as the invitation from Bray Studios in 1918 to produce films on mineralogical subjects.

The final area involved AMNH-sponsored expeditions.[22] Two notable expeditions from the 1920s that used film were the 1927 Woodcraft Indian

---

[19] "Lending of Motion Pictures," *AR* 58 (1926): 19.

[20] "Public Education," 49.

[21] Ibid., 126.

[22] *AR* 50 (1918): 37; and *AR* 51 (1919): 62 and 68. The Bray Studio project resulted in the late teens in the production of *Gem Cutting and Polishing, Mysteries of the Snow, Dew, In Nature's Treasure House,* and *Window Frost.*

expedition (cosponsored by the League of Woodcraft Indians, a youth organization founded by Ernest Thompson Seton) and the 1926 Asiatic Expedition led (and funded) by William J. Morden and James L. Clark. The latter expedition returned with "not only a fine series of skins, complete skeletons and full scientific measurements of the large game of the country which they visited, but a complete record of the trip in motion pictures [actually only 2,300 feet of film], still photographs and field notes."[23] The Woodcraft Indian expedition was led by education curator Clyde Fisher and famous naturalist Ernest Thompson Seton, cofounder of the Boy Scouts of America. The expedition produced four reels of film as part of the summer visit to the Southwest, with Fisher operating the camera).[24] The film depicts a variety of Native American dances (buffalo, hood, war, eagle, corn, deer, and snowbird) performed by members of the Tusque, Taos, Acoma, and Santa Clara Pueblos. Fisher also filmed other activities of the local peoples, including an intertribal ceremony in Gallup, New Mexico. He recorded the dances, material culture, and cultural practices of several tribes in a systematic way, foregrounding some of the most popular dances as important cross-cultural events within the community. Some of the dances, especially those featuring children, were performed for the camera, while others were part of large public celebrations.

On two occasions in 1927, Fisher screened at least some footage, which he called *Camping Among the Indians*. The first was part of a "Saturday Afternoon Program for Children and Parents" at the museum and the second included in the "Free Lectures for the Children of Public Schools" series. His lecture was one of eight that fell under the rubric "Nature and Industries" and was entitled "The American Indian of Today." The AMNH's promotion read: "Visit the Indian Reservation from North Dakota to Arizona with Dr. Fisher, Ernest Thompson Seton and their friends. Learn how the Indian talks by signs, put up their tipis, make pottery, and bake their bread. See the Navajo, Pueblo, and Sioux Indians do their ceremonial dances in fantastic dress of beads and feathers."[25] The three active verbs—*Visit, Learn,* and *See*—position virtual travel, knowledge, and vision as the pedagogical payoff and offer us clues as to how the lecture was organized. The first two parts of the lecture—native sign language and tipi building—could not, however, have been illustrated by footage from *Camping Among the Indians* since there is no footage of these activities in the extant version of the film. The reference made to sign language and tipi making in the

---

[23] "Morden-Clark Expedition," *AR* 59 (1927): 72.

[24] For more on *Camping Among the Indians* and the Woodcraft Movement, see my essay "The 1920s Museum Sponsored Expedition Film: Beguiling Encounters in All But Forgotten Genre," *Early Popular Visual Culture* 9 (Dec. 2011).

[25] "Free Lectures for the Children of Public Schools," Spring 1928 brochure, description of lecture on page 6, box 1267, CA-AMNH.

lecture, suggests one of three possibilities: that footage of these cultural practices *was* shot by Fisher and Seton but edited out of the extant twenty-one-minute version; that magic lantern slides were substituted for film at this point in the lecture; or that footage acquired by the AMNH or a film made by another curator was used instead.

But how did Fisher's lecture and *Camping Among the Indians* fit into the museum program of visual education? Why, for example, was the film never screened on its own, as many other films were at the museum, but instead submerged within lectures or excerpted in the Dramagraph? We don't know with certainty how much of the footage Fisher shot was used in any of the lectures at the AMNH or elsewhere—the extant film, at just twenty-one minutes, could easily have been screened in its entirety. But the footage brought home from the field was obviously edited to suit the needs of the event, as indicated by a reference in the 1927 *Annual Report* to the motion picture's having been "edited and used in several lectures for the public schools."[26] What *Camping Among the Indians* makes clear is that the filmic text is far less precise (or useful) an arbiter of meaning in contexts such as museums— where lecturers and curators inserted the film into customized programs that integrated slides, music, and the spoken word, thus sharing more in common with ephemeral performances—than it seems to be in traditional theatrical screenings.

The museum's employees received sneak previews of AMNH-sponsored expedition footage, such as *Camping Among the Indians,* as well as a broad mix of other films that wound up at the museum and that were linked, sometimes only tangentially, to the work of the various departments. Memos to heads of departments announcing daytime screenings in either the auditorium, which accommodated 1,500 people, or more commonly in the Education Hall in the School Service Building, which accommodated 500 people, were sent out sometimes only a day before or on the day of the screening. The sources of the films shown were varied, from the latest footage shot by a famous commercial travelogue exhibitor, such as Burton Holmes; by the museum's own taxidermist-explorer Carl Akeley; or by individuals who were presented as experts in their specific fields. For example, in September 1927, department heads were informed that a special screening of a film made in Africa by naturalist M. P. Greenwood Adams would be shown, depicting "accurately and in detail the life of David Livingston as missionary, doctor, and explorer in Africa, including his rescue by [Sir Henry Morton] Stanley" in Tanzania. While there doesn't appear to be much information on this film other than this terse description, its focus on a famous historical event of 1871 and link to a colonial Africa that was certainly

---

[26] "Distribution of Motion Pictures," *AR* 25 (1927): 99.

represented in the museum, and to which expeditions had traveled, gives us some sense of the broad mission the AMNH cast for film. Here was a film that came the way of the museum by a credentialed individual; the decision to screen it may simply have been motivated by a "why not" mentality, perhaps a demonstrative display of politeness not to offend Adams. Given the relatively large number of these internal screenings, this was not an ad hoc policy decision but more likely an attempt to expose curators to the possibilities of cinema as a research and pedagogical tool, to showcase film that had been shot both by AMNH curators and by affiliated professionals, and maybe even to provide a welcome respite from the daily grind. The museum also regularly scheduled films for its staff, heralded by free public lectures that were also organized at the AMNH under the auspices of the Board of Education and that served as a forum where professional lecturers could show their latest slides and films. In the fall of 1927, for example, Harry C. Ostrander showed his colored stills and motion pictures of Italy; August Post exhibited "aviation views" and films; and Burton Holmes delivered a lecture on "Angkor the Great," featuring stereopticon and motion picture views of the fortified city of Angkor Thom located on the Mekong River in Cambodia.[27]

In fall 1921, the museum inaugurated its "film only" program, screening eight motion pictures illustrating literary classics, including previews of *Silas Marner* (Frank P. Donovan, 1922) and *The Last of the Mohicans* (Clarence Brown and Maurice Tourneur, 1920). The AMNH found such commercial feature films attracted "a larger attendance than usual at other lectures." Henry Fairfield Osborn, president of the museum from 1908 to 1933, opined that while the movies "were not all that could be desired, the experiment [showing films without a lecture] proved very much worthwhile."[28] Aside from establishing the museum's stance on the value of stand-alone screenings, the comment about the films not being "all that could be desired" is telling. It points up a longstanding concern among curators about the relevance of certain film topics to the mission of the museum; they argued that it had no connection to the institution's overarching mission. We find additional ambivalence toward film in the 1924 annual report, where the problem again concerns the difficulty of securing appropriate content. According to the "Report of the President," "our lantern slide and film work has been handicapped because of the lack of the right kind of pictures to portray the life of the people of foreign countries, even the countries of Europe . . . it is not easy to find good pictures of historical buildings, famous streets, or important shrines in the cities of foreign countries, it is not easy to find good pictures

---

[27] Announcement of Free Public Lectures in file N-O1927/1267H, box 1267, CA-AMNH.

[28] *AR* 54 (1922): 44.

that will show the common, homely, everyday activities of the people at large—their industries and their children."[29] This complaint testifies to the improvised status of ethnographic filmmaking in the 1920s, resulting in museums being forced to rely upon either commercially produced films or footage that had been shot as part of their own expeditions in support of lectures and other public programs. However, Osborn's tepid response to film-only programming in the early to mid-1920s can be contrasted with his enthusiasm for classroom-based film years later. "In the teaching of many subjects," he wrote, "the motion picture is of much greater value than the lantern slides or pictures in a book, provided that the motion pictures are good, that they are suitable, and that the story is well told."[30]

As part of its commitment to civic uplift in the early 1920s, the AMNH also began showing a series of motion pictures during the Christmas holidays, the purpose of which was twofold: to give children "wholesome entertainment to keep them off the streets, and second, to get them into the habit of visiting the museum."[31] The museum's broader mission of acculturating the lower classes and immigrants to museumgoing as a vital tool in self-education and betterment can be considered a third goal of these free motion picture screenings. Like other museums, the AMNH worked toward the ideal of "rational entertainment" and a self-defined role as a civilizing instrument for New York City's burgeoning population.[32] But the AMNH's decision to show films during the holidays also brands the institution as a place of fun, relaxation, and free movies, where young people would have to walk past exhibits to reach the auditorium. The AMNH took no chances with the programming, showing a print of Robert Flaherty's hit *Nanook of the North*, which Revillon Freres (the French fur company and film's sponsor) and Pathé Exchange donated to the AMNH. A staggering 2,915 people turned up the first day to see the film, making it necessary to screen it three times and to show it again the next day, when 3,083 children were admitted. Any fears the AMNH might

---

[29] "Report of the President," *AR* 57 (1925): 80. The report goes on to identify the progress made in this area, including films made by Philip H. Pratt and his wife Gladys L. Pratt, who "very kindly volunteered to go to France last summer [1924] and take pictures of this character." The Pratts' trip to France was underwritten by the French Consul General in New York, the General Secretary of the Compagnie Géneral Transatlantique, and the Office Francais du Tourisme. The AMNH was very pleased with the fifteen reels (of positive and negative film) entitled *Everyday Life of People in France*, stating that "for the first time we were able to give the school children of New York a true idea of the life of the people of Brittany, Normandy, the Provinces of Central France, the Pyrenees, and along the Mediterranean coast."

[30] "Report of the President: Public Education in Schools," *AR* 56 (1926): 100.

[31] "Public Education," 44.

[32] For more on this see Tony Bennett's book on late-nineteenth-century museum culture, *The Birth of the Museum: History, Theory, Politics* (New York: Routledge, 1995).

have had about unruly behavior at these capacity film screenings were entirely mitigated: "Although the auditorium was repeatedly crowded to overflowing, there was no disorder. On the contrary, the children were more quiet and gave better attention than when they were accompanied by their teachers."[33] Here was filmgoing powerfully resignified by the reputation and physical architecture of the museum (which perhaps accounts for the good behavior). The rules and etiquette of reception were redrawn—there was no popcorn or soda, for one thing—and the free admission to the film might have precipitated a longer stay at the museum, to wander the galleries or perhaps visit the museum shop on the way out. Invoked here also is the idea of more decorous behavior and serious response to the film being more likely outside the context of an organized school trip, with the "mob mentality" of the class somewhat abated.

The AMNH was also used as a venue for lectures in media education, often spearheaded by outside organizations, such as the "Visual Aids to Instruction" series mentioned earlier. Fisher delivered the second lecture in the series (the first meeting in December 1926 was held at the Metropolitan Museum of Art)[34],

Figure 5.3. Children attending a lecture, AMNH Auditorium, 1916. (Courtesy Department of Library Services, AMNH.)

---

[33] "Public Education," 44.

[34] For more on film's role within the Metropolitan Museum of Art, see Elias Katz, "Educational Possibilities of Motion Pictures in Art Courses," *International Review of Educational Cinematography* 6 (1934): 29–35. Also see Haidee Wasson, *Museum Movies: The Museum of Modern Art and the Birth of Art Cinema* (Berkeley: University of California Press, 2005), 78.

"The Future of Motion Pictures in Education," and though this was six months before he shot *Camping Among the Indians*, it is likely he made some reference to the role of expeditionary filmmaking in public education.[35] Motion pictures had become such an accepted part of the institution's public service mission by the mid-1920s that when groups requested an introduction to the museum and its work, as the Municipal Club of Brooklyn did in November 1928, the AMNH rounded off the evening's activities with a screening of Martin Johnson's films showcasing the museum's role in sponsoring expeditions. In a letter asking Johnson for loan of the films, Sherwood thanked him for "making a program for this group of business men from Brooklyn attractive and interesting," a sentiment mirrored in the thank-you letter from Municipal Club secretary Almet R. Batson Jr., in which he praised the film for "illustrating the explorations conducted under the auspices of the museum in a little known region of the world."[36]

The AMNH obviously had to deal with the cost of securing, storing, and maintaining films (by 1927 the film library contained 463 reels). The problem of flammable film stock became such a serious challenge by this time that the museum was renting space for 100 reels at Lloyds Film Storage in Manhattan, paying a monthly rate of $2 per reel for the first 5 reels and $1 per reel thereafter. The problem of film storage at the AMNH is a refrain in a great deal of the internal memoranda compelling overseers of film at the museum to cull the collection for what was generically referred to as "poor material." A memo from October 5, 1927, recommended that they "pass on film which may be presented to the Museum in the future." In an attempt to resolve the flammable film stock issue, the AMNH hired a motion picture operator (with added responsibility for the physical care of films) at a cost of $2,500.[37] Such expenses were nevertheless not a disincentive to the museum's acquisition of new film material, as gleaned from the fact that almost every expedition underwritten by the AMNH involved someone responsible for documenting the expedition cinematographically.

---

[35] Letter to Sherwood from Pam Klapper, Apr. 27, 1927, in file 1267F (1927), box 1267, CA-AMNH.

[36] The evening consisted of a behind-the-scenes tour; dinner in the restaurant; a lecture by Sherwood on the museum's School Service; a lecture by Dr. Kingsley Noble, curator of Herpetology and Experimental Biology; and the Johnson films. Quotes from letter to Johnson from Sherwood, November 19, 1928, and letter from Batsob to Sherwood, November 27, 1928, both in file I-M 1928/1267M, box 1267 (1928–1931), CA-AMNH.

[37] Minutes from Luncheon Meeting of Trustees and the Educational Committee, October 5, 1927, 1, box 1237.3; George Sherwood, "Report to the Committee on Education," 1927, 2, both in CA-AMNH.

"By-Products of the Entertainment Film": Cinema and Visual Education in the 1920s[38]

> [M]ake every classroom and every assembly hall a movie show, a show where the child learns every moment while his eyes are glued to the screen.
> —*School Life,* 1919[39]

By the mid-twenties, the concept of visual education had gained sufficient traction in educational and museum discourses that coming to its defense was no longer necessary. Books and articles targeting educators, policymakers, curators, and public intellectuals had appeared in print. As Haidee Wasson notes, "Museums themselves were being reshaped through a pervasive set of ideas and discourses catalyzed particularly from the 1920s forward through a range of mass media."[40] The National Education Association (NEA) had a Committee on Visual Education that worked closely with Eastman Kodak, targeting the fourth through eighth grades and honing in on geography, health and hygiene, civics, fine and practical arts, and general science.[41]

In May 1928, Kodak established Eastman Teaching Films, Inc., which would develop a program of motion pictures to be used "for instruction in schools, colleges, universities, technical institutions, and medical schools." The development of cheaper, safer, and more portable 16mm prints had a significant impact on the educational possibilities of film. In 1925, Eastman Kodak and the NEA enlisted 176 teachers and 12,000 pupils from cities across the United States to take part in a study on the impact of motion pictures in education. Not surprisingly, the study authors concluded that "films contribute elements to the experiences of the children which it is difficult and often impossible to secure by any other method available to the school."[42] A letter from philanthropist John L. Porter, trustee of the Carnegie Institute, to AMNH president Osborn in 1926 referred specifically to the impact of the past ten years on young people:

---

[38] The phrase "by-products of entertainment" is from Carl E. Milliken, "Increasing General Usefulness of Films," *Motion Picture* 4, no. 8 (Aug. 1928): 6.

[39] "Edison Urges Educational Use of Motion Pictures," *School Life* (Feb. 1919): 5.

[40] Wasson, *Museum Movies*, 71. According to F. Dean McClusky, by 1931 "the reports of a total of thirty-six important research studies of visual instruction" had been published. McClusky, *Visual Instruction: Its Value and Its Needs; A Report* (New York: Mancall Publishing Group, 1932), 16. McClusky was president of the National Academy of Visual Instruction. The report was completed for Will H. Hays, head of the Motion Picture Producers and Distributors of America (MPPDA).

[41] Letter to Sherwood from Jason S. Joy [director of the MPPDA's Studio Relations Committee], July 15, 1928, 1, box 1237, CA-AMNH.

[42] "A Climactic Development in Education," *Movie Makers* 3, no. 6 (1928): 380.

Education in the past decade has taken on so much of the visualizing methods, that our Museums are fast becoming the greater and greater adjuncts, annually to our educational program, and if I judge rightly, it will not take more than a generation to bring most of our younger element to a point where there will be very little of Natural History, which will be to them a wonderland, such as it has been to most of us, as the knowledge they will gain during their school days will have started them off on their own journey, through the universe, with a very broadened conception of it.[43]

Porter's point, if a bit buried in this wordy proclamation, seems to be that museums of natural history will be beneficiaries of the stellar job schools are doing introducing students to the natural world through visual means, implying that the introduction to natural history via film and lantern slide will trigger a life-long, self-guided, and expansive journey of discovery. Porter's letter casts the AMNH's relationship to the larger visual education movement in an interesting light, suggesting even a circularity where the AMNH promotes film to schools by providing free films, the films shown in classes ignite a lifelong interest in natural history, and this development in turn draws people back to the source of the impetus, the AMNH. If the AMNH was never entirely explicit about what was in it for them in terms of a motivation for using film (we can identify a cluster of reasons in the presidential summaries in the *Annual Reports*), it would be remiss to assume that the AMNH wasn't aware of how film shown both behind its own doors and distributed through its lending service would ultimately cast the institution in a favorable light and further the museum's mission through visual educational means.

However, the substantial increase in slide and motion picture loans made to schools during the 1920s had a deleterious effect on the circulating collection of natural history specimens. The 1924 *Annual Report* offered that "the important branch of the work [in this area] has fallen off this year on account of a lack of messenger service for transferring the collections. . . . As has been true during the past two years, the lending of lantern slides has taken precedence over this work, although in visual instruction it is believed that *the real object is of greater service than any still picture of it*."[44] And yet the real object, what Barbara Kirschenblatt-Gimblett calls "first order" materials, could not reach as many students as still or moving pictures, nor could these material objects reveal much about culture in the absence of explanations as to their use, context, and symbolic significance. Museum extension work began with the circulation of collections of objects,

---

[43] Letter to Osborn from Porter, July 14, 1926, box 1248.1 1925, CA-AMNH.

[44] "Public Education," 133.

specimens, and models, usually accompanied by descriptions and suggestions for classroom use. The AMNH clearly felt that these were more valuable as introductions to natural history and related scientific areas than lectures with drawings or no illustrations at all.[45]

By 1927 the AMNH felt completely at ease appropriating industry-driven motion picture marketing in its *Annual Reports*, even when referring to slides; the rhetoric used, for example, in "Report of the President" in the *Annual Report* from that same year about the distribution of lantern slides could very well have been lifted straight from *Moving Picture World* or any other industry magazine: "Thousands of pupils," we are told, "are enabled to visit the haunts of birds, mammals, and other creatures; to see how their neighbors live in other hemispheres as well as their own, and to grasp, in a more comprehensive way, the story of life, past and present, the world over."[46] Noting an "ever-increasing demand for motion pictures," the president described the films as supplementing the slides, a clear indicator, I believe, of the added difficulties of exhibiting films in schools where projectors were less readily available in classrooms versus lantern slides.[47] While it would be shortsighted to slight the differences between lantern slides and films as circulating objects, they were viewed through a very similar epistemological lens by the AMNH, discursively constructed as legitimate alternatives to habitat groups in the museum, hugely expensive diorama-type displays where fauna and flora would be exhibited in illusionistic glass cases. Both slides and film provided cheap alternatives to these 3-D displays that contextualized objects in their proper environment.

We therefore see considerable investment by the AMNH in the lure of indexicality, the idea of film "stopping short only of the actual experience" in the words of *Educational Screen* contributor Annette Glick. For Glick, this indexicality shares an affinity with the experiences of children—she says that the motion picture is rendered "almost with childlike naiveté," since its reality amounts to a "vicarious experience," and in her mind, "children who come from a motion picture have lived the scenes portrayed, not merely viewed them."[48] Of course, given the often inflated rhetoric surrounding the pedagogical uses of motion pictures at this time (and even earlier during the silent cinema period), we should interpret cinema's lauded status as driven as much by self-serving agendas as by genuine beliefs in its elevated status above the other related arts. In some instances, the hyperbole is part and parcel of a broader industry-driven effort to recuperate film from its lowbrow, mass culture connotations and to legitimize

---

[45] Barbara Kirshenblatt-Gimblett, "Objects of Ethnography," in *Exhibiting Cultures: The Poetics and Politics of Museum Display,* ed. Ivan Karp and Steven D. Lavine (Washington, DC: Smithsonian Institution Press, 1990), 394.

[46] "Museum and School Service," 98.

[47] *AR* 59 (1927): 98–99.

[48] Annette Glick, "The Habit of Criticizing the Motion Picture," *Educational Screen* 8, no. 1 (1934): 10.

film use in schools. The AMNH doubtless felt quite comfortable appropriating this rhetoric to further its institutional mandates and in many respects had few other options given its status as a high cultural institution of refined entertainment; all of the films shown under the auspices of the AMNH had to confer a set of brand associations to the public, because otherwise the stakes in appropriating the medium to further the AMNH's mission would have simply been too high, especially if it meant alienating some of the museum's wealthy stakeholders.

Even Thomas Edison threw his weight behind the aggrandizing of film (for obvious reasons), entering the fray to extol the virtues of cinema as both an illusionistic *and* an educational tool, describing it as the "closest possible approximation to reality" and "almost the same as bringing that object itself before the child or taking the child to that object."[49] In addition to the convenience of neither having to bring the object before the child nor the child before the object— although paradoxically, this was precisely what museums did—other virtues were bestowed upon cinema, including Glick's argument that it was "through the power to supply experience as well as simply to convey ideas and thoughts and emotions, that the motion picture accomplishes what the poet or sculptor cannot do."[50]

One advantage the natural history object had over film was its ability to be used in the classroom as opposed to the auditorium, as Ramsey explains: "A great drawback to the more common use of the thirty-five millimeter film as a teaching aid was the necessity of providing a licensed operator and taking the prescribed fire precautions. This practically prohibited the classroom use of films and restricted their showings to assemblies where both teachers and pupils thought of the films more often as a form of entertainment than as an integral part of a lesson."[51] To address this problem, in 1914 the museum inaugurated lecture centers in New York City high schools with large-capacity auditoriums that could be used to host illustrated lectures for elementary schoolchildren (Washington Irving High School was among the first to allow its 1,500-seat auditorium to be placed at the disposal of local elementary schools).[52] Whether viewing the film in a high school auditorium or an assembly hall in an elementary school made any difference in how students perceived the screening is obviously hard to assess, although the expense of transporting students across the city surely played a role in curtailing this practice. With the introduction of 16mm film stock by Eastman Kodak in 1923 the situation improved, as the AMNH was able to lend the narrow-gauge films to those schools that were equipped with portable 16mm projectors, which could be used in classrooms, as opposed to 35mm, which could only be shown in school auditoriums. This clearly had an impact on both the circulation of AMNH-owned films, which exponentially increased, as well as on

---

[49] "Edison Urges," 5.

[50] Glick, "Habit of Criticizing," 11.

[51] Ramsey, *Educational Work,* 183.

[52] Ibid., 188

museum-sponsored expeditions that used the Akeley camera, described in the 1924 AMNH *Annual Report* as "so perfect that the small film negative one inch square is capable of being enlarged to display the finest details of an animation in full motion [such as] as animal moving at a speed of 40 miles per hour."[53]

According to Ramsey, the AMNH "kept pace with the changes in visual education . . . which resulted in the extension of its film circulation to schools and other educational organizations all over the country [except Pacific coast states]." In 1937, the AMNH circulated "34,700 reels to 1,706 borrowers in forty-five states, with an audience of 13,102,368 people reported at the 80,532 showings."[54] Despite these impressive numbers and the not inconsiderable research on film that had taken place by 1937, it was still difficult to know with certainty how film was being used in schools, an issue raised by J. Frederic Andrews, who argued that "nowhere is there any great uniformity of practice, nowhere does there exist any significant scientific research to guide these organizations." Drawing upon data generated by 241 questionnaires sent to public schools known to be using visual aids in 241 cities (with a 59 percent response rate) in 1934, Andrews concluded that 83 percent of these schools were using motion pictures in the classroom; 86 percent in assembly halls; and 70 percent in special meetings or activities (slides exceeded films only in the classroom [89 percent]).[55]

Museums such as the AMNH and the Field Museum in Chicago were pivotal in providing the infrastructure for free motion pictures and slide distribution to public schools from the teens through today. Cinema was the darling if controversial child not only of an emerging visual education movement but also in other fields such as religion and medicine that were keen to experiment with film either as a recruiting device in the case of churches or to train medical students. Another reason to use film was simply to appear modern and "with the times." For the natural history museum this was obviously a less pressing concern (recall that the AMNH had shown no interest in cinema whatsoever until 1907); permanent galleries were literally that, fixed spaces where little changed. Film therefore entered the AMNH on the back of lantern slides, which created the conditions of possibility and a framework of reassurance that the visual experience would be similar yet different.

Few would dispute the pivotal role played by the AMNH in audiovisual-based education in the 1920s. The museum stuck with a costly program to promote the AMNH's collections, vouchsafe cinema as a legitimate mode of educating young people, and advance such vital tenets of American progressivism as anthropologist Franz Boas's theory of cultural relativism. The Depression slowed the museum's activities down but did not halt the development of film at the AMNH, and sponsored expeditions were cut more deeply than public programs.

---

[53] *AR* 56 (1924): 15.

[54] Ramsey, *Educational Work,* 184, citing *AR* 69 (1937).

[55] Milliken, "Increasing General Usefulness of Films," 6.

Generations of children growing up in New York City saw the AMNH delivery vans and motorcycles pulling up at their schools, bringing the magic of the cinema into the classroom. In 2009, I saw one of the AMNH's mobile museum buses stopped at a red light in Brooklyn and thought about some of the wondrous objects that lay inside. The "Moveable Museum Program," launched in 1993, has four buses providing educational outreach to "schools, libraries, camps, and community centers in the New York City area." Buses are devoted to paleontology, anthropology, and astronomy; parked outside schools, they offer "state-of-the-art, walk-in exhibition spaces."[56] Given the focus of this chapter, it is ironic, though hardly surprising, that they no longer deliver film (and don't even bring objects into the classroom) but instead attempt to recreate a miniature AMNH on the doorstep of the school. The Moveable Museums have provided a new lease on life for the taxidermy specimens and other objects, which, while highly valued as artifacts, were displaced on the New York City school circuit by cinema during the 1920s and 30s. While the AMNH no longer delivers films to schools (although films housed in Special Collections can be borrowed via interlibrary loan), the museum has consolidated its interest in cinema into four enterprises: IMAX films screened in the Samuel J. and Ethel LeFrak Theater (a lucrative funding stream in the repurposed 1900 auditorium); the annual Margaret Mead Film and Video Festival (which no longer has access to the auditorium during the festival since it would cut into the weekend IMAX box office); the production of high-definition natural history video programming for the *Science Bulletins* division of the Education Department; and gallery-based plasma screens and video interactives. As for the place of film in New York City's public schools, except for the occasional documentary on a specific curricular topic such as the history of slavery, the civil war, or the Depression, film has taken on something of a Foucauldian role, used during inclement weather to keep large numbers of children under control in the auditorium. Who knows what Ramsay, Osborn, and Fisher would make of a hundred or so elementary schoolchildren sitting watching *SpongeBob SquarePants* and *High School Musical*, a far cry from the "broadened conception of the universe" envisioned by Porter in his 1925 letter to Osborn about the relationship between museums and visual education.

Filmography

Camping Among the Indians (1927) 22 min., 16 mm
SPONSOR: American Museum of Natural History. PHOTOGRAPHER: George Clyde Fisher. Documents the AMNH Woodcraft Indian trip to the American Southwest, led by Ernest Thompson Seton. ACCESS: AMNH Library Special Collections, Film collection no. 22; on ¾" U-matic videotape.

---

[56] "Moveable Museum," AMNH website (2009), www.amnh.org/education/school_groups/program.php?id=33.

The Chronicles of America: The Pilgrims (1924) 30 min., 35mm
PRODUCTION: Chronicles of America Picture Corp.
DIRECTOR: Edwin L. Hollywood. WRITER: William B.
Courtney. CAST: Robert Gaillard, Harry Simpson, John Hopkins.
ACCESS: Library of Congress (LOC).

The Chronicles of America: The Puritans (1924) 30 min., 35mm
PRODUCTION: Chronicles of America Picture Corp.
DIRECTOR: Frank Tuttle. WRITER: Evangeline Andrews. CAST:
Arthur Hohl, Audrey Hart. ACCESS: LOC.

Jungle Life in India (1923) 20 min., 16mm
SPONSOR: AMNH. PHOTOGRAPHER: Commander George M.
Dyott. Documents the Faunthorpe-Vernay Indian Expedition to India,
Nepal, and Burma (1922–23). Made for designers of dioramas in the
Hall of South Asiatic Mammals. ACCESS: AMNH Library Special
Collections, Film Collection no. 198; on ¾" U-matic videotape.

The Morden-Clark Asiatic Expedition (1926), 73 min., 16mm
SPONSOR: American Museum of Natural History. PHOTOGRA-
PHER: James Lippitt Clark. Documents the AMNH Morden-Clark
Asiatic Expedition, which crossed the Himalayan and Karakoram
mountains to a restricted territory called the Pamirs (in Tajikistan).
ACCESS: NARA (Records of the Central Intelligence Agency, under
the title *Morden-Clark Asiatic Expedition of the American Museum of
Natural History, India*); Internet Archive, www.archive.org/details/
gov.archives.arc.617938.r1 (reel 1) and www.archive.org/details/gov.
archives.arc.617938.r2 (reel 2).

Related Films

Every Day Life of People in France (1924). Directed by Philip H. Pratt and
Gladys L. Pratt.

The Last of the Mohicans (1920). Directed by Clarence Brown and Maurice
Tourneur.

Nanook of the North (1922). Directed by Robert Flaherty.

Silas Marner (1922). Directed by Frank P. Donovan.

Trailing African Wild Animals (1923). Directed by Martin and Osa Johnson.

6 GLIMPSES OF ANIMAL LIFE: NATURE FILMS AND THE EMERGENCE OF CLASSROOM CINEMA

JENNIFER PETERSON

> Dissect him how I may, then, but I go skin deep; I know him not, and never will.
>
> —Herman Melville, *Moby-Dick*

In a 1923 article in the *New York World*, an aging Thomas Edison extolled motion pictures not for their entertaining or artistic attributes but for their educational potential. The article explained Edison's proud belief that with cinema, "education can be manufactured wholesale like any other product of the factory."[1] Although Edison had been making similar proclamations for many years—and he himself had recently tried and failed to popularize educational subjects with his short-lived Conquest Pictures series (1917–1918)—this time his ballyhoo contained a larger quantity of truth.[2] The dream of an educational role for cinema, always an undercurrent in discourses about film since its inception, was finally becoming a reality in the early 1920s. So-called educational cinema was burgeoning not in commercial movie theaters, as some had hoped, but in the growing nontheatrical circuit of schools, churches, libraries, and museums. Moving pictures, once scorned as a bad influence for children, were becoming a new feature of the classroom in the 1920s. By the 1930s, what had been suspiciously viewed by

I am grateful to Dino Everett, Archivist at the Hugh M. Hefner Moving Image Archive at the University of Southern California, for his invaluable help with the 16mm educational films I researched for this article. I would also like to thank Tim Wilson of the UCLA Film & Television Archive's Stanford Theatre Lab for helping with research on paper materials at the George Eastman House.

[1] "Education by the Movies," *New York World*, May 17, 1923.

[2] On Conquest Pictures see Jennifer Horne, "Nostalgia and Non-Fiction in Edison's 1917 Conquest Program," *Historical Journal of Film, Radio, and Television* 22, no. 3 (2002): 315–31.

the previous generation as a tool for pouring information into passive spectators was now being hailed as a "magical master teacher."[3]

This article examines the emergence of the classroom film in the 1920s by focusing on one prominent classroom genre: the nature film. I first explore the emergence of classroom cinema as an institution separate from commercial cinema, and the concurrent history of the nature film as one of the most popular early "educational" genres. I turn next to early debates about educational cinema, exploring the nature film's role in those debates and in the history of science education. Finally, I examine several examples of classroom nature films, outlining their wide range of visual approaches to education. Nature films were already a fully developed commercial film genre when classroom films emerged, and because of this, the classroom version incorporated both popular and scientific tropes. These films present simple information about organisms and their habitat, directed at an audience of students at the elementary school, high school, or college level. Although they were hailed as efficient tools for modern learning, in fact nature films did not so much teach current scientific ideas as present an older model of natural history; rather than introducing lessons on modern zoology, anatomy, or genetics, most early nature films simply pictured and described the natural world. These films follow what science historians Lorraine Daston and Peter Galison call the Enlightenment "truth-to-nature" standard of representation, marked by idealization and simplification, rather than the new standard of "mechanical objectivity" that arose in the late nineteenth century, which forbade aestheticizing or idealizing manipulations in scientific representation.[4] While the medium may have been modern, the motion pictures themselves often followed an older nature-study paradigm.

The Emergence of Classroom Cinema

Although Thomas Edison proudly described them as factory merchandise, educational films in the 1920s were not exactly standardized products. Many genres and styles were still being developed, and the question of how motion pictures might best educate viewers—or whether they were capable of educating viewers at all—was not yet settled. In fact, educational cinema had been hotly contested terrain in the previous decade. Edison may have been its most high-profile advocate, but as a businessman he was not engaged with the same issues as educators. The inventor was one of several important film industry figures who had championed educational cinema for nickelodeon theaters in the 1910s. These efforts

---

[3] George F. Zook, foreword to Cline M. Koon, *Motion Pictures in Education in the United States: A Report* (Washington, DC: U.S. Department of the Interior, 1934), iii.

[4] Lorraine Daston and Peter Galison, *Objectivity* (New York: Zone Books, 2007).

had been largely unprofitable, however, and by the beginning of the 1920s, the dream of a popular educational cinema for commercial moving picture theaters had all but died. Film distributor George Kleine explained in a 1921 letter to Edison, "Your own experience . . . to popularize so-called educational films . . . demonstrated that the field was not profitable. Of late, however, the purchase and use of smaller projecting machines have increased greatly."[5] By the time educational films became successfully established, it was in a manner quite different from what Edison, Kleine, and other motion picture moguls had imagined.

Kleine's letter anticipated an important change in the early 1920s, when small-gauge film formats were about to become a key factor in the success of educational cinema in the nontheatrical field. Although many in the industry considered small-gauge formats "substandard" (Kleine himself would only distribute films on 35mm throughout the 1920s), small-gauge formats were cheaper. Some small-gauge formats were already in use, such as Pathéscope (28mm), used from 1911 to the mid-1920s, and Edison's own 22mm format for the Edison Home Kinetoscope, introduced in 1912.[6] However, it was the hugely successful 16mm gauge, introduced in 1923 by Eastman Kodak, that enabled the large-scale success of the classroom film. It was economical (about one-sixth the price of 35mm) and nonflammable (unlike most 35mm, which used a highly flammable nitrate film base until 1952), and it became the dominant format for the nontheatrical market until the ascendancy of video in the 1980s.[7] Perhaps even more important than small-gauge formats, it was in the 1920s that a distinct distribution network for the nontheatrical circuit was established. Nontheatrical exhibition was at this time a relatively noncommercial enterprise. Schools did not show films to make money, of course, but to educate students, and where there were any profits to be made, these flowed to the producers, distributors, and equipment manufacturers, not the exhibitor. Although the profits may not have been spectacular, short subjects did not cost much to make, and some producers and distributors managed to carve out a modest business in the nontheatrical niche; even the big commercial studios produced short subjects that reached the nontheatrical market.[8] The era of mass-mediated visual education had begun.

---

[5] Letter from George Kleine to Thomas Edison, Apr. 20, 1921, box 18, George Kleine Collection, Library of Congress.

[6] See Anke Mebold and Charles Tepperman, "Resurrecting the Lost History of 28mm Film in North America," *Film History* 15, no. 2 (2003): 137–51.

[7] Anthony Slide, *Before Video: A History of the Non-Theatrical Film* (New York: Greenwood Press, 1992), 35. The fact that 16mm projectors required no projection booth or licensed operator was also a boon to the classroom film movement.

[8] Metro-Goldwyn-Mayer placed ads in *1001: The Blue Book of Non-Theatrical Films* in 1929 and 1930; Universal advertised its Nontheatrical Department there in 1931. MGM had the largest shorts department of the Hollywood studios and even published an in-house journal, *MGM's*

Films produced for the emergent classroom market in the 1920s and early 1930s contain several conventions that mark them as unique. First, classroom film subjects were organized along the lines of school curricula, which meant that educational movie genres fell into a different taxonomy than commercial genres. Second, these films were often released in a series by companies expressly dedicated to the production of classroom materials (such as Eastman Teaching Films or DeVry School Films), and thus certain "house styles" emerged. In this way, they do indeed begin to resemble Edison's vision of factory-manufactured products. Third, classroom films have a different style than movies produced for the commercial market: freed from the burden of turning a profit, they pursue an educational mandate. Educational cinema was not necessarily old-fashioned or boring, as stereotype would have it. Instead, these films carve out an alternative style that engages the spectator differently. Educational films do not present self-contained diegetic worlds, as commercial films do, but instead they rely on outside context (a teacher's lecture, a class project) to activate the material on screen. Finally, unlike educational films made for theatrical release in the 1900s and 1910s (which were documented only sporadically), there was a huge amount of information about classroom films generated in the 1920s and 1930s. Numerous academic studies on the effectiveness of visual education were conducted as classroom films began to be adopted by many schools. These studies, which I will discuss below, contain a wealth of data about how the films were used, including rare spectator feedback in the form of student testing and answers to questionnaires.

Early Nature Films: From the Theater to the Classroom

One of the most consistently popular classroom genres was the nature film. Motion pictures depicting animals, insects, plants, and other natural history subjects have been a staple since the beginning of film history, but the genre's divergent history on theatrical and nontheatrical screens has not previously been addressed.[9] Some of the first subjects ever filmed were animals. Indeed, as Derek Bousé suggests, "the history of wildlife film must begin at the beginning of

---

Shorts Story, from 1937 to 1941. On short subjects in Hollywood see Richard Ward, "Extra Added Attractions: The Short Subjects of MGM, Warner Brothers and Universal," *Media History* 9, no. 3 (2003): 221–44.

[9] Despite increasing scholarly interest in animals and media, to date there has been no study of the "educational" nature film. Four books and several important articles on wildlife films have been published since 1999. See Gregg Mitman, *Reel Nature: America's Romance with Wildlife on Film* (Cambridge, MA: Harvard University Press, 1999); Derek Bousé, *Wildlife Films* (Philadelphia: University of Pennsylvania Press, 2000); Jonathan Burt, *Animals in Film* (London: Reaktion Books, 2002); and Cynthia Chris, *Watching Wildlife* (Minneapolis: University of Minnesota

all film."[10] The well-known experiments in animal locomotion using series photography by Eadweard Muybridge and Étienne-Jules Marey in the 1870s and 1880s are the canonical starting point in most histories of the emergence of cinema, although these were largely scientific experiments. In a more popular vein, beginning in 1891, Thomas Edison's employees W. K. L. Dickson and William Heise made numerous films of animals for viewing in Edison's peephole Kinetoscope viewer, such as *The Cock Fight* (1894).[11] These early Edison films, like most commercial animal films, commonly featured animals fighting—either trained vaudeville animal acts such as *The Boxing Cats* (Edison, 1894), or staged bloodsport films such as *Fight Between a Lion and a Bull* (Lubin, 1900) or *Fight Between Spider and Scorpion* (American Mutoscope and Biograph, 1900). As these film titles indicate, a particularly violent vision of animals in conflict proved popular in the early years of cinema, and in fact, this quasi-Darwinian view of nature as a field of endless competitions constitutes a major trope of the nature film to this day.[12]

These earliest nature films, each consisting of a single shot, were not exactly natural history documentaries depicting animals in their habitat; they simply featured animals. Nonetheless, the earliest animal films established three key themes that remained central to the genre throughout the silent era and beyond: fighting, hunting, and feeding.[13] It wasn't until around 1907 that nature films began to depict animal and plant habitats more carefully, with the release of British wildlife photographer Oliver Pike's film *In Birdland*. The success of this film garnered Pike a production deal with the major French company Pathé, which released more Pike films of animals in their habitat such as *Glimpses of Bird Life* (1910).

Press, 2006). See also Scott MacDonald, "Up Close and Political: Three Short Ruminations on Ideology in the Nature Film," *Film Quarterly* 59, no. 3 (2006): 4–21; Jan-Christopher Horak, "Wildlife Documentaries: From Classical Forms to Reality TV," *Film History* 18, no. 4 (2006): 459–75.

  [10] Bousé, *Wildlife Films*, 41.

  [11] Other very early Edison Kinetoscope films featuring animals, all made by Dickson and Heise, include: *[Monkey and Another, Boxing]* (1891), *Horse Shoeing* (1893), *[Trained Bears]* (1894), *The Wrestling Dog* (1894), and *Rat Killing* (1894). See Charles Musser, *Edison Motion Pictures, 1890–1900: An Annotated Filmography* (Washington, DC: Smithsonian Institution Press, 1997).

  [12] *When Animals Attack*, a 1996–1997 series on Fox, and *Animal Face-Off*, a 2004 series on Animal Planet, are just two of many recent TV series to exploit the persistent trope of animals fighting. And of course, these subjects thrive on YouTube. For a comedic account of this Internet phenomenon, watch infoMania's "Animal Fights: Viral Video Film School," May 19, 2011, youtube.com/watch?v=Erz2r0MIQr4.

  [13] See Bousé, *Wildlife Films*, 44–45.

In 1908, British-based producer and distributor Charles Urban, who specialized in educational films of travel and science, began releasing films with plant, animal, and insect subjects made by Percy Smith, who was later to become famous for his "Secrets of Nature" series in the 1920s (many of which were photographed by Oliver Pike).[14] Smith's films, such as the stop-motion *Birth of a Flower* (1910) and *The Acrobatic Fly* (1910), were hugely successful, although at this point it was Pike's films that made a more conscious effort to depict animals in their natural habitat, while Smith's films played up the sensationalistic aspects of their subject matter.

The depiction of natural setting, whether real or simulated, became perhaps the most important characteristic of the genre by the 1910s. As more films were released with an emphasis on natural habitat, the nature film—which was variously referred to as a *nature study film, natural history film,* or *natural science film*—began to take shape as a cinematic genre with its own conventions and iconography. "Cute" animal films of puppies and kittens also became popular at this time, and it is important to distinguish between films of domestic animals and films of wildlife, as indeed most catalogs of nontheatrical film later did. At the beginning of this era, it was still unclear what business practices or movie subjects would be the most profitable, and there was a brief moment when some in the industry (such as Edison and Kleine) hailed educational film subjects as the commercial future of cinema. The efforts to establish educational films as profitable theatrical subjects were largely unsuccessful, however. By the time educationals found nontheatrical success in the 1920s, industry leaders from an earlier generation, such as Edison, Kleine, and Urban, were nearing the end of their careers.[15]

By the 1920s, rather than the Progressive-Era dream of a commercial cinema loaded with "uplifting" and "moral" educational subjects, educational film exhibition was shifting to the nontheatrical field. At this time, the history of the nature film splits in two directions: theatrical and nontheatrical. On commercial movie screens, short-format nature subjects became less common as wildlife was the subject of feature films such as *Chang: A Drama of the Wilderness* (1927) and *Simba: The King of the Beasts* (1928). While theatrical wildlife films exploited nature as a sensationalistic domain, on the nontheatrical circuit the nature film

---

[14] A number of these films were recently released on DVD (Region 0/PAL format). See *Secrets of Nature: Pioneering Natural History Films, 1922–1933* (London: British Film Institute, 2010).

[15] For more on the efforts of George Kleine and Thomas Edison to promote educational films in the United States in the 1910s, see Jennifer Peterson, "'The Five-Cent University': Early Educational Films and the Drive to 'Uplift' the Cinema," chapter 3 in *Education in the School of Dreams: Travelogues and Early Nonfiction Film* (Durham, NC: Duke University Press, forthcoming).

became one of the dominant genres of the schoolroom, its subject matter modeled loosely after the canonical educational subjects of biology and zoology. However, as we shall see, classroom nature films also used many of popular cinema's sensationalizing tropes. Produced by newly formed companies such as Eastman Teaching Films and DeVry School Films, as well as established commercial outfits such as the Bray Studios and the German Ufa studio, classroom nature films combined the popular cinematic trope of animals fighting with more sober attempts to depict and describe organisms in their habitat. Some, such as *Struggle for Existence* (1925), *A Murderous Midget Fish* (ca. 1920s), and *Wing, Claw, and Fang!* (1946) presented nature as a strange and ferocious domain: a space to be tamed, or a space in the process of being tamed. Other films with more plainly descriptive titles such as *Beavers* (1930), *Trees* (1928), or *Bees and Spiders* (ca. 1927) were less sensationalistic, but they still relied on techniques of popular cinema, albeit reconfigured to suit classroom use.

By the early 1930s classroom films were becoming less of a novelty and more of a "standard piece of instructional technology."[16] One study estimated that in 1931 "there were 350,000 non-theatrical projectors in the United States. About 6/7 of the total were 16 mm. projectors."[17] A 1934 U.S. government study found that thirty-two states had "film libraries of varying qualities under the supervision of educational directors." This same study also reported that "more than thirty-five reliable commercial companies produce nontheatrical films, and nearly two-hundred companies distribute them."[18] Film journals such as *Educational Screen* and *Visual Education* were launched to cater to this emergent wing of the motion picture industry. The nontheatrical field may not have been as profitable as the theatrical side of the movie business, but it was in some ways more stable. In fact, classroom films constitute one of the most significant and durable alternatives to the theatrical conception of cinema.

Early Debates about Motion Picture Education

Educational motion pictures were a hotly debated topic in the 1910s and 20s. Many educators were at first skeptical about the new medium as a tool for learning. The most common criticism of educational films (as opposed to commercial cinema, which was often dismissed outright) centered on the perception that cinema creates passive spectators, inert viewers who quickly forget

---

[16] Kenneth P. King, "The Motion Picture in Science Education: 'One Hundred Percent Efficiency,'" *Journal of Science Education and Technology* 8, no. 3 (1999): 216.

[17] F. Dean McClusky, *Visual Instruction: Its Value and Its Needs* (New York: Mancall Publishing, 1932), 125, quoted in Koon, *Motion Pictures in Education*, 7.

[18] Koon, *Motion Pictures in Education*, 7, 8.

what they see on the screen. One educator, for example, warned in 1913 that educational films were "dangerously convenient adjuncts of the old 'pouring-in' method of teaching."[19] However, a standard defense of educational films quickly emerged, hinging on two points: film's efficiency (it was thought to educate students more quickly than reading or lecturing), and its realism (film's lifelike quality of representation was celebrated particularly in nature films and travel films). Praise for educational films in the popular press tended to uncritically celebrate visual education as an easier and faster method of communicating information with unsubstantiated claims such as, "The eye is far quicker than the ear."[20] While the terms of this debate emerged quite early, the questions surrounding educational cinema were not seriously grappled with until the 1920s. The question of cinema's popularity—always an issue for the film industry, which was unsure of the market value of educational films—clashed with the question of how motion pictures could best be used as an educational tool, which was the main question concerning educators. In a sense, the nontheatrical sector solved the first problem by marketing classroom films not to potential audiences (in this case, students) but to the teachers and educators who showed them.

As educational films moved into classrooms, the institutional forces of newly professionalizing academic departments of education stepped in to examine visual education more thoroughly. In 1922, the National Education Association (NEA) began appointing an annual Committee on Visual Education.[21] By the late 1920s, a number of research studies had been conducted to examine the effectiveness of films in the classroom, and by the mid-1930s, a flood of new publications exploring the subject of visual education appeared—at least thirty-three books, according to one bibliography.[22] In 1927, the NEA authorized what would become one of the most important of these early studies, conducted by Ben D. Wood of Columbia University and Frank N. Freeman of the University of Chicago, the results of which were published in 1929 as *Motion Pictures in the Classroom*. Unlike the vague and sometimes contradictory efforts of commercial film industry figures such as Edison and Kleine, this two-year study by two professors of education followed a clear methodology, asking teachers specific questions such as, "Do these films have a measurable value in supplementing class

[19] Leonard P. Ayres, "Ladling Learning into Children," *The Survey*, Sept. 6, 1913: 686.

[20] "Films for Class Work," *Rochester Democrat and Chronicle*, Apr. 13, 1927, Manuscript Collection, George Eastman House (hereafter GEH).

[21] Ben D. Wood and Frank N. Freeman, *Motion Pictures in the Classroom: An Experiment to Measure the Value of Motion Pictures as Supplementary Aids in Regular Classroom Instruction* (Boston: Houghton Mifflin, 1929), xvii.

[22] Edgar Dale et al., *Motion Pictures in Education: A Summary of the Literature* (New York: H. W. Wilson, 1937), 459–62.

instruction? What are the values and influences of these films?"[23] The study involved nearly 11,000 children in grades four through nine in twelve cities across the country. The children were taught the same basic curriculum, but half of the teachers—the "experimental" teachers—were given classroom films to supplement their lessons. The published study contains forty-four tables comparing test scores and other attributes of those children who watched classroom films and those who did not. The study concluded that the students who learned with motion pictures gained more knowledge than those who did not:

> The foregoing analysis has shown that the motion picture film
> contributes to both [direct and indirect] aspects of the child's
> education. It shows, however, that the film contributes by a much
> larger amount to the direct than to the indirect aspects. In other
> words, the film gives the child clear-cut notions of the objects and
> actions in the world about him.[24]

By "indirect" education the writers meant abstract ideas requiring reflection. These conclusions, despite being supported by a large amount of data, are perhaps unsurprising given the study's financial backing: the Wood-Freeman study was sponsored by the Eastman Kodak Company, and its findings resulted in the founding of Eastman Teaching Films, Inc. The Wood-Freeman study is even obliquely mentioned in the company's first advertisements (see fig. 6.1). (In this ad and elsewhere, the names "Eastman Teaching Films" and "Eastman Classroom Films" are used interchangeably, although the company itself officially went by the former name.)

The Wood-Freeman study's positive conclusions were consistent with other early research studies on classroom films, which also found that motion pictures helped students learn. Even more traditional educators reached similar conclusions. Prominent biologist George W. Hunter, whose *Civic Biology* (1914) was the "best-selling text in the field," published a 1934 book called *Science Teaching at Junior and Senior High School Levels,* which surveyed the use of visual education in science classrooms.[25] Hunter takes up the concerns of previous educators, but his arguments are more systematically explained and supported.

---

[23] Wood and Freeman, *Motion Pictures in the Classroom,* xx.

[24] Ibid., 221.

[25] Edward J. Larson, *Summer for the Gods: The Scopes Trial and America's Continuing Debate over Science and Religion* (New York: Basic Books, 1997), 23. Incidentally, Hunter's 1914 textbook was at the center of the "Scopes Monkey Trial" of 1925; *Civic Biology* was used by John Thomas Scopes to teach evolution in a Tennessee high school. Larson, *Summer for the Gods,* 231, documents that a revised edition, published after the trial as *A New Civic Biology* (1926), excised all mention of evolution.

Pupils' standings are raised
—the cost of education is reduced
—by the use of

Eastman Classroom Films

A SCIENTIFIC ten weeks' test in one hundred schools proved that *Eastman Classroom Films:*

    1. Arouse and maintain greater interest.
    2. Increase the quantity and improve the quality of reading, project work, classroom discussion and writing.
    3. Help pupils to correlate materials more thoroughly.
    4. Increase the richness, accuracy and meaningfulness of experience.
    5. Facilitate the teacher's work of organizing lesson materials, and add to the pleasure and interest of teaching.

Learn more about this new and helpful classroom agency. Write for the booklet that tells the story of *Eastman Classroom Films.*

EASTMAN TEACHING FILMS, INC.

Subsidiary of
EASTMAN KODAK COMPANY, ROCHESTER, N. Y.

Figure 6.1. Ad for Eastman Teaching Films. *1000 and One: The Blue Book of Non-Theatrical Films*, 6th ed. (Educational Screen, 1929), 96.

He concludes that students learn better and more quickly with the use of visual aids: "Children with high I.Q. learn by word quickly because they have adequate mental imagery, but the lower I.Q.'s have to be stimulated by visual aids." He also argues the familiar point that the motion picture saves time and effort: "It takes the place of the field excursion and the visit to the manufacturing plant." In addition, Hunter argues that films could visually capture natural phenomena in a way that would be otherwise impossible:

> They can use slow motion picture and time-lapse effects. Cell division, growth, and movement of unicellular animals, yeasts, bacteria, and so forth, are examples of such usage. . . . Animal life histories, such as the development of the frog or the life cycle changes of insects are summed up as in no other way.

Finally, Hunter expresses reservations which echo earlier concerns: Watching science films "is an easy way to go to school. There is no effort to see and to absorb."[26]

All of these studies of visual education had the effect of validating film as a tool for the classroom. The pros and cons expressed by earlier generations were systematically explored by dozens of educators, and classroom films were found, on balance, to be beneficial. This institutional endorsement of film undoubtedly helped transform educators' attitudes from skepticism to acceptance. This academic institutionalization could never have been achieved by the commercial film industry. But what specific issues were raised by the discipline of natural history? And how did nature films engage with this discipline?

Natural History as Popular Science in the 1920s

Among scientists, natural history was not well respected in the 1920s. Biologist Charles Elton wrote in his important book *Animal Ecology* (1927), "It is a fact that natural history has fallen into disrepute among zoologists." Elton disparages local natural history societies, characterizing their work as a "mania" and writing that "however much pleasure they may give to their members, [they] usually perform no scientific function."[27] This attitude is indicative of general scientific trends in the early twentieth century. Historians of science point to a major shift in biology that took place at the end of the nineteenth century.

---

[26] George W. Hunter, *Science Teaching at Junior and Senior High School Levels* (New York: American Book Company, 1934), 296, 301–2, 305.

[27] Charles Elton, *Animal Ecology*, rev. ed. (1927; reprint ed., Chicago: University of Chicago Press, 2001), 1–2.

"After reaching a peak in the first half of the nineteenth century" with the establishment of natural history museums and zoological gardens, one historical account argues, "the social status of natural history underwent a relative decline with the rise of laboratory biology in the second half of the century."[28] By the early twentieth century, natural history was often considered the province of amateurs. By mid-century, biologist G. F. Ferris could fondly mock the pre-1900 natural historian archetype—one who conducted the observational work in the field rather than in the laboratory: "He was the man who is referred to now, sometimes with respect, sometimes with a sort of envy, and sometimes with a slightly condescending air, as the 'Old Time Naturalist.'"[29] The "Old Time Naturalist," interested in "the organism as a functioning whole and as a part of the living world," was not a specialist but a generalist.[30] This type had been superseded in the twentieth century by specialized professionals committed to what Daston and Galison call "mechanical objectivity."

What is significant about this shift is that natural history films for the classroom made during the 1920s and 30s still participate in the Old Time Naturalist version of the discipline: collecting, displaying, generalizing. The films present animals in their habitat, but with a minimum of detail about their physical characteristics or behavior, and completely independent of experiments then being conducted in biochemistry, anatomy, and genetics. For a practicing biologist in the 1920s, these films would have appeared to present anachronistic natural history, not contemporary science. In fact, several studies of science education conducted in the 1920s came to the conclusion that science instruction in schools (without motion pictures) was stunted in just this way. "Observation and identification have become the predominant notes in nature study," one writer concluded, saying, "hence, with the vital elements of both scientific method and content lacking, nature study has become, in many cases, a conglomeration of busy work and object lessons."[31] Similarly, another report concluded that "the kind of knowledge which children have of elementary science is largely of an observational and factual type, such as 'what is,' 'name,' and 'tell about.' It is the

---

[28] Jean-Marc Drouin and Bernadette Bensaude-Vincent, "Nature for the People," in *Cultures of Natural History,* ed. N. Jardine, J. A. Secord, and E. C. Spary (Cambridge, UK: Cambridge University Press, 1996), 408.

[29] G. F. Ferris, "The Contribution of Natural History to Human Progress," *A Century of Progress in the Natural Sciences, 1853–1953* (San Francisco: California Academy of Sciences, 1955), 76.

[30] Ibid.

[31] Gerald S. Craig, "Certain Techniques Used in Developing a Course of Study in Science for the Horace Mann Elementary School," PhD diss., Columbia University, 1927, excerpted in Francis D. Curtis, *Second Digest of Investigations in the Teaching of Science* (Philadelphia: P. Blakiston's Son, 1931), 41.

kind of knowledge which could be acquired incidentally, in the course of normal experience, with little or no regard to systematic classroom instruction."[32]

In fact, nature films for the classroom made in the 1920s fit into an older curricular model: nature study. Nature study was introduced into American public schools as part of the progressive school reforms of the 1890s, which updated school curricula and expanded elementary- and grammar-school education to reach a larger percentage of the population. As Sally Gregory Kohlstedt has shown, the nature study movement built upon new developments in child psychology, urging a child-centered approach that would "pique natural curiosity, build basic observational skills, and utilize materials familiar to children."[33] New in this method was an emphasis on what Kohlstedt calls "nature, not books"—learning through direct experience with nature via classroom terrariums, field trips, and the like. As Kohlstedt points out, with its emphasis on direct observation and participation, nature study "emphasized visual and other sensual experiences."[34] (With its emphasis on organisms interrelating within habitats, the nature study paradigm is most closely related to what we now call ecology.)

Elementary school science does of course lag behind the cutting edge of scientific research. As the examples below make clear, classroom nature films remain within the realm of observational knowledge rather than advanced scientific experimentation. As Daston and Galison observe, "Mechanical objectivity did not drive out truth-to-nature, but nor did it leave truth-to-nature unchanged."[35] What we see in early classroom films is a range of visual appeals that borrow heavily from the old nature study model but occasionally utilize the tropes of mechanical objectivity. Science historians have argued that natural history's "longstanding success seems to distinguish [it] as the most popular of all the sciences."[36] Perhaps what these nature films demonstrate is not so much the shortcomings of the early classroom cinema curriculum but rather a difficulty in bridging the split between colloquial and academic knowledge that grew deeper as educational disciplines professionalized in the early twentieth century.

---

[32] James Elgan Hillman, "Some Aspects of Science in the Elementary Schools," PhD diss., George Peabody College for Teachers, 1924, excerpted in Curtis, *Second Digest of Investigations in the Teaching of Science,* 35.

[33] Sally Gregory Kohlstedt, "Nature, Not Books: Scientists and the Origins of the Nature-Study Movement in the 1890s," *Isis* 96, no. 3 (2005): 330.

[34] Kohlstedt, "Nature, Not Books," 342. For an overview of the historical nature study method see the influential book by Anna Botsford Comstock, *Handbook of Nature-Study* (Ithaca, NY: Comstock Publishing, 1911). This became a popular textbook for teachers, and was reprinted many times; a new edition from 1939 was still being reprinted in the late 1950s. The later edition can be downloaded at www.archive.org.

[35] Daston and Galison, *Objectivity,* 111.

[36] Drouin and Bensaude-Vincent, "Nature for the People," 409.

"A Land of Strange Contrasts": Nature Films as a Classroom Genre

As a genre, nature films display characteristics that appear regularly: setting (natural habitat), "character" types (animals and plants), and dramatic incidents (fighting, hunting, feeding). And, as in all film genres, these conventions are often broken. Indeed, there is a great deal of variety in nature films from the twenties and thirties, given that the genre was hypothetically capable of documenting the entire natural world according to scientific taxonomy. Some films were made to illustrate individual scientific concepts, such as *The Struggle for Existence* (1925), which loosely deals with one part of Charles Darwin's theory of evolution. Others focused on a group of organisms populating a given region, such as *Wildlife on the Deserts of America's Great Southwest* (a.k.a. *Wildlife on the Desert*, ca. 1920s), which documents plant and animal life in the Colorado Desert of southern California. But the largest number of nature films in this era focus on just one organism, or several closely related organisms, as in *Frogs, Toads, and Salamanders* (1932). These films present the life cycle, physiology, and environment of organisms in the style of a biology textbook of the old natural history mode. Within these various kinds of nature films, there is also a variety of approaches to scientific popularization.[37]

The Struggle for Existence, released the year of the infamous "Scopes Monkey Trial," was produced by the Bray Studios (also known as the Bray Pictures Corporation), a company known primarily for its animated films. After making a series of successful World War I instructional films for the U.S. Army, animator John Randolph Bray decided "the future of his company lay in expansion from the realm of entertainment into the production of industrial and educational pictures."[38] Like Edison and Kleine before him, Bray discovered that educational films were not the financial bonanza he had hoped. Bray had its own nontheatrical distribution department handling educational subjects.[39] Perhaps because of the company's drive for commercial success, *The Struggle for Existence* is filled with sensationalized scenes of animals in conflict. Indeed, a reviewer from *The Educational Screen* underscored the film's popularizing style by calling the film "an acceptable reel of the popular science variety."[40]

---

[37] For an account of scientific popularization in French educational cinema of the 1910s see Oliver Gaycken, "'A Drama Unites Them in a Fight to the Death': Some Remarks on the Flourishing of a Cinema of Scientific Vernacularization in France, 1909–1914," *Historical Journal of Film, Radio and Television* 22, no. 3 (2002): 354–74.

[38] Mark Langer, "The Reflections of John Randolph Bray: An Interview with Annotations," *Griffithiana* 53 (1995): 105.

[39] *1000 and One: The Blue Book of Non-Theatrical Films,* 3rd ed. (Chicago: Educational Screen, 1924), 107.

[40] Review of *The Struggle for Existence, Educational Screen* (Apr. 1925): 247.

"Struggle for Existence" is the title of a chapter from Darwin's *Origin of Species* (1859), but rather than exploring Darwin's theory, the film uses the idea of "struggle" as an excuse for staging scenes of conflict between animals and plants. The film announces with its first intertitle that "life is a perpetual struggle, particularly in the animal kingdom, where one animal preys on another, and the law is to hunt, catch, kill, and eat."[41] A dozen examples of this "perpetual struggle" are visualized in the film, which moves hierarchically from simple to more complex organisms—from the plant and insect worlds to birds and finally mammals. The film not only uses the popular cinematic trope of animals fighting, but it even anthropomorphizes its animals at one point when a seal feeding is shown and an intertitle provides dialogue: "Stop shoving, it's mine." Clearly, this film is less invested in science than in capturing the attention of young audiences.

These images of animals in conflict might be dramatic, but *The Struggle for Existence* has a concept to explain, for which it relies on intertitles. To explain Darwin's idea, the film makes a nursery rhyme reference: "It is a kind of 'House that Jack Built.' Each creature is the 'dinner pail' of some other. What is death to one is life to another." This intertitle is followed by a staged fight between a weasel and a snake that resembles the animal fight films of early cinema. As an explanation of Darwin's complex theory of species interconnectedness and time unfolding, this nursery rhyme model is strikingly inadequate. But as a strategy for appealing to children, a nursery rhyme presentation of information seems appropriate. Students who viewed this film may not have learned any specifics about evolution or natural selection, but they would have viewed a loose interpretation of Darwin's concept that shares more in common with the fairground than the classroom.

Wildlife on the Desert, in contrast, uses fewer sensationalizing tropes and instead follows the tradition of the "romantic" documentary made famous by Robert Flaherty's *Nanook of the North* (1922).[42] The desert in this film is a "grim ... land of strange contrasts," where the environment is "harsh" and nature is "stern," the intertitles tell us. Unlike *Nanook,* however, the film does not present any maps, and instead only gestures broadly toward a vague "great southwest." Taking a traditional natural history approach, the film presents a variety of flora and fauna living in the region, such as the ocotillo plant, the cholla cactus, the gila monster, and the ringtail cat. The film contains some beautiful photography, moving from extreme long shots of the landscape to close-ups of

---

[41] In contrast, Darwin concludes his chapter by saying, "When we reflect on this struggle, we may console ourselves with the full belief, that the war of nature is not incessant, that no fear is felt, that death is generally prompt, and that the vigorous, the healthy, and the happy survive and multiply." Charles Darwin, *The Origin of Species* (1859; reprint ed., New York: Penguin, 1958), 87.

[42] I have not been able to identify *Wildlife on the Desert*'s year of production, although it was certainly made before 1938, as I have found it in one filmography from that year. Judging from the film's visual style, it was probably made in the mid-1920s.

animals. A segment on the gray fox uses slow motion, allowing the viewer to focus on the fox's tail, which, we are told, serves as a balance when running. Even though it precedes by decades Walt Disney's acclaimed feature *The Living Desert* (1953), which documents this same region, *Wildlife on the Desert* uses many of the same conventions that proved popular in later theatrical nature films. The film presents simplified information, brought to life by compelling film imagery. We see various wildlife specimens, but we learn only a few details about them: what they look like, how they move, and what they eat.

This film, like most classroom films before the mid-1930s, is silent. Synchronized sound technology was available in commercial theaters beginning in 1927, but classroom films lagged several years behind. No 16mm sound-on-film projectors were available until 1934, and then they were expensive.[43] The lack of synchronized sound would have given the teacher more room to tailor and adapt the film, however, by lecturing as the film unspooled. This lack of sound also means that each specimen is typically represented twice, first linguistically (by intertitles) and then photographically. In *Wildlife on the Desert*, the intertitles feature artistic renderings of idealized desert scenes, so that when the photographic images of wildlife subsequently appear, the animals are in a sense projected into a preexisting fantasy landscape (see fig. 6.2). This film may not resemble a fairground attraction as much as *Struggle for Existence* does, but it still popularizes science. Classroom nature films were becoming accepted as useful educational tools; however, as films, they still catered to popular expectations about entertainment.

In fact, the most "modern" nature films—by which I mean films that were conceived according to the most current ideas in visual education at that time—were the least sensationalistic. In an attempt to move toward modern scientific objectivity, which by definition runs counter to the fairground tradition of visual attractions, some nature films attempted to avoid the tropes of theatrical animal films. Eastman Teaching Films' output exemplified this modern, scientific approach. In May 1928, Eastman Teaching Films, Inc. was incorporated and began selling (not renting) prints to schools.[44]

As a commercial venture, Eastman Teaching Films was expected to make money, as one Eastman Kodak executive explained in 1927: "If [this] is a success . . . it will have to be justified to our stockholders as being an enterprise that will yield a reasonable profit to the company."[45] However, the company was

---

[43] Slide, *Before Video,* 89–90.

[44] "Use of Films for Teaching Is Launched," *Rochester Times-Union,* May 5, 1928, GEH. "Eastman Classroom Films Are Not Offered on the Rental Plan," in *Eastman Classroom Films: A Descriptive List including Latest Releases* (Rochester, NY: Eastman Kodak Company Teaching Films Division, n.d.), 2.

[45] "Educational Movies Made by Kodak Company," *Rochester Democrat and Chronicle,* Apr. 22, 1927, GEH.

Figure 6.2. Popular science: fantasy landscape and subsequent photographic image have equal status. Frames from *Wildlife on the Deserts of America's Great Southwest* (a.k.a. *Wildlife on the Desert*) (n.d.). (University of Southern California Hugh M. Hefner Moving Image Archive.)

headed by educators rather than businessmen, and accordingly followed different principles of production, distribution, and exhibition than commercial promoters such as Bray.[46] Wood and Freeman explained:

> The films were written with definite pedagogical goals in view. . . . The films tell no story and present no drama other than that which inheres in motion pictures of concrete things, places, and actions. They are not entertainment films, though all who view them find them exceedingly interesting. The films were designed to stimulate close observation and to provoke, in the minds of the pupils, insistent questions. . . . The classroom film with which we are here concerned is not a self-contained unit carrying its own story which the student is to receive passively, and least of all is it a story which has a definite and satisfying end. On the contrary, it is an instrument which the teacher is to use and not a substitute for the teacher, textbooks, maps, drawings, or other time-honored instrumentalities of the classroom.[47]

Filmmakers attempted to keep intertitles to a minimum, and educators were instructed to show their pupils each film twice, at least during the experimental phase.[48] Study guides accompanying each film were written by education theorist Edgar Dale, whose widely used 1933 book *How to Appreciate Motion Pictures* was one of the first to envision spectators as potentially engaged, critical participants in film viewing.[49] This series of classroom films thus demonstrates some of the most up-to-date ideas of 1920s visual education, and it includes a number of nature films. One Eastman Classroom Films pamphlet listed twenty-nine titles under the category "Nature Study."[50] The films and guides were widely circulated in schools across the country, and quite a few of them survive in libraries and archives today.

A characteristic example is *Frogs, Toads, and Salamanders* (1932), which was made for classes at junior-high, senior-high, and college levels.[51] As its title indicates, the film depicts three different (but related) organisms. Unlike the previous

---

[46] Slide, *Before Video*, 40–41.

[47] Wood and Freeman, *Motion Pictures in the Classroom*, 36–37.

[48] Ibid., 20–21, 36.

[49] For an analysis of Edgar Dale in the context of the early visual education movement, see John Nichols, "Countering Censorship: Edgar Dale and the Film Appreciation Movement," *Cinema Journal* 46, no. 1 (2006): 3–22.

[50] *Eastman Classroom Films: A Descriptive List*, 21–25. Although this catalog is undated, it was clearly published before World War II.

[51] Dorothy E. Cook and Eva Cotter Rahbek-Smith, *Educational Film Catalog: A Classified List of 1175 Non-Theatrical Films with a Separate Title and Subject Index* (New York: H. W. Wilson, 1936), 29.

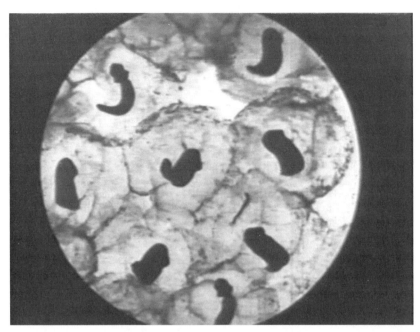

Figure 6.3. Modern science: microscopic image of frog eggs. Frame from *Frogs, Toads, and Salamanders* (1932). (University of Southern California Hugh M. Hefner Moving Image Archive.)

two films I have discussed, this one strives for scientific objectivity, depicting the life cycle of each amphibian from egg to tadpole to adult. The film even uses representational techniques of "mechanical objectivity" at several points. Microscopic photography, for example, is used to depict frog eggs (see fig. 6.3). This image is framed with the circular matting of early cinema days, a convention often used to denote objects deserving special visual attention, shown in close-up (as in the film *Grandma's Reading Glass* [G. A. Smith, 1900]). While a similar circular matting was also used in nineteenth-century scientific photographs by Auguste-Adolphe Bertsch and others (because it replicates the human eye's perspective when looking through a microscope), for viewers familiar with the visual sensibility of popular cinema rather than scientific photographs, the matting in this film might have had the effect of hearkening back to the conventions of popular cinema, rather than connoting scientific objectivity.

Unlike *Wildlife on the Desert,* which devotes just a couple of shots to each specimen, *Frogs, Toads, and Salamanders* devotes approximately three minutes to each of its organisms, which allows the film to present more detail about each specimen than the previous two titles discussed above. However, the film still presents only the most basic information, certainly covering less ground than a textbook would: "only the [frog's] hind feet are webbed," "when the toad winks the eyes are pulled into the head," and so on. What's more, the film contains

Figure 6.4. The animal feeding trope: toad devours worm. Frame from *Frogs, Toads, and Salamanders* (1932). (University of Southern California Hugh M. Hefner Moving Image Archive.)

moments reminiscent of the animal fight and animal feeding tropes when it depicts birds hunting for tadpoles to eat and, in particular, when it displays a toad eating a worm (see fig. 6.4). This brief segment also utilizes a technique of continuity editing, a hallmark of fiction film, by cutting from a master shot of the toad and its prey to a close-up of the toad, and back out to the first shot again, to increase the dramatic tension of the moment.

We can see, then, that even the more academically oriented Eastman Teaching Films productions used some devices of popular cinema to convey their information. Another Eastman Teaching Film, *Some Seashore Animals* (1930), features close-up shots that have clearly been staged in a controlled laboratory environment, as one can see from the careful, artistic backlighting in this image of marine tube worms (see fig. 6.5). It was certainly acknowledged in the 1920s that some stage management was necessary to film nature study specimens. Especially when recording discrete events such as a butterfly molting, a 1921 article in *Visual Education* said, "it is . . . vital that the stage be so ingeniously arranged beforehand as to make it possible to operate lights, camera, and focusing device on the instant."[52] However, as the tube worm image demonstrates, it can be difficult to draw the line between capturing an "objective" image of

---

[52] Jean Ramsey, "Nature-Study Films in the Making," *Visual Education* 2, no. 6 (June 1921): 15.

Figure 6.5. Stage-managed habitat: marine tube worms. Frame from *Some Seashore Animals* (1930). (University of Southern California Hugh M. Hefner Moving Image Archive.)

nature and an "artistic" image of nature. Interestingly, I found the tube worm film in an archive on the same reel with a much more sensationalistic film called *The Cuttle Fish* (ca. 1920s). While *Some Seashore Animals* feels careful and controlled, *The Cuttle Fish* focuses on its subject's propensity to shoot ink while in conflict with other sea life, and it features a more obviously staged mise-en-scène along with more fight scenes. All this is to say that nature films have a difficult time moving away from the domain of popular science and into the realm of academic science. Some films popularize more than others.

Animals and other natural history topics were ideal subjects for uniting the competing needs of education and entertainment in the classroom film. As one of the most enduring popular science topics, and as a favorite subject for children, animals were, not surprisingly, a cornerstone of classroom cinema. As Akira Lippit writes, "Animals had found a proper habitat or world in the recording devices of technological media."[53] Theorists since John Berger in 1980 have been arguing that animals appear in representations more frequently as they disappear from everyday life in the modern world.[54] More often than not, as

---

[53] Akira Mizuta Lippit, *Electric Animal: Toward a Rhetoric of Wildlife* (Minneapolis: University of Minnesota Press, 2000), 25.

[54] See John Berger, "Why Look at Animals?" in *About Looking* (New York: Pantheon, 1980), 1–25.

these critics have pointed out, animals serve as metaphors for human behavior.[55] And yet early natural history films—particularly the more academic ones such as Eastman Classroom Films—strove to represent animals not as metaphors but as scientific subjects, as animals in themselves. While these films may not have entirely succeeded in modeling scientific objectivity for their young audiences, it is worth noting that this goal of pure objectivity was by definition unattainable even in the realm of advanced scientific practice. "Was mechanical objectivity ever completely realized? Of course not," Daston and Galison write.[56] But the fact that children and young adults were exposed to a cinematic version of natural history in the classroom as early as the 1920s is in itself a remarkable development, and should remind us that encounters with film at school may have been as significant for young viewers as going to the movie theater.

Filmography

The Cuttle Fish (ca. 1920s) 2 ½ min., 16mm
DISTRIBUTOR: Film Featurettes, Inc. ACCESS: www.archive.org/details/some_seashore_animals_1930. NOTE: *The Cuttle Fish* is found at the end of this video file. This is likely a film made by the German Ufa studio, as Film Featurettes, Inc. distributed Ufa educationals in the United States at this time.

Frogs, Toads, and Salamanders (1932) 9 min., 16mm and 35mm
PRODUCTION: Eastman Teaching Films, Inc. ACCESS: www.archive.org/details/etf_frogs_toads_and_salamanders.

Some Seashore Animals (a.k.a. *Seashore Animals*) (1930) 7 min., 16mm and 35mm
PRODUCTION: Eastman Teaching Films, Inc. ACCESS: www.archive.org/details/some_seashore_animals_1930.

The Struggle for Existence (1925) 5 min., 16mm
PRODUCTION: Bray Studios. ACCESS: www.archive.org/details/struggle_for_existence_1925.

---

[55] For a useful overview, see Susan McHugh, "One or Several Literary Animal Studies?" *Ruminations* 3, H-Animal Discussion Network, May 19, 2011, www.h-net.org/~animal/ruminations_mchugh.html.

[56] Daston and Galison, *Objectivity*, 121.

Wildlife on the Deserts of America's Great Southwest (a.k.a.
Wildlife on the Desert) (ca. 1920s) 11 min., 16mm
PRODUCTION: William and George Allen. ACCESS: www.
archive.org/details/wildlife_deserts_americas_southwest.

Related Films

The Acrobatic Fly (1910). Directed by Percy Smith. Production
company: Charles Urban Trading Co. Access: www.youtube.com/
watch?v=8hlocZhNc0M (posted by BFIfilms, January 29, 2008).

Beavers (1930). Production company: Eastman Teaching Films, Inc.
Access: www.archive.org/details/beavers_1930.

Bees and Spiders (circa 1927). Directed by G. Clyde Fisher, American
Museum of Natural History. Distributed by DeVry School Films.
Access: www.archive.org/details/bees_and_spiders.

Birth of a Flower (1910). Directed by Percy Smith. Production
company: Charles Urban Trading Co. Access: www.wildfilmhistory.
org/film/21/clip/796/Blooming+flowers.html.

Chang: A Drama of the Wilderness (1927). 67 min. Directed by
Merian C. Cooper and Ernest B. Schoedsack. Production company:
Famous Players-Lasky. Distributed by Paramount Pictures. Available
on DVD from Milestone Films.

Glimpses of Bird Life (1910). Directed by Oliver Pike. Distributed by
Pathé. Access (only if you are at a registered school or library location
in the UK): www.screenonline.org.uk/film/id/1271010/index.html.

In Birdland (1907). Directed by Oliver Pike. Film is no longer extant.

A Murderous Midget Fish (ca. 1920s). Distributed by Film Featurettes,
Inc. Access: www.archive.org/details/murderous_midget_fish.
NOTE: This film was produced by Ufa and distributed in the United
States by Film Featurettes, Inc.

Simba: The King of the Beasts (1928). 83 min. Directed by Martin and
Osa Johnson. Production company: Martin Johnson African Expedition Corporation. Available on DVD from Milestone Films.

Trees (a.k.a. *Planting and Care Of Trees*) (1928). Production company:
Eastman Teaching Films, Inc. Access: www.archive.org/details/trees_
planting_and_care_of_1928.

Wing, Claw, and Fang! (1946). Distributed by Castle Films (no. 612).
Access: www.archive.org/details/wing_claw_and_fang_1946.

7 MEDICAL EDUCATION THROUGH FILM: ANIMATING ANATOMY AT THE AMERICAN COLLEGE OF SURGEONS AND EASTMAN KODAK

KIRSTEN OSTHERR

Fictional representations of doctors regularly top the television ratings charts. But while programs like *Grey's Anatomy* and *House, M.D.* may captivate the viewing public, they also frequently provoke irritated medical professionals to publish editorials debunking these depictions as potentially harmful fantasies. Though some medical students and physicians admit to enjoying the mass culture versions of their profession, since the earliest days of film and television official medical societies have dedicated considerable effort to correcting the public record whenever seemingly damaging distortions have appeared. At the same time that these organizations were critiquing the exploitation of medicine for entertainment, however, they were also actively engaged in producing their own versions of scientifically accurate, educational images for both experts and the laity. The American College of Surgeons (ACS) was a leading national force in the standardization of medical education and the use of educational motion pictures in the early twentieth century.[1] To pursue these entwined goals, the ACS formed a Committee on Medical Motion Picture Films in 1926, under the guidance of two major institutions of the film industry: the Eastman Kodak Company and the Motion Picture Producers and Distributors of America (MPPDA, also known as the Hays Office), a trade association formed by the major Hollywood studios in 1922 to regulate film content and to promote and protect the industry's interests. While the topics of health and medicine were already popular in the repertoire of early cinema, they received haphazard treatment often backed by dubious expertise in the years

The author gratefully acknowledges the assistance of Susan Rishworth, director of the American College of Surgeons Archives in Chicago.

[1] On the standardization of medical education in the United States, see Paul Starr, *The Social Transformation of American Medicine* (New York: Basic, 1982); as well as Kenneth M. Ludmerer, *Time to Heal: American Medical Education from the Turn of the Century to the Era of Managed Care* (New York: Oxford University Press, 1999).

prior to ACS involvement in this field. The health film movement that emerged established the American College of Surgeons as a central institution in the development of nontheatrical, educational cinema in the United States. But the physicians' collaboration with Hays and Eastman also posed several problems for their emergent field of specialization: How would ACS films clearly distinguish themselves from the lowbrow entertainment and health quackery often promoted by commercial entertainments and associated generally with the mass medium of motion pictures? And how would the filmmakers justify the investment of time and money in this new form of medical visualization and display, when adequate older forms of education were already available?

In explaining how the ACS overcame these obstacles to using motion pictures in medicine, this chapter will chronicle the evolution of educational film in the United States from 1912 to the post–World War II era. Through close analysis of the pivotal collaboration between the ACS and Eastman Kodak in the late 1920s, I will argue that the ACS placed medical motion pictures at the center of surgical training and thus established moving images as fundamental to the practice of medicine—a legacy that still shapes health care today. Ironically, these medical films made extensive use of animation, even as their producers and promotional materials adamantly rejected any commonality between surgical films and mass entertainment, including the burgeoning field of animation, whose popularity exploded at the same time that the first ACS-Eastman films were released. Starting with *Feline Follies* (1919), Felix the Cat cartoons were popular throughout the 1920s, and Mickey Mouse made his debut in the 1928 film *Steamboat Willie*.[2] The first film exhibited at an ACS meeting, in 1927, made extensive use of animated drawings to present surgical sequences that were otherwise impossible to capture on film. Highlighting the medium's unique capacity for resolving difficult representational problems, cultural critic Gilbert Seldes hypothesized in a 1932 discussion of animated cartoons that "something in the form itself is a satisfaction to us. And that satisfaction, I think, is the childish . . . pleasure in magic, in seeing the impossible happen."[3] By simultaneously defending the use of animation as a vehicle for medical education and refusing to differentiate between the documentary status of animated and live action footage, the American College of Surgeons attempted to resolve the contradictory linkage of this "pleasure in seeing the impossible happen" with both childish pastime and scientific visualization. As we will see, the adoption of the motion picture as an educational tool required the ACS physician-filmmakers to both foreground and disavow their active participation in constructing medical

---

[2] Donald Crafton, *Before Mickey: The Animated Film, 1898–1928* (Cambridge, MA: MIT Press, 1982), 3–5.

[3] Gilbert Seldes, *New Republic*, June 8, 1932, quoted in Crafton, *Before Mickey*, 12.

reality through representations that depended on artifice to convey objective scientific truths.

"The Cinematograph as an Aid to Medical Education and Research"

Much has been made of the scientific appeal of cinema as a research tool. The medium's ability to slow down, speed up, enlarge, and replay images of organic processes as they change over time has been widely acknowledged as the impetus for the "invention" of the motion picture.[4] This celebrated capacity to manipulate temporal and spatial relations also played a crucial role in cinema's initial appeal for medical education, as it solved several key logistical problems for the field. By the early twentieth century, many surgical procedures had been adequately described in textbooks and medical journals, but live demonstration in "wet clinics" was considered a more effective method of teaching and learning. Seeing expert surgeons perform before one's eyes allowed viewers to comprehend perspective and continuity in ways that the framing and abstraction of individual anatomical illustrations or photographs could not, even if they were presented in sequence. Not surprisingly, then, wet clinics provided the main attraction at the first Clinical Congress of Surgeons of North America in 1910.[5] However, the popularity of these sessions meant that the operating amphitheaters were packed full of physicians craning their necks to get a decent view of the surgery. The difficulty of predicting the timing of uncommon surgical procedures further undermined the pedagogical efficacy of the live demonstration model, as cases could not easily be scheduled for observation. By the third Clinical Congress in 1912, these time and space limitations demanded resolution; a new system of visual pedagogy was needed.

That same year, physician Rudolph Matas delivered the presidential address to the annual meeting of the Southern Surgical and Gynecological Association in New Orleans. His talk was titled, "The Cinematograph as an Aid to Medical Education and Research: A Lecture Illustrated by Moving Pictures of Ultramicroscopic Life in the Blood and Tissues, and of Surgical

---

[4] See Virgilio Tosi, *Cinema Before Cinema: The Origins of Scientific Cinematography*, trans. Sergio Angelini (London: British Universities Film and Video Council, 2005); Timothy Boon, *Films of Fact: A History of Science in Documentary Films and Television* (London: Wallflower, 2008); Lisa Cartwright, *Screening the Body: Tracing Medicine's Visual Culture* (Minneapolis: University of Minnesota Press, 1995); Hannah Landecker, "Microcinematography and the History of Science and Film," *Isis* 97 (2006): 121–32.

[5] John S. O'Shea, "Motion Pictures and the College: A History of 'Learning By Seeing,'" *Bulletin of the American College of Surgeons* (Aug. 2003): 17.

Operations."[6] As he chronicled the early contributions of medical men to chronophotography, Matas emphasized the pioneering role of filmed studies of pathological motion. He singled out the work of Ètienne-Jules Marey and Jean Comandon, in particular the latter's work in cinemicroscopy and the research potential contained in serial images of cellular movement that could be studied repeatedly and in slow motion. Highlighting "the value of cinematography in teaching ultramicroscopic pathology in the classroom," Matas enumerated the logistical benefits of film-based instruction, comparing surgical training to "the problem of imparting individual instruction in the trades." Citing a 1909 article in *Scientific American* that proclaimed the value of cinema for technical training, Matas asked his fellow surgeons, "Why could we not profit by this suggestion and inaugurate cinematographic courses that would illustrate all the operations of surgery covering a complete course of operative surgery as contributed by the most noted and greatest specialists in the surgical profession?"[7]

Matas went on to explain the origins of his film enthusiasm: he had recently visited Paris, where the renowned (and in some quarters notorious) surgeon Eugène-Louis Doyen had impressed Matas with some of his own surgical films, several of which were projected on the occasion of the New Orleans lecture.[8] Doyen was an early and strong proponent of the pedagogical efficacy of motion pictures. By filming and reviewing his own procedures together with the rest of his surgical team, he argued, "the cinematograph helped me to perfect my surgical technique considerably."[9] Matas noted that Doyen had already begun work on a series of films to accompany his own medical textbooks, and he urged the American audience to follow the French doctor's example. However, apart from a few early adopters in the audience, the surgeons generally ignored this plea until

---

[6] Rudolph Matas, "The Cinematograph as an Aid to Medical Education and Research: A Lecture Illustrated by Moving Pictures of Ultramicroscopic Life in the Blood and Tissues, and of Surgical Operations," *Southern Medical Journal* 5 (1912): 511–27. American College of Surgeons, Committee on Medical Motion Pictures, Correspondence and Data on Films, 1926–1997, RG5/SG2/S2, box 7, folder— "Visual Education in Surgery," Bulletin, May 1976 (source material), American College of Surgeons Archives, Chicago, Illinois (hereafter ACS Archives).

[7] Matas, "Cinematograph as an Aid," 19–20; *Scientific American* 67 (1909), quoted in Matas, 20–21.

[8] Matas, "Cinematograph as an Aid," 21–22. Doyen infamously performed the operation that separated the conjoined twins Doodica and Radica, who had previously been displayed as spectacles in the Barnum & Bailey Circus. See José van Dijck, "Medical Documentary: Conjoined Twins as a Mediated Spectacle," *Media, Culture and Society* 24 (2002): 537–56; and Thierry Lefebvre, *La Chair et Le Celluloïd: Le Cinéma Chirurgical du Docteur Doyen* (Brionne, France: Jean Doyen, 2004).

[9] Eugène-Louis Doyen quoted in Tiago Baptista, "'Il faut voir le maître': A Recent Restoration of Surgical Films by E.-L. Doyen (1859–1916)," *Journal of Film Preservation* 70 (2005): 44.

many years later. Their hesitation may have been due in part to the ambiguous status of the motion picture as a technology of both serious scientific investigation and frivolous amusement. In a discussion of Doyen's film of the surgical separation of Siamese twins, *Séparation des soeurs xiphopages Doodica et Radica* (1902), Oliver Gaycken has observed, "The proximity of [Doyen's] film to the world of sideshow exhibitions crystallized a pre-existing suspicion about cinema held by many members of the medical community. This film's complex history demonstrates how the tendency of medical images to drift into spaces and contexts neither envisioned nor sanctioned by their creators would come to haunt Doyen (and others)."[10] Indeed this sort of "drift" had troubled scientific cinema since its inception. Timothy Boon recounts the programming of early scientific visual novelties amid ballet and magic performances, as well as the memorable accompaniment of "Belloni and the Bicycling Cockatoo" at the first British screening of Lumière films in 1896.[11] Given the clear aim of entertainment implied by such pastimes, it is no wonder that many early medical men greeted the idea of medical motion pictures with some skepticism.

After all, the practice of surgery was just becoming a legitimate specialty in the early twentieth century, after years of debate about the accuracy and function of X-ray images had finally consolidated into a degree of professional acceptance of the technology and its potential for transforming the physician's ability to "see" inside of a living human body, gaining them a previously "impossible" viewpoint.[12] As Bettyann Holtzmann Kevles has demonstrated, the use of X-rays during the Spanish-American War in 1898 greatly elevated the specialty of surgery: "Operations to remove bullets and shrapnel after seeing them in radiographs produced dramatic results, and, because the patients were otherwise in good shape and usually recovered, they made the specialty look good." She continues, "Thanks to antisepsis and anesthetics, surgery was already on the rise from the bottom of the medical hierarchy. The X-ray completed the trio of discoveries that pushed it to the top."[13] Historical studies have identified the coemergence of X-rays and cinema as central to modern conceptions of the body and visuality. Both imaging technologies also played important roles in securing and maintaining the prestige of surgery as a medical specialty, but the motion picture's capacity to legitimate and disseminate innovative surgical techniques was not yet proven. In the late nineteenth century, cinema's public image was

---

[10] Oliver Gaycken, review of *La Chair et le celluloïd: le cinéma chirurgical du docteur Doyen* by Thierry Lefebvre, *Medical History* 52, no. 1 (2008): 155–56.

[11] Boon, *Films of Fact*, 14.

[12] See Barron Lerner, "The Perils of 'X-Ray Vision': How Radiographic Images Have Historically Influenced Perception," *Perspectives in Biology and Medicine* 35, no. 3 (1992): 382–97.

[13] Bettyann Holtzmann Kevles, *Naked to the Bone: Medical Imaging in the Twentieth Century* (New Brunswick, NJ: Rutgers University Press, 1997), 40.

more clearly associated with low-culture entertainments such as live animal acts than with medical research and training. With the field of surgery in a tenuous state of public acceptance, doctors could hardly afford to be seen as acquiring their professional expertise from sideshow amusements.

Nonetheless, the scientific appeal of motion studies was clear from the earliest days of chronophotography. Boon concisely summarizes the early period: "After the Lumière Brothers demonstrated the technology in 1895, doctors and scientists very soon began to experiment with it, applying it as an instrument for scientific research. L. Braun filmed the mammalian heart, Paul Schuster produced studies of patients with conditions including Parkinson's disease, Robert Watkins made microcinematographic renderings of blood corpuscles, John Macintyre—a consultant Ear, Nose and Throat surgeon—created a stop-motion X-ray film of a frog's legs flexing, and the surgeon Dr. Eugène-Louis Doyen started making surgical films."[14] By 1907, the American showman Charles Urban had acquired the rights to distribute Doyen's films alongside his own *Unseen World* series of microcinematographic films for the general public. Despite the novelty of some of the films in his collection, Urban promoted the scientific value of all of his films, perhaps strategically cultivating the mystique of prohibition by announcing in his catalog, "IMPORTANT: Under no circumstances can Surgical or Medical Film Series be supplied for exhibition except to Medical Colleges, Hospitals and Cognate Institutions."[15] (This exhortation appeared in a section of Urban's catalog that advertised the value of motion pictures for surgical training, with special emphasis on the films of Doyen.) However, American surgeons seemed skeptical of such ballyhoo and remained largely unconvinced that they should begin using motion pictures as instructional tools at this time.

The American College of Surgeons was founded in 1913, only one year after Matas first attempted to convince his colleagues that moving pictures were the future of surgical education. As the primary professional organization for surgeons in the United States, the ACS has always dedicated a significant portion of its annual meeting time to continuing medical education, including presentations on innovative surgical techniques. Thirteen years after Matas first recounted his enthusiasm for the medical motion picture programs he witnessed in Europe, ACS founder Franklin H. Martin was also influenced by a trip to the Continent; this time, the excitement led to concrete action. The surgical films Martin saw in

---

[14] Boon, *Films of Fact*, 8. On early scientific uses of motion pictures, see also Hannah Landecker, "Cellular Features: Microcinematography and Film Theory," *Critical Inquiry* 31, no. 4 (2005): 903–37.

[15] Charles Urban, *General Catalogue of Classified Subjects* (London: Charles Urban Trading Company, 1909), 83, quoted in Boon, *Films of Fact*, 24. For a full discussion of Charles Urban's early science films, see Oliver Gaycken, "Devices of Curiosity: Cinema in the Field of Scientific Visuality," PhD diss., University of Chicago, 2005.

Paris led him to propose a plan for medical motion picture production in the United States. In 1925, he presented the plan to the ACS Board of Regents, under the auspicious leadership at the time of president Dr. Rudolph Matas, and received authorization to proceed.[16] The inaugural event was a 1926 meeting between MPPDA president Will Hays, Eastman Kodak founder George Eastman, and the next ACS president, George D. Stewart, at Eastman's home in Rochester, New York. This gathering led to a series of coproductions that would shape health films and the broader field of educational film for decades to come.[17]

"The entire medical profession is becoming 'film conscious'": Collaboration at ACS and Eastman Kodak

In 1929, three years after the initial meeting between Eastman, Hays, and the ACS, a pamphlet called *Announcing Eastman Medical Films* was published to promote the fruits of the collaboration. The booklet lists completed films as well as works in progress with projected dates of availability. It begins by recounting the origins of the collaboration: In 1926 Eastman Kodak "undertook an extensive experiment to determine the teaching value of films made expressly for classroom instruction," the results of which "were so gratifying that a separate company, Eastman Teaching Films, Inc., was formed to produce teaching films." Meanwhile, the American College of Surgeons was interested in producing medical teaching films, so Kodak and the ACS joined forces to lend technical photographic skill to the cinematic presentation of scientific medicine.[18]

Descriptions of the logistics of the Eastman-ACS project indicate the full participation of both parties at the levels of development and production. The ACS Medical Motion Pictures Committee initiated new projects by selecting a topic for a film and a board-approved surgeon to develop an outline for the surgical sequences. Once the basic technical features were established, Eastman Teaching Films developed a draft of a shooting script, which was then reviewed and revised by numerous medical advisers before the final scenario was approved. The ACS continued to participate actively throughout filming and postproduction,

---

[16] Eleanor K. Grimm Records, vol. 20: Motion Pictures, reel I/1, page 1, ACS Archives. Grimm was secretary to ACS founder Franklin H. Martin. Hereafter vol. 20: Motion Pictures citations abbreviated as EKG 20.

[17] George Stephenson, "Visual Education in Surgery," *Bulletin of the American College of Surgeons* 60 (1976): 9.

[18] Committee on Medical Motion Pictures, Correspondence and Data on Films, 1926–1997, RG5/SG2/S2, box 3, folder—Eastman-Kodak Co., Correspondence and Catalogs, 1931–1955. *Announcing Eastman Medical Films*, n.d., 3, ACS Archives. The pamphlet was most likely printed in 1929, as it makes reference to a film that "will be released for distribution about November 1, 1929," 12.

supervising the editing of intertitles and subtitles, and reviewing publicity prepared by Eastman Kodak as well as the Hays Office before going to press. This systematic review process enforced ACS ethical standards, especially its prohibition on commercialism, and ensured consistency among the finished products, a central goal of medical education at this time.[19]

Following the brief history of the Eastman-ACS collaboration, each page of the catalog provides a description and a film still for each title: *The Technique of Blood Transfusion; Intestinal Peristalsis; Indirect Inguinal Hernia; Rabies; Diagnosis and Treatment of Infections of the Hand; Ectopic Heart; Benign Prostatic Hypertrophy; Amyotonia Congenita; Simple Goiter; The Normal Heart; The Treatment of a Normal Breech Presentation; The Development of the Fertilized Rabbit's Ovum; Tests of Vestibular Function; Acute Appendicitis (Lay Public);* and *Acute Appendicitis (Professional).*[20] While the catalog only includes one title designated appropriate for nonexpert viewers, the collaborators intended to produce an entire series for the general public that would emphasize the importance of preventative medicine for maintaining health and detecting diseases such as cancer. These films were never produced.

The catalog emphasizes the "ingenious and difficult animations" present in many of the films, and the incorporation of these artistic renderings highlights the difficulty of simply capturing on film an ideal surgical performance. Consider, for instance, the 1927 film *Diagnosis and Treatment of Infections of the Hand.* As noted in the promotional pamphlet, the film is based on a book by Allen Buckner Kanavel, a future ACS president (1931–1932).[21] Skipping over the basic introductory sections of the text, the film begins with "the most important and serious types of infections of the hand . . . lymphangitis, fascial-space abscesses, and tenosynovitis." After several lengthy intertitles define these terms, a photograph of a man's extended arm appears onscreen. The image is animated with labels as well as moving lines demonstrating the flow of the lymphatic system from the fingertips up the arm, and subsequently, the photograph dissolves into a drawing to demonstrate the temporal process of swelling of the fingers that occurs with infection. Intertitles describe the treatment regimen, and a

[19] EKG 20, reel I/1, pp. 6–7, attachments, 1930 ACS *Yearbook*, 91; Minutes of Board of Regents meeting, Oct. 4, 1927, ACS Archives.

[20] Production dates are not included in the catalog, but alternate sources indicate that they were all produced between 1927 and 1930. Committee on Medical Motion Pictures, Correspondence and Data on Films, 1926–1997, RG5/SG2/S2, box 3, folder—Eastman-Kodak Co., Correspondence and Catalogs, 1931–1955. *Announcing Eastman Medical Films*, 4–19, ACS Archives.

[21] Allen B. Kanavel, *Infections of the Hand: A Guide to the Surgical Treatment of Acute and Chronic Suppurative Processes in the Fingers, Hand, and Forearm*, 5th ed. (Philadelphia: Lea Febinger, 1925).

brief live-action sequence shows the left side of a man (from below the neck) in a hospital bed. His arm is completely wrapped in hot dressings, as indicated in the preceding intertitle. The arms and skirt (but not the face) of a nurse enter the frame and she applies hot compresses to the bandaged arm, covers it, and exits.

In the next section of the film, on "fascial-space abscesses," another photograph of a hand and forearm appears onscreen, then animated skeletal features of the hand are superimposed with explanatory labels to indicate where the abscess may occur. Later, an animated image of the hand's bone structure is presented alone, without the underlying photography. Onto this image are drawn sequential layers of musculature, as indicated by intermittently appearing labels assisted by a pointer. Finally, the same spaces (the middle palmar and thenar spaces) that had been superimposed above the photograph reappear, this time as the culmination of the animated sequence. On top of this already layered drawing are added the tendons, sheaths, and fascia that cover the sites of potential infection. As the sequence concludes, the animation dissolves back to the original photograph, and the internal structures of the hand are again covered with skin.

The next intertitle introduces a new orientation for the same anatomical structures: "The relation of these spaces to surrounding structures is well shown in a cross section." The hand is initially pictured in close-up, laying flat, palm facing the camera, as a pointer draws an animated line across the hand to indicate the location of the cross-section we are about to see (figs. 7.1 and 7.2). After a subtle cut to a different shot of the hand in the same position, this sequence

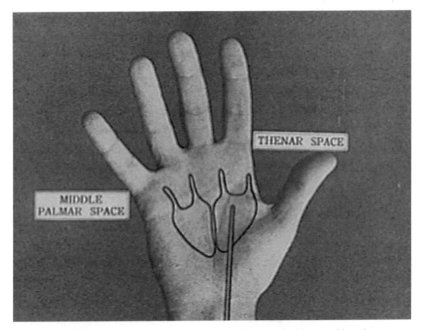

Figure 7.1. Frame from *Diagnosis and Treatment of Infections of the Hand* (1927). (Eastman Kodak Company.)

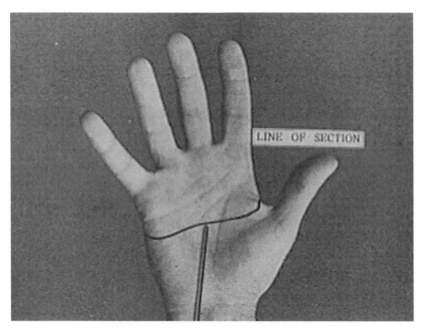

Figure 7.2. Frame from *Diagnosis and Treatment of Infections of the Hand* (1927). (Eastman Kodak Company.)

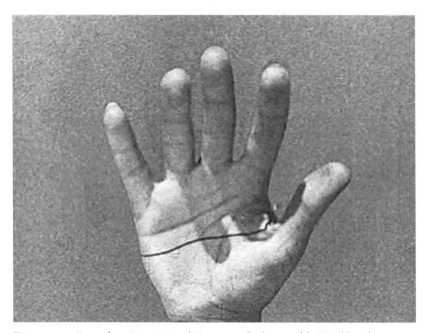

Figure 7.3. Frame from *Diagnosis and Treatment of Infections of the Hand* (1927). (Eastman Kodak Company.)

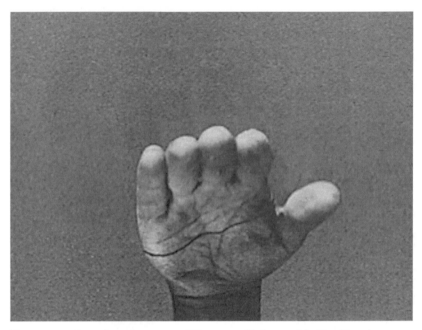

Figure 7.4. Frame from *Diagnosis and Treatment of Infections of the Hand* (1927). (Eastman Kodak Company.)

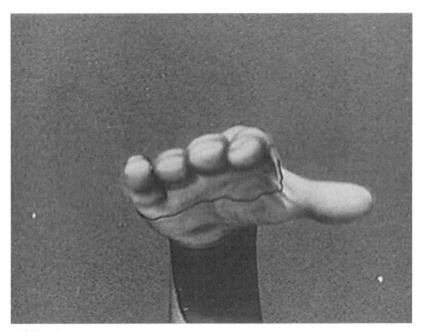

Figure 7.5. Frame from *Diagnosis and Treatment of Infections of the Hand* (1927). (Eastman Kodak Company.)

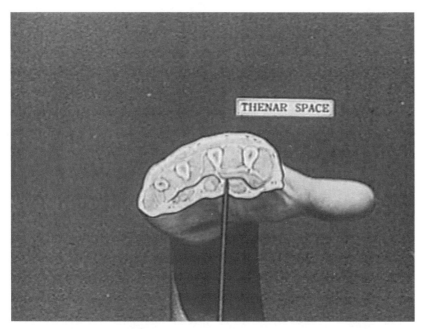

Figure 7.6. Frame from *Diagnosis and Treatment of Infections of the Hand* (1927). (Eastman Kodak Company.)

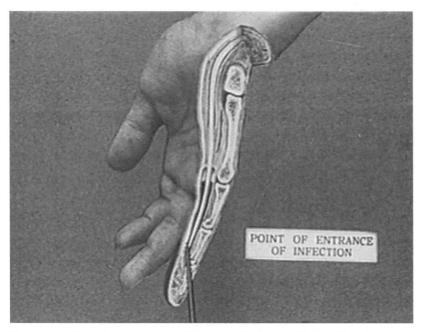

Figure 7.7. Frame from *Diagnosis and Treatment of Infections of the Hand* (1927). (Eastman Kodak Company.)

maintains viewer orientation by showing the hand flip its fingertips up toward the camera through three shots, so that the final shot shows the fingertips in the foreground, with the hand extended back behind it at the same angle that the cross-section will display (figs. 7.3, 7.4, and 7.5). Obstructive shadows clearly reveal that this hand is a three-dimensional object rather than a two-dimensional animation, and yet, the movements of this hand from flat to perpendicular are shown through three slightly awkward jump-cuts rather than continuous moving pictures. The resulting sequence appears more characteristic of stop-motion animation than live-action cinematography.

Why use this somewhat jarring representational technique? Possibly to animate a lifeless specimen without calling attention to its mortal state; possibly to preserve aesthetic continuity with the preceding sequences that seamlessly blend animation with profilmic anatomy while simultaneously drawing just enough attention to the postproduction enhancements of the image for viewers to become aware—and appreciative—of the sophisticated representational techniques employed in this film. A dissolve superimposes an animated cross-section onto the corresponding parts of the hand, and the four fingers slowly fade out, leaving only the cross-section and the photographed thumb extending outward to preserve the viewer's spatial orientation by anchoring the animation in an indexical image (fig. 7.6). (This extraordinary sequence essentially accomplishes through rudimentary analog media what it took millions of dollars and decades of international scientific collaboration to accomplish through the digital integration of external photographs of a human body with computerized tomography [CT] sections of that human body in the Visible Human Project, completed in 1994.)

In the "tenosynovitis" sequences that follow, different types of infections are displayed by dissolving from a photograph of the hand to a drawing of that hand, differentiated only by the erasure of some visual detail, such as creases and attached shadows on the palm and fingers of the hand. Once animated, the hand undergoes infection through various points of entry, and the obscuring layers of that part of the hand dissolve to reveal the anatomy and pathology that lie beneath. The standard, palm-up positioning of the hand is occasionally replaced with a different orientation to show a partial cross-section, but only the affected section of the hand is exposed in this manner, leaving the remaining fingers in their original photographic state to preserve spatial orientation (fig. 7.7). Other animations show the photographed hand swell up as infection spreads. When treatment calls for an incision, animated, not photographed forceps appear to open up the infected hand.

When an intertitle describes the sheaths of the flexor tendons extending "a thumb's breadth into the palm," a cutout photograph of a hand with extended thumb is inserted from the side of the frame to clarify the spatial relationships between the parts of the partially exposed hand onscreen. After a few seconds, the paper cutout is removed from the frame. Here again, the representational technique seems deliberately calculated to call attention to its own "ingenious"—and aesthetically pleasing—mode of production, while still preserving the verisimilitude of the sequence. Although a living arm could have reached into the frame to accomplish the desired comparison, such an intrusion would have disrupted the streamlined aesthetic of animated realism that the film has established thus far. Subsequent intertitles also call for demonstration of "a thumb's breadth" between various anatomical features, and the same cutout is employed. These sequences serially invest the diegetically animated photograph with scientific objectivity as it becomes a standardized tool of measurement precisely through its identical appearance in each sequence—a feat that not even the steadiest hand model could accomplish without introducing at least a modicum of subjective performativity into the display. By inserting the flat photograph into the frame just above and parallel to the plane of animation, which lies at a 90-degree angle to the camera, the image of the thumb accomplishes maximal visual comprehensibility while also establishing its two-dimensional plane of movement as impossible for a living hand to traverse. Thus, by employing consistent techniques of animation even when live action would provide a simpler solution to the representational problem, *Diagnosis and Treatment of Infections of the Hand* cultivates an aestheticized rendering of surgical intervention. In contrast to live-action depictions of dissections that graphically peel back the layers of skin and subcutaneous fat as the scalpel intrudes, this film neatly dissolves those layers to provide a clear view of only the most essential elements of the operative field. While these renderings only abstractly resemble the appearance of living tissue stained with blood that would be present in a real surgery, they nonetheless provide clear instruction, a central goal of the Eastman Teaching Films series. Only at its conclusion does the film revert to live action, demonstrating postoperative care for what appear to be "real" patients suffering from infections of the hand. In these final sequences, several men and women in street clothes appear onscreen as nurses splint their arms and dress their wounds.

Despite the celebration of artistic animation in such films by both Eastman and the ACS, the frequent emphasis in ACS publications on the challenges of visually rendering surgery onscreen suggests that the physicians were not wholly at ease with the varied means employed to enhance the depictions of their performances. The tension between displaying surgical skill in an instructional, documentary format and relying on animation to achieve adequate representation comes across in the 1931 ACS *Yearbook*, which presents a curious blend of self-congratulatory boasting and defensive justification: "Most of the technical films now being made under the auspices of the College are largely animated drawings of a high order seldom if ever heretofore seen in medical films, and much of this type of work is of a pioneer nature, requiring considerable experimentation. Many mechanical problems and special methods will be worked out in films now in production, which will facilitate future production."[22] This account seems calculated to circumvent critiques of the time spent and expense incurred by medical motion picture production, especially postproduction techniques such as animation, and indeed may also reflect the anticipated loss of Eastman Kodak funding that seemed increasingly likely after the stock market crash of 1929.

These comments may also be seen as referring to the ambiguous status of animation as a scientific mode of visualization. While emphasizing its instructional capacities, theories of visual pedagogy in this period often implied that animation held an intrinsic appeal for "simple-minded" audiences, because this mode of representation minimized the amount of visual information that the image conveyed, and was therefore deemed easier to comprehend and consequently more "entertaining" as well.[23] While the ACS embraced the medium's facility for revealing bodily processes invisible to the naked eye, the College was strictly opposed to associating its medical motion pictures with entertainment or childish cartoons. The status of animation was further complicated by the artistry inherent in its mode of production. Unlike the noninterventionist mechanical reproduction that placed motion pictures squarely in the domain of scientific imaging, the creation of hand-drawn animated sequences was no more objective than the illustrated anatomical atlases that motion pictures were meant to supersede.[24] Paradoxically, while moving pictures were often described as superior to illustrated print media due to their combination of movement and dense visual detail, the films' reliance on animation—which would seem to undermine the medium's claim to verisimilitude—highlights a truism of medical education: that more visual detail is not necessarily more pedagogically effective. In fact, animation's ability to selectively highlight the important elements in the visual field while omitting distracting details may not have produced the most accurate rendering of the human body, but it may nonetheless have provided the best training for the surgeons who viewed them. In other words, the very quality that gave animated cartoons their magical properties for childlike

---

[22] EKG 20, reel I/1, page 7, attachment, 1930 ACS *Yearbook*, 91, ACS Archives.

[23] For more on the ambiguous scientific status of animation, see Kirsten Ostherr, "Cinema as Universal Language of Health Education: Translating Science in *Unhooking the Hookworm* (1920)," in *The Educated Eye: Visual Culture and Pedagogy in the Life Sciences,* ed. Nancy Anderson and Michael R. Dietrich (Hanover, NH: University Press of New England, 2012). See also Ostherr, *Cinematic Prophylaxis: Globalization and Contagion in the Discourse of World Health* (Durham, NC: Duke University Press, 2005), especially chap. 2, "'Noninfected but Infectible': Contagion and the Boundaries of the Visible."

[24] On the presumed objectivity of mechanical reproduction of images in contrast to the subjectivity of the medical illustration, see Lorraine Daston and Peter Galison, "The Image of Objectivity," *Representations* 40 (1992): 81–123.

viewers was also responsible for the surgeons' privileging of animation as an educationally powerful special effect within their own films.

Viewing the "Medical Teaching Films" as a historic turning point in both educational film and medical education, ACS president Franklin Martin attempted to persuade George Eastman to continue funding the series despite the economic downturn in 1929. Though ACS guidelines sought to promote professional production values, Martin invoked the figure of the amateur film hobbyist to cite the physician-filmmaker's ancillary role as consumer of Kodak products for home moviemaking.[25] Thus, surgical film production became an entry point for a continuing revenue stream and a rationale for Eastman to continue investing in this benevolent but financially unprofitable realm of production. Acknowledging the disproportionate cost of medical filmmaking given the relatively small profit margin for educational films, Martin wrote:

> We appreciate the fact that our developmental work may not be fully reflected in the present rentals and sales of films. All medical institutions and organizations must be educated to use motion pictures, and we see convincing evidence of satisfactory progress in this direction. The entire medical profession is becoming "film conscious" and we believe that when a considerable number of good films are available the approximately 7000 hospitals, 3000 medical societies, and all the medical schools in this country will become regular users of these films. . . . May I emphasize the fact that the Eastman Medical Films approved by the American College of Surgeons are recognized as a standard for scientific films in this country today, and the medical profession is looking to us to continue the production of such films.[26]

The plea was unsuccessful, however, and the ACS immediately sought alternate sources of funding. Fox Film and ERPI Classroom Films (a subsidiary of Western Electric and its parent company, AT&T) both expressed interest. The ERPI company underwrote the costs of the film screenings at all of the ACS Sectional Meetings in 1930.[27] After the death of George Eastman in 1932, the collaboration was never revived.

---

[25] In 1951 an Amateur Motion Picture League was formed within the Committee on Medical Motion Pictures at the ACS. For more on the history of the Amateur Cinema League, see Charles Tepperman, "Communicating a New Form of Knowledge: Tracing the Amateur Cinema League and Its Films (1926–1954)," PhD diss., University of Chicago, 2007.

[26] Letter from Franklin H. Martin to George Eastman, Dec. 4, 1930, EKG 20, reel I/1, pages 10–11, ACS Archives.

[27] EKG 20, reel I/1, page 10, ACS Archives.

Despite the abrupt end to ACS-Eastman film production, medical motion pictures had become immensely popular teaching tools, just as Matas had predicted in 1912. From their 1927 debut at the ACS annual meeting, standing-room-only crowds gathered all week long, from morning until night, to see the latest surgical innovations on the big screen.[28] The ACS kept up with the latest technological innovations in motion pictures, eagerly adopting synchronized sound and color film as they became available.[29] By 1938, descriptions of the convention sounded more like a film festival than a medical meeting: "The almost continuous projection of motion pictures on surgical subjects was a feature of the Congress that attracted large audiences and again emphasized the educational advantage of this medium."[30] Large crowds continued to gather for the motion picture screenings at the Clinical Congresses, and new formats developed over time as the presentations became increasingly sophisticated.

"On a par with our accepted textbooks": Overcoming Skepticism amongst Medical Professionals

The enthusiastic reception of the motion picture screenings at the annual ACS Clinical Congress proves that the initial reluctance of many surgeons to engage with the medium of film had been handily overcome. How had this skeptical crowd been persuaded to embrace motion pictures? In order to achieve widespread professional acceptance, the ACS films had to prove their pedagogical superiority over earlier (and less expensive) forms of medical visualization and display. In addition to celluloid's rich visual detail (notwithstanding the complications of animation), another critical distinction between medical motion pictures and the still images that comprised anatomical atlases was the latter's capacity to depict the human body's movement through space and time. Unlike a series of illustrations or photographs depicting the same procedure, the motion picture could provide continuous representation of the movements of the surgeon's hands as well as the response of the body under the knife. Moreover, the portability of film—as compared to the busy surgeons themselves, who as "residents" literally lived in the training hospitals—meant that classes could be conducted anywhere the film could be shipped, in any language, and at any time that a projector and screen were available.

Distancing medical motion pictures from the commercialism of popular cinema was the second crucial step in securing professional acceptance of the ACS films. The fields of medicine and cinema were rapidly developing in the

---

[28] Ibid.

[29] EKG 20, reel I/1, pages 9 and 13, attachment, 1932 ACS *Yearbook*, 37, ACS Archives.

[30] EKG 20, reel I/2, page 2, citing "Notes on 1937 Clinical Congress," Feb. 15, 1938, *Surgery, Gynecology & Obstetrics*, ACS Archives.

early twentieth century, but despite surgeons' and cinematographers' claims of specialization, the boundaries of their domains were blurry, and crossover occurred with some frequency. Indeed, the popularity of both X-ray and motion picture demonstrations in department stores in this period typifies the ambiguity of these professional identities.[31] As the scientific invention of motion picture technologies gave way to the scientific development and dissemination of new surgical procedures through motion pictures, the field of medical filmmaking increasingly became populated by amateur hobbyists, whose films sometimes promoted idiosyncratic surgical techniques of questionable ethical standing. In an attempt to curtail such practices, the American College of Surgeons set forth guidelines in 1928 for evaluating the quality of films submitted for the ACS seal of approval. Written as a set of directive questions, the guidelines attempted to enforce medical ethics and the ideal of objective instruction by asserting, "The films shall not depict anything which may be construed as undue personal advertisement, or commercialism," and "Films of operations which represent a 'hobby' of the operator and which are not generally accepted by the profession will not be approved by the College for general distribution."[32]

Films like Doyen's surgical separation of Siamese twins seem to haunt the framers of these objectives, whose emphasis on "suitable" subjects, ethical principles, and "accepted" techniques all seem to have particular versions of inappropriate filmed procedures in mind. In keeping with the prohibition on "undue personal advertisement," the filmmakers who produced the first ACS-sponsored film, *Diagnosis and Treatment of Infections of the Hand,* were not credited when the film premiered at the 1927 Clinical Congress. Because "it was then considered unethical to publicize the name of the author of a film," the surgeons, Kanavel and Koch, were not identified and their faces never appeared onscreen.[33] Since the invention of moving pictures, the discourse on scientific cinematography had emphasized the promise of objectivity seemingly embedded in mechanical reproduction, and this prohibition seems intended to support the ideal of objectivity. However, the ACS also celebrated the medium's ability to capture for posterity the unique skill of the master surgeon's hands, a goal that would be difficult to attain while preserving that surgeon's anonymity. The aspect of mechanical reproduction that seemed most significant to the ACS was the film's capacity to provide uniform instruction through the distribution of identical copies of images depicting the movements that comprise a single, well-executed surgery. And yet, it was precisely the nonmechanical, individualized human touch of the great surgeon that the ACS films sought to reproduce, so that

---

[31] Kevles, *Naked to the Bone,* 25.

[32] EKG 20, reel I/1, page 7, attachment, ACS *Yearbook,* 89–90, ACS Archives.

[33] EKG 20, reel I/1, page 7, ACS Archives.

future generations could learn proper surgical techniques by repeatedly watching exemplary performances. Unlike illustrated atlases or live performances at wet clinics, motion pictures seemed capable of rapidly and repeatedly producing uniform results among vast numbers of viewers, thus enabling modern medicine to join the ranks of high-speed industrial enterprises. The automation of the photographic mechanism, coupled with its capacity for speed, positioned the motion picture at the technological and philosophical center of state-of-the-art medical training.

The tension between celebrating and suppressing subjectivity in these films comes through in the College's attitude toward the field's famous personalities. The policy prohibiting the representation of the surgeon's face onscreen seems initially to respond to the professional organization's desire to distance its work from that of Hollywood film stars, whose faces appeared onscreen to provoke an affective, not an intellectual, response. The rapid reversal of the ACS policy in 1930 seems to acknowledge the irresistible appeal of celebrity, even among such serious-minded audiences. However, the prohibition on personal publicity was replaced with a prohibition on publicizing the name of a film's commercial underwriter in the early 1930s; this restriction was relaxed in the late 1930s, but even then, sponsors were only permitted a brief appearance at the very end of the film. In contrast, over the next several decades the status of celebrity surgeons grew to the point that, starting in 1960, ACS annual meetings culminated in an evening screening called "Spectacular Problems in Surgery" that served both to publicize unique surgical solutions to particularly difficult and unusual cases and to entertain the gathering after dinner and drinks.[34] While ostensibly educational, these screenings also provided a form of cinematic pleasure that was designed for—and only comprehensible *as* pleasure to—an audience trained in highly specialized modes of viewing that authorized their delight in representations of the human body that were strictly prohibited in commercial films.

In 1928, before most of the ACS-Eastman medical films had been completed, Dr. Martin described the lofty goals of the ACS film program by firmly situating medical motion pictures within the realm of high culture, quite apart from commercial amusements: "An artistic appreciation of the motion picture has been developed through its use in the drama, and we will not be satisfied with the commonplace in subject, or even the worth-while in conception, if the material is presented inartistically or ineffectively. Our pictures must represent the highest conception in artistry and workmanship, and be on a par with our accepted textbooks, before the College can release them with its stamp of

---

[34] EKG 20, reel I/1, pages 9 and 12; reel I/2, page 2, ACS Archives. Committee on Medical Motion Pictures, Correspondence and Data on Films, 1926–1997, RG5/SG2/S2, box 1, folder—Medical Motion Picture Committee—Chronological, ACS Archives.

approval."[35] In essence, then, the ACS films were meant to function as aestheticized teaching instruments that conveyed a standardized set of surgical methods. This seemingly self-contradictory ideal straddles the line between scientific objectivity and aesthetic pleasure that had vexed medical illustrators since the sketches of Vesalius helped to shape the modern era of anatomy in the sixteenth century. As Catherine Waldby has argued, the purpose of the anatomical atlas "is to standardize both the vision and interpretation of scientific objects. The atlas eliminates what it considers superfluous detail in order to maximize intelligibility, so that it can mediate between raw, material objects and communities of scientific interpretation."[36] The "artistry and workmanship" that Martin sought in ACS films centered on finding a balance between documenting the surgery as it really happened and selectively highlighting through postproduction processing (that is, animation) the most important aspects of the procedure, while strategically obscuring the distraction of the inessential elements of the visual field.

Martin's comments show that despite its enthusiastic collaboration with emissaries of Hollywood, the ACS took pains to distance its medical motion pictures from the perceived degradation of popular culture. One key strategy for protecting the status of ACS films was the institutionalized prohibition on exhibiting surgical films to general theatrical audiences. The MPPDA included "surgical operations" in its 1927 list of "Don'ts and Be Carefuls" as well as in the prohibitions of the 1930 and 1934 Production Codes. Enforced by both the Production Code Administration (beginning in 1934) and ACS regulations restricting audiences for medical films to physicians and medical students, the limitations on where and by whom these films could be seen amounted to what Martin Pernick has called "aesthetic censorship."[37] However, these prohibitions were not only restrictive, they were also productive. The ACS consultations with the Hays Office suggest a strategic engagement with Hollywood that highlights an important aspect of the restrictions on medical film exhibition. Far from merely reflecting moral or ethical standards as the organizations claimed, audience segmentation produced two distinct ways of seeing the body that supported the objectives of these two institutions. By restricting audiences for ACS films to medical specialists, the College cultivated a form of medical vision accessible only to an elite, highly trained viewership; meanwhile, by ensuring that

---

[35] The 1928 "Blue Book," i.e., ACS *Yearbook*, "Report of the Director General, Franklin H. Martin, MD," 79, EKG 20, reel I/1, page 5, ACS Archives.

[36] Catherine Waldby, "Virtual Anatomy: From the Body in the Text to the Body on the Screen," *Journal of Medical Humanities* 21, no. 2 (2000): 98.

[37] Martin Pernick, *The Black Stork: Eugenics and the Death of "Defective" Babies in American Medicine and Motion Pictures since 1915* (New York: Oxford University Press, 1999).

its audiences could reliably experience entertainment free of biologically unsettling images, the MPPDA cultivated a form of "visual pleasure" that would appeal to the broadest possible viewership. Moreover, by identifying the appropriate domain for the excessively realistic documentary images (and their attendant animations) presented in ACS surgical films, this alliance left Hollywood free to imagine a more idealized version of the medical encounter in its films and, later, in its television programs.[38] The arrangement benefited both sides, allowing Hays to assure the surgeons gathered for the annual ACS meeting in 1931 of the "sympathetic cooperation of the organized motion picture industry" when he addressed the assembly.[39]

Conclusion: A Production Code for Medical Films

What were the long-term effects of the American College of Surgeons' commitment to medical motion pictures, for medicine and for cinema? In addition to the coproductions with Eastman Medical Films, the ACS Medical Motion Pictures Committee also evaluated and reviewed films. Beginning in the early 1930s, any producer of health or medical films could submit a copy of their film to the ACS for review.[40] Films for specialists and the general public were reviewed by committees of experts and evaluated on the basis of their "teaching value" as well as "professional technique" and "photographic quality."[41] Films that met "basic standards" in these areas were approved by the College, and their producers were allowed to insert a title card at the beginning of the film, which read: "Passed by the Committee on Medical Motion Pictures of the American College of Surgeons." The list of approved films was first published in the ACS *Bulletin* in 1935 and annually thereafter, alongside the criteria for evaluation discussed above in the 1928 formulation, which was revised in 1935 and titled, "Fundamental Principles in Evaluating Medical Motion Picture Films."[42] In this capacity, the ACS Medical Motion Pictures Committee had far-reaching influence among producers and consumers of health and medical films. Because the committee reviewed films for medical as well as lay audiences, their imprimatur circulated through a wide range of nontheatrical film networks, much as the Production Code seal of approval was required on release prints of all MPPDA members' films. The ACS seal was a clear and

---

[38] For an excellent discussion of medical representations under the Production Code, see Susan Lederer, "Repellent Subjects: Hollywood Censorship and Surgical Images in the 1930s," *Literature and Medicine* 17, no. 1 (1998): 91–113.

[39] EKG 20, reel I/1, page 13, attachment, 1932 ACS *Yearbook*, 37, ACS Archives.

[40] Stephenson, "Visual Education in Surgery," 11.

[41] "Medical Motion Picture Films," *Bulletin of the American College of Surgeons* 34, no. 4 (1949): 381.

[42] EKG 20, reel I/2, page 1, ACS Archives.

potent symbol of quality that could function immediately to assure viewers that the following film was backed by legitimate, board-certified medical expertise. As a guarantee against quackery, exploitation masquerading as education, or otherwise untoward content, the ACS list of approved films could provide programming guidance to a general public interested in issues of health and hygiene. Moreover, the celebrity status that accrued to surgeons who made widely viewed films meant that the ACS seal also advertised a level of professional accomplishment that could boost a doctor's career. (It is notable how often members of the Committee on Medical Motion Pictures became presidents of the ACS.) A review of producers who submitted their films for approval demonstrates that lone filmmakers in search of publicity as well as large, well-established film studios were equally desirous of the ACS seal of approval, and this coveted quality both reflected and perpetuated the importance of the seal itself.

Rhetorically and systematically, then, the ACS created a "Production Code" for medical films. The parallel systems of standardization and evaluation at the MPPDA and the ACS may have been influenced by MPPDA president Will Hays's participation in the formative years of the ACS-Eastman collaboration, as "honorary president" of the Medical Motion Pictures Committee. Knowing that a finished product would be submitted for ACS approval undoubtedly shaped the production values of unaffiliated filmmakers, especially when the successful distribution of the film would depend, as it did for Hollywood films, on public display of the seal of approval. Professional medical societies, including the ACS itself, viewed the seal as sufficient evidence that a film deserved a place on a screening program, and such exhibitions were often scheduled sight unseen in this era of scarce celluloid copies of popular titles. Given the preponderance of educational films produced in these years, discriminating exhibitors and viewers needed reliable evaluations of films by uninterested parties. The high standards evident in the Eastman-ACS coproductions, which were widely distributed to medical audiences by the early 1930s, allowed viewers to safely assume that other films approved by this organization would display similar levels of professionalism and polish.

Of course, the assumption that the ACS was a purely disinterested party may have been inaccurate. While the College was indeed committed to health education in general, it was also invested in maintaining and promoting its status as the preeminent national and international arbiter of excellence in surgical specialization. Dedicating resources to developing the motion picture as a leading innovation in medical visualization and display can be seen as a strategy for securing the ACS reputation at the forefront of its field. Fellows of the ACS were explicitly cognizant of the publicity gained by international distribution of films bearing the College seal when, in 1939, the U.S. State Department asked the ACS to cooperate in producing and distributing medical films to Latin American countries. This program, under the Office of Inter-American

Affairs, expanded to include countries in Asia and Eastern Europe during the Cold War.[43]

The greatest contribution of the ACS medical motion picture program thus lay not in the excellence of any single teaching film the College produced but rather in the long-term effects that the institutional support of this prestigious organization had on all varieties of educational motion picture production. While many producers of educational films in the early and mid-twentieth century were small studios dedicated to making commissioned films rather than specific types of educational films, the ACS provided a model for specialization.[44] By emphasizing a systematic and integrated approach to selecting topics for films and evaluating production procedures, surgical technique, and artistic proficiency, the ACS set a high standard for medical and health film production that impacted producers and distributors of all sorts of educational films. The widely accepted social authority of physicians as emissaries of scientific discovery in the postwar era endowed the ACS film reviews with an irrefutable appeal, especially at a time when educational film itself was often described as a scientific approach to pedagogy. Moreover, the ACS set a standard for incorporating visual pedagogy into medical training that remains an integral part of medical instruction today. While medical visualization had been inseparable from medical training since the earliest days of anatomical illustration, the ACS approach to medical motion pictures established a professional role for this particular form of representation that served as a model for other fields of specialization as well. The ACS thus ensured that the new medium of moving pictures was not dismissed as a sideshow amusement or as a mode of representation too tainted by its association with crass commercialism to be of objective scientific value in the training of medical specialists. Instead, medical imaging came to define advanced health care in the twentieth century.

Filmography

Diagnosis and Treatment of Infections of the Hand (1927) 48 min., 16mm

PRODUCTION: Eastman Teaching Films and American College of Surgeons. SPONSOR/DISTRIBUTOR: Eastman Kodak Company. DIRECTOR/SURGEON: Allen B. Kanavel, MD (uncredited).

---

[43] For more on this phase of ACS film history, see Kirsten Ostherr, "Health Films, Cold War, and the Production of Patriotic Audiences: *The Body Fights Bacteria* (1948)," in *Useful Cinema,* ed. Charles Acland and Haidee Wasson (Durham, NC: Duke University Press, 2011).

[44] Some studios developed expertise in medical filmmaking and medical animation as a result of their collaboration with the ACS, such as Mervyn LaRue Studio in Chicago and Churchill-Wexler in Los Angeles.

ASSISTANT: Sumner L. Koch, MD (uncredited). ACCESS: Film print and viewing copy at History of Medicine Reading Room, National Library of Medicine, National Institutes of Health, Bethesda, Maryland.

Séparation des soeurs xiphopages Doodica et Radica (1902) 8 min., 35mm

PRODUCTION: Eugène-Louis Doyen, MD. DISTRIBUTOR: Société Géneral des Cinemathographes Eclipse (the French branch of the Charles Urban Trading Company). DIRECTOR: Eugène-Louis Doyen, MD. CAMERA: Clement Maurice and Ambroise-François Parnaland. EDITOR: Eugène-Louis Doyen, MD. ACCESS: *The Origins of Scientific Cinematography* DVD (dir. Virgilio Tosi, 99 min., 2006), distributed by BUFVC. NOTE: Only two minutes of the reportedly eight-minute-long original film are recorded on this DVD. Another brief fragment is archived at the Paris Institut de la Cinématographie.

Related Films

Acute Appendicitis (Lay Public) (1929). Eastman Teaching Films and American College of Surgeons. Distributed by Eastman Kodak Company. 10 min. Archival print available at History of Medicine Reading Room, National Library of Medicine, National Institutes of Health, Bethesda, Maryland (HMD-NLM).

Acute Appendicitis (Professional) (1929). Eastman Teaching Films and American College of Surgeons. Distributed by Eastman Kodak Company. 21 min. Archival print available at HMD-NLM.

Amyotonia Congenita (1930). Eastman Teaching Films and American College of Surgeons. Distributed by Eastman Kodak Company. 6 min. Archival print available at HMD-NLM.

Benign Prostatic Hypertrophy (1929). Eastman Teaching Films and American College of Surgeons. Distributed by Eastman Kodak Company. 11 min. Archival print available at HMD-NLM.

The Development of the Fertilized Rabbit's Ovum (1929). Eastman Teaching Films and American College of Surgeons. Distributed by Eastman Kodak Company. 10 min. Archival print available at HMD-NLM.

Ectopic Heart (1929). Eastman Teaching Films and American College of Surgeons. Distributed by Eastman Kodak Company. 8 min. Alternate title: *Ectopia Cordis*. Archival print available at HMD-NLM.

Feline Follies (1919). Pat Sullivan Studios. Distributed by Paramount. 4 min. Public domain. Available at www.archive.org/details/FelixTheCat-FelineFollies1919.

Indirect Inguinal Hernia (1929). Eastman Medical Films and American College of Surgeons. Distributed by Eastman Kodak Company. 41 min. Archival print available at HMD-NLM. Excerpt (16 min.) at www.wellcomecollection.org/explore/mind--body/topics/dissection/video.aspx.

Intestinal Peristalsis (1930). Eastman Teaching Films and American College of Surgeons. Distributed by Eastman Kodak Company. 12 min. Archival print available at HMD-NLM.

The Normal Heart (1929). Eastman Teaching Films and American College of Surgeons. Distributed by Eastman Kodak Company. 8 min. Alternate title: *Mechanism of the Normal Heart.* Archival print available at HMD-NLM.

Rabies (1929). Eastman Teaching Films and American College of Surgeons. Distributed by Eastman Kodak Company. 20 min. Archival print available at HMD-NLM.

Simple Goiter (1929). Eastman Teaching Films and American College of Surgeons. Distributed by Eastman Kodak Company. 11 min. Archival print available at HMD-NLM.

Steamboat Willie (1928). Produced and Distributed by Walt Disney Studios. 8 min. Available on DVD *Walt Disney Treasures—Mickey Mouse in Black and White* (Walt Disney Video, 2002).

The Technique of Blood Transfusion (1929). Eastman Teaching Films and American College of Surgeons. Distributed by Eastman Kodak Company. 30 min. Archival print available at HMD-NLM.

Tests of Vestibular Function (1929). Eastman Teaching Films and American College of Surgeons. Distributed by Eastman Kodak Company. 11 min. Alternate title: *Vestibular Tests.* Archival print available at HMD-NLM.

The Treatment of a Normal Breech Presentation (1929). Eastman Teaching Films and American College of Surgeons. Distributed by Eastman Kodak Company. 29 min. Archival print available at HMD-NLM.

The Unseen World: Revealing Nature's Closest Secrets by Means of the Urban-Duncan Micro-Bioscope (1903). Produced and Distributed by Charles Urban Trading Company. Approximately 20 min.

8 DR. ERPI FINDS HIS VOICE: ELECTRICAL RESEARCH PRODUCTS, INC. AND THE EDUCATIONAL FILM MARKET, 1927-1937

HEIDE SOLBRIG

In 1930, a Chicago high-school student skipping school to attend her first talking picture may not have escaped a little educational fare. It was possible that her neighborhood theater would have begun the program with the Western Electric animated film short *Finding His Voice* (1929), which described exactly how sound-on-film technology worked.[1] The cartoon, codirected by Max Fleischer, was shown widely in theaters for promotional purposes and also in nontheatrical trade exhibitions where sound film technology was sold. The short featured a scientist, Dr. Western, explaining to a silent strip of film, named Mutie, how optical sound-on-film technology works "just like a telephone." Dr. Western's explanation of sound technology was part of an attempt to define film sound as a telephonic rather than a filmic technology. This was by no means an innocent comparison. This early "educational" sound film foreshadowed the ideological frame that Western Electric and its subsidiaries used to fight RCA and Hollywood over who would control sound film equipment. By arguing that talking pictures were a telephone technology, Western Electric sought to add sound film equipment to the Bell Telephone monopoly in the communication industry.

This essay is informed by my research in the AT&T Archives and History Center in Warren, New Jersey, during 2000–2001. The archives, according to Sheldon Hochheiser (corporate historian for AT&T until 2004), house 15,900 films and videos. "The earliest titles are from the 1920s, the latest from the early 1990s. They are all by or about AT&T. In addition to training films, we have recruiting films, public relations films, informational films for employees, research seminars, video news clips, speeches, advertisements, and no doubt other types." E-mail to the author, June 27, 2000. Papers concerning these films are filed under the heading "Docupub Corporate Films."

[1] Arthur Edwin Krows later wrote of *Finding His Voice:* "When completed it became one of the most popular short subjects of the time, and was screened in virtually every important theatre in the country. Today a print of it is kept at the Museum of Modern Art as a milestone of progress in motion picture development." Krows, "Motion Pictures—Not for Theatres," *Educational Screen* (Feb. 1944): 70. All subsequent citations of Krows refer to this series of columns.

Integral to this fight was an effort waged throughout the 1930s to reshape the educational and nontheatrical film industries in the image of the Telephone Company, as a potential public utility organized around a communication technology.

In the 1920s and 1930s, the Bell System was the largest corporation in the world. It held a near-total monopoly over telephone utilities and related goods and services in the United States. The Bell System of the 1920s and 1930s had four operating areas with distinct functions: the twenty-two Bell Regional Operating Companies, which served local telephone service markets; Western Electric; AT&T Long Lines; and Bell Labs. As one corporate history describes it, "Bell Laboratories designed the network, Western Electric manufactured the telephones, cable, transmission equipment, and switching equipment, the operating companies installed the phones and billed customers, and AT&T long lines operated the long distance network."[2]

Electrical Research Products, Incorporated (ERPI), a subsidiary of Western Electric, was a part of the Bell System responsible for researching nontelephonic sound technologies, including the talking picture. In 1929, when it became obvious what a huge influence sound would have on the film industry, ERPI commissioned *Finding His Voice* through Paramount. Its opening credits read "Story by W. E. ERPI" above the directors' credit for F. Lyle Goldman and Max Fleischer. The story line contrasts two rolls of film as characters, Mutie and Talkie. Mutie asks Talkie to set him up with Dr. Western, the scientist who gave Talkie a voice. This lab-coated scientist then walks the two through the basics of the optically printed sound-on-film production process. He starts with a performance on a sound stage, recorded through a soundproof camera booth and a microphone controlled in a mixing booth, then demonstrates printing sound tracks onto film, and, finally, shows the reproduction and amplification of sound through the projector. Many of these technical operations described for the audience were specifically the patented technologies of the Bell Company and Western Electric. This instructional film ends with Mutie getting his voice and joining Talkie in a round of the traditional tune "Good Night, Ladies" as they morph into a rowboat and are eaten by a whale. The explanation of how motion picture sound works is comprehensible to laypeople,

[2] David C. Massey, "Western Electric History," Bell System Memorial Home Page, Porticus Centre website (ca. 2009), www.porticus.org/bell/westernelectric_history.html. See also John Brooks, *Telephone: The First Hundred Years* (New York: Harper & Row, 1975), as well as books in the AT&T Series in Telephone History, including George David Smith's *The Anatomy of a Business Strategy: Bell, Western Electric and the Origins of the American Telephone Industry* (Baltimore: Johns Hopkins University Press, 1985) and Robert W. Garnet's *The Telephone Enterprise: The Evolution of the Bell System's Horizontal Structure, 1876–1909* (Baltimore: Johns Hopkins University Press, 1985).

Figure 8.1.   Dr. Western explains to Mutie and Talkie: "This is the picture and sound projector. One motor drives both the picture and sound equipment." Frame from *Finding His Voice* (1929).

while the animation is quirky and whimsical. Despite its popular appeal, this film was not produced for the general public. It was made to market sound-film technologies to theater owners, nontheatrical producers, corporate film units, and educational institutions.[3]

Finding His Voice was one of the first ERPI-produced films, but it was followed by nearly a decade of educational sound film production, experimentation, and industrial struggle funded by the Bell System. Why did ERPI frame its pitch to control sound technologies through the educational film genre? And why did ERPI's educational genre develop the way it did rather than through more conventional, more emotionally appealing narrative or Hollywood genres? Making sense of *Finding His Voice*, and ERPI itself, requires the reconstruction of a formative yet understudied moment in the history of

---

[3] Animation historian Ray Pointer notes of *Finding His Voice*: "It came about because 1) the Fleischer Studio was a prominent producer of animated films in the 1920s, 2) Fleischer had previously produced two Industrial Films for Western Electric [*Einstein's Theory of Relativity* (1923) and Darwin's *Theory of Relativity* (1925)], and 3) Max was a student of the latest scientific and technical advancements." E-mail from Poynter to the author, May 14, 2009. See also, Richard Fleischer, *Out of the Inkwell: Max Fleischer and the Animation Revolution* (Lexington: University Press of Kentucky, 2005).

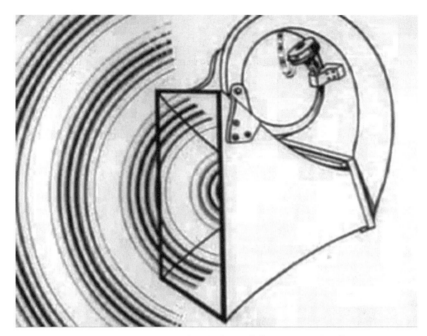

Figure 8.2. "The receivers, connected to the horns [of the loud speakers], convert the electrical vibrations back into sound waves—exactly the way the telephone receiver operates." Frame from *Finding His Voice* (1929).

nontheatrical film. The company's approach grew out of complex relationships among scientists, businessmen, educators, and filmmakers. While ERPI executives sought to define nontheatrical film for their own gain, scientists and educators saw an opportunity to produce new forms and production practices based in educational research and scientific method. Filmmakers, on the other hand, saw an opportunity to make higher quality films for the nontheatrical field. Despite different interests that went into shaping the ERPI educational picture, its nascent style and institutional standards were fundamentally shaped by the efforts to create a monopoly on the market of nontheatrical sound technologies for the Bell System. To do this, ERPI executives needed to distinguish educational sound film from Hollywood entertainment and to frame it as primarily a communication technology, thus within the Bell corporate purview. Although they ultimately failed to monopolize motion-picture sound technologies, ERPI left a lasting imprint on the form and function of the educational film.

On December 30, 1926, ERPI was established to market nontelephonic technologies, including sound film, the reproduction of sound from acetate discs, submarine cables, and public address systems, as well as to exploit patents that might develop from these. According to the initial incorporation documents, ERPI's stated goals were to see sound technologies patented by Western Electric and Bell become useful and profitable. At the same time, the company sought to use its patent dominance in other fields to fend off competitive business interests in the telephonic industry.[4] Beginning in 1927, through research and development of these audio technologies, ERPI's Western Electric sound systems became the first widely adopted for theatrical films.[5] Many in the film industry, ERPI included, were taken by surprise by the runaway popularity of the talkies. With broad control over patents in sound film, aggressive leverage of those patents, and Bell Company prestige, Western Electric/ERPI quickly gained a lucrative equipment market in Hollywood, as talkies rapidly replaced the silents in the theatrical exhibition sector.

From 1927 to 1931, ERPI struggled against RCA to establish both a technological standard and dominance as the provider of sound systems for the major studios. The company's first industrial conflict with RCA centered on which technology would become the standard. In the late 1920s, three systems competed. Two were Western Electric technologies: Vitaphone (a sound-on-disk system first licensed to Warner Bros.) and Fox Movietone (a sound-on-film system). A third, RCA Photophone, was a sound-on-film technology developed by General Electric. Again, that "Dr. Western" was explaining a sound-on-film technology in *Finding His Voice* had significance, pointing toward sound-on-film as the industry standard. All of the major Hollywood studios had a stake in who would control these new technologies. After a short-lived deal with Warner Bros. to distribute its sound technology through Vitaphone discs, and fearing industry resistance to having a single studio control sound equipment, ERPI reacquired rights to their sound systems.[6] Most contentious for ERPI's equipment licensing was its policy of exclusivity, in which both producers and exhibitors were required to use only ERPI products and services. Just as the Bell Telephone monopoly licensed telephone sets and required users to depend upon Bell technical support, ERPI sound systems remained the property of the company, not the theater. This required licensees to use ERPI repair technicians and Western Electric parts and to show only movies produced

---

[4] Bell Telephone, in its disputes with RCA and General Electric, held patents in these other fields, which they used as bargaining tools to fend off competitive challenges in telephony. As the Radio Group illustrates, Bell would trade pool patents in the electrical industry (with GE, for instance) to limit its entry into telephony. See U.S. Federal Communications Commission, *Proposed Report: Telephone Investigation,* Pursuant to Public Resolution No. 8, 74th Congress (Washington, DC: GPO, 1938), 792 pages [hereafter, FCC *Telephone Investigation* (1938)]. See esp. chap. 1, "Electrical Research Products, Inc.: Its Organization, Activities and Place in the Bell System," 1–25.

[5] Donald Crafton, *The Talkies: American Cinema's Transition to Sound, 1926–1931* (New York: Scribner's Sons, 1997), 127–33.

[6] Crafton, *The Talkies,* 101–18, 130–31.

on Western Electric sound-recording devices. Although by 1930 these practices had given ERPI a competitive advantage in Hollywood, this position soon began to slip. In response to a confluence of legal battles over patents, technical standards, and resistance to monopoly practices from Hollywood studios, ERPI's strategy took a different direction.[7]

Legal battles with RCA over radio sound technologies in the early 1920s left little doubt that the Bell Company would encounter strong resistance when entering the entertainment sector. The Bell System's own corporate policy restricted the company's activities to the communications sector, defining itself as both a public utility and a for-profit private enterprise.[8] In early 1927, J. E. Otterson, a Western Electric manager, was appointed president of ERPI. Despite Bell's official policy, Otterson had a broader agenda for ERPI, using its patents for both film sound and radio to expand out from the telephone field toward the motion picture and broadcasting industries.[9] Otterson believed the nontheatrical film field held financial potential equivalent to Hollywood. The nontheatrical sector had the added advantage of being an underdeveloped market that could be loosely construed as more akin to communications than to entertainment; it also lacked any major industrial challengers to ERPI's dominance. In these areas, external to Hollywood, including educational and industrial film, Otterson's expansionist ambitions were most clearly expressed. Otterson envisioned mapping the successful centralized communication and public utility model of the Bell System onto the field of nontheatrical sound film technology. One enormous opportunity for this model of sound film was the public education system. Officials of ERPI hoped that a substantially research-driven, audiovisual curriculum based on sound pictures could create a huge demand for a centralized equipment service provider, reproducing the telephone monopoly model in a new market. With corollaries in the regional Bell operating companies, school systems and their audio/visual infrastructures were often centrally organized at both city and state levels with the potential for significant economies of scale for both equipment and film purchasing.[10]

---

[7] Milton Anderson, *The Modern Goliath: A Study of Talking Pictures, with a Treatment of Non-Theatrical Talking Pictures Especially Talking Pictures for Schools and Churches* (Los Angeles: David Press, 1935), 40.

[8] Brooks, *Telephone*, 143–52.

[9] Frank C. Waldrop and Joseph Borkin, *Television: A Struggle for Power* (New York: W. Morrow, 1938); N. R. Danielian, *A.T. & T.: The Story of Industrial Conquest* (New York: Vanguard Press, 1939). Both Waldrop and Danielian believed Otterson intended to create a monopoly in the film industry.

[10] It might be noted that the public address system, which by the 1970s had become ubiquitous in public schools, was in fact an ERPI sound patent.

The market for sound equipment installation in Hollywood studios and theaters became saturated by 1931. Executives at ERPI, hoping to create a similarly broad market in nontheatrical sound installation, paid special attention to popularizing educational sound films in school systems. The company's earliest direct involvement in production took place through an educational sound research department established in 1929 and located in ERPI's New York headquarters, around the corner from Bell Labs.[11] Increasingly ERPI became involved in the creation of nontheatrical film materials—especially educational and industrial films, slide-films, and supporting documentation—as well as production facilities, distribution systems, and equipment for small, independent film companies. The deepening Depression threatened the economic stability of the independent production companies in which ERPI had stakes. Otterson had invested in these independents in order to encourage production in the nontheatrical field and to increase demand for Western Electric equipment and services. As the economy failed, many of these companies were unable to support sound film production. The company used Bell's substantial resources to gain a controlling interest in these independent production houses while also developing a film financing house, a small-format equipment manufacturer, and the production of an educational film library produced in concert with the research of ERPI experts. This broad structural investment in the nontheatrical film industry would ultimately lead the Federal Communications Commission (FCC), established in 1934, to impose the first divestiture order on the Bell System in 1937.

Otterson's efforts to affect an institutional and ideological distinction between "entertainment" and "communication"—with ERPI as the dominant source of film communication products, systems, and services—ultimately failed. From its inception ERPI was besieged by patent disputes and legal battles, and the nontheatrical market did not provide adequate cover to sidestep these obstacles. In 1937, the FCC ordered Bell to divest itself of its sound film technology patents, as well as other motion picture interests, including companies important to educational film production and distribution, such as Erpi Picture Consultants, Audio Productions, Inc., General Service Studios, and Eastern Service Studios.[12] Despite ERPI's failures, its efforts spawned production companies, distribution systems, technologies, and a substantial body (hundreds) of educational films. Many of these ventures would survive divestiture and continue to influence the nontheatrical and educational film fields for decades.

---

[11] "Quiet on the Set," *The Reporter* (May/June 1965): 28–31, clipping in "Docupub Corporate Films, #346 ERPI Classroom Films," AT&T Archives.

[12] FCC *Telephone Investigation* (1938), 3:580.

Erpi Picture Consultants, Inc.: Divisions of Labor and the Public Education Utility

An organization on the razor's edge of antitrust violation, ERPI did not advertise that it had put together a film production facility at the ERPI headquarters.[13] Arthur Edwin Krows, a producer and writer in nontheatrical productions in the 1920s and 30s, wrote a long-running account of the nontheatrical film field for the trade periodical *Educational Screen* titled "Motion Pictures, Not for Theatres." In this series, he devoted several columns to his experience working with ERPI, including his work in the educational sound film department. In this rare description of an educational film unit at work, Krows writes about his first encounter with the "ERPI operation."

> The flourishing Electrical Research Products, Inc., of this period was an enterprise the magnitude of which inspired awe. There were about seven hundred Erpi (sic) employees in the Fisk Building alone, and many departments, each bustling with actual and potential business and with its own ideas of new developments. The lines dividing these departments however were becoming more sharply defined.[14]

Krows lists increasingly segmented industrial divisions. After years of working in the disorganized nontheatrical field, he imagined his profession was finally achieving stability by mimicking the specializations found in the Hollywood studio system. With this state-of-the-art facility ERPI organized production around divisions of labor that emulated both Hollywood and corporate America. Krows further notes that "an experimental testing section was growing rapidly, with strong ties to Bell Laboratories; the so-called educational division was steadily qualifying to speak within the Bell System, for the entire non-theatrical field."[15]

Despite outward trappings that mimicked Hollywood production, scientific discovery drove the Bell Company, which, by capitalizing on its patents,

---

[13] The caution in regards to maintaining ERPI's "experimental" status is illustrated by the story told by Krows about shooting church film for Milton Anderson at Bell Labs in order to retain the experimental appearances. See Krows, June 1944, 250. Anderson, in *Modern Goliath,* would later note: "Electrical Research Products, Inc. (Western Electric) is financially related to the big telephone monopoly. The have unsuccessfully attempted to sell their high-priced but quality equipment in the nontheatrical field without pictures (except experimentally) because they fear that Congress will accuse the monopoly of proselytizing in school, church, and home" (40).

[14] Krows, Apr. 1944, 162. For a contemporary account of how Erpi Classroom Films were made, see H. A. Gray, "Social Science and the Educational Sound Picture," *Historical Outlook* 23 (May 1932): 211–17.

[15] Krows, Apr. 1944, 162.

kept Western Electric and ERPI in business. The executives and engineers who ran ERPI were technocrats, convinced that science narratives were a logical choice for a nontheatrical film genre. From the first Western Electric promotional short, *Finding His Voice*, the scientific bias of corporate engineers drove the aesthetic decisions at ERPI's educational division. Krows noted in his *Educational Screen* column:

> When most of those Bell engineers . . . became specific in their ideas, they thought of non-theatrical pictures in their own terms, namely, moving graphs and charts. They thought next of the men who had made a great deal of this sort of product—Carpenter and Goldman, whose scientific animation ranked high, and who actually had produced some intricate screen demonstrations of the sort for the Telephone Company[16]

Bell executives' and engineers' faith in communication technology as a way to popularize the rational discourses of science influenced their investment in educational film. Their bias toward a centralized, research-based communication industry characterized the Bell culture and shaped the direction of Western Electric's educational sound film division controlled by ERPI. This privileging of scientific method shaped the educational film department and its emphasis on school research and experimental method. The company focused on scientific and social-science subject matter and emphasized collaboration between academic and production personnel in the making of the first decade of educational talkies. As early as 1929, ERPI's first educational films such as *Administrative Departments of the Federal Government* were designed around academic lectures and widely survey-tested for a school curriculum. The early films produced by ERPI in this period included many one-reelers with graphic diagrams of scientific subject matter (often about audio or electrical technologies) or actuality footage of industrial processes or nature, done with postsynchronized sound.[17]

Experts from ERPI's educational department decided to produce a series of "Teacher Training" films in the early 1930s. It was the flagship series based on this institutional model of collaborative research and production. These training films would support the development of the relationships needed for building an educational film market, as they aimed to predispose teachers to the use of

---

[16] Krows, Feb. 1944, 22.

[17] William Lewin, "First Experiments with Talkies in American Schools," *Educational Screen* (Feb. 1930): 248. Lewin refers to the 1929 film as *Administrative Departments of the Federal Government*, which might be the same short movie as *Our Government at Work* (1929), which ERPI commissioned the Fox film studio to shoot. See Paul Saettler, *The Evolution of American Educational Technology* (Englewood, CO: Libraries Unlimited, 1990), 104.

educational technology. The teacher training series was the first of the ERPI educational film products used in research to reinforce the vision for the production of films in the public service.[18]

Krows's account of how these films were made highlights some of the inefficiencies of the public utility/research model. These ERPI executives, visual education specialists, and film producers hoped to create a new body of educational talking film distinguished from Hollywood film. This production environment led to the development of a set of realist stylistic conventions, mandated by educational experts who believed that film was particularly good at reproducing one's experience of the world, as well as by ERPI administrators who hoped to produce a distinct sound genre for a large institutional market—the public school system—in order to sell sound equipment. Visual education specialists, in particular, were anxious to get films made that demonstrated pedagogical value, which they could screen instead of the plethora of second-run Hollywood features available. Both educational specialists, who imagined genuine experimentation in the creation of educational films, and filmmakers, who thought a financially viable nontheatrical film studio might aim for high production values, ended up being disappointed. Krows's descriptions of filmmaking practices at ERPI reveal directors and cameramen who worked in frustrated collaboration, and often in conflict, with teams of educational experts. Frederick L. Devereux was the first manager of ERPI's educational department and would become the vice president of Erpi Picture Consultants, Inc. In his book *The Educational Talking Picture* (1933), Devereux optimistically anticipated a process that would combine budget-driven managerial efficiencies with efforts to organize the production around the most recent, pedagogically sound research. Krows, on the other hand, described ongoing conflicts over narrative versus realism, production values versus experimentation, and the limitations of early sound technology in the production films used for teacher education:

> Waller [a cinematographer with Hollywood experience] and his
> camera crews had been sent to an experimental school in Bronxville to
> photograph actual situations without rehearsal. If scenes were not
> spontaneous, the committee said, they would be valueless. Not
> knowing how the action might develop, all Waller could do was to
> light the room in its entirety, set up a number of cameras to cover

---

[18] See, for example, Richard D. Allen et al., *Modern Trends in Education: Syllabus for a Teacher Training Course Utilizing Educational Talking Pictures* (New York: Erpi Picture Consultants, 1933); and Laura Krieger Eads, *The Educational Talking Picture In Teacher Training* (New York: Erpi Picture Consultants, 1936).

every angle of visibility and shoot. What might become usable thereafter was just a matter of luck.

Waller, who had been accustomed to the most rigid budget economics in production stood by helplessly in this fantastic situation, while, to his everlasting disgust, the cameras ground out in one afternoon upwards of 16,000 feet.[19]

Though Krows dismisses this particular film project (saying it was "quietly shelved"), these classroom scenes would ultimately become *Classroom Demonstrations from Grade I to Grade VI,* a part of ERPI's Teaching Training series. It was screened for the NEA convention in 1930 and cited throughout the 1930s as exemplary of ERPI's new approach to the educational genre.[20] During the first year of production, Krows wrote in 1944, "a rule was promulgated that story form was thenceforth prohibited in any teaching film that we might make."[21] In Krows's account, practices in the production division were primarily focused on scientific approaches to creating films. They relied on eager young educational specialists like Edgar Stover and William Lewin, who had been writing about visual education since the 1920s. However, in addition to the ideals of young educators, it was crucial to ERPI staff and executives that these films remain "experimental" so as not to appear to compete with movies produced by either Hollywood or their own licensees.

The anticipated boom in educational films in the early years of sound simply did not materialize. Krows reported that producers who approached ERPI's nontheatrical distributors were deeply discouraged by the licensing fees imposed by ERPI. Absent a substantial catalog of films or affordable access to the equipment to display them, it is difficult to imagine how ERPI could have successfully marketed sound equipment to schools.[22] In addition, before 1934, ERPI's educational sound films (including *Finding His Voice*) were primarily produced and distributed on 35mm, prohibitively expensive for many schools.[23] Nevertheless, starting in 1929, the educational sound research division produced short reels. Its

---

[19] Krows, May 1944, 207.

[20] The film series is mentioned in demonstrations of teacher education in the pages of *Educational Screen* in the 1930s but with reference to a voiceover lecture rather than recorded sound. "Among the Producers," *Educational Screen* (May 1930): 152; Dean McClusky, "The School Department: Real Educational Talking Pictures," *Educational Screen* (Mar. 1931): 89.

[21] Krows, June 1944, 248.

[22] Ibid., 250. Krows reported that nontheatrical film initially ground to a halt when sound film first became popular. The ERPI licenses were prohibitively expensive, yet the popularity of talkies rapidly made sound seem a necessity.

[23] "16mm Talking Pictures Released by Victor," *Educational Screen* (Feb. 1934): 58.

main researchers, Devereux and V. C. Arnspiger, screened these experimental films for the company's school sites and educational organizations throughout the country.[24]

In 1932, ERPI transferred its educational research department over to its new acquisition, Erpi Picture Consultants, Inc., along with most of the research staff. As part of ERPI's attempt to create a market for its sound technologies, it had begun to invest in the nontheatrical film industry. The company spun off its distribution, financing, research, and production departments into separate but still entirely dependent entities. Erpi Picture Consultants "was created for the purpose of rendering services to prospective users of sound motion pictures . . . promoting programs of pictures to be undertaken by outside interests."[25] The new films, production practices, and bureaucratic structure conceived by Erpi Research Consultants, in cooperation with visual educational experts at major universities, were designed for education. They were distinct from entertainment films in their aims, aesthetics, and model of production. Devereux authored an Erpi Picture Consultants study, *The Educational Talking Picture* (1933), which begins with a description of how the production of educational film was fundamentally different from Hollywood movies. Devereux anticipated a production model where films were made by a collaborative team of researchers who worked toward a collective vision rather than by a single director with an aesthetic vision. Studio professionals and educational specialists would work side-by-side. Devereux described this process as follows:

> The evolution of the educational talking picture has been accompanied by rapid and revolutionary changes in production techniques. No longer does an individual educator "make a picture" entirely according to his own ideas. No longer does a lone writer produce a scenario and expect it to be translated into film just as he wrote it. No longer does a director take a scenario script and interpret it as his own peculiar experience or capabilities may dictate. The new educational talking picture grows from start to finish as a result of research and conference; group judgment based upon objective considerations and approved standards shapes its development. The building of the new educational picture is marked by a close integration of the work of research and production specialists, an integration that insures the

[24] Krows, May 1944, 208–9; McClusky, "School Department," 89; "Among the Producers: Summary of Erpi Activities," *Educational Screen* (Feb. 1934): 56.

[25] FCC *Telephone Investigation* (1938), 3:583.

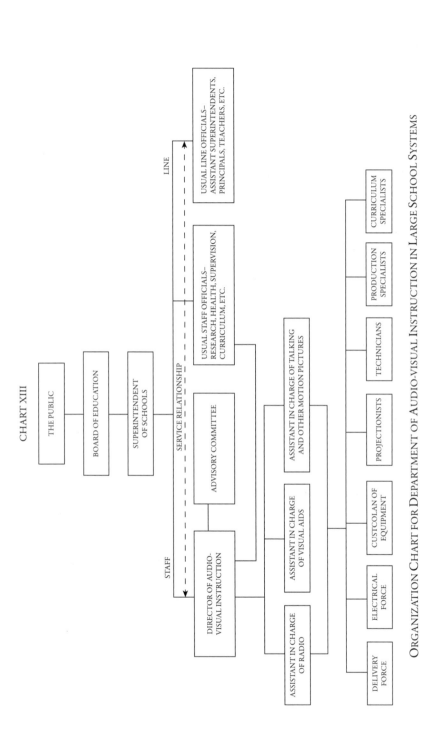

Figure 8.3. Organization Chart for Department of Audio-Visual Instruction in Large School Systems. Source: Frederick L. Devereux's book *The Educational Talking Film* (1933), 21.

maximum contribution of each in attaining the educational objectives of the picture.[26]

Erpi Picture Consultants, Inc., became the intellectual leader in producing educational film research, envisioning the proliferation of educational sound films through a new audiovisual bureaucracy. The strategy laid out in *The Educational Talking Picture* was for producers to design audiovisual curricula for public schools, universities, and adult-centered organizations. Devereux's research provided expert testimony, outlining an administrative plan for production, distribution, and exhibition on the state and local levels. Geared toward public education officials and educational specialists, *The Educational Talking Picture* proposed the implementation of a detailed audiovisual administration that would require the creation of new jobs, including audio-visual director, assistant to the director, subject-matter specialists, clerical staff, technicians, delivery staff, and production specialists (some of whom—due to ERPI's licensing demands—would presumably be ERPI employees or trained through ERPI production staff). Equipment maintenance and standard license fees were included in the bureaucratic structure and funding of an educational film program. Erpi Picture Consultants laid out a bureaucratic model for a public communication system similar to Bell's public utility system, which if implemented on a state or county level (as regional Bell Operating Companies were) would create an enormous market for educational films and equipment. This public communications market could rival Hollywood's dominance as a private entertainment market.[27]

Devereux proposed that every public school district in the United States develop a standardized audiovisual department responsible for the management of visual curricula. These departments would be in charge of everything from curriculum research to technical support. If ERPI maintained its licensing system, the latter group of employees (the entire bottom rung in fig. 8.3) would have to be either contracted or trained by ERPI to operate sound film equipment. School systems would be potentially subject to the restrictive licensing practices ERPI had implemented in Hollywood. Devereux was, in fact, proposing an enormous state-by-state system of interconnected audiovisual departments with an army of technicians employed by the Bell System and funded

---

[26] Frederick L. Devereux et al., *The Educational Talking Picture* (Chicago: University of Chicago Press, 1933), 21.

[27] This potential did not go unnoticed by Hollywood. *Film Daily* opined: "We now find this ERPI-Western Electric combine practically closing the windows as far as this industry is concerned and reorganizing forces and shock troops for a powerful offensive on the nontheatrical front. Installations in Hotels, Clubs, Churches, Schools, Colleges, Institutions, etc. is the objective [*sic*]. . . . Would this hurt the legitimate picture business? Answer yourself, for we haven't the heart." *Film Daily*, Apr. 13, 1931, quoted in Crafton, *The Talkies*, 133.

through public coffers with standardized sound equipment installed in schools. The company was well placed to be a primary provider of equipment if this genre should take off in the way that theatrical sound film had.

The executives at ERPI, with roots in Bell's research and development culture, thought they needed to prove that their educational films "worked." They hoped this would create a widespread market for educational talkies while distinguishing these audiovisual "experiments" from entertainment films, so as not to risk antitrust violation.[28] As a result, in addition to producing several films, the educational division developed research projects, installing sound film equipment in schools in the Northeast for the sake of showing educators that ERPI films, equipment, and curricula were effective. The company funded experimental studies in school systems in New York, New Jersey, Connecticut, and Rhode Island. It set up audiovisual departments in these schools complete with ERPI films, Western Electric Sound Systems, and technical staff. In addition, ERPI's research staff published several important studies of educational sound film in the 1930s. These included Devereux's *The Educational Talking Picture*, V. C. Arnspiger's *Measuring Effectiveness of Sound Pictures as a Teaching Aid* (1933), and M. R. Brunstetter's *How to Use Educational Sound Film* (1937).

Lecture film overlaid with on-location sound, accompanied by graphically rich, explanatory animations, would ultimately define the ERPI educational film, much to the frustration of production personnel. Educational specialists, according to Krows, wanted visual media to create rational subjects, not viewers who were absorbed by the medium.[29] The ERPI executives, producers, and researchers worked together to develop a model for educational production practices that followed the managerial and aesthetic forms of corporate research rather than Hollywood style. This kind of film would also find an audience within corporate communication. In addition to these efforts to create an educational film market based on a public utility model, ERPI worked simultaneously to foster a market for its technology among existing nontheatrical film producers who could serve the needs of the school system.

From Entertainment to Communication: The Voice of the Bell System

In the 1930s, Walter Gifford, then president of AT&T, publicly adhered to Bell's policy of abstaining from nontelephonic industry while discreetly supporting the pursuits of John Otterson, president of ERPI. In 1935, in hearings

---

[28] David Bordwell, Janet Staiger, and Kristin Thompson, *The Classical Hollywood Cinema: Film Style and Mode of Production to 1960* (New York: Columbia University Press, 1985), 299; Krows, Jan. 1944, 12.

[29] Krows, June 1944, 248.

before the FCC, Gifford claimed that he had not been paying attention to Otterson's aggressive attempts to control sound film technology in the theatrical or nontheatrical film industry.[30] Otterson saw possibilities for extending the uses of sound technology by expanding the reach of the communications industry. The emphasis by ERPI on educational films in the nontheatrical field was a response to the ways that Hollywood had resisted ERPI's efforts to reshape that industry on the model of the Bell monopoly. Public education—already state and federally funded—lent itself to the possibility of a large, centralized organization of film equipment, service, and distribution along the lines of a public utility.

The company's public discourse, expressed through Otterson's public presentations at Lowell Academy in Massachusetts, characterized sound film technology as a development of amplification technology, such as the telephone.[31] Otterson emphasized two points in his presentations about ERPI's role in motion pictures: first, sound film was an outgrowth of the telephone; and second, film had a greater social purpose than entertainment. In May 1931, *Educational Screen* summarized Otterson's presentation for the Halsey, Stuart and Co. radio series "The Future of Talking Motion Pictures": "Mr. Otterson pointed out the interesting fact that motion pictures are the product of telephone research. He also showed that the entertainment field . . . is only one of many fields in which the pictures will be used in the future," said the journal. "Mr. Otterson visions the talking picture as a factor of outstanding importance in the fields of education, religious teaching, politics, and industrial training."[32]

In Otterson's own words, restated in a speech at the Lowell Academy:

> The transition from the old to the new method of recording and reproducing sound was made possible by the scientific developments in the fields of telephone and radio research. . . . However important and significant has been the introduction of talking pictures into the entertainment field, we are confronted today with an infinitely more important and far-reaching application of this new found medium of expression. I refer to the use of talking pictures in the fields of education, religious teaching, politics, industrial training, and advertising.[33]

[30] Brooks, *Telephone,* 143–52.

[31] Crafton, *The Talkies,* 61.

[32] "The Future of Talking Motion Pictures," *Educational Screen* (May 1931): 144.

[33] John Otterson, "Talking Pictures and Other By-Products of Communication Research," in *Modern Communication,* ed. Arthur W. Page (Boston: Houghton Mifflin, 1932), 110, 114.

Since telephones were the progenitors of sound film, an argument was implicitly made that the medium belonged with a company that could operate as a "common carrier" throughout society, serving a communication function as telephones did already. Early sound projects made this seem like a reasonable option: Fox put news stories into films with Movietone Newsreels, while the earliest sound experiments by ERPI focused on the lectures of well-known public intellectuals, civic responsibilities, and educational curricula. Sound engineers themselves saw the explication of scientific principles or experiments as the ideal use for the talking film. As its substantial investment in educational film indicates, ERPI executives had high hopes for how the talking film could be used in public "communication" discourse through vocational training in education, science, and industry.[34]

Otterson's message was consistent when he spoke to Lowell educators or to a radio audience about the future of business. Positing film's primary role as one of education rather than entertainment, he found support from several sectors. During the 1920s and 30s, an active public and academic discourse emerged over the role of motion pictures in society, with particular concerns about the negative impact movies had on youths. Civic activists, government officials, prominent educators, and religious leaders called for using the new medium for purposes other than distracting the young.

Most of the audience listening to Otterson's presentations no doubt had never seen an educational sound film, other than perhaps *Finding His Voice*. In 1931, there were very few educational talking films in circulation largely because the producers who worked in nontheatricals could not afford the investment in equipment and licensing to show the films. It was a boon for educators that Otterson and the Bell System, one of the few financially viable large corporations in the 1930s, were supporting this different vision of film. Still, in order for ERPI to successfully reframe the form and function of sound film as a dynamic new educational technology, ERPI and Bell would have to break with some basic tenets of Bell policy, becoming materially involved in the production of nontheatrical sound film. This is exactly what Otterson did.

Making Markets: Between the Studio System and the Research Lab

Accustomed to the massive economies of scale of the Bell Company and the Hollywood studio system, ERPI executives were unfamiliar with the limitations of the underdeveloped nontheatrical industry. They mistakenly believed that the industrial and educational market for sound projectors and other sound film equipment would grow as rapidly and become as profitable as it had

---

[34] Krows, Mar. 1944, 116.

in entertainment film production.[35] Starting around 1930, ERPI began to market their sound production technologies more aggressively to nontheatrical production studios through a sales division that, according to Krows, was initially unsuccessful because of prohibitively high licensing fees. At the cost of "$300,000 a piece per year," few producers could afford sound recording technology. This price was calculated on the basis of a single production company shooting six hundred reels of finished films a year and ERPI's belief that each of these films would gross about $500 in royalties. At this time, however, there were few nontheatrical production companies unaffiliated with major corporations that produced films at anywhere near this scale. Krows (April 1944) points to this problem:

> It was supposed that picture production, apart from the making of school subjects which were going to require an unprecedented attention, would be cared for by non-theatrical licensees. Licensees, however, were not signing up as readily as had been expected. Nontheatrical producers generally were interested in talking picture equipment, of course, and many came to inquire about terms, usually to bow themselves out again promptly when they heard the originally stiff stipulations. Beside, the Erpi management was very particular. It did not wish to do business with firms which could not or would not produce evidence of their capacity to develop the field and pay royalties. The rub was that, in Erpi's opinion, only two or three could so qualify.[36]

Clearly ERPI did not believe that developing a field at below this scale of production was worth the effort, nor were they willing to lower their fees for sound licenses for independent or nontheatrical production for fear they would be forced to do the same for Hollywood. However, around 1930, based on the cost of a sound production license, it was simply not feasible for small educational producers to make sound films or for nontheatrical venues to screen them. While a few independent producers did license equipment from ERPI, as the economic realities of the Depression hit, these production

---

[35] Krows's narrative states this, but more to the point, ERPI continued to invest in independent studios, films, and small-format projector companies despite evidence of their lack of profitability. Many of these companies collapsed under the expense of ERPI licenses, only to become the property of ERPI. Additionally, the FCC reported that Otterson hoped to develop the nontheatrical field despite resistance from the bankers, who believed that this was not a good investment. FCC *Telephone Investigation* (1938), 2:403.

[36] Krows, Apr. 1944, 162.

houses found themselves in significant debt to ERPI, unable to meet their contractual obligations.

By 1931, in contravention of Bell directives that restricted the monopoly from entering noncommunication industries, ERPI began investing in independent theatrical film companies and production studios and financing struggling nontheatrical companies.[37] As ERPI's markets were threatened by the Depression, they stepped in to support these nontheatrical and independent film companies, using their financial resources either to pressure banks to finance studios or to subsidize productions themselves. The company also organized a financing company, Reliance, using Bell funds for their production enterprises.

The story of Christie Films and Metropolitan Studios, which would eventually become a General Film Studios subsidiary called General Talking Pictures Corp., is illustrative. Initially ERPI underwrote productions and pressured the Bank of America (unsuccessfully) to finance the Christie Film Company, an independent firm that produced comedy shorts. Christie subsequently invested in a sound production studio, Metropolitan Studios, to produce industrial sound films. While ERPI approved of this investment, it held Christie responsible for Metropolitan's licensing fees. Thus ERPI used their financing as leverage to gain control of the company when the Christie-Metropolitan combination struggled in the early years of the Depression. In this case, as in others, ERPI reorganized independents by investing enough for them to retain a controlling interest in the company to ensure the use of Western sound equipment. The control over a sound studio was significant for the nontheatrical field since few independent producers had the resources for their own studios.[38] When another acquisition, Educational Talking Pictures Company, Ltd., struggled, ERPI restructured it with Christie-Metropolitan as Western Studios, organized to produce industrial films using Western Electric equipment.[39] In 1935, Western Studios became General Studios, a wholly owned subsidiary of ERPI. General Studios would ultimately sue ERPI for its insistence on the exclusive licensing of Western/ERPI equipment. As the FCC later noted:

> In order to stimulate the exploitation of his company's sound apparatus . . . Otterson intended to create out of the Christie Film–Metropolitan situation a facility for the effectuation of his plan to exploit the non-theatrical field. The proposed Educational-Christie

---

[37] The FCC documented ERPI's break with Bell policy when it examined the history of ERPI's involvement in the nontheatrical film field. FCC *Telephone Investigation* (1938), 2:399, 403.

[38] Ibid., 422.

[39] "Production Notes," *Educational Screen* (May 1931), 144.

combination was intended to be the nucleus around which was to be built a comprehensive producing and distributing organization in the non-theatrical sound motion picture field.[40]

It is worth noting that it was the FCC, and not the courts, that stepped in to regulate ERPI's film industry trade violations, since the FCC generally regulated broadcasting. These proceedings were meant to keep the Bell System from overstepping the recently established legalized monopoly, rather than to protect the motion picture industry.

Otterson's effort to monopolize the production and distribution of nontheatrical film, while at the same time spearheading an educational research company, appeared to be an effort to reshape the sound film market in the Bell System's image as a research-based public utility. If this effort had been successful, ERPI would have been able to secure for themselves a vastly increased market for their sound film technologies without jeopardizing their identity as a communication industry.

Conclusion: ERPI Meets Its Legal Limit

The Communication Act of 1934 was the beginning of the end for ERPI's effort to recreate the film industry in its own image. With this act, Congress gave legal sanction to Bell's monopoly; however, it simultaneously put explicit federal sanction on its access to other industrial fields, especially sound film technology. The Bell Company had built the largest corporation in the world and had received exclusive access to U.S. telephone markets. Nevertheless, Otterson's burgeoning hope of extending this communication empire into film technologies would ultimately lead to the FCC's investigation into the company's far-reaching activities, resulting in a federal consent decree requiring Bell to divest itself of film production–related subsidiaries, including Erpi Picture Consultants, Exhibitors Reliance Corporation, Modern Talking Pictures, Audio Productions, General Studios, and Eastern Service Studios.[41] The sound-equipment division of ERPI became Altec Service Corporation, a privately held company with Roswell C. Tripp as the president. The newly formed Altec remained affiliated with ERPI, with essentially the same operating executives from Bell, who invested private funds into the newly formed company. Roadshow licensees would become Modern Talking Pictures, an

---

[40] FCC *Telephone Investigation* (1938), 2:401.

[41] Anthony Slide, *Before Video: A History of Non-Theatrical Film* (New York: Greenwood Press, 1992). Corroborated by Robert Finehout, former executive at Modern Talking Pictures, who provided me with his unpublished manuscript about the company in 2001.

educational and industrial distribution company headed by Frank Arlinghaus and owned wholly by the previously ERPI licensees. Similarly, ERPI's service and equipment department was spun off into Altec Service, owned by the previous company executives. Audio Productions would spin off to distribute industrial pictures. Under the direction of Victor Shumaker, once president of Victor Phonographs, what was left of the ERPI subsidiary would focus entirely on educational film and curricula until 1943. That year, the newly formed Encyclopaedia Britannica, Inc., acquired Erpi Classroom Films (then still owned by the Bell Company) and launched Encyclopaedia Britannica Films, which became an influential producer-distributor of educational films.

Nonetheless, Bell did not entirely divest many of these separate companies, nor did they divest their ownership of sound patents that retained aspirations of sound and broadcasting. It was not until 1956, with a new Western Electric and AT&T consent decree, that the courts successfully prohibited Bell from using sound patents to retain a foothold in the entertainment field. Western Electric and Bell were "enjoined and restrained from engaging, either directly, or indirectly through its subsidiaries other than Western and Western's subsidiaries in any business other than the furnishing of common carrier communications services."[42]

The story of ERPI may seem a cautionary tale of failed monopolistic ambitions. However, it is a mistake to allow this failure to be ignored in the history of media consolidation. The history of ERPI illustrates another way that a national film infrastructure might have been organized. If the federal government had not shutdown ERPI when it did, the Bell System, with its deep pockets, might have significantly reshaped the form and content of the nontheatrical film industry. At the time, ERPI had begun to conceptualize an alternative infrastructure for nontheatrical film in the image of corporate managerial expertise. Although this failed to reshape either Hollywood or the nontheatrical sector, Bell's influence over postwar educational film institutions deserves analysis. Many of the ERPI spinoffs survived the Depression, continued to thrive during World War II, and became major figures in the production, distribution, and exhibition of educational and nontheatrical films after the war. Many of the films produced by these companies were influenced by the scientific stylistic conventions of educational film research in the 1930s, much of which was implemented through the ERPI enterprise. The history of Electrical Research Products, Inc. allows us to imagine a different set of dominant genre conventions for the educational film; it also offers a case study for understanding how complex industrial structures beyond the movie industry shaped the nontheatrical film sector.

---

[42] Consent decree, *U.S. v. Western Electric Co.*, Civil Action No. 17–49 (D. NJ 1956).

Filmography

Finding His Voice **(1929) 11 min., 35mm**
PRODUCTION: Western Electric Co., Inc. DIRECTORS: F. Lyle
Goldman, Max Fleischer. WRITER: W. E. Erpi [Charles W. Barrell].
NARRATOR: Carlyle Ellis. ACCESS: GEH, LC/Prelinger,
MacDonald, UCLA (film prints); DVD *History of Motion Pictures*
(A2ZCDS.com, 2005); Internet Archive, www.archive.org/details/
FindingH1929.

9 EDUCATIONAL FILM PROJECTS OF THE 1930S: SECRETS OF SUCCESS AND THE HUMAN RELATIONS FILM SERIES

CRAIG KRIDEL

The 1930s was an especially interesting time for the development of educational film in the United States. Distinguished social science researchers from the country's leading universities were attempting to ascertain the effects of film on youth, and the Rockefeller Foundation was channeling substantial funding to various organizations as a way to encourage the production, dissemination, and evaluation of film in schools, libraries, churches, and community centers. Further, educational theory and school experimentation during this period was at a zenith as advances in progressive education were making their way into the classroom. The emerging fields of curriculum design and development, student testing, and program assessment were rapidly evolving as professors, school administrators, and teachers searched for new conceptions of secondary education. While "traditional education" focused on textbooks, lectures, and recitations, "new education," also called progressive education, was generating excitement among educators. This heightened interest was due, in part, to the use of innovative curricular and instructional materials—including film.

Many questions remain today, however, as we examine the dynamics among those educators who sought to harness "sight and sound" in the classroom.

This work was supported by a research grant from the Rockefeller Archive Center. I appreciate the assistance of James Allen Smith, Carol Radovich, Thomas E. Rosenbaum of the Rockefeller Archive Center, Nancy Cricco of the New York University Archives, and R. V. Bullough, Jr. of Brigham Young University.

Abbreviations used in notes:

AVK   Alice V. Keliher Papers, New York University Archives, Bobst Library, New York University

GEB   General Education Board Collection, Record Group 632.1, Rockefeller Archive Center, Sleepy Hollow, New York

HRSF   Human Relations Series of Films

In GEB and AVK citations, S = series, B = box, and F = file number.

Common funding sources complicate our understanding of the collaborations of educational media leaders who were determining the future of film in American schools when, in fact, many of their beliefs clearly conflicted. Similarly, common terms used during the period—such as "human relations," "progressive education," and "character education"—are difficult to fully comprehend as they now receive deceivingly simple definitions that mask dramatically diverse practices.

Within this mosaic of obscured educational film efforts, two important projects call for closer examination. Now often noted in film histories with just a few sentences, the "Secrets of Success" and "Human Relations Series of Films" programs are often referred to interchangeably to describe edited Hollywood film shorts that were used to teach character education and human relations in schools. Both projects are often identified as sponsored by the Progressive Education Association and funded by the Rockefeller Foundation. While somewhat accurate, these descriptions are also at times misleading according to what I have learned from the examination of archival documents and interviews with the programs' staff and teachers.

During my research on the Progressive Education Association, I read accounts of the Human Relations series and became suspicious of its connection with Secrets of Success. After looking at classroom transcripts, I found myself even more perplexed that Human Relations series film staff, who would have been selecting lynching footage from the film *Fury* for use in middle-school and high-school classrooms, could be confused with Secrets of Success committee members, who would have been discussing the impact of *Huckleberry Finn* as a way to foster Christian character. But I must admit that I became more "motivated" after hearing, at a recent conference, a dismissive comment maintaining that the Human Relations series was merely part of the Teaching Film Custodians' Secrets for Success series. I knew that while some of the Human Relations Series films were later included among the holdings of the Teaching Film Custodians, an organization that distributed rather drab, traditional 1940s and 50s school films throughout the United States, the radical, innovative spirit of the human relations film work seemed to have been obscured and overlooked.

This essay will illustrate the dramatic differences between these two film series; however, I will not engage in an analysis of the twelve- to twenty-four-minute edited excerpts of Hollywood films. Unlike other chapters in this collection that present detailed examinations of specific films, I will discuss the Human Relations Series of Films as an integral component of one of the most important, groundbreaking educational experiments of the twentieth century, the Progressive Education Association's Eight Year Study. While we will always wonder what caused the Secrets of Success and Human Relations series to become connected administratively, as they clearly were, I wish to introduce the more innovative efforts of the Human Relations Series of Films as their staff sought to integrate film into the educational culture of the secondary schools.

Secrets of Success: "A Series of One Reel Motion Pictures about Interesting People and How They Behave"

The Secrets of Success series arose from discussions in Boston at the 1929 Use of Motion Pictures for Religious Education Conference and the data from a 1930 nationwide questionnaire distributed to Protestant clergy who were screening motion pictures at their churches, primarily during their Sunday evening services. The survey described the use of film in religious education and identified specific titles that had been "used with success," although later the phrase "used with success" would represent the project as a way "to re-interpret success in terms of social values."[1] Recommending the formation of an independent motion picture committee to represent the movie producers and to edit existing materials for use by the church, the Committee on Social Values in Motion Pictures was formed in 1931 and sponsored by the Motion Picture Producers and Distributors of America (MPPDA), a conservative agency administering the Hays Code (the Motion Picture Production Code of 1930) by which the decency of films was judged.[2]

The Committee on Social Values, while committed to character education and moral teachings, also began to consider an administrative topic of great importance: the distribution of photoplays—films—to schools. Hollywood producers questioned whether films could be introduced into public education since few schools owned projection equipment. In many respects the future of educational film was being decided by issues of access and distribution as well as by the potential for curriculum design and development. The MPPDA provided funding and obtained permission from studios so that excerpts could be taken from "noncurrent theatrical films" and edited into the Success Series, "one reel motion pictures about interesting people and how they behave," to determine whether there was use for and interest in such photoplays in education. Ultimately, a total of twenty one- and two-reel edited 35mm films were produced and distributed to schools and colleges, churches, social agencies, and community organizations throughout the United States. Between fall 1934 and spring

---

[1] Secrets of Success Manual, front cover; GEB:S1–2:B284:F2966. In terms of the title, the director of the project stated, "We call these pictures Secrets of Success, although no one seems enthusiastic about the name. Youngsters like secrets; they are interested in success. We did not wish to suggest to groups seeing the pictures any effort to improve them." Howard LeSourd, "The Films in a New Field," *National Board of Review Magazine* 10, no. 3 (Mar. 1935): 5.

[2] Summary of Secrets of Success (1936); GEB:S1–2:B284:F2964.

1936, over 47,000 students and adults attended presentations and participated in over one thousand discussion groups.[3]

With strong Protestant beliefs and clear definitions of "proper character," the Success series distinguished between true educational experiences for youth and mere entertainment for the general public, thereby easing the MPPDA's concerns that such film presentations would become too similar to commercial moviegoing. (Since no proceeds were offered to the producers, no admission fees would be charged.) Further, the Success materials quoted self-proclaimed progressive educators of the period who underscored the importance of learning as "experience" rather than the mere presentation of facts. The use of popular film represented a powerful curricular and instructional resource, and Secrets of Success staff maintained that the series was "the first attempt to construct film materials for educational purposes out of feature pictures that were made for entertainment."[4] The Success series' pedigree could certainly be construed as within a progressive education tradition, and selections were edited to encourage discussion among students. Yet, merely being distinct from mainstream school practices does not suggest that a program would embrace the qualities of a progressive classroom and be worthy of sponsorship by the Progressive Education Association (PEA). For many members of the PEA, the Success program would have been seen merely as "sugar coating the curriculum," John Dewey's distinctive criticism of superficial attempts to construct child-centered educational experiences. More upsetting would have been the "fixed ends" of the character education series. Leaders of the PEA would have sought to forge a personal/social vision of character, defined through students' experiences and conceived as being in a constant state of growth, as opposed to the somewhat rigid (and Christian-based) conceptions of self-control, duty, self-reliance, loyalty, and the general teaching of ideals embedded in the Success series. In fact, some educators would have viewed character education as merely a way to introduce a form of civic religion into the schools rather than a redefinition of personal and social conceptions of democracy, a mission of progressive education.

Secrets of Success Instructional Methods

When educators and clergy requested a Success photoplay, they received not only the film print but also four to five posters of illustrated scenes and accompanying dialogue to help discussion leaders review specific topics. The narrative displays a rather narrowly conceived view of good character, returning regularly

---

[3] Report of the Committee on the Use of Motion Pictures for Religious Education, Boston (1930); GEB:S1–2:B284:F2964.

[4] Mark A. May, "Educational Possibilities of Motion Pictures," *Journal of Educational Sociology* 11, no. 3 (Nov. 1937): 155.

to the fundamental principles of the character education movement. The manual's instructional methods tell discussion leaders to introduce the film excerpt by reading aloud the accompanying synopsis and not to imply that the subsequent discussion will be "a chore." The following prologue was then to be announced: "The picture you are about to see is a one-reel excerpt taken from a photoplay of eight or ten reels. It is unfinished but you will find it interesting, so enjoy it. You all like to discuss pictures you have seen and we will talk about this one after it is shown. If we had the time and facilities, it would be pleasant to see the whole picture, but you will find in this twelve-minute movie some of the most interesting situations in the story."[5] Apart from the manual's predefined assessment of the viewers' positive experience (considered a progressive education "sin"), such structured curricular materials appeased a significant concern: the fear of inexperienced teachers improperly presenting the films. Teachers were told not to preach or moralize and, instead, to use precise words—"wise, sensible, useful, charitable"—rather than making more general "right and wrong" judgments. The solution, common then as well as now, resulted in instructional materials prepared in a "teacher-proof" format.

Within the context of mid-1930s secondary school education, the Success series represented a progressive teaching method by using film to present in "vivid form" the conflicts of life. Yet, here we are confronted with the complexities of terminology since progressive education proved to be a banner that anyone could wave. "Learning by doing" and "teaching the whole child" became simple-minded slogans available to any self-proclaimed progressive.[6] Progressive education–oriented experiences would not have been conceived with such established, predefined ends. The Success production of *Huckleberry Finn* was edited "to cultivate a spirit of social democracy in contrast to intellectual snobbishness." *There's Always Tomorrow* (1934) sought to "to facilitate family adjustments in terms of mutual obligation," and *Sign of the Cross* (1932) was shown "to perpetuate the best traditions of the past in our present social order as exemplified by the idealism of the Early Christians."[7] To envision this character education

---

[5] Secrets of Success Manual, 13.

[6] The term "progressive education" is, for some, considered to be vacuous and no longer appropriate to use as a descriptor. Nonetheless, certain fundamental beliefs defined progressive educators during the 1930s: attending to the experience, interest, needs, and growth of the students; viewing schools as a venue to define democracy as a social/political construct and form of community; seeking to integrate knowledge and to develop a more exploratory conception of knowledge for both teacher and student; drawing upon the scientific method as a means for educational and cultural experimentation; and accepting the dynamic, evolving quality of knowing. Self-proclaimed progressives, such as educational film researchers Edgar Dale, W. W. Charters, and Ben Wood, would never be considered progressives by today's educational historians, and few of their contemporary colleagues viewed them as such.

[7] Secrets of Success Manual, 36–37.

program—with its scripted materials, limited view of the abilities of teachers, and predefined ends—as falling under the jurisdiction of the Progressive Education Association was possible, perhaps, but highly unlikely. The leaders of the PEA were confronting issues of open-ended school experimentation, social imposition, curricular fragmentation, and democratic action. At their 1932 conference, PEA members were driven to a frenzy with the keynote presentation by George Counts who "dared schools to change society" and who reprimanded those in attendance for being politically inactive. By the mid-1930s and the time of Secrets of Success, the PEA leadership was engaged in a struggle for the mission of the American high school rather than developing a character education program that openly embraced Christian teachings and values.[8]

The Human Relations Series of Films, the Commission on Human Relations, and the Eight Year Study

A number of individuals and committees of the Progressive Education Association came together to form the Human Relations Series of Films. Specifically, the project was a component of the Commission on Human Relations, one of the three commissions that constituted the Eight Year Study (1930–1942), a national program that sought to reconceive the purposes of secondary school education. Sponsored by the PEA and funded by the General Education Board of the Rockefeller Foundation, the study consisted of full-time staff members who worked directly with the faculty of 42 high schools and 26 junior high school programs and assisted tangentially the efforts of 200 other secondary schools. Through "exploration and experimentation," what became a motto for the study, the Commission on the Relation of School and College (formed in 1930) addressed how the high school could serve youth more effectively. The Commission on Secondary School Curriculum (formed in 1932) designed general education materials (in science, mathematics, social studies, arts, and language) and, recognizing that further study of youth needed to be undertaken, established the Study of Adolescents project. The Commission on Human Relations (formed in 1935 and chaired by Alice Keliher) prepared social science–related curriculum materials—incorporating the then-innovative use of radio and motion pictures—and examined human problems faced by youth. The staffs of the commissions overlapped greatly, and their research, publications, and implemented programs served to completely transform educational practices in the

---

[8] George Counts, *Dare the School Build a New Social Order? A Challenge to Teachers and to the Present Social Order* (New York: John Day, 1932). I will accept criticism for this claim since some PEA members were interested in character education and since the PEA was known to initiate projects based upon funding. If the Rockefeller Foundation had offered the organization $200,000 for a character education project, a commission would have been formed.

Figure 9.1. Alice V. Keliher, ca. 1936. (New York University Archives.)

fields of curriculum studies, instruction, teacher education, educational research, and evaluation throughout the remainder of the twentieth century.[9]

Alice Keliher, an early childhood educator with considerable experience in film, gathered a loose-knit collective of progressives who viewed education not as an occasion to focus on the interests of the student but instead who focused on academic content as a way to forge a synthesis of personal and social values. They configured schools around a conception of "democracy as a way of life" and introduced a carefully designed method of teacher–pupil planning and a distinct conception of general education (core) curriculum.[10] Keliher and her colleagues, unlike the Success staff, trusted the ability of teachers to reason through complex issues, and they maintained faith in thoughtful inquiry and experimentation to create ways of making education more life-enhancing for students and teachers.

---

[9] Craig Kridel and Robert V. Bullough Jr., *Stories of the Eight Year Study* (Albany, NY: SUNY Press, 2007).

[10] Too often progressive education has been described as the tension between a child-centered and a subject-centered curriculum. Keliher and her colleagues were distinct from today's commonly used categories of social meliorists, administrative, pedagogical, and child-centered progressives. They represent what is now being called "Eight-Year Study progressives" who were academically oriented while also seeing student needs as both personal and social in nature and not merely as expressions of individual interests. The Eight Year Study represented the importance of educational exploration and served as an experiment in support of school experimentation, implicitly asserting that a healthy school was an experimental school.

The Eight Year Study's conceptual foundation allowed Keliher to explore the use of edited Hollywood film in ways that differed greatly from the Success series.

Human relations, as conceived by Keliher and others, represented more of a "culture and personality" approach to adolescent development with some allegiance to psychoanalytic thought and a strong faith in political and community participation. The simple progressive education slogan of "attending to the interests of the child" was transformed into a much more sophisticated vision of the personal/social needs of students and society. Human relations was situated in an emerging conception of adolescence, redefined in intellectual, physical, social, and emotional terms as a process with no definite moment of beginning and with no clear break between childhood and adulthood.[11] The adolescent was seen "as a functioning whole"—and not in isolated emotional, social, and intellectual dimensions, as conceived by the character education movement. This served as a guiding focus for the selection of Hollywood films as Keliher and her staff identified problems—personal and social—facing youth.

A Copyright Connection of the Secrets of Success and Human Relations Film Series

While the MPPDA had obtained permission from Fox, MGM, RKO, and Warner Bros. to prepare 35mm excerpts of noncurrent Hollywood films, the Committee on Social Values knew that to increase distribution to schools would be difficult if not impossible unless the footage was transferred to 16mm in what was becoming the standard film projector format for classroom use. With the costs of distribution, film editing, and duplication, and upcoming contractual negotiations with the studios, financial support was requested from the Rockefeller Foundation. Funding was forthcoming; however, the committee decided in 1936 "that the Secrets of Success should not be further developed as an isolated undertaking; that it ought to be related to the work Miss Kelleher [*sic*] is doing for the Foundation and that any subsequent pictures made in the series should be keyed to youth problems as revealed by her research."[12] Reasons for this decision are somewhat mysterious. The educational film world was aware of Keliher even though she was not involved in any ongoing project. Yet, why did they turn to her when she was fully immersed in other PEA committee work? I suspect Keliher served as "a cleaner," swooping into settings with administrative acumen and organizational directness—she was once described as "hard-boiled" in *Time* magazine—and maintaining focus and forcefulness until tasks were completed. This was the role she had adopted in the Eight Year Study, a reason many gave for her receiving recognition and leadership in the PEA.

---

[11] K. W. Taylor, *Do Adolescents Need Parents?* (New York: D. Appleton-Century, 1938), 70.

[12] Summary of Secrets of Success, 4.

The MPPDA and the Committee on Social Values anticipated difficulties in the copyright negotiations with Hollywood producers. Much was at stake, financially, educationally, and politically, in light of the "tremendous power" of box office films during the Depression: "The American people in unprecedented numbers are flocking to the movies to enjoy their brief moment of identification, finding such release from the actualities about them as they may. The life of the American adolescent (including the adult adolescent) is colored markedly by his movie experiences."[13] In fact, when the Human Relations series was completed in 1941, the first major accomplishment noted was that of obtaining the producers' contracts as "the opening wedge in securing the release to schools and colleges of films made in Hollywood for theatrical showing."[14] The MPPDA's administrators complimented Keliher's successful negotiations with the studios, a feat that warranted their decision to affiliate with her program.

While funding was assigned to the PEA, Keliher indicated that she would have no interest unless the film project was related to the work of the Commission on Human Relations. Her Commission at this point had redefined itself as an integral component of the Eight Year Study and was preparing a series of human relations books that would begin to transform educational practice during this period. Her publication, *Life and Growth*, written in the second person, introduced human relations as a way for secondary school students to understand themselves as well as others, thus creating a crucial balance between the personal/social dimensions of adolescence. Louise Rosenblatt's *Literature as Exploration* was another Commission work that helped to introduce her celebrated reader-response theory and transactional theory (an instructional practice significantly related to the film series discussion activities and curricular materials). Other books by psychoanalysts brought new dimensions for the understanding of adolescence to the field of secondary education.[15]

During the next five years (with total funding for the film component at well over $1,000,000 in current dollars), Keliher and her staff produced, distributed, and assessed the use of feature film excerpts in high school classrooms as a way to engage students in discussing issues of human behavior and in defining themselves in relation to family and society. Throughout the life of the Commission, Keliher consistently and specifically distinguished its work from the Success series. Conceived as a way to integrate the curriculum and not to serve as an alternative "sugar-coating" instructional method, she maintained, "We are dealing with a type of film material which primarily builds attitudes and

---

[13] Alice Keliher, correspondence to GEB/PEA (May 27, 1936), 1; GEB:S1–2:B283:F2960.

[14] Appraisal: Motion Picture Project (Jan. 1940), 1; GEB:S1–2:B284:F2962.

[15] Alice Keliher, *Life and Growth* (New York: D. Appleton-Century, 1938); and Louise M. Rosenblatt, *Literature as Exploration* (New York: D. Appleton-Century, 1938).

emotional responses and only secondarily teaches facts."[16] Adolescent needs provided the framework for preparing over sixty Human Relations shorts with themes centering on the family, an individual's adjustment to life, group relations, and the relation of the individual to society. In contrast to the Success series of character education, the Human Relations series' educational ends remained more open-ended and less deterministic, maintaining that behavior and the development of personality was guided by societal mores and varied among cultures and groups.[17] Unlike the character education movement with its predefined ends and predetermined definition of good character, few established norms were embedded in the Human Relations series as Eight Year Study progressives resisted any accusations of indoctrination and imposition of values. Film permitted educators to establish a safe instructional setting for youth to confront personal and societal problems. Classroom groups worked together in a progressive tradition of "democracy as a way of life" to forge common visions for a better and more thoughtful conception of society.

All of the Human Relations films were edited and framed in such a manner as to elicit questions from students (referred to as "the free entertaining of ideas"). Similar to the Success series, the shorts were prepared so that the issues were complex and not easily resolved. Students were placed in situations where they must "work out possible solutions and attacks on the problems."[18] The term "problem" takes on additional significance during this period since student "needs" were being articulated into personal and social problems as a way to move the curriculum away from a simplistic focus upon students' personal interests. This work was leading the way in attempting to resolve one of the field of education's greatest dilemmas: the conception of needs—an issue that had plagued progressive educators through the 1930s.[19] The Eight Year Study's companion group, the Commission on Secondary Curriculum, was developing "the resource unit" as a way to counter the rigid (teacher-proof) curriculum manuals and teaching plans typically used in schools. Keliher's film committee incorporated the resource unit in their materials and, rather than providing teacher-proof scripts similar to the Secrets of

---

[16] Petition to GEB (ca. Apr. 1938), 23; GEB:S1–2:B284:F2961.

[17] Petition to GEB (ca. Apr. 1938), 29.

[18] Alice Keliher, "Human Relations Education and American Democracy," *New England Educational Film Association* (n.d.), xi; AVK:MC-139:B17:F7,

[19] While this publication focuses on educational film, the conception of needs proves to be one of the more important curricular issues for the role of film in the classroom. For more information about this classic curricular (and instructional) dilemma, see these essays in the journal *The Social Frontier:* Boyd H. Bode, "Education and Social Reconstruction," 1, no. 4 (1935): 18–22; John L. Childs, "Professor Bode on 'Faith in Intelligence,'" 1, no. 6 (1935): 20–24; Boyd H. Bode, "Dr. Childs and Education for Democracy," 5. no. 39 (1938): 38–40; John L. Childs, "Dr. Bode on 'Authentic' Democracy," 5, no. 39 (1938): 40–43.

Success, maintained a faith in the abilities of teachers and students to use the film shorts in fruitful, open-ended ways.

The initial selections of Human Relations film productions represent a rather dramatic shift in content from the Success series. Both programs, running simultaneously, sought to portray personal and social relations topics, but Keliher's group ultimately emphasized social issues as a venue to help adolescents explore their beliefs and values. *Fury* (1936) proved to be the most widely distributed film and was edited into three separate excerpts, each displaying issues stemming from an attempted lynching. The *Private Jones* (1933) short portrayed a nonconformist drafted into the army; *Captains Courageous* (1937) addressed aspects of competition and its effects on individual and groups; *Cavalcade* (1933) illustrated war seen through the eyes of a mother; and *Black Legion* (1936) revealed the evils of intolerance toward foreigners.

Encouraging action among students was, for Keliher, the most important aspect of the Human Relations series: "These solutions and attacks on the issues should involve actually doing something about them wherever possible to prevent either the frustrating feeling that nothing can be done, or the feeling that talking is sufficient."[20] She described students forming a welcoming committee after seeing *The Devil Is a Sissy* (1936), a film about the difficulties of an adolescent entering a new school; conducting a housing survey after viewing an excerpt from *Dead End* (1937), which depicted a social-class housing incident; and planning a community recreation center after seeing *Alice Adams* (1935). Keliher maintained that youth "need to sense their responsibility for assuming action as a part of their citizenship in a democracy!" A distinct sense of involvement—"activity with meaning"—became the intent of the series.[21] The human relations shorts were field-tested in selected Eight Year Study schools and other educational settings, and transcripts were submitted to Keliher's staff to determine "how films are best used in the study of human relations as an integral part of a more effective general education."[22] While the project focused initially upon Eight Year Study schools, by 1941 the Human Relations Series of Films was distributed to over 3,000 schools throughout the United States.[23]

One of the more intriguing (if not astonishing) aspects of the Human Relations series is Keliher's staffing decisions. A 1940 Rockefeller Foundation document notes "the social views of some of the members of the Commission's staff resulted in a majority of its films' dealing with social problems."[24] Keliher secured

---

[20] Alice Keliher, "Human Relations Series of Films," *New England Educational Film Association* (n.d.), xi; AVK: MC 139:B17:F7.

[21] Ibid., xii.

[22] Appraisal, 4.

[23] Alice Keliher, Commission on Human Relations Report (Jan. 7, 1941); GEB:S1–2:B283:F2959.

[24] Appraisal, 4.

the services of Dutch filmmaker Joris Ivens as the first production director and later technical adviser and included his films into the series. Ivens, considered one of the most important documentarists of the twentieth century, proves to be a rather startling selection by a group of educators who sought to edit mere classroom films. Well known for his documentary short *Rain* (1929), Ivens was subsequently granted leave from the project to film *The Spanish Earth*, a 1937 documentary about the Spanish Civil War, and he would continue his distinguished career with *Indonesia Calling* (1946), *7th Parallel: Vietnam in War* (1967–1968), and *How Yukong Moved the Mountain* (1971–1977). Irving Lerner, another production director, was simultaneously filming the documentary *China Strikes Back* (1937). Helen van Dongen, who worked as a film editor with Ivens on many of his documentaries and also with Robert Flaherty on *The Land* (1942) and *Louisiana Story* (1948), served as the Human Relations series sound and film editor. The production supervisor, Joseph Losey, was active in New York City's agitprop theater while spending the majority of his Human Relations series time talking with members of the Hollywood companies. Both Ivens and Losey were later named members of the Communist Party and blacklisted by the House Un-American Activities Committee (as were other members of the PEA). All of Keliher's staffing decisions occurred in 1936 and represented a dramatic social, cultural, and political break from the religious leanings of the Success series whose board members, while contractually integrated into the project, were placed on a separate "special advisory committee."[25]

A Complicated Tale of Two Educational Film Series

The Secrets of Success series arose from a religious education conference and was sponsored by an agency monitoring and determining the decency of films. In contrast, the Human Relations Series of Films was staffed by many devoted radicals and communists as well as others who had been members of Freud's Vienna Circle. One program taught character education, the other experimented with a complex, evolving conception of human relations. While any published classroom transcript is merely a snapshot of the intention of an educational project and certainly not a comprehensive overview, what follows is a teacher-student

---

[25] Ibid., 3; Helen van Dongen, interview with author (July 20, 2005); Louise Rosenblatt, interview with author (May 2, 1998). Keliher's social and cultural views are intriguing as well. In 1937, she responded to frantic requests from a junior colleague who was in Vienna at the time with Freud for affidavits to sponsor Austrian Jews who wished to immigrate to the United States. She sponsored three émigrés and proudly used her American Film Center title to establish credibility with the State Department. Keliher's participation in national and community social causes increased greatly after she befriended Eleanor Roosevelt, who rented office space next to her residence in Greenwich Village. See "Alice V. Keliher (1903–1995): Fate, Frank, and Film," in Kridel and Bullough, *Stories of the Eight Year Study*, 113–19.

discussion excerpt (from 1935) resulting from the viewing of the Secrets of Success production of *Huckleberry Finn*:

MISS BAXTER: Huckleberry Finn did have to have his face washed. He didn't seem to like it very much. . . . Why do people have to wash their faces and hands?

PAUL: Because, if you notice on your hands, there's little holes. You breathe in—

BOBBY: (interrupting) Those are pores.

MISS BAXTER: One of the reasons you think you should keep your hands and faces clean, then, is because it is good for your health. Is there another reason?

MARGARET: Nobody likes to see one with dirty face and hands.

BOY: It looks terrible.[26]

Such comments are remarkably different from an excerpt of a 1937 class discussion following the screening of the Human Relations' Series of Films production of *Fury*:

LEADER: How could we eliminate the situation which leads to lynching? . . .

BOY: If you take the ring-leaders of a former mob,—put them in jail, it wouldn't take any effect because he doesn't know what he is doing. —I mean the people in the mob, any mob, even if he isn't ignorant, even if he is following the crowd . . . he doesn't see anything that would make him ashamed. . . .

BOY: Another solution would be if public officials would take a different attitude. In California after the recent lynching, the Governor issued a statement saying this was a lesson to the world that kidnapping isn't tolerated here. That is an encouragement to lynching; that acts as the sanction of the public officials. They do it then with a free conscience.[27]

For these two programs, years later, to be merged together proves most odd and unfortunate especially in light of the dramatic differences in intent, mission, conception, and purpose.

When the Rockefeller Foundation decided in the early 1940s to withdraw major funding of general education projects, the work of the Eight Year Study and the Human Relations Series of Films would end. The Teaching Film Custodians had been established in 1937, with some involvement from Keliher, and its films were available to schools by 1939. While today's account maintains that the Teaching Film Custodians assumed distribution of the Success series and Human Relations series, the Custodians 1941 catalog, with its array of content-specific

---

[26] Secrets of Success Manual, 16.

[27] Motion Picture Project (Dec. 24, 1937), 71; GEB:S1–2:B284:F2966.

instructional films, is culturally and politically quite different from the 1939 Human Relations catalog with social issues films and a theoretical discussion of human needs and relationships. No reference is made to Keliher's series in the 1941 Custodians catalog; however, the 1954 edition does include certain Human Relations series shorts alongside the training films, considered by some as "the curricular deadwood" of the twentieth century.[28] Alice Keliher seems to have disappeared from any references in the Teaching Film Custodians materials by this time. Clearly, the spirit of the Human Relations film group remained of some interest to educators even if not embraced by the Teaching Film Custodians. In the 1950s, a close colleague of Keliher's, Louis Raths of New York University, received a small grant from the Rockefeller Foundation to edit ten noncurrent theatrical films for classroom use that were similar in conception to the Human Relations series.[29]

This complicated relationship between the Secrets of Success and the Human Relations Series of Films and the many other Rockefeller Foundation–funded film groups of the 1930s and 40s warrants further study by researchers.[30] Similarly, the Hollywood producer's contracts obtained by Keliher and others call for further investigation as we attempt to ascertain the impact of profits and copyrights on the development of these educational materials. We must continue to explore and unravel the relationships and complexities among those educators working during the golden age of educational film in the United States.

Films in the Human Relations Series of Films

Alice Adams (1935). RKO.
Black Legion (1936). Warner Bros.
Broken Lullaby (1932). Paramount.
Captains Courageous (1937). MGM.
Cavalcade (1933). 20th Century–Fox.
Dead End (1937). Goldwyn.
The Devil Is a Sissy (1936). MGM.
Fury (1936). MGM.
Huckleberry Finn (1931). Paramount.

---

[28] Paul R. Klohr, interview with author (April 26, 2008); George Stoney, interview with author (May 20, 2008). Klohr served as an assistant for the Human Relations film project and later as director of the Ohio State University Laboratory School where he was a colleague of educational film expert Edgar Dale and educational radio legend I. Keith Tyler.

[29] Louis E. Raths, The Human Relations Training Films Project (July 1, 1950); GEB: S1–2:B226:F 2165. Robbins Barstow, interview with author (March 7, 2009).

[30] A more detailed essay, "Examining the Educational Film Work of Alice Keliher and the Human Relations Series of Films and Mark A. May and the Secrets of Success Program," appears on the Rockefeller Archive Center Publications website, www.rockarch.org/publications/resrep/kridel.php.

Private Jones (1933). Universal.
The Sign of the Cross (1932). Paramount.
There's Always Tomorrow (1934). Paramount.

Films excerpted for the Secrets of Success series

Alias the Doctor (1932). Warner Bros.
The Band Plays On (1934). MGM.
Broken Lullaby (1932). Paramount.
Christopher Bean (a.k.a. *Her Sweetheart*) (1933). MGM.
Cradle Song (1933). Paramount.
Gentlemen Are Born (1934). Warner Bros.
Huckleberry Finn (1931). Paramount.
Lucky Dog (1933). Universal.
No Greater Glory (1934). Columbia.
One Night of Love (1934). Columbia.
The Sign of the Cross (1932). Paramount.
Skippy (1931). Paramount.
Sooky (1931). Paramount.
There's Always Tomorrow (1934). Universal.
Tom Brown of Culver (1932). Universal.
Tom Sawyer (1930). Paramount.
Wednesday's Child (1934). RKO.
Young America (1932). Fox.

10 "AN INDIRECT INFLUENCE UPON INDUSTRY": ROCKEFELLER PHILANTHROPIES AND THE DEVELOPMENT OF EDUCATIONAL FILM IN THE UNITED STATES, 1935-1953

VICTORIA CAIN

Throughout the 1910s and 1920s, producers struggled to find a market for educational films. However eager educators were to show their work, few libraries, schools, or churches could afford to purchase projection equipment or pay substantial rental fees for prints. The commercial market was equally inhospitable to educational film, though for different reasons. Theater owners, convinced that free screenings by educational institutions would whittle away at their own earnings, demanded that theatrical distributors refuse to deal in educational films. Distributors complied, and "the result was stagnation," wrote educational filmmaker George E. Stone in a 1925 article for the *Educational Screen*. Without hope for distribution, many producers did not bother to make high-quality educational films. According to Stone, this stalemate explained why the vast category of educational film consisted largely of corporate advertisements, heavily edited versions of aging commercial photoplays, and worn-out reels of "some writhing grotesque of plant or animal behavior photographed and titled for sensational purposes."[1]

Convinced of film's educational potential, officers at the nation's most powerful philanthropic foundations spent the next two decades searching for

---

Abbreviations used below:

RAC   Rockefeller Archive Center (Sleepy Hollow, New York)
RF   Rockefeller Foundation Archives, collection held by RAC
GEB   General Education Board Archives, collection held by RAC
RG   record group

[1] George E. Stone, "Visual Education: A Retrospect, an Analysis and a Solution," *Educational Screen* 4, no. 6 (1925): 330–34.

solutions to the problem Stone had articulated. While the Carnegie Corporation, Sloan Foundation, Rosenwald Fund, Payne Foundation, and Twentieth Century Fund all sponsored research and experimentation in the genre during the Depression and World War II, it was the Rockefeller-funded General Education Board (GEB) and the Humanities Division of the Rockefeller Foundation (HD) that assumed the most prominent roles in exploring and sustaining the educational film sector. The Rockefeller philanthropies' initial approach to educational film reflected their faith in both the free market and the rationality of the public. In the mid-1930s, officers of the GEB and the HD sponsored small-scale programs designed to iron out existing inefficiencies in the production, distribution, and exhibition of educational films so that the industry might eventually sustain itself and perhaps even persuade Hollywood studios to enter the field. After just a few years, officers admitted that their relatively market-based approach to educational film had not produced the results they anticipated. Neither GEB nor HD officers were prepared to produce educational films themselves, however, so Rockefeller philanthropies instead pinned their hopes upon a nonprofit organization that promised to streamline and centralize American educational film.

The Rockefeller philanthropies' efforts to promote educational film are instructive for historians. Officers' debates and decisions offer us a window into the difficulties of penetrating what contemporaries called the "school market." Their embrace of film's pedagogical promise and their corresponding fears of its persuasive powers provide insight into how Americans of this era perceived the nebulous, ever-expanding category of educational film. Their evolving visions of how the market for educational film did and should work illustrates the importance of private foundations to the educational film sector in this period, and the reasons that the American educational film industry developed differently from its counterparts in other nations. Finally, policy-makers currently considering a market-based approach to education may find it useful to reflect on foundation officers' ultimate conclusion that such an approach undermined, rather than improved, the quality of educational film.

Tinkering with the Market: Rockefeller Philanthropies' Early Relationship with Film

In order to put his enormous wealth to use, John D. Rockefeller chartered several philanthropic organizations in the 1900s and 1910s. Chief among them were the General Education Board, charged with improving education in the United States and abroad, and the massive Rockefeller Foundation, which aimed to promote "the well-being of mankind throughout the world." The foundations' priorities and policies reflected Rockefeller's own nineteenth-century liberalism, his pragmatic embrace of capitalist realities, and his conviction that an educated public was critical to a well-functioning democracy.[2] The philanthropies directed millions to education and research. To the family's dismay, both foundations faced savage criticism almost immediately. Critics denounced them as tax-free efforts to whitewash the sins of Standard Oil, and labor leaders accused them of attempting to "Rockefellerize" political opinion through payments to scientists, economists, and other experts.[3]

Wary of sponsoring projects that might excite controversy or incite accusations that the family was "propagandizing," officials at both foundations tried to keep a safe distance from film. Americans embraced film's pedagogical possibilities, but they also associated movies with overt commercialism and disgraceful behavior. (The Rockefeller name had already been exploited by promoters of a scandalous commercial film, *The Inside of the White Slave Traffic* [1913], who claimed affiliation with the Rockefeller-sponsored Bureau of Social Hygiene.)[4] After World War I, many citizens also linked the medium of film with manipulative political propaganda. Understandably, officials of the Rockefeller philanthropies steered clear of film and its unsavory connotations. As one family adviser delicately phrased it, the Rockefeller interest in motion pictures "was not so great as in other phases of education."[5]

The Rockefeller Foundation did fund a few films in the 1920s on subjects officials pronounced "noncontroversial," and they met with mixed success. In 1920, for instance, the foundation's public health division commissioned *Unhooking the Hookworm,* which helped eliminate hookworm in the American South and tropical regions abroad. In contrast, two of the three agricultural education films sponsored by the foundation were rejected as unusable by

[2] Brett Gary, *The Nervous Liberals: Propaganda Anxieties from World War I to the Cold War,* ed. Alan Brinkley and William E. Leuchtenburg, Columbia Studies in Contemporary American History (New York: Columbia University Press, 1999), 1–14, 85–130. Also see William J. Buxton, "Reaching Human Minds: Rockefeller Philanthropy and Communications, 1935–1939," in *The Development of the Social Sciences in the United States and Canada: The Role of Philanthropy,* ed. Theresa Richardson and Donald Fisher (Stamford, CT: Ablex, 1999), 177–92.

[3] See, for instance, United States Commission on Industrial Relations et al., *Final Report of the Commission on Industrial Relations* (Washington, DC: United States Commission on Industrial Relations, 1915), 262–64. Cited in Kenneth Prewitt et al., *The Legitimacy of Philanthropic Foundations: United States and European Perspectives* (New York: Russell Sage Foundation, 2006), 68–69.

[4] Arthur Edwin Krows, "Motion Pictures—Not for Theatres," *Educational Screen* 18, no. 1 (1939): 15.

[5] Arthur W. Packard, "Memorandum on Talking Picture Epics," Nov. 15, 1929, folder 115, box 11, series III2E, Cultural Interests, Rockefeller Family Archives, Rockefeller Archives Center (hereafter RAC). The Bureau of Social Hygiene published George J. Kneeland and Katharine Bement Davis, *Commercialized Prostitution in New York City* (New York: Century, 1913). Krows recollected the scandal attached to Rockefeller in his *Educational Screen* column.

the U.S. Department of the Interior.[6] Occasionally, John D. Rockefeller Jr. personally financed productions he thought worthwhile. In 1919, for instance, he quietly provided $15,000 to Outlook Photoplays, a company said to make films to "combat the tendency to radicalism, socialism etc., by presenting in a popular way to audiences of farmers, working men, etc., the real function of capital and the underlying principles of sound economics."[7] In general, though, the Rockefeller family and its philanthropic arms kept a decided distance from the film industry.

In the early 1930s, a new mission to democratize information inspired Rockefeller officials to reconsider their aversion to motion pictures. Both the GEB and the Rockefeller Foundation's new Humanities Division resolved to participate in the general education movement, an effort that attempted to prepare Americans of all ages and backgrounds to become productive workers and citizens.[8] In this context, film seemed an ideal teaching tool. American suspicions of film had softened throughout the 1920s, and movies were more popular than ever. Additionally, psychologists and educational researchers had published several studies demonstrating film's educational potential. Professors at the University of Chicago, an institution founded and funded with Rockefeller money, had conducted a number of those studies, making the philanthropies all the more receptive to their findings that film, more than other media, had tremendous persuasive power. Aware that cinema had the potential to reach the very audiences they most hoped to educate, officers at the GEB and the HD agreed that educational

---

[6] The foundation's International Health Board was responsible for the foundation's brief foray into film production in the 1920s. In addition to *Unhooking the Hookworm,* the board commissioned and funded *What a Girl Can Do* (1924), a film about girls' agricultural clubs, and, less successfully, *A Boy's Interest* and *Better Homes,* respectively intended to educate rural boys and women about the contributions they could make to farm life. *Malaria and the Mosquito* (1925), a public health film produced by George E. Stone and acquired by the International Health Board, was more successful, proving almost as popular as *Unhooking the Hookworm.* "Resolution for Funding," July [16?], 1924, and W. W. Brierley to Register of Copyrights, Jan. 30, 1925, folder 222, box 15, series I–1, RG 26, International Education Board, RF, RAC.

[7] Starr J. Murphy to John D. Rockefeller Jr., June 25, 1919, folder 120, box 11, series III2E, Cultural Interests, Rockefeller Family Archives, RAC. In 1928, the Cambridge-based University Film Foundation requested aid from the Rockefeller Foundation in order to expand its attempts to produce films for Harvard courses. Though Rockefeller Jr. refused to allow any foundation money to be used for the purpose, after considered analysis of the plans and reassurance about the organization's close ties to Harvard, he personally donated $20,000 for production equipment in December 1929.

[8] Raymond B. Fosdick, *Adventure in Giving: The Story of the General Education Board* (based on an unfinished manuscript prepared by Henry F. Pringle and Katharine Douglas Pringle) (New York: Harper & Row, 1962), 240–41, 316–17. Fosdick, *Story of the Rockefeller Foundation,* 137–38, 240–42.

film was worth exploring. By 1935, the trustees of both organizations announced they were going to "strike out experimentally" into the wide-ranging world of educational film.[9]

Yet the production and distribution of educational film remained deadlocked. Though more than 350,000 nontheatrical projectors were estimated to exist in the United States, educational film remained unprofitable.[10] "Producers cannot afford to make films until a sufficient number of projectors is sold to make the work profitable, and the projector concerns cannot sell their apparatus because there is no comprehensive library of suitable films available for their use," visual education expert Clive Koon wrote in 1934.[11] A "vicious circle" crippled attempts to use films in schools, explained Robert Kissack, director of visual education at the University of Minnesota.[12]

To solve this problem, Rockefeller officers first contemplated sponsoring a public-private agency designed to nourish the fragmented field of educational film through consolidation and ongoing financial support. In 1935, they considered funding an ambitious proposal submitted by George Zook, former U.S. Commissioner of Education (1933–1934) and the current head of the American Council on Education, an advocacy group for higher education. Zook asked the GEB to fund the creation of a national film institute, one that would function along the lines of the recently established British Film Institute, a national clearinghouse for film production, distribution, exhibition, and research that relied on a combination of public and private support.[13] The American Film Institute would involve itself in everything from preparing scripts to shipping film reels, Zook promised, and in doing so, would expand "the potential contribution of the motion picture to the cultural life of America."[14] Zook's proposal,

---

[9] John Marshall, "Memorandum," Dec. 1, 1932, folder 50, box 5, series 911, RG 3, RF, RAC.

[10] The major studios invested little in the educational sector. There were a few notable exceptions. In 1931, for instance, Fox Film Corporation launched the Movietone School Series, producing ten short sound films for classroom use. The Movietone series was short-lived, as Fox was bankrupted by the Depression. This kind of educational production was piddling in comparison to studios' feature film work, however. Paul Saettler, *The Evolution of American Educational Technology* (Englewood, CO: Libraries Unlimited, 1990), 105.

[11] Clive Koon, *Motion Pictures in Education in the United States: A Report Compiled for the International Congress of Educational and Instructional Cinematography* (Chicago: University of Chicago Press, 1934), 81.

[12] Robert A. Kissack to David H. Stephens, June 5, 1936, in folder 2171, box 226, series 1.2, RG 377, GEB, RAC.

[13] "A Proposal for the Establishment of an American Film Institute," Apr. 1935, folder 2131, box 222, subseries 2, series 1, GEB, RAC. The proposed American Film Institute of 1935 is unrelated to the current AFI, founded in 1967.

[14] Ibid., 1; Report on New Programs in the Humanities of the Rockefeller Foundation, 1935, 17, folder 50, box 5, series 911, RG 3, Program & Policy, RF, RAC.

wrote an intrigued foundation official, offered "the best answer to the question of how we are to improve understanding on the part of the general public by direct methods."[15]

It is not entirely clear why the General Education Board refused to fund Zook's proposal, but it seems likely that officers were put off by Zook's sweeping vision of nationalizing educational film production and distribution.[16] Fiscally pragmatic and committed to free-market economics, foundation officials had no intention of establishing such an institute without the support of the commercial film industry.[17] Unless Hollywood cooperated, they agreed, the experiment would fail.[18] But the movie industry was adamantly opposed to Zook's idea. The major studios chafed against the idea of more government oversight, and they disliked Zook's determination to protect nontheatrical film from commercial pressures.[19] "They fear that the Institute might enter the field with a predisposition to be antagonistic to the industry—that it would have a militant reform attitude," reported GEB director Edmund Day.[20] These objections sounded a death knell for the institute. The plan to sponsor film production may also have unnerved Rockefeller officials, who rarely provided direct funding for the creation of media material so as to avoid accusations of political participation. Finally, the Rockefeller philanthropies provided seed funds, not maintenance funds, and believed organizations should become self-sustaining within three years or so. Rockefeller officers were uncertain the institute could accomplish such a feat, especially if entangled in film production.[21] Rather than sponsor a single bold program that might encroach upon Hollywood's territory and upend the free market, Rockefeller philanthropies instead elected to fund a series of smaller programs that they hoped would overcome the impasse in the

---

[15] Report on New Programs in the Humanities, 17–18.

[16] William J. Buxton, "Rockefeller Support for Projects on the Use of Motion Pictures for Educational and Public Purposes, 1935–1954," *Rockefeller Archive Center Research Reports Online* (2001): 2; Paul Saettler, *The Evolution of American Educational Technology* (Englewood, CO: Libraries Unlimited, 1990), 233–35.

[17] Buxton, "Reaching Human Minds," 183. John Marshall, "Memorandum on Humanities Program," p. 22, Jan. 1936, folder 51, box 5, series 911, RG 3.1 RF, RAC. For more on the political and economic ideologies governing Rockefeller philanthropy, see Gary, *Nervous Liberals*.

[18] Edmund E. Day to George F. Zook, Nov. 9, 1935, folder 2131, box 222, subseries 2, series 1, GEB, RAC.

[19] John Marshall officer's diary, Aug. 19, 1935, RF, RAC.

[20] Edmund E. Day, "Interview with Dr. Mark A. May, Subject: Proposed American Film Institute," Oct. 22, 1935, folder 2131, box 222, subseries 2, series 1, GEB, RAC.

[21] Haidee Wasson, *Museum Movies: The Museum of Modern Art and the Birth of Art Cinema* (Berkeley: University of California Press, 2005), 112–13.

educational film market through indirect tinkering. The GEB began by backing a series of programs designed to expand the production, distribution, and consumption of school films. Under the auspices of the more modestly titled Educational Motion Picture Project, the GEB provided the American Council of Education with a series of grants totaling nearly $200,000—more than three million dollars in today's money—to survey the state of school film equipment, publish reports on relevant literature, and examine what kinds of commercially produced motion pictures worked best in the classroom. Officials of the GEB hoped producers and distributors would change their work accordingly. The GEB tried to educate consumers as well. Each year, librarians at state and city departments of education, university extension programs, and school systems had to scan through thousands of film titles to decide what reels were worth buying. To help them make informed choices, in 1938, the GEB granted $47,000 to the Association of School Film Libraries, which published a catalog of movies that, according to the association, "recognized authorities have found to have real educational value."[22]

The GEB also worked directly with the Motion Picture Producers and Distributors of America (MPPDA), a group formed to advance Hollywood's interests, to transform existing theatrical films into appealing educational fare. In 1936, the GEB placed $75,000 in the hands of Alice V. Keliher, a professor of education at New York University.[23] With the reluctant blessing of the MPPDA, Keliher oversaw the preparation and distribution of the Human Relation Series, a collection of sixty excerpts from Hollywood feature films designed to foster discussion among high school students about conflict resolution.[24] Emboldened by the success of the Human Relations series, Rockefeller officials next pushed MPPDA chief Will Hays to persuade studios to allow a wider selection of theatrical film excerpts to circulate through the nation's classrooms. Despite protests from exhibitors, the major studios, with the exception of Metro-Goldwyn-Mayer, eventually agreed to accommodate this request. The resulting program was slow-moving but vast: throughout 1939, fifty educators reviewed 1,800 theatrical shorts, designating 360 appropriate for school use.

Officials in the Rockefeller Foundation's Humanities Division agreed that stimulating demand for high-quality documentaries and other educational attractions would be the best way to improve the market for educational film outside of school walls. "Informed public opinion has its own function to perform

[22] Report, "Conference on Motion Pictures," Oct. 5, 1939, folder 2160, box 226, subseries 2, series 1, RG 337, GEB, RAC.

[23] Robert McG. Thomas Jr., "Alice V. Keliher, 92, Authority on Childhood Education, Dies," *New York Times*, July 14, 1995.

[24] Saettler, *Evolution of American Educational Technology*, 113.

by exerting indirect influence upon the industry," explained a 1935 HD report.[25] Officers believed that, with the proper exposure and training, American audiences would develop an appetite for educational films, and would ultimately demand more and better examples. This demand, the report promised, "will have salutary effects upon producers" and production, and, eventually, the market for educational film would thrive on its own.[26]

As a result, the foundation's Humanities Division funded a number of programs, the most successful of which was the film library established at the Rockefeller-backed Museum of Modern Art (MoMA), which collected "historically and aesthetically important" films. Inspired by the example of the London Film Society, MoMA's librarians organized films into thematic series, which they rented at a nominal cost to subscribing universities, museums, and film-appreciation groups. The library also mounted international retrospectives of documentary films during the Christmas holidays in order to attract wide audiences, and especially educators and students. These programs delighted foundation officers, who noted that they not only generated revenue but also served to train the tastes of moviegoers. "The values gained in this way [will] without question have direct influence on the kinds of film to be exhibited in the commercial houses," officers predicted. Best yet, confident officers believed, the students watching movies today would be making them tomorrow, for "several of the present leaders in the British film industry came from these study groups, which in effect were laboratories for the development of critical judgment."[27] In educational terms, the library was a triumph, legitimizing documentary, instructional, and other film genres among college-educated American audiences and a broad swath of New Yorkers.

The Promise and Peril of Production: From ERPI to Minnesota (1937)

Though it had only been two years since the HD and GEB entered the world of educational film, by 1937 officers felt mounting pressure to take a more aggressive approach. While many officers still believed in letting the market drive the improvement of educational film in the United States, others felt that the nation could not afford to wait. Foundation officers and the experts they consulted were increasingly terrified by dictators' successful use of propaganda films in classrooms, movie theaters, and public squares abroad. Extreme political ideologies also boiled up in the Depression-wracked United States, and Americans fumed as they listened to radio broadcasts and newsreel speeches delivered by

---

[25] Report on New Programs in the Humanities, 18.

[26] Ibid., 15–16.

[27] Ibid., 18–19; Tino Balio, *Grand Design: Hollywood as a Modern Business Enterprise, 1930–1939* (Berkeley: University of California Press, 1993), 351; Wasson, *Museum Movies*, 150–84.

angry politicians and populists of many stripes. In this intensely political world, foundation officers agreed that intervention in education and educational film was ever more important—and ever more politically explosive.

Officer John Marshall soon became the philanthropies' most ardent cheerleader for more direct participation in the educational film market. A Harvard-trained medievalist, Marshall had joined the Rockefeller Foundation in 1933 to serve as an officer for the GEB and as assistant director for the HD, and pushed the Rockefeller philanthropies to invest in mass communication initiatives. As early as January 1936 he had urged Foundation director David H. Stevens to lead the national effort to develop film's educational potential by funding film production directly.[28]

Marshall's impatience to enter the field was understandable. The Human Relations series notwithstanding, visual education experts regularly pronounced that films intended as commercial entertainment made poor pedagogical tools. Studies commissioned by Marshall and Stevens in 1936 and 1937 reinforced this belief, asserting that films produced with profit in mind could never realize their full educational potential.[29] Moreover, Rockefeller officers increasingly admitted to themselves that the improvement of public taste through bottom-up efforts would take decades, and the dearth of first-rate educational films undermined programs designed to promote the genre in educational and commercial settings. "With the motion picture industry organized as it is, no one seems ready to run the risks of an experiment," Marshall complained in 1937. "The public has little opportunity to see films of types other than what Hollywood believes will succeed." Independent producers who did manage to create good educational films lacked access to the studios' wide distribution channels. As a result, even the best nontheatrical films were "apt to begin life in a smallish radical or art theater and end it in a lecture hall," observed critic and MoMA Film Center affiliate Archibald MacLeish.[30]

Prodded by Marshall, officers at the GEB and the HD began to flirt with a new strategy for promoting educational film: the direct sponsorship of film production. This approach caused considerable tension among foundation officers, especially because Raymond B. Fosdick, an attorney and longtime family adviser who assumed the presidency of the Rockefeller Foundation and the GEB in 1936, was adamantly opposed to the idea. For ideological and pragmatic reasons, official policy still forbade foundations from directly sponsoring film production, and Fosdick believed the prohibition was a wise one.

---

[28] See, for instance, John Marshall to David Stevens, Jan. 22, 1936, in folder 5, box 5, Series 911, RG 2, Program & Policy of Films, Radio and Motion Pictures, 1914–1940, RF, RAC.

[29] Buxton, "Rockefeller Support for Projects on the Use of Motion Pictures," 3.

[30] John Marshall, "Interview of George Gallup," officer's diary, June 23, 1937; Archibald MacLeish, "The Cinema of Joris Ivens," *New Masses*, Aug. 24, 1937, 18, cited in Balio, *Grand Design*, 355.

With very few exceptions, film production ran counter to the fundamental mission of the Rockefeller philanthropies, Fosdick maintained. The foundations should attempt to provide the public with thoroughly researched information to help citizens make educated decisions, not try to sway public opinion through direct appeals via mass media.[31] Entering the scrum of film production could lead to the accusation that the philanthropies were producing propaganda to further the Rockefellers' private economic or political interests. Fosdick, sensitive to the era's economic populism, had no intention of exposing the foundations to such allegations. If accused of politicking via film production, Rockefeller philanthropies could lose their tax-exempt status as charitable organizations devoted to public welfare. "*No foundation* would ever be allowed by public opinion to get too close to activities which had to do with the shaping of government objectives," film production included, Fosdick pointed out to Marshall. While foundations could legitimately fund experimentation in and study of moving pictures, film production represented "an area which a foundation could, with impunity, touch only indirectly, if at all." "This is not logical," Fosdick admitted in 1939, "but we are not living in a logical world."[32]

Fosdick also opposed the idea of sponsoring film production for financial reasons. The production of mass media was extraordinarily expensive, and equipment and production practices changed quickly. Successful Rockefeller-sponsored public health films produced in the early 1920s had to be pulled from public circulation just a few years later because they seemed so out-of-date.[33] Rather than gambling on specific films whose contents, styles, and technologies would become obsolete within a decade, the philanthropies would serve society better by funding research on educational film, argued Fosdick.[34] Personal experiences had made Fosdick wise to the perils of film production, for he had invested his own money in an educational film corporation in 1920. "We all of us lost our shirts," he later wrote. "The road back to 1920 is lined with the skeletons of organizations that thought they were going to sweep the field in educational moving pictures."[35] Scarred by the experience, Fosdick was determined to spare the philanthropies the embarrassment and fiscal devastation he had personally suffered.

---

[31] Gary, *Nervous Liberals,* 1–14, 85–130.

[32] Raymond B. Fosdick to John Marshall, Mar. 6, 1939, Rockefeller Foundation, Humanities Division, Program and Policy, RG 3, series 911, box 5, folder 50, RAC.

[33] See, for example, Rollin C. Dean to the American Medical Association, July 30, 1931, and Rollin C. Dean to EWS, Aug. 21, 1935, RF, RG 1, series 100, box 5, folder 39, RAC. For more on the history of the Rockefeller Foundation's public health films see Marianne Fedunkiw, "The Rockefeller Foundation's 1925 Malaria Film," unpublished conference paper, Quinnipiac / Rockefeller Archive Center Workshop, Nov. 2003.

[34] Raymond B. Fosdick to Ernest M. Hopkins, Mar. 14, 1938, folder 2128, box 222, subseries 2, series 1, GEB, RAC.

[35] Ibid.

Both officers and family members nonetheless continued to toy with the idea of making educational films. In 1937, Foundation officer David H. Stevens commissioned University of Chicago–trained educational psychologist F. Dean McClusky to review the history of educational film production in order to determine what factors were responsible for companies' successes and failures. Simultaneously, family advisers hired the industrial engineering firm of Ford, Bacon & Davis to analyze the economic status of ERPI, an AT&T–owned educational film company with a production arm at the University of Chicago, and determine whether it would be a worthwhile financial acquisition.[36] As officers had anticipated, both reports concluded that the educational market had tremendous potential, but current producers could not make high-quality educational films and still turn a profit. With no financial incentive to make good films, commercial studios tended to produce dull dreck, or ignore educational film altogether.

In order to balance educational needs and private interests, McClusky recommended a system whereby commercial companies, supervised by nonprofit advisory boards of educational leaders, would create films for American classrooms. Though production companies would operate for profit, the service motive would be dominant, and they would market only those films validated by advisory boards. Alternately, he proposed, production companies could be based at the nation's top private universities, ensuring their focus would be scholarly.[37]

These reports caught the imagination of Junior's sons, Nelson and Laurance, and the young scions began to investigate what it would take to acquire ERPI. As foundation officers had, friends and family advisers came down on both sides of the issue. Some pressed the young Rockefellers to enter the field. "The more I think of it, the more I realize its importance. It will have tremendous bearing on

[36] Though McClusky's report has now vanished from the archives, the information it provided proved extremely useful in the family's economic analysis of the industry's past and future. Fortunately, it is still possible to piece together at least some of the report's contents from other sources. Rockefeller philanthropic officers urged McClusky to keep his research a secret, and became furious when he publicly described his work. While they circulated his report among themselves and Rockefeller family members, they never distributed or published his findings, though correspondence routinely described his report as astute, thorough, and useful to those thinking about investing in the field of educational film. On the reports, see Saettler, *Evolution of American Educational Technology*, 106–8; Ford, Bacon & Davis, Inc., "Preliminary Report: Educational Motion Pictures," Jan. 8, 1937, folder 127, series 12, RG II2E, Cultural Interests, Rockefeller Family Archives, RAC. On the Rockefeller philanthropies' desire for discretion, see John Marshall to F. Dean McClusky, Sept. 20, 1937, folder 2913, box 243, series 200, RG 1.1, RF, RAC;. John Marshall to Lyman Bryson, Aug. 14, 1939, box 233, folder 2672, series 200, RG 1.1, RF, RAC.

[37] F. Dean McClusky, *Motion Pictures for the Schools* (Rockefeller Foundation, 1937), 25–26, cited by Saettler, *The Evolution of American Educational Technology*, 107–8.

the future and events to come," wrote one friend.[38] Others were less enthusiastic. The reports "point unquestionably to the existence of a market and potential great demand for the right kind of pictures," admitted family financial adviser Arthur W. Packard. But, he cautioned, the acquisition of ERPI would be an expensive gamble. "One or a group must be prepared to advance anywhere from $4,000,000 to $8,000,000 and be ready at least to write [this] off as a loss," Packard warned. If they hoped to turn a profit, Packard advised, the brothers would do well to hold onto their money for a few years more, until the field of educational film was more mature. Otherwise, they shouldn't expect to make anything "but more and better knowledge."[39] Their plans came to naught: when the young men approached their father for the money, he flatly refused to fund the venture.

Chastened but still intrigued by film's educational promise, Nelson Rockefeller next attempted to transform ERPI into the kind of nonprofit McClusky had described. To do so, he enlisted the help of University of Chicago president Robert Hutchins, former advertising executive William Benton, and University of Chicago dean Beardsley Ruml (for good measure, Nelson persuaded a friend, architect Wallace Harrison, to join them). The group proposed that the GEB finance the purchase of ERPI, but turn control of the business over to them and a handpicked group of representatives from select private universities. The resulting company would not only produce educational films but also distribute those films to educational institutions and, later on, to broader audiences. Under their expert guidance, the group declared, ERPI would become "an aggressive business enterprise with the advantages of direct ownership, but with its primary purpose the serving of American education."[40]

The group's proposal appealed to the economic hopes and political fears of GEB officials. "Every indication is that the interest in educational pictures is now gathering enough momentum to sweep across the educational world," they wrote. "The opportunity is being studied by various groups, some interested in the money-making possibilities, others in indoctrinating the young with their own political and economic theories. There is danger that a group may enter the field whose self-seeking motives may turn this powerful medium into an instrument [that is] harmful rather than beneficial. The opportunity should be seized by those whose primary and only interest is the welfare of the American educational system."[41]

---

[38] David H. Stevens interview with F. Dean McClusky, Jan. 20, 1937, folder 2913, box 243, series 200, RG 1.1, RF, RAC.

[39] J. C. Rowevsky to Nelson A. Rockefeller, June 7, 1937, folder 126, box 12, series III2E, Office of Mssrs. Rockefeller, RAC.

[40] Arthur W. Packard to Nelson A. Rockefeller, Mar. 24, 1937, folder 126, box 12, series III2E, Office of Mssrs. Rockefeller, RAC.

[41] Robert Maynard Hutchins, Nelson Rockefeller, Laurance Rockefeller, Beardsley Ruml, Wallace Harrison, and William Benton to the General Education Board, memorandum, 1937, folder 126, box 12, series III 2E, Office of Mssrs. Rockefeller, RAC.

Straightaway, Fosdick dismissed the ERPI plan as financially impractical. The economy had recently plunged back into a deep recession, and officials would have had to dip into the foundation's principal in order to purchase the production company. This, Fosdick maintained, was unthinkable.[42] Dartmouth president Ernest Hopkins, a personal friend, begged him to reconsider. "With the growing technique of propaganda and the growing influence of propaganda, truth every day becomes less and less effective in determining men's opinions and beliefs," he wrote.[43] The Rockefeller philanthropies, he asserted, had a duty to produce films that would counteract such propaganda, for the foundations were among the only organizations in the United States that could both finance and wisely guide the production of competing messages. But Fosdick held firm. "You have a feeling of urgency about this matter which frankly I do not share," he wrote. "Why should we finance the mistakes and discouragements which other organizations are bound to make anyway?"[44] Accordingly, the GEB declined to fund ERPI's purchase.

But ongoing lobbying by Marshall and Stevens, the Rockefeller sons, and various advisers eventually succeeded, and the foundations began to experiment with film production, albeit on a much smaller scale than its advocates originally envisioned. By December, reiterating their commitment to invest only in programs that could become self-sustaining within a few years, Rockefeller officers agreed to sponsor a handful of experiments in educational film production.[45] The GEB granted $134,000 to Robert Kissack, director of the University of Minnesota's Visual Education Unit, to produce "dramatic and emotionalized" alternatives to the dry instructionals that flickered on the nation's classroom screens in the 1930s.[46] If Kissack's project succeeded, officers optimistically conjectured, universities across the nation might be induced to serve as centers for the production of educational film.

Rockefeller officers also experimented with the sponsorship of documentary, a thriving new form of educational film. Hoping to promote "a new profession or, perhaps better, a kind of working guild" of documentary filmmakers in the United States, officers in the Foundation's Humanities Division encouraged filmmakers to learn more about international developments in their field, and funded a series of visits by French and British documentary filmmakers to the film library at MoMA and other sites around the nation.[47] Rockefeller philanthropies also

---

[42] Ibid.

[43] Raymond B. Fosdick to Ernest M. Hopkins, Mar. 14, 1938, folder 2128, box 222, subseries 2, series 1, GEB, RAC.

[44] Ernst M. Hopkins to Raymond B. Fosdick, Mar. 2, 1938, folder 2128, box 222, subseries 2, series 1, GEB, RAC.

[45] Fosdick to Hopkins, Mar. 14, 1938.

[46] Cited in Buxton, "Rockefeller Support for Projects on the Use of Motion Pictures," 3.

[47] Robert Kissack to David H. Stevens, Mar. 16, 1937, folder 2171, box 226, subseries 2, series 1, RG 377, GEB, RAC.

funded American photographers and documentarians who wished to travel to European film institutes and university drama departments for inspiration, exhorting grant recipients to "develop the medium, to work out new techniques appropriate to purposes other than entertainment."[48]

The American Film Center Fiasco, 1938–1946

Increasingly anxious about the power of propaganda, Marshall continued to push the GEB and the HD to consider new approaches to the promotion of educational film, even if these required deviating from established practices. Yet Fosdick and other foundation officers remained committed to the idea that the market would eventually take care of educational film, and, ever concerned about the expense and political ramifications of directly funding film production, they remained hesitant. In 1938, a proposal submitted by the charming Donald Slesinger, formerly a dean at the University of Chicago and the current head of the Department of Education of the 1939 New York World's Fair, seemed to provide a solution. Slesinger proposed founding an American Film Center (AFC), a public-private organization whose structure closely resembled the venture Zook had outlined just a few years earlier.

The philanthropies' officers were now more willing to consider funding a national film clearinghouse because of their recent conversations with leaders of educational film in Great Britain. In the winter of 1938, Rockefeller funds had paid for British documentarian Paul Rotha and London Film Centre director John Grierson to lecture at MoMA and Columbia University for six months. Marshall and HD officers had taken the opportunity to attend their lectures and speak at length with both about the state of educational film in the United States and abroad. According to Rotha, Britain's integrated system of government and private support had allowed its educational film industry—and the production of documentaries in particular—to flourish. The lack of participation by "educationalists," the fractured infrastructure of educational film production, and the absence of a similar public-private partnership, he argued, had crippled educational film in the United States.[49] "How ripe the time is here," Marshall mused in his diary after conversations with Rotha and Grierson. "What seems to be needed is a film center comparable to Grierson's in London."[50]

---

[48] John Marshall memo to TBA, Jan. 19, 1939, folder 50, box 5, series 911, RG 3, Program & Policy, RF, RAC. Buxton, "Reaching Human Minds," 185–86.

[49] Memorandum to David H. Stevens, Jan. 22, 1936, 1, folder 50, box 5, series 911, RG 3, RF, RAC.

[50] Balio, *Grand Design*, 374–76; Paul Rotha, "The Outlook for Documentary Films," *New York Times*, May 1, 1938.

As a result, in June, when Donald Slesinger asked Marshall and David Stevens if they would consider funding a centralized consulting agency for educational and documentary film production, they agreed to look at his proposal. "What film needed," Slesinger declared, "was not another producing unit but some central thinking and planning unit."[51] The agency would charge low fees for its assistance to producers, and this revenue would allow it to become self-sustaining. Slesinger proposed creating an American Film Center (AFC), which, he promised, would do "what Hollywood would not."[52] By "keeping its single aim—the promotion of the production and use of films of educational value—constantly before it," he promised that the Film Center would limit itself to "education, broadly interpreted."[53] Slesinger assured them he had no interest in producing propaganda, but simply wanted to help furnish Americans with "the common experience basic to democratic government."[54]

Rockefeller officials were open to Slesinger's proposal, and assured by his self-presentation. Such a center would let the Rockefeller philanthropies guide the course of educational film production without engaging in it directly. It would encourage the conditions under which democracy could flourish, but still permit the foundations to maintain their status as objective research institutions while at the same time encouraging the conditions under which democracy could flourish. Finally, it would allow Rockefeller officers to resuscitate their original vision of stimulating public demand for educational film. And the charismatic Slesinger seemed to have the ideal credentials to helm such an operation. In November 1938, the HD sent the center the first installment of what would come to almost $300,000 in grants over the next ten years.

The American Film Center provided educational film producers with the resources to see their films from idea to exhibition, serving as an informal studio system for educational film. It took on tasks large and small, estimating costs for prospective producers, making suggestions on films' contents and forms, recommending production units and staff, writing and reviewing scripts, editing footage, and advising and assisting with distribution.[55] In its first two years, the AFC planned a documentary on higher education for women; assisted the New

---

51 John Marshall, "Developments in Humanities Program in Motion Pictures," RG 1.1, series 200, box 199, folder 2383, RF, RAC.

52 Donald Slesinger to David H. Stevens, Dec. 28, 1938, folder 2383, box 199, American Film Center Papers, RAC.

53 American Film Center Report, Nov. 2, 1939, folder 2393, box 200, American Film Center, cited in Gary, *Nervous Liberals,* 110.

54 Donald Slesinger to John Marshall, July 9, 1938, folder 2383, box 199, American Film Center Papers, RAC.

55 Joan Ogden, "Rockefeller Foundation and the Film," 1964, 22, folder 52, box 5, series 911, RG 3, RF, RAC.

York Zoological Society with natural history documentaries; helped to prepare training films for the National Association of Housing Officials; and pieced together school films on farming out of reels originally shot for farmers by the U.S. Department of Agriculture. It provided similar services to the Progressive Education Association, the Greater New York Fund, the United States Children's Bureau, the State of Missouri Conservation Commission, and the Bureau of the Census.[56] It supported independent filmmakers as well, coproducing *Day after Day* (1940), a short documentary about the Henry Street Settlement's Visiting Nurse Service in New York, and assisting with other films intended to raise social awareness. Following the lead of other Rockefeller-sponsored programs, the AFC also worked to improve the distribution of educational films to libraries and schools. As well, it attempted to facilitate the international market for such films, organizing an exchange of cultural and educational films with Latin America.[57]

Though it served as an alternative to the commercial film industry, the AFC attempted to collaborate, rather than compete, with Hollywood studios. After a trip to Los Angeles with Slesinger in April 1939, Marshall enthused that the AFC "has an opportunity in Hollywood that was by no means evident to us in New York." "People in the industry, having gone serious themselves, believe that the audience is ready to take much more serious stuff than what it is getting," Marshall and Slesinger wrote in a joint memorandum. The AFC might be useful not only to independent producers but also to Hollywood bigwigs newly concerned about the state of the world and the nation. The AFC could help Hollywood filmmakers make their films more accurate, more meaningful, and more educational—everything "that Hollywood lacks experience in handling." The AFC, they suggested, could serve as an intermediary between Hollywood and academics, and help studios work within documentary's constraints.[58] The AFC subsequently consulted on films like *So Gallantly Gleaming*, an unrealized United Artists feature about the opening of the American West, and Warner Bros.' *Dr. Ehrlich's Magic Bullet* (1940), which dramatized scientists' struggle to develop antimicrobial drugs.

As the United States drew closer to war, Slesinger's vision of the AFC's future became grander and more political. He frequently hinted that the AFC should assume the power of a government agency, in order to centralize and coordinate the production and distribution of the nation's film propaganda. By the time the United States began to fight, Slesinger and his assistant, John

---

[56] Donald Slesinger, "American Film Center Mid-Term Report," Nov. 5, 1938, and "American Film Center, Report of Work," Nov. 2, 1939, folder 2393, box 200, series 200, RG 1.1, RF, RAC.

[57] Buxton, "Rockefeller Support for Projects on the Use of Motion Pictures," 6; Gary, *Nervous Liberals*, 110.

[58] Memorandum on Hollywood visit, John Marshall and Donald Slesinger, Apr. 1939, folder 50, box 5, series 911, RG 3, Program & Policy, RF, RAC.

Devine, had assumed almost total control of the motion picture efforts of the Office of Civilian Defense. The AFC also contracted with the overseas Office of War Information, advising the department on films intended for propaganda abroad.[59] Rockefeller officials increasingly worried that Slesinger had ceased to distinguish between propaganda and education, but held their tongues, for the AFC was earning high praise from government officials for its contributions to the war effort. Slesinger himself was well respected by government officials, who frequently consulted him for advice. What's more, the AFC was earning its keep; between 1940 and 1942 the Film Center earned as much or more from clients for its services as it received from the foundation.[60]

Officials of the HD, pleased with the organization's success and persuaded by Slesinger's vision, ignored indications that all was not well at the AFC. Slesinger had successfully cultivated relationships with government officials, but his angry denouncements of communism alienated many of the nation's best documentary filmmakers, whose politics leaned left. He couldn't seem to keep a full staff, and departing employees bitterly described his frustrating management style and readiness to stretch financial truths to get what he wanted.[61] Facing the loss of his primary clients after Congress dissolved the Office of Civilian Defense in 1943, Slesinger imperiled the AFC's reputation for ideological and financial independence by turning back to Swift & Company for funding. At the firm's suggestion, the Film Center produced *Red Wagon* (194?), a hagiographic biopic of Swift company founder Gustavus Swift.[62] While these films pleased the Swift company, critics dismissed them as little better than advertising. Nonetheless, through the force of his personality and the strength of his longstanding relationship with Rockefeller officials, Slesinger won continuing support from the HD as well as grants from other foundations. But by 1945, it had become clear to HD officers that the AFC was on shaky financial ground. Rockefeller officials decided to see their original grant through, but they agreed that the Film Center would be on its own after 1947.

In 1946, however, the extent of Slesinger's mismanagement became impossible to ignore. In January, the managing editor of the AFC magazine, *Film News*, resigned over what she tactfully called Slesinger's "misrepresentations of fact."[63] Marshall, still eager for the center to succeed, looked the other way. But in June, Edwin Embree, head of the Rosenwald Fund, sent the Rockefeller Foundation an urgent telegram: to cover administrative costs, Slesinger had

---

[59] Gary, *Nervous Liberals*, 112–13.

[60] John Marshall, memorandum, Dec. 1, 1942, p. 1, folder 51, box 5, series 911, RG 3, Program & Policy, RF, RAC.

[61] See, for example, Jeannette Samuelson to Thomas Baird, Jan. 5, 1946, folder 2392, box 200, series 200, RG 1.1, RF, RAC.

[62] Ogden, "Rockefeller Foundation and the Film."

[63] Jeannette Samuelson to Thomas Baird, Jan. 5, 1946, folder 2392, box 200, series 200, RG 1.1, RF, RAC.

misappropriated a $30,000 Rosenwald grant intended for the production of a film on race relations. Inquiring further, Marshall learned the AFC was bankrupt, and had already spent the money it was expecting from the Rockefeller Foundation for the second half of the year. Rockefeller officials promptly cut off the AFC's funding and closed its offices at Rockefeller Plaza.[64]

Though educational film production had surged as a result of wartime demands for training films and increasing interest in audiovisual education, immediately after the war educational film remained economically marginal. "Sponsors, distributors, and film users would do well to assume that the future of nontheatrical films lies mainly outside the Hollywood orbit," announced a 1949 report on educational film sponsored by the Twentieth Century Fund. According to the report, studios found the tiny profit margins, specialized techniques, and complicated distribution issues of educational film off-putting: "Hollywood companies find the nontheatrical water too chilly for more than a brief footwetting."[65] Yet Hollywood inadvertently continued to hinder the production of educational film. As a dejected John Marshall wrote in an interoffice memo that same year, Hollywood studios tended to cannibalize successful experiments in educational film, for they "absorbed and turned to their own purposes talented personnel which has developed outside industry, as they have ordinarily been able to at the salaries they can offer."[66]

Burned by his experience with Slesinger, frustrated by the sluggish pace of change in the market for educational film, Marshall slowly backed away from the many programs he had championed in the 1930s. The AFC's troubled efforts to sponsor film production during the war had changed the officer's outlook on the foundation's role in the sector. Film, if it was good, produced an "immediate and decisive impression" in the viewer, he wrote. To intentionally elicit this kind of reaction ran perilously close to the production of propaganda, Marshall continued, which the foundation refused to support, "however meritorious the purpose or disinterested the intention." Finally, the magnitude of production costs demanded more than the foundation could responsibly provide, and "less expensive proposals seldom can involve first-rate talent, with the result that their outcomes are at best second or third-rate," he declared.[67] The HD and the GEB followed Marshall's lead, refusing to extend grants to the organizations they had funded throughout the 1930s and 1940s.

---

[64] James V. Hatch, *Sorrow Is the Only Faithful One: The Life of Owen Dodson* (Champaign: University of Illinois Press, 1995), 128–29.

[65] Gloria Waldron, *The Information Film: A Report of the Public Library Inquiry* (New York: Columbia University Press, 1949), 47–48.

[66] John Marshall, memorandum on Barclay Leathen's letter of June 1, to CIB, June 14, 1949, folder 51, box 5, series 911, RG 3, RF, RAC.

[67] John Marshall, "Draft—RF Practice with Respect to Radio, Film (and Television) Production," Nov. 2, 1953, folder 51, box 5, series 911, Program & Policy, RF, RAC.

The Rockefeller vision of a centralized model for the production and circulation of films had come to naught. Officials concluded that no single nonprofit corporation would come to coordinate the development of educational film in the United States. Nor would Americans be willing to establish an official public agency to generate such films. "Individual and institutional initiative seemed to prevail in this country with a corresponding distrust of any attempt to impose coordination," Marshall observed. "All one could do," he believed, "would be to hope that enterprises would grow together."[68] The Twentieth Century Fund report concurred with Marshall's assessment: Americans, "much more than the British or Canadians, are loath to undertake 'public' projects when private funds and energy are available."[69] Though the report continued to urge the creation of a subsidized national production center, funded "by one or several of our leading foundations," the Rockefeller Foundation had little interest in donating to another such organization. And in the anticommunist decades following World War II, there was little chance that either government or foundations would attempt to create a centralized structure to assist with the production of mass media.[70]

In the early 1950s, educational media once again seemed to be on the verge of realizing its long-heralded promise, but this time Rockefeller officers bowed out. Postwar efforts to educate the booming number of American students and to promote the American way of life internationally seduced educational film producers, who visualized vast new audiences for their films and scrambled for government and corporate production contracts. The nascent medium of television promised to solve the knotty problems of national distribution, as well as to provide an enormous new market for educational film. Yet officers of the HD and the GEB were happy to leave experimentation in educational television to other nonprofit organizations. "With the Ford Foundation and its subsidiaries active in the field, there is perhaps less need than earlier for Rockefeller Foundation aid," Marshall wrote in 1953.[71] After nearly two decades of experience in the sector, Rockefeller officials agreed that the development of an independent industry for educational film, uncorrupted by commercial motivations but profitable enough to stand without the crutch of public or foundation funding, was as improbable as a Hollywood plot.

---

[68] John Marshall, memorandum of Interview with Dr. Adolf Nichtenhauser, Apr. 15, 1942, folder 841, box 70, series 200, RG 1.1, RF, RAC.

[69] Waldron, *Information Film*, 41.

[70] Such structures did eventually take hold in the late 1960s. Public-private corporations and services established a new American Film Institute in 1967 and began to provide educational content for much smaller screens through PBS /CPB. Ultimately, the vision of Zook, Slesinger, and Marshall was best realized not in the realm of film, but in the world of educational television.

[71] Marshall, "Draft—RF Practice."

11 CORNERING *THE WHEAT FARMER* (1938)

GREGORY A. WALLER

> All motion pictures are educational if education is thought of as life experience. However, distinctions exist between films prepared for entertainment purposes, those assembled for novelty or survey presentation, and the *teaching film* produced specifically for classroom use.
>
> —Erpi Classroom Films, *Instructional Sound Films for the Classroom Produced under the Sponsorship of Leading Educators* (1939)

While Hollywood may not have focused on rural subjects during the 1920s–1930s, except in the production of animated cartoons, the occasional feature like *State Fair* (1933), and certain B-Westerns, for the nontheatrical market, the American farmer and the farm family, the business and technology of modern agriculture, and the farm as a culturally resonant site were prime motion picture material. Farm machinery companies like International Harvester sponsored an array of motion pictures, as did the American Farm Bureau and—most notably—the United States Department of Agriculture (USDA). The USDA was the government agency that made the most extensive use of film as a key part of its extension program and its broader mission of public-service outreach primarily, though not exclusively, directed toward rural audiences.[1] By the later 1930s, *The Plow That Broke the Plains* (1936), the now-canonical, U.S. government–produced documentary about the catastrophic state of American agriculture during the Depression, attracted considerable public attention and even garnered a fair share of theatrical bookings.

---

[1] Gregory A. Waller, "Free Talking Picture—Every Farmer Is Welcome: Non-Theatrical Film and Everyday Life in Rural America during the 1930s," in *Going to the Movies: Hollywood and the Social Experience of the Cinema*, ed. Melvyn Stokes, Robert Allen, and Richard Maltby (Exeter, UK: University of Exeter Press. 2008), 248–72.

It is not surprising, therefore, that when Erpi Classroom Films, the emerging leader in educational film production, looked to expand its primarily science-oriented list of instructional films specifically designed for school use, it produced several titles about American agriculture, including *The Wheat Farmer* (1938). Such films were not prompted by the pressing sense that American agriculture was in crisis but rather by the idea that farming was a thriving and diverse aspect of the United States economy. Though I have not been able to locate any specific information about the number of prints of this particular title that were sold to schools and libraries, nor information about the precise distribution and screening of these prints, by all accounts *The Wheat Farmer* had a long shelf-life as a notably successful product designed specifically for the educational film market. It remained in release after Erpi was acquired by Encyclopaedia Britannica Films (EBF) in 1943. In fact, it was featured in EBF's *Using the Classroom Film,* a 1945 production intended to be used for teacher training (and for promoting the virtues of the classroom film) that documented the screening and discussion of *The Wheat Farmer* in a seventh-grade social studies class.[2] In 1956, EBF rereleased *The Wheat Farmer* in a second, significantly revised edition.

In addition to being a widely available example of a larger corpus of non-Hollywood motion picture production about U.S. agriculture, *The Wheat Farmer* merits attention as an exemplary test case for how we might analyze, historicize, and perhaps even appreciate the films of a company like Erpi and early 16mm instructional sound film more generally. To that end, this essay examines *The Wheat Farmer's* formal qualities and ideological emphases, its pedagogical strategies and its mode of delivering information, its "movie"-like aspects, and even what might be called its measure of excess.[3] By taking into account Erpi's own promotional material, the teacher's study guide provided for *The Wheat Farmer,* and the period discourse about educational film, I contextualize this interpretive analysis by considering the marketing, circulation, exhibition, programming, reception, and utilization of a "teaching film" like *The Wheat Farmer.*

The Wheat Farmer: Sound and Image, Information and Ideology

In ninety-eight shots spread over eleven minutes, *The Wheat Farmer* follows the planting, harvesting, and transporting of wheat, detailing the role of machinery

---

[2] "Motion Picture Demonstrates How to Teach with Films," *Educational Screen* 24, no. 8 (Oct. 1945): 351. Erpi Classroom Films, Inc. was the production division of ERPI–Electrical Research Products, Incorporated, itself a subsidiary of Western Electric and AT&T.

[3] On the concept of "excess" in film studies, see, for example, Kristin Thompson, *Breaking the Glass Armor: Neoformalist Film Analysis* (Princeton, NJ: Princeton University Press, 1988); and Kristin Thompson, "The Concept of Cinematic Excess," in *Film Theory and Criticism: Introductory Readings,* 5th ed., ed. Leo Braudy and Marshall Cohen (New York: Oxford University Press, 1999), 487–98.

and suggesting how modern agricultural practices enable urban consumption. The process on display is notably direct, leading from seeded field to ripening wheat to grain elevator to loaves of bread. At the same time, and quite unlike *Wheat* (1928), an earlier film on the subject produced by Eastman Classroom Films, *The Wheat Farmer* portrays—in the words of a 1939 Erpi catalog—"the life of a wheat farmer and his family in a typical Midwestern area." The farm family is figured as a married couple with two children, appropriately named "the Whites," all played by uncredited and what appear to be nonprofessional performers. Are these people "real" rural Midwesterners? Are the Whites an actual family? A composite? A representative construct? A random sample? Such questions, related to issues of verisimilitude, representation, and responsibility, would come to preoccupy later nonfiction filmmakers, but they were not explicitly of interest to Erpi in 1938, judging from the film itself or its accompanying study guide.

The Wheat Farmer's season-by-season narrative of one crop and the life of an ostensibly prototypical family is presented via footage shot on location, expository voiceover commentary, and enacted vignettes that frequently include spoken dialogue. These elements are efficiently combined and contained within an episodic structure that allows for some measure of comic relief, a modicum of suspense, and even certain stylistic flourishes. The film's ideological message is mixed but nonetheless clear: Modern farming is a family affair, dependent on the labor, equipment, and expertise of farmer White and, notably, his son Tom. The contributions of the father are essential to this enterprise, best captured in images of the solitary, experienced wheat farmer ritualistically walking waist-deep into his field of grain to gauge the ripeness of his crop by touch and taste (see fig. 11.1). Yet this family farm—tied to a national commodities market and subject to the vagaries of the weather—also requires seasonal workers ("harvest hands") and ready access to a larger distribution-transportation network. Waylaying late-Depression-era anxieties, *The Wheat Farmer* depicts an American heartland in which the crop thrives, the male wage-earner fulfills his role, the family farm prospers, and U.S. agriculture runs as smoothly as the massive combine that sweeps the Whites' shimmering fields of grain.

Always operating in concert with the film's quickly passing images, the voiceover narration provides an essential fabric of continuity to *The Wheat Farmer*. Predictably, the voiceover supplies what we assume is vital information, for example, clearly marking the passage of time, identifying the stages of this agricultural process, explaining in simple terms the operation of a combine and a grain elevator, and even indicating how much the men who work the fields appreciate a chance to wash up and go inside to sit at the dinner table for a fortifying meal. Repetitive phrases, delivered in measured tones and rhythmic cadence, sometimes render wheat farming a poetic if not a spectacularly exciting activity: "This is the harvest field routine from dawn to dusk,

Figure 11.1. Mr. White tests his wheat.

from field to combine, from combine to truck. From combine to truck and from truck to elevator." While the voiceover can be humorous ("There are no finicky appetites among a group of harvest hands . . . woe to the expectant harvester whom the pie plate reaches last!"), it is never arch, condescending, or hyperbolic in the manner, say, of certain commentators for major studio travelogues. Free of any immediately identifiable aural traces of region and class, the disembodied voiceover speaks from a position of authority and oversight while also remaining appreciative—of wheat ripening in the field, of human labor and farm machinery, of the complex process that provides us with our "staff of life."

The voiceover conducts no interviews in *The Wheat Farmer*, but on several occasions it does hand over the soundtrack, as it were, to the Whites and even to other folks in this paradigmatic wheat country, speakers whose Midwestern words are always presented as dialogue, wedded to the image track. The bits of dialogue are often spoken in a stiff and halting manner that contrasts with the voiceover's polished delivery and likely signifies that Erpi has relied on the performances of amateurs or nonactors—and perhaps thereby, paradoxically, gaining a measure of realism for *The Wheat Farmer*.

The dialogue scenes that actually picture the Whites matter-of-factly articulate a conventional gender economy, focusing on the outdoor work of Mr. White and Tom, with the domestic labor of the "womenfolk" foregrounded in a brief scene set in the kitchen. Interestingly, dialogue figures most prominently in a sequence inserted between the planting and the harvesting of the wheat crop. As he repairs a tractor, Tom is interrupted by his (unnamed) sister, who brings a letter from the local 4-H Club, asking whether she and Tom want to be on the program at the next meeting. She jokingly chides him about getting his face clean in time, and then the film moves to the gathering, where a dozen or so teenagers and younger adolescents listen attentively as Tom recounts raising a calf that he plans to show at the fair, another boy describes raising strawberries, and a girl explains why sifting flour makes for a better cake. In each instance, spoken language prompts illustrative inserts. The girl's account, for example, includes a shot of her sifting flour in a kitchen, then of her freckle-faced younger brother puckishly enjoying a large slice of cake, reinforcing the film's clear articulation of gender roles.

Like the classroom where *The Wheat Farmer* was intended to be shown, the 4-H meeting is a site of instruction, with the farm kids themselves reporting on their highly practical "projects" and passing on knowledge to their peers, thereby sharing and pooling their individual efforts toward improving agricultural practices, enriching farm life, and taking personal initiative (see fig. 11.2). This interpolated sequence hints at a larger, cohesive, harmonious, and smoothly functional social framework beyond the farm, which is also briefly glimpsed from a quite different angle when Mr. White at harvest time goes to town to hire laborers. These men don't seem to be desperate and weary victims of a dispiriting cycle of unemployment but instead look to be merely two fellows relaxing while waiting for the opportunity to work (see fig. 11.3). Neither on the farm nor in the

Figure 11.2. Tom at the 4-H meeting.

Figure 11.3. Mr. White hires workers in town.

town are there any traces, in other words, of the Depression we have come to know through *The Grapes of Wrath*, Farm Security Administration photographs, and retrospective oral histories.

The 4-H meeting also includes one of the three or four instances when the film turns lightly comic, a strategy that seems geared to reach the intended (and captive) classroom audience. Proponents of visual education in this period worried that students and teachers alike regarded the classroom film as merely an entertaining time-filler. As late as 1948, two researchers in an article for *Child Development* concluded that "most Americans, both teachers and learners, come to a [classroom] motion picture 'show' wrapped up in their theatrical motion picture habits and expect to be entertained."[4] One solution to this pedagogical dilemma would be to acknowledge and exploit these very "habits." *The Wheat Farmer*'s images of, for instance, a young boy enjoying his sister's cake and of Mr. White squirting milk from a cow's udder into the mouth of the family cat ("a quick dinner for the cat"; see fig. 11.4) might be seen as an attempt to make this teaching film more entertainingly movie-like and less soberly factual, without, however, lapsing into what a 1940 guidebook to educational films from Teachers

---

[4] Stephen M. Corey and Virginia E. Magidan, "Dissemination of Child Development Information through the Use of Motion Pictures," *Child Development* 19, nos. 1–2 (Mar.–June 1948): 95.

Figure 11.4. A quick dinner for the cat.

College, Columbia University, called the "bad taste" endemic to ostensibly "funny" travel films.[5] As much as any direct voiceover reference to the market, these humorous moments help *The Wheat Farmer* set its ideological bearings. The film's comic vignettes render U.S. agriculture more human and more mundane while implicitly countering the idea that the farm and the farm family is or could be caught in the death grip of a natural or market-driven disaster.

What about the visual style of *The Wheat Farmer* in this regard? When Frederick L. Devereux, then vice president of Erpi Picture Consultants, published a handbook cum apologia entitled *The Educational Talking Picture* with the University of Chicago Press (1933; 2nd ed. 1935), he took pains to enumerate what he claimed were certain empirically tested standards by which to measure the quality of a classroom film. Beyond the choice of an appropriate subject, the reliance on professional experts as advisers, and the availability of a thorough study guide, other factors were also relevant, Devereux insisted: "Even the child in the elementary school is a keen critic of technical matters," and so "technical aspects" of the classroom film must "approximate the best theatrical standards." Relying on "original and artistic expression" and careful attention to camera position, composition, and "dramatic value," the successful classroom film will avoid "monotonous

[5] William H. Hartley, *Selected Films for American History and Problems* (New York: Bureau of Publications, Teachers College, Columbia University, 1940), 18.

Figure 11.5. Approximating classical Hollywood style.

regularity" and instead offer viewers a "vivid, rich, and satisfying experience."[6] We may not be able to rate such an experience on a scale of one to five as Devereux suggests in the formal checklist that concludes his book, but the aesthetic criteria evoked in *The Educational Talking Picture* might help explain certain formal aspects of an Erpi product like *The Wheat Farmer,* which offers considerable stylistic variety.

Shot on location, each of the scenes in *The Wheat Farmer* featuring the Whites, the 4-H members, and the hired hands has a clear beginning and end—and contains little that is surprising, superfluous, or unmotivated. At the same time, none of these scenes unrolls in a single take from a stationary camera. Erpi's production team abides by the rules of continuity editing, with camera movement limited to reframing the action, following onscreen movement. Dissolves bridge jumps in time and space. Individual images in these scenes typically favor the sort of balanced, uncluttered compositions and frontal, roughly eye-level setups common to theatrical feature films of the period (as in fig. 11.5, for example). One key exception is the recurring image of Mr. White or another man shot alone, framed against the bright, expansive sky from a slightly low but never notably extreme or unusual angle (never, that is, in the manner of Soviet-style agitprop or socialist realism, for example). The overall result of these choices in

---

[6] Frederick L. Devereux, *The Educational Talking Picture* (Chicago: University of Chicago Press, 1935), 40, 46–48.

The Wheat Farmer is a technically proficient approximation of the classical Hollywood style, but—significantly—without elaborate lighting effects and visible markers of glamour that could undercut a sense of the film's ordinariness and verisimilitude.

What might possibly qualify *The Wheat Farmer* as a "vivid, rich, and satisfying [classroom film] experience" is not its depiction of the Whites at work or the 4-H meeting, but rather the film's flashy final montage sequence, as well as its many images of wheat and machinery. Once the Whites' crop has been deposited at a grain elevator, *The Wheat Farmer* rushes to a conclusion with a sequence that packs seventeen shots into twenty seconds of screen time. This montage encapsulates what happens next in a process that moves from field to table: kneading, weighing, rolling, baking, and slicing bread at a commercial bakery leads to a consumer buttering and eating the final product. A brief shot or two stands in for each of these actions, which are also verbally identified by the voiceover narrator: "Processed and mixed and kneaded. Mixed and kneaded and weighed. Weighed and rolled, and put into pans and baked." On striking display here is the speed and efficiency of modern production techniques (the bakery as factory) and the almost miraculous transformation of grain to tasty morsel. Accelerating the process even more—and adding another measure of surplus aesthetic value—are eight split-second inserts of a canted neon sign flashing the word "BREAD" that punctuate each step, from kneading to eating (figs. 11.6–11.8). With the inclusion of this montage sequence, it is as if *The Wheat Farmer* has suddenly and

Figures 11.6, 11.7, 11.8. Details from the final montage.

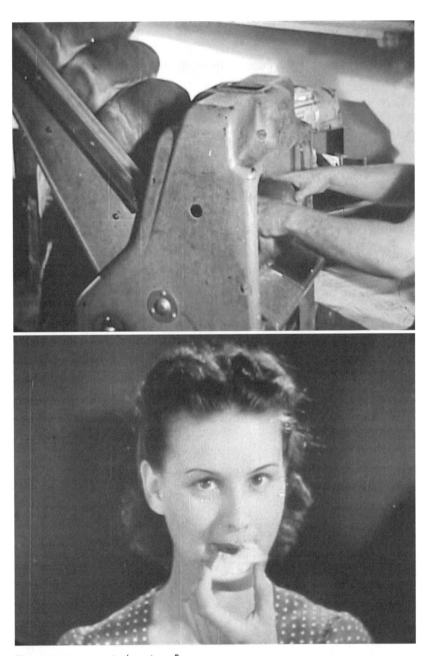

Figures 11.6, 11.7, 11.8. (*continued*)

inexplicably entered a different modality of American modernity, evoked by familiar signifiers of speed, mass production, advertising, consumption, and the urban. And this montage sequence makes the formal possibilities of the classroom film, circa 1938, seem suddenly more varied and interestingly open to an array of cinematic influences and possibilities.

The conclusion of *The Wheat Farmer* stands out even more emphatically when contrasted with the way the film has previously represented the natural crop and the formidable machinery required to harvest it. The film's first image, for example, is a slow tracking shot looking up through what the voiceover calls "heavy-headed grain." Lightly swaying wheat stalks are framed diagonally across a cloud-filled sky (see fig. 11.9)—pure natural fecundity as far as the eye can see. (This image will be briefly reprised later in the film.) But within seconds this striking tableau dissolves into a ground-level shot of a tractor approaching and passing the camera, indicating the sort of labor and technology required to grow a field of wheat. The various vehicles that are essential for the operation of this family farm get special visual attention for the rest of the film, most notably in the presentation of the combine, the largest and most complex piece of farm machinery in *The Wheat Farmer*. Once the grain has ripened, panoramic views stress the expansive scope of the Whites' farm, while from a much closer perspective the film captures the combine in action, with the camera tracking parallel to it from the side, then mounted on the combine as it rumbles through the field, then positioned in front of it as it approaches (see fig. 11.10). Unlike the final montage sequence, here the shots linger, focusing on the revolving eight-spoke cutting wheel mechanism and nicely reflecting the pace of the combine as it methodically cuts the wheat and separates the grain from the chaff. Of course, it is ideologically telling that the combine—the most sophisticated piece of machinery on the White farm—merits such lingering: there is no farming without powerful and efficient technology, no preindustrial agrarian space in *The Wheat Farmer*. At the same time, I would suggest that these interestingly composed and "vivid" images of the combine offer a measure of aesthetic excess well beyond what might be required to illustrate the voiceover narrator's description and to satisfy the rather modest expository ambitions of a classroom film.

When Encyclopædia Britannica Films prepared the second edition of *The Wheat Farmer* (hereafter *The Wheat Farmer 2*) for distribution in 1956, it maintained the focus on a single nuclear family planting and bringing in one harvest, but it retained none of the actual footage from the first edition. Dialogue again is kept to a minimum, though *The Wheat Farmer 2* features an intermittent score, a more extensive use of ambient sound (particularly of the various vehicles and machines), and a virtually nonstop voiceover commentary that glosses and explains almost every image. A number of scenes from the original are revised and reshot, including the 4-H meeting. *The Wheat Farmer 2* also adds a family trip to a nearby bustling town, where the kids head for the public swimming pool while their parents window-shop and check out the latest farm equipment. In their 1950s incarnation, the Whites are mobile, up-to-date, at home in the town, and ready to recycle their income as consumers. In contrast, the 1938 family looks almost quaintly rural.

Figure 11.9. From field to tractor.

Figure 11.10. The combine.

Missing from the second edition is the bakery-to-consumer montage of *The Wheat Farmer*, replaced by an equally eye-catching sequence that also dramatically puts accelerated noncontinuity editing on display: suddenly, on the last day of the harvest, a hail-storm looms, depicted in twenty-five shots that together run a little over a minute. As the wind whines and engines roar and clank, fragmentary images of wheat, machines, sky, Mr. White, and Tom shot from different angles and distances abruptly collide, conjuring a moment of narrative danger and visual excitement à la Sergei Eisenstein. The natural threat soon passes, sparing this "lucky" family, leaving the combine to continue its methodical harvesting and American agriculture to maintain its high level of prosperity. Aesthetic excess, however, has had its moment.

The Wheat Farmer as Human Geography

It would be interesting to examine whether the differences between the two versions of *The Wheat Farmer* point to a change in educational films from the late 1930s to the mid-1950s or, perhaps, to a difference in "house style" between Erpi and Encyclopaedia Britannica Films. At least for the 1938 production, this corporate/studio identity was extremely significant. *The Wheat Farmer* was not simply any "classroom film" hitting the burgeoning 16mm market. It was an Erpi Instructional Sound Film—a brand with high visibility and status in the late 1930s and into the 1940s, when the United States' involvement in World War II spurred unprecedented interest in the role and availability of all forms of educational and "useful" cinema. For example, when the American Council on Education in 1942 published its *Selected Educational Motion Pictures: A Descriptive Encyclopedia*, covering five hundred "valuable" titles, almost 30 percent were Erpi films.[7]

Around the time of *The Wheat Farmer*'s release, Erpi had 122 titles available—all described in some detail in the company's 1939 catalog, *Instructional Sound Films for the Classroom Produced under the Sponsorship of Leading Educators*. Virtually all of these films were one-reel productions, and most were available only for purchase, not rental. By this date, Erpi still sold 35mm as well as 16mm

---

[7] *Selected Educational Motion Pictures: A Descriptive Encyclopedia* (Washington, DC: American Council on Education, 1942). By way of contrast, this bibliography included eighty-two Eastman Teaching Films and thirty-eight titles produced by the USDA.

Thanks to David Shepard for sharing with me his copy of *The Wheat Farmer* (1938). His talk, "Through the Alimentary Canal with Gun and Camera," addresses the history of ERPI and provides an introduction to a screening of *The Wheat Farmer* at the Fifth Orphan Film Symposium ("Science, Industry and Education"), University of South Carolina, Mar. 25, 2006. An audio recording of Shepard's talk is available at www.sc.edu/filmsymposium/Orphans_Sound/orphans.htm.

prints; at $100 per single reel, the 35mm prints were twice as expensive as those in 16mm. These prices were not cheap, but in promoting their films and educating educators in the uses of motion pictures in the classroom, Erpi emphasized that its Instructional Sound Films were based on extensive research into audiovisual pedagogy as well as on the expert advice of "leading educators"—with the University of Chicago especially well represented. *The Wheat Farmer*, for instance, was "produced in collaboration with Dr. H. P. Hartwig of Cornell University." Other Erpi titles relied on accredited representatives of the Museum of American Natural History, Bell Telephone Laboratories, and the Boston Museum of Fine Arts.

Erpi brought this expertise to bear on films about child psychology and teacher training as well as a number of titles designed solely for use in primary schools. But the company's focus by the end of the 1930s was on classroom films geared toward more advanced grades, particularly in three principal areas of study: biological science, physical science, and human geography. *The Wheat Farmer* fell within Erpi's Human Geography Series, which included seventeen other titles, ranging from *Clothing* (1937) and *The Development of Transportation* (1939) to *People of Mexico* (1939) and *A Backward* [!] *Civilization: The Berbers of Northern Africa* (1937). Such films, Erpi claimed, could in fact meet the needs of both elementary social studies classes and also more specialized instruction in sociology, geography, or economics. Contemporary agriculture in the United States was covered in titles like *The Cattleman* (1939), *The Truck Farmer* (1939), and *Irrigation Farming* (1939), as well as *The Wheat Farmer*. Underscoring the prominence of American agriculture as a key film subject for the classroom, Erpi debuted *The Corn Farmer* (1939), *The Orange Grower* (1939), and *Science and Agriculture* (1939) late in 1939, a time that saw a widely manifested heightening of media interest in U.S. history, American values, and the present state of the nation, as war loomed.

While all of its human geography films claimed to offer "the presentation of actual situations taken from human living" in specific "national and cultural areas,"[8] Erpi's catalog synopses point to a striking distinction between films about "archaic" cultures and societies (Mexicans, Navajo, Berbers) and films that present the world of progressive, productive, technologically sophisticated white modernity. In titles such as *The Wheat Farmer* and *The Truck Farmer*, American agriculture is usually seen through and embodied in the successful work life of a white, land-owning, self-reliant, and therefore "typical" family. For Erpi, this enterprise is intimately bound up with region and place, but it is also, as *The Wheat Farmer* makes clear, fully modern in that it participates in an interdependent system linked by communication, transportation, and the market-driven distribution of goods and resources.

---

[8] *Instructional Sound Films for the Classroom Produced under the Sponsorship of Leading Educators* (Long Island City, NY: Erpi Classroom Films, 1939), 29.

Making the Most of *The Wheat Farmer*

The broad rubric of "human geography" provides one way of situating *The Wheat Farmer* and imagining its place not so much literally in a classroom as in a curriculum. Even their titles indicate that *The Wheat Farmer* might be effectively paired with *The Corn Farmer* and *The Truck Farmer* in a teaching unit on agriculture. Erpi's 1939 catalog enumerated a host of other possible classroom uses for *The Wheat Farmer*: in courses on geography, elementary science, general science, and sociology; and in vocational guidance programs, where it could be shown with Erpi films like *New England Fisherman* (1938) and *Shell-Fishing* (1938). Other, more precisely defined programming options for *The Wheat Farmer* were laid out in *ERPI Classroom Films Correlated with School Programs*, a pamphlet that by 1945 was in its sixth edition. According to this guidebook, *The Wheat Farmer* could, for instance, be used—along with films such as *Science and Agriculture*—in an "intermediate grade" unit on the "Central States" as part of a larger study of "Americans at Work." Erpi's account of the White farm could also be included in a sociology unit on "People and Their Environments," an economics unit on "Production and Technology," a geography unit on "Productive Resources," a junior high school biology unit on the "World of Plants," and a senior high-school unit on "Economic Biology," as well as general courses on home economics or agriculture. In each of these instances, *The Wheat Farmer* could be combined with a different array of Erpi films.[9]

What Erpi's own promotional material clearly indicates, then, is that titles like *The Wheat Farmer* were marketed as multipurpose motion pictures, a good investment not just because they could be screened again and again, but more importantly because they could be slotted into the curriculum—programmed— in a variety of different ways. "Programming," I would argue, is a crucial, historically specific aspect of all film exhibition. As related to theatrical cinema, programming usually refers to the grouping of two or more individual films (and, potentially, other elements like slides, lectures, or live musical performances) for a particular presentation. This type of program was also sometimes presented in churches, tent shows, school auditoriums, and other nontheatrical venues, but not in the classroom. What Erpi is promoting, in contrast to this "movie-style" presentation, is the program as a series of linked but separate screenings, with the expectation that the same classroom audience over a certain time period will watch all six films about vocations, for example, or all ten films about agriculture. Erpi's classroom program is in some ways analogous to other nontheatrical exhibition

---

[9] H. A. Gray, *Erpi Classroom Films Correlated with School Programs*, 6th ed., rev. M. Brodshaug and M. Bittmann (Chicago: Encyclopaedia Britannica Films, 1945).

strategies introduced in this period, for example, the Museum of Modern Art's circulating film series or the thematically organized film forums sponsored during World War II by the Rockefeller Foundation–funded American Film Center.[10]

While I have not found any evidence of teachers following Erpi's advice for how to incorporate *The Wheat Farmer* into a curriculum as part of a multifilm series, a 1941 report published by the American Council on Education noted that "the interesting thing about films like *The Wheat Farmer* is that teachers in the many grades rate them uniformly good or excellent." In the Santa Barbara, California, schools, *The Wheat Farmer*

> was used successfully from the kindergarten through the eleventh grade. The kindergarten teacher used the film to acquaint the children with a different kind of farm and farmer than could be found around Santa Barbara. The third- and fourth-grade teachers used the film to help the children to understand our great dependence on workers who make plants serve us, and to answer the question of what has to be done before plants can be of use to us. A fifth-grade teacher used the film to show methods of farming and types of machinery used, and a ninth-grade teacher used it to present the steps and methods used in raising and processing wheat. In the eleventh grade, the film was used to develop an appreciation of the need for conserving both natural and human resources.[11]

This testimonial, viewed in demographic terms, offers a compelling scenario, attesting that an Erpi title could be screened successfully for a number of different age groups or micro-audiences. All the more reason, then, for a school to purchase a print. In being able to serve so many pedagogical purposes, *The Wheat Farmer* in this account becomes not only a good investment but also an unlikely example of the polyvalent film text, open to various appropriations and different emphases depending on the context within which it is screened.

Using *The Wheat Farmer*

The other major point to be made about the American Council on Education's report from Santa Barbara is its unequivocal belief that classroom films like *The Wheat Farmer* should be judged as investments and evaluated as media products

---

[10] See Haidee Wasson, *Museum Movies: The Museum of Modern Art and the Birth of Art Cinema* (Berkeley: University of California Press, 2005); also see the regular coverage of American Film Center programs in *Film News*.

[11] *Motion Pictures in a Modern Curriculum: A Report on the Use of Films in the Santa Barbara Schools, Motion Pictures in Education*, series 2, no. 6 (May 1941): 173.

in terms of their *use* value. Such films were not merely to be screened, but utilized—as Erpi's promotional material and the many guides to visual education like Charles F. Hoban Jr.'s *Visualizing the Curriculum* (1937) and *Movies that Teach* (1946) never tired of reiterating. "No one will deny the educational value of selected feature pictures when shown in the theatre or school auditorium," declares the 1939 Erpi catalog:

> Certainly travelogues, newsreels, documentary subjects, novelties and the like possess general, and in many cases, great, educational value and may be used to vitalize auditorium assemblies or provide material for noon hour recreation and club activities. However, the properly prepared *teaching film* is produced as an integral part of a unit of instruction that has a definite relation to a course of study being taught by the individual teacher . . . obviously, such a film should be utilized quite differently, and more frequently, than "just a motion picture" if optimum benefits are to accrue.[12]

According to the period discourse concerning teaching films, "utilization" is not the same thing as exhibition, or at the very minimum it is a specific way of presenting film, quite distinct from anything resembling theatrical exhibition. When it comes to the "entertainment" film, writes Frederick L. Devereux, "the objective . . . is realized largely while the picture is in the process of being seen and heard," thus the screening experience is self-contained and self-explanatory, and "no preparation needs to be made for the showing and no follow-up is essential." In contrast, he continues, "the educational talking picture is not intended to be a complete experience in itself. It is the middle part of an educative process and is related both to a preparation and to a follow-up."[13] As carefully planned and professionally produced as Erpi titles might have been, their value as classroom films depended on how they were introduced, mediated, and mined by teachers. Hence the supreme importance of the comprehensive study guides—sometimes called "teacher's handbooks"—that Erpi (like Eastman Classroom Films) produced for its films.[14]

The considerable amount of "background" information and detailed pedagogical advice contained in these study guides make plain Erpi's commitment to a particular version of film-enhanced, active learning that by the late 1930s still required considerable explanation, if not outright justification. For example, the

[12] *Instructional Sound Films for the Classroom*, 1.

[13] Devereux, *Educational Talking Picture*, 113–14.

[14] The Erpi-style study guide can be fruitfully contrasted with another type of utilitarian, "official" paratext, the standard Hollywood pressbook of the same period, which was designed to explain to the exhibitor how best to get the most profit out of a specific film.

same year that *The Wheat Farmer* was released, Elizabeth Laine, in *Motion Pictures and Radio: Modern Techniques for Education*, complained that "lack of experience on the part of the teacher contributes profoundly to the inept handling of film material. Uncertain as to what is expected of the film, teachers frequently ... employ it as they would a substitute teacher."[15] *Life on the Wheat Farm: Teacher's Handbook For Use with the Instructional Sound Film, "The Wheat Farmer"* addresses the anxiety that even the most carefully wrought and built-for-the-classroom instructional film could easily be underused or misused—treated, for instance, as a time-filler or, worse, as "'just a motion picture'" rather than as a valuable educational component to be integrated into a curriculum. Thus *Life on the Wheat Farm* takes pains to enumerate several "practices to avoid," which I assume were common enough to warrant policing:

> do not show the film apart from the larger curricular unit
> do not screen this film with other films during the same class meeting
> do not fail to include follow-up work
> do not mistake this film for "an entertainment device"

It is worth noting that all these rules will definitely be broken when and if the educational film outlives its usefulness in the classroom and resurfaces years or decades later as a nostalgic throwback, unintentionally campy relic, or newly prized orphan film.

On the positive side, as might be expected given these particular prohibitions, *Life on the Wheat Farm* offers teachers a long list of "introductory activities" to set up a larger "unit of study," including but not limited to screening *The Wheat Farmer*. This unit was also supposed to involve various individual or group student projects, like the creation of maps, graphs, stories, illustrations, displays, or reports. For example, one such activity the study guide describes is to have students "write the story that the land would tell if it could talk of its misuse in connection with the cultivation of wheat"—a topic of great currency in the 1930s, but one never actually mentioned or referenced in the film. While there is, according to the study guide, more to wheat farming than *The Wheat Farmer* covers, nothing in the guide suggests that students should be encouraged to think critically about the film, for example, by identifying its point of view or noting its particular emphases and absences in the treatment of U.S. agriculture.

Erpi's principal concern is rather that this film become an "an integral part of the work in the [curricular] unit." To this end, the study guide insists on a quite specific form of exhibition. First, the preliminary screening of *The Wheat*

---

[15] Elizabeth Laine, *Motion Pictures and Radio: Modern Techniques for Education* (New York: McGraw-Hill, 1938), 48.

Farmer must be prefaced by the teacher's "leading questions," which will arouse students' curiosity and focus their attention when they initially see the film, complete and uninterrupted. Discussion should follow this screening, preparing the way for a second viewing, but "not until there has been a definite purpose" established for "repeating the film." Then might come a third screening with the sound turned off so that the teacher or pupils can provide spoken commentary, in effect demonstrating command of the visual material by replacing (or mimicking?) the male voiceover. Whatever else it might accomplish as cost-effective pedagogy, this strategy renders the classroom experience of film absolutely distinct from the theatrical experience, well beyond the simple fact that in the classroom the projecting apparatus is usually there for all to see and hear.

Erpi assumes that to make maximum—and correct—use of *The Wheat Farmer,* teachers need more than a list of potential student activities and certain guidelines for how best to screen and rescreen the film. Thus a quarter of the study guide's twenty-six pages constitute what amounts to an extended encyclopedia entry on wheat and wheat farming, covering agricultural machinery; the "community life" of the farm family; and the planting, harvesting, and marketing of this crop. This information is offered as the necessary background and context for *The Wheat Farmer,* attesting to the film's accuracy while also acknowledging that a one-reel treatment of a complex subject is inevitably incomplete or partial. In addition, though the guide offers no information at all about the production of *The Wheat Farmer,* it does include a full transcription of the film's dialogue and voiceover narration, along with a shot-by-shot "description": "Scene 1—Wheat . . . Scene 2—Tractor and Plows . . . Scene 3—Closeup Gangplows," and so on. Such a transcription presumably made using *The Wheat Farmer* more manageable for the teacher, who thus would have been able to check dialogue and locate specific scenes without examining a 16mm print (or perhaps to forego previewing the film). The transcription also, I think, serves as an implied testament to the Erpi way of making instructional sound films. That is, the availability of the transcription itself gives the impression (tautologically) that this carefully wrought and well-informed film merits transcription, encouraging the teacher—and us—to attend closely to precisely how *The Wheat Farmer* deploys sound and image, relays its information, and achieves its various instructional ends.[16]

Of course, there is no guarantee that the study guide's instructions were followed in practice and that the promised pedagogical payoff was delivered in the form of students' greater understanding or appreciation of wheat farming. And we can never get a full sense of whether Erpi's desired instructional ends were achieved—if, in fact, it is even possible to measure this sort of "achievement."

---

[16] *Life on the Wheat Farm: Teacher's Handbook for Use with the Instructional Sound Film, "The Wheat Farmer"* (Long Island City, NY: Erpi Classroom Films, 1938).

The American Council on Education's national "film evaluation program" did, however, report in 1942 that *The Wheat Farmer* was "found useful in (1) developing an appreciation of the progress that has been made in agricultural methods and equipment, (2) showing the life of a wheat farmer and his family, and (3) stimulating an interest in the farmer's problems."[17] On the basis of its usefulness and "excellent" sound and photography, the film was deemed "very good," a rating also awarded to Pare Lorentz's *The Plow That Broke the Plains* and *The River* (1938), as well as other Erpi titles about U.S. agriculture, including *The Corn Farmer*, *Irrigation Farming*, *The Orange Grower*, and *The Truck Farmer*.

The American Council on Education provided a quite different glimpse of the reception of *The Wheat Farmer* in a 1942 report, *Focus on Learning: Motion Pictures in the Schools*, authored by Charles F. Hoban, one of the principal academic promoters of audiovisual education in the period.[18] This report summarized the findings of the "Motion Picture Project," a five-year study funded by the American Council on Education, which in 1936 had established a Committee on Motion Pictures in Education.[19] Interviews with students were essential for this project, and *Focus on Learning* reprints what it calls the "unedited description" of *The Wheat Farmer* by a ninth-grade female student, written after a classroom screening:

> The movie we had yesterday has shown much progress toward agriculture. It gave the various things people have had time to do to make living worthwhile. For instance, the man with that lovely little cow; he took such good care of the little calf. When the calf had grown a bit it was fed from a bucket. Then the cow produced the best milk. Another man explained how his wheat came out big and tall and pretty. The little girl who baked the cake, which her little brother thought was very good.
>
> One day a man planted wheat along so many acres of land. After a while he tested his wheat to see whether it was ready for cutting. It looked pretty much like rain was coming along. This man had to

---

[17] *Selected Educational Motion Pictures*, 324.

[18] Hoban was, for instance, coauthor, with Samuel B. Zisman, of *Visualizing the Curriculum* (New York: Cordon, 1937). See Alan Januszewski, *Educational Technology: Development of a Concept* (Englewood, CO: Libraries Unlimited, 2001), 13–15.

[19] Lindsay Pattison, "Taking the Movies to School: Science, Efficiency and the *Motion Picture Project*, 1929–1939," *History of Intellectual Culture* 6, no. 1 (2006): 1–15; Paul Saettler, *The Evolution of American Educational Technology* (Englewood, CO: Libraries Unlimited, 1990), 230–38. American Council on Education pamphlets in its Motion Pictures in Education series included *The Motion Picture in Education: Its Status and Its Needs* (Apr. 1937) and *A School Uses Motion Pictures* (Sept. 1940).

hurry up and get his wheat cleared before it rained. He hired men to come and help him. They started at once to cut the wheat with large machines. His wife was working hard also getting supper ready for the men working.

The men worked very hard in the dusty field of wheat, though it was worth a fortune to the one who planted the wheat.

The wheat was already to go to market. He received his money and paid the men who worked for him. They had done all this before the rain came that would have been the ruination of that little family.

Who knows, we are probably eating bread made from the wheat this man working so hard to save.

I liked this movie very much because it wasn't only a movie to look at. It had a good story in back of it.[20]

Hoban observes that even if this girl expresses certain "misconceptions" arising from "errors in accuracy and extent of interpretation," *The Wheat Farmer* succeeded in arousing her interest and therefore "presented fertile opportunity for the development of critical thinking and for the re-formulation of some of her understandings of and attitudes toward the economics of large-scale wheat farming."[21] The necessary next step, Hoban explains, is for a well-prepared teacher to develop, correct, and refine the impressions generated by this viewing.

For my purposes, it is the student's account itself that make this rare glimpse into the historical reception of *The Wheat Farmer* so intriguing. For her there is no question that this particular instructional sound film is a "movie"—and what's more, one with a "good story in back of it." Is she actually placing *The Wheat Farmer* in the same category as all those motion pictures shown theatrically? Can Erpi make anything else but a movie, given its commitment to framing a "story" of U.S. agriculture—one complete with a typical family, a crop that must be harvested, a girl working on her cake-baking, and so on. This student retells the "good story" of *The Wheat Farmer* as a Depression-era fable: a man plants and harvests a lucrative wheat crop under the threat of a rainstorm that might spell the "ruination" of his "little family." The workings of the larger economic process are straightforward and encouraging: the farmer succeeds, his hired workers are paid, we have bread. At the same time, this student pays particular attention to the activities described at the 4-H meeting (raising a calf,

---

[20] Charles F. Hoban, *Focus on Learning: Motion Pictures in the Schools* (Washington, DC: American Council on Education, 1942), 105–6.

[21] Ibid., 107.

baking a cake), which to her are not directly related to pressing economic concerns. These achievements, she states, signify "the various things people have had time to do to make living worthwhile." This resonant phrase powerfully underscores, I think, just how much a film like *The Wheat Farmer* offers instruction not only in how agricultural machinery operates but also in what makes a life worthwhile and successful. Like the American Council on Education's evaluations of best classroom motion-picture practices and Erpi's own discourse concerning how its products should be used, this ninth-grader's report helps to open up the range of formal, ideological, and historical questions we should be asking about a film like *The Wheat Farmer*, including questions about the relation between classroom films and theatrical movies. And at this stage of our consideration of educational cinema, the more questions, the better.

Filmography

The Wheat Farmer (1938) 11 min.; b&w; 16 and 35mm
PRODUCTION: Erpi Classroom Films Inc. ADVISER: Herbert B. Hartwig. NARRATOR: James A. Brill. STUDY GUIDE: *Life on the Wheat Farm*. ACCESS: LOC; Internet Archive, www.archive.org/details/wheat_farmer_1938 (running time 9:44).

The Wheat Farmer, 2nd ed. (1956) 13 min.; color; 16mm
PRODUCTION: Encyclopaedia Britannica Films. ADVISER: H. P. Hartwig.
PRODUCTION SUPERVISOR: Nicholas Dancy. With film guide.
ACCESS: LOC; University of South Carolina; Southeastern Oklahoma State University; Internet Archive, www.archive.org/details/wheat_farmer_1956.

Wheat Farmer (1951) 35mm filmstrip, 82 frames
PRODUCTION: Encyclopaedia Britannica Films. ACCESS: Coppin State University.

12 THE FAILURE OF THE NYU EDUCATIONAL FILM INSTITUTE

DAN STREIBLE

In 1939, the Alfred P. Sloan Foundation funded the creation of the Educational Film Institute at New York University (NYU). A group of the nation's best-known progressive documentarians and artists (Willard Van Dyke, Irving Lerner, Ben Maddow, Roger Barlow, Joris Ivens, John Ferno, Julian Roffman, Marc Blitzstein, and members of the Group Theatre) made three short teaching films about the economic and educational needs of rural and working-class America. *The Children Must Learn*, *And So They Live*, and *Valley Town* were all produced in 1940, but they displeased the conservative Alfred Sloan, who withdrew funding from the NYU Educational Film Institute (EFI), shortly after ordering major changes be made to *Valley Town*.[1]

As essays in this book demonstrate, a full-fledged educational film enterprise developed throughout the 1930s, as educators created curricula that integrated movies into classrooms. When New York University created its Educational Film Institute in 1939, it was not launching a bold new venture so much as contributing to the national movement toward that integration. What was new was the conception of the institute as a comprehensive entity that

---

Nancy Cricco (University Archives, NYU), Richard Angelo (University of Kentucky), the wise Craig Kridel (University of South Carolina), and the matchless Rick Prelinger shared their knowledge and perspectives during my research. This essay is informed by reading the extensive documentation about the Educational Film Institute (EFI) found in the Administrative Papers of the Chancellor Harry Woodburn Chase, 1933–1951, Record Group 3.0.5, Series II: Administrative Correspondence, Box 39, Folders 4–9 (1938–1946), New York University Archives (hereafter NYU Archives). I use the acronym EFI, although the institute was not referred to this way in its day.

[1] The political and cinematic contexts in which the EFI films and filmmakers must be understood are well defined by William Alexander, *Film on the Left: American Documentary Film from 1931 to 1942* (Princeton, NJ: Princeton University Press, 1981); Russell Campbell, *Cinema Strikes Back: Radical Filmmaking in the United States, 1930–1942* (Ann Arbor, MI: UMI Research Press, 1982); and Charles Wolfe, "The Poetics and Politics of Nonfiction: Documentary Film," in *Grand Design: Hollywood as Modern Business Enterprise, 1930–1939*, ed. Tino Balio (Berkeley: University of California Press, 1996), 374–76.

would integrate all sectors of the movement. It would have a well-endowed production unit, hiring accomplished nonfiction filmmakers; it would serve as a national distributor for its own productions and others; and it would exhibit films for NYU classes in a purpose-built theater. Scholars at the institute would measure the effectiveness of individual motion pictures, surveying student and teacher responses. Developing a library of film prints for loan, it would publish catalogs and generally advocate for the importance of well-made, effective educational films.

Some of these ambitious plans did materialize and endured for a generation, notably the distribution library. However, the most compelling part of the historical narrative about the NYU Educational Film Institute is the quick launch of a well-funded production unit, the creation of three short documentaries in 1940, followed by Alfred Sloan's withdrawal of all production funding upon seeing these films, which displeased him politically and aesthetically. How did such a high-level venture, with talented producers working under relatively optimal conditions, rise and fall so swiftly?

Creating the Educational Film Institute and Library at New York University was Alfred Sloan's own idea. In 1934, while chair of General Motors, he used his personal fortune to create the Alfred P. Sloan Foundation, giving it considerable influence in 1937 with a $10 million gift. The "single objective" of his largesse, according to his public announcement, was "the promotion of wider knowledge of basic economic truths generally accepted by authorities of recognized standing and as demonstrated by experience."[2]

For nine years, the executive director of the foundation was his brother. Dr. Harold S. Sloan was previously a professor of economics at Montclair College and author of the textbook *Today's Economics* (1936).[3] Shortly before lobbying NYU to house the institute, he published in the *New York Times* a bold assertion of the foundation's plans for 1938–1939. In order "to make America a nation of economic literates," the organization would begin a "bombardment of the American mind with elementary economic principles," funding college programs willing to participate. "By radio, motion pictures, forums, classes, clinics, university fellowships, pamphlets, news stories, and, ultimately, in text books," these institutions would "attack the everyday American's economic problems."

---

[2] David R. Farber, *Sloan Rules: Alfred P. Sloan and the Triumph of General Motors* (Chicago: University of Chicago, 2002), 210–12.

[3] Although Farber in *Sloan Rules* dismisses Alfred's younger brother as an untalented "yes man" (212), Harold Stephenson Sloan accomplished much in his one hundred years. He coauthored *Farming in America* (1947) and *A Dictionary of Economics* (1949), as well as four studies with Harold F. Clark: *Classrooms in the Factories* (1958), *Classrooms in the Stores* (1962), *Classrooms in the Military* (1964), and *Classrooms on Main Street* (1966). See "Harold S. Sloan, 100, Former Manufacturer," *New York Times* [hereafter *NYT*], Nov. 9, 1988.

"Most ambitious perhaps of all the foundation's plans," Harold Sloan announced, was "the creation of entertaining motion pictures on live social problems, such as displacement of men by machines."[4]

An Experimental Study of Machines and Men

Sloan's allusion to a motion picture about the displacement of men by machines was a specific one. In 1938, the foundation had already commissioned an "experimental film" on the subject before "selecting an educational agency." Initially entitled *The Challenge*, the sixteen-minute economics lesson was not so subtly renamed *The Machine: Master or Slave?* when it was finally put into distribution in 1941. In fall 1938, Dr. Sloan approached NYU chancellor Harry Woodburn Chase about creating the institute. They screened *The Challenge* for select administrators the following January. Sloan pressed Chase to release it with NYU's imprimatur rather than the foundation's. The chancellor and his advisers were wary, however—not because the film was underwhelming (though they did find it so) but because they did not want the university to endorse any particular school of economics.

The chancellery's reaction to the film paralleled that of test audiences. Before NYU agreed to set up the institute, the Sloan Foundation had enlisted the help of the National Education Association (Visual Education Department) and the U.S. Office of Education, screening *The Challenge* in schools and civic clubs in New York and Washington. Viewer response was highly negative. High-school students snickered at the bad acting. Adults viewed the film's proposed solution to unemployment as one-sided propaganda. Having spent five months to complete a script (revised based on experts' critiques) and another five months to produce the 1938 edition of *The Challenge,* the foundation revised it further in response to audience feedback. *The Machine: Master or Slave?*, as the surviving version is called, includes the added voiceover narration, revised dialogue, and retakes with different actors.[5]

Nevertheless, compared with the three films NYU produced in 1940, *The Machine* is a substandard production. With a budget of $25,000 (considerable for an educational short at the time), the foundation hired an ad hoc production team. Director Walter Niebuhr had coordinated motion picture photography for the U.S. Army's Signal Corps during World War I and had recently directed a nontheatrical documentary for the Peace Films Foundation, *Must War Be?*

---

[4] Harold S. Sloan, "Sloan Foundation Aids Research in Attack on Economic Problems," *NYT,* Aug. 21, 1938.

[5] *Report Covering the Motion Picture Operations of the Alfred P. Sloan Foundation Inc. February 1938–December 1940,* in folder "April '38–December '40," correspondence file #2, Sloan Foundation office records (kindly provided by Richard Angelo).

(1932). Writer Charlton Ogburn Jr. was knowledgeable of the effects of machines on labor. His uncle, an eminent scholar, had published three books on the subject; his father was counsel for the American Federation of Labor automobile unions. The journeymen cinematographers had credits ranging from Hollywood features to striptease films.[6]

The Machine: Master or Slave? alternates between scenes dramatizing the unemployment of a typical worker-machinist (Tom) and a generic executive (R. B. Palmer) overseeing his generic factory (which manufactures "product"). These are framed by overwrought montage sequences, composed of stock shots signifying industry, commerce, and consumerism, and a voiceover asking how we might "untangle the web of prices and buying, of costs and income, of machines and of men." A male voice begins: "America is busy now. Factories hum and millions of men, formerly idle, now work night and day on tanks, airplanes, defense orders." Certainly this opening was added to the original cut for the 1941 release. The rest of the film, however, addresses a Depression audience. "New labor saving machines will be invented. Must they again throw men out of work?"

Talk of layoffs reaches the factory floor. Meanwhile, Palmer and his personnel manager fret about the human impact of "the new labor-saving machines." What's "good news for the stockholders," the manager says, will be hard on the families of the men terminated. We see Tom reading a notice of termination, telling a fellow machinist, "High-speed machinery goes in; men like you, me, go out." A three-minute montage follows, with a frenetic orchestral score and shots of speedy conveyor belts and monstrous machines working "faster, ever faster," with no human workers onscreen.

Next we see Palmer talking to his sales manager in overly didactic terms, symptomatic of the written-by-committee script. The new machines produce goods faster than the market can sell them. What to do? Their first answer is aggressive advertising. Meanwhile, Tom arrives home after a fruitless job search. He verbalizes his frustrations and announces to his wife that they are going to live on his cousin's farm. When Palmer's ad campaign fails, his executive committee proposes lowering prices. An optimistic capitalist logic reasons that lower prices will mean more customers, which will allow the company to expand and then to create new jobs and raise wages.

The Machine: Master or Slave? concludes with a sequence posing open-ended questions, but is dominated by a confusion of visuals and music. "How shall

---

[6] George Creel, *How We Advertised America* (New York: Harper and Brothers, 1920), 119. Journalist-filmmaker Walter Niebuhr was the brother of theologian Reinhold Niebuhr. Charlton Ogburn Jr.'s study guide for *The Challenge* referred viewers to books written by his uncle, William F. Ogburn: *Living with Machines* (1933), *You and Machines* (1934), and *Machines and Tomorrow's World* (1938). See *Charlton Ogburn Papers, 1898–1998*, Manuscript, Archives, and Rare Book Library, Emory University, http://marbl.library.emory.edu/findingaids.

these conflicting factors be arranged," the narrator asks, "to provide better living and abundance for all?" A bewildering series of dissolving shots show us houses being built, then washing machines, vacuum cleaners, tractors plowing, threshers harvesting, children in a park, a woman taking snapshots, men fishing, beaches, amusement parks. "And so we find our problem at the crossroads," we hear, while seeing an incongruous image of a family picnic, "broad highways leading in all directions."

Clumsily presented with wooden acting and contrived dialogue, the film was admittedly an "experiment," a dry run for what the Sloan Foundation hoped would be part of an expertly conceptualized educational campaign. Accompanying *The Challenge/The Machine* were guidebooks with discussion questions and an advanced-level annotated bibliography. The script plays to a high-school level, but the literature refers to the likes of J. K. Galbraith and Karl Marx. A Sloan report later declared the study guide "a complete failure," finding that viewers wanted to discuss only the film.[7]

Despite Sloan's lobbying, NYU did not embrace the film. However, after some hesitancy, the chancellor accepted the Sloan Foundation money and in June 1939 set up the Educational Film Institute of New York University. Its mandate was (1) to produce and disseminate short films designed to teach principles of economics to a general audience, and (2) to measure the impact of these films on viewers. The institute completed only three films, but it did gather a significant number of written comments from test audiences. With the EFI's short lifespan, however, this data was never analyzed.

To set up the EFI, the university sought a scholar with credentials in economics and knowledge of motion pictures. Harold Sloan led them to a twenty-nine-year-old Harvard PhD candidate, Spencer D. Pollard, who was teaching economics at Harvard and writing a dissertation on labor unions.[8] Pollard told the search committee he had some vague "field" experience in film production at Oxford, where he had been a Rhodes scholar, and that he fancied writing a book about movies in education. Chancellor Chase reported to Sloan that Pollard

---

[7] *Motion Picture Operations of the Alfred P. Sloan Foundation.*

[8] Spencer Drummond Pollard (1910–1989) taught economics at the University of California Berkeley (1943–1945), Whittier College (1945–1946), and the University of Southern California. One of his few publications bears the Sloanian Cold War title *How Capitalism Can Succeed: A Primer of Economic Choices for People Who Want to Be Both Prosperous and Free* (Harrisburg, PA: Stackpole Books, 1966). The only item Pollard published while EFI director was his letter to the *New York Times* ("Film Sketches by Milestone," Sept. 22, 1940), assaying the need for better books about filmmaking. "Here at our institute we have as good a shelf of books as is available to the serious student of films, but all of us know how unspecific and unrewarding practically all of this material is. Except for [Soviet cinematographer] Vladimir Nilsen's work on *The Cinema as a Graphic Art* [1936], I do not know of a single book upon which one could base a satisfactory course in film directing."

made a "good impression in New York, including with the Wall Street group." New York University hired him in June, giving him the luxury of six months to survey the field of educational films.[9]

An Artful Study of Machines and Men

By late 1939, Pollard commissioned three short films. The first, *Valley Town: A Study of Machines and Men,* attempted to put the concept of *The Machine: Master or Slave?* into a more effective documentary. Pollard hired Documentary Film Productions, Inc., which director Willard Van Dyke had recently formed after splitting with Ralph Steiner. Together they had codirected the landmark film *The City* (1939), widely seen at the New York World's Fair as well as in theatrical and nontheatrical releases. The critical and popular success of *The City* put Van Dyke in demand as a maker of artful nonfiction films. In 1940 alone, he directed six sponsored films: the two NYU educational films plus *Design for Education* (a portrait of Sarah Lawrence College), *New Hampshire's Heritage* (for the state's Savings Bank Association), *Tall Tales* (for musicologist Alan Lomax), and *The Year's Work* (for General Mills, Inc.).[10]

On *Valley Town,* Spencer Pollard shared credits with Van Dyke on the script, and with "David Wolff" (an alias used by Ben Maddow) on voiceover commentary. The rhetoric of the film sticks to the theme of *The Machine,* driving home the point that automation displaces workers and asking what can be done about systemic unemployment. Pollard's job may have been to keep the film focused on Sloan's men versus machines question, but the production is dominated by the experimental style and populist critique that Van Dyke and Maddow impose on the material. Cinematographer Roger Barlow (*The City*) and editor Irving Lerner contribute to this aesthetic. Originally running thirty-five minutes, *Valley Town* was shot in New Castle, Pennsylvania, and debuted at a Steel Workers' convention in Chicago on May 14, 1940.[11] But as chair of General Motors, Alfred Sloan was angered that his foundation money had been used to make a film blaming corporations for not aiding workers who were casualties to the machine age. Further, *Valley Town* included avant-garde sequences, which challenged Sloan's sensibilities. The Sloans ordered a recut that deleted the most downbeat

---

[9] Chancellor Chase letter ("writing a book") to Harold Sloan, Apr. 3, 1939; Chase ("good impression") to Sloan, Apr. 10; Sloan ("six months") to Chase, Apr. 11, NYU Archives.

[10] James L. Enyeart, *Willard Van Dyke: Changing the World through Photography and Film* (Albuquerque: University of New Mexico Press, 2008), 207. See also *Living Films: A Catalog of Documentary Films and Their Makers* (New York: Association of Documentary Film Producers, 1940); and Richard M. Barsam, *Nonfiction Film: A Critical History* (Bloomington: Indiana University Press, 1992), 168.

[11] [Rick Prelinger], *Valley Town* shotlist, Internet Archive, www.archive.org/details/ValleyTo1940.

sequences and heavily revised the narration. The press reported the "extensive revisions" would delay the June 22 premiere at the New York World's Fair.[12] The more widely seen reedited version of *Valley Town* runs nearly ten minutes shorter, with major changes evident in the opening and closing sequences.

Both versions begin with a series of panning and dissolving shots looking down through smoky air at rows of chimneyed houses. A folksy voice (performed by actor Ray Collins) identifies himself as the longtime mayor of this unnamed American industrial town, narrating the community's bittersweet past. He tells of the "men and women who lived by machines." The narrator's distant but sympathetic telling of the lives of "the people" (a term repeated throughout) resonates with Thornton Wilder's play *Our Town*, which played on Broadway throughout 1938 and was being adapted in Hollywood at the time Van Dyke's film was being made. An even closer parallel: narrator Ray Collins was a member of Orson Welles's Mercury Players, who performed *Our Town* as a CBS radio drama in 1939. Less than half of the elegiac opening sequence survived the reedit. As the mayor tells of the generations of immigrants who "came a thousand miles" to "work the machines," we see enormous empty buildings and rusting oversized machine parts. Expressively lighted and composed images of gravestones follow, bearing a dozen European languages and birthplaces. (Wilder's narrator similarly introduces *Our Town* by referencing the graveyard and the neighboring "Polish town.") The mayor's somber rhetoric underscores the loss, as "machines were changed and the people were changed. It happened once in every man's lifetime, and sometimes twice. And then he got too old to move." The gravestones and dinosaur machine parts are not in the revised edition, nor are most of the mayor's words. Instead, he says that "smoke over these houses" meant "good times."

A loud chime abruptly begins an energetic workday, as we see the town clock at 6:00 a.m. (see also *Our Town*). We meet in close-up a steel worker leaving home with his lunch pail, an unnamed man who becomes the focus of a later scene. After showing the morning activity, *Valley Town* transitions to the factory floor. The mayor tells us that the older men we see operating machines are retrained "skilled hands." A music-driven montage of the steel rolling mill in action illustrates the three thousand jobs that fed as many families while the narrator explains, "The machines brought life to our town." Composer-critic Paul Bowles saw the first cut of *Valley Town* and praised Marc Blitzstein's scoring of this "machine sequence." He also insightfully referred to it as "the traditional 'second movement' of social documentaries: mechanization of industry."[13]

---

[12] "'Valley Town' to Be Revised," *NYT*, June 21, 1940. *And So They Live* began its fair run the following week. "Program for Today at the World's Fair," *NYT*, June 28, 1940.

[13] Paul Bowles, "On the Film Front," *Modern Music* (Nov.–Dec. 1940), in *Paul Bowles on Music*, ed. Timothy Mangan and Irene Herrmann (Berkeley: University of California Press, 2003), 33.

Another montage follows, showing Main Street shoppers reaping the benefits of a thriving economy. But "the wheels stopped" with the coming of the Depression, illustrated by empty storefronts on a gray, snowy day. "Two thirds of the town on relief." When economic recovery brings new steel orders, the latest "automatic, high-speed strip mill" does the work of thirty men. As we see the machinery in action, the mayor's voice switches from folksy to mechanical, speaking a staccato recitative: "Automatic. High-speed. Powerful. Accurate. Never gets tired. Never gets sick."

Now midway through the film, *Valley Town* follows this cue into a radical and unexpected change in register. Blitzstein's modernist musical score moves into a Brechtian mode. Like Van Dyke, Bertolt Brecht admired the composer's *The Cradle Will Rock* (1937), a leftist labor drama set in Steeltown, U.S.A., which ran on Broadway and in steel towns and union halls in 1938.[14] Blitzstein repeats its technique of "proletarian opera," with vernacular dialog sung or chanted throughout an extended scene.

The anonymous steel worker from the 6:00 a.m. sequence is now unemployed, walking home to his wife and children. We hear his interior monologue: "What the devil am I going home for? Just to walk in the door and say, 'No job again'?" He comments on the idle neighbors he passes: "They're thinkin' and I'm thinkin' when is that mill gonna open again? When do we work? There's nothing wrong with me! I can still work!" As he dejectedly enters the house, his wife is mentally calculating the pennies they will need for food. Her voice too is an interior soliloquy, but it intensifies the Brechtian effect by being sung. "What happens after all you saved is gone? . . . Oh, far away, there's a place with work and joy and cheer. . . . The dream, it ends somehow, with never here or now." As they eat in silence, Van Dyke shows the couple's forlorn faces in alternating tight close-ups (fig. 12.1).

The woman's more devastating second song was shortened from the original, in which we hear her sing, "They say they're tearin' down the mill soon. Why if that were so, I know then, some day he'd walk right out of here and never come back to us again." On screen, we see her weep. "Tell me, where is that place with work and joy and cheer?" she asks, looking at parts of her decaying house. Meanwhile, her husband, thinking facetiously about the "wonderful" "age of machines and gadgets," smuggles their electric toaster under his coat and slips out to hock it.

Abandoning the pair, *Valley Town* cuts to its best-known sequence. A couple dozen men solemnly gather to watch the demolition of a mill's smokestacks. Van Dyke intercuts shots of the idle men looking up with six shots of dismantled

---

[14] Michael Denning, *The Cultural Front: The Laboring of American Culture in the Twentieth Century* (New York: Verso, 1997), 285–90.

Figure 12.1. From left to right: Frames appearing in both editions of *Valley Town* (1940). The unemployed steel worker arrives home to his wife. Their voices are heard as interior monologues and song over these images.

towers crashing to the ground (fig. 12.2). (As he later pointed out, the men were not present at the demolition. He filmed them at a different location.) Accompanied by a suspenseful timpani roll, the scene functions as a climax. The dying town is now dead. Five men wander through the ruins of a factory ground, huddling around a small fire.

The mayor's narration returns, speculating about what will happen now that the company has "cut those smokestacks out of the sky." A revised text replaces most of the mayor's lines in this final section. In Pollard and Maddow's first version, the mayor heaps blame on "the company": "These men should have had notice. They should have been given dismissal wages." In *Valley Town*'s only instance of onscreen characters speaking aloud, each of these real displaced workers offer isolated comments. "But what good are the machines if they throw

Figure 12.2. From left to right: Frames 1 through 5 from *Valley Town*'s climactic montage sequence, as the dying steel company "cut those smokestacks out of the sky." The last image (bottom, right) is the final one in the film.

us out of work?" and "Prosperity for who? Not for him, not for you, not for me!" are typical of the critical, even resentful tone of these lines, most of which were deleted from the more widely seen version.

"They're being wasted and thrown away," the mayor protests in his final statement. His argument in the long edition sounds more like a populist harangue against a never-named U.S. Steel (or General Motors) than a Sloan-funded educational film: "Let's think about the people. New machines are coming. . . . But what about the men they replace? . . . Let's look to the people. Let's not forget the people." These words too were eliminated. However, as a critique *Valley Town* falls short of even mentioning the role of labor unions, something on the minds of all steel and autoworkers in these years.

The revised *Valley Town* replaces the corporate critique with the mayor's simple plea for worker retraining. In its final moments, the recut (done in June and July 1940) brings the national defense emergency to the fore. The lament for the unemployed is replaced by a flurry of help-wanted ads for tool-and-die men.[15] Footage of older, retrained men at lathes returns, accompanied by narration: "We're meeting a crisis now. Government and industry are working together to retrain these men." The culminating shots show mechanics working on aircraft engines. However, a poetic final shot (in both versions) returns to the melancholic image of the unemployed. The camera lingers on a low-angle close-up of one of the idle men first seen during the smokestack demolition, the face of the steel worker who afterward says, "I'm only 25 years old. *I'm* not obsolete." Now he is silent, looking pensively off-screen while a strong wind blows through his hair.

The Kentucky Films

When Spencer Pollard learned that the crew he sent to Kentucky to shoot his script for *The Children Must Learn* was having difficulty, he had Willard Van Dyke suspend production of *Valley Town* to join them on location. Pollard had hired John Ferno and Julian Roffman to codirect a related pair of films, shooting both in Kentucky. According to Van Dyke, he and cinematographer Bob Churchill ignored the work Ferno and Roffman were doing, found a new location, and shot everything for *The Children Must Learn* in a week.[16] Ferno's team finished production of the more ambitious *And So They Live*.

Running thirteen minutes, *The Children Must Learn* demonstrates a director working creatively with a limited budget. Like *Valley Town*, it was filmed silently in 35mm, then edited in New York, where its soundtrack was created. For this piece, members of the Group Theatre provided the sound elements. Actor Myron McCormick delivers the low-key voiceover narration. Fred Stewart created a music track with a small mixed-voice ensemble providing textless melodies, humming, whistling, and parts of two traditional songs.

The first of the two principal sections of *The Children Must Learn* introduces the home of a family of five unnamed "mountain people" who, the narrator tells us, scrape out a living on deforested land and depleted soil. A father and mother tend to their three children on a winter morning, sending the eldest off to school after breakfast. As the man chops firewood, the narrator describes

---

[15] In a particular irony, the coauthor of *Valley Town*'s commentary, Ben Maddow, had only months earlier written *United Action Means Victory* (1939, Frontier Films), a documentary about the Tool and Die Makers strike against General Motors. The United Auto Workers sponsored the militant film.

[16] Enyeart, *Willard Van Dyke,* 217–18.

him as representative of the descendents of pioneers. Throughout, the commentary struggles to balance a respect for these "cousins of the people who built America" with its argument that "new ideas" are needed for these people "lost in old ways." (This harsh assessment escalates in a coda, which presents shots of unidentified "old folks" and concludes "It's too late now for the old ones. The children must learn.")

As the father enters his cabin, the plaintive music transitions to a lament sung by a high tenor: "O, man, O poor man, come tell me true / how you may take your family / your children who are small / how you may take your family / and how you'll bring them through." The mother enters to dress the baby boy, while a chorus sings a folk song: "What do you want for your breakfast? Oh, Willie, tell me." The cheerful tune, however, intimates a child's death, with the rejoinder "I don't want nothin,' mother / Fix my bed soon / I'm sick in my heart / I want to lie down."[17]

We follow mother to the kitchen, where she stoically prepares breakfast. Her nuclear family gathers round a table, heartily eating sausage with corn pone and gravy. But the voiceover offers a bleak assessment: "Often there isn't enough to eat, never the right things to eat. No green vegetables and milk. . . . Weak bones from poor food; poor food from poor land. Kids growing up to the same years of hunger." Still, we see mother pack a lunch for her daughter, who sets off to school in the snow.

As the second part begins, the daughter enters the schoolhouse with other children. Their teacher begins and the students take out books. We see samples of what the students are reading. The first is a lesson in stamp collecting. The second, a passage from a fairy tale about a golden bowl on a silver table. Third comes a poem beginning "It's very hard to spend a penny / The kinds of candy are so many. . . . But, oh! you feel so rich and grand / To hold a penny in your hand."[18] The final reading is a poignant performance. The daughter stands to read aloud. For the only time in the film, we hear a character's voice. A young girl with an authentic-sounding accent reads haltingly from a Horatio Alger–like story. As

---

[17] The lyrics are from "Lord Randall," an Appalachian folk song, derived from an English-Scottish ballad. The children's song "(Oh Where Have You Been) Billy Boy" is another variation—as is Bob Dylan's "A Hard Rain's A-Gonna Fall" (1962). See James M. Hylton, 1941 notes on "Lord Randal" [sic], James Taylor Adams Collection, Ferrum College (Nov. 17, 2007), www.ferrum.edu/applit/texts/LordRandal.htm.

[18] "Beginning a Stamp Collection," in Ullin W. Leavell, *Trails of Adventure* (New York: American Book Co., 1936), 282. The story of thrift is from the same textbook, which was related to the American Book Company's McGuffey Reader, famous for espousing thrift. The fairy tale is "Wishing Wishes" by Maud Lindsay, originally published in her book *More Mother Stories* (Springfield, MA: Milton Bradley, 1906); the students are reading the tale from the primer by Bessie Blackstone Coleman, Willis Lemon Uhl, and James Fleming Hosic, *The Pathway to Reading* (New York: Silver Burdett, 1932), 26–36. The poem "A Penny to Spend" is in the same primer (59).

with the other texts, the passage underlines how alien the textbook rhetoric and subject matter are to these children. She declaims:

> "There's no doubt of it," said Mr. Curtis one day, "that one of the greatest factors in success is for a young fellow to learn thrift. . . . Take a young man who follows his policy of saving. He gets a little nest egg in the bank. He gets a chance to buy some good investment on a share in the business in which he is engaged as an employee. There is the nest egg in the bank which he can fall back upon. Suppose he wants to buy his first home and has not enough money. There again comes the value of a bank account, in that he can go to a banker, show him what he has saved, demonstrating that he is thrifty."[19]

As she reads, Lerner cuts away to Van Dyke's composed shots in the schoolroom (fig. 12.3). Three times we see low-angle shots of the girl holding her book. The other shots alternate between affectionate depictions (a girl in a tiny rocking chair, a tight close-up of a boy reading intently, girls trading smiles and whispers) and images connoting poverty (worn shoes and tattered clothing). The most conspicuous of these begins with the reader in medium close-up, then slowly tilts down the length of her body, stopping on her shoes. Van Dyke makes this a motif, earlier inserting shots of these same shoes, not fit for snow, during the daughter's trek to school.

The cruel irony of penniless rural children being taught subject matter irrelevant to their needs is similarly highlighted in *And So They Live*, whose script was loosely the source for *The Children Must Learn*. Two extended schoolhouse scenes set up the argument for curricular reform. Recorded with synchronous sound, they have an almost verité quality. The regional accents are distinctive and particular, cutting against the aestheticization that a studied close-up and a mellifluous soundtrack create elsewhere. First, the teacher has seventh and eighth graders take turns reading couplets from *The Canterbury Tales*. ("An eleventh-century legend," [fourteenth-, actually] the narrator says afterward, "remote in the lives of even city children, but stranger still to children who live on the land, who help their fathers work in the fields.")

Second, a geography lesson has the teacher talking about the windmills of Holland and the bounteous food Dutch children enjoy. The implication that Holland would be an alienating subject is undercut in the next sequence, where the narrator offers that the men who came to this place a hundred years before "were Scotch and Irish, Dutch and German." Further, the subjects of the film were working with a Dutch director, John Ferno, who had recently come to the

---

[19] The passage is from Edward W. Bok's *A Man from Maine* (New York: C. Scribner's Sons, 1923).

Figure 12.3. From left to right: Frames from *The Children Must Learn* (1940). The unnamed mountain family's daughter at home finishes an unhealthy breakfast (top, left). The remaining five images appear in the final schoolhouse sequence. The daughter stands and reads aloud a lesson about thrift.

United States from Holland with Helen van Dongen and Joris Ivens. The Dutch American Van Dyke was filming down the road.

The Kentucky films do not have the cutting irony or bewildering ambiguities of Luis Buñuel's *Land Without Bread* (1937), but the schoolhouse scenes beg comparison. Buñuel's narration comments on the education of impoverished kids in a remote region of Spain: "To these starving children, the teacher explains that the sum of the angles in a triangle equals two right angles." The brightest student writes from memory, we are told, the aphorism "Respect the property of others." And referencing the portrait of an eighteenth-century noblewoman hanging in the schoolhouse, the narrator asks, "Why is this absurd picture here?" The commentary in *And So They Live* is restrained, but a cutaway shot of a poster, "Hawaii by the Sea," invites a similar response. The makers of the Kentucky films had likely seen *Land Without Bread* quite recently. Buñuel deposited a print with the Museum of Modern Art in 1940 and personally introduced a screening there. A 1940 catalog published by the new Association of Documentary Film Producers offered that *Land Without Bread* "earned the enthusiastic praise of leaders of the documentary film movement." All of the principal personnel on Educational Film Institute productions were members of the association, as was Luis Buñuel.[20]

The structure of *And So They Live* mirrors its companion: a portrait of a malnourished family living on deforested land with poor soil, followed by scenes shot in a one-room schoolhouse. However, it also includes a remarkable third section, set in the family's home at twilight. An omniscient voiceover narration remains, performed with sympathy and restraint by Storrs Haynes.

Otherwise, *And So They Live* uses sound quite differently. The film delivers an open ending, the didactic narration supplemented by location sound recording. Haynes's final voiceover shifts into telegraphic rhythm. As we see the family eating supper, we hear, "Nothing but potatoes: skin infections. Only fat pork: dysentery. Nothing but cornbread and biscuit: pellagra." What follows is practically an ethnographic recording. Inside the darkening cabin, the family gathers to hear father play his banjo. He sings a traditional song, "Going Across the Sea," with the "high lonesome" timbre characteristic of Kentucky mountain music. His wee son, dressed in overalls, buck-dances to the music, his father shouting encouragement. Then, in a moment that no doubt alarmed its Eastern audiences, the father rewards the boy with a cigarette, which he lights and puffs like an experienced smoker. No commentary follows. *And So They Live* ends serenely, showing the exterior of the home at dusk, music slowly fading.

From Film Institute to Film Library to Film Society

With such nondidactic, artistic moments and persistent sympathy with working people, the experimental films lost their key audience: Alfred P. Sloan. Yet they would secure another in the expanding group of cinephiles who supported the film societies and art houses that flourished after World War II. Although Spencer Pollard, the economics scholar, shared the Sloan Foundation's goals, he also supported the concept of the documentarian as artist. He consented to the revisions that took some of the sting out of the films' critiques of industrial capitalism, but stood by the artistic innovation. "We've made three films our way, to good effect," he wrote to Chase on August 26, 1940, "[but we] disagree on methods." He asked the chancellor to intervene in the "stalemate." Pollard officially was on leave for the fall, but he never returned to NYU or to educational films.

---

[20] *Living Films*, 6.

Figure 12.4. Screen logo, ca. 1940s. Added to the head of distribution prints, it shows the Washington Square Arch, with NYU buildings in the background. The Film Library itself was in the main library, adjacent to Washington Square South.

Alfred Sloan had already cut off his support for Pollard and movie production. On June 24, 1940, the institute shut down two units in the field. Joris Ivens and his Frontier Film crew were shooting a feature-length EFI film in Colorado; John Ferno's team, a three-reeler in Illinois. The two directors ineffectually served legal notice on the Sloan Foundation for "discontinuance of production funds." Ivens told the press his action was to "defend the prestige of the documentary field."[21] Without Sloan money, the Educational Film Institute was closed after only one year of operation. However, the foundation extended some support to a more limited effort. The NYU Film Library lived on for another five decades, distributing 16mm prints of hundreds of educational films and publishing catalogs (fig. 12.4).[22]

With distribution beyond the classroom, the three EFI productions gathered an audience not as educational films but as artistic documentaries. The

---

[21] Thomas M. Pryor, "Pot Shots at the News," *NYT*, July 28, 1940. See also Hans Schoots, *Living Dangerously: A Biography of Joris Ivens* (Amsterdam: Amsterdam University Press, 2000).

[22] See "New York University Film Library," *Journal of Educational Sociology* 16, no. 4 (1942): 251–53; Esther Speyer, "Movies and Children: A Challenge to Parents," *Journal of Educational Sociology* 20, no. 7 (1947): 422–24; and Irene F. Cypher, "Filmstrips," *Educational Screen* (Jan, 1961): 31–34. In the late 1980s, NYU Libraries phased out its Film Library distribution. In the 1990s, much of the material went to Pennsylvania State University Audio-Visual Services. Some 16mm prints, including editions of *The Children Must Learn* and *Valley Town*, went to Rick Prelinger in exchange for laserdisc and CD-ROM copies of his series *Our Secret Century* (Voyager, 1996).

Association of Documentary Film Producers presented a public series called "Living History" throughout the fall of 1940. It included a screening of *And So They Live* and "lectures on the art of the documentary film" by Van Dyke and Ivens, as well as presentations by Robert Flaherty and John Grierson. Eleanor Roosevelt plugged *And So They Live* and *Valley Town* in her syndicated column, advocating their theatrical distribution. A year later, the Ferno-Roffman film was added to Columbia's required Contemporary Civilization course. After the war, the University of Chicago included both documentaries in its social science curriculum.[23]

The movies also became part of the earliest programs by Cinema 16, the influential New York film society that presented innovative screenings from 1947 to 1962. For a week in 1947, Amos Vogel programmed *And So They Live* ("John Ferno's powerful and moving commentary on the lives of simple people") between experimental animated films. In 1950, *Valley Town* headed a five-film program that epitomized Vogel's alchemical approach to intermixing documentary, educational, scientific, and experimental cinemas. As Vogel declared in his Cinema 16 notes, "This powerful and deeply moving portrayal of unemployment is a documentary film classic." He followed *Valley Town* with *Hypnotic Behavior* (1949, a clinical recording), *The Making of a Mural* (1947, with painter Thomas Hart Benton), Sidney Peterson's avant-garde *The Petrified Dog* (1948), and *Hausa Village* (1946), an ethnographic film shot in Nigeria for Britain's Colonial Office.[24] Ironically, having recontextualized the straight educational films as experimental art pieces, Vogel helped return them to the classroom: rather than serving the Sloan mission, the films were shown in NYU's first course devoted to avant-garde cinema. In 1950–1951, Vogel and professor George Amberg used Cinema 16 screenings to teach "New Frontiers in Cinema."[25]

---

[23] Douglas W. Churchill, "Screen News Here and in Hollywood," *NYT,* Oct. 28, 1940; Eleanor Roosevelt, "My Day," Dec. 2, 1940, electronic edition of Roosevelt's papers, George Washington University, www.gwu.edu/~erpapers/myday; "Movies Form Part of Columbia Study," *NYT,* Oct. 5, 1941; "Educational Films Plan of U. of Chicago," *Chicago Tribune,* Dec. 29, 1946.

[24] Thomas F. Brady, "Of Local Origin," *NYT,* Dec. 2, 1947; Scott MacDonald, *Cinema 16: Documents towards a History of the Film Society* (Philadelphia: Temple University Press, 2002), 135. Also in 1950, at the Institute of Contemporary Arts in Washington, DC, Amos Vogel programmed *And So They Live* between a British documentary on primates, *Monkey into Man* (1940), and the French cine-poem *La Rose et le Reseda* (1945). Richard L. Coe, "A Masterpiece Of Simplicity," *Washington Post,* May 5, 1950. Given that Vogel lived one block from the NYU Film Library, and that Cinema 16 screenings took place in the Provincetown Playhouse (also a block away), he doubtless had the university in mind when he said that the society was founded on the premise that "there were scores of superior nonfiction films gathering dust on film-library shelves." Amos Vogel, "Cinema 16: A Showcase for the Nonfiction Film," *Hollywood Quarterly* 4, no. 4 (1950): 420–22.

[25] MacDonald, *Cinema 16,* 21; David O'Neill, *Guide to the George Amberg and Robert Gessner Papers,* NYU Archives.

The migration of the EFI productions from economics lessons to art pieces made sense for the artist Willard Van Dyke, but not for the institute's underwriters, who thought films of fact could and should be delivered free of artistry. In March 1939, an NYU advisor had forewarned the chancellor about the "too aesthetic" problem. Chase asked Donald Slesinger, head of the American Film Center, about the feasibility of making films to teach economics. Slesinger replied with a caveat: "The motion picture is the perfect medium for such a presentation, but the motion picture alone is not enough." He cited Pare Lorentz's *The River* (1938, with cinematography by Van Dyke) as a documentary that "used all the cinematic arts" but which lacked any follow-up to generate social action. If NYU made films that were "too aesthetic," he wrote, they could even have a "negative effect on action."[26]

While the aestheticization of unemployment and malnutrition may have distracted from the EFI mission, the films could not be measured as having a negative effect on attempts to teach economics. For two years, the NYU Film Library kept detailed records of audience feedback from dozens of screenings. All three films were rented regularly to schools and other nontheatrical venues. Most written responses were positive. Few viewers complained about style, though they noted the "depressing" nature of the films. Lacking the follow-up of a sustained, cross-media educational campaign, the trio of documentaries had no measurable impact on the problems they addressed.

In fact, the coordinators of the EFI contradicted themselves in statements published in *Educational Screen*. Harold Sloan said the foundation conceived of them as a longitudinal study, something EFI planning documents never mentioned. "The original idea in making these pictures," Sloan suggested "was to put them in vaults [!] for the present and add to them from time to time as the studies developed, releasing them when the experiments themselves showed positive results." In contrast, Chancellor Chase rationalized that the institute, by design, made each film "according to different documentary techniques." Sounding more like an aesthete than an administrator, he concluded, "Our hope is that the differences will help advance the art of documentary film production." But by September 1940, production had ceased and Pollard had departed NYU.[27]

Another mischaracterization of the EFI project appeared in that same *Educational Screen* article. Both Kentucky films begin with scrolling titles announcing they were produced "in cooperation with the University of Kentucky," but there is no record of the school being directly involved. In fact, there is no record that the films were ever shown in Kentucky at all. What was true, in part,

---

[26] Donald Slesinger, letter to Chase, Mar. 24, 1939, NYU Archives.

[27] "Educational Film Institute Uses Motion Pictures to Report Educational Experiments," *Educational Screen*, Sept. 1940, 304–5; "Documentary Film Programs," *Educational Screen*, Dec. 1940, 431, 433.

was the claim that the EFI productions were linked to Sloan Foundation projects conducted by state universities and coordinated by Columbia Teachers College professor Harold F. Clark. He worked with educators in Kentucky, Florida, and Vermont to investigate how (or if) local schools could improve (respectively) diet, clothing, and housing for people in the communities they served. Motion pictures were seldom mentioned in his research. To the contrary, Clark most often addressed the need to increase experiential learning, especially in poor and rural areas.

Although his name does not appear on *The Children Must Learn* or *And So They Live* (nor in EFI documentation), Clark's ideas shaped the scripts. Both films include an identical piece of footage: a close-up of hands flipping through a hand-drawn picture book, *Let's Learn about Goats.* "Next year the children will study materials prepared in their own community," both narrators say, "about facts of soil and food, along with reading and writing." These "food bulletins" were produced as part of the larger Sloan Project in Applied Economics between 1941 and 1949.[28] Clark (himself from eastern Kentucky) headed the long-term study and later coauthored a series of books with Harold Sloan. Some ideas in the EFI films derived from Clark's prior work. In particular, he made headlines as early as 1929 for inveighing against the teaching of thrift, an unpopular idea dramatized in *The Children Must Learn*. Other Clark ideas translated to the screen included his critique of teaching *The Canterbury Tales* and the geography of Switzerland and Holland, as well as his advocacy for teaching malnourished children about milking goats.[29]

The Artless, Sponsored Educational Film

Donald Slesinger's advice—that educational films should avoid being "too aesthetic" and that a motion picture alone could not effect change—jibed with Harold Clark's pragmatic, multifaceted approach to education reform.

As historian David Farber puts it in *Sloan Rules: Alfred P. Sloan and the Triumph of General Motors*, although the industrialist "was particularly interested

---

[28] Marie Goodwin Halbert, *Let's Learn about Goats* (Lexington: Bureau of School Service, University of Kentucky, 1942), one of a score of Food Bulletins (1941–1947) prepared for the Sloan Project in Applied Economics. Clara M. Olson and Norman D. Fletcher coauthored a summary of the project, *Learn and Live* (1946), for the Sloan Foundation.

[29] "Thrift Is Harmful, Economist Asserts," Nov. 13, 1929; Harold F. Clark, "A Child's Handling of Money Weighed," Feb. 14, 1932; Clark, "To Educate All Youths," July 17, 1932; Benjamin Fine, "New Teaching Improves Living," Apr. 27, 1941, all in *NYT*. See also Harold F. Clark and Maurice F. Seay, "An Effort to Extend the Measurement of the Results of Schooling into the Social and Economic Fields," *Journal of Educational Research* 33 (May 1940): 685–91; Seay and Clark, *The School Curriculum and Economic Improvement*, Bulletin of the University of Kentucky Bureau of School Service (Sept. 1940).

in exploring the utility of film in spreading the free-enterprise gospel," the philanthropist's designs for an NYU Educational Film Institute "saw little clear success in his efforts to change the public's perception of the free enterprise system." Sloan failed to affect classroom education, but while head of General Motors from 1937 to 1956, he deployed a powerful production and distribution system for sponsored films. Before Sloan's reign, the company, like most big businesses, was making films, such as *General Motors around the World* (1927), which promoted its status. He also supported the motion picture efforts of the influential National Association of Manufacturers. Its short *Men and Machines* (1936) was a forerunner of Sloan's attempt to foist the subject on NYU. The film featured celebrity newsreel narrator Lowell Thomas extolling the mechanization of the workplace as good for both labor and business.[30]

As Rick Prelinger shows elsewhere in this book, General Motors, working with the Detroit-based filmmakers at the Jam Handy Organization, had a formidable motion picture operation, which was designed to promote belief in free-market capitalism as much as to sell cars. Its penetration extended into the theatrical realm, as demonstrated by *We Drivers* (1936), a safety film that reached thousands of theaters and millions of viewers—and by 1941 was distributed by the NYU Film Library to boot. The symphonic *Master Hands* (1936) is now regarded as one of the most artfully crafted industrial films of the era. In response to successful union strikes against GM, the company produced *From Dawn to Sunset* (1937), depicting a harmonious day in the life of a typical autoworker. *'Round and 'Round* (1938) simplistically explains the supply-and-demand marketplace, using stop-motion toys. Coinciding with the modest EFI efforts, General Motors was making films on a grand scale (including Technicolor sequences) for the New York World's Fair. *On to Jupiter* (1939) showed a fantasy of corporate economic progress. *To New Horizons* (1940) celebrated the company's noted Futurama exhibit at the fair.

Lessons Learned

Given Alfred P. Sloan's success with General Motors–sponsored films, the failure of his foundation's Educational Film Institute at New York University was hardly a blow to his fortunes or influence. Rather it demonstrated the tensions between the aesthetics of documentary cum educational film and a motion picture's demonstrable power to educate. The discrepancies between artful documentary and the prosaic classroom film were not necessarily irreconcilable.

---

[30] Farber, *Sloan Rules,* 211. The National Association of Manufacturers (NAM) distributed *Men and Machines* in a "multimedia package" as part of its "Business Facts Program," according to Rick Prelinger, *The Field Guide to Sponsored Films* (San Francisco: National Film Preservation Foundation, 2006), 62. See also *Men and Machines,* Booklet no. 2 (New York: NAM, 1937).

Artists and educators were both cognizant of the tensions. Paul Bowles articulated for the avant-garde Slesinger's "too aesthetic" warning. Of *Valley Town*, whose song-soliloquies he praised, Bowles noted as problematic "the ascribing to the wife of a steelworker a song which in 1940 is still of a subtlety that limits its intelligibility to the sophisticated, politically or otherwise."[31]

Ultimately, it was more than political differences between the conservative industrialist Sloan and *Valley Town*'s critique of capitalism that proved the undoing of the institute. From the beginning, Alfred and Harold Sloan found incompatibilities among the cultures of business, philanthropy, art, and education. Shortly before getting NYU's commitment in 1939, Harold told Alfred, "As you say, the project may be a flop." More telling was Alfred's response to Harold's announcement that the NYU deal was done. Betraying his foundation's supposed nonpartisanship, he complained of "the difficulty" that "these educational projects" had in getting "the job done the way we think it ought to be done." Anticipating the EFI project would fail him, Alfred wrote: "We are trying to sell an idea, rather than to set up an educational debate," adding "it is hard for me to appreciate this so-called 'educational' approach."[32]

Although the Sloan reaction to *Valley Town* triggered the shutdown of EFI, Harold's assessment of the EFI project in 1941 reported there had been "many troubles" and "vexations" throughout. However, he also expressed pride in the films the institute had made. *And So They Live* and *The Children Must Learn* "received universal approbation," his report said. "One critic predicted that they would prove to be the most remarkable American documentaries ever produced." They were "on the market" and in demand. While the first cut of *Valley Town* "proved rather unsatisfactory," viewers of the revised version found the film "carried conviction" and was of "uniformly great interest."

Finally, the Sloan Foundation's report on lessons learned from the Educational Film Institute experiment echoed the field's struggle to define formal criteria for effective educational productions. Harold Sloan could only offer trite conclusions: educational films should be objective documentaries about real people in specific situations, rather than acted pieces in generic settings. Ideally, he concluded, "a pure documentary type of technique" made for the most effective educational form, by which he meant the technique seen in the EFI films. Given the failure of the ambitious enterprise, particularly its inability to evidence any impact on viewers' knowledge of economics, it was a stunning and contradictory conclusion, one that did little to advance "educational film," even if it aided the art of documentary.[33]

---

[31] Bowles, "On the Film Front," 32.

[32] Harold S. Sloan memo to Alfred P. Sloan Jr., Mar. 24, 1939; Alfred memo to Harold, June 8, 1939. (Richard Angelo generously provided copies of both.)

[33] *Motion Picture Operations of the Alfred P. Sloan Foundation.*

Filmography

And So They Live (1940) 22 min., 35mm

PRODUCTION: Educational Film Institute, New York University; University of Kentucky. DIRECTORS: John Ferno, Julian Roffman. WRITERS: John Ferno, Edwin Locke, Julian Roffman. MUSIC: Lee Gron. EDITOR: Irving Lerner. NARRATORS: George Tiplady, House Jamison. ACCESS: LC/Prelinger; NARA; MacDonald and Associates; Indiana University Wells Library (DVD); Rutgers University (16mm); Internet Archive, www.archive.org/details/AndSoTheyLive.

The Children Must Learn (1940) 13 min., 35mm

PRODUCTION: Educational Film Institute of New York University and Documentary Film Productions, Inc. DIRECTOR: Willard Van Dyke. WRITER: Spencer Pollard. CAMERA: Bob Churchill. MUSIC: Fred Stewart. EDITOR: Irving Lerner. NARRATOR: Myron McCormick. ACCESS: Library of Congress; NARA; DVD *Historic Appalachia Culture Films* (Quality Information Publishers, 2007); Internet Archive, www.archive.org/details/Children1940.

The Machine: Master or Slave? (1941) 14 min., 16mm

SPONSOR: Alfred P. Sloan Foundation. DISTRIBUTOR: Educational Film Institute, New York University. DIRECTOR: Walter Niebuhr. WRITER: Charlton Ogburn Jr. CAMERA: Dan Cavelli, Frank Zucker. NARRATOR: Don Goddard. ALTERNATE VERSION: The first version was entitled *The Challenge* (1938) when it was test screened. ACCESS: Library of Congress; MacDonald and Associates; Internet Archive, www.archive.org/details/machine-master_or_slave.

Valley Town: A Study of Machines and Men (1940) 35 min.; 25 min. rev. ed.; 35mm

PRODUCTION: Educational Film Institute of New York University and Documentary Film Productions, Inc. DIRECTOR: Willard Van Dyke. WRITERS: Spencer Pollard, Willard Van Dyke, Daniel Wolff [Ben Maddow]. CAMERA: Robert Barlow, Bob Churchill. EDITOR: Irving Lerner. MUSIC: Marc Blitzstein. NARRATOR: Ray Collins. ACCESS: Original version available for video purchase or 16mm rental, Museum of Modern Art Circulating Film and Video Library. Internet Archive includes both the uncut version (www.archive.org/details/ValleyTown-AStudyOfMachinesAndMen) and the revised release version (www.archive.org/details/ValleyTo1940).

Related Films

From Dawn to Sunset (1937) 24 min., 35mm
SPONSOR: Chevrolet/General Motors. PRODUCTION: Jam Handy
Organization. ACCESS: Internet Archive, www.archive.org/details/
FromDawn1937.

General Motors Around the World (1927) 38 min., 35mm
SPONSOR: General Motors Export Co. PRODUCTION: Newspapers
Film Corp. [Jam Handy]. ACCESS: www.archive.org/details/
GeneralM1927.

Men and Dust (1940) 17 min., 35mm
SPONSOR: Tri-State Survey Committee. DIRECTOR: Lee Dick.
WRITER/CAMERA: Sheldon Dick. MUSIC: Fred Stewart.
NARRATORS: Storrs Haynes, Will Geer, Eric Walz. ACCESS:
MoMA; NARA; MacDonald and Associates.

Men and Machines (1936) 10 min., 35mm
SPONSOR: National Association of Manufacturers. PRODUC-
TION: Audio Productions, Inc. NARRATOR: Lowell Thomas.
ACCESS: MacDonald and Associates.

On to Jupiter (1939) 20 min., 35mm
SPONSOR: General Motors. PRODUCTION: Sound Masters Inc.
ACCESS: General Motors Media Archives; University of Georgia
Media Archives; MacDonald and Associates.

'Round and 'Round (1938) 6 min., 35mm and 16mm
SPONSOR: General Motors. PRODUCTION: Jam Handy
Organization. ACCESS: Internet Archive, www.archive.org/details/
Roundand1939.

To New Horizons (1940) 23 min., 35mm
SPONSOR: General Motors. PRODUCTION: Jam Handy
Organization. ACCESS: Available on video compilations, beginning
with Rick Prelinger's *To New Horizons: Ephemeral Films 1931–1945,*
VHS and laserdisc (Criterion, 1987) and CD-ROM (Voyager, 1994).
Lesser-quality versions on DVD include: *Historical World Fairs, New
York,* vol. 4 (AtoZcds.com, 2004); *Futurism & Kitchen of the Future
Film Collection* (Historical Archive Corporation, 2006); Quality
Information Publishers' *Vintage Highways & Roads* (2006); and
Historic World's Fair Films, New York, 1939–1940 (2007). Internet
Archive, www.archive.org/details/ToNewHor1940.

We Drivers (1936) 10 min., 35mm and 16mm.
SPONSOR: General Motors. PRODUCTION: Jam Handy
Organization. ACCESS: George Eastman House; Internet Archive,
www.archive.org/details/WeDriver1936.

The Year's Work (1940) 3 reels, 35mm
SPONSOR: General Mills. PRODUCTION: Documentary Film
Productions. DIRECTORS: Willard Van Dyke, Herbert Kerkow.
CAMERA: Willard Van Dyke, Bob Churchill. ACCESS: None
known.

13 SPREADING THE WORD: RACE, RELIGION, AND THE RHETORIC OF CONTAGION IN EDGAR G. ULMER'S TB FILMS

DEVIN ORGERON

Nontheatrical Material and the Legacy of Authorship

There has been and to some degree there remains a substantial culture of blindness and resistance within the evolving field of cinema studies. The largest academic film organization in the United States, the Society for Cinema and Media Studies (SCMS), adopted the "M" for "media" rather late in life (2003), though its annual conferences have always featured much broader research interests than the "C" ever indicated. The same organization's quarterly publication is still called *Cinema Journal*, though the pages of this publication have routinely explored a wide range of visual media—cinematic and otherwise—that push against the traditionally defined parameters that have long hemmed our understanding of *Cinema* with a capital "C." In spite of these advancements, it is clear that the work film scholars did in the 1960s and 1970s to justify their object of study had the not entirely unrelated effect of closing off that field of inquiry to marginalized, though certainly never marginal, media.

Industrial, military, and most especially educational films, if considered at all, are typically relegated to a footnote in nonfiction film or documentary scholarship. This elision arises in part from the mistaken notion that these so-called ephemeral films have simply disappeared into the ether, somehow proving their truncated shelf-life or their questionable relevance beyond the initial, purely functional point of contact.[1] This critical neglect, however, stands in the face of

---

[1] This oversight is key because sponsored films have historically been central objects of inquiry within documentary studies, though the terms of sponsorship are infrequently examined. With regard to educational films, the first wave of documentary scholarship, which continues to exert considerable force over our contemporary definitions, was well aware of the pedagogical potential of nonfiction film. See, for example, Erik Barnouw, *Documentary: A History of the Non-Fiction Film* (New York: Oxford University Press, 1993). The breadth of Barnouw's

the sometimes begrudgingly acknowledged volume of material known to have been produced within nontheatrical realms. It also challenges the even more uncomfortable fact that, like the mountains of lost silent-era films mourned by scholars and fans, these materials, whose academic value remains to be assessed, face an uncertain future.

Film studies, in the sixties and seventies, was marked by a surge of interest and faith in the auteur. Directors "on the margins" of the Hollywood mainstream were frequently lionized in both European and North American criticism for their ability to imprint their unique authorial signature on works produced within a factory-like system focused on the bottom line, not personal style. In some of this criticism, a comparatively well-known filmmaker's "lesser" works were exalted over studio showpieces or "masterworks" for the presumed access these seemingly negligible films granted to authorial intention. In short, an overly romantic and difficult to shake addiction to directorial identification and evaluation was established during these years. This addiction has had its casualties.

There is no doubt that some previously underappreciated American directors—Sam Fuller, Nicholas Ray, and Howard Hawks are a few of the most celebrated—were "discovered" in this climate. Another of these rediscoveries was the Austrian-born Edgar G. Ulmer, sometimes called the "King of PRC," after Producers Releasing Corporation, the sub-low-budget, Poverty Row studio where he directed eleven pictures. As early as 1956, French critic Luc Moullet wrote adoringly of Ulmer's work, lamenting its relative invisibility and charting the progression of a set of thematic and formal obsessions that characterized it. A cult of American critics and scholars (Andrew Sarris, Peter Bogdanovich, John Belton, and others) would follow suit in the ensuing years.[2] As Ulmer's career

---

"nonfiction" category, however, has resulted in an impasse. Categories of nonfiction media seem to fit into this unwieldy container but are seldom written about because they are "other" than documentary. Michael Renov and Bill Nichols provide a blueprint for understanding and theorizing about the particular rhetorical position educational, industrial, and military films occupy in the nonfiction realm, though that blueprint has remained underutilized. See Michael Renov, *The Subject of Documentary* (Minneapolis: University of Minnesota Press, 2004); and Bill Nichols, *Representing Reality: Issues and Concepts in Documentary* (Bloomington: Indiana University Press, 1991).

[2] See Luc Moullet, "Edgar G. Ulmer," *Cahiers du Cinema* 58 (April 1956): 55–57. Also see Andrew Sarris, *The American Cinema: Directors and Directions 1929–1968* (1968; reprint, Cambridge: Da Capo Press, 1996), 142–43. Sarris begins his entry on Ulmer with what has been historicized as an indirect citation of Moullet's piece, writing, "The French call him *un cineaste maudit*, and directors certainly don't come any more *maudit* [cursed]." Moullet's entry only obliquely refers to Ulmer's "curse," although he and fellow *Cahiers* critic François Truffaut likely used the phrase elsewhere. Truffaut attended the first and second Festivals independent du Film Maudit in Biarritz in 1949 and 1950 and gave talks about them. See Antoine de Baecque and

came into focus, however, so too did its enormous, almost stupefying scope. Auteur critics and their scholarly progeny agreed that entertainment, no matter its presumed caliber, could harbor creativity and was worthy of scholarly attention. But what to do with a filmmaker whose career was built around what might be seen as a more practical brand of image-making?[3]

Along with an impressive roster of theatrical films, the best known of which are *The Black Cat* (1934) and *Detour* (1945), Tag Gallagher estimates that Ulmer directed forty-two industrial films, several military training films, and a few advertisements for the Coca-Cola Bottling Company.[4] Bogdanovich, in his 1970 interviews with the filmmaker, acknowledged material scarcely visible to Moullet and Sarris: some of the sponsored films, the Yiddish and Ukrainian features, and a nudie picture. The strands of Ulmer's career, however, were held together with material most film scholars—and, for that matter, Ulmer himself—simply glossed. Making ends meet and making meaning were conveniently imagined to be mutually exclusive categories, and as the years passed, this "marginal" work and any hope of engaging with it seemed to recede further into the background of Ulmer's already complex career.

Some of this material, however, has begun to surface, and my aim here is to unearth a body of neglected Ulmer films that fall under the educational rubric. From the late 1930s through the early 1940s, Ulmer directed what appears to be

---

Serge Toubiana, *Truffaut: A Biography,* trans. Catherine Temerson (Berkeley: University of California Press, 2000), 47–57. Instrumental in cementing Ulmer's stateside cult status were Peter Bogdanovich, "Edgar G. Ulmer," in Bogdanovich, *Who the Devil Made It* (New York: Ballantine Books, 1997), 558–604; John Belton, *Hollywood Professionals,* vol. 3, *Howard Hawks, Frank Borzage, Edgar G. Ulmer* (New York: A. S. Barnes, 1974); and Belton, *Cinema Stylists* (Metuchen, NJ: Scarecrow Press, 1983). Noah Isenberg has pieced together a less "embellished" and more complete version of Ulmer's career than has been previously available in "Perennial Detour: The Cinema of Edgar G. Ulmer and the Experience of Exile," *Cinema Journal* 43 (Winter 2004): 3–25.

[3] Dan Streible, Martina Roepke, and Anke Mebold discuss issues of nontheatrical authorship, suggesting (à la Rick Prelinger) that the sector had its own auteurs and that many otherwise well-known directors "moonlighted" in this realm. See "Nontheatrical Film," *Film History* 19, no. 4 (2007): 339–43.

[4] Tag Gallagher, "All Lost in Wonder," *Screening the Past* 12 (2001): www.latrobe.edu.au/screeningthepast/firstrelease/fr0301/tgafr12a.htm. The online version is an English translation of the Swedish original, "Förtrollad av ett under: Edgar G. Ulmer," *Filmhäftet* 27, no. 4 (1999): 30–39. Ulmer's detailed, typewritten sketch of this period (provided to me by daughter Arianné Ulmer Cipes) reports the same figure, indicating also that from 1940 to 1941, he directed eight commercials. The numbers game, I hasten to add, is a dangerous one to play when attempting to get a handle on Ulmer's career. Ulmer's penchant for hyperbole coupled with the perceived disposability of many of the materials in question makes an accurate count all but impossible. I suspect that he directed "many" industrial and educational films.

eight educational health shorts for the National Tuberculosis Association (NTA). The dates attached to these films vary from source to source, though something close to a chronology might be ascertained based largely on Ulmer's own press clippings, his contracts and itemized budgets for the films, and the Tuberculosis Association's rather detailed promotional catalog entries.[5] The films include: *Let My People Live* (1938); *Cloud in the Sky* (1939); *They Do Come Back, Goodbye Mr. Germ,* and *Diagnostic Procedures* (all 1940); *Another to Conquer* (1941); and a mysterious pair of undated, unconfirmed Fox Movietone films, *Mantoux Text* and *Life is Good*.[6] These films, which serve quite admirably the educational function they were designed for and should by no means be separated from the historical context that gave rise to them, shift our traditional, staid understanding of cinematic authorship. Guided by the hand of a media-savvy sponsoring body with a clearly defined mission, these films are the product of the NTA's guiding efforts. They are also, however, the work of a director with a unique understanding of the role germs—literal and metaphorical—play in the American social fabric. This understanding is evidenced in the films Ulmer made outside of the NTA-sponsored films.

Recall, for example, the fact that Vera (Ann Savage), the cruel but pathetic femme fatale in Ulmer's *Detour*, made several years after the TB campaign, is dying of tuberculosis. While holed up in cheap rented room, Vera starts coughing. Her hostage, Al (Tom Neal), says to her, "You've got a mean cough . . . you oughta do something about it." Vera snaps back, with visible though wounded hostility, "I'll be alright," to which Al replies, not skipping a beat, ". . . s'what Camile said . . ." and then, under his breath, an insult aimed at his captor: "nobody you'd know." Looking unusually concerned, even fragile, Vera asks, "Wasn't that the dame that died of consumption?"

---

[5] Bogdanovich's Ulmer filmography, based on his conversations with the filmmaker, contains some inconsistencies that have been handed down. These inconsistencies—including a story recounting the success of *Let My People Live* at the 1939 World's Fair, followed by a 1942 production date for the film—are compounded by varying dates, for example, in the National Archives catalog. I am grateful to Arianné Ulmer Cipes for providing a paper trail that has shed some light on this period of her father's career. More valuable still have been references to some of the films in educational and medical trade publications from the period Ulmer was making these films.

[6] *Let My People Live* was completed in 1938 and appears to have been selectively screened that year, but it was shown most actively at the New York World's Fair in 1939. Additionally, *Cloud in the Sky* was completed and copyrighted in 1939, but appears to have been released in 1940. The later dates recorded in the National Archives catalogue are probably dates of accession, not of copyright or release. Finally, Ulmer's typed, personal account of these years list *Life is Good* and *Mantoux Text* along with the other TB films he directed, though I have yet to encounter references to either film elsewhere and the films have yet to be located. It is quite likely that the latter of these was actually called *Mantoux Test*. My thanks to Arianné Ulmer Cipes for providing these notes.

Recall too that conceptually disease had been a subject of Ulmer's since his literal investigation of it in his Hollywood debut, the syphilis exploitation melodrama *Damaged Lives* (1933). Like Ulmer's career-long interest in fate and predetermination, germs and a generalized notion of contagion seem to form the very foundation of this director's narrative logic. Again, an exemplary moment from *Detour* stands out. Early in the film, after his girlfriend Sue (Claudia Drake) has left him to make a go of it in California, Al is glimpsed pounding out his living on the piano at the Break O' Dawn Club. After a jazzified Brahms number performed at a customer's request, said customer flags a waiter, hands him a bill, and the waiter makes his way to deliver it to Al. Al narrates his thoughts on the exchange, saying, "When this drunk handed me a ten spot after a request I couldn't get very excited. What was it, I asked myself? A piece of paper crawling with germs."

Germs, then, and a unique notion of fate's communicability and the hand human beings have in the chain of actual or conceptual contagion, unite Ulmer's fiction films to his films for the NTA, suggesting a larger, scholarly need to consider this (and perhaps any) filmmaker's nontheatrical film efforts as a central part of the director's career. Lisa Cartwright, for example, in an otherwise engaging discussion of the represented tubercular body in *Let My People Live, Another to Conquer, Diagnostic Procedures*, and *They Do Come Back*, manages not to acknowledge in any way that all four films were directed by Ulmer and were part of a series of films the NTA sponsored in an effort to reach specific communities where the disease still lingered.[7] Educational films, as Cartwright's work demonstrates, are often considered to be unauthored texts, overdetermined by their sponsor or purpose. This essay hopes to demonstrate the value of contextualizing Ulmer's NTA campaign both in relation to the history of social engineering in American cultural history and within the filmmaker's larger body of work.

Missionary Medicine: Fighting Disease One Population at a Time

Ulmer's TB films were made in the midst of what might justifiably be called the filmmaker's East Coast Ethnic Melodrama period, his post–*Black Cat* and pre-PRC years. Noah Isenberg refers to this span of years as Ulmer's "Ethnic Intermezzo," though Isenberg is careful not to overly romanticize what was also one of a string of difficult episodes in Ulmer's long career.[8] Ulmer had experienced a brief period of success working in the Hollywood system. *The Black Cat*, like *Damaged Lives*, was a studio film. Where *Damaged Lives* was a lurid VD exploitation film

---

[7] Lisa Cartwright, *Screening the Body: Tracing Medicine's Visual Culture* (Minneapolis: University of Minnesota Press, 1995), 149–52.

[8] Isenberg, "Perennial Detour," 10–15. Isenberg has also published a book that sheds historical light on *Detour* (1945). *Detour*, BFI Classics (London: British Film Institute, 2008).

that Columbia opted to remove its name from (the credits list the invented "Weldon Pictures" as the studio), *The Black Cat*, made for Universal, was a somewhat controversial but also highly successful studio product that showcased Ulmer's German studio style. The picture's popularity seemed to guarantee the enthusiastic young filmmaker's initiation into the exclusive club of Hollywood émigrés. As Isenberg indicates, however, Ulmer's A-studio tenure would be very brief indeed. Along with a successful horror picture, Ulmer made an adulterous romantic connection with the boss's nephew's wife, script supervisor Shirley Castle (born Kassler); and said boss, Carl Laemmle, had pull well beyond Universal. Ulmer would eventually marry Shirley, but Laemmle's response to the infraction made Ulmer virtually unemployable in Hollywood. Ulmer would leave the town and its promise (the artifice of this promise is explored bitterly in *Detour*) for New York.[9]

Ulmer's subsequent East Coast theatrical film career coincided with and would prepare him for his educational shorts for the National Tuberculosis Association. While in New York and New Jersey, he directed two Ukrainian-language films (*The Girl from Poltavia* [1937] and *Cossacks in Exile* [1939]); four Yiddish films (*Green Fields* [1937], *The Singing Blacksmith* [1938], *The Light Ahead* [1939], and *American Matchmaker* [1940]); and a black musical drama (*Moon over Harlem* [1939]) featuring legendary jazz musician Sidney Bechet. This work established Ulmer's professional reputation as a filmmaker especially capable of reaching niche or ethnic audiences, and this ability meshed with the NTA's newly focused, late-Depression-era campaign. Ulmer's unique perspective on minority communities and the role they might play in their own fate suited him to the campaign. As we will see, however, Ulmer's perspective and the NTA's were not always in lockstep.

Founded in 1904 by a group of physicians and concerned laymen, the NTA (originally the National Association for the Study and Prevention of Tuberculosis) was the first national voluntary health agency to focus its efforts on a specific health threat. The organization recognized from the outset that their crusade against tuberculosis was part medical and part social, though these two arms of the anti-TB campaign were not always of equal strength.[10] While the germ that

---

[9] For more on the intricacies of this relationship and Ulmer's subsequent exile, see Isenberg, "Perennial Detour," 10–11.

[10] For more on the social/medical distinction (and the NTA's work in both categories), see James Harvey Young's review of Richard Shyrock's history of the NTA in *American Historical Review* 63 (Jan. 1958): 445–46; as well as the more specialized Richard Harrison Shyrock, *National Tuberculosis Association, 1904–1954: A Study of the Voluntary Health Movement in the United States* (Manchester, NH: Ayer Publishing, 1977). Also see James E. Perkins, "The National Tuberculosis Association: Fiftieth Anniversary," *Public Health Reports (1896–1970)* 69 (May 1954): 513–18.

caused tuberculosis was known in the early 1900s, the science deployed to eradicate it lagged behind. The NTA, then, began a large-scale and largely unprecedented social education mission that stressed prevention and successfully kept the disease itself foremost in the public consciousness.[11] By the late 1930s and into the 1940s, as medical science caught up with the organization's grassroots zeal and as TB mortality rates were steadily declining, the NTA's emphasis shifted away from spreading the anti-TB gospel toward research.[12] The organization determined, however, that popularly held misconceptions about the disease lingered within and about certain populations, justifying its continued production of educational media. Ulmer's contributions to the campaign, then, were produced at a transitional moment for the NTA, though they hark back to the organization's earlier educational campaigns.

The series of films Ulmer directed for the NTA was defined by the organization's desire to respond to the spread of misinformation and fear regarding racial susceptibility to the disease. This sense of panic was bolstered by statistics indicating that, while the fight against TB had been quite successful, the disease still had a formidable grip on nonwhite American communities. While the NTA managed to promote a fear of germs and contamination, a consequence of its efforts was a mounting fear of the people carrying those germs, and these fears expanded exponentially when the presumed carriers were people of color.[13] Three of Ulmer's films would be produced for exhibition within these communities. *Let My People Live*, aimed at African Americans, was shot at and used drama students from Tuskegee Institute, and the Health Department prominently featured the film at the 1939 World's Fair. *Cloud in the Sky*, targeting Mexican Americans, was produced both in Spanish and English. Boasting the assistance of the Navajo Service and the U.S. Office of Indian Affairs, *Another to Conquer*

---

[11] For more on the evolving focus of the organization see Young's review, 446; and Shyrock, *National Tuberculosis Association*, 286–97. For an outstanding discussion of the NTA's media savvy and the organization's enviable ability to "[make] their disease newsworthy," see Nancy Tomes, "Epidemic Entertainments: Disease and Popular Culture in Early-Twentieth Century America," *American Literary History* 14 (Winter 2002): 630–31. For one of only a few discussions of the organization's use of film, see esp. 642–47. In addition to Miriam Posner's essay in this volume, see Martin S. Pernick, "Thomas Edison's Tuberculosis Films: Mass Media and Health Propaganda," *Hastings Center Report* 8 (June 1978): 21–27.

[12] For more on this shift in focus and on the near-religious zeal of anti-tuberculosis reformers see Nancy Tomes, *The Gospel of Germs: Men, Women and the Microbe* (Cambridge, MA: Harvard University Press, 1998), 243–44. For more on shifts in mortality rates see Barbara Bates, *Bargaining for Life: A Social History of Tuberculosis, 1876–1938* (Philadelphia: University of Pennsylvania Press, 1992).

[13] Claudia Marie Calhoon discusses the manner by which the knowledge of germs sparked increased racial fear and misunderstanding in "Tuberculosis, Race, and the Delivery of Health Care in Harlem, 1922–1939," *Radical History Review* 80 (Spring 2001): 101–19.

was created for a Native American audience and features the most stunning location shooting of the series.

No doubt because of Ulmer's theatrical work in this area, Ulmer scholars refer to these ethnically focused TB films more frequently than the others.[14] The NTA, however, also hoped to inoculate against misinformation within the white community: in white schoolyards, within the white medical establishment, and in predominantly white factories. All produced in 1940, three films focused on white characters: *Goodbye Mr. Germ*, *Diagnostic Procedures*, and *They Do Come Back*. Theses films make their appeals differently and are intriguing for the alternate light they shed on the NTA's ostensibly progressive approach to the question of race.

In the three ethnically focused films, TB's death-grip on the community is imagined to be a consequence of an outmoded, dangerously traditional way of thinking. The disease first strikes key figures within the community's older generation. The young are then left to make a decision: follow along the traditional, typically faith-based path of their (often deceased) elders or, as *Another to Conquer* has it, "heed the wisdom of the white doctors' ways." Religion plays a key role in all three films. It is partly to blame, rooted as it is in tradition and faith rather than science. However, religious belief ultimately becomes a mechanism by which to smuggle science and medicine into the community. *Let My People Live,* in this respect, goes a bit further than the others in its realization of this concept. Rex Ingram plays an African American doctor who speaks about tuberculosis from the pulpit of a black church in the film's opening scene and later analyzes X-rays and sputum tests (see fig. 13.1). The halls of religion, these images suggest, are the place to begin spreading the gospel of medicine, and African American physicians themselves are envisioned as the conversionary conduit. The other two films, for all of their interest in and respect for "other" cultures, imagine the intervention of benevolent white doctors.

Shot largely at and prominently featuring the Tuskegee Institute in Alabama, *Let My People Live* was produced at a critical moment for the NTA, when the organization was reaching out directly to black institutes of higher education where the disease was on the rise. Citing a 1937 NTA report, Heather Munro Prescott writes that "prevention programs in black colleges grew out of the NTA's Committee on Tuberculosis Among Negroes, whose major goal was to overturn 'the attitude all too prevalent that tuberculosis in the Negro is invariably fatal'; rather, TB in blacks, like that in whites, could be 'effectively combated by health education.' 'Knowledge is power,' wrote one Committee report, 'and until we have given the Negro race a knowledge of tuberculosis, its

---

[14] Isenberg, in fact, lumps the three racially specific TB films (the only nontheatrical materials he mentions) with the other films comprising the Ulmer's "Ethnic Intermezzo." Isenberg, "Perennial Detour," 15.

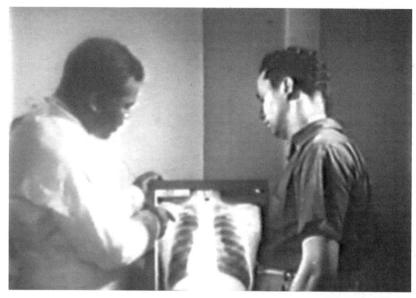

Figure 13.1. Dr. Gordon (Rex Ingram) points to the suspicious spot on George's lung. *Let My People Live* (1938). (National Archives and Records Administration, NARA.)

cause, prevention, and a knowledge of the fact that it can be cured, our other control measures will be ineffective.'"[15] It is precisely how the organization sought to spread this knowledge in *Let My People Live* that is of interest here.

Let My People Live concerns George and Mary, young siblings from a family affected by the disease. As George listens to Dr. Gordon's address in the school chapel, he is summoned to take a call from his sister, who reports that their mother has fallen ill and that he must return home at once. Their mother dies shortly thereafter. Mary, afraid that she's stricken as well (she manifests several of her mother's symptoms), seeks the advice of her minister, who has just presided over her mother's funeral and who demands that she see a *real* doctor. From the opening images of Dr. Gordon speaking before an enraptured congregation through the end of the film, *Let My People Live* is intent upon using organized religion to promote science. It is equally committed to questioning the efficacy of what is viewed to be a dangerously immobile community tendency toward traditional faith.

The real conflict between science and its alternatives occurs on the street. On her way to see Dr. Gordon and just outside of his office, Mary runs into her friend

---

[15] Heather Munro Prescott, "The White Plague Goes to College: Tuberculosis Prevention Programs in Colleges and Universities, 1920–1960," *Bulletin of the History of Medicine* 74 (Winter 2000): 757. Prescott cites *National Tuberculosis Association, Report of the Committee on Tuberculosis Among Negroes: A Five-Year Study and What It Has Accomplished* (New York: National Tuberculosis Association, 1937), 48. For more on the struggle against TB in the African American community, see Calhoon, "Tuberculosis, Race."

Minnie, who looks her up and down and says "Um-hum. I knowed it. You got the same thing your mama had, ain't you?" Minnie advises that she take some of her grandma's considerably less expensive tea, intimating that, after all, no doctor is going to cure her, a widely held myth the NTA hoped to eradicate along with the disease. The erroneous "hoodooism" of the older generation is foregrounded in this pivotal exchange, its belief in the heredity and inevitable fatality of the disease systematically taken apart. A previous generation's presumed subscription to folk traditions is cautiously dismantled as Mary thinks twice and makes the right decision, entering Dr. Gordon's office as her minister had suggested.

Mary learns that she has the disease and cheerfully and logically accepts her treatment, recommending that her brother George, who is visiting her bedside at the sanatorium, see Dr. Gordon as well. George does as he is told, and after Dr. Gordon examines the tuberculin test he has administered, he informs George that he has hosted the germ but that his good health fought it successfully. Viewers would surely note the environmental differences: Mary lived in her family's impoverished country home and George has been away at school where, in the logic of the film, his body and, one suspects, his mind as well, stood a better chance against the germ. Dr. Gordon recommends a path of continued fitness that involves diet, rest, and exercise. Science is key in *Let My People Live*, but the film suggests that the NTA's mission in the African American community begins and ends with belief. The film opens on the doctor speaking from the pulpit and ends with Mary at the sanatorium, listening to the radio and trying to pick out George's voice in the transmission of the Tuskegee Institute choir's "Hallelujah Chorus." The film, then, literalizes the NTA's missionary stance even as the organizational emphasis was beginning to swing toward research.

Like their campaign for African Americans, the NTA's campaign for Mexican Americans targeted not only the spread of TB but also the equally rampant spread of misinformation regarding the disease. Writing about unfair medical and border policies during these years, Emily Abel contends that "because Mexicans lived and worked in dangerous surroundings, it is likely that they bore a very high burden of tuberculosis. Contemporary statistics, however, tell us less about the prevalence of disease than about the attitudes of health officials." Turning to these statistics and the rhetoric encasing them, Abel demonstrates the manner by which TB, especially in U.S. border towns, came to support a large-scale policy of racial intolerance masquerading as a health crusade. The result: claims of racial susceptibility to the disease and wildly inflated "diagnoses" within the community, often resulting in deportation.[16]

Cloud in the Sky, in the face of these actions, is even more frank in its rhetorical conjoining of science and religion. A rapidly moving montage of Mexican

---

[16] Emily Abel, "From Exclusion to Expulsion: Mexicans and Tuberculosis Control in Los Angeles, 1914–1940," *Bulletin of the History of Medicine* 77 (Winter 2003): 831, 833–48.

factory workers, field laborers, and enlisted men is accompanied by narration informing viewers that America's Spanish-speaking citizens "bear more than their share of the crushing burden of tuberculosis." This montage of labor and contribution fades into images of a lively Mexican dance where we are introduced to a critical pair of white characters who will play a determining role in the fate of the community. Seated in the middle of the celebration, a doctor and another man (called "a wise Padre" in the promotional materials) watch the festivities, chat briefly about "these people," and part ways.

As in *Let My People Live*, the older generation in *Cloud in the Sky* is depicted as being skeptical of medicine's usefulness, and this skepticism has a heavy price. At the film's center is the Lopez family, now motherless because of tuberculosis. They fear the worst when the daughter, Consuelo, begins to show symptoms of the disease. Consuelo's only response is to pray more frequently and more earnestly. The Padre, whom she runs into after one of these sessions, offers Consuelo the comforts of religion, but urges her to see a medical doctor at once and to avoid patent medicine or home remedies. He tells her, in a manner that quite plainly links medical progress to religious faith, that God has given us science and that we are obligated to use it.

Convinced, Consuelo goes to the white physician, bringing her father with her. Mr. Lopez, who once feared doctors, learns so much during this visit that he becomes, as the NTA's publicity has it, a "missionary" of tuberculosis prevention. He has his other children tested and, even as his neighbors chide him about his "conversion" (one friend tells him that he believes he's sold his soul to the Devil), he urges his comrades not to spit on the ground and exalts the medicine that will eventually save his daughter. The film ends with the Padre and the doctor, seated once again at an evening dance, celebrating Consuelo's marriage to a young serenading caballero, Pedro. All are satisfied that their unified efforts have insured the health of the community.

Targeted at Native Americans, *Another to Conquer* is similarly themed. Nema and Don, the promotional materials for the film explain, are made orphans by tuberculosis. Their parents taken by the disease, they are left on the reservation following the wisdom of their science-fearing grandfather and the community's respected leader, Slow-Talker. Robert, their neighbor and friend, has gone away to school—forsaking tradition, according to his detractors—and has learned the scientific ways of the white man. He has also learned that he has TB and, through rest and treatment, is cured.

That the film focuses on the spread of knowledge to stop the spread of disease among the Navajo is no coincidence. Christian W. McMillen, writing about the extraordinary spread of the disease among Native Americans and the determining role that myths of racial susceptibility played in this decimation, writes that "better knowledge of TB did not lead to better care [for Native Americans]. Halfway through the twentieth century, when TB in the general

U.S. population was at a historic low, and racial explanations were in steep decline, TB among Indians was alarmingly high. The Navajo, for example, were infected with tuberculosis at a rate of 302.4 per 100,000 while the rate among the general population was 33.4 per 100,000—a figure all the more astonishing because in a 1909 survey of TB among Indians, Aleš Hrdlička found the Navajos to be the 'natives most free from tuberculosis.'"[17]

As with the other films under discussion here, the issue is not played cheaply in *Another to Conquer*. The doctors are aware of and interested in Native customs and use them as points of comparison. This, in fact, is the crux of Ulmer's ethnically focused TB films. Science must, like the germ itself, take root within the supposed belief structures of the given minority group and use those structures to disseminate outward. In *Another to Conquer*, which obliquely references the many struggles of the Native American, it is Don's death and the threat of Nema's that finally makes Slow-Talker bend, only to learn that he has been the carrier all along. The final shot captures him regarding the heavens and, in voiceover, committing to be a *warrior* for the cause of tuberculosis prevention (see fig. 13.2).

Where tradition and faith become medicine's entrée in the productions focused on American minorities, the films featuring white characters are somewhat differently pitched. *Goodbye Mr. Germ*, for example, is geared toward very

Figure 13.2. Slow-Talker (Howard Gorman) resolves to be a warrior for the cause of tuberculosis prevention in Edgar Ulmer's *Another to Conquer* (1941). (NARA.)

---

[17] Christian McMillen, "The Red Man and the White Plague: Rethinking Race, Tuberculosis, and American Indians, ca. 1890–1950," *Bulletin of the History of Medicine* 82 (Fall 2008): 616.

young children and features the perhaps-too-adorable animation of H. L. Roberts. The film, like those explored above, also features a generation gap that must be bridged. Here, however, the older generation's near-fanatical faith in science needs to be passed to the younger, still ideologically pliable generation. Without the container of religion, science as such is on offer and the white children grasp it in a manner that may well warrant a reconsideration of the other films. The implication here is that white children absorb what adults of color need to be more actively convinced of: the scientific realities of the disease and its treatment.

On a rainy, dreary evening at home, John and Mary, desperate for their father to take them to the movies, tease him about his old-fashioned attachment to his science books and mock his interest in an image of the tubercle bacillus. This sends their father into a strange and, to the children, deeply engaging scientific reverie. What if, he wonders, we could talk to this fascinating germ? What story would he tell?

Father imagines himself in his lab (he now dons an eye patch), where he will demonstrate his latest invention, a fantastic two-way "Germ Radio" that will allow him to interview Tee Bee, whose animated "Lungland" is beautifully realized (see fig. 13.3).[18] Tee Bee tells the story of his "tribe's" invasion of young Edgar's lungs via Aunt Matilda, who insisted on tasting Edgar's food before feeding him. Here they

Figure 13.3. Tee-Bee, broadcasting live from Lungland, in Ulmer's *Goodbye Mr. Germ* (1940). Here and in the other films ostensibly intended for white audiences, technology and not faith is the "missionary" conveyance. (NARA.)

---

[18] Tee Bee had made his screen debut about eight years earlier in another NTA film called *The Story of My Life by Tee Bee*. It is likely that the character was familiar to children from the association's printed material as well.

resided, waiting for a moment of weakness to attack. Tee Bee's story, however, soon becomes the story of his own tribe's inevitable genocide. Edgar, now a teen-ager, grows sick, gets frightened, and of his own accord seeks immediate medical attention. "The man in the white coat" sees to Edgar's recovery. He makes a culture of the invading germ; this culture includes our dear narrator, Tee Bee.

As in all of the films, science is triumphant. Edgar marries and has learned enough from his experience to have his own child tested. The film is unusual, however, in its sympathetic racializing of Tee Bee, whose once powerful tribe now faces extinction. *Goodbye Mr. Germ* also depicts a rather easy relationship between the patient and the medicine that will be his salvation. Edgar is, until he coughs blood, complacent, but never frightened of "the man in the white coat," which stands in direct contrast to the skeptical nonwhite communities in the previously examined films. Though the admittedly unthinking Aunt Matilda is a carrier, her negligence is not villainized, in part because it is not passed down. The generation gap, in fact, is reversed. Father (a man of science whose enthusi-asm is near-religious) passes his, albeit fanciful, wisdom along to his children, who are delighted by his story and confident that they will never be stricken by the disease. The missionary rhetoric so apparent in the films focused on non-white characters, in other words, is packaged differently.

This missionary rhetoric is also reconfigured in *Diagnostic Procedures*. Aimed at the medical establishment, *Diagnostic Procedures* moves dryly and me-thodically through the stages of diagnosis and analysis. It is, not surprisingly, like *Goodbye Mr. Germ* in its lack of any obvious missionary posturing. Its alternative rhetorical positioning, however, is equally revealing. As its title suggests, the film is tediously academic, though fascinating, in part, for the fact that Ulmer's direc-torial credit in the film reads "Edgar G. Ulmer, PhD."[19] Aimed as the film was at medical practitioners, the initials are likely an attempt on the part of the NTA to lend to this material a degree of credibility.

Regardless of Ulmer's fraudulent credentials, however, the film is set up as a lecture headed by Dr. Kendall Emerson, managing director of the NTA. In the film, this learned and experienced physician trains a group of newcomers not from the pulpit, but from its academic equivalent, the podium, including the assistance of visual aids. Dr. Emerson's lesson is supported by the appearances of his colleagues, Dr. Ralph S. Muckenfuss (a real expert, though his name seems as fictional as Ulmer's credentials), Director of the Bureau of Laboratories of the New York City Department of Health; Dr. Esmond Ong, Director of the Henry Phipps Institute; and Dr. Edgar Mayer, Assistant Professor of Medicine

---

[19] Additional research into Ulmer's educational background and some discussion with daughter Arianné revealed Ulmer's lifelong belief that honorary degrees should be bestowed upon anyone walking past the gates of a university. Arianné also kindly reminded me of her father's somewhat legendary truth-stretching abilities.

at Cornell University Medical School and formerly on staff at the Trudeau Sanatorium. Rather like preaching to the converted, *Diagnostic Procedures* demonstrates the latest scientific methods to young white physicians and once again reverses the generation gap imagined in the ethnically focused films. As with *Goodbye Mr. Germ*, an uncontaminated faith in science is clearly on display.

The most curious of the films dealing with white characters, however, is *They Do Come Back*. Aimed at spreading the word to young, working, or college-aged white Americans, the film is interesting both for its differences from and its similarity to the other Ulmer TB films. Taking place in "EVERY TOWN USA" (the film is shot in Philadelphia), *They Do Come Back* borrows much from Ulmer's *Damaged Lives*. Romance, here in the form of a kiss, leads to disaster. As the title suggests, however, there is redemption. Our characters do come back.

In its focus on working-class young people, not children or would-be physicians, *They Do Come Back* is thematically most like Ulmer's ethnically focused films for the NTA. A brief preamble solidifies the similarities. Before we meet our protagonists, we are introduced to the town as a whole and are told that, like every town in the country, tuberculosis has a foothold here among its hard-working inhabitants. As our narrator, voiced by radio announcer Alois Havrilla, describes the ravages of the disease and its effect on the community at large, a shadowy pair of figures mourns the passing of a loved one. The image cuts to a young girl standing alone, enveloped in chiaroscuro lighting, as our narrator announces that the disease is a "maker of orphans." This concise introduction suggests that, while the disease may not be hereditary or necessarily fatal, ignorance about it is. And this ignorance is a deadly germ indeed.

Roy and Julie, the film's protagonists, are romantically attached factory workers. They are also careless. That aforementioned kiss is a conduit for tuberculosis. Roy manifests symptoms first, and quite violently. After showing off his strength at a public pool, Roy, seemingly out of nowhere, coughs up blood. He seeks medical treatment immediately. Piecing together the young man's social connections, medical professionals seek out Julie, who will also need treatment and care.

In a manner that would seem to separate it from the minority-focused films, our young couple in *They Do Come Back* seems to accept, without question, the science that will be their salvation. Their absorption into the sanatorium seems as natural as their eventual and titular absorption back into society, a process that involves a change of jobs for Roy, the cheerful abandonment of a careerist future for Julie, and, of course, marriage. No adherent to an outmoded, science-fearing way of life stands in the way of their treatment. Alois Havrilla's enthusiastic narration lends to Julie and Roy's narrative a brisk sense of urgency and importance. Like the other films focused on white characters, traditional faith is absent, replaced by a secularized faith in medicine and science. The missionary message, however, remains. In an elaborate concluding montage of NTA media including radio announcements, films, leaflets, and flyers, we learn that spreading the word can arrest the spread of the disease. The NTA gospel, in other words, is spread through secular, technological channels.

Authorship Revisited . . . and Revised

This, at least, is what I thought *They Do Come Back* was about. When I visited the National Archives (NARA) to view Ulmer's NTA films, the staff pulled *They Do Come Back* from the vaults and I viewed the print just described. It begins with an unambiguous directorial credit, "Edgar G. Ulmer," and ends with a plea to "BUY CHRISTMAS SEALS." The film matched almost word-for-word the script Ulmer's daughter had provided for me, and it corresponded perfectly to the NTA's own publicity materials. It also seemed to be a fine candidate for screening at the Orphan Film Symposium. The 35mm materials were, I was told, in outstanding condition. The archive staff kindly arranged for a new 35mm print to be made from the negative. The print that was struck, however, quite literally tells a different story from the access copy I had studied.[20]

While composed largely of the same parts, the handsome new print, also titled *They Do Come Back* though produced by United Films, is a different film: a different narrator (uncredited and much calmer) presides, a different story is told, and different "heroes" emerge. Even Ulmer's beloved Brahms Fourth Symphony (the same piece Al embellishes in *Detour*), which opened the program, has been replaced. While a satisfactory explanation remains elusive, it is likely that the NTA recut and renarrated the film at a later date, either for a particular market or possibly for ideological reasons.

This mix-up helps to establish a critical point about the unknowable fate (Ulmer would've loved this!) of orphaned, nontheatrical material. It also raises interesting questions about what we might call "sponsored authorship." The earlier version of *They Do Come Back*, where Ulmer's directorial credit is still intact, is, like Ulmer's other TB films, thoughtfully sensational. Havrilla's dramatic narration lends to this effect. It is also consistent with the films focused on nonwhite communities in its attention, albeit technologically focused, to the NTA's missionary project. Julie, Roy, and all Americans, the film suggests, need to be told about the dangers of tuberculosis; it is not knowledge inherent to any race, and the germ of ignorance must still be fought.

In all of the films featuring white characters, technology and not religion is the imagined missionary vehicle. In *Goodbye Mr. Germ*, the children are indoctrinated

---

[20] The print, made by Colorlab for screening at the fifth Orphan Film Symposium (2006) at the University of South Carolina, was made from NARA's preservation negative, which itself was created using the original nitrate materials. NARA received this film, along with eight other titles totaling thirty-four reels, on May 23, 1945 (based on an offer letter of Jan. 4, 1945, from Martha E. Pouech for the Committee on Archives of the National Tuberculosis Association).

by their obviously hallucinating father's scientific vision, a vision involving Germ Radios. In *Diagnostic Procedures,* young physicians are treated to a dry but technologically sophisticated demonstration of cutting-edge science's role in the battle against tuberculosis. Radios, along with other media, figure prominently in the earlier version of *They Do Come Back* as well. That the film is narrated by Havrilla is certainly key, but the radio also functions sermonically, replacing the pulpit and the preacher from the other films. Julie and Roy enter the sanatorium without question, in part because of the omnipresence of their technologically mediated and secularized faith in the medical establishment; images of them "receiving the word" via radio while in the sanatorium pepper the latter portion of the film.

Media obviously played an important role in the fight against and even the treatment of the disease. Motion pictures, audio broadcasts, and narrated slideshows were part of the training of nurses and physicians. As early as the 1920s, widely circulating nursing publications reviewed films that were deemed useful teaching tools.[21] A 1940 issue of *Chest: Official Publication of the American College of Chest Physicians* also extolled the virtues of film, suggesting that "an excellent practice carried out by some schools during the first or second year is the showing of some of the National Tuberculosis Association educational pictures such as *Behind the Shadows, Let My People Live, On the Firing Line,* and *Cloud in the Sky.* Pictures such as these may, and no doubt do, stimulate in some students, at least, an interest which they will maintain throughout their work."[22] This practice carried over to the treatment of patients themselves, for whom radio broadcasts, of the sort Julie and Roy listen to, and screenings were an important means of keeping the word alive and transforming the patient into a public servant (see fig. 13.4).[23]

But even this revised missionary science is lacking in the NTA's reedit of *They Do Come Back,* as is any sense that the characters at the film's center are in real danger. The narration is calm, almost sleepy, and Julie and Roy, who are fleshed-out characters in the earlier version, are merely "examples" in the reedit, replaced by a more heroic army of physicians and reformers whose lives are dedicated to fighting the disease. The NTA, in fact, is the hero in this later version. Julie decides that, once she recovers, she will volunteer for the organization. More curious is the erasure of the deaths that open the earlier version or any sense that this community of white, working-class urbanites is quite as desperately in need of the education so vividly on display in Ulmer's ethnically focused TB films or even in his original version of *They Do Come Back.*

---

[21] Review, "Health Films by Health Films Committee of the National Health Council," *American Journal of Nursing* 23 (Aug. 1923): 995–96.

[22] Ed. W. Hayes, "Schedule for Teaching Chronic Diseases of the Lungs in Medical Schools," *Chest: Official Publication of the American College of Chest Physicians* 6, no. 7 (July 1940): 203.

[23] See, for example, Alta Kressler, "Teaching Patients with Tuberculosis," *American Journal of Nursing* 59 (Aug. 1959): 1116–18.

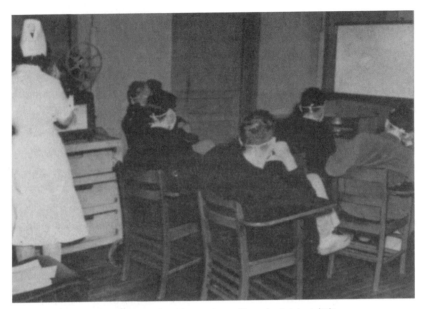

Among the teaching aids used are films about tuberculosis.

Figure 13.4. In an article titled "Teaching Patients with Tuberculosis," Alta Kressler, as late as 1959, discusses the importance of film. Here, patients at Valley Forge Army Hospital view two TB films: a cartoon called *Rodney* (1951) and *The Inside Story* (NTA, 1952). (*American Journal of Nursing*, August 1959.)

Spreading the word in an effort to stop the spread of disease was, obviously, the NTA's primary task, and the films examined here played a decisive role in this multifaceted, multimedia defense strategy. The NTA, proud of its successes in the 1930s and 40s and eager to promote its campaigns in previously neglected populations, focused on the production of educational films designed to reach those communities. The organization's renewed campaign, undertaken at the height of its push for advanced research, focused on the indoctrination of ethnic minorities who, in the logic of the campaign, remained medically skeptical and scientifically unknowing. Ulmer's films, which he claimed were prepared and written in his free time and with very little oversight, fit the bill perfectly.[24] Culturally sensitive and not dismissive of tradition and faith, the films use these systems of belief to spread the newly invigorated gospel of medical science.

With *Goodbye Mr. Germ* and *Diagnostic Procedures*, the new campaign also preached effectively to children and future health-care professionals. There is, in fact, ample evidence that several of Ulmer's films were shown routinely in K–12

---

[24] Ulmer's typed notes on this period of his career indicate the faith the NTA had in his ability to deliver and his relative autonomy in making these films: "The films for the National Tuberculosis Association & U.S. Health Department were documentaries of varying lengths

as well as advanced medical classrooms.[25] The religious conveyance is absent in these films focused on white characters, replaced by a secular and unquestioning faith in science that may have prolonged the notion of racial susceptibility, though here the perceived vulnerability is based on antiquated beliefs rather than inferior biology. Children and students must be taught about the disease, these films collectively argue, but science doesn't work in conjunction with or come to replace another system of belief.

Religion or a dangerous sense of tradition is also lacking in Ulmer's *They Do Come Back*, though similarities to the ethnically focused films abound. Chief among these is a sense of panic that the disease is on the rise and that the spread of information (religious or secular) is the only way to stop it. The NTA's revised version strips the film of this sense of panic, removing any impression that adult white Americans might need to be educated, opting instead for a distinct and puzzlingly blameless vision of the disease.

That Ulmer's version implies the culpability of white Americans and suggests, however subtly, that ignorance might destroy this community as well, may have sat uneasily with the NTA, with viewers, or both. The notion that the disease was in decline among white Americans was key to the rhetoric aimed at nonwhite communities. *They Do Come Back*, in its original form, lumps its white protagonists with the other groups in need of salvation, and effectively equalized the NTA's unwittingly divisive rhetoric. Like the ethnic minorities targeted in the NTA campaign, Ulmer's white characters have a hand in their own fate, but need to be convinced to use it.

Ulmer's position on fate and predetermination is the stuff of controversy, though the long-maintained notion that his fictional characters are merely victims of

---

promoting the fight against TB on a national basis. These films were prepared, written, etc., in my spare time as a service and when available I was hired to produce and direct them—between my feature assignments and during layoff periods while I was under contract to Springer. Time: Balance of free time 1937, 1938, 1939, 1940." Ulmer's notes indicate that he had a hand in the preparation and writing of some films he did not direct, although this has yet to be confirmed. My thanks to Arianné Ulmer Cipes for providing this material.

[25] See, for example, Charles Hoban Jr., *Focus on Learning: Motion Pictures in the School* (Washington, DC: American Council on Education, 1942), 53–59, for repeated references to the classroom use of *Let My People Live*. References to this film's use in largely white classrooms abound in the educational literature of the period, often for the teaching of racial tolerance. Hoban's findings indicate that, sometimes, the film had precisely the opposite effect, creating in white children a sense of social superiority to the racially susceptible characters in the film. Several of Ulmer's TB films receive high ratings in *Selected Educational Motion Pictures: A Descriptive Encyclopedia* (Washington, DC: American Council on Education, 1942), though again, the films seem to serve purposes beyond the original intention. Racial tolerance becomes a central, perhaps unexpected pedagogical repurposing. The American Council on Education's second series, *Motion Pictures in Education*, devotes much of its attention in 1940 to the classroom use of *Let My People Live* (second in popularity only to *The Plow That Broke the Plains* [1936]).

fate's malevolence continues to erode. The two versions of *They Do Come Back*—all of his TB films, in fact—do not stand in the way of this erosion. Al Roberts, Ulmer's best-known character, narrates his own dilemma at the end of *Detour*. Disheveled and quite a bit worse for the wear, he says, "Whichever way you turn, Fate sticks out a foot to trip you." Looking back at Ulmer's theatrical films through the peculiar lens of his work for the NTA, his career-long investigation of characters who *blame* fate for their misfortunes —instead of actively rerouting the course of their lives to avoid the foot—is most apparent.[26] Ulmer's educational films, in this respect, fit into a much larger cycle of films with similar pedagogical designs—films that attempt to instruct viewers, regardless of race, to take an active role in their own future.

Filmography

Another to Conquer **(1941) 20 min., 16mm /35mm**
DIRECTOR: Edgar G Ulmer. SPONSOR: National Tuberculosis Association/U.S. Office of Indian Affairs. PRODUCTION: Springer Pictures, Inc. CAMERA: Robert Cline. EDITOR: H. E. Mandl. CAST: Howard Gorman, Sammy Day, Geraldine Birdsbill, Richard Hogner, W. W. Peter MD. ACCESS: National Archives and Records Administration (NARA); Internet Archive, www.archive.org/details/another_to_conquer_1941.

Cloud in the Sky **(1939) 20 min., 16mm /35mm (English and Spanish)**
DIRECTOR: Edgar Ulmer. SPONSOR: National Tuberculosis Association. CAMERA: J. Burgi Contner. EDITOR: Marc Asch. SOUND: Dean Cole. ACCESS: NARA, National Library of Medicine (NLM); Internet Archive, (English) www.archive.org/details/cloud_in_ the_sky_1939 & (Spanish) www.archive.org/details/cloud_in_the_ sky_1939_esp.

Diagnostic Procedures in Tuberculosis **(1940) 20 min., 16mm /35mm**
DIRECTOR: Edgar Ulmer, PhD. SPONSOR: National Tuberculosis Association. PRODUCTION: Motion Picture Service Corporation. CAMERA: William Miller. PRODUCTION. SUPERVISER: J. Burgi Contner. CAST: Dr. Kendall Emerson, Managing Director of the NTA. ACCESS: ACCESS: NARA; Internet Archive, www.archive.org/details/diagnostic_procedures_in_tuberculosis_1940.

---

[26] For more on the reconsideration of Ulmer's understanding of fate, see Gallagher, "All Lost in Wonder."

Goodbye Mr. Germ (1940) **14 min., 16mm /35mm**
DIRECTOR: Edgar Ulmer. SPONSOR: The National Tuberculosis
Association. PRODUCTION: DeFernes Studios. CAMERA:
Joseph Noble. ANIMATION: H. L. Roberts. SETTINGS: Stanley
Levick. EDITOR: Hans Mandl. CAST: James Kirkwood. ACCESS:
NARA, *Edgar G. Ulmer: Archive* (David Kalat/All Day Entertain-
ment, 3 DVD anthology); Internet Archive, www.archive.org/details/
goodbye_mr_germ_1940.

Let My People Live (1938) **15 min., 16mm /35mm**
DIRECTOR: Edgar Ulmer. SPONSOR: The National Tuberculosis
Association. PRODUCTION: Motion Picture Service Corporation.
CAMERA: William Miller. SOUND: Nelson Minnerly. DRA-
MATIC ASSISTANTS: S. E. Walker, Edward Lawson. CAST: Rex
Ingram, Peggy Howard, Merritt Smith, Erostine Coles, Christine
Johnson. Jackson Burnside. ACCESS: George Eastman House, NARA;
Internet Archive, www.archive.org/details/let_my_people_live_1938.

They Do Come Back (1940) **17 min., 16mm /35mm**
DIRECTOR: Edgar Ulmer. SPONSOR: National Tuberculosis
Association. PRODUCTION: DeFernes Studios. CAMERA:
Joseph Noble. EDITOR: Hans Mandl. NARRATOR: Alois Havrilla.
CAST: Wilma Caspar, Edward Mulhern. ACCESS: NARA, NLM;
Internet Archive, www.archive.org/details/they_do_come_back_1940.

They Do Come Back (n.d.) **15 min., 35mm**
DIRECTOR: None credited. SPONSOR: National Tuberculosis
Association. PRODUCTION: United Films. NOTE: No record
associated with this alternate version has been uncovered. ACCESS:
NARA; Internet Archive, www.archive.org/details/they_do_come_back.

Related Films

Damaged Lives (1933). 61 min., 35mm
PRODUCTION: Columbia (as Weldon Pictures). DIRECTOR:
Edgar Ulmer.

Life is Good (n.d.). 35mm
PRODUCTION: 20th Century–Fox, Movietone studio.
DIRECTOR: Edgar Ulmer (unconfirmed).

Mantoux Text [or *Test?*] (n.d.). 35mm
PRODUCTION: 20th Century–Fox, Movietone studio.
DIRECTOR: Edgar Ulmer (unconfirmed).

14 EXPLOITATION AS EDUCATION

ERIC SCHAEFER

The term "exploitation film" conjures up vivid connotations for most people: images of low-budget and lurid genres such as women-in-prison films, soft-core melodramas played out in anonymous motel rooms, nihilistic biker dramas, and bottom-of-the-barrel horror movies featuring monsters with ping-pong ball eyes and dime-store fangs, all served up with a generous helping of exposed female flesh.[1] They were the motion picture's poor relations, the disreputable kin of cinema's more refined and responsible betters. But for several generations, exploitation films meant something else: education. For a time, learning with the lights off—at least when it concerned certain subjects, such as sex and drugs—was more likely to take place in a commercial theater than in a classroom.

From the late teens to the late 1950s, "classical" exploitation films operated at the fringes of the mainstream motion picture industry in the United States.[2] Exploitation movies initially emerged in the mid- to late teens, at about the same time that film began to be used in the classroom as an educational tool. Health professionals grappled with rising rates of venereal diseases and tried to combat their growing numbers in the armed services and civilian population by using films. Some of the films designed to combat the scourges of syphilis and gonorrhea were manufactured by independent producers (*The Scarlet Trail* and *Wild Oats*

---

[1] "Exploitation film" originally referred to any movie that, because of its unusual genre or lack of stars, required special promotion (or "exploitation") over and above the usual trailers, posters, and newspaper advertising to reach an audience. The term came to mean low-budget movies made outside of the Hollywood studio system that defied the Production Code. By the late 1950s "exploitation movie" had expanded to include almost any cheap genre picture, and soon became more descriptive, e.g., "sexploitation" and "blaxploitation" in the 1960s and 70s.

[2] "Classical" exploitation films are so designated because they paralleled the "classical Hollywood cinema" from the late teens through the late 1950s, operating as a shadow industry to mainstream motion picture practice in the United States. For a full history of these films see Eric Schaefer, *"Bold! Daring! Shocking! True!": A History of Exploitation Films, 1919–1959* (Durham, NC: Duke University Press, 1999).

[both 1919]). Others were made by quasi-governmental services (*Fit to Fight* and *The End of the Road* [both 1919]), and later received theatrical releases. Public outcry followed. The backlash against sex hygiene movies ultimately led to their excision from the mainstream motion picture industry and to the development of the smaller, parallel exploitation industry that embraced censorable subjects.

Through the Motion Picture Producers and Distributors of America (MPPDA, later the Motion Picture Association of America [MPAA]), Hollywood attempted to regulate the content of films with the "Don'ts and Be Carefuls" (1927) and eventually the Production Code, adopted in 1930 and enforced through the MPPDA's Production Code Administration in 1934. As self-regulation of content took hold in Hollywood, a variety of controversial subjects and imagery was banned from mainstream movies, including sex hygiene, childbirth, venereal disease, drug use, and nudity. Feature films with explicit educational aims were also shunned, viewed as antithetical to the commercial screen's primary role as an entertainment medium. Indeed, the preamble to the Production Code stated that motion pictures were to be regarded "as entertainment without any explicit purpose of teaching or propaganda."[3] Several years later, Martin Quigley, coauthor of the Code and publisher of the *Motion Picture Herald*, reiterated this stance when he said, "The entertainment motion picture is not to be considered a deliberate agency of propaganda and reform in any province, including that of moralities."[4] Topics forbidden by the Code became the domain of the makers of exploitation films, small-time independents who made movies on the cheap that provided forbidden spectacle—nudity, scenes of childbirth, striptease dances—that could not be found in mainstream motion pictures.

Exploitation films were barred from the lavish first-run theaters owned or booked by the majors, and they frequently ran into trouble in those states and communities with censorship boards, such as New York, Pennsylvania, Ohio, and Chicago. But that still left thousands of unaffiliated movie houses willing to take a break from their usual program of Hollywood fare, whether for a few days or a week, to play an exploitation film. They did so because the movies inevitably provided a boost to the box office, drawing ticket buyers with their promise of "adults only" fare.[5] In order to justify the inclusion of such risqué material, exploitation movies assured ticket-buyers and the community that they were, first and foremost, educational.

---

[3] For the text of the original Motion Picture Production Code of 1930 as well as addenda and amendments, see the appendices of Thomas Doherty's *Pre-Code Hollywood: Sex, Immorality, and Insurrection in American Cinema, 1930–1934* (New York: Columbia University Press, 1999), 347–67.

[4] Martin Quigley, *Decency in Motion Pictures* (New York: Macmillan, 1937), 14.

[5] Although labeled as "adults only," there was never any set age limit (e.g., 18 or 21 years of age), or definition of who constituted an adult. That definition differed from place to place and was based on policies of distributors and exhibitors. Some distributors used the rubric of "high school age and older"—knowing that the age at which one entered high school differed by community, and that they could snag ticket-buyers as young as 13 or 14 in some locales.

One could easily assume that moviegoers only attended exploitation films for a cheap thrill, but this would be incorrect. It is important to recall that information about subjects like reproduction and venereal diseases was difficult to obtain during the heyday of exploitation movies. Not until 1937 did the American Medical Association officially resolve that birth control was an important part of physician training and medical practice. Some exploitation films were actually made in cooperation with health and law enforcement agencies, but others fabricated official-sounding sponsors. The information contained in exploitation films could range from relatively current and accurate to misleading. Exploitation films were an amalgam of now recognized and relatively distinct categories: fiction and nonfiction, entertainment and education, lowbrow appeal and high-minded ideals. They could be many different things to different people, and for some they were a combination of all of those categories. Even if a portion of the exploitation film audience attended merely to enjoy the lure of forbidden sights, they ultimately learned something in the process.

While a small handful of classroom films dealt with aspects of sex education as early as 1920, it would be decades before they became staples in American schoolrooms.[6] Until that happened, theatrical exploitation movies provided lessons on sensitive, often controversial, subjects. For several generations "exploitation" and "education" were synonymous. As we will see, the educational messages in exploitation films were often at odds with their lurid advertising. They were also undermined by the lack of coherence and intelligibility brought about by the films' low budgets, abbreviated shooting schedules, and exhibition contexts that were different from both theatrical motion picture entertainment and classroom films. But if controversial subject matter and slapdash approaches employed by exploitation producers would seem to consign them to the realm of mere cinematic mercenaries, chasing a quick buck, we should bear in mind that most manufacturers of educational films were in the business of making money as well. I will focus here on several films by way of example: the sex hygiene movies *Human Wreckage*, a.k.a. *Sex Madness*[7] (1938) and *Because of Eve* (1948); and the drug films *Reefer Madness* (1936) and *The Narcotics Story* (1958). But my observations on these films can be generalized to apply to many exploitation movies from the 1920s to the late 1950s.

---

[6] *The Gift of Life* (1920) and *The Science of Life* (1922) are two examples. See Robert Eberwein, *Sex Ed: Film, Video, and the Framework of Desire* (New Brunswick, NJ: Rutgers University Press, 1999), 102–8. See also Martin S. Pernick, "More Than Illustrations: Early Twentieth Century Health Films as Contributors to the Histories of Medicine and of Motion Pictures," in *Medicine's Moving Pictures: Medicine, Health, and Bodies in American Film and Television,* ed. Leslie J. Reagan, Nancy Tomes, and Paula A. Treichler (Rochester, NY: University of Rochester Press, 2007), 19–35.

[7] Although *Human Wreckage* is now more frequently known as *Sex Madness*, in part due to its circulation on the midnight movie circuit in the 1970s, I will refer to it by its original title here.

Exploitation Prototypes

Exploitation movies developed from a series of anti–venereal disease movies that, in turn, were rooted in the social hygiene movement that emerged in the United States in the early part of the twentieth century and had links to other Progressive causes. A collection of municipal vice commissions that studied the social impact of prostitution, coupled with emerging diagnostic and treatment options for syphilis, gradually penetrated Victorian rectitude to draw attention to the twin problems. Venereal diseases had been cloaked in what was referred to as the "conspiracy of silence." As Dr. Prince A. Morrow, who would lead the early fight against venereal disease (VD) in the United States, claimed in 1906, "Social sentiment holds that it is a greater violation of the properties of life publicly to mention venereal disease than privately to contract it."[8] Historian Jeffrey P. Moran explains that the conspiracy of silence was slowly eroded as "medical experts joined with moralists and professional educators in what came to be known as a movement for 'social hygiene,' or the eradication of venereal disease and prostitution."[9] At least some measure of this concern stemmed from growing anxieties about urbanization and increased immigration that appeared to portend a decline in the white Anglo-Saxon Protestant middle-class ideal. Morrow and his followers emphasized clean living and high moral standards, while also stressing that the victims of venereal disease included innocent wives and children to whom men passed their maladies. When the American Social Hygiene Association was founded in 1913, its work was built on the foundation of morality and medical treatment.[10] Similarly, within exploitation films education had two main aims: moral lessons and clinical instruction.

The dual aim of moral and clinical education was evident in some of the earliest sex hygiene films. *Damaged Goods* (1914), based on Eugène Brieux's play and one of the first hygiene films, emphasized moral education in its story of a successful lawyer who contracts syphilis at his bachelor party and then passes the disease on to his wife and child. The film was widely viewed as an exemplary lesson, one that directed men to avoid streetwalkers and other corporeal temptations and to confine sexual relations to the marital bond. The moral instruction of exploitation films was firmly rooted in the dominant Judeo-Christian, bourgeois ideology, as well as capitalist demands for a productive citizenry. The titles of exploitation movies succinctly summed up their lessons: straying from the moral path made one "damaged goods," which led to "damaged lives" or "wasted lives"; the "wages of sin" sent one down the "road to ruin" clutching a

---

[8] Quoted in Alan M. Brandt, *No Magic Bullet: A Social History of Venereal Disease in the United States since 1880*, rev. ed. (New York: Oxford University Press, 1987), 23.

[9] Jeffrey P. Moran, *Teaching Sex: The Shaping of Adolescence in the 20th Century* (Cambridge, MA: Harvard University Press, 2000), 26.

[10] See Brandt, *No Magic Bullet;* and Moran, *Teaching Sex.*

Figure 14.1. A handbill for one of the earliest exploitation films, *Damaged Goods* (1914).

"one-way ticket to hell."[11] But as the exigencies of World War I dictated that American soldiers avoid disease and be kept "fit to fight," clinical information about how venereal diseases were contracted and the prophylactic measures that could be used to prevent them became part of the mix in social hygiene films. It was often this clinical component that drew the wrath of censors and religious figures because it appeared to provide an easy out from the physical toll that had been seen as the price for moral lapses. Clinical footage, which provided the forbidden spectacle in the form of diagrams of the body and sex organs, microscopic photography of pathogens, and images of diseased sexual organs, was also considered offensive—even if the graphic images of the wages of sin usually provided the most vivid deterrent to the behaviors the films condemned (see fig. 14.1).

New York distributor Samuel Cummins's *The Naked Truth* (1924, a.k.a. *T.N.T.*) provides an archetypal example of an early exploitation film that combined moral and clinical education. The six-reel core of *The Naked Truth* was a 1919 feature originally titled *The Solitary Sin* that concerned three boys—Bob,

---

[11] These were all titles of exploitation movies: *Damaged Goods* (1914 and 1937), *Damaged Lives* (1933), *Wasted Lives* (a 1943 short, and 1959 retitle of an Italian film), *The Wages of Sin* (1938), *The Road to Ruin* (1928 and 1933), and *One Way Ticket to Hell* (1954).

John, and Edward—who live in the same neighborhood.[12] Bob's father takes the time to explain the facts of life to his son, even escorting him to a hospital to show him the effects of venereal diseases. John and Edward's parents neglect their children's sexual education. As adults all the boys become engaged to girls they have known since childhood. John discovers that he has syphilis. Told by Dr. Stone that it will take years to treat, John instead sees a quack, who claims to cure him. Dr. Stone stops John's wedding, pronouncing him unfit for marriage. Meanwhile, Edward loses his mind from masturbating too much, commits a crime, and is declared insane. Only Bob marries and lives happily, thanks to the education he received as a youth.

The fictional component of the film served to convey a lesson by tracing the "moral careers" of characters who are corrupted by temptation and face the consequences of their dubious decisions. Edward and John, like the characters who would follow in their footsteps in so many exploitation films, become stigmatized, only to suffer shame and damaged reputations that leave them cast out to the margins of society.[13] Bob, whose father has the foresight to impart proper sex instruction, is saved from a similar fate. Exploitation films emphasized the crucial role that mothers and fathers played in educating their children about matters of sex, drugs, prostitution, and other pleasures of the flesh. They suggested that parents who neglected that role through "false modesty" were guilty of endangering their children. Of course the irony was that the films usurped the instructional role that at least some parents had played in the past, and for which they advocated so strongly in their narratives. As we will see below this trend increased over time, to the point where motion pictures operated in loco parentis.

To the fictionalized moral lesson about premarital sex and masturbation that constituted the core of *The Solitary Sin*, Cummins added three one-reel documentary subjects, "The Male Reel," "The Female Reel," and "The Clinical Reel," to make up his presentation titled *The Naked Truth*. These clinical reels may have been of European origin or acquired from the American Social Hygiene Association.[14] Extant footage of "The Female Reel" features diagrams and animation of the female reproductive system, fertilization of the egg and development of the embryo, and footage of venereal disease. The "Clinical Reel" includes numerous graphic shots of the effects of syphilis and gonorrhea: diseased genitals

---

[12] Exploitation films were frequently retitled and rereleased, sometimes with footage deleted or new material added. Many exploitation movies were in release for years, even decades, often in a variety of forms.

[13] See Erving Goffman's classic study *Stigma: Notes on the Management of Spoiled Identity* (New York: Simon & Schuster, 1963).

[14] This conclusion is based on documents in the file on *The Naked Truth* (Box 2565) in the Motion Picture Division of the New York State Archives, as well as other reviews from the time.

and limbs, oozing sores, patients suffering from paralysis, and blind and mentally disabled children born to parents afflicted with the diseases. For instance, an intertitle that says "Gonorrhea (Clap) causes blindness, not only in adults, but in the babies of those who have it" is accompanied by shots of blind babies on rocking horses. Another intertitle states, "Syphilis can be contracted in other ways than sexually. We had a case the other day which we found had been contracted through indiscriminate use of toilet articles." The intertitle is followed by nine separate shots of diseased breasts, eyebrows, faces, and close-ups of ulcerated flesh.

These clinical reels served to reinforce the moral education of the narrative by depicting the negative, often nauseating, results of moral infractions. Even childbirth is framed as a pathology that requires medical intervention—not surprising given that at the turn of the century the rate of obstetrical death was still about one in one hundred. Images of flesh stretched to the breaking point during vaginal deliveries, or the deep, bloody cleaves of Caesarian operations, served as stern reminders that sex and the resulting possibility of childbirth were not to be entered into lightly. Movies like *Damaged Goods* and *The Naked Truth* established the classical exploitation template in which moral and clinical lessons were combined within a palatable and commercially exploitable framework of conventional narrative or documentary technique (which often involved reenactments) through which educational imperatives could be communicated. This model would come to be the standard for classroom films in the years ahead.

Pedagogic Methods in Exploitation Movies

From the late 1910s there were several methods by which exploitation movies attempted to convey their educational aims. Some of these were contained within the films, while others came through their advertising and through various exhibition strategies. For most moviegoers, the educational elements of exploitation movies were encountered long before they arrived at the theater. One thing that the advertising for all exploitation movies stressed was that they were for "adults only." At a time when Hollywood films were designed so they could be seen by people of any age, the "adults only" tag served as both a warning about the mature nature of the subject matter and a lure for those seeking racy content. But after the "adults only" label, advertising for exploitation movies usually stressed their educational components as a way of balancing their more lurid or sensational aspects.

Education was presented as occurring through the presentation of truths and the act of revelation in a character, which was then imparted to the spectator. These truths were most often framed as exposés. Potential ticket-buyers were assured that they would *see* sights they had never seen before. Print ads for *Marihuana* (1936) stressed that audience members would "See the truth about drug addicts." The trailer stated that viewers would "See and hear what goes on—Behind closed doors!" Ticket buyers were also assured of the film's veracity ("It's True!") and of its claims to legitimate information ("Made with the co-operation of Federal, State and Police Narcotic Officials"). Radio spots for *The Narcotics Story* (1958) screamed "*The Narcotics Story* reveals for the first time the hideous history of a girl mated to heroin! The real facts of *The Narcotics Story*, stripped of its gloss, exposing on the motion picture screen the flesh and bone of the truth!"[15] Ads for *Because of Eve* promised "The Hush-Hush Facts of Life Revealed in Every Detail!" One of the prepared stories in the film's pressbook, designed to be planted in local newspapers, made claims of authenticity and education: "The picture contains many scenes taken in hospitals—like two birth scenes, both of which make audiences gasp, then sigh with relief when they hear the first cry of the newborn children. These scenes, and many others, are sex education at its best." Radio-spot copy inveigled parents, "Bring your sons and daughters to *Because of Eve* and give them the right start in life. Equip them with an intelligent understanding of hygiene, childbirth and the dangers they face. The film treats these subjects with deserving dignity and taste" (see fig. 14.2).[16]

Figure 14.2. Crowds gather to see "the stark naked facts of life!" in *Because of Eve* (ca. 1948).

---

[15] Print ads for *Marihuana*, collection of the author. Radio ad for *The Narcotics Story* (1958, Police Science Productions), on Something Weird Video Triple THC Feature Special Edition, DVD (Something Weird Video, 2000).

[16] *Because of Eve* pressbook, 1948. Collection of the author.

Patrons frequently found that their education began on the sidewalk in front of the theater, or as soon as they entered the lobby, as they were greeted by elaborate displays that were delivered by distributors to theaters prior to the film's opening. Exhibits of narcotics paraphernalia such as opium pipes, syringes, and marijuana cigarettes accompanied drug films. Sex hygiene movies might come with wax or plaster models showing the physical effects of syphilis and gonorrhea, as well as the processes of gestation and childbirth. Items were labeled with descriptive tags and explanations. Such exhibits evoked classroom displays or the models that one might encounter in a physician's office or a museum. Thus they helped to transform a space associated with entertainment and escape into a more serious site in which learning could, at least in theory, take place. Some distributors contractually forbade the exhibition of co-features, cartoons, and short subjects with their films because they might counter the sobriety of their educational message.

Many exploitation films—especially sex hygiene films—stopped midway through for a live lecture, at times accompanied by slides or other visual aids. The lecturer would spout statistics and expand on the lessons of the films. These "eminent hygiene commentators," as they were often billed, were typically carnival talkers, schooled in the art of parting rubes from their cash. Their main charge was hawking "pitchbooks," cheap paper-covered pamphlets with titles such as "Facts about Motherhood," "The Art of Love," and "Father and Son" or "Mother and Daughter." Sold in sets of two for a dollar or two, the illustrated booklets might contain basic information about sexual anatomy, puberty, menstruation, warnings about masturbation, venereal diseases, and so forth. Moviegoers were urged by lecturers to buy the books so they could sate their desire for further knowledge in the privacy of their own homes, as well as use them as an aid in instructing their children. Women dressed as nurses were often on hand to help with the sale of the books and to further lend an air of edification to the proceedings. They were occasionally called on assist viewers made woozy by the raw images of Caesarian operations or venereal sores.[17] Although exploitation films contained titillating elements, they were always held in some check by the educational trappings that surrounded their exhibition.

When a classical exploitation film began to unspool on the screen it invariably opened with a prefatory statement known as a "square-up."[18] The square-up served as an apologia for the tawdry subject on the screen—drug use, VD, or

---

[17] If the primary purpose of the "nurses" was to sell pitchbooks, they were often called upon to help sickened patrons. Even in today's blasé been-there-done-that environment of media consumption, the footage of births and VD in decades-old sex hygiene films is still capable of eliciting agonized groans from spectators and can cause some viewers to flee the screening room.

[18] The only form of feature-length exploitation between the 1920s and the late 1950s that regularly eschewed the square-up was the burlesque film.

prostitution—and then underscored the necessity to bring it to the public's attention as a means of exposing and correcting a social ill. They announced the edifying nature of the film, while at the same time insulating distributors and exhibitors against charges of exploiting a distasteful topic or pandering to moviegoers' baser instincts. Square-ups worked in no small measure because of the pompous tone and earnest entreaties of their words. For instance, the square-up for *Human Wreckage* concludes with the line, "The subject of syphilis must no longer remain hushed, but must be fought in the open like any other dangerous contagious disease. . . . Humanity must be enlightened! Ignorance must be abolished! Young and old . . . Rich and poor . . . They Must Be Told!" *Because of Eve's* square-up suggested that the three short films shown within its framing narrative were intended for use in high schools and colleges, but added:

> Doctors and teachers felt that such vital facts should be made available
> not only to the school children, but to their mothers and fathers as
> well . . . in other words, to the whole family. This is the story behind
> the STORY OF LIFE, a motion picture conceived, produced, and
> brought to you in the name of social progress, AS AN HONEST
> EFFORT at making our beloved America a cleaner, healthier, happier
> place in which to live.[19]

The square-up for *Reefer Madness* stated in part, "The scenes and incidents, while fictionalized for the purposes of this story, are based upon actual research into the results of Marihuana addiction." And the one that prefaced *The Narcotics Story* asserted, "This motion picture was produced as a contribution to narcotics education." Although the film was filled with staged scenes, the square-up claimed: "It is not fiction. These are facts, true and authentic, based on actual cases taken from enforcement files." Appeals to the authority of science and research, facts and rationalism, were erected as a counter to any protests against the movies that attempted to frame them as being based on emotion, superstition, and outdated moralism.

 Within their narratives and documentary frames, and through their square-ups and advertising, exploitation films encouraged parents to teach their children "the facts of life" and warn them about the dangers of narcotics and other vices. The films also extolled the value that would come from such lessons in the form of clean, productive lives. As noted above, the moral education in exploitation films was usually delivered by showing characters who, through failed moral careers, fall prey to corrupting influences and their own innate weaknesses. For

---

[19] *Because of Eve* was apparently to be called *The Story of Life* originally. "The Story of Life" appeared as a prominent subtitle in the film's advertising. Why the title change took place is unknown.

instance, *Reefer Madness*—certainly the most famous exploitation film of the 1930s—begins with Dr. Carroll, a high school principal, addressing a group of parents. He warns them about marijuana, the "frightful assassin of our youth." The film foregrounds the necessity for parents to guide their children's moral education because of what it asserts is the detrimental impact marijuana has on self-control. What follows in flashback is the story of a group of young people who fall under the smoky spell of a local dope peddler, Mae. The clean-cut, middle-class kids are involved in hit-and-runs and attempted rape, murder and suicide, all committed with either glassy-eyed stares or lunatic giggling. The wildly overblown lessons of *Reefer Madness* are presented with such dour earnestness that they are now valued as prime examples of camp. But with virtually no accurate information about the effects of marijuana available in the 1930s, they were accepted as fact.

Coming two decades later, *The Narcotics Story* adopted a semidocumentary format using dramatizations and a stentorian narrator to convey authority. A lack of parental supervision is again shown as the key to poor moral choices made by teens. As the narrator cautions, "The unsupervised adolescent playing the make believe role of adult, easily finds companions to join in the game—and perhaps introduce new rules." Those "new rules" include recreational barbiturate use. "She has found a crutch to see her through her difficulties," says the narrator, referring to a girl presented in the movie, admonishing that "in time she may be willing to try something different, something *better*." A series of vignettes showing pusher and addict behaviors, stakeouts, searches, and busts illustrate the toll illegal narcotic use takes on society and individuals. Warnings about personal degradation are the strongest, and the film concludes suggesting, "The addict will sell all her possessions, and finally herself in her drive for drugs," as we see a young woman outside a cheap motel with a john. A final shot shows an addict on the floor suffering withdrawal as the narrator intones, "This is the end of the world."

Another example from the 1930s illustrates how moral education was deployed. *Human Wreckage* opens with several parallel stories that converge at a big city burlesque show. Young James Winthrop watches the show with his date; Peggy, an office worker, makes sexual overtures to her coworker Betty whom she has convinced to see the show; Tom Lorentz, son of a reformer, and his pals ogle the performers; and finally, a dissipated patron smacks his lips as he glares at the women onstage. After the show, James and his date check in to a seedy hotel under assumed names for a tryst, Tom and his friends wait at the stage door of the burlesque theater to go out with the dancers, and the dissipated man attacks and murders a little girl in an alley. Although not shown, presumably Betty succumbs to Peggy's lesbian advances. The sexualized entertainment of the burlesque review is shown to have broken down and perverted the moral resolve of those under its influence. The story then shifts to Millicent,

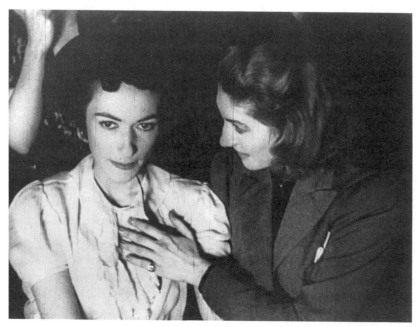

Figure 14.3. Peggy makes sexual overtures to her friend Betty as they watch a burlesque show in *Human Wreckage* (a.k.a. *Sex Madness*, 1938).

one of the burlesque dancers, who visits Dr. Harris and tells him how she came to the big city and met a producer who took advantage of her and left her with syphilis. The doctor takes Millicent on a tour of hospital wards to show her the effects of the disease. She begins her treatment, but then moves home where she takes a quick cure from a quack, passing the disease on to her new husband, and then their baby. Back in the city Tom Lorenz admits to his father that he has VD and joins him in his reform efforts. Millicent decides to poison her now blind husband and herself, but a last-minute phone call from a friend who is being treated for syphilis stops her and makes her realize she has the strength to go on living.

Along with the moral messages, clinical education continued to be the other key educational component of the exploitation film. Sometimes it was woven into an exploitation feature, such as in *Human Wreckage*. In that film Dr. Harris takes Millicent, the showgirl who succumbed to a shady producer, to a hospital where he shows her the effects of syphilis. Stock medical shots, some of silent vintage, are inserted as illustration. The clinical elements in *Reefer Madness* include documentary shots during Dr. Carroll's introduction, showing the making of cigarettes and methods of smuggling, and sequences illustrating the supposed violence-inducing effects of the drug. In *The Narcotics Story* clinical elements include details about the characteristics of drugs (such as the shape, serrations, and sticky resin of marijuana leaves) and police procedures used for searches and arrests ("Toilets provide numerous hiding places" as the narrator explains). Much of the latter part of the film deals with verbal descriptions and visual depictions of the symptoms of narcotics withdrawal.

Very often, clinical instruction came in the form of separate short films that were played in the middle of the feature or added on at the end. For instance, *High School Girl* (1934), a comparatively tame exploitation movie, was about a high school girl who through a momentary moral lapse is impregnated by her boyfriend. It was later paired with a birth reel and peddled on the exploitation circuit as *Dust to Dust* in the early 1940s.[20] Many short movies with titles such as *The Truth about Sex* (1928), *Sinister Harvest* (1930), *The Story of Birth* (ca. 1940), and *Wasted Lives* (1943) produced during the period were designed to be shown with exploitation features.

These shorts tended to incorporate extant clinical footage created for medical colleges, nursing schools, or military and police training rather than using new footage with expensive, specialized sequences. The footage was usually purchased from stock houses or other sources, and there is ample evidence to suggest that it was frequently pirated. Once a producer or distributor had a birth reel, venereal disease shots, or other clinical material, he would use it over and over again, at times recutting it or including new intertitles or narration in an effort to keep up with scientific or medical advances. For instance, at some point in the 1930s distributor Samuel Cummins acquired a Swiss film titled *Birth* (1930) that dealt primarily with abortion. By 1949 he was issuing it under the title *Miracle of Birth* with additional clinical footage. A reviewer for *Variety* speculated that *Miracle of Birth* "appears to be a patchup of three different stories" and said that cut into the picture was "a hospital scene of an actual Caesarian birth," which he labeled the best thing in the film and the other Cummins film with which it was paired, *Miracle of Life*.

Miracle of Life, in turn, was cobbled together from other clinical reels and included footage of a horse giving birth from the 1936 Hungarian movie *Hortobágy*. It is safe to speculate that audiences were unconcerned about the source of the clinical footage as long as it seemed to support the educational charge of the film and to provide the requisite spectacle.[21] Because the clinical footage in exploitation movies may have been made years, if not decades, earlier, and because footage from other countries often contained cues that made it look "foreign," clinical material often stood out from the remainder of a film whether it was integrated into the middle or simply tacked onto the end. By the postwar period,

---

[20] *High School Girl* was the inspiration for Kroger Babb's exploitation blockbuster *Mom and Dad* (1944). Babb toured with *Dust to Dust*.

[21] In the 1989 documentary *Sex and Buttered Popcorn*, Dan Sonney, son of exploitation pioneer Louis Sonney, states that he "never had to give anyone their money back." David F. Friedman, who was a roadshowman from the late 1940s, agrees. This, and other evidence, would seem to indicate that ticket buyers seldom complained about the content of the films.

these clinical reels continually tried to up the ante. Tired of black-and-white childbirth footage? See the birth of a baby in color! Bored with standard deliveries? See the birth of twins! Twins are passé? See the birth of triplets!

From their emergence in the late teens into the post–World War II period, exploitation movies offered a new version of "the talk" for parents, a convenient, modern surrogate for awkward and uncomfortable conversations about difficult subjects. They also positioned themselves as superior to mere verbal information about sex and drugs because of their ability to present such lessons in a moving, visual, and scientific form. Where a parent might show a child some drawings of sexual anatomy, fertilization, and gestation, an exploitation film could offer animated diagrams. Where a mother or father could describe the process of childbirth, a film could show it, in close-up, from crowning to afterbirth. Where a child or teen could be warned of the devastating health effects of syphilis, gonorrhea, or drug use, several shots in a motion picture could implant an indelible image of that damage in their minds. Even if moral, medical, and educational authorities often questioned the legitimacy of exploitation movies, the films themselves consistently asserted the superiority of motion pictures as a tool for moral and clinical education for parents and for children old enough to gain admittance to see them.

Watching People Watching Educational Films

During the post–World War II years, the moral lessons of exploitation films diminished and the clinical elements increased in importance. This was due to several reasons. During the war moral standards were relaxed, a trend that only deepened through the 1950s and 60s as the "sexual revolution" took hold. Also, there was a tremendous desire on the part of postwar couples for family planning information that was linked to the developing importance of science and therapeutic culture. Finally, exploitation films were in competition with an increasingly sexualized popular culture, which meant that they were forced to rely on greater amounts of spectacle provided by clinical footage to remain competitive within the changing exploitation marketplace. A growing trend in exploitation movies during the postwar years was to show films within films—a ploy that served to heighten the spectacle, while at the same time emphasizing the educational nature of the films.

Movies had already proved to be a critical teaching tool during World War II. Hundreds of films were produced for the U.S. armed forces by the Signal Corps, the major studios, and small concerns, demonstrating everything from the use of bombsights to setting up mobile laundry units. A number of these movies were directed at maintaining the health of soldiers, covering familiar territory that exploitation films had during the 1920s and 30s. Perhaps the most famous was director John Ford's *Sex Hygiene* (1941). Estimated to have been seen by every man in the armed forces within days of his induction—and then many times afterward—the film was credited as "a powerful factor in maintaining the relatively low venereal disease rate in the army during the war."[22] By most accounts the repulsive imagery in *Sex Hygiene* made for some of the most vivid noncombat-related memories of those who served in World War II.

The efficacy of using film as a teaching tool to impart clinical lessons during the war appears to have been one of the main reasons for its prominent place within the diegesis of postwar exploitation films. The first of these was Kroger Babb's *Mom and Dad* (1944), a sex hygiene blockbuster about yet another high school girl who winds up "in trouble." In the film a progressive biology teacher, fired for speaking frankly about youthful romance in class, is eventually rehired to offer a social hygiene class. As part of his effort he shows his students 16mm films on venereal diseases and childbirth, which the audience for *Mom and Dad* see in their entirety. These films constituted the clinical portion of Babb's movie, and the conceit of showing educational films within an exploitation feature was popularized through *Mom and Dad*'s enormous success.[23] Three films released in 1948 to compete with *Mom and Dad*—*Street Corner*, *The Story of Bob and Sally*, and *Because of Eve*—all used the same technique.[24]

Because of Eve opens with a young married couple, Bob and Sally, waiting with Dr. West to learn the results of Sally's pregnancy test.[25] A flashback shows them a year earlier as they complete their premarital health exams. Dr. West tells Sally, "That first baby didn't hurt you a bit," and he says to Bob, "There's no trace of your old VD." The husband and wife-to-be look at each other, aghast. Sally runs out of the room. Bob tells the doctor that a buddy who was killed in the war, Nick Wilde, introduced him to a shady woman who left him with a venereal disease. Unlike in the earlier films, Dr. West does not launch into a long sermon about the wages of sin. Instead, he asks Bob what he knows about VD. When Bob admits that he's no expert, West proclaims, "Well here's where you're going to get a liberal education on the subject . . . I'm going to show you some pictures that we put together on VD." He turns to the handy 16mm projector, loaded and

---

[22] Quoted in Eberwein, *Sex Ed,* 71. For more on *Sex Hygiene* and other anti-VD films used by the armed forces during the war, see ibid., 64–86.

[23] *Mom and Dad* was estimated to have taken in $8 million from twenty million moviegoers by 1949. "Something for the Soul," *Time,* Apr. 18, 1949, 102. The film-within-a-film technique was apparently used as early as Dwain Esper's lost *Modern Motherhood* (1934), but it did not catch on until after World War II.

[24] Clinical films could also be lifted out of a feature leaving only the moral education. Babb did this to *Mom and Dad*, calling the new presentation *Side Road*, which was able to play in censorship territories that refused to license *Mom and Dad*.

[25] Joseph Crehan, who plays Dr. West, also appeared as the physician in *Street Corner*. Complicating this confusing intertextuality, the main characters in *Because of Eve* and *The Story of Bob and Sally* are both named Bob and Sally.

Figure 14.4. In *Because of Eve* (1948) Bob (John Parker) consults with Dr. West (Joseph Crehan), who sits with his 16mm projector at the ready.

ready to play the self-contained short *The Story of V.D.* "Shows you what it is, how to spot it," the doctor explains, "and what to do about it." He invites Bob to click off the light and pull up a chair. The film unspools for Bob, and the audience for *Because of Eve*, in its entirety.

Sally returns and tells the doctor that she was engaged in college—to Nick Wilde—who had impregnated her. He was drafted and killed in the war. Sally failed at attempting abortion and suicide, and she subsequently delivered a baby that died at birth. Dr. West asks the couple, "Do you know anything about the facts of life?" They admit they know nothing. He tells them that they "better learn something about sex, right now. I have some pictures here that were made for folks just like you. You're going to sit quietly and look at them. And never again, will you ever think of sex as anything but something wonderful, miraculous, almost divine." He flips on the projector for *The Story of Reproduction*. (The live, pseudonymous lecturer, "Alexander Leeds," would have taken the stage for the book pitch following *The Story of Reproduction*.) As *Because of Eve* resumes, we find the couple returning to the doctor's office a week later. He confirms that Sally is pregnant and shows them *The Story of Birth*. When Dr. West asks if they will teach their child the facts of life, Bob promises, "He'll be the most educated little rascal in the whole neighborhood."

Because of Eve's moral lessons are imparted through Bob and Sally's flashbacks to their premarital indiscretions which led to physical and emotional scars that almost derail their wedding. But the moral education is far less important than the clinical education, which is neatly compartmentalized in the three short films that Dr. West shows on his 16mm projector. They feature charts, diagrams, and explicit footage ranging from childbirth to diseased genitals. Indeed, the "hot" version of *Because of Eve* was notable for its full-frontal nude shots of male and female models used in the clinical reels.[26] The visuals in the short films were supported with descriptive voiceover narration. For instance, in *The Story of Reproduction* the process of fertilization is accompanied by images of sperm and narration that says, "Here come the sperm cells, racing like little fish upstream to spawn." There was also practical advice. In *The Story of V.D.* the narrator admonishes viewers to "see any reliable doctor for such [a VD] examination. Or if you can't afford a doctor go to your local health clinic."

In *Because of Eve* the films, and the projector that Dr. West treats with an almost totemic reverence, are accorded tremendous power. Robert Eberwein notes "the authority of the doctor who controls the projector and the film legitimates diegetically the gaze at sexual information." While Dr. West spends time fulminating about the ignorance of youth regarding sexuality, he never offers explicit instruction to Bob and Sally. In fact, he has completely ceded his authority and role as educator on sexual subjects to the short films. His final act of relinquishing his influence comes when he recommends that Bob and Sally buy a good book on the subject, a clear prompt to *Because of Eve*'s audience to purchase the pitchbooks available in the theater.

The films-within-films may also have helped naturalize the notion of sex education within the classroom setting at a time when it was just beginning to take root in the United States. Eberwein points out that

> the observers within the film play an interesting role vis-à-vis the audiences at the exploitation film. On the one hand, they serve as a relay for the viewers observing them and the film they watch, thus establishing at one remove the validity of what everyone is observing as a result of the union of school, medical authority, and government. On the other hand, though, the disparity between the actual conditions of reception at a grindhouse and those depicted in the film suggest one criterion that might be used to differentiate exploitation films from nonexploitative sex education films. That is, with one or two exceptions the latter seem to be distinguishable when the conditions of reception externally for them are similar to or consonant

---

[26] "Hot" versions of exploitation films, with more nudity or other forms of spectacle, were used in locales without censorship. Cold versions, for areas that had harsher censorship, substituted tamer footage, or cut material entirely. The "cold" version of *Because of Eve* substituted drawings of male and female figures for the nude photographs.

with those depicted in the film being watched by the interior audience.[27]

While exploitation films were not always shown in grindhouses[28]—they usually played in neighborhood and small-town theaters—Eberwein is correct in suggesting that even though the content of exploitation films and standard educational films was much the same, the conditions of reception had the potential to influence the ways in which they were greeted by an audience and how their information was received. And yet by showing images of people soberly watching education films (be it in a doctor's office or a classroom) within the framework of an exploitation feature, the scenes may have served as a model for the behavior of some exploitation audiences. Moreover, the deployment of such scenes helped to validate the use of film as a tool for teaching sensitive or controversial topics.

Conclusion

During the postwar period the classroom rapidly began to replace the motion picture theater as the space in which lessons about sex and drug use were imparted.[29] This can be attributed to the continuing lurid nature of promotion of "adults only" exploitation films and the fact that during the late 1940s and 50s exploitation films as a whole began to move away from ostensibly educational topics to those that were more overtly titillating, such as nudist camp films and burlesque movies. It can also be credited to a growing number of school systems around the country that began to include elements of sex and drug education as part of their curricula. Postwar anxieties about juvenile delinquency and family dysfunction led to the growth of sex education in classrooms, even if "'education for personal and family living' continued to mean a strongly prescriptive program for sexual restraint."[30] Warnings about drug use also became fixtures. Biology and health classes became the most frequent venue for drug and sex

---

[27] Eberwein, *Sex Ed*, 93.

[28] The term "grindhouse" originally referred to theaters that were grinding continuously from early morning into the late night hours. As the term developed it came to connote a marginal house that showed exploitation movies and other low-end product. In the postwar years there were probably only a hundred or so grindhouses in the United States.

[29] The theater reemerged as a place to learn about sex again in the late 1960s and early 1970s as a series of illustrated "marriage manual" films, sometimes referred to as "white coaters," were released. Showing a variety of sexual practices and positions, the films offered up hard-core imagery within an educational context. *Man and Wife* (1969), *He and She* (1970), and *Sexual Freedom in Denmark* (1970) are just several examples. However, narrative hard-core pornography quickly displaced the educational sex instruction film in theaters.

[30] Moran, *Teaching Sex*, 131.

education, in the case of the latter further cementing the bond between sex and science in the minds of the masses that began with the publication of Alfred Kinsey's pioneering studies, *Sexual Behavior in the Human Male* (1948) and *Sexual Behavior in the Human Female* (1953).

Films such as *Human Growth* (1948), made by actor Eddie Albert's small production company, rode a wave of army surplus 16mm projectors into classrooms across America during the postwar years. Although it was clearly designed for adolescents rather than adults, the film had many commonalities with exploitation films from the time (anatomy lessons, animated diagrams, and representations of birth—albeit the latter was in animated form rather than real birth footage). It even included the film-within-a-film conceit of having students in a classroom watching a film called *Human Growth*.[31] While *Human Growth* was designed to stimulate questions and discussion in the classroom, we might wonder how many teachers actually used the film in such a manner—or if they, like the fictional Dr. West in *Because of Eve*, simply abdicated their responsibility as educators to the clattering machine at the back of a darkened room.[32]

As tools for education, exploitation films were seriously flawed. Their tawdry nature, shrill moral preachments, and sometimes outdated clinical information might not have concerned those who only came to the theater simply for a cheap thrill. For some desperately seeking knowledge about subjects that were rarely spoken of with frankness in a physician's office, much less in polite society, their lack of currency and muddled messages may have done a decided disservice. But for others who hoped to at least begin to attain a modest amount of knowledge about sex, venereal diseases, drug use, and other difficult subjects, for many years they served as an introductory lesson at a time when such information was difficult to find.

Filmography

Because of Eve (1948) 72 min., 35mm
PRODUCTION: Crusade Productions. DISTRIBUTOR: Crusade Productions. DIRECTOR: Howard Bretherton. WRITER: Larry Allen, Walter A. Lawrence, Arthur Martinelli. CAST: Joseph Crehan (Dr. West), John Parker (Bob Stephens), Wanda McKay (Sally Stephens), Sam Balter (Segment Narrator), Hy Averback (Segment Narrator). ACCESS: DVD available from www.somethingweird.com.

---

[31] Eberwein, *Sex Ed*, 113–18.
[32] "Sex in the Schoolroom," *Time*, Mar. 22, 1948, 71–72.

Damaged Goods (1914) 7 reels, 35mm
PRODUCTION: American Film Manufacturing Company.
DISTRIBUTOR: Mutual Film. DIRECTOR: Thomas Ricketts.
WRITER: Harry A. Pollard, Richard Bennett, Thomas B. Middleton.
CAMERA: Thomas B. Middleton. CAST: Richard Bennett (George
Dupont), Adrienne Morrison (A Girl of the Streets), Maud Milton
(Mrs. Dupont), Olive Templeton (Henriette Locke). ACCESS: No
versions known to survive.

Human Growth (1948) 19 min., 16mm
PRODUCTION: Eddie Albert Productions. DISTRIBUTOR:
E. C. Brown. PRODUCERS: Eddie Albert, Jack Fletcher.

Human Wreckage (1938) 57min., 35mm
PRODUCTION: Cinema Service Corp. DISTRIBUTOR: States
Rights. DIRECTOR: Unknown. PRODUCER: Unknown. WRITER:
Joseph Seiden, Vincent Valentini. CAST: Vivian McGill (Millicent
Hamilton), Rose Tapley (Mrs. Hamilton), Al Rigali (Mr. Hamilton),
Stanley Barton (Wendel Hope). ALTERNATIVE TITLE: *Sex Madness*. ACCESS: www.archive.org/details/sex_madness_ACM.

Mom and Dad (1944) 96 min., 35mm
PRODUCTION: Hallmark Productions. DISTRIBUTOR:
Hallmark Productions. DIRECTOR: William Beaudine. WRITER:
Kroger Babb, Mildred Horn. PRODUCER: Kroger Babb, J. S. Jossey.
CAMERA: Marcel Le Picard. MUSIC: Dave Torbett. EDITOR:
Richard C. Currier, Lloyd Friedgen. CAST: June Carlson (Joan
Blake), Lois Austin (Sarah Blake), George Eldredge (Dan Blake),
Jimmy Clark (Dave Blake).

The Naked Truth (1924) 7 reels, 35 mm
PRODUCTION: Public Welfare Pictures. DISTRIBUTOR: Public
Welfare Pictures. PRODUCER: Samuel Cummins. WRITER:
George D. Walters. CAST: Jack Mulhall (Bob), Helene Chadwick
(Mary), Leo Pierson (Bob's Playmate), Charles Spere (Another
Playmate). ALTERNATIVE TITLE: *T.N.T.* ACCESS: No versions
known to survive.

The Narcotics Story (1958) 75min., 35mm
PRODUCTION: Police Science Productions. DISTRIBUTOR:
Harry Stern. DIRECTOR: Robert W. Larsen. PRODUCER: Robert
W. Larsen. WRITER: Roger Emerson Garris. CAMERA: Jerry May.

MUSIC: Alexander Laszlo. EDITOR: Charles Henkel Jr. NAR-
RATOR: Art Gilmore. CAST: Herbert Crisp, Officer Joe Delro,
Darlene Hendrick, Bob Hopkins. ACCESS: DVD available from
www.somethingweird.com; http://blip.tv/free-media/the-narcotics-
story-1958-4533661.

Reefer Madness (1936) 66min., 35mm
PRODUCTION: G and H Productions. DISTRIBUTOR: States
Rights. DIRECTOR: Louis Gasnier. PRODUCER: George A.
Hirliman. WRITER: Lawrence Meade, Arthur Hoerl, Paul Franklin.
CAST: Dorothy Short (Mary), Kenneth Craig (Bill), Lillian Miles
(Blanche), Dave O'Brien (Ralph). ACCESS: www.archive.org/details/
reefer_madness1938.

Sex Hygiene (1941) 30 min., 35mm
PRODUCTION: U.S. Army Signal Corps. DISTRIBUTOR: U.S.
Army Signal Corps. DIRECTOR: Otto Brower and John Ford.
PRODUCER: Darryl F. Zanuck. WRITER: W. Ulman. CAMERA:
George Barne, Charles G. Clarke. EDITOR: Gene Fowler Jr. CAST:
Kenneth Alexander (Soldier), Robert Conway (Soldier), Robert
Cornell (Soldier), Richard Derr (Soldier). ACCESS: www.archive.org/
details/SEX.HYGIENE.

The Solitary Sin (1919) 6 reels, 35mm
PRODUCTION: The Solitary Sin Corporation. DISTRIBUTOR:
States Rights. DIRECTOR: Frederick Sullivan. PRODUCER:
George D. Watters. WRITER: George D. Watters. CAMERA: King
D. Gray. CAST: Jack Mulhall (Bob Meredith, as an adult), Helene
Chadwick (Mary McMillan), Gordon Griffith (Bob Meredith, age
14), Pauline Curley (Dorothy Morton). ACCESS: No versions
known to survive.

Street Corner (1948) 73 min., 35mm
PRODUCTION: Wilshire Pictures Corp. DISTRIBUTOR: Viro
Pictures. DIRECTOR: Albert Kelley. PRODUCER: Jim Doane.
WRITER: Jack Jungmeyer (Screenplay), Albert Kelley (Story), Edwin
Roth (Adaptation). MUSIC: Bernard Katz. CAMERA: Virgil Miller.
EDITOR: John Faure. CAST: Joseph Crehan (Dr. James Fenton),
Marcia Mae Jones (Lois Marsh), Jean Fenwick (Mrs. Marsh), Don Brodie
(Arnold Marsh). ACCESS: DVD available from www.somethingweird.
com.

The Story of Bob and Sally (1948) 71min., 35mm
PRODUCTION: Social Guidance Productions. DISTRIBUTOR:
States Rights. DIRECTOR: Earle C. Kenton. PRODUCER: J. G.
Sanford. WRITER: Mary C. Palmer. MUSIC: Milton Rosen.
CAMERA: Ellis Carter. EDITOR: Paul Landres. CAST: Gloria
Marlen (Sally Wright), Ralph Hodges (Bob Jordan), Rick Vallin (Jim
Cooper), Mildred Coles (Helen Cooper). ACCESS: No versions
known to survive.

Related Films

Birth (1930). Produced by Praesens Film Co. (Zurich, Switzerland).
Distributed by Culture Films, Inc. and Public Welfare Films. 6 reels.

The End of the Road (1919). Produced by U.S. Public Health Service;
American Social Hygiene Association. Distributed by Public Health
Films. 6–7 reels.

Fit to Win (1919). Produced by U.S. Public Health Service; American
Social Hygiene Association; War Department Commission on
Training Camp Activities. Distributed by Public Health Films. 6 reels.

High School Girl (1934). Produced and distributed by Brian Foy
Productions. 55min.

Marihuana (1936). Produced and distributed by Roadshow Attractions. 57 min.

Miracle of Birth (1949). Produced by Jewel Productions and distributed by Public Welfare Pictures. Running time unknown.

The Miracle of Life (1949). Produced by Jewel Productions and
distributed by Public Welfare Pictures. 50 min.

The Scarlet Trail (1919). Produced by G. and L. Features Inc. and
distributed by States Rights Independent Exchanges. 6 reels.

Sinister Harvest (1930). Produced and distributed by Roadshow
Attractions. 1 reel.

The Story of Birth (ca. 1940). Produced by Nathan Cy Braunstein. 2 reels.

The Truth about Sex (1928). Produced and distributed by Dwain
Esper. 3 reels.

Wasted Lives (1943). Produced by Louis Machat. 3 reels.

Wild Oats (1919). Produced by Samuel Cummins. Distributed by
Social Hygienic Films of America Inc. 6 reels.

15 SMOOTHING THE CONTOURS OF DIDACTICISM: JAM HANDY AND HIS ORGANIZATION

RICK PRELINGER

For half a century portraits memorializing a score of "showmen, educators, business exponents and patriots" graced the walls of the Jam Handy Organization's (JHO) main lobby in Detroit. Hung by order of company founder Henry Jamison ("Jam") Handy (1886–1983) and rotated in and out as their birthdays came and went, this eclectic group of thinkers and makers represented Handy's intellectual and commercial influences. Judging from their frequent appearance in his interviews and letters, they were his role models as well. Manufacturers like John H. Patterson of National Cash Register and Charles F. Kettering of General Motors shared the wall with promoters and showmen like George M. Cohan and Phineas T. Barnum, and a group of educators so diverse as to confound anyone looking for a clear thread in Handy's own development: Horace Mann, Froebel, Goethe, Dewey, Pestalozzi, Rousseau, Florence Nightingale, Susan B. Anthony, and, perhaps less enigmatically, John Comenius, the early exponent of education through images. The pictures remained until the dissolution of the organization in 1984.[1]

Accompanying the portraits were short quotations whose flavor is shown by these examples:

JEFFERSON: "Educate and inform the people. They are the only sure reliance for the preservation of our liberty."
JOHN H. PATTERSON: "Visualize. Dramatize. Make it so a 12-year-old can understand."
MEDILL MCCORMICK: "To exteriorize the viewpoint. To advertise the features. To popularize all presentations."

The Jamison Handy Papers (referenced below) are part of the Burton Historical Collection at the Detroit Public Library.

[1] Folder of memoranda and birthday lists in author's possession.

Figure 15.1. Headquarters of the Jam Handy Organization, 2900 East Grand Boulevard, Detroit, Michigan, ca. 1935. (Author's collection.)

In many interviews, oral histories, and recurrent stabs at autobiography, Handy repeatedly credited the members of this group for his ideas about education and visual instruction.[2] While there is no doubt that their works and philosophies informed Handy's own, Handy's theories of visual education look more like a diffuse mash-up of ideas from many sources than a structured approach to pedagogy. Nonetheless, this admitted autodidact and unconscious dilettante influenced the development of audiovisual education and corporate speech more than anyone else working with moving images.

Charismatic founder of what was perhaps the longest-lived American media production company, Jam Handy made educational, training, and promotional films for a wide spectrum of businesses, associations, and government agencies. The many thousands of films and filmstrips JHO produced pioneered countless experiments and innovations and, in many cases, represented key moments in the evolution of commercial and institutional communication. Handy taught corporations new ways of communicating with their employees and customers, merging discourses of education with the practices of business and the disciplines of salesmanship.

---

[2] Though wall portraits were rotated throughout the year and certain ones waxed and waned in favor, the list, as far as I can determine, is as follows:

Showmen: George M. Cohan, B. F. Keith, Florenz Ziegfeld, Phineas T. Barnum, Lee Shubert, David Belasco, James B. Turbett, and John Ringling.

Educators: Horace Mann, J. W. Goethe, Friederich Froebel, Herbert Spencer, John Dewey, Johann Pestalozzi, John Comenius, Jean-Jacques Rousseau, Florence Nightingale, and Susan B. Anthony.

Business Exponents: Benjamin Franklin, Medill McCormick, T. J. Watson, Charles F. Kettering, John H. Patterson, John Wanamaker, Andrew Carnegie, George M. Pullman, Richard H. Grant, and W. E. Holler.

Patriots: George Washington, Abraham Lincoln, and Thomas Jefferson.

Figure 15.2. "Jam Handy Picture Service—Central Organization and Branch Heads on Stage 'A,'" Dec. 14, 1935. (Author's collection.)

Though Handy himself foregrounded his role as visual educator, there has been little work tracing his media production in the context of the history of education. The dearth of scholarship on Handy and his work points more broadly to the lack of attention that has been paid to ephemeral film genres. To date, only scattered mentions of his work appear in monographs written by historians and little or none occurs in cinema studies literature. This article hopes to begin to address that gap by looking at his influences and revisiting a few of his statements on education.

Handy came early in a long line of educator-entrepreneurs who sought to produce audiovisual media informed by preexisting educational theories. Unlike the builders of educational film colossuses like Eastman Teaching Films (founded in 1927) and Encyclopaedia Britannica Films (whose ancestor, Erpi Classroom Films, dates back to 1929), both of which solicited regular input and evaluation from scholars and teachers, Handy—who began making films around 1914—did not maintain roots in or relationships to organized educational institutions or academic experts. As we will see, his early life was marked by rebellion against the orthodox educational system that summarily rejected his presence. His work was financed by eminent industrialists and some of the wealthiest American corporations, and his pedagogical experiments were realized as a direct part of his corporate

Figure 15.2. (*continued*)

and industrial production, not as an adjunct. Assessing Handy's particular claim
to fame within the realm of education will reveal that his greatest contribution
was to link educational concerns and strategies with corporate and institutional
objectives, often in an idiosyncratic manner. And even though he clearly played
a major role in the articulation of American corporate speech and public relations (though historians have yet to seriously evaluate his work), it may be most
revealing to think of him as a gifted maker of sponsored media who managed to
modulate prosaic productions with an unusual blend of ideas that were inspired
by the examples, if not the word-by-word theories, of eminent educational
thinkers.[3]

---

[3] A brief treatment of some of the JHO films for General Motors in the 1930s appears in
Roland Marchand, *Creating the Corporate Soul* (Berkeley: University of California Press, 1998),
241–45. More detailed information on commercial speech during the 1930s through the 1950s,
including discussion of some Handy films and a filmography of sponsored motion pictures, can be
found throughout William L. Bird's *Better Living: Advertising, Media and the New Vocabulary of
Business Leadership, 1935–1955* (Evanston, IL: Northwestern University Press, 1999).

Besides Jam Handy Organization's estimated 7,000 motion pictures and perhaps as many as 100,000 slidefilms (later known as filmstrips, slidefilms combined still images onto a one-meter-long strip of film that could be shown with a folding pocketsize projector), JHO produced trade shows, industrial theater productions, multimedia training aids, and communication kits.[4] The company proudly offered its clients complete, vertically integrated media production, distribution, and exhibition services. Handy men drove mobile projection vans across the country, presenting films at meetings, conventions, and public events. In essence, JHO was a factory for the production of didactic media, using every delivery platform known at the time, developing new technologies like simulation and 3-D, and integrating diverse media forms into sales, training, persuasive, and educational campaigns. Aiming to bridge the class divides of the early twentieth century, optimize industrial education, and standardize sales training, Handy linked industrialists with consumers and management with workers, articulating a relatively new discourse of corporate and commercial speech. Bill Sandy, who worked for JHO for many years and took over his Chevrolet media production business, credited Handy with being the first person to imagine distance learning.[5]

Unlike the canonical educational film, most JHO films were not originally produced for showing in classrooms. Rather, they were sponsored by corporations, associations, and organizations and targeted primarily at adult audiences. Some, such as training and orientation films, were made for in-house corporate and industrial screenings. Others were aimed toward the general public. These films fell into three rough categories:

- Films promoting specific products or product lines, such as *The Car of Tomorrow, Today* (1948), advertising the first Oldsmobile fully designed after World War II. Some of these films were produced for theatrical release, others for point-of-purchase screenings (such as in mini-theaters within automobile dealerships).
- Films promoting a corporate image or brand, known in the trade as institutional advertising. Examples might include *Master Hands* (1936), showing the assembly of Chevrolets at the Flint, Michigan,

---

[4] The count of 7,000 is the author's estimate, based on entries contained in a checklist (in the author's possession) of JHO productions between 1935 and 1968, plus vault index cards covering some earlier motion pictures. Since most JHO corporate records apparently do not survive (a handful of corporate records are held with Jamison Handy's personal papers at the Detroit Public Library), I have found no authoritative tallies of slidefilm production. The figures cited in contemporary press accounts vary from hundreds of thousands to millions, but it is likely that these counts refer to prints rather than titles.

[5] Bill Sandy, quoted in Robert T. Eberwein, "The Contributions of the Jam Handy Organization to American Commerce and Culture," *Oakland Journal* 4 (Spring 2002): 91.

plant; and *American Look* (1958), an homage to American industrial, interior, and product designers. Institutional films might often incorporate implicit advertising of a company's products, but the films ordinarily did not support specific sales campaigns.

- Advocacy films promoting particular positions, such as *Give Yourself the Green Light* (1954), a General Motors–sponsored film urging the public to support legislation authorizing the Interstate Highway system. Some of these were shown theatrically and on television, which played sponsored films for new audiences, sometimes in the tens of millions per film.

Many films in the second category were produced without explicit sales pitches so that they could be shown in classrooms and, beginning in the late 1930s, on television. The suitability of a film for classroom use was based on a number of considerations, notably the absence of direct advertising and its evaluation by educational film reviewers, who tended to be critical of films they felt introduced undue commercialism into the educational environment. *Master Hands,* originally produced as a tribute to General Motors' highly evolved system of assembly-line production, had a second life as a "vocational subject," shown in trade schools and industrial education programs. Relatively few Handy films, however, were produced primarily for direct school showings, though there are conspicuous exceptions, like *The Tip-Tops in Peppyland* (1936), made by the New York State Bureau of Publicity to teach nutrition to elementary school students.[6]

What little work that has been done on Handy and JHO tends to look at the productions piecemeal, rather than as a body of work sharing common and often novel characteristics, and also tends towards sociocultural criticism rather than analysis of the works themselves. Hopefully, this will change as access to his works becomes more widespread, especially online. We can also hope that emerging and future scholars will begin to critically examine the vast and intimidating corpus of educational film and compare the widely divergent representational styles and strategies that distinguish the work of different producers. It is my belief that many trails will link back to Handy.

The Transfer of Experience

In an autobiographical fragment, Jamison Handy wrote:

As a young man it seemed to me that the most important use I could make of my life was to find better ways for the transmission of

---

[6] *The Tip-Tops in Peppyland* bears little resemblance to other JHO films. It combines somersaulting clowns, stock footage, and Max Fleischer–like animation showing the benefits of vitamins into an unusually fragmented whole.

instructions, and the transfer of experience. It seemed a shame that so many instructions were misunderstood, that information offered was so hard to understand, that the experience of my elders was so hard to get at, and so many good ideas lost.[7]

Handy's life as well as his sensibilities linked two centuries. Though his mid-century films showed freeways, mass-produced suburbs, and space shots, their narration sometimes sounded like late-nineteenth-century industrial promotions, and their images looked like magic lantern slide shows with sound. Even if sometimes stagy and verbose, Handy's work was conceived in rebellion against educational orthodoxy, and constituted one man's attempt to make learning an attribute of daily life and to make education happen outside schools.

Handy's father Moses Purnell Handy (1847–98), a former Confederate army major, was editor-in-chief of the *Chicago Times-Herald* and later organizer of publicity for the World's Columbian Exposition. An innovative and aggressive promoter, he brought many prominent industrialists, inventors, and media people home to family dinners, which young Jam would reminisce about for the rest of his life. The Handy children were allowed to pose a few questions to their renowned guests, and much was made of the quality of their questions. When Jam was six, there ensued a family debate as to whether to send him to public or private school. Instead Handy asked his father to allow him to "learn on the job" at the 1893 World's Columbian Exposition. He won his wish. For the next two years he visited the Expo and talked to exhibitors, spending the same time that school would have occupied. Later he would write that the explanatory, illuminative labels in the machinery exhibition inspired the lantern slides and the frames of the slidefilms he would make some twenty years later, and it's likely that his visual and rhetorical sensibilities were formed at the fair.[8] Bill Sandy said, "After a spring and summer immersed in the sights, sounds, color, splash and showmanship of a World Fair, Handy forevermore chafed under the limitations of the classroom and the blackboard."[9]

Handy would not do well in organized education. In one of the many unfinished autobiographical fragments in his personal papers, he said that he ran into trouble with the traditional-minded teachers in the Chicago public schools because he loudly advocated a shift toward visual education, influenced by

---

[7] Undated autobiographical fragment, Jamison Handy Papers, box 3, 1.

[8] Information on Handy's childhood is largely drawn from an untitled autobiographical fragment (ca. 1975–1977). Jamison Handy Papers, box 4, 1–30.

[9] Ibid., 84. Handy describes his World's Columbian Exposition experience in many places; an example is "Biographical Material—Mr. Handy," unpublished outline, Jamison Handy Papers, box 1.

Goethe's "desire to 'speak only in pictures.'"[10] Graduating from high school at fifteen, he matriculated at the University of Michigan in September 1902, age sixteen, standing 4'11" and weighing eighty-six pounds. He went out for the football team but was only accepted as the team mascot. At Michigan he tried to find excuses to advocate visual education, but he would quickly achieve notoriety through other means. As a stringer for the *Chicago Tribune*, he filed a story in May 1903 describing Professor Thomas C. Trueblood's Elocution 2 class, where students dramatized scenes from plays and novels and Trueblood demonstrated how to propose marriage on bended knee. Ignoring Trueblood's request to keep the class off the record, Handy characterized it as a "course in lovemaking." The next day, a mocking cartoon by John T. McCutcheon appeared in the *Chicago Herald*, and Handy, despite his enthusiasm for this innovative method, was suspended from Michigan for a year. Admitted to Wharton College at the University of Pennsylvania, he was soon called in by a dean and told that Michigan had pressured Penn to ask Handy to leave. At that point, Handy gave up his plans for higher education.[11]

Through a family friend, Medill McCormick, owner of the *Chicago Tribune*, a job materialized for Handy. Handy later claimed to have worked jobs in every *Tribune* department until he left the paper to work with advertising man and inspirational writer Herbert Kaufman in about 1910. While working for Kaufman, he met and quickly fell under the influence of inventor Charles F. Kettering and industrialist John H. Patterson, the charismatic, paternalistic autodidact who founded National Cash Register (NCR), the highly successful manufacturing company and pioneer of scientific salesmanship.

Patterson's "talk to the eye" precept and passionate interest in the processes of selling and distribution led him to experiment with photography as a means of worker education and sales training. As far back as 1896, Patterson had organized a photographic department, building a glass slide collection that would ultimately total some 68,000 images. Each depicted a particular moment of interaction between management and worker, sales trainer and salesman, or salesman and customer. This massive matrix of imagery functioned both as a proto-semiotic dissection of everyday business activity and a base of images that could be assembled into didactic or training sequences. It was only a short step from this to the slidefilm, and from the slidefilm another short step to the motion picture. Patterson also built the "NCR School House" in downtown Dayton, used for training employees, and was the originator of the national sales

---

[10] Autobiographical manuscript, July 14, 1975, Jamison Handy Papers, box 4, 30–36.

[11] The canonical retelling of Jam Handy's suspension is Linda Robinson Walker, "The Suspension of Jam Handy," *Michigan Today* (Mar. 1995): 1–3.

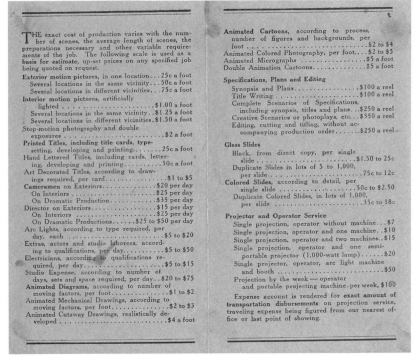

THE exact cost of production varies with the number of scenes, the average length of scenes, the preparations necessary and other variable requirements of the job. The following scale is used as a basis for estimate, up-set prices on any specified job being quoted on request.

Exterior motion pictures, in one location...25c a foot
Several locations in the same vicinity...50c a foot
Several locations in different vicinities...75c a foot
Interior motion pictures, artificially lighted.....................$1.00 a foot
Several locations in the same vicinity..$1.25 a foot
Several locations in different vicinities.$1.50 a foot
Stop-motion photography and double exposures....................$2 a foot
Printed Titles, including title cards, type-setting, developing and printing........25c a foot
Hand Lettered Titles, including cards, lettering, developing and printing.........50c a foot
Art Decorated Titles, according to drawings required, per card...............$1 to $5
Cameramen on Exteriors..............$20 per day
On Interiors ....$25 per day
On Dramatic Production............$35 per day
Director on Exteriors.................$15 per day
On Interiors ....$25 per day
On Dramatic Productions......$25 to $50 per day
Arc Lights, according to type required, per day, each ....$5 to $20
Extras, actors and studio laborers, according to qualifications, per day.........$5 to $50
Electricians, according to qualifications required, per day...................$5 to $15
Studio Expense, according to number of days, sets and space required, per day..$20 to $75
Animated Diagrams, according to number of moving factors, per foot...............$1 to $2
Animated Mechanical Drawings, according to moving factors, per foot..............$2 to $3
Animated Cutaway Drawings, realistically developed ....$4 a foot

Animated Cartoons, according to process, number of figures and backgrounds, per foot ....$2 to $4
Animated Colored Photography, per foot....$2 to $5
Animated Micrographs ....$5 a foot
Double Animation Cartoons.............$5 a foot

Specifications, Plans and Editing
Synopsis and Plans................$100 a reel
Title Writing ....$100 a reel
Complete Scenarios of Specifications, including synopsis, titles and plans...$250 a reel
Creative Scenarios or photoplays, etc...$350 a reel
Editing, cutting and titling, without accompanying production order......$250 a reel

Glass Slides
Black, from direct copy, per single slide ....$1.50 to 25c
Duplicate Slides in lots of 5 to 1,000, per slide ....75c to 12c
Colored Slides, according to detail, per single slide ....50c to $2.50
Duplicate Colored Slides, in lots of 1,000, per slide ....35c to 18c

Projector and Operator Service
Single projection, operator without machine...$7
Single projection, operator and one machine..$10
Single projection, operator and two machines..$15
Single projection, operator and one semi-portable projector (1,000-watt lamp).....$20
Single projector, operator, arc light machine and booth $50
Projection by the week — operator and portable projecting machine.per week, $100

Expense account is rendered for exact amount of transportation disbursements on projection service, traveling expense being figured from our nearest office or last point of showing.

Figure 15.3. Detail from JHO promotional booklet, ca. 1926–1927. (Author's collection.)

convention, where he dramatized sales procedures with "mock up" and "act it out" drills, turning outstanding salespeople into instructors.[12]

Though the slidefilm seems low-tech and antiquated today, its particular attributes made it an ideal medium for teaching, training, and instruction. Inexpensive to produce and reproduce, slidefilms were well suited for both one-to-one and group presentations. Portable pocketsize projectors facilitated small-scale teaching; larger and brighter projectors blew up images to room size. The slidefilm's character as a serial assembly of quickly accessible discrete frames that contained both word and image also permitted a high degree of modularity; a salesperson or instructor could choose points of entry and exit or build a customized presentation. Since frames were advanced by the presenter, instruction could take place at any speed, though synchronized phonograph records (ultimately replaced by reel-to-reel tapes and,

---

[12] The best-known (and authorized) biography is Samuel Crowther, *John H. Patterson: Pioneer in Industrial Welfare* (Garden City, NY: Garden City Publishing, 1926). The broader context of Patterson's visual education work is covered in Judith Sealander, *Grand Plans: Business Progressivism and Social Change in Ohio's Miami Valley, 1890–1929* (Lexington: University Press of Kentucky, 1988). Interestingly, Patterson's nineteenth-century sensibility has recently been enthusiastically revived by a modern salesmanship educator, whose book reprints many original documents from the NCR Archives. See Jeffrey Gitomer, *The Patterson Principles of Selling* (Hoboken, NJ: Wiley & Sons, 2004).

Pictures Show Them How

Lighted pictures of the right kind will show your salesmen just how to do it. They tell your sales story with interesting pictures that take your salesman straight through, from approach to order. They give him a picture pattern of the right way, exactly as the executive office wants it presented, without variations.

Sales Managers' Service offers you all the experience our organization has gained in successfully picturizing the plans of a number of progressive sales promotion clients for more than ten years—experience which has skilled us in using the picture method to show salesmen just how. We are organized to give comprehensive service to progressive companies that wish to train the retail salesman by a simple, easy method that saves expense.

 Lighted Pictures Are Exact

6

Figure 15.4. Detail from JHO production pricelist, ca. 1926–1927. (Author's collection.)

even later, audio cassettes) appeared sometime in the 1930s, locking presentations into specific soundtracks and speeds, thus bringing the slidefilm closer to the motion picture. The low cost of the slidefilm enabled frequent updates, and in fact Jam Handy produced a monthly *Sales Managers' Series* for circulation to Chevrolet sales managers. Though figures are lacking, it would appear that the slidefilm business financed a significant portion of JHO's overhead.

"The more you say the less it means."

Bringing Patterson's innovations into the corporate mainstream, Handy's work evolved into the production of sales materials and industrial shows for many large and small corporations.[13] His first film, an unknown title made in 1910, was for NCR; and soon afterward he joined the organization headed by pioneer animator John R. Bray, who specialized in filmstrips and animated films for government agencies, corporations, and classrooms. At that time, the poor state of literacy in America was emerging as a national concern. Some 25 percent of the 1.5 million World War I draftees were either totally or functionally illiterate, and many new immigrants were not yet fluent in English. Illiteracy was perceived as a threat to national security and an obstacle to Americanization, and the drive to abolish it legitimized the efforts of visual educators like Bray and Handy. At the start of the European war in 1914, Handy went to Washington to meet with Interior Secretary Franklin Lane, urging him to use pictures to improve safety and increase output in mines and factories. He also met with Secretary of Agriculture Henry Wallace and suggested that moving pictures could help increase production of food and fibers. Handy apparently also worked on illustrated posters bearing just a few words to reach draftees with low reading levels, yet another example of his interest in relocating education outside the classroom.[14]

By America's entry into the war in 1917, Handy was producing motion pictures. He worked with animators Max Fleischer, Frank Lyle Goldman, and Rockwell Barnes to make animated technical education films about naval weaponry and especially electricity, which had just recently come aboard U.S. naval vessels. He also worked with Bray to make educational animations. Perhaps because of an apparent dispute with Bray over the invention of the slidefilm, Handy's chronology of events during this period is imprecise and difficult to follow. It seems likely, however, that Handy was Bray's "idea man" and Bray was Handy's film teacher. Until about 1920 Handy continued to work with Bray

---

[13] Quote in subheading is from Jamison Handy, motto from undated slidefilm still in the author's possession.

[14] Autobiographical fragment, Apr. 11, 1975, 1–4, Jamison Handy Papers, box 4.

until they fell out, making films in collaboration with newspaper companies for syndication in theaters, and also producing a number of films for National Cash Register.[15] Concurrently, in January 1919 Handy joined the staff of Interior Secretary Lane "to assist in Americanization education among foreign speaking people and among illiterates." One of Handy's early projects, which seems highly motivated by his own concerns, was a letter-writing campaign to all editors, publishers, and recognized authors, calling attention to the high percentage of illiteracy in adults and urging the wider use of pictures in textbooks and the press. The goal was, quite simply, to turn writers and publishers into advocates of visual communication.[16]

In the early 1920s, after a period apparently marked by searching and striving, his various activities merged into the Newspapers Film Corporation (known as "Newspapers," later the Jam Handy Picture Service, and, even later, the Jam Handy Organization), first headquartered in Chicago. This vertically integrated enterprise offered a full range of production, promotion, and training services to its clients, and was modeled on the Patterson educational and training machine. Handy's big break came in 1923, when Richard H. Grant summoned him to Detroit for a consultation. Grant, who had been general sales manager of the Delco Light and Frigidaire divisions of General Motors, was already a Handy customer, but he faced a major problem: 270,000 unsold cars. He engaged Handy to help dealers with their retail sales problems and to train wholesale salespeople as well. Though Handy continued to operate Newspapers out of Chicago, he ultimately moved his headquarters to Detroit, where the company operated until its demise. Beginning about 1923, Newspapers/JHO became a prolific motion picture producer.

By the late 1930s, JHO operated a large studio complex in Detroit, less than a mile from General Motors headquarters, said to employ up to six hundred people. The complex occupied eight buildings and included slidefilm and motion-picture production departments, a full film laboratory, and an animation department. Many "Handy men" worked in the distribution and exhibition departments; they drove mobile projection vans throughout the country and presented films at sales meetings, corporate events, and the World's Fairs of the 1930s. Every month anywhere from several dozen to more than a hundred motion pictures and perhaps hundreds of slidefilms were in various stages of production.[17] Very few of these were intended for immediate classroom use, but many were repurposed after their

---

[15] "Fighting Waste with Movies," *Literary Digest*, May 1, 1920; reproduced with annotations in a Bray Pictures Corporation advertisement, *Associated Advertising*, Aug. 1920, 1.

[16] Autobiographical fragment, 4.

[17] A detailed portrait of JHO is in M. R. McKeown, "Detroit: The Commercial Hollywood," *Barron's*, June 19, 1936, 11.

Figure 15.5. Film inspection room at the Newspapers Film Company plant, Chicago, ca. 1927. (Author's collection.)

Figure 15.6. Frame from *Master Hands* (1936).

initial releases into theaters or corporate venues. *Master Hands* (1936), an institutional promotion film originally produced for Chevrolet Motor Company that showed the process of manufacturing Chevrolets at the Flint, Michigan, plant, was shown soon after its completion at a ceremony celebrating the 100th anniversary of the United States patent system, and may also have been shown as a theatrical short subject and at a stockholder meeting. Later, it was repurposed as a "vocational subject," meant to be shown in trade schools and industrial education programs.[18]

Though there is a vast historical literature regarding the use of commercially sponsored films in the classroom, much of it focusing on the controversial issue of whether commercial messages had a place in an educational environment, a detailed study of their educational deployment is beyond the scope of this paper. In the meantime, it would be worthwhile to mention two distinctive characteristics of JHO's films in this regard. First, Handy saw education as a lifelong learning process that could happen in any venue; he was not schoolroom-bound. This attribute encourages us to look at a majority of JHO's films as educationally focused films, even if they shared little with other classroom-focused educational films. Second, JHO was a master of the soft sell. Entire series of films, such as Chevrolet's *Direct Mass Selling* series (1935–1941), were produced without explicit mentions of products precisely in order that their sponsors could arrange showings in schools in schools and, later, on television before July 1941, when commercial television was greenlighted. Though the *Direct Mass Selling* films are mostly auto-centric and replete with drive-on appearances of current-model Chevrolets, the name of the car itself is almost never mentioned, save for a main-title appearance and a rotating Chevrolet hubcap under the end title.

Though JHO is best known for its film work (and especially for its longevity and the number of films it produced), it makes little sense to consider the films in isolation. Many, perhaps most, were not produced as standalone products but were coordinated with concurrently produced materials in other media, such as slidefilms, live shows, press articles, study guides, and training materials. The company constantly promoted itself as a "full-service organization" and expressed an agnostic attitude toward specific media forms. As Handy once said, "If a specific audio-visual device is better than any other material for our specific purpose, we use it; if it is not better, its use is not justified."[19]

As with many similar producers, World War II refocused JHO away from the production of corporate-sponsored media and almost immediately turned it into a major producer of training materials for the war effort. The company joined thirty-five other contract producers in making films on shop training and aircraft assembly under the sponsorship of the U.S. Office of Education. These films were made freely available for the cost of reproduction and sold many thousands of prints. In addition, they made at least 168 specialized training motion pictures for the U.S. Navy, and perhaps 70 for other branches of government, plus

---

[18] "Auto Plant Noises to Fuse with Music," *New York Times*, Nov. 14, 1936, 9.

[19] McKeown, "Detroit," 11.

thousands of slidefilms. The company also became renowned for its work with "special training devices," which today we would call simulators. They experimented with single-person display systems and immersive, anamorphic 360-degree cinematography, developing a process that after the war was marketed as "Cinesphere."[20]

As has often been noted, World War II fully legitimized moving images as educational tools. Surplus projection equipment made its way into U.S. schools; surplus films entered educational film libraries; and wartime-trained production people fanned out into the industry, many starting new production companies. The new receptivity toward audiovisual media, combined with hundreds of thousands of projectors in schools, caused the distribution market for educational films to grow dramatically and drove both new and old producers into the educational film production business. Though JHO did not specifically become an educational film producer, it extended its filmstrip business into the educational sector, starting the "Jam Handy School Service," which produced slidefilms and occasional motion pictures for sale to schools. Though the School Service lasted at least until the 1970s, it does not appear to have been a great financial success vis-à-vis other companies, perhaps because the filmstrips were not coordinated with a motion picture production program that would have permitted cross-promotion of 16mm and filmstrips.

Well into the 1960s, JHO was a busy shop, making television commercials as well as the usual sponsored and training films. Even while Handy continued to expound his theories of education through the eye and ear in interviews and public speeches, his company's management aged and some key departments disappeared or downsized (especially laboratory and sound). Its creative development began to slow, and its films became increasingly formal and static, falling out of touch with the dynamism of U.S. visual culture during the late 1960s. During 1968 and 1969, JHO split into three companies, and for its last fourteen years of formal existence it ceased to be a major force in the industry. Jamison Handy died on November 13, 1983, aged ninety-seven, and the company dissolved the next year. Its memory lives on largely through its many alumni, and in recent years in an emergent fan culture sustained by the availability of some three hundred titles on the Internet.[21]

---

[20] "Producers of the USOE Film Program," *Business Screen* 7, no. 3 (1946): 20. Figures on government film production are derived from production records in author's possession.

[21] The largest collection of JHO films online can be accessed at www.archive.org/details/prelinger. Many of these films have been cross-posted on YouTube and other web video services, though often in shorter or degraded versions.

While Handy stressed his commitment to "making pictures in people's minds," he tended to recycle familiar aphorisms. His assimilation of educational theory found its embodiment in the selective deployment of quotations, like the mottoes that decorated JHO's walls. In this idiosyncrasy he was not alone. Patterson and Thomas Edison, two spectacularly successful autodidacts and frequent enunciators of sound bites, broke a path for Handy's highly personal assemblage of theory and representational strategy, and in fact the very young worlds of instructional and industrial film were populated by self-educated and occasionally eccentric personalities, such as the flamboyant Carlyle Ellis, who produced health films whose style resembled French Surrealist films.[22] In a time when national learning standards were implicit rather than explicit and student progress was still measured by the mastery of McGuffey Readers, there was considerable room for experimentation and empire building based on personal preference.

Handy was a brilliant showman and skilled synthesist, and his employees at JHO made many hundreds of memorable films that far outshine the work of other producers. As we begin to investigate the poorly known sponsored film "genre," though, we need to remember that no corporation stands alone. Industrial film producers actively monitored one another's work (not to mention one another's clients). Then, as now, representational innovation occurred through emulation and recombination. Other great didactic producers, such as the Ford Motor Company's motion picture production unit and Watterson S. Rothacker's companies, kept pace with JHO's work for a time and often appear to have influenced it. Handy's company produced the *Chevrolet Leader News* (1935–1939) and *Laughs and Flashes* (1936–1937), another newsreel-like series for Chevy, long after Ford set the pace with the *Ford Educational Weekly*. Rothacker experimented with mainstreaming narratives of industrial production to mass audiences while Handy was still making training films for in-house audiences. The automobile styling sequence in Handy's *American Look* (1959), made for Chevrolet, bears a striking resemblance to the styling sequence in *The Human Bridge* (1950), made by Raphael G. Wolff Productions for Ford.

As Bill Sandy once noted, "Many young people had the mysteries of the business system, of managing, selling, making a profit, stripped away and made hospitable. Jamison Handy captured the romance of commerce and showed how products like automobiles and appliances could be mechanisms of liberation."[23] Sandy's words point to Handy's particular innovation—grafting a sense of romance, utopianism, and theatricality onto the transmission of prosaic but essential information. As one of the first and certainly the longest-lived stylists of

---

[22] Carlyle Ellis's film *The Calorie Counter* (ca. 1925) takes place on a tabletop and features stop-motion animation of different foods moving around the table, fighting one another and dramatizing their caloric content.

[23] Eberwein, "Contributions of the Jam Handy Organization," 91.

audiovisual education, Handy set standards for presentation and production value that have outlived him and migrated into other media. Though it would be a considerable stretch to credit Handy for the web's assimilation of moving images, animation, sound, and 3-D simulation, today's didactic media continues to seek richer and more immersive ways of fulfilling its often quotidian mission. As we grapple with the contradictions and uneven development of what many call the postindustrial age, it is striking how we, like Handy and JHO, continue to gravitate toward idiosyncratic ways of getting messages to audiences.

Filmography

The largest group of JHO films is held by the Library of Congress, at its National Audiovisual Conservation Center, Packard Campus, in Culpeper, Virginia. Until the collection is processed and opened for research, the primary access point for Handy films remains Prelinger Archives (www.archive.org/details/prelinger), which holds approximately 400 JHO titles transferred to videotape. About 270 of these are available for free viewing and download as digital video files at the Internet Archive. A smaller collection of JHO films, mostly sponsored by Chevrolet, was given by JHO to the Bill Sandy Company and is represented for stock footage sales by Historic Films (historicfilms.com).

American Look (1958) 28 min.; 35mm
PRODUCTION: Jam Handy Organization. SPONSOR: Chevrolet Division, General Motors Corporation. DIRECTORS: W. F. Banes, John Thiele. CAMERA: Roger Fenimore, Pierre Mols, Robert Tavernier. ART DIRECTORS: Robert Mounsey, Charles Nasca, Otto Simunich. EDITORS: V. L. Herman, Harold Rogers. MUSIC: Samuel Benavie, James Higgins, Milton Weinstein. ACCESS: www/archive.org/details/American1958.

The Car of Tomorrow, Today (1947) 2 reels; 16mm
PRODUCTION: Jam Handy Organization. SPONSOR: Oldsmobile Division, General Motors Corporation. ACCESS: Preprint elements at Library of Congress.

Chevrolet Leader News (1935–1939) 15 issues, 1 reel each, 35mm
PRODUCTION: Jam Handy Organization. SPONSOR: Chevrolet Motor Company. ACCESS: www.archive.org/details/Chevrole1935.

Direct Mass Selling Series (1935–1941), 110 films, varying lengths; 35mm
PRODUCTION: Jam Handy Organization. SPONSOR: Chevrolet Motor Company. ACCESS: Most titles at www.archive.org/details/prelinger.

Ford Educational Weekly (1916–1921) **approx. 200 issues, 1 reel each; 35mm**
PRODUCTION/SPONSOR: Ford Motor Co. ACCESS: Film prints at Library of Congress, National Archives, and UCLA Film and Television Archive.

Give Yourself the Green Light (1954) **24 min.; 16mm**
PRODUCTION: Jam Handy Organization. SPONSOR: Dept. of Public Relations, General Motors Corp. ACCESS: www.archive.org/details/GiveYour1954.

The Human Bridge (1949) **27 min.; 16mm**
PRODUCTION: Raphael G. Wolff Studios. SPONSOR: Ford Motor Co. ACCESS: www.archive.org/details/HumanBri1949 (incomplete; excerpt runs 12 min.).

Laughs and Flashes (1936–1937) **15 issues, 1 reel each; 35mm**
PRODUCTION: Jam Handy Organization. SPONSOR: Chevrolet Motor Company. ACCESS: No issues known to survive.

Master Hands (1936) **32 min.; 35mm**
PRODUCTION: Jam Handy Organization. SPONSOR: Chevrolet Motor Company. CAMERA: Gordon Avil. MUSIC: Samuel Benavie. EDITOR: Vincent Herman. An alternate version superimposes captions over select scenes, describing the manufacturing processes. ACCESS: Library of Congress (includes restored 35mm version); www.archive.org/details/MasterHa1936.

The Tip-Tops in Peppyland (1934) **11 min., silent; 35m and 16mm**
PRODUCTION: Jam Handy Organization. SPONSOR: New York State Bureau of Milk Publicity. ACCESS: www.archive.org/details/TipTopsi1934.

Related Films

The Calorie Counter: A Lesson in Nutrition (ca. 1925) 14 min., silent; 35mm and 16mm
PRODUCTION: Carlyle Ellis. EDITOR: Arthur Edwin Krows.

National Cash Register (ca. 1910s–1920s) 15 min., silent; 16mm
PRODUCTION: Unknown. SPONSOR: National Cash Register Company. Compilation of historic film clips depicting activities and events at the NCR Company, probably edited using excerpts from other films. ACCESS: Library of Congress.

16 MUSEUM AT LARGE: AESTHETIC EDUCATION THROUGH FILM

KATERINA LOUKOPOULOU

> [Film] remains predominantly a machine for seeing better, a remote
> cousin of the magnifying lens, a periscope, a pair of opera glasses. Small
> wonder then that it should also be used to enable more people in more
> places to see more paintings and sculpture . . . and to see them clearer
> or . . . at least to see them in a new and different way than heretofore.
>
> —Iris Barry, "Pioneering in Films on Art" (1952)

Is it "small wonder" that film was used to show more paintings to more people,
so that the paintings could be seen "in a new and different way"?[1] Before the
1940s, film was utilized to record works of art but not, in general, to provoke
alternative ways of seeing them. Barry's statement suggests a crucial shift in the
way photography and film were used to remediate the fine arts—especially modern art—for educational purposes. It reflects the "supervening social necessity"
of the postwar expansion of art education and the construction of a nationally
and internationally recognized "American" art, factors which accelerated the
production and exhibition of films about art and artists.[2] These films began to be
seen as a distinct genre. In the relevant literature, this genre was also referred to
as the "art film" or the "art documentary." Although there are certain historical
and national differences between these terms, they were generally treated as syn-
onyms, but "film on art" was the term most frequently used.[3]

---

[1] The source of the epigraph for this chapter is Iris Barry, "Pioneering in Films on Art," in
Films on Art 1952, ed. William McK. Chapman (New York: American Federation of Arts, 1952), 1.

[2] Brian Winston, *Technologies of Seeing: Photography, Cinematography and Television*
(London: BFI, 1996). Winston argues that specific social and political exigencies determine when
an existing technology can be promoted successfully. His term for this, "the supervening social
necessity," can be usefully applied to developments in film genres and specialized uses of film.

[3] Theodore Bowie, "About Films on Art," *College Art Journal* 14, no. 1 (1954): 28–37.

The use of the comparatively new medium of film for the remediation of the older media of painting, sculpture, architecture, and other "high" arts is of special interest to the historiography of the educational film in the United States. With its roots in the photographic reproduction of works of art, the film on art developed in tandem with changing attitudes about the place of the visual arts in education, culture, and society. An educator advocating the usefulness of films on art in the classroom sketched the broad picture of the state of art education in the early 1950s: "As short a time as twenty-five years ago, art in the majority of school systems was a subject for the dilettante or the technician in training. Today [1952], art is considered as a necessary and even a fundamental part of education for all."[4] Similarly, films about the visual arts gradually shifted away from their initial specialized function—to record and dramatize exhibitions in the 1920s and 30s—and became a legitimate genre that aimed to advance aesthetic education from the late 1940s onward. It was after World War II that film was propagated at large as the ideal medium to carry the visual arts out of the museum, the artist's studio, and the gallery to new locations, such as educational institutions (mainly art schools), nontheatrical venues, and, momentarily, even commercial cinemas.[5] Better than photographic reproductions and slide shows, which fix images, film was regarded as an exciting new way to analyze paintings and works of sculpture in order to reveal their plasticity and in the case of the latter their three-dimensionality. The camera's mechanical eye could do more than the human eye: it could dismantle, resize, and synthesize works of art as well as shift from a bird's-eye view to a worm's-eye view of a sculpture across a single edit.

This essay aims to historicize the origins and developments of the film on art in the United States. The central position in this story is occupied by *Jackson Pollock* (1951), a film by photographer Hans Namuth and documentarian Paul Falkenberg about the abstract expressionist painter. This was not the first American film on a modern artist, and, initially, it was not well received. However, its subsequent impact on the art world and art education—catalyzed by Pollock's mythical status after his death in 1956—played a significant role in the legitimization of films on modern art that proliferated in the 1970s. This was the first collaboration between Namuth and Falkenberg, who later set up Museum at Large, a nontheatrical production and distribution company specializing in art documentaries, and continued to work together until the mid-1980s.

---

[4] Charles D. Gaitskell, "The Art and Craft Film in General Education," in Chapman, *Films on Art 1952*, 21.

[5] Publications which indicate that the film on art was a post–World War II genre: UNESCO, *Films on Art: A Specialised Study* (Paris: UNESCO, 1949); Arthur Knight, *The Liveliest Art: A Panoramic History of the Movies* (New York: New American Library, 1959), 263–67; Siegfried Kracauer, *Theory of Film: The Redemption of Physical Reality* (New York: Oxford University Press, 1960), 193–201.

Although *Jackson Pollock* has been discussed in the context of art historical accounts of Pollock's work, abstract expressionism, and postwar American art, its role as an educational film on art, seen by thousands of art students, has been overlooked. Equally neglected is this film's historical context, especially the concurrent developments in the expansion of the educational uses of films to propagate the relevance of modern art in contemporary society. This essay will argue that *Jackson Pollock* exemplifies some of the key conventions in the development of films about modern artists and their educational potential. By foregrounding the mechanics of the creative process, this film exercised unprecedented influence on the aesthetic education of art students, teachers, and critics.

A well-established view in debates about cultural value is the distinction between the "autonomy" of the fine arts and the "function" of mass-produced, mechanical "low" art, such as film. Films on art problematize this historically contingent distinction. With the postwar increase in art education, the dissemination of knowledge about art was deemed useful for the creation of new audiences and the ideological promotion of a national American art. As Sidney Berkowitz, a trustee of the American Federation of Arts and advocate of the employment of films on art at all levels of education, put it in 1950: "By the time . . . students reached college level they would have a background of Documentary film appreciation that would greatly simplify the efforts of College Art teachers. The least possible result of such a plan would be the constant development of a growing art audience without which the artist is but a voice crying in the wilderness."[6] However, training new audiences to appreciate the visual arts through film had an impact beyond this pedagogic function. It had political dimensions that echoed the progressive discourses emanating from the Federal Arts Project (1935–1943): the experiential understanding of art and the demystification of the creative process.[7]

From "Motion Photography" to "Films" on Art

The main postwar developments in films about the visual arts were their cinematic dynamism and their increasing focus on modern artists. By the early 1950s films on art were directed and produced by professional filmmakers, many of whom were veteran documentarians who found new inspiration in the genre. These films need to be distinguished from the type of instructional film that was previously known as "motion photography" of the pictorial arts, mainly produced

---

[6] Sidney Berkowitz, "The Information Film in Art," *College Art Journal* 10, no. 1 (1950): 49.

[7] For a comprehensive collection of contemporary documents, see Francis V. O'Connor, ed., *Art for the Millions: Essays from the 1930s by Artists and Administrators of the WPA Federal Art Project* (Greenwich, CT: New York Graphic Society, 1973).

by museums, which did not necessarily exploit filmic techniques, such as editing, voiceover, variation of shot types, and camera movements.[8]

These early records of museums' collections through "motion photography" originated in one of the first applications of still photography: the reproduction of works of art. By the turn of the century, photographic reproductions of the collections of the Louvre in Paris, the Victoria and Albert Museum in London, and the Metropolitan Museum of Art in New York were widely sold and circulated for publicity and popular education.[9] As a continuation of this tradition, museums began to use film to document and disseminate their collections and exhibitions in the United States from the 1920s, with the Metropolitan at the forefront. The National Gallery of Art in Washington, DC also employed film in its educational activities from its opening in 1941, to address the wide range of visitors from across the world. Film's "universal popularity" was seen as a guarantee that people of different educational, cultural, and national backgrounds could all be addressed and that the older fine arts could be made to look appealingly modern.[10] However, as the film critic Arthur Knight noted, these films had limited uses: "During the twenties and thirties, many museums were supplementing their lantern slide collections with motion pictures. More often than not, these were amateur productions hastily shot in the museum's basement by someone with more enthusiasm than skill. Their purpose was invariably instructional ... There was an inescapable uniformity both in the subject matter and the mediocrity of these museum productions."[11] Postwar films on art became more

---

[8] For one of the earliest uses of the term "motion photography" to designate educational films as opposed to "amusement films," see George W. Stevens, "The Use of Motion Photography in Museums," *Metropolitan Museum of Art Bulletin* 11 (Sept. 1916): 203–4. For an indication of the shifts in educational films about the arts, see David A. Wilkie, "Still Pictures into Motion Pictures," *College Art Journal* 7 (Winter 1947–1948): 96.

[9] Revisionist historians of photography and documentary film have highlighted the educational and social significance of this often overlooked, but popular, early use of photography to reproduce works of art. Anthony J. Hamber, *"A Higher Branch of the Art": Photographing the Fine Arts in England (1839–1880)* (Amsterdam: Gordon and Breach, 1996); Elizabeth A. McCauley, *Industrial Madness: Commercial Photography in Paris, 1848–1871* (New Haven, CT: Yale University Press, 1994), 265–300; Brian Winston, "The Documentary Film as Scientific Inscription," in *Theorizing Documentary*, ed. Michael Renov (New York: Routledge, 1993), 39. For an account of reactions against the early uses of photography to reproduce works of art, see Lawrence W. Levine, *Highbrow/Lowbrow: The Emergence of Cultural Hierarchy in America* (Cambridge, MA: Harvard University Press, 1988), 160–64.

[10] Grace Fisher Ramsey, *Educational Work in Museums of the United States* (New York: H. W. Wilson Company, 1938), 184–86; Katrina Van Hook, "Educational Activities in the National Gallery of Art," *College Art Journal* 3 (May 1944): 130–31; Haidee Wasson, "Mobilizing the Museum: Film at the Metropolitan Museum of Art in the 1920s," *Framework* 46 (Spring 2005): 83–92.

[11] Arthur Knight, "A Short History of Art Films," in Chapman, *Films on Art 1952*, 8.

sophisticated both in terms of their production values and their educational scope.

The post–World War II increase in educational films on art needs also to be seen in relation to the precedential boost of the arts and art institutions during the 1930s and 40s. Popular interest in the visual arts—especially modern art—increased dramatically during the 1930s, due to the Federal Art Project's extensive state patronage of unemployed artists. This was one of the four art programs (the other three being music, theater, and literature) created by the Works Progress Administration to provide work relief to artists affected by the Depression. This unprecedented state intervention had two long-term effects: the reinvigoration of art education at all levels; and the emergence of coordinated discourses and practices in schools and other institutions to "educate a democratic and cultured citizenry through the principles and practices of modern art and liberal humanism."[12]

In 1931 the New York Museum of Modern Art (MoMA) started a scheme of circulating exhibitions of modern art, in response to demand from local museums and colleges that were unable to meet the costs of setting up substantial exhibitions of modern art from scratch. The report that MoMA published about its circulating exhibitions during the period 1931–1954 provides convincing evidence of the dramatic increase of interest in contemporary art from 1935 onward. This report also shows that modern art was in considerably higher demand by institutions of higher education rather than museums, galleries, art associations, and schools (see fig. 16.1).

During the postwar period the study of art in higher education increased more than in any other subject. Its purpose and pedagogy were debated at large and a new emphasis on the creative process became the focal point for an understanding of the meaning of modern art.[13] Alongside this changing role of the visual arts in education, a new interest in visually articulating the mechanisms of artistic production started gaining ground, evident in MoMA's circulating exhibition "How the Modern Artist Works" (1947–1949). It was dedicated to the visual demonstration of the ways modern artists work, deploying "sketches and photographs to supplement original paintings and to show how four contemporary artists plan and carry out their work."[14] The popularity of this exhibition

---

[12] Camilla Best, "Applications of the Film in Art," in *Film and Education: A Symposium on the Role of the Film in the Field of Education*, ed. Godfrey M. Elliott (New York: Philosophical Library, 1948), 189–202; Nancy Shaw, "Modern Art, Media Pedagogy and Cultural Citizenship: The Museum of Modern Art's Television Project, 1952–1955," PhD diss., McGill University, 2000, ii.

[13] James S. Ackerman, "The Arts in Higher Education," in *Content and Context: Essays on College Education*, ed. Carl Kaysen, Laurence R. Veysey, and Carnegie Commission on Higher Education (New York: McGraw-Hill, 1973), 219.

[14] MoMA, "Circulating Exhibitions 1931–1954," *Bulletin of the Museum of Modern Art* 21 (Summer 1954): 4, 9, 29.

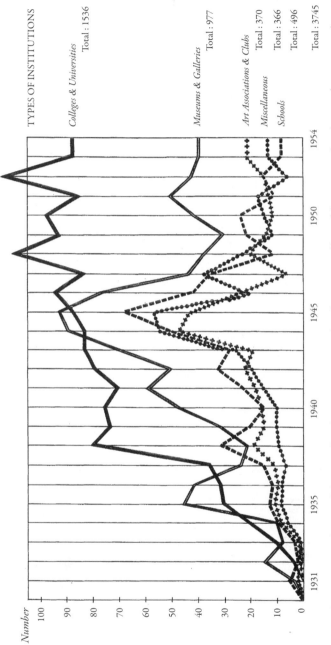

Figure 16.1. Graph of MoMA's Circulating Exhibitions of Modern Art, Design, and Architecture. *Bulletin of the Museum of Modern Art* (Summer 1954): 29.

evidences the growing educational interest in the documentation of the processes of art-making, which had also started to be explored through film (see fig. 16.2).

The growing demand for exhibitions about modern art in higher education institutions led MoMA to set up educational visual aids for teachers, such as specially prepared slide talks, filmstrips, and, gradually, films about modern artists. One of the first films MoMA supported was *Alexander Calder: Sculpture and Constructions* (1944). Filming Calder's mobile sculpture was deemed to be the ideal way of reproducing it, and the visually compelling outcome led to many more films on Calder to be made in the ensuing decades. Another successful film of the time, with more emphasis on the cinematic technique of editing, was *Grandma Moses* (1950), about the self-taught painter Anna Mary Robertson Moses, which juxtaposed scenes from her life in the countryside with shots of her paintings. The aim was to show the sources of her inspiration and to invite the viewer to see through the eyes of the painter.

A wide range of rhetorical and pedagogical techniques were mobilized through film style in order to concretize and explicate abstract ideas, such as artistic inspiration, creative process, aesthetics, and art appreciation. These developments of the film on art exemplify the different approaches in educational films identified by Cecile Starr in her essay "Films for Learning" (1951). Starr categorized educational films according to their corresponding pedagogical purview—education by formula and education by experience. The former "demonstrates prescribed techniques, and makes of learning an almost automatic process," while the latter motivates the students "with emphasis on their active participation in the learning situation" and directs them to follow up what they have been taught with activities.[15]

The above taxonomy aptly describes the development of "motion photography," which filmed exhibits and art techniques for education by formula, into the film on art, which deployed a wide range of cinematic devices and documentary styles to promote understanding of the creative process, privileging the visual demonstration of artistic experience and practice. The film on art aimed at

Figure 16.2. MoMA's circulating panel exhibition, *How the Modern Artist Works* (1947–49). *Bulletin of the Museum of Modern Art* (Summer 1954): 9.

---

[15] Cecile Starr, "Films for Learning," in *Ideas on Film: A Handbook for the 16mm Film User,* ed. Cecile Starr (New York: Funk & Wagnalls, 1951), 89–92.

the mobilization of multiple senses, promoting an understanding of art similar to that advocated in John Dewey's influential philosophical treatise *Art as Experience* (1934). Dewey's progressive ideas had been widely debated in educational and political circles in the 1930s, and they continued to be influential for Jackson Pollock and other abstract expressionist artists for whom paintings became the index of the process.[16] For Starr, film was equally an index of experience: "The film has literally been exposed to certain experiences, and it reproduces those experiences for the audience."[17] Films about modern artists at work thus aimed at conveying the sense of process and production rather than an appreciation of the final work of art. This was interrelated with the new institutional and critical apparatus, which aimed to explicate the mechanisms of the at-first-sight "simplistic" and "incomprehensible" formalism of cubism, surrealism, and abstract expressionism for wider audiences, as evidenced in MoMA's circulating exhibition "How the Modern Artist Works" and continuing with the use of film and television. This move to make modern art "legitimate" was ultimately an act of self-preservation; it offered tools and techniques for engaging with modern art that could be passed down to future generations.

Another key change in the postwar films on art was their development beyond the aegis of museums. More educational film production and distribution companies, documentarians, and independent filmmakers became attracted to the idea of making films about living artists and American modern art. These films were often commissioned and used for cultural propaganda purposes. For example, Willard Van Dyke's film about Edward Weston, *The Photographer* (1948), was made at the behest of the U.S. Department of State, but later it came to be considered as a landmark in the historiography of the genre.[18] Another key factor that helped the distribution and exhibition of films on art was the increased availability of projection equipment for nontheatrical spaces. As Arthur Knight points out, "The estimated 400,000 16mm projectors used during the war to show training and morale films created an unprecedented market for nontheatrical pictures."[19] The growing demand for films on art was also facilitated by the growing importation of European films on art by distributors like A.F. Films, Brandon Films, British Information Services, and Robert Snyder. These imported films, alongside the high technical quality of films on art produced by Encyclopaedia Britannica, McGraw-Hill, Young America, and Castle Films, contributed to the shift toward more complex styles (see fig. 16.3).

---

[16] Stewart Buettner, "John Dewey and the Visual Arts in America," *Journal of Aesthetics and Art Criticism* 33 (Summer 1975): 383–91.

[17] Starr, "Films for Learning," 91.

[18] Richard M. Barsam, *Nonfiction Film: A Critical History* (Bloomington: Indiana University Press, 1992), 295.

[19] Knight, *The Liveliest Art,* 255.

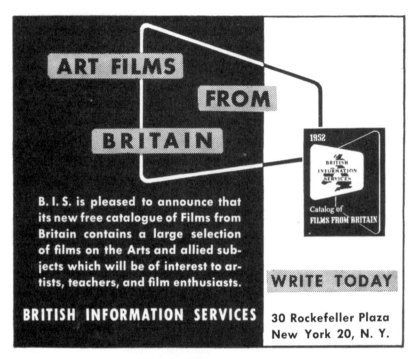

ART FILMS FROM BRITAIN

B. I. S. is pleased to announce that its new free catalogue of Films from Britain contains a large selection of films on the Arts and allied subjects which will be of interest to artists, teachers, and film enthusiasts.

BRITISH INFORMATION SERVICES

1952

Catalog of FILMS FROM BRITAIN

WRITE TODAY

30 Rockefeller Plaza
New York 20, N. Y.

FILMS ON ART

"RUBENS"
An unparalleled work of film art creatively analyzes and interprets the master and his painting techniques. Through juxtaposition, this study opens new avenues of critical approach to Rubens and his work. 45 minutes.

3 FILMS IN COLOR
INTRODUCING: "THE WORLD OF THE ARTIST." A new series of films in COLOR about famous paintings, with commentary and music.
1—"PAINTINGS BY HIERONYMUS BOSCH." 1 reel.
2—"BALLET BY DEGAS." 1 reel.
3—"CRUCIFIXION, THEME AND VARIATIONS." 1½ reels.

"LOOKING AT SCULPTURE"
A visit to the Sculpture Room of London's Victoria and Albert Museum, with pointers on the most rewarding way to view the works of art on display. Narration by Michael Redgrave. 11 Min.

Apply for rental and sale on above films.

BRANDON FILMS, INC.
DEPT. A, 200 WEST 57TH ST.,
NEW YORK 19, N. Y.

Images Medievales

IS AVAILABLE

1. American version with commentary by
JAMES JOHNSON SWEENEY.

2. Original French version.

3. French language-study version prepared by teachers for the classroom.

A.F. FILMS
1600 BROADWAY
NEW YORK 19, N. Y.

Figure 16.3. Advertisements for European films on art available for distribution in the United States. It is worth noting the advertisement addressed a wide-ranging audience: "artists, teachers, and film enthusiasts." *Films on Art 1952* (American Federation of Arts), 162.

What also distinguished these professionally made films on art was their appeal to wide-ranging institutions and viewers: teachers, museums, film societies, art and film critics, commercial producers, and even, momentarily, theatrical audiences. For example, Hans Richter's feature-length art film, *Dreams That Money Can Buy* (1948), about a young man who starts a business selling his dreams, had been released theatrically and was a critical success. The film comprised six long dream sequences in color, each designed by a modern artist: Max Ernst, Marcel Duchamp, Alexander Calder, Man Ray, and Richter himself, accompanied by music from experimental composers, such as John Cage and Edgard Varèse. An even more successful film on art was Robert Flaherty's American version of *The Titan* (1950), a 1939 Swiss film about Michelangelo, which told the story of the artist solely with paintings, drawings, pictorial material, and a voiceover commentary. This film won an Academy Award and gained theatrical distribution by United Artists.

Moreover, the dissemination of knowledge about the visual arts through film was promoted by the United Nations Educational, Scientific and Cultural Organization (UNESCO) with the establishment of the International Federation of Art Films in 1949, which supported the circulation of films and information about them as a means of "international understanding." Due to the internationalism of the film on art and UNESCO's campaign to reach an agreement to facilitate the international circulation patterns of educational films by lifting custom taxes and restrictions, a wider range of films on art became available to U.S. distributors, who until then "offered more technical films than any other kind."[20] (See fig. 16.4.)

Under the joint influence of European films on art, the American documentary tradition, and the proliferation of instructional and guidance films, postwar U.S. audiences were exposed to four main types of films: films about artists at work, such as *A Visit to Picasso* (Paul Haesaerts, 1950); pictorial films on art, which reconstructed historical events with the use of paintings and drawings as main visual sources, such as *Lincoln Speaks at Gettysburg* (Lewis Jacobs and Paul Falkenberg, 1950); dramatizations of famous paintings (for example, the films by

Figure 16.4. The "filmic" logo of UNESCO's campaign for the international circulation of educational, scientific, and cultural films. *UNESCO Courier* 3, no. 2 (1950): 2.

---

[20] J. P. Urlik, "Films Bring Art to the People," *UNESCO Courier* 2, no. 12 (1950): 6–7; "UNESCO Helps Educational Films over Frontier Barriers," *UNESCO Courier* 3, no. 2 (1950): 2; Arthur Knight, "Art Films in America," in UNESCO, *Films on Art*, 45.

the Italian pioneers Luciano Emmer and Enrico Gras, distributed in the United States by the MoMA Film Library); and artists' biographies, reconstructed from their own art, like *The Titan*. The main champion of this new genre was the *Magazine of Art,* published by the American Federation of Arts, a nonprofit educational association. This magazine was the "first" to publish regular reviews of films on art and announcements of the educational film activities of museums (see fig. 16.5).

According to Haidee Wasson, the use of film by museums like the Metropolitan in the 1920s was part of "a distinct lineage, one that has less to do with film's contribution and aesthetic cross-pollination with the other arts, and much more to do with cinema's utility as a mobile classroom and an efficient reproduction system for conventional art objects."[21] However, the boundaries between the two lineages started to blur with the expansion of the film on art as a genre addressing more general audiences. Arthur Knight, in his essay "A Short History of Art Films" (1952), written for the first American critical guide on the genre, promoted educational films on art for their aesthetic merit:

FIRST to bring you the LATEST Information on Art Films

MAGAZINE OF ART

Published by The American Federation of Arts

- *Authoritative reviews and critical articles on films by expert specialists*
- *Monthly listing of all art films as soon as they become available*

and, of course,

- *Informative articles on all the arts of all countries and every period*

MAGAZINE OF ART

22 East 60th Street, New York 22

$6 per year   *professional rate $5*

Figure 16.5. Advertisement of the *Magazine of Art's* commitment to films on art. *Films on Art 1952* (American Federation of Arts, 1952), 160.

---

[21] Wasson, "Mobilizing the Museum," 85.

It was the application of film art, the aesthetic of cinema, to art films that turned them from pedestrian, routine teaching reels and art travelogues into a stimulating, visually exciting art experience. Not until works of art were interpreted in terms of the motion picture medium did they begin to come alive on the screen—and to attract both new audiences and new creative talent to the field.[22]

Thus the film on art's increasingly cinematic and aestheticized take on its subject meant that the two lineages described by Wasson—film's aesthetic "cross-pollination with the other arts" and "cinema's utility"—productively merged. This was made most evident in films about modern artists at work, where the formalism of the represented artists influenced the films' style.

Filming a Modernist Artist at Work

Jackson Pollock decisively marks the emergence of the film on art from "motion photography." As David Wilkie had noted a few years earlier, films were needed that showed more than the "know-how" of the craft: "How tempera paintings in general are made can be very well shown in motion pictures. How Fra Angelico and Botticelli worked in tempera are more difficult undertakings."[23] The film on Pollock was indeed a more difficult undertaking: How to film a living artist at work, especially one whose unorthodox way of stretching the canvas on the floor and utilizing enamel paints had created a sensation? In August 1949, *Life* magazine had published its third feature about Pollock, with the heading, "Jackson Pollock: Is He the Greatest Living Painter in the United States?"

Namuth and Falkenberg were both German émigrés who had fled Nazi Germany and met in New York. Although this was Namuth's first venture into filmmaking, Falkenberg was a veteran. In Germany, Falkenberg had edited *M* (dir. Fritz Lang, 1930) and worked alongside G. W. Pabst and Carl Dreyer. When he moved to New York, he worked at MoMA's Film Library alongside Luis Buñuel, where he wrote scripts and edited propaganda films for the Office of Inter-American Affairs (1941–1945).[24] He then established his own company, Educational Documentary Films (E.D. Films), specializing in cultural subjects and making films for the United Jewish Appeal. He made educational films for McGraw-Hill and a documentary about the new United Nations building. He collaborated with Lewis Jacobs on the prizewinning *Lincoln*

---

[22] Knight, "A Short History of Art Films," 6.

[23] Wilkie, "Still Pictures into Motion Pictures," 97–98.

[24] For an account of the MoMA Library's involvement in cultural propaganda films during World War II, see Richard Dyer MacCann, *The People's Films: A Political History of U.S. Government Motion Pictures* (New York: Hastings House, 1973), 147–51.

Speaks at Gettysburg, which became popular in many film societies and colleges.[25] With this background in propaganda, educational, and instructional films, Falkenberg was open to suggestions for new subjects or techniques. So when Namuth approached him to support his film on Pollock, Falkenberg provided the working capital of $2,000 for the film and acted as advisor and coproducer.[26]

Having already photographed Pollock at work during the summer of 1950, Namuth realized that film could offer a more accurate recording of Pollock's kinesthetic method of dripping paint on the flat, huge canvas stretched on the floor. His experience as a photographer determined his initial approach: "I started this film as one starts still photography . . . I suddenly realized that a film is a different kettle of stew and that one needed to have a different complexion of things."[27] Falkenberg, an experienced film editor, turned Namuth's "motion photography" of Pollock at work into a highly structured film about the artist. Falkenberg watched the rushes and made suggestions about close-ups and specific shots to be taken: Pollock's paint-spattered shoes, his cigarette, his hands mixing the paint. The result was a rhythmic montage of alternating wide shots and close-ups, which created the cinematic equivalent of Pollock's continuous movement while painting.

The film is structured around a staple type of documentary narrative, "a day in the life," incorporating elements of the industrial process film, showing how paintings are made and with what tools. We watch Pollock walking toward his work site; changing into his paint-spattered shoes; starting a new painting; and talking about his routines, tools, and techniques. Films about both creative and industrial processes rely on a narrative of progress and analysis of the mechanics of work. In *Jackson Pollock*, every sequence shows moments of progression, culminating in the longest sequence, when Pollock starts and finishes a painting on a glass pane. The development of a painting on glass is then recorded, with Namuth filming from underneath the glass, showing the development to the final work.[28] This final sequence of the film can be considered the most educational in terms of persuasive cinematic rhetoric and visual elucidation of Pollock's radical decision to shift from the perpendicular to the horizontal canvas.

---

[25] For details about Falkenberg's wide-ranging career, see "Paul Falkenberg," *Variety*, Jan. 29, 1986, 94; a special tribute to Falkenberg in the German film magazine, *Filmexil* 8 (Nov. 1996): 45–56; Cecile Starr, "Paul Falkenberg (1903–1986)," *Sightlines* 19 (Spring–Summer 1986): 30.

[26] Steven Naifeh and Gregory White Smith, *Jackson Pollock: An American Saga* (New York: Clarkson N. Potter, 1989), 648.

[27] Oral history interview with Hans Namuth, Aug. 12–Sept. 8, 1971, Archives of American Art, Smithsonian Institution, www.aaa.si.edu/collections/oralhistories/transcripts/namuth71.htm.

[28] For a still of Pollock painting on glass and more of Hans Namuth's photographs, see the National Gallery of Art Web site, www.nga.gov/feature/pollock/pollockhome.shtm.

The glass pane replacing the canvas had a clear instructive function: to demonstrate the gravity of the paint.

Instead of reiterating myths about the "mystery" of the creative process and abstract notions about art, the film utilizes techniques and rhetoric that emphasize industrial processes. Pollock's own voiceover about his training under Thomas Hart Benton, his materials, and his tools is grounded and functional: "I like to use a dripping fluid paint. I also use glass, pebbles . . . ." The commentary is as lucid as the images. If this film is viewed with a fresh eye, devoid of the mythical, biographical, and ideological connotations of Pollock's life and work, it is an educational film about the creative process, not dissimilar in intention from instructional films about art techniques, yet more elaborate and cinematic in execution and scope. Morton Feldman's specially composed experimental music heightens the effect and echoes similar uses of modernist music to accompany modern art, as in the film about Calder and Richter's *Dreams That Money Can Buy.*

Jackson Pollock premiered at MoMA in June 1951 and was subsequently distributed by MoMA's Film Library and A. F. Films, both nontheatrical distributors connected with a wide network of film societies and educational institutions. In September of that year, it was shown at the first American Art Film Festival in Woodstock (N.Y.), where, according to Falkenberg, it was not well received: "What we considered self-evident visual analogues of Jackson Pollock's emotion did not work for an audience in 1951. . . . Today [1980] nobody would take exception to our film as did George Grosz in 1952 . . . when he berated me for promoting 'inhumanity in the arts.'"[29]

The predominant type of art film shown at this festival and championed at the time in the *Magazine of Art* was that about the great masters of the past. However, *Saturday Review*'s Film Forum column, which promoted nontheatrical and educational films, recognized the film's cinematic achievements: "Pollock and his paintings are well suited to motion picture treatment, both being highly photographic, sharp, and interesting in close-up. Definitely worth seeing."[30] This mixed initial reception explains the distributor's strategic promotion of *Jackson Pollock* alongside a film about a great master, Fra Angelico, and a film by László Moholy-Nagy, a more established modernist designer and artist (see fig. 16.6).

Discussions of *Jackson Pollock* by art historians have tended to overemphasize the destructive impact that the strains of the filming process had on the artist's creativity, leading him fatally to resume alcohol consumption.[31] Scholars often

---

[29] Paul Falkenberg, "Notes on the Genesis of an Art Film," in *Pollock Painting,* ed. Barbara Rose (New York: Agrinde, 1980), n.p.

[30] Cecile Starr, review of *Jackson Pollock,* a film by Hans Namuth and Paul Falkenberg, *Saturday Review,* June 25, 1952, 32. That week's column was dedicated to "Art on Film."

[31] Rosalind E. Krauss, *The Optical Unconscious* (Cambridge, MA: MIT Press, 1993), 294–303; Ellen G. Landau, *Jackson Pollock* (London: Thames and Hudson, 1989), 196–205.

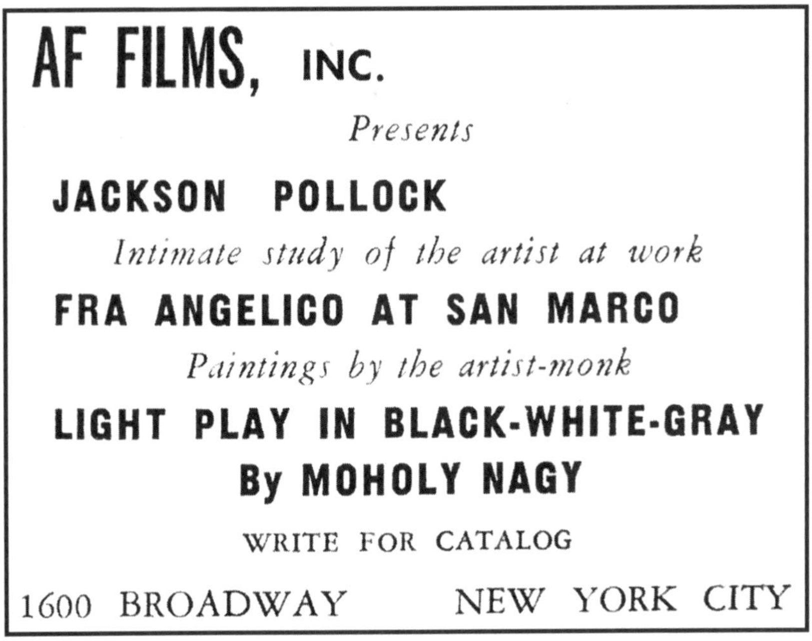

AF FILMS, INC.

Presents

JACKSON POLLOCK

Intimate study of the artist at work

FRA ANGELICO AT SAN MARCO

Paintings by the artist-monk

LIGHT PLAY IN BLACK-WHITE-GRAY By MOHOLY NAGY

WRITE FOR CATALOG

1600 BROADWAY   NEW YORK CITY

Figure 16.6. Promotional advertisement of A. F. Films, distributor of *Jackson Pollock*. *Magazine of Art* 45, no. 1 (1952): 43.

quote Pollock's superstition that "when a photographer takes your picture he steals your soul."[32] Although it is contestable whether Namuth's photographs and the film indeed "destroyed" Pollock's creativity, it is beyond doubt that this film generated concrete evidence of the intrinsic value of Pollock's creative process. *Jackson Pollock* is a public document whose educational impact and influences on future generations of artists and new art forms needs to be researched and debated anew by taking into account the historical context within which Namuth and Falkenberg worked. It is also important to highlight that Pollock himself was more familiar with films and filmmaking than is often suggested. His influential teacher and artist, Thomas Hart Benton, had collaborated on an Encyclopaedia Britannica educational film demonstrating the steps in planning and completing a mural composition, *The Making of a Mural* (1947). More directly, Pollock had helped his friend, the photographer Herbert Matter, make his film on then prominent artist Alexander Calder, *Works of Calder* (1951). During 1948–1949 Pollock carried the tripods and heavy equipment and acted as a guide for Matter, who shot the film's ocean sequences at East Hampton near Pollock's home.[33] His interest in and familiarity with the media of photography and film are evidently visible in the naturalness of his performed unawareness of the camera's intrusiveness, giving the film a tone of an observational documentary.

---

[32] Landau, *Jackson Pollock,* 204.

[33] Naifeh and Smith, *Jackson Pollock,* 561–62.

Namuth and Falkenberg's film has offered concrete visual evidence about Pollock's action painting to innumerable students, teachers, critics, theorists, art historians, and even scientists. Allegedly no one before Namuth had seen Pollock in the act of painting. Newman's photos of Pollock, published in *Life* in 1949, only showed him mimicking some gestures. It is worth asking whether art criticism about action painting and Pollock's kinesthetic paint-dripping methods would have been different without the influence of Namuth and Falkenberg's film. *Jackson Pollock* revealed the artist's methods in a way that no critic—not even Pollock himself—could have visualized.

Barbara Rose has noted that when art critics of the time wrote about Pollock's paintings, they actually discussed Pollock at work as seen in the film, rather than the paintings themselves. Unconsciously, their prose followed the film's editing, even if no mention of the film was made. Rose emphasizes that it was in Namuth's images, and "not in Pollock's deliberately controlled paintings," that art critics and artists saw the "liberating possibility of uninhibited acting out."[34] Subsequent and recent scholarship about Pollock has consistently reproduced photographs of filmstrips from *Jackson Pollock*. Once positioned alongside Pollock's paintings, the filmstrips were used to emphasize the kinetic action of the creative process, while familiarizing fine art students and critics with celluloid film's materiality and fragmentation of time.[35] This is an added dimension of this film's long-term educational value.

Moreover, the film has provided evidence of the artist's statement that "there is no accident, just as there is no beginning and no end." By analyzing the glass pane sequence, scientific research in fractal analysis has shown that "Pollock used a remarkably systematic method capable of generating intricate patterns that exhibit fractal scaling criteria with precision and consistency," raising the more general question of how a human being could create fractals.[36]

This ten-minute film is generally considered one of the main influences on process art, performance, and the use of film by artists themselves to document and reflect on their own performance: Allan Kaprow, Bruce Nauman, Richard Serra, Joseph Beuys, and Yoko Ono. According to Caroline Jones, *Jackson Pollock* was more influential than Pollock's paintings, "in the sense that no one could copy Pollock's dripped skeins of paint . . . without committing forgery, while the implications of his painting method were widely and consciously pursued by younger artists active in performance art, happenings, body art."[37] The same can

---

[34] Barbara Rose, "Namuth's Photographs and the Pollock Myth," in *Pollock Painting*, n.p.

[35] See, for example: Rose, *Pollock Painting*; Krauss, *Optical Unconscious*, 294–303.

[36] Richard P. Taylor, Adam P. Misolich, and David Jonas, "The Construction of Jackson Pollock's Fractal Drip Paintings," *Leonardo* 35, no. 2 (2002): 203–7.

[37] Caroline A. Jones, *Machine in the Studio: Constructing the Postwar American Artist* (Chicago: University of Chicago Press, 1996), 72.

be argued for the subsequent films by Namuth and Falkenberg, showing Willem de Kooning and Joseph Albers at work and enacting onscreen the idea that "paintings became records of movement rather than merely visual compositions."[38] What needs to be stressed in terms of the educational impact of *Jackson Pollock* and ultimately Pollock's legacy is that the film's wide circulation in educational institutions was due to an existing nontheatrical network of educational producers and distributors, the availability of 16mm projectors, and a long history of film in the American classroom. Art history thrives on accounts of artistic influence. However, the practicalities and historical contexts of art students and artists' visual education remains an underresearched area. The extensive use of films on art in art education should not be overlooked; it arguably played an instrumental role in developments in postwar American art by enabling a different experiential study of art.

Museums at Large and on Film

"Museum at Large," the name of Falkenberg and Namuth's company, which led to a thirty-five-year partnership, can be understood in two ways. First, it puts into practice André Malraux's thesis that photographic reproductions of art can create a "Museum without Walls."[39] They made numerous films about single-artist exhibitions in world-renowned museums. Falkenberg and Namuth not only filmed the actual exhibits but also authenticated them with historical and contextual material and sequences of the artists at work. Thus, the second connotation of the name "Museum At Large" is that their films would untether the museum not only geographically but also historically and materially. By filming artists at work, they expanded the idea of what art exhibited in museums can be. Their films showed that works of art are not ossified monuments of mystical creativity but the products of work, often mechanical and repetitive, performed by artists as producers. "Museum At Large" implied "works of art at large"; it thus moved away from an object-oriented idea of the museum and toward the concept of the living museum. Hence, the contribution of Museum at Large to the world of educational filmmaking can be summed up in its consistent focus on the working practices of modern artists shown in their studios and working environments. In their films the creative process of making modern art was dissected, demystified, and presented in terms similar to the visualization of industrial processes.

---

[38] Michael Kirby, "Happenings," in *Happenings and Other Acts*, ed. Mariellen R. Sandford (London: Routledge, 1995), 15.

[39] Malraux's work was translated from French into English in 1949 and quickly became popular in the United States. André Malraux, *The Psychology of Art*, 3 vols. (Princeton, NJ: Princeton University Press, 1949).

Films about modern artists that aimed at "suturing the spectator" into their world played a significant role in the substantiation of theories about art as experience, action painting's indexicality, and what Caroline Jones calls "the performative aspect of postwar industrial aesthetic" of American art, perhaps even more than the books or articles that propagated these ideas.[40] The director of the Metropolitan Museum of Art recognized this crucial role of film in art education in his introduction to the first dedicated critical guide, *Films on Art 1952*. His introductory note endorsed Arnold Hauser's argument in *Social History of Art* (1951) that the medium of film defined the era after impressionism, which Hauser called the "Film Age." The director of the Metropolitan urged all those engaged in art education to familiarize themselves with the tools and techniques of art films and emphasized that "the possibilities of the art film . . . are unlimited."[41]

This shows considerable progress in the use and understanding of the medium of film by the Metropolitan, the stalwart of cultural authority, since the 1920s. The dominant view then was that "quiet contemplation" was "the keystone of aesthetic enjoyment, and [that] with this the motion picture [had] little in common."[42] Similar skepticism was also voiced during the postwar period. The most common criticism by opponents of films on art was that filmic reproduction and contextualization of a work of art distorted its spatial and formal integrity by imposing a temporality unintended by its creator.[43] However, this kind of criticism was counterbalanced by a new direction in the 1960s in the philosophical and academic study of aesthetics and aesthetic experience, which embraced film. The new learned *Journal of Aesthetic Education* dedicated one of its first issues to film and the moving image in 1969. This journal published the research of the Institute for Advanced Study in Aesthetic Education at the University of Illinois, where Falkenberg had been invited to lecture on film and aesthetics in 1967. He went on to teach about the subject at many universities in the late 1960s and 70s, while continuing to make films.

Falkenberg's long experience in editing and educational filmmaking made him prioritize the viewer's perception in his understanding and analysis of film. Hence he argued that:

> The viewer's eyes are not his own any more as they are in the theatre, or in a museum or art gallery. The painter hangs a painting and it is up to the individual to approach it. He either keeps his distance, turns his back, inspects it closely, or glances at it in passing. But in film, it is the

---

[40] Jones, *Machine in the Studio*, 345.

[41] Francis Henry Taylor, "Introduction," in Chapman, *Films on Art 1952*, i.

[42] Huger Elliot, "The Educational Work of the Museum," *Metropolitan Museum of Art Bulletin* 21 (Sept. 1926): 216, cited in Wasson, "Mobilizing the Museum," 92n10.

[43] Beatrice Farwell, "Films on Art: A Report from Ottawa," *Art Journal* 23, no. 1 (1963): 38.

director who determines and controls what one sees. The viewer may be bored, turned off, manipulated, brainwashed, propagandized, used, or misused. In any case, the responsibility lies with the director or editor.[44]

This neatly summarizes in retrospect the control that Falkenberg and Namuth's film on Pollock exercised in the critical and popular perception of Pollock's techniques and his paintings. *Jackson Pollock* and subsequent Museum at Large films on artists at work played integral roles in the wider shift toward emphasis on the creative process, thus expanding, in a truly Deweyan way, the viewers' experiential understanding of works of art. More than mere documentations of the "behind the scenes" world of artists, their films had an unprecedented impact on visually positioning the creative process in the public sphere of general education. The Pollock film and other Namuth and Falkenberg productions marked the ways of understanding and teaching what modern artists do in an appropriately modernist manner: by filming it.

Filmography

Films codirected and coproduced by Paul Falkenberg and Hans Namuth. Production and distribution by Museum at Large Ltd. All films shot on 16mm in color. For a list of university and public libraries in the United States with Museum at Large productions in their holdings, consult www.worldcat.org.

Alexander Calder: Calder's Universe (**1977**) **30 min.**
WRITER: John Russell. NARRATORS: Tom Armstrong, Louisa Calder. Made with a grant from Exxon. VHS distribution by Kultur International Films (ca. 1998), Collector Series, Museum of Modern Art.

Alfred Stieglitz: Photographer (**1982**) **30 min.**
NARRATOR: Marthe Jacobs. EDITOR: Susanne Jasper. Supported by grants from the National Endowment for the Arts, New York State Council on the Arts, Polaroid Foundation, Mobil Foundation. VHS distribution by Kultur International Films (ca. 1998), Collector Series, Museum of Modern Art.

---

[44] Paul Falkenberg, "Notes on Film and Film History," *Journal of Aesthetic Education* 3 (July 1969): 60. Special Issue: Film, New Media, and Aesthetic Education.

Balthus (also *Balthus at the Pompidou*) (**1984**) **30 min.**
COPRODUCER: George Freedland. COPRODUCTION: Centre
National d'Art et de Culture Georges Pompidou, Musée National
d'Art Moderne, Paris. VHS distribution by Kultur International Films
(1994), Collector Series, Museum of Modern Art.

Brancusi: Retrospective at the Guggenheim Museum (**1971**) **25 min.**
NARRATOR/WRITER: Sidney Geist. CINEMATOGRAPHER:
Jon Wing Lum. MUSIC: Gheorghe Zamfir. VHS distribution by
Kultur International Films (1998), Collector Series, Museum of
Modern Art (as *Bancusi* [*sic*]: *Retrospective at the Guggenheim
Museum*).

Homage to the Square (also *Josef Albers: Homage to the Square*)
(**1970**) **25 min.**
A Chelsea House Publishers production for University-at-Large
Programs. DISTRIBUTION: Released in 16mm by Association-
Sterling Films, 1973. ACCESS: VHS release in Great Minds of Our
Times Series.

Jackson Pollock (**1951**) **10 min.**
DISTRIBUTION: Initially distributed by MoMA Film Library and
A. F. Films. MUSIC: Morton Feldman. ACCESS: Pacific Film
Archive. Two short extracts are posted on the website of the National
Gallery of Art, Washington, DC. One of them is a compilation of the
close-up shots of the film that Falkenberg suggested to Namuth:
www.nga.gov/feature/pollock/process3qt.shtm. Longer clip at
www.youtube.com/watch?v=CrVE-WQBcYQ.

Louis Kahn: Architect (**1972**) **28 min.**
NARRATOR: Vincent Scully. CINEMATOGRAPHER: Jon Wing
Lum. NOTES: Interviews with Louis Kahn by Peter Blake. ACCESS:
Released on VHS and DVD.

Matisse: Centennial at the Grand Palais (**1970**) **55 min.** (a.k.a. *The
Henri Matisse Centennial at the Grand Palais*)
WRITER/NARRATOR: Pierre Schneider. MUSIC: Tom Glazer.
CINEMATOGRAPHER: Henri Alckan. Production coordinator:
George Freedland. VHS distribution by Kultur International Films
(ca. 1998), Collector Series, Museum of Modern Art.

Willem De Kooning: The Painter (**1964**) **13 min.**
MUSIC: Morton Feldman. DISTRIBUTOR: Museum of Modern Art Circulating Film & Video Library. ACCESS: VHS, 2004.

Willem De Kooning's Studio (a.k.a. ***Willem de Kooning at the Modern***) (**1972**) **26 min.**

Related Films

Alexander Calder: Sculpture and Constructions (1944). 11 min. Hartley Studios for MoMA. Distributed by MoMA Film Library.

Dreams That Money Can Buy (1947). 99 min. Directed by Hans Richter. Production: Art of This Century Films. Distribution: Films International of America.

Grandma Moses (1950). 21 min. Directed by Jerome Hill. Falcon Films. Distributed by A. F. Films.

Lincoln Speaks at Gettysburg (1950). 10 min. Produced, directed, and written by Lewis Jacobs and Paul Falkenberg. Distributed by A. F. Films.

The Making of a Mural (1947). 10 min. Production and distribution by Encyclopaedia Britannica Films. Thomas Hart Benton demonstrates the steps in planning and completing a mural composition.

The Photographer (1948). 25 min. Directed by Willard Van Dyke. Produced by Affiliated Film Producers and U.S. Office of Education. Distributed by Brandon Film and U.S. Department of State (later USIA).

The Titan: The Story of Michelangelo (1950). 70 min. Directed and photographed by Curt Oertel in 1939. U.S. version presented by Robert Flaherty, produced by Robert Snyder. Distribution: United Artists; Classic Pictures (nontheatrical).

A Visit to Picasso (1950, Belgium). 18 min. Written and directed by Paul Haesaerts. Produced by R. A. Cinema. Distributed by Film Advisory Center, New York.

Works of Calder (1951). 20 min. Produced and narrated by Burgess Meredith. Directed by Herbert Matter. Music by John Cage. Distributed by MoMA Film Library.

17 CELLULOID CLASSROOMS AND EVERYDAY PROJECTIONISTS: POST–WORLD WAR II CONSOLIDATION OF COMMUNITY FILM ACTIVISM

CHARLES R. ACLAND

In *Making Films That Teach* (1954), a solitary employee in the dark offices of Encyclopaedia Britannica Films (EBF) struggles after hours to write a script on the contributions of motion pictures to education. He is not completely alone. A helpful ghost named Mr. McGuffey Reader materializes from a framed photograph hanging on the wall. Together, the literarily inclined figure from the past and the more technologically advanced character from the present discuss the multiple advantages of film, taking time to compare filmic attributes with the traditional textbook. Illustrating various aspects of film production, including editing, sound, and color, our guides reassure the audience that film programs are produced with the cooperation of, and are reviewed by, qualified educational consultants and that the work of EBF is to help teachers make the best film selections for themselves. Scenes demonstrating the variety and adaptability of motion pictures include recreations of historical events; easy-to-remember nutritional information; presentations of industrial and scientific processes; images of family life worldwide; close-ups of the natural world; and views of the internal workings of the human body, including the larynx, eardrum, and joints. The film suggests that the textbook is improved upon by the visual malleability of a cinematic supplement, with dramatic examples of animation, microphotography, and time-lapse sequences, revealing what would otherwise not be visible.

Encyclopaedia Britannica Films produced *Making Films That Teach* to commemorate its twenty-fifth year of producing motion pictures for schools and teaching contexts. It explicitly narrates not only the wonders of filmic

I wish to acknowledge Louis Pelletier's expert research assistance, and the funding support received from the Social Sciences and Humanities Research Council of Canada. Versions of this paper were presented in 2006 at the fifth Orphan Film Symposium (University of South Carolina), Society for Cinema and Media Studies Conference (Vancouver), and the History and Epistemology of Moving Image Studies Seminar (Concordia University, Montreal).

construction and plasticity but also the regularized and noncontroversial presence of movies in classrooms. Mr. McGuffey Reader, far from a stodgy champion of the printed page, is comfortable with this technological addition to instructional situations. *Making Films That Teach* reasons that film pedagogy does not usurp the authority of teachers but rather supplements and enhances their existing role and materials. After all, quality resources from EBF still rely upon conventionally recognized experts in various subject areas.

Making Films That Teach is one example of a subgenre of information films designed to promote the use of motion pictures for instructional purposes. Others include *Teaching with Sound Films* (EBF, 1936), *Using the Classroom Film* (EBF, 1945), *Film Tactics* (U.S. Navy/Castle Films, 1945), *Projecting Motion Pictures* (UCLA, 1951), and *Film Research and Learning* (W. A. Wittich, 1956). Even into the 1960s, such films were still being produced and released, including *Choosing a Classroom Film* (McGraw-Hill Text Films/Centron, 1963), *How to Use Classroom Films* (McGraw-Hill Text Films/Centron, 1963), *New Dimensions through Teaching Films* (Coronet, 1963), and *Motion Film in the Classroom* (EML, 1968). In addition to providing technical advice, these films focus on the advantages of motion pictures as illustrators, bringing the distant or microscopic into the classroom. They typically offer examples of subjects, using excerpts from the company's catalog to demonstrate uses to which the teaching film might be put, highlighting the photographic manipulation of scenes and presenting general stages of film production.

Most strikingly, film-use films include material on proper selection, the screening skills of educators, and their incorporation into lessons and public forums. These films, then, reveal something of the supposed location and deployment of motion pictures in educational and informational settings, at least as imagined and promoted by the production companies themselves. Such films are often not just about film use but about the organizational and corporate entities themselves. *Making Films That Teach*, for instance, in addition to its treatment of instructional film, is both a marketing and commemorative device for Encyclopaedia Britannica Films.

This essay documents the institutional and discursive structures for informational film in the United States and Canada during the1940s and 50s, with emphasis on the film-use instructional film. How did these education shorts imagine and present a comfortable place for motion pictures alongside text books and chalkboards, in gymnasiums and community halls? I discuss material features that shaped how the factual film moved about in the world, the agencies that advanced this circulation, and the situations for cinematic engagement they developed. Significantly, it is clear that the role of film in pedagogical and community contexts was not automatically appreciated by all. Agencies interested in the advancement of film in instructional and training venues—most notably, the film council system—launched an enterprise to assess and recommend "proper" modes of film adoption, with postscreening discussions becoming the pedagogical standard, thus educating educators and community leaders about a new media environment.

The forties and fifties were not the first decades to witness investment in the public service dimensions of motion pictures. Entrepreneurs and teachers had exploited, or at least talked about exploiting, film for instructional purposes since the first decades of motion pictures, intensifying their activities in the 1930s.[1] The interwar period was primarily a moment of experimentation, one that began to settle by the end of the 1930s into generally recognized, at least among modern educators, priorities and procedures. The use of film for mass mobilization in World War II further solidified the favorable view toward functional applications of motion pictures. John Grierson noted the success of mobilization activities as a vital resource for civic development and progressive educational programs by writing in 1943, "There is more seating capacity outside theaters than there is inside them."[2] The wartime experience left many Canadian and American educationalists and community leaders interested in continuing similar efforts in a civilian capacity after the cessation of hostilities, hoping to seize upon the contemporary enthusiasm for the community and pedagogical advantages of film as wartime federal support receded. Consequently, a rapid augmentation of the use of classroom and community films followed World War II. The postwar period is distinct for the normalization of the place and operations of informational film on a mass basis. A number of organizations emerged to promote and guide that wave of activity, circulating information on access to films, evaluation of instructional potential, and methods of incorporation into various classroom and community locations.

Attention to agencies directing that film education activity reveals the interconnectedness of sites and institutions incorporating motion pictures into their operations after World War II. The deployment of motion pictures muddied the boundaries of the classroom, redefining what counted as an educational context, and extended the reach of community authority into schools. This is a crucial aspect in the history of instructional film: one cannot understand the rise of the classroom film without understanding the related rise of film use in community, institutional, and industrial contexts. Not only was film taken up simultaneously in these extratheatrical locations, but often the same films and film-usage materials (such as catalogs, discussion guides, programs and screening ideas, notes and

---

[1] For example, Edgar Dale, Fannie W. Dunn, Charles F. Hoban Jr., and Etta Schneider, *Motion Pictures in Education: A Summary of the Literature* (New York: H. W. Wilson, 1938); and Charles F. Hoban Jr., *Focus on Learning: Motion Pictures in the School* (Washington, DC: American Council on Education, 1942).

[2] John Grierson, "Propaganda and Education," in *Grierson on Documentary*, ed. Forsyth Hardy (1943; reprint, New York: Praeger, 1971), 291.

essays) traveled between them. Moreover, the organizations and industrial concerns advancing instructional film did so for both formal and less conventional educational situations. For example, the 1950 catalog for the New York University Film Library made clear its services were for "schools and organizations."[3]

One outgrowth was the film council movement, a network of community-based organizations promoting proper use of informational and instructional film by all potential users. This movement built upon other community councils and local chapters of voluntary societies, including women's, adult education, religious, and labor groups. Local chapters might be linked to form national organizations, like the YMCA, 4-H, and Rotary Clubs. The special role of voluntary organizations in American civil society has been regularly noted by commentators and historians, beginning with de Tocqueville. Lizabeth Cohen points to the key function voluntary societies had on the initiation of contemporary consumer advocacy.[4] These civic groups had a structuring influence on the public sphere. They delineated constituent-defined access to informational and deliberative agencies and drew formal institutional paths between local and national contexts.

The film council movement, then, had a double role with respect to these societies. First, it provided a technologically defined service to these groups, furthering group usage of motion pictures; and second, it was itself a constituency of technologically invested educators and activists, championing the place of film in the future of democracy.[5] These media education activists held the belief that film was a valuable instrument for learning about this "rapidly changing world," as Film Council of America director Glen Burch put it, and that people "must learn to choose for themselves, from among all the films available, those best suited to their individual needs and interests."[6]

In a major and immediate order of business, both the Canadian and U.S. councils responded to perceived community problems in accessing, evaluating, and deploying informational films. In the United States, the Film Council of America (FCA) was founded in 1946.[7] According to its constitution, it was a

---

[3] *New York University Film Library, A Catalogue of Selected 16mm. Educational Motion Pictures* (New York: NYU, 1950), 4.

[4] Lizabeth Cohen, *A Consumers' Republic: The Politics of Mass Consumption in Postwar America* (New York: Vintage, 2003), 33.

[5] The postwar council movement is not to be confused with prewar councils, such as those emerging from the National Board of Review, which primarily focused on feature films and theatrical exhibition, rather than informational and educational films in extratheatrical situations.

[6] Glen Burch, "Film Councils at Work," in *Ideas on Film*, ed. Cecile Starr (New York: Funk and Wagnalls, 1951), 62.

[7] For a fuller account of the FCA, see Charles R. Acland, "Classrooms, Clubs, and Community Circuits: Reconstructing Cultural Authority and The Film Council Movement, 1946–1957," in *Inventing Film Studies*, ed. Lee Grieveson and Haidee Wasson (Durham, NC: Duke University Press, 2008), 149–81.

nonprofit educational association whose mission was "to increase the information and work toward the general welfare of all people by fostering, improving and promoting the production, the distribution, and the effective use of audiovisual materials."[8] It was to pursue these ideals by coordinating and supporting the activities of community-based councils, its own local chapters, and national audiovisual organizations.[9] To this end, the FCA was an active producer of catalogs, discussion guides, material on how to run a council, and informational film news. By June 1951, the FCA had more than 150 local chapters, and had developed information centers in more than 1,200 towns. These materials were widely circulated, and the priorities for instructional film usage were acted upon by the gamut of formal and informal educational organizations.

The National Film Society of Canada (NFS), founded in 1935, acted in a manner similar to the FCA, and its affiliation as a member organization of the FCA assured an easy flow between the two countries for programs and publications on informational film utilization. The coordination of the distribution of information about educational film utilization, and the council system on the whole, was a few years more advanced in Canada than in the United States. Consequently, American film educationalists kept close watch on Canadian developments.[10] Though education was always part of its mandate, in its early years the NFS was modeled on the British Film Institute, and it operated very much as a conventional film society, helping to organize screenings of exemplary and rare works of world cinema. But the NFS became more engaged in informational film during and after World War II. At the time, the National Film Board of Canada (NFB) had been operating its own distribution circuit. Seen as a success, this circuit "took on substance, becoming a part of the nation's life, communities themselves responded with energy," establishing their own film councils.[11] In actuality, postwar cutbacks to the NFB led to a reduction of this focus, and staff progressively declined.[12] As a result, NFB representatives provided the information and

---

[8] "FCA Constitution," Mar. 4, 1947, Film Council of America [hereafter FCA], Iowa State University, Ames, Iowa, Ms. 351, box 1, folder 1, 1.

[9] Letter, Evans Clark to Carnegie Corporation, Mar. 1950, Columbia University, Rare Book and Manuscript Library, Carnegie Corporation Grants, box 144.12, folder "Film Council of America, 1947–1957," 2.

[10] As a point of comparison, the FCA had 130 affiliated councils in July 1949, while the NFS boasted more than 250 councils in Canada. "Summary Report on the Second Annual Meeting of the Film Council of America," *Film Counselor* 3 (July–Aug. 1949): n.p. Though FCA and Ford Foundation executives repeatedly referred to the more highly developed Canadian community film scene, these tallies reflect the more centralized organizational structure of the U.S. agency and not the size of educational film audiences.

[11] Memorandum, NFB Sept. 1953, *Film and You* file, National Film Board Archives [hereafter FAY], Montreal, 15.

[12] Staff declined from a peak of 787 in 1945 to 540 in 1949. Ibid., 20.

arguments needed to encourage communities to take this activity up for themselves. The NFB representative had "been called many things, not all of them complimentary and ranging from 'film peddler' to 'adult educator'" but was in fact a "'demonstrator, organizer and promoter of films and filmstrips for their informational values and as tools of adult education.'"[13] These individuals facilitated the formation and operation of local councils, and though NFB-operated rural circuits fell from 85 to 67 in 1946–1947, 90 new circuits had been created by departments of education and agriculture, school boards, and Wheat Pools among other organizations.[14] Thus, even as state support for informational film usage dwindled with the end of World War II, the general investment increased, and along with it, increasingly specified modes of film utilization by educators and community leaders. The NFS executive noted, "The growth of interest in the educational film throughout Canada during the past year has been remarkable." They felt that had the NFS "not prepared itself to give extended service to these many new converts to audio-visual education, the growth of film use in Canada would have been retarded or the Society might have lost its enviable place of pioneer leadership."[15]

Like the FCA, the NFS worked with other educational organizations, pooling resources and coordinating the nationalist energy that was apparent among the cultural authorities of the day. Members compiled evaluations of films in catalogs, produced status reports on usage, published a newsletter on quality international films, wrote practical guides like *How to Organize a Film Library*, helped produce radio talks to be used in conjunction with screenings, and collaborated with the NFB on films demonstrating cross-media information events.[16] Typical for the period's blurred boundary between commercial and educational interests, the NFS circulated films from private as well as public sources, and eventually used sponsorship films to begin screenings.[17] Many of these local councils in turn pooled resources to form provincial structures like the Ontario Association of Film Councils and the Manitoba Film Association. The NFB measured council activity as reaching half a million people a month by

---

[13] NFB Representatives' Manual, ca. 1952, FAY, 1.

[14] Memorandum, NFB Sept. 1953, 20.

[15] NFS, "Report of the Executive Secretary for the Fiscal Year, 1946–47," FAY, 1.

[16] NFS, "Film Library and Depot Membership Services," Mar. 1948, FAY, 2; Donald Buchanan, *Educational and Cultural Films in Canada* (Ottawa: National Film Society, 1936); Donald Buchanan and D. S. McMullan, "Report to the Executive of the National Film Society of Canada" (1938), Rockefeller Archives Center, Rockefeller Foundation Collection, record group 1.1, series 427R, box 27, file 270; O. C. Wilson, *How to Organize a Film Library* (Ottawa: NFS, ca. 1945). Their catalogs include *Canadian Films Reviewed, 1939–1941*, and *Educational Sixteen Millimetre Films Distributed by the NFS* for both 1947 and 1948.

[17] NFS Bulletin, 1946, "Distribution Plan for Sponsored Films," FAY.

1950 with their documentary and educational programs.[18] This would have been about half the NFB's total monthly audience at this time, according to its own measurements. In short, volunteer work of the NFS and the film councils established a formidable system of film and information circulation.

The preceding description of activity gives a sense of the magnitude of the film councils, a seriously underappreciated distribution and exhibition apparatus. And, most essential to the topic at hand, they were key to the organization of ideas about how motion pictures were to be incorporated into educational and informational contexts. Their presence following World War II marked the widespread energy devoted to normalizing the place of factual film in ordinary public, pedagogical, and cultural life. And with the emphasis on user guides, assessment committees, and catalogs to assist in particular forms of usage, it is clear that the movement was not just about access to films but also about the production and circulation of material about film. The advancement of this brand of motion picture education was varied. For example, W. S. Jobbins designed a film utilization workshop in 1950, covering such topics as using a film for discussion and staging a screening. Jobbins described that 90 percent of people using film, whether community council members or teachers, had never had any training. The workshop included two films on utilization (*Film Tactics* and *Projecting Motion Pictures*) and two example forum topics (*Seed Growing in Grand Forks* [NFB, 1947] and *Worth the Risk* [Central Office of Information, United Kingdom, 1948]). Common for film educators of the period, Jobbins's workshop emphasized discussion questions and preparation of technological aspects of screening situations.[19]

The advancement of "proper" informational film usage appeared in radio addresses, often supplementing written argument and cataloging to assist informational film users in discernment. Canadian educationalists, building on Farm and Citizen Radio Forums, promoted joint programs of group-listening to radio talks, watching films on a topic, followed by related discussion. The Canadian Broadcasting Corporation (CBC) broadcast a radio series called "Speaking of Films." One program dramatized the work of film councils, with characters including a bored boy looking for entertainment other than the movie house, pool hall, and skating rink; a schoolteacher looking for "closer cooperation between teachers and parents"; a doctor saying, "It's been pretty tough getting folks interested in health campaigns and clinics"; and a clubwoman wanting to "stimulate discussions at our church meetings."[20] The announcer then recommends, and defines, a film council, whose end result, in this broadcast, is the

---

[18] Memorandum, NFB Sept. 1953, 21.

[19] W. S. Jobbins, "Capsule Workshop: An Outline for a Two and One-Half Hour Course in Film Utilization," Dec. 1950, *Let's Talk about Films* File, National Film Board Archives [hereafter LTAF], Montreal.

[20] "Speaking of Films," Radio script, FAY, 2.

confrontation with issues of racial intolerance and juvenile delinquency. The ultimate objective of a film council's work was the creation of "the rarest of all types of citizens . . . world citizens, discovering that the world does not end at their city limits, nor their country's borders. That what happens in a village in Hungary or Greece or Palestine sooner or later affect every one of them. These films are dispelling the bonds of ignorance and prejudice."[21] This radio documentary captures a dominant set of ideas and ideals for motion pictures in postwar life, one that is evident among educational, community, and film progressives throughout the period, namely that motion pictures indisputably played a productive role in a media-dominated era. If handled properly, they could help the full flowering of a liberal public sphere, technologically structured, but in which debate and discussion still reigned and world citizenship might still emerge.

Other material advising educationalists on the liberal public potential of wisely deployed film included trailers demonstrating motion pictures as part of a multimedia community event. For example, the three-minute *Film and Radio—A Word About Citizen's Forums* (NFB, 1943) presents three civically engaged individuals—Neil Morrison from the CBC, Edith Spencer from the NFB, and Ralph Wright, who was studying rural health—sitting around a radio after listening to a talk on reconstruction that had aired on the CBC series *All Things to Come* and having watched Paul Rotha's *World of Plenty* (1943) (see fig. 17.1). They

Figure 17.1. A film discussion demonstrated in *Film and Radio—A Word about Citizen's Forums.* (Courtesy of the NFB.)

---

[21] Ibid., 3–4.

say a few words about the film, but on the whole, the trailer depicts the demeanor of knowledgeable individuals engaged in cross-media consumption and evaluation. It highlights discussion about issues of concern, following media consumption. Spectators see one image of the appropriate mode of active engagement with mass media, with the sleek portable 16mm projector hovering in the background as a visible reminder of the technological means of expert exchange.

Nowhere are these ideas about motion pictures' democratic impulse better represented than in the films made about the functional and educational uses of film. Several of the most widely circulated ones came from the NFB. A notable example, *Film and You* (NFB, 1948), demonstrates the work of councils, showing how one might be formed and depicting the progressive possibilities of nontheatrical screenings. The producer, Donald Fraser, had been an executive secretary of the NFS and had worked with the wartime film circuits. Early in production, Fraser was convinced of the multiple objectives of this film: as a prestige project for the NFB; a document of Canadian educational film usage; and a way to link production staff, field staff, and general audiences.[22] Fraser conducted an extensive survey of the state of the film council movement in Canada and the United States during the course of production, ensuring that the content would be accurate and up-to-date. The survey equally had the effect of assessing the market for the finished product.

During production, Margaret Carter, head of the U.S. office of the NFB, circulated a script to individuals in U.S. extension departments, the FCA, and educational film companies.[23] The most common recommendation she received was to minimize the Canadian information and also to include more dramatic subject matter to suggest urgency, such as images of famine and atomic blasts (a recommendation, incidentally, the filmmakers did not follow). One comment from Scott Fletcher, president of Encyclopaedia Britannica Films and an FCA board member, disapproved of the current community-oriented nature of the script—which indeed would become the focus of the film—proposing that "film excerpts deal with the significant problems of nutrition, hygiene and medicine, child welfare, public health, social planning, conservation, international responsibilities rather than those outlined in the present script which deal with community planning, industrial safety, weed control, farm home improvement and the like."[24] Stephen M. Corey, professor of educational psychology at the University of Chicago, and president of the FCA Board of Trustees, concurred with this view, feeling that even more film excerpts might be included.[25] Publisher of *Business Screen* O. H. Coellin

---

[22] Memorandum, Don Fraser to Ross McLean, May 12, 1947, RE: Film Council Film Project—Prod. 15—023, FAY.

[23] Memorandum, J. Margaret Carter (Chicago) to Donald Fraser (cc. Jack Ralph), Oct. 16, 1947, FAY, 1.

[24] Memorandum, J. Margaret Carter (Chicago) to Ralph Foster (cc. Jack Ralph and Jean Palardy), Oct. 24, 1947, FAY.

[25] Memorandum, Carter to Fraser, Oct. 16, 1947, 1.

suggested that the filmmakers be careful to not display makes of projectors in their films in order to avoid charges of "commercial favoritism."[26]

These notes notwithstanding, the response Carter received was supportive and gave her the impression that this film would be a much sought-after work. C. R. Reagan, first president of the FCA, went so far as to declare that "as usual Canada leads out in significant factual films."[27] Carter encouraged making the production of *Film and You* a priority, speeding up the process and assuring it would be of superior quality. As Carter wrote, "I have given the film so much advanced publicity here among leaders of the FCA movement that it would be extremely bad form to come forward with an inferior film. A really good film offers National Film Board a tremendous opportunity for prestige and good will."[28] In the end, the FCA did abundant publicity for *Film and You*, published a discussion guide, and produced its own introductory trailer providing specifically U.S. information.[29] The NFB, on their part, made the film available on a cost-recovery basis, hopeful it would both sell other NFB films and expand the market for nontheatrical productions with each council created.[30]

Film and You begins with a screening in a community hall setting, showing excerpts of actual NFB films, including *Kitchen Come True* (1948), *Get Rid of Rats* (1948), and *Canada Dances* (1947), and presenting individual, intergenerational, and stereotypically gendered audience reactions. A father looks mindfully at a child following a scene from *Lessons in Living* (1944) in which a boy pours boiling water on himself. Watching a film of energetically dancing women, a male spectator displays a lascivious grin, the woman next to him is scowling and purse-lipped, and an adolescent's face alternates between interest and disbelief. Images of rats make some women yelp and a scene about new kitchens makes Grandpa nod off, though he bolts up, clapping, when a movie about square dancing commences. Following this screening scene, people wonder how they can be certain such films will always be available to them. The narrator, to whom the characters respond directly, introduces the idea of a film library and council. To illustrate the idea, animated sequences, including abstract electronic sound effects, represent the forming of community groups, group representation on a regional council, and the sharing of materials. The film goes on to depict a council's basic functions—fund raising, projector care, cataloging, and preview committees (see figs. 17.2 and 17.3). The final third dramatizes additional screenings igniting lively community debate, leading to solutions to local problems. A rural community sees *Just Weeds* (1945) and decides to pool resources to invest in a

---

[26] Ibid., 2.

[27] C. R. Reagan to Margaret Carter, Oct. 3, 1947, FAY.

[28] Memorandum, J. Margaret Carter (Chicago) to Jack Ralph, Nov. 5, 1947, FAY.

[29] "'The Film and You'—A 16mm Film about Films—and You," Feb. 1949, FAY, 2.

[30] Memorandum, Carter to Fraser, Oct. 16, 1947, 1.

Figure 17.2. Film resources at a community library in *Film and You*. (Courtesy of the NFB.)

Figure 17.3. A projection tutorial in *Film and You*. (Courtesy of the NFB.)

chemical sprayer. A film on workplace safety screens in an industrial setting, prompting those watching to form a committee to investigate their own factory. And a movie on community beautification sparks what appears to be a massive groundswell of painting and litter collection. Thus, a film about film councils presents motion pictures igniting social action and is itself designed to produce interest in forming councils. *Film and You* illustrates the combined interest in civic duty, choices for modernization, and the careful incorporation of film to these ends.

For a test panel assessing its potential applications just prior to release, *Film and You* was seen as timely for the promotion of community projects. The panel suggested questions for postscreening discussion including "How can a community use film to best advantage?" and "Is a Film Council needed?"[31] The NFB discussion guide for *Film and You* provided information on documentaries, councils, and libraries, highlighting the work of the NFS and the Film Board itself. The stated intention was to develop interest in "films which rouse our will to be doing."[32] The discussion guide divided recommended questions into those for rural audiences, those for urban audiences with a film council, and those for urban audiences without a council. Rural audiences faced questions probing key community concerns, how motion pictures might help, how films might be accessed, and if a regional committee might be more useful than a local council. The guide recommended that urban audiences with a council contrast the representation of the screening scene in *Film and You* with their own experience, and to think about how films might be better deployed to match community interests. Urban communities without councils were asked to consider how a council might serve the community and what the first issues to tackle might be. It appears that the contribution of film was a given, and that it was only through a community's lack of energy that it would miss out on the benefits.

A U.S. pamphlet promoted the film. The redundantly titled "'The Film and You'—A 16mm Film about Films—and You," from February 1949, was a reprint of an article from *See and Hear: An International Journal of Audio-Visual Education*. Providing a synopsis and information on how to acquire prints, the pamphlet offered a sketch of U.S. film council work in general. The discussion questions focused upon getting audiences to think about community problems first, then to think about how motion pictures might be a useful resource and catalyst to the related solutions:

1. Is there any issue before the community now where films could be used profitably?
2. Do you feel that you are able to get the films you need—when you need them?

---

[31] "Film and You"—Evaluation Sheet, 1950, FAY.

[32] "Let's Discuss It!: A Film Discussion Guide, *Film and You*," NFB 1948, FAY, 2.

3.   What assets has the community which would serve as the beginning for a local council?

4.   Would a regional or district plan be better than a local setup?

5.   Would other films of this type stimulate more interest generally?

6.   What do you feel is most lacking in your use of films?

7.   Canada's problem of local film handling is different from our own in many respects. How many film libraries exist in your own area? Do you keep in regular touch with them?[33]

The *Australian Monthly*'s enthusiastic review wondered, "Why haven't we got councils like the Canadian ones?"[34] A review in "Film Council Corner" of the U.S. magazine *Film News* was less complimentary; the author was skeptical about the amount of community activity film might be able to activate. Arguing that "a thorough and balanced assimilation of films in the community" should have been depicted, the assessment continued, "One sequence in particular conveys the impression, at least to this reviewer, that a community was well-nigh revolutionized after a film screening. Maybe it happened somewhere *once*, but that it is typical seems pretty doubtful." In what appears to be a reference to the communication research of Paul Lazarsfeld and his cohort, this same reviewer criticized the film for an "over-evaluation" of the effects of mass media, pointing out that "latest research gives greater value to the role of face-to-face relations in influencing the individual directly, the community activity through him, than it gives to the press, radio and films."[35] Given that the film *does* set as a priority the face-to-face discussion and evaluation of films, I understand this comment as a sign of just how widely accepted this "new" understanding of media use must have been, such that *Film and You* could be criticized for not prioritizing it enough. *Ideas on Film,* the 1951 source guide for nontheatrical film comprised mostly of selections from the *Saturday Review of Literature*, reproaches *Film and You* for not being as exciting as it might be, but concludes that "it gives the best all-around coverage on the nontheatrical field yet available on film."[36] Gloria Waldron made favorable mention of its use by the FCA in her 1949 *The Information Film.*[37]

Spurred on the by the success of *Film and You*, the NFB produced a companion film titled *The Gentle Art of Film Projection* (1950). It had some of the same crew as the earlier film, including director Peters, composer Eldon Rathburn, and cinematographer Lorne C. Batchelor, though this one was produced

---

[33] "'The Film and You'—A 16mm Film about Films—and You," 2.

[34] Review, *Australian Monthly* (Dec. 1950), FAY.

[35] Review of *Film and You*, *Film News* (Feb. 1949), FAY.

[36] Cecile Starr, ed., *Ideas on Film* (New York: Funk and Wagnalls, 1951), 153.

[37] Gloria Waldron, *The Information Film* (New York: Columbia University Press, 1949).

by a future head of the Canadian Film Development Corporation, Michael Spencer. Designed to improve showmanship in nontheatrical settings, with an accompanying lithograph pamphlet, it contains material on how to set up and run projectors.[38] The necessity of such good projection practices is reinforced by the hapless George Beasley, the quintessential bad projectionist. He is a clumsy, Walter Mitty–like character, who alternately dreams he is a dandy schoolboy in ruffles, tights, and oiled hair; an orchestra conductor; and a love-struck romantic, mooning over Alice the film librarian. He sets the volume too high or too low, he runs the film upside down, and he doesn't notice when celluloid misses the take-up reel, burying him (see fig. 17.4). It ends with him crashing down a flight of stairs, off-screen, while overloaded with film reels and a projector. The narrator/film expert turns to the camera and pointedly says, "George Beasley will never be a showman. But you could."

The response to *The Gentle Art of Film Projection* was not as favorable as it had been for *Film and You*, and some powerful figures wanted the film scrapped. The High Commissioner for Canada in Australia wrote to complain of the "burlesque treatment" of the topic.[39] The NFB staff documented problems with the

Figure 17.4. George Beasley learning the finer aspects of film screenings in *The Gentle Art of Projection.* (Courtesy of the NFB.)

---

[38] Memorandum from Michael Spencer, May 11, 1951, *Gentle Art of Film Projection* File, National Film Board Archives [hereafter GAFP], Montreal.

[39] Letter from the Office of the High Commissioner for Canada, Canberra, Nov. 28, 1951, GAFP.

film's light touch, pointing to *Film Tactics* as an appropriately serious film, which is a striking assessment given that the latter film now appears surreal, and perhaps even absurdist.[40] Negative comments felt *The Gentle Art* was "directed to people with a low I.Q.," "it is unbelievable that taxpayer's money is spent on such rubbish," and that the straight man was seen as too much like a Gestapo officer. [41] A full survey showed that it did in fact please film council members, projectionists, and rural audiences, and was seen unfavorably primarily by urban audiences. Still, complaints led to a temporary suspension of distribution in 1951.[42]

One of the problems with the film, aside from tone, was that it didn't deal with discussion. Spencer proposed to make another film, more explicitly a practical guide to instructional film for community use, rather than revise *The Gentle Art of Film Projection*.[43] Distribution and field officers also expressed a desire for a short on film discussion.[44] Their findings contributed to the NFB's *Let's Talk about Films* (1953). This film illustrates techniques to generate questions and debate following a film screening, showing the importance of a skilled group leader. Again using a diegetic film instruction context, this time an unsuccessful forum following a film on rehabilitation of ex-convicts called *After Prison What?* (NFB, 1951), *Let's Talk about Films* argues for an active and authoritative leader. Film discussion leaders were not to be blustery authorities, but to become members of the group, watching films with audiences and posing questions. Forum leaders were directed to express their personal opinion on film topics, thus encouraging audiences to do the same. Rather than dominating a discussion, leaders prompt audience members "to share their feelings," seeing this as the best way to get people to make up their minds about something and then, once convinced, to be prepared to act.[45] The goal of *Let's Talk about Films* was to convey "the *feeling* of a warm group atmosphere" as an essential component to effective discussion and utilization.[46]

Looking Beyond . . . Story of a Film Council (NFB, 1957) was an ode to the success of the councils. It presents the contributions to "the welfare and enlightenment" of citizens made by the over four hundred councils through which "people gather together, discussing, arguing, learning—with the aid of film," as

---

[40] Memorandum from Vaughan Deacon, "Observations of NFB Toronto Staff on Gentle Art of Film Projection," June 11, 1951, GAFP.

[41] "*The Gentle Art of Film Projection*: A Report on Audience Reaction as Reported by NFB Representatives," Nov. 1951, GAFP, 4.

[42] Memorandum from T. V. Adams, "RE: *The Gentle Art of Film Projection*," May 3, 1951, GAFP.

[43] Memorandum from Michael Spencer, July 20, 1951, GAFP.

[44] Memorandum from Glen Byford, "Film Utilization," Jan. 20, ca. 1953, LTAF.

[45] Vaughn Deacon, "Getting the Most out of Your Film Showing," Dec. 29, 1952, LTAF.

[46] Memorandum from E. W. Bovard Jr., University of Toronto, June 23, 1953, LTAF, 1.

the NFB information notice puts it.[47] Where nine years earlier *Film and You* chronicled the process by which communities form film councils, *Looking Beyond* begins with a montage of councils already in operation. In the first scene, a council has just watched a film and they begin to discuss the politics of aid to developing nations. Next, a gathering of older women argue about childcare. This leads to a "New Canadians" club wondering about what is left behind by the progressive education of their new country. As presented here, groups are typified by gender, interest, ethnicity, and language, with the rather obvious imperative of Canadian citizenship enforced. The New Canadians declare, "We agreed to speak English," which is followed by a French-speaking council from Montreal. This opening montage includes a 16mm projector or screen, or both, standing watch over each of these screening scenes. There is no highlighting of the film titles, with the exception of *L'homme aux oiseaux* (English version: *The Bird Fancier*) (NFB, 1952) watched by the francophone group. The overarching element is discussion and debate. Moreover, discussion is calm, civic, and ordered, with measured turn-taking and meaningful contributions respected by other members.

Looking Beyond then flashes back, presenting a reminiscence of a particular council's formation, beginning with the needless death of a child from diphtheria, and a doctor's campaign to promote an immunization plan. A representative from a neighboring film council arrives to describe how a community can be mobilized behind a general health concern through film programs. The movie ends by presenting a forum celebrating the fifth anniversary of the council's establishment. Echoing the reference to the politics of international development in the opening scene, the final forum topic depicted is an appeal to global significance of their activities, including excerpts from *The War on Want* (NFB, 1954), a film about Canadian contributions through UNESCO to the development in Southeast Asia. Thus, *Looking Beyond* moves from localized communities of difference, enacting a common mode of national citizenship, to the cosmopolitan ideal of world citizenship at the conclusion.

The depiction of activity in this cycle of film-use films makes it evident that the path of progress toward a stable informational and instructional media scene involved certain ideas about motion pictures, education, and citizenship. Examining these largely forgotten works now provides access to some of the presumptions of the day as popular ideas about educational media were in process of being set in place. Represented is a link between local participation in community activity and international civic responsibility, with film as the crucial vehicle for this connection. Further, these film-use films indicate a desire for the promotion

---

[47] NFB Information Bulletin for *Looking Beyond . . . Story of a Film Council* (1957), *Looking Beyond . . . Story of a Film Council* File, National Film Board Archives, Montreal.

of *guided group discussion* as the ideal form of film utilization. The film-within-a-film structure of the film-use films shows the sort of topics available, which were of interest for community and classroom contexts, rural and urban audiences, and serious and light programming. Along with these ideas ran particular modes of serious consideration of community and curricular topics via motion pictures as well as related uses of classroom and community space for gatherings, screenings, and discussions. Put differently, cultural leaders deployed the mobile media of film to gain access to and influence in locations for the molding of civic participation. In addition to the discourse of democratic life and volunteerism advocated here, there is also a reconfiguration of the relationship between government and industry in the arena of education and media, with private citizens taking a leadership role in the integration of media with existing institutions. On the matter of the media industries, take note that this is also partly a tale of the expansion of the extratheatrical market as businesses readied themselves to pry open classrooms and other quasi-educational sites as targets for their new media wares.

Film educationalists and their organizations worked to coordinate how decisions were made about film, offering a framework for a public mediated by screens, which were in turn mediated by community leaders, teachers, and cultural authorities. The forum/discussion idea blended less traditionally authoritative educational tactics with ideas about participation in democratic life. This enactment of citizenship appeared in other films, including Encyclopaedia Britannica's *How to Organize a Discussion Group* (1954), *How to Conduct a Discussion Group* (1954), and *Room for Discussion* (1953). Together these represent an effort to situate a technological apparatus in a vaguely Deweyian educational idea. The guided group discussion model offered a reasonable supplement to an existing understanding of progressive education, and in so doing, it established comfortable ground for screen education and a film-inflected public to grow. The place of group discussion in mass media echoes the founding paradigm of the field of communication studies, the contemporaneously developing "limited effects" or "two-step flow" model. In the existing historical material on the discipline, this paradigm is presented as the product of research, albeit sponsored research, from sociologist Paul Lazarsfeld's studies of media influence or psychologist Kurt Lewin's research on group dynamics.[48] In light of the priorities evident in the film-use film, in the activities of film educationalists, in similar

---

[48] See, for example, Paul Felix Lazarsfeld, Bernard Berelson, and Hazel Gaudet, *The People's Choice: How the Voter Makes Up His Mind in a Presidential Campaign* (New York: Duell, Sloan and Pearce, 1944); Elihu Katz and Paul Felix Lazarsfeld, *Personal Influence: The Part Played by People in the Flow of Mass Communications* (New York: Free Press, 1955); and Kurt Lewin, *Resolving Social Conflicts: Selected Papers on Group Dynamics [1935–1946]* (New York: Harper, 1948).

initiatives with other media, and in the philanthropic foundations that supported these projects, I am convinced that the two-step flow model was equally the product of policy. In other words, the limited effects hypothesis of the impact of mass media emerged from an organized and concerted effort to establish a postwar liberal consensus built upon relations between ideas about mobile technology and group discussion.[49]

The film council movement, and its advancement of screen-mediated citizenship, was a major force directing the incorporation of film into diverse educational locations. *The Unique Contribution* (EBF, 1959), a film about Encyclopaedia Britannica Films' successful role in modernizing classrooms, ends with an encapsulation of the dominant sentiment about technological futures, though with a post-Sputnik anxiety in the subtext. Narrator Maurice B. Mitchell, then president of EBF, declares that films used by "forward looking teachers" are part of the nation that has "never before turned its back on a challenge to use the modern devices, the most advanced techniques, to solve its problems. Certainly in education we have a critical problem, and certainly in education we will make our greatest contribution to provide to those who deserve the most, our teachers, the tools that help them do the job that is so important to us." As the sites and occasions of education expanded, and as officially sanctioned curricula confronted novel community forms, authorities acting in the name of public interest sought to occupy that terrain, filling it with what they deemed to be appropriate tactics, subjects, and materials. Thus, a brand of vernacular film knowledge about the instructional and information genre was emerging, one that expressed a hierarchy of authority about a modern mass-mediated public sphere.

Filmography

Film and Radio—A Word about Citizen's Forums (1943) 3 min.
PRODUCTION: NFB. ACCESS: NFB.

Film and You (1948) 21 min.
PRODUCTION: NFB. PRODUCER: Donald Fraser. DIRECTORS: Jean Palardy, Donald Peters. CAMERA: Lorne C. Batchelor. MUSIC: Eldon Rathburn. A French-language version, *Conseil du Film,* was also produced. ACCESS: NFB.

---

[49] Anna McCarthy, *The Citizen Machine: Governing by Television in 1950s America* (New York: The New Press, 2010) develops this argument with respect to middlebrow, educational television.

Film Tactics (1945) 22 min. and 15 min. sd. b&w. 35mm and 16mm
PRODUCTION: U.S. Dept. of the Navy. PRODUCER: Harry Joe Brown. NOTE: In 1947, the U.S. Office of Education released this for public educational use; distributed by Castle Films. Released in 1974 by National Audiovisual Center (Washington, DC). ACCESS: University Libraries of Maryland, North Texas, Pittsburgh, South Carolina, and Idaho State; State Library of New South Wales, Australia.

The Gentle Art of Film Projection (1950) 21 min.
PRODUCTION: NFB. PRODUCER: Michael Spencer. DI-RECTOR/WRITER: Donald Peters. CAMERA: Lorne C. Batchelor. SOUND: Roger Beaudry. EDITOR: Pierre Bruneau, Victor Jobin. ANIMATION: Wolf Koenig. MUSIC: Eldon Rathburn. CAST: John Pratt. A French-language version, *Les joies innocentes de la projection,* was also produced. ACCESS: NFB.

Let's Talk about Films (1953) 18 min.
PRODUCTION: NFB. PRODUCER/DIRECTOR/WRITER: Julian Biggs. CAMERA: John Foster. SOUND: Joseph Champagne. EDITOR: Fergus McDonell. A French-language version, *Ciné-forum,* was also produced. ACCESS: NFB.

Looking Beyond . . . Story of a Film Council (1957) 18 min.
PRODUCTION: NFB. PRODUCER: Tom Daly. DIRECTOR/WRITER: Stanley Jackson. CAMERA: Robert Humble. SOUND: Clarke Daprato. EDITOR: William Greaves. ACCESS: NFB.

Making Films That Teach (1954) 18 min.
PRODUCTION: EBF. PRODUCER: Hal Kopel. ACCESS: Prelinger Archives; www.archive.org/details/MakingFi1954.

Projecting Motion Pictures (1951) 10 min., sd., b&w, 16mm
PRODUCTION: UCLA (Motion Picture Division, Dept. of Theatre Arts). DIRECTOR/WRITER: William E. Jordan. PHO-TOGRAPHER: Gabriel Hachigian. EDITOR: Tamara Webster. ACCESS: UCLA Film and Television Archive; Pacific Film Archive.

The Unique Contribution (1959) 28 min.
PRODUCTION: EBF. ACCESS: Prelinger Archives/LOC; www.archive.org/details/UniqueCo1959. www.archive.org/details/UniqueCo1959_2.

Related Films

After Prison What? (1951). NFB. 11 min.

Canada Dances (1947). NFB. 9 min.

Choosing a Classroom Film (1963). McGraw-Hill Text Films/Centron. 18 min. www.archive.org/details/Choosing1963.

Film Research and Learning (1956). W. A. Wittich. 12 min. www.archive.org/details/FilmRese1956.

Get Rid of Rats (1948). NFB. 10 min.

L'homme aux oiseaux (English version: *The Bird Fancier*) (1952). NFB. 29 min.

How to Conduct a Discussion Group (1954). EBF.

How to Organize a Discussion Group (1954). EBF.

How to Use Classroom Films (1963). McGraw-Hill Text Films/Centron. 14 min. www.archive.org/details/HowtoUse1963.

Just Weeds (1945). NFB. 21 min.

Kitchen Come True (1948). NFB. 18 min.

Lessons in Living (1944). NFB. 23 min.

Motion Film in the Classroom (1968). EML Corp. (Educational Media Laboratories, Austin, TX).

New Dimensions through Teaching Films (1963). Coronet. 27 min.

Room for Discussion (1953). EBF.

Seed Growing in Grand Forks (1947). NFB.

Teaching with Sound Films (1936). EBF.

Using the Classroom Film (1945). EBF.

The War on Want (1954). NFB. 15 min.

World of Plenty (1943). Paul Rotha. 42 min. www.screenonline.org.uk/film/id/560335/index.html.

Worth the Risk (1948). Central Office of Information, UK.

18 SCREEN CULTURE AND GROUP DISCUSSION IN POSTWAR RACE RELATIONS

ANNA McCARTHY

In 1954, when the United States Supreme Court's *Brown v. Board of Education* decision abolished racial segregation in public schools, many socially liberal community organizations began to develop techniques and strategies to help parents, teachers, and students cope with the demands of integration. The individuals and groups involved in this effort were known as the "intergroup relations movement," and one of the movement's first priorities was a focus on establishing contexts for group discussion. The technique of guiding group discussions occupied a privileged place in postwar liberal conceptions of civic practice. Political scientists described it as a "cultural prerequisite of democracy" and practitioners in applied fields such as social work saw it as a realization of the antitotalitarian mandate shaping postwar political psychology.[1] Guided group conversations, many integrationist reformers believed, would help individuals come to terms with the new racial reality. If blacks and whites engaged in constructive and frank dialogue, airing their hopes and fears about desegregation in a supportive and controlled context, they might better work together to identify and resolve problems that arose in the integration process. But creating these dialogues was not an easy task. For one thing, there was no guarantee that participants would cooperate; indeed, there was always the chance that face-to-face conversation might increase levels of alienation and resistance to change. How, reformers wondered, could they manage these discussions so that they arrived at a productive conclusion? The sheer scale of the endeavor was daunting, involving millions of people located in communities spread across large regions of the United States. Under these conditions, training discussion leaders and coordinating and monitoring discussions seemed at times inconceivable.

---

[1] Ernest S. Griffith, John Plamenatz, and J. Roland Pennock, "Cultural Prerequisites to a Successfully Functioning Democracy," *American Political Science Review* 50 (Mar. 1956): 108. Paul Bergevin and Dwight Morris, *A Manual for Group Discussion Participants* (New York: Seabury Press, 1965), 9. The classic articulation of the problem of authoritarianism in U.S. political culture is T. W. Adorno, *The Authoritarian Personality* (New York: Harper, 1950).

One solution was to enlist the help of the media. Along with educators and other nonprofit organizations, groups such as the National Conference of Christians and Jews (NCCJ) turned both to television and to 16mm film in their search for a method of outreach that might touch the largest number of people, providing citizens with tutelary texts that would help them talk about integration in their own neighborhoods and towns.[2] The screen technique they favored was the staged discussion session, in which a group of actors, often nonprofessional, modeled the act of interracial discussion for an audience that would then engage in discussions of its own. As an educational film technique, the onscreen discussion had shortcomings, most notably a tendency toward wooden acting styles and artificial, even preachy dialogue, which potentially diminished the technique's pedagogical effects. But these stylistic deficiencies should not obscure the broader cultural import of the onscreen discussion sessions. Through this dramatic technique, members of the governing classes imagined they might influence the minds and conduct of others. The didactic scripts and amateur performances in these filmed sessions modeled a particular kind of civic personhood in the *Brown* era, one based in Cold War ideals of personal sovereignty, centrist rationality, and civic virtue.

These postwar scenes of interracial dialogue may strike today's viewers as highly contrived, but in their very artifice they provide important historical insight into postwar liberalism and its contradictions. They not only staged templates for racial interaction but also, in their iconography and ideology, made visible some key racial assumptions in the liberal imagination. Indeed, the genre of screen discussion may have offered the intergroup relations movement a means for wide dissemination of its visions of citizenship. But it was also—at least in one memorable instance, discussed at the end of this essay—a powerful means for the critique of the mainstream liberal ideals on which these visions rested.

When approaching the question of how civic racial fellowship groups understood the pedagogical value of onscreen discussion, it is important to note at the outset that they did not consider film and television to be wholly separate spheres of moving image production and distribution; correspondingly, historians hoping to understand onscreen discussion as a particular technique in civic education cannot afford to apply criteria of medium specificity in assembling texts for analysis, at least where post-*Brown* integrationist education is concerned.

---

[2] For an explanation of the benefits of film and television for intergroup relations discussions, see J. L. Moreno, "The Concept of Sociodrama: A New Approach to the Problem of Inter-Cultural Relations," *Sociometry* 6 (Nov. 1943): 440, 449. For two helpful analyses of the strategic use of film discussion in broader programs of governmentality, see Heide Frances Solbrig, "Film and Function: A History of Industrial Motivation Film" (PhD diss., University of San Diego, 2004), 156; and Ronald W. Greene, "Y Movies: Film and the Modernization of Pastoral Power," *Communication and Critical/Cultural Studies* 2, no. 1 (Mar. 2005): 20–36.

To do so would not only obscure the broader political import of the form, it would also mischaracterize the culture of the moving image in which scenes of interracial discussion circulated. Groups like the NCCJ, the Southern Leadership Council, and others treated film and TV as complementary and contiguous arenas through which they could make contact with the community. The films they sponsored were not only distributed through 16mm rental catalogs, they were also sent to local television stations for airing in their (federally mandated) public service and educational programming hours.[3] Sometimes the two venues were combined. For example, the 16mm distribution agreement for *A City Decides*, a 1956 documentary about the successful integration of schools in St. Louis, Missouri, included local television rights for civic groups that purchased a print.[4] Moreover, many programs produced for public service broadcast were destined to enjoy a second life in the nontheatrical sphere. The 1957 discussion program called *Free Assembly*, for example, was initially presented as a live remote broadcast on KETC-TV (the St. Louis educational television station), but its producers planned to shoot subsequent episodes on 16mm film, allowing them to "edit out the dull and weedy and . . . make a half-hour package for other uses," including distribution to civic groups for use in their own discussions.[5] Even live broadcasts might be recorded on 16mm, via the Kinescope process, and sent out to civic groups and other nontheatrical, community-oriented venues for additional screenings. In short, when we talk about educational television in this pre-PBS era we are often, necessarily, talking about nontheatrical film at the same time, at least when it comes to civic education.

---

[3] As Steve Classen's excellent study *Watching Jim Crow: The Struggles over Mississippi TV, 1955–1969* reveals, public service was a highly elastic category, expanding to encompass such sponsors as the White Citizens Council in the South (Durham, NC: Duke University Press, 2004). Heather Hendershot uncovers other examples of illiberal civic speech in "Cold War Right-Wing Broadcasting: H. L. Hunt, Dan Smoot, and the Unraveling of Consensus Culture," paper presented at the annual meeting of the American Studies Association, Oct. 12, 2006.

[4] Leo Dratfield [nontheatrical film distributor] to Edward Reed, Mar. 21, 1957, Fund for the Republic Records, box 108, folder 10, Public Policy Papers, Dept. of Rare Books and Special Collections, Princeton University Library.

[5] Martin Quigley [Jr.] to W. H. "Ping" Ferry, Jan. 30, 1957, Fund for the Republic Records (per n. 4, above). If St. Louis figures large in the story of public service television program in this chapter, it is in part a result of archiving and preservation. Quigley, the producer of *A City Decides* and a former KETC station manager, had strong personal connections to the civil rights and civil liberties philanthropy group the Fund for the Republic. The Fund sponsored a number of film and television projects aimed at supporting integration, several in St. Louis. The organization's papers, held at the Seeley G. Mudd library in Princeton, are extensive. Because they contain many documents recording frank conversations about techniques and imagery for reaching "the masses," they are an invaluable source for understanding the terms in which elites understood television and other media as tools for governance. Quigley is not to be confused with his father, Martin J. Quigley, prominent film industry publisher and coauthor of Hollywood's Production Code of 1930.

A good example of how intergroup relations organizations approached the process of staging onscreen discussions in the wake of the *Brown* decision is a locally produced program from St. Louis entitled *Soap Box*, also produced by KETC-TV. In February 1955, the series devoted four episodes to staged discussions concerning the integration of the city's high-school system scheduled for that fall. The last episode, "Teacher's Meeting on Integration," is archived in the Peabody Awards Collection at the University of Georgia, a collection that contains many kinescoped examples of the period's socially progressive ambitions for television. *Soap Box* was one of numerous public discussion forums designed to bring together white people and Negroes (the terminology of the time) and facilitate the transition to integration in 1955 St. Louis. Some of these community dialogues were teacher workshops and parent meetings organized by the St. Louis school board. Others were administered by groups such as the Urban League, the Parent Teacher Association (PTA), and the National Conference of Christians and Jews. These last two groups were sponsors of this particular episode, and their members played various roles in the discussion that enfolded onscreen. Quite likely, judging by its highly pedagogical mode of address, a Kinescope of the episode was distributed to local chapters for additional screenings that might be supplemented with discussion among the audience members.

The program began with a message from *Soap Box*'s host, a lanky thirty-year-old with a crew cut named Ranlet "Ran" Lincoln. The St. Louis PTA sponsored this particular episode and, as Lincoln explained, the evening's broadcast was somewhat unusual. Four PTA members were going to role-play community concerns about integrated classrooms for the home audience, acting out "typical ideas, feelings, and attitudes in a more concentrated form than we would find in real life." Their role-play was facilitated by a trained intergroup relations consultant from the NCCJ, a visibly nervous woman named Dr. Jean Grams. As the program progressed it quickly became clear that its participants weren't accustomed to theatrics. But although they stumbled on their words and glanced uncomfortably at cue cards, the sincerity of their performances communicated the PTA's commitment to television as a vehicle for democratic pedagogy. The PTA's members were active in the Educational Television Commission, the civic body that administered station KETC-TV (known locally as the "panel channel"). The group also raised $100,000 in door-to-door donations to help build the studio in which *Soap Box*'s guests were sitting, a converted women's gymnasium housing two cameras, a control room, and the kinescope machine on which the episode was recorded.[6]

The televised enactment that evening centered on the preconceptions teachers and parents might bring to a particular situation: a Negro fifth-grade teacher's decision to award a low conduct mark to Johnny Jones, a little white

---

[6] Martin Quigley, "Home Grown TV in St. Louis," *Harpers*, July 1955, 39–44.

boy. The performances were staged against a stylized map of the Americas that might well remind viewers of the international scrutiny surrounding the *Brown* decision. But the content of the PTA's pedagogical drama was highly localized, foregrounding the difficulties of parent-teacher communication. To address the problem, Dr. Grams asks the role-playing parents and teachers to talk with each other about solutions. Throwing himself into the part, the man playing Johnny's blustery father confronts the Negro teacher, Mrs. Smith, saying that "Mrs. Clark" (a white teacher) had never contacted him about problems with Johnny in *her* classroom. "Mrs. Smith" listens patiently, then responds quietly and respectfully. Her speech focuses on their commonalities, offering the ecumenical observation that "we both are fearful," and concludes with the suggestion that she and he meet on an individual basis to discuss the problem. The discussion stretches on, touching on the pros and cons of large and small meetings, letters and phone calls, home visits, open houses, voluntarism, and other ways that teachers and parents might interact. Dr. Grams tries not to glance at the camera as she offers her summation, explaining that face-to-face interaction was the only way to achieve "understanding" in this "stressful" period. At the end of the program, Lincoln steps in and suggests to the viewer that watching the preceding role-play was one way of starting such conversations. "You've been participating in the last of three teachers meetings on education," he announces in voiceover, making it clear that watching *Soap Box* was not passive entertainment but a form of active democratic involvement.

If Lincoln seemed sure of this alignment of broadcasting and civic governance, it was undoubtedly a reflection of his own experience. After serving in the navy during World War II he attended St. John's, the "Great Books" college in Annapolis, Maryland. While there he produced an FM radio discussion show called *Backgrounds in Democracy,* in which guests like Secretary of the Army Frank Pace Jr. discussed John Locke's "Second Essay on Civil Government" (1690) and other classic liberal texts.[7] *Soap Box*'s PTA role-players, uncredited in the KETC-TV broadcast, would certainly not have questioned his equation of viewership and democratic participation. Although they were clearly uncomfortable in front of the camera, they undoubtedly viewed the reenactment of social problems as a crucial therapeutic tool for group governance. Psychologist Jacob Moreno developed role-playing, or sociodrama, as a sociometric technique in the 1920s. By the late 1940s it was flourishing, adopted by schools, social service organizations and civic bodies, along with labor unions and corporations, to solve collective problems and educate participants on topics ranging from alcohol abuse to world peace. Role-play was usually coupled with discussion in these situations, and Dr. Grams's performance as *Soap Box*'s discussion leader reflected current thinking on how such conversations should proceed.

---

[7] Sidney Lohman, "News of TV and Radio," *New York Times,* Apr. 23, 1950.

Focusing not on abstract concepts but on concrete situations, her interjections moved the dialogue toward active problem-solving, in order that the group might collectively identify possible courses of actions.[8] As a representative of the intergroup relations movement, she readily voiced its key suppositions. Located at the nexus of psychology, sociological research, social work, civic practice, and school and adult education, the intergroup relations movement aimed at the abolition of prejudice and inequality through concerted forms of interpersonal contact.[9] Talking and listening across racial lines was, the technique's advocates believed, a vehicle for reconciliation through which participants would uncover their common humanity and learn to see beyond skin color to the person "beneath."

Soap Box, with its tutelary style, its use of nonprofessional role-players rather than actors, and, as I'll eventually explain, its mobilization of a figure of saintly outreach in the form of Miss Smith, encapsulates the template for progressive racial governance that liberal groups hoped onscreen discussion would provide. These elements of the technique reflected the epistemological tenets and practical agendas defining liberal social science in the first decades of the Cold War, when pressing questions about individual and mass psychology, as well as the relation of the extremes to the center, dominated debates about popular self-governance in mainstream political culture. Some of the intergroup relations movement's suppositions about racial difference are easy to criticize. The issue here is not so much the failings or shortcomings of the movement but rather the way its contradictory or ambivalent ideas about postwar race relations found expression in the visual and verbal rhetoric of onscreen discussion, along with definitions of the problems in racial governance that discussion scenes in film and television were supposed to solve.

Discussion Films and Postwar Political Culture

The combination of screenings and group discussions appealed to intergroup relations professionals for a number of reasons, all of which reflected the dominant Cold War conception of good citizenship as a personal, ethical responsibility based in the reasoned exercise of individual sovereignty and located at a remove from the potentially oppressive matrix of state power (identified, in this period, with the dehumanizing state apparatus of the Soviet system). In the prevailing view, racial reconciliation through discussion was a process that required,

---

[8] William Vickery, "Ten Years of Intergroup Education Workshops: Some Comparisons and Contrasts," *Journal of Educational Sociology* 26 (Mar. 1953): 293–302.

[9] Walter A. Jackson, *Gunnar Myrdal and America's Conscience: Social Engineering and Racial Liberalism, 1938–1987* (Chapel Hill: University of North Carolina Press, 1994), 280.

in one participant's words, "personal contact and personal participation."[10] But handbooks and manuals also acknowledged the many ways that personal interaction through discussion might serve to entrench, rather than overcome, particular attitudes and roles. Recounting an awkward encounter between a protestant minister and a rabbi watching television together at an intergroup relations conference, the authors of the 1955 *Manual of Intergroup Relations* noted that "persons inexperienced in intergroup relations frequently alienate minority persons with whom they wish to be friendly by inadvertently using the language of prejudice."[11]

Role-play was seen as a potent tool for overcoming the attitudes that gave rise to such awkward and alienating social interactions. Although it involved the adoption of false personae, it seemed at the time to provide a means for discovering social truths that conformed closely to broader ideas about representative democracy. Political culture in the United States during the decade following World War II moved away from the agonistic New Deal model of civic life as a dynamic of forces and fronts and headed toward the technocratic conception of the polity as an aggregation of interest groups.[12] Role-play, coupled with group discussion, embodied the postwar idea of democratic deliberation as a process of voicing, and balancing, *interests*, an approach quite distinct from the model of group discussion associated with the prewar Forum Movement, which focused less on mobilizing abstract categories like the interest group and more on activating a local community's potential for active self-governance.[13] As sociologist Claude C. Bowman explained in a 1949 issue of the left-liberal journal *Social*

---

[10] H. H. Giles, "The Present Status and Programs of Private Intergroup Relations Agencies," *Journal of Negro Education* 20, no. 3 (Summer 1951): 418.

[11] John P. Dean and Alex Rosen, *A Manual of Intergroup Relations* (Chicago: Phoenix Books/University of Chicago Press, 1963 [1955]), 12, 10.

[12] David Truman outlined the theory of interest groups in his 1951 classic *The Governmental Process: Political Interests and Public Opinion* (New York: Knopf, 1951). For a critique, see Theodore J. Lowi, *The End of Liberalism: The Second Republic of the United States* (Ann Arbor: University of Michigan Press, 1969). Lowi sees the 1960s and 70s as the period of ascendancy for interest group politics, but the seeds are evident in conceptions of power-sharing in the Eisenhower years—consider, for example, the manufactured professional, economic, and cultural diversity embodied in the memberships of the proliferating boards and committees that made up the infrastructure of establishment networking. See also Ira Katznelson, "Was the Great Society a Lost Opportunity?" for a critique of labor leadership's assimilation into interest group politics in this period (in *The Rise and Fall of the New Deal Order, 1930–1980*, ed. Steve Fraser and Gary Gerstle [Princeton, NJ: Princeton University Press, 1989], 185–211).

[13] On Progressive-Era and New Deal conceptualizations of democratic group discussion, see David Goodman, "Democracy and Public Discussion in the Progressive and New Deal Eras: From Civic Competence to the Expression of Opinion," *Studies in American Political Development* 18 (2004): 81–111. See also William M. Keith, *Democracy as Discussion: Civic Education and the American Forum Movement* (Lanham, MD: Lexington Books, 2007).

Forces, "Situations involving thousands or millions of persons can be reduced to a relatively few type-roles."[14]

Given the centrality of the technique for postwar conceptualizations of the governance process, it is not surprising that role-play should appear in *Soap Box.* Its inclusion as a dramatic technique signaled a commitment to social science as a resource for civic pedagogy. Moreover, in its obvious artifice, role-play positioned viewers as observers of behavioral examples rather than as spectators identifying with naturalistic characters. This distinction is important to maintain. For Moreno, who invented role-play and was consequently its most vocal advocate, one of the advantages of the technique was the commitment to impartiality it required of the role-player. The participant, he explained, must "detach himself as far as possible from everything in his own collective life which might bias him toward one or another of the cultures portrayed."[15] In drawing on role-play's distinctive style of nonnaturalistic acting, the discussion film engineered exposure to multiple viewpoints and used its actors to model for viewers a kind of selfhood based not in emotional immediacy but rather in rational, detached reflection. Thus, although films that used nonprofessional actors to role-play discussion methods are easily criticized for their bad acting, it is important to consider that part of their educational value lay in the manifestly antinaturalistic performances they contained. Role-play's wooden acting provided viewers with a tangible reminder of the valued sociological distinction between individuals and their social roles. (The overacted performance of Johnny's insinuatingly prejudiced father in *Soap Box* is a case in point.) This disconnect between the role-player and the social position he or she ventriloquized conformed to a Cold War ideal of personhood: the rational citizen, who was a centrist capable of understanding more than one perspective, rather than a single-minded extremist; and a subject capable of transcending personal interests in the service of self-governance on an individual and group level.[16]

---

[14] Claude C. Bowman, "Role Playing and the Development of Insight," *Social Forces* 28 (Dec. 1949): 199.

[15] Moreno, "Sociodrama," 448, 446. Role-play was, in other words, the *opposite* of the "method acting" coming into prominence in the dramatic arts at the time. For more on this, see Jon Mackenzie, *Perform or Else: From Discipline to Performance* (New York: Routledge, 2001); Rebekah Kowal, "Modern Dance and American Culture in the Early Cold War Years" (PhD diss., New York University, 1999); Louis Scheeder, "American Performance and the Cold War, 1947–1961," (PhD diss., New York University, 2004); Marianne Conroy, "Acting Out: Method Acting, the National Culture, and the Middlebrow Disposition in Cold War America," *Criticism* 35, no. 2 (Spring 1993): 239–63.

[16] For a discussion of this civic figuration, see Ronald Walter Greene and Darren Hicks, "Lost Convictions: Debating Both Sides and the Ethical Self-Fashioning of Liberal Citizens," *Cultural Studies* 19 (Jan. 2005): 121. On its role in the development of rational choice theory, see S. M. Amadae, *Rationalizing Capitalist Democracy: The Cold War Origins of Rational Choice Theory* (Chicago: University of Chicago Press, 2003).

But role-play and discussion were not enough by themselves. Expert guidance was crucial to this process of exemplifying citizenship. The presence of people like kindly Dr. Grams, listening to and guiding the heated conversation staged by the role-players of *Soap Box*, was essential to the pedagogical outcome of group discussion both onscreen and off. This conceptualization of expertise was not new: Walter Lippmann had argued in *Public Opinion* (1922) that deliberative discussion must always moderate "partisan voices" with reasoned and knowledgeable expert opinions. In ensuing decades, broadcast discussion, promising to distribute specialist advice and opinion on a mass scale, bolstered this technocratic ideal. As a 1947 handbook accompanying recordings of the radio program *America's Town Meeting of the Air* explained, "Adult discussion groups may through recordings secure the direction of experts, and find in them stimulation for thinking and study."[17] But in the era of *Brown*, a period when social scientists began to focus more and more on the place of individual identity and group identification in civic governance, Lippmann's top-down fantasy of expert social engineering was not enough.[18]

In addition to experts, onscreen discussion about integration needed some means to help viewers identify with and internalize the process of reconciliation being acted out onscreen. One pathway to achieving this affect involved ensuring that onscreen discussion was always complemented by discussion among the audience.[19] Another involved providing viewers with positive exemplars with whom they might identify, and who might model the kinds of reparative speech acts necessary for the radical restructuring of the racial order. Each was an application of a point of consensus in the realm of social practice formed at the intersection of social scientific research and social work: the idea that individuals are the product of a group environment, that they learn from their peers and from the immediate social contexts in which they circulate.[20]

This focus on the individual's environment was immensely important in the context of integration. The *Brown* decision drew heavily on the findings of Kenneth Clark, Gunnar Myrdal, E. Franklin Frazier, and other social and behavioral scientists when it asserted that living in a segregated environment generated among Negro children "a feeling of inferiority as to their status in the community

---

[17] *Recordings for Classrooms and Discussion Groups* (New York: New Tools for Learning, 1947), n.p.

[18] On the rise of identity in postwar social science and in mainstream cultural forms, see Leerom Medovoi, *Rebels: Youth and the Cold War Origins of Identity* (Durham, NC: Duke University Press, 2005).

[19] Giles, "Present Status and Programs," 415.

[20] Kurt Lewin's "action research" paradigm in the study of group dynamics, and the "two-step flow" model devised by Elihu Katz and Paul Lazarsfeld, are two examples of this conception of individual-group relations. See Lewin, *Field Theory in Social Science* (New York: Harper, 1951); and Katz and Lazarsfeld, *Personal Influence* (New York: Free Press, 1955).

that may affect their hearts and minds in a way unlikely ever to be undone."[21] A tainted civic environment enforcing negative role models threatened both the practice of democratic citizenship and the development of the healthy individual. However, interactive social experiments like role-play, combined with group screenings and discussions, allowed intergroup relations experts the opportunity to rebuild the damaging social environment from the bottom up. Screen culture was crucial for this process of social rebuilding because the visual language of the moving image encouraged emotional identification on the part of the spectator. "Through movies, panel discussions, and bull sessions we soon learned what it felt like to be a Negro in this country," recalled one intergroup relations trainee, who felt that this awareness would never have been awakened were participants simply required to "sit through all the lectures ever given on theoretical race relations."[22]

Discussion films and television programs thus triangulated the expertise of trained professionals with the intimate learning context of the small group, encouraging empathic awareness. They allowed intergroup relations professionals to coach viewers by example, showing them how to create an interpersonal environment in which democracy, and the sovereign individuals comprising it, might flourish. However, as will shortly become clear, the pedagogical examples installed in the onscreen discussion group sometimes signified more than they were supposed to, laying bare in the process some of the ambivalences and shortcomings of liberal race talk in the *Brown* era.

The Burden of the Example

Leading by example is a seemingly straightforward and transparent pedagogical tool, but in the postwar period it was a process that took on complex meanings. Its presence in the media of discussion was a discursive and material link to broader tensions and conflicts, extending beyond the interpersonal scale on which intergroup relations professionals sought to effect meaningful change. In the case of *Soap Box*, the ethics of exemplarity so evident onscreen reflected a broader sense of example-setting associated with a specific historical context: the 1955 desegregation of the St. Louis school system. Widely upheld as a model for other school districts, the city's relatively untroubled process of integration was, for many observers, the product of tireless efforts to promote intergroup

---

[21] *Brown v. Board of Education* quoted in Ellen Herman, *The Romance of American Psychology: Political Culture in the Age of Experts* (Berkeley: University of California Press, 1995), 198. For a thorough treatment of social scientists' role in the *Brown* decision, see John L. Jackson, *Social Scientists for Social Justice: Making the Case against Segregation* (New York: NYU Press, 2001).

[22] Dean and Rosen, *Manual of Intergroup Relations*, 47.

discussion in the community on the part of civic groups like the PTA and the NCCJ.[23] The national impression of the city as an exemplar in desegregation was heightened by the success of *A City Decides*, the aforementioned 1956 television documentary on the topic. Although there is no evidence that it was released theatrically, the film was nominated for an Academy Award in the documentary short subject category; it was also broadcast in public service time on NBC stations in 1957 and distributed widely to civic and educational groups for screening and discussion. It was funded by a grant from the Fund for the Republic, a group devoted to education and research in civil liberties and civil rights and wryly described by Dwight Macdonald as a "wholly disowned subsidiary" of the Ford Foundation. The film included in its cast at least one of *Soap Box*'s PTA-member performers. It was produced and written by Charles Guggenheim, the first station manager of KETC-TV, who would later go on to become a prominent documentarian.

Discussion groups and the complexities of group social processes figure prominently in the film, and the examples (positive and negative) that they set play a central role in the pedagogical mission of *A City Decides*. Ten years after its release, film librarian William J. Sloan observed that although the film was noteworthy in revealing "the fears of Negro parents in having their children attend school with white children," it was "aimed primarily at preparing the white community for integration."[24] Writing at a point when the cinema verité style was ascendant, Sloan judged this goal as a limit on the film's progressive political value, even though mainstream liberal thinking at the time *A City Decides* was made located the full political potential of such films as much in the postviewing discussion process as in the material onscreen.[25] Still, the film clearly strived to set the agenda from which conversations about the film would proceed, heavily emphasizing the responsibilities of the individual and suggesting that the interpersonal scale is where democracy succeeds or falters. In one notable scene, the

---

[23] As a *New York Times* editorial noted, "a campaign of public education by community leaders" was crucial in ensuring that integration was "effected quietly and without incident." "St. Louis Sets an Example," *New York Times,* Feb. 2, 1955. See also Monroe Billington, "Public School Integration in Missouri, 1954–1964," *Journal of Negro Education* (Summer 1966): 253.

[24] William J. Sloan, "The Evolution of the Integration Film," *Journal of the Society of Cinematologists* 4 (1964–65): 67.

[25] Like many documentaries from this period, *A City Decides* was a dramatized essay that relied extensively on reenactment, hoping to set examples for other communities facing integration by showing how St. Louis citizens collectively addressed potential problems in the process. Its claim to documentary status is therefore very much a product of the period; *A City Decides* and other films using reenactment located the documentary idea not in the emergent cinema verité or Direct Cinema aesthetic, but in the combination of a manifestly educational objective with the use of a nonprofessional cast playing either themselves or representative community members.

camera visits a crowded meeting hall where parents are gathered to pose questions about integration to a panel of teachers, school administrators, educational psychologists, and intergroup relations specialists. The parents' blushing performances and hesitant speeches indicate that they are not actors but participants recruited from the community; the officials on the panel, on the other hand, play themselves.[26] As the parents recite their half-memorized lines, the film's main character, a teacher, interprets in voiceover the meanings of their questions for the viewer. "I'd like to know what our school plans on doing about things like social dancing," a white man asks, clutching his infant son out of nervousness. The voiceover whispers the subtext underlying his words: "He's worried about intermarriage." The panel members forthrightly address these hidden worries when they answer the parents' questions. In thus airing examples of the kinds of disingenuous or mealy-mouthed speech acts that might arise in interracial discussion, the film worked to encourage candor and transparency in discussions that might take place around its own screening.

But example-setting worked on another level in the film too. Perhaps more significant, however, at least in relation to the broader shortcomings of *Brown*-era liberal humanism, is the way black participants figure in its interracial discussions. Each unfailingly enacts an authoritative and authentic modeling of humanity and civic depth. After listening to the concerns of some white teenagers, a poised young black woman has the last word at an intergroup youth meeting: "I think it's the individual that counts. How are you going to get to know a person unless you meet them?" she asserts, echoing the intergroup relations movement's ethos of interpersonal contact. This focus on the interpersonal dimensions of race relations was no doubt crucial for getting people to cooperate with *Brown*, but it stifled any possible questions about the roles of social institutions and underlying structural inequalities in the process of racial oppression. Conforming closely to the tenets of sacred individualism on which the so-called Free World defined its opposition to other political systems, most pressingly communism, the interpersonal focus made it easy to sidestep questions of white privilege. *A City Decides* further disavowed the force of racial difference in its final scene, in which black and white teens reconcile and the voiceover asserts their universal commonalities as teenagers.

---

[26] The Urban League representative is introduced as "Mr. Bohannon." An oral history of Vivian Dreer mentions that Leo Bohannon was head of the local Urban League chapter in the 1950s. Vivian Dreer, interview by Doris Wesley, University of Missouri–St. Louis, 1995, in Western Historical Manuscript Collection, University of Missouri–St. Louis, www.umsl.edu/~whmc/guides/oral.htm. Reba Mosby's oral history records that Virgil Border, who runs the meeting in the film, was the head of the regional branch of the National Conference of Christians and Jews. Reba Mosby, interview by Dr. Richard Resh, St. Louis, Missouri, July 9, 1970, in Western Historical Manuscript Collection, www.umsl.edu/~whmc/guides/bclp.htm.

In asking black discussion participants to carry the moral weight of the integrationist message, exemplifying the kind of humanity to which all should aspire, *A City Decides* drew on the contradictory racial logic that shaped U.S. efforts to exemplify nationhood in the Cold War. According to George F. Kennan, architect of the diplomatic policy of containment, the United States should endeavor to demonstrate the value of freedom and democracy to totalitarian nations by displaying "its own confidence and patience, but particularly the integrity and dignity of its example." The latter, for many liberal internationalists of Kennan's mindset, included the example of improved race relations.[27] It is interesting, moreover, to note that the exemplary qualities he ascribes to the United States—patience, dignity, and integrity—were also embodied in the performances of individuals like Miss Smith, the Negro teacher who serves as the voice of reason and conciliation in *Soap Box* and whose thoughtful concern sets an example for the rest of the group. These same qualities were often ascribed to figures like Ralph Bunche, whose overseas visibility in the postwar years helped counteract the negative international image of the United States created by Southern segregation. Bunche, along with hundreds of black artists, athletes, and writers sent overseas by the State Department, was meant to exemplify the artistic and intellectual opportunities black Americans enjoyed in the system of capitalist democracy.[28] Instrumentalized because of their race, such figures embodied a paradoxical mode of exceptionalism that was central to the characterization of blacks in white liberal race-talk in the 1950s.

The authoritative examples set by black participants in interracial discussion onscreen in the *Brown* era mobilized an enduring trope in the visual culture of progressive racial reform: the "exemplary Negro." A figure familiar to us today from the spate of Hollywood films in which, as K. Anthony Appiah notes, black characters embody a deeper "ethical principle," the exemplary Negro has occupied a privileged place in the liberal humanist imagination since the abolitionist movement.[29] Not simply a "model minority" accepted and approved of by whites—think of the Negro persona associated with Sidney Poitier in this period, indelibly

---

[27] George F. Kennan quoted in John Lewis Gaddis, *Strategies of Containment* (New York: Oxford University Press, 2005), 49. See also Anders Stephanson, *George Kennan and the Art of Foreign Policy* (Cambridge, MA: Harvard University Press, 1989), 95.

[28] Penny Von Eschen, *The Cold War and the Color Line: Black Americans and Anticolonialism, 1937–1957* (Ithaca, NY: Cornell University Press, 1997), 128. For an extended treatment of the role of black Americans in U.S. cultural diplomacy, see her *Satchmo Blows Up the World* (Cambridge, MA: Harvard University Press, 2004). See also Melinda M. Schwenk-Borrell, "Selling Democracy: The United States Information Agency's Portrayal of American Race Relations, 1953–1976" (PhD diss., University of Pennsylvania, 2004).

[29] K. Anthony Appiah, "'No Bad Nigger': Blacks as the Ethical Principle in the Movies," in *Media Spectacles,* ed. Marjorie Garber, Jann Matlock, and Rebecca Walkowitz (New York: Routledge, 1993), 80. On the problematic exemplarity of Frederick Douglass in abolitionism, see Gustavus T. Stadler, *Troubling Minds* (Minneapolis: University of Minnesota Press, 2006).

stamped with the adjective *dignified*—the exemplary Negro is also a figure of therapeutic reparation whose oratorical self-presence facilitates white liberal self-realization, setting an example of authenticity and "civic depth."[30] For black intellectuals of the postwar period, the demands of serving as the moral conscience of the social microcosm and a figure of exemplarity for humanity as a whole were grating. Historian J. Saunders Redding, the first black professor hired by an Ivy League school, raged against such expectations in his anguished 1951 memoir *On Being Negro in America*. He condemned "the specialization of the sense and talent and learning…expected of Negroes by other members of their race and by whites," calling it "tragic and vicious and divisive." As Ross Posnock notes, Redding's memoir was "one of the frankest confessions of disgust with exemplarity and the 'obligations imposed by race.'"[31] To be seen only as a figurehead or a mouthpiece was to experience a profoundly one-dimensional life, flattened by the pressure not only to look perfect in white eyes but also to help white interlocutors hone their own self-awareness for personal enrichment and the greater social good.

Such critiques of the exemplary Negro figure gathered force within the broader U.S. discourse on race and racialization throughout the 1950s. However, they remained largely absent from onscreen discussions of intergroup relations, with one notable, and vigorously critical, exception: a 1959 essay film, part narrative and part lecture, called *The Cry of Jazz*. Produced by four black men from Chicago, the film was an attack aimed with ferocious directness at the liberal discussion culture that programs like *Soap Box* and *A City Decides* sought to foster. Indeed, we can see in its exploitation of the screen practices of the intergroup relations movement a point of frictional contact between the emerging color consciousness that would come to define black activism in the 1960s and the currents of Cold War era political thought, each struggling for ownership of the exemplary language of freedom, responsibility, and individualism.

The Examples Talk Back

The narrative portion of *The Cry of Jazz* is fairly simple: an interracial discussion at a meeting of the Parkwood Jazz Club explodes with conflict when white members claim that rock and roll is a form of jazz. The wooden acting of the

---

[30] See Christopher Castiglia, "Abolition's Racial Interiors and the Making of White Civic Depth," *American Literary History* 14, no. 1 (2002): 32–59, for a detailed account of this process in the nineteenth century. See John Nickel, "Disabling African American Men: Liberalism and Race Message Films," *Cinema Journal* 44 (Autumn 2004): 27–28, for an account closer to the period under discussion here.

[31] J. Saunders Redding, *On Being Negro in America* (New York: Charter Books, 1951), 27; Ross Posnock, *Color and Culture: Black Writers and the Making of the Modern Intellectual* (Cambridge, MA: Harvard University Press, 1998), 32.

semiprofessional cast is highly reminiscent of an educational film's staged role-play, but the dialogue exudes a level of antagonism rarely, if ever, encountered in the genre. Whites protest the idea that only Negroes could have created jazz, accusing blacks of "always singing the blues." Blacks tell whites that they have no

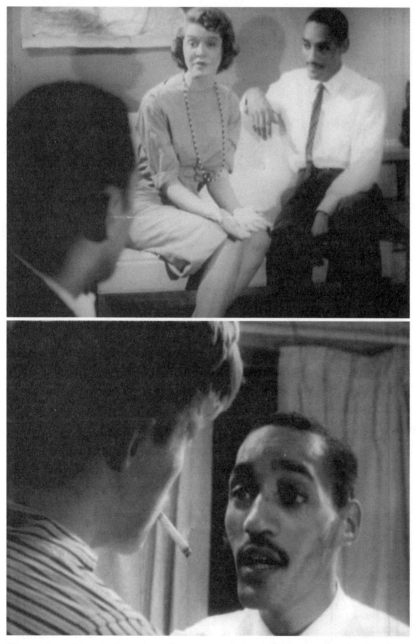

Figure 18.1. Onscreen discussions of intergroup relations. Alex lectures the white jazz fans at a meeting of the Parkwood Jazz Club. (Courtesy of Ed Bland.)

Figure 18.1. (*continued*)

souls, that they are not and never can be human. Alex, a black jazz arranger who serves as the de facto narrator of the film, lectures the young white audience in the film with acid condescension, demolishing their suppositions about rock and roll, the liberal idea of sameness under the skin, and the authenticity of white jazz. These didactic discussions are interspersed with scenes in which the camera roams lyrically through the vernacular landscape of black Chicago life, visiting jazz clubs, barbershops, churches, and pool halls, as well as apartments that bear witness to the degradations of poverty. Alex's voiceover annotates these scenes with a complex and esoteric theory, at once musicological and cultural, which locates both jazz and Negro experience in the tension between structure and play, the "escapist reward" of the "eternal present," and the legacy of suffering.

The de facto expert within the film, Alex also embodies the figure of the Negro truth-teller, but he transforms the role entirely. Instead of serving as the liberal exemplar of common humanity, he takes the position of the provocateur, doggedly asserting that American Negroes' experience of suffering and oppression renders them fundamentally different from white Americans. It is a schism that the film never resolves. Bemoaning exemplarity, "the terrible burden the Negro has in trying to teach American whites how to become human," Alex proposes that "America's soul is an empty void," asking, "Where else does its future image as a world power reside but in the dark soul of the Negro?" This concluding question, posed over a slow zoom into the face of a carved African statuette, references the Cold War politics of expediency in which the need to solve America's international image problem motivated the push to solve its segregation problem, the image serving as a reminder of the rising tide of decolonization and the new demands of nonaligned nations. But the instrumentalist logic of expediency has been inverted by this point in the film. Invoked at the

Figure 18.2. Silhouette of the Sun Ra Arkestra in *The Cry of Jazz* (1959): bassist Ronald Boykins and Sun Ra's hands at the piano. (Courtesy of Ed Bland.)

Figure 18.2. (*continued*)

conclusion of Alex's invective, the mainstream Cold War liberal argument for integration seems to serve primarily as a legitimizing vehicle for black expressions of rage, demonstrating the falsehood of the assimilationist liberal creed of sameness under the skin.

The Cry of Jazz was produced by khtb Productions, a group of four men whose lowercase initials made up the title of their company. Mark Kennedy, Nelam Hill, Eugene Titus, and Edward Bland met in the navy during World War II. After the war, all four moved to Chicago, where Bland, Titus, and Hill took classes at the University of Chicago. Bland, a native of the city, worked in the local jazz scene and composed music for independent films. Hill, born in Gary, Indiana, worked as a planner for the city. Titus, originally from Selma, Alabama, was a doctoral student in mathematics working on an air force missile project. Kennedy, born in Kansas City, was a writer whose first novel, *The Pecking Order* (1953), recounted a day in the life of a Chicago youth gang. After its publication Kennedy moved to New York to write his second novel (never published), although he collaborated with Bland and Hill from afar on *The Cry of Jazz*. Bland is credited as the director of the film, and the titles announce that the film is based on *The Fruits of the Death of Jazz,* his unpublished book manuscript. However, their frequent correspondence in this period, along with other materials documenting the film's production and reception archived with Hill's papers at the New York Public Library, indicate significant levels of collaboration, particularly in the writing process.[32] More importantly, the khtb archive provides remarkable insight into the way that the politics of exemplarity that circumscribed intergroup relations might be read from the perspective of black participants, preserving in the producers' correspondence hugely entertaining eye-level accounts of actual discussion sessions surrounding the film.

The khtb team hoped to get airtime on television, but only a few TV broadcasters were willing to screen their film. Although a number were interested in looking at it, only one, WHDH-TV in Boston, put it on the air, as an excerpt. Educational stations were the most willing to program it, but they couldn't afford the fee, and indeed, given that such films as *A City Decides* were available in a weekly quota from the Educational Television Center that supplied them with film programming, they had little incentive to generate controversy.[33] NBC executives previewed the film but decided to pass—hardly a surprise given the network's policy of "integration without identification," that is, using black performers without commenting on their race.[34] However the film circulated widely in overseas TV markets and domestically in 16mm circles, where it attracted interest from college campuses, film and jazz clubs, and civic organizations.

Critics were divided in their opinions about the film's social and aesthetic value.[35] The *Christian Science Monitor*'s Robert Colby Nelson echoed the views of many. Quoting its producers' goals—*The Cry of Jazz* was a critique of "'northern liberals'" and 'their sentimental romanticisms'"—he noted that "some viewers—Negro and white—have indignantly walked out on showings," and asked, nervously, "will this bring enlightenment or just more upset thinking about racial affairs?"[36] Those individuals who rented the film from khtb through its distributor, Ideal Pictures, occasionally conveyed similar assessments in their

---

[32] Emile de Antonio, "Credits and Cast: *The Cry of Jazz*," n.d. (draft of program notes for the New Yorker Theater), box 4, folder 25, Nelam Hill Papers, New York Public Library Schomburg Center (hereafter NHP). Eugene Titus seems to have played only a minor role in the production and distribution of the film, although I noticed when going through the files that the breakup of his marriage, his subsequent depression, and the matter of his original $1,000 investment in the film, find occasional mention in the correspondence.

[33] Of the seven stations interested in broadcasting *The Cry of Jazz*, two of them were not affiliated with a national network and four of them were educational. The one that actually aired an excerpt was WHDH, the ABC affiliate in Boston, on its highly regarded public affairs program *Dateline Boston*. See box 3, folders 14, 15, 18, 19, 20, NHP. On overseas screenings see box 4, folder 23.

[34] On NBC race policy see Dianne Brooks, "They Dig Her Message: Opera, Television, and the Black Diva," in *Hop on Pop: The Politics and Pleasures of Popular Cultures*, ed. Henry Jenkins, Tara McPherson, and Jane Shattuc (Durham, NC: Duke University Press), 306–7.

[35] Jazz critics were united in their objections to its claims about the form's essential blackness, and its death. Bland to Hill, n.d. (circa 1960), box 1, folder 8, NHP.

[36] Robert Colby Nelson, "The Negro in the City," *Christian Science Monitor*, June 6, 1960.

correspondence with Bland, Hill, and Kennedy. Marsha R. Porte, a Dallas librarian, typed comments on the back of her print return slip, complaining about the sound quality and concluding that "on the whole, the film would antagonize viewers rather than enlighten them or enlist their sympathy and understanding."[37]

Not surprisingly, educators were especially concerned about this possibility. John O. Fritz, audiovisual director of the University of Chicago's Department of Education, voiced his reservations in a letter to Hill. Fritz acknowledged that "this film can serve an exceedingly useful purpose in stimulating discussion and reflection among a viewing audience," but only, he cautioned, if "an exceedingly experienced and competent person (discussion leader) is present to ameliorate different and conflicting viewpoints."[38] In invoking the need for an expert presence, such criticisms articulated a sense that the progressive political utility of the film depended upon the transfer of authority away from its own authority figure, Alex, to the figure of the discussion leader. Even those sympathetic critics who saw the film's racial fireworks as a learning experience invoked as touchstones the values of the intergroup relations movement, ignoring the possibility that the film was an implicit critique of these values. *Film Quarterly*'s Ernest Callenbach and Dominic Salvatore, for example, saw in *The Cry of Jazz* a pressing moral message with the figure of the "exemplary Negro" at its center: "In society as in personality growth, conscience is forced upon us; and the Negro must politically teach the new conscience to the whites."[39]

What blocked the learning process, for Callenbach and indeed for virtually every other critic, was the poor quality of the discussion scenes. Jazz writer Leonard Feather described them as "clumsy (especially the girls)" and "offensive."[40] When Kennedy screened the newly completed film for arts patrons and industry figures in New York, in the hopes of publicizing it and securing sponsors for the group's next (and never completed) project, he explained afterward in a letter to Hill and Bland that these viewers denounced the discussion group scenes as propaganda. Leave it in, they warned, and "we are doomed to fritter and fade away in the dusty little emporia of off beat art people . . . our other uh, avenue you might say is what is dismissingly referred to as the 'intellectual and educational' medium." Despite this discouraging reception, Kennedy was gleefully enthusiastic about the film's ability to stir up its audience members: "The strange and inexplicable thing about this film is its impact. People may become enraged but they're under no observable circumstances bored."[41] Indeed, it seems clear from

---

[37] Ideal Pictures receipt with comments, n.d., box 3, folder 29, NHP.

[38] John O. Fritz to Nelam Hill, May 20, 1960, box 3, folder 8, NHP.

[39] Ernest Callenbach and Dominic Salvatore, "The Cry of Jazz," *Film Quarterly* 13 (Winter 1959): 60.

[40] Lennie to Barbara, Apr. 15, 1959, box 4, folder 25, NHP. See also Callenbach and Salvatore, "Cry of Jazz," 58.

[41] Mark Kennedy to Bland et al., Apr. 23, 1959, box 3, folder 14, NHP.

the archival record surrounding *The Cry of Jazz* (and, I would argue, the style of the film itself) that it adapts for its own purposes the format of the discussion-heavy intergroup relations film. And central among these purposes was the goal of shaking people up.

The relationship between *The Cry of Jazz* and educational film is a somewhat contradictory one. The film both satirized the intergroup discussion technique and seized its authority, exploiting the form's association with expertise by ventriloquizing its didactic voice, while borrowing its truth-telling exemplary Negro in order to re-voice the movement's ethical principles entirely. Announcing the completion of the film toward the end of 1958, Bland wrote to Kennedy, boasting, "It's an overwhelming profound masterpiece. It's a discussion starter. . . . Greater than 'The Quiet One.'" It might seem strange for Bland to compare *The Cry of Jazz* to *The Quiet One* (1948), an acclaimed documentary about a poor Negro city boy's therapy at a school for troubled youth, which eschews didacticism in favor of a lyrical, open-ended psychoanalytic portrait. But *The Quiet One*'s humanism, rendering one person's healing as the basis for the reform of a society, made it a signal example of the liberal focus on individual consciousness over structural inequality or racial difference, a story through which white viewers might experience both empathy and personal growth. It is far easier to identify with silent suffering than with the musically discordant cry that Bland's film produced. Bland may well have been thinking of *The Quiet One* and the ethical preoccupations of the intergroup relations genre when shortly after the release of *The Cry of Jazz* he told the *Chicago Defender* that the film avoided "the usual pitfalls of the problem picture and the brotherhood film."[42] This is a curious pronouncement, given that the discussion scenes were wholly of a piece with the genre. There is, indeed, a distinct possibility that Bland and the khtb production team deliberately sought to exploit the wooden acting and cardboard roles associated with the genre. This is an irresolvable question, although it is interesting to note that throughout the writing process, Kennedy repeatedly cautioned Bland about the flatness of the characters. Bland and Hill did incorporate some of Kennedy's ideas as they revised the script, most notably his proposition that *Jazz*'s eternal present "reflects and symbolizes this improvised life," but the Chicago members of the production team doggedly retained the one-dimensional characterization he had repeatedly criticized.[43]

The motivation for including the discussion group scenes was no doubt in part strategic. Although they were maddeningly contrived, they were a recognizable educational film format, and in keeping them in the film the khtb team ingeniously managed both to attract and antagonize a cluster of target audiences in the 16mm film distribution market. Indeed, the Parkwood Jazz Club's northern,

---

[42] "Chicago Produced Film 'The Cry of Jazz' Due Soon," *Chicago Defender*, Mar. 16, 1959.
[43] Mark Kennedy to Edward Bland, Aug. 10, 1958, box 3, folder 14, NHP.

middle-class, college-age whites (Parkwood is clearly Hyde Park, the mixed South Side neighborhood surrounding the University of Chicago) are a mockery of the very demographic that would comprise the bulk of the film's viewers. It was apparent to khtb from early on that screenings at jazz clubs and film societies in educational institutions would outnumber all others by far.[44] The khtb team gave the group's white actors ridiculously pat lines of dialogue that reduced them to mouthpieces of liberal orthodoxy: "America needs the Negro to teach us how to be American, right?" asks sympathetic, moderate Faye, later proposing that "Jazz and the Negro could win friends for this country more readily than other things we're doing in the Cold War." The unpleasant Natalie is the most cartoonish figure of the lot: "What's this, a mau mau meeting?" she shouts, "This is nothing but black chauvinism!" "It's black Americanism," Alex spits back. Such hostile depictions of the film's viewing demographic, along with the lyrical scenes of Chicago life, distinguished *The Cry of Jazz* from standard intergroup relations films. But perversely, they actually helped the film achieve the intergroup relations goal of setting an example, albeit on an entirely different level: judging from the accounts of participants and eyewitnesses, the group discussions that took place around screenings of the film uncannily mirrored those modeled within it: strident and defensive, with everyone talking at once.

The khtb team relished the arguments that erupted at screenings of the film. Their letters back and forth between New York and Chicago are full of gleeful anecdotes recounting pitched discussions in which the object is clearly not group understanding but victory in a battle of wits. "I was quite jovial and polite in kicking their asses," Bland told Kennedy after a particularly heated discussion at the Playboy Jazz Festival.[45] When Ralph Ellison indignantly criticized the film on multiple counts in the discussion following a screening at Cinema 16 in New York, Bland wrote to Hill with a triumphant summation of his and Kennedy's verbal skill: "I killed the music points and Mark, in the most brilliant move I've seen him do, completely demolished the other crap Ellison spoke of." In Bland's depiction and in that of critic Kenneth Tynan, present at the same screening, the discussion was not so much an exchange of ideas as a heated battle between profoundly incompatible points of view: "When they went musical I scared them off and when they went cultural Mark scared them off + at times Mark and I switched roles," Bland wrote. "After a while [jazz historian Marshall] Stearns sat there mouth ajar as Kennedy and I poured point after point after point."[46]

---

[44] By my estimate, the extant materials from the khtb office show a total of 75 requests or receipts for screenings; 33 are from educational institutions, and the next-largest category is public library audiovisual departments with a total of 12.

[45] Edward Bland to Mark Kennedy, Aug. 14, 1959, box 3, folder 14, NHP.

[46] Bland to Hill, n.d. (but ca. 1960), box 1, folder 8, NHP. See also Kenneth Tynan, "A Contrast in Black and White," *The Observer* [UK], Mar. 20, 1960, clipping in box 3, folder 15, NHP.

Approaching the concept of roles in discussion not as vehicles for increased interracial understanding but as tools for scoring points, Bland communicates the degree to which *The Cry of Jazz* was an attack on, rather than a contribution to, the discussion culture in which it circulated.

In light of this possibility, it is worth quoting at length from Hill's account of the discussion following a screening of the film at a "Funference" in Lake Geneva, Wisconsin. It is not entirely clear what the word *Funference* meant in this context. The term was associated with the interracial youth recreation programs organized a decade earlier by Chicago social worker Glenford Lawrence, which one observer described as embodying "in miniature what society today is struggling to achieve."[47] Lake Geneva was a largely white town located eight miles northwest of Chicago; a popular location for summer camps, it is possible that the Funference at which *The Cry of Jazz* screened was part of a youth intergroup relations program of some sort. If this was in fact the case, the film's screening ended up radically undermining the conciliatory ethos of such programs. As Hill explained to Bland:

> The people were in a very argumentative mood and of course threatened to discontinue working for brotherhood. . . . I was called irresponsible, fascistic, and ungrateful. . . . Other people told me that I had to document what was said in the film. How could they believe this without some support from an authority. I was told also that the film had no scientific base. I told all these people that they were idiotic, insane, and simple. One girl said she was so angry that she couldn't see straight. . . . One woman, a social worker, said that we should take a lesson from Richard Wright. Seems some years ago in the '30s she had read Wright's 13,000,000 voices (I think I heard her say 13, 000 she was so mad) and she reported what a beautiful job he had done in presenting the subject matter. One Negro fellow there . . . said that this was the strangest argument he had ever heard in the field of race relations. They were still talking when I left.

Hill's irreverent account touches on the cardinal pieties within liberal race talk in the period, namely, its enshrinement of social truths in "authorities" and the desire to anoint Negro exemplars, here embodied in Richard Wright's 1941 classic *Twelve Million Black Voices*, an ur-text of exemplarity (one that Saunders Redding's 1951 memoir railed against). His delight in provoking scenes of outrage among *The Cry of Jazz*'s white audience members suggests that these

---

[47] Lucy P. Carner, "Why New Settlements?" in *Readings in the Development of Settlement Work*, ed. Lorene M. Pacey (New York: Association Press, 1950), 273.

discussions were, in fact, an arena in which to seek revenge against the pressures of exemplarity with which white liberals frequently burdened their black interlocutors.

If such descriptions are accurate, white liberal reactions to the film often came close to total rejection. Indeed the audience whose consciousness was most likely to be affected by the film was other black people who, like the khtb team, were weary of being asked to set good examples. In a letter telling Bland he would try to come to Chicago for one of the film's premiere screenings, Kennedy registered his distaste at the idea of entering the screening space, a community organization on the South Side called the Abraham Lincoln Center: "Ugh! Horrid joint! Full of social workers and Unitarians, or is it the social group workers in the vineyard and fellowship for ethical reconciliation? We may be compelled to crawl, but must we actually creep, before walking?"[48] This dissatisfaction with the culture of liberal race relations was radicalizing black intellectuals elsewhere. Harold Cruse, the prominent black intellectual with whom Bland and Hill coauthored a treatment for their never-produced second film, was one of them; Amiri Baraka, was another. Interviewed in 1984, Baraka credited the film with raising his consciousness of the relationship between racial identity and aesthetics.[49]

After *The Cry of Jazz*, Bland and Hill worked for ten years on the script for a feature film, *The American Hero*, each draft of which annotates changes in radical consciousness over the course of the 1960s. The first draft was written around the time they were shopping *The Cry of Jazz* to the New York cultural elite; their experiences in this arena clearly shaped the plot of the film, which recounted the struggles of a black composer assigned to write the score for a television documentary about "the new Negro" by a hypocritical and racist white liberal network executive. By the last draft, completed in the early 1970s, the cast of characters included young militants speaking out in hip jargon against the Vietnam war and the white man's oppression—a revision that suggested that the film's social critique now encompassed the internal divisions within the movement itself. Confrontational rap sessions abound in the later versions, these scenes suggesting the degree to which the racial politics of interpersonal discussion had shifted away from the conciliatory ethos of ecumenical fellowship associated with the discussion group to encompass the cathartic act of expressing black anger.[50]

---

[48] Mark Kennedy to Edward Bland, "March equinoc '59," box 3, folder 14, NHP.

[49] Interview with Amiri Baraka quoted in Lorenzo Thomas, "'Communicating by Horns': Jazz and Redemption in the Poetry of the Beats and the Black Arts Movement," *African American Review* 26 (Summer 1992): 292.

[50] The early drafts of the script are contained, pages out of sequence, in folders 2, 4, 5 and 6; the 1971 final draft is in box 5, folder 1, NHP.

The Cry of Jazz was not the only work of independent cinema to chart this transformation in the meaning of interracial conversation. It is also evident in the powerful cinema verité film *A Time for Burning*, a documentary about a white Lutheran pastor in Omaha and his failed attempt to integrate his congregation. Released in 1966 by Lutheran Film Associates, the film's goal, like that of *The Cry of Jazz*, was not fellowship but critique. It too failed to get airtime on a national television network. This was no doubt in part because of the anger displayed in the film's interracial discussions, particularly those involving the eloquent and utterly damning soliloquies of black Lutheran and future Nebraska state senator Ernie Chambers. These discussion scenes testify both to the ultimate radicalization of onscreen discussion as a pedagogical form and the degree to which—at least in Lutheran circles—the institutions of intergroup media education were capable of absorbing the rap session's irresolvable antagonisms. That a church group was willing to provide a voice to this critique provides us with an encouraging picture of the intergroup relations movement's capacity to change with the times. The networks' refusal to air it, on the other hand, indexes the extent to which the media establishment could not. Praising the educational television network for airing it when commercial broadcasters refused, *New York Times* TV critic Jack Gould observed, "If ever the value of an alternative system of non-commercial television needed demonstration, 'A Time for Burning' would serve as an example."[51] A year later, this wish would be granted with the founding of PBS, never more radical than in its earliest years. As Laurie Ouellette notes, early PBS programs like *Black Journal* (which ran from 1968 to 1976) blended discussion and entertainment and employed activists as experts, "[c]ollapsing the artificial boundary between reason and emotion," to construct a black counterpublic sphere.[52] This was a far cry from the patient, didactic, and exemplary Negro performances of *Soap Box*, but it was an effort to effect self-governance through television that could not have happened without the latter, if only as a consequence of the negative example it set.

Filmography

A City Decides (1956) 27 min., b&w, 16mm
PRODUCTION: Charles Guggenheim & Associates. SPONSOR: Fund for the Republic. SUPERVISOR: Fleishman-Hillard, Inc. (a St. Louis–based public relations firm). PRODUCER: Richard Heffron. DIRECTOR: Charles Guggenheim. SCRIPT: Mayo Simon.

---

[51] Jack Gould, "The High Price of Serenity on Sunday," *New York Times*, Oct. 30, 1966.
[52] Laurie Ouellette, *Viewers Like You? How Public TV Failed the People* (New York: Columbia University Press, 2002), 132.

CINEMATOGRAPHER: Victor Duncan. ORIGINAL TELEVI-SION AIRDATE: Saturday, Feb. 3, 1957, 4:00 pm EST, National Broadcasting Company (NBC). Distributed on 16mm by McGraw-Hill Text Films. ACCESS: Charles Guggenheim Collection, Academy Film Archive; available on VHS (Guggenheim Productions, 2005). NOTE: Aired on NBC as part of the National Council of Christians and Jews' Brotherhood Week. Academy Award nomination, Best Documentary Short Subject.

The Cry of Jazz (1959), 35 min., b&w, 16mm; 35mm restoration
PRODUCTION: khtb Productions DIRECTOR/MUSICAL DIRECTOR: Edward O. Bland. WRITERS: Edward O. Bland, Nelam L. Hill, Mark Kennedy; PHOTOGRAPHY: Hank Starr. EDITOR: Howard Alk. MUSIC: Le Sun Ra, Paul Severson, Eddie Higgins, Julian Priester, Norman Leist, (uncredited) Ronald Boykins. CAST: George Walker, Dorthea Horton, Linda Dillon, Andrew Dunean, James Miller, Laroy Inman. ORIGINAL TELEVISION AIRDATE: June 23, 1959 (WHDH-TV, Boston). ACCESS: DVD *The Cry of Jazz*, featuring Sun Ra and His Arkestra (Atavistic and Music Video Distributors, 2004). Restored 35mm version (2010) at Anthology Film Archives, New York.

Soap Box, "Teachers Meeting on Integration" (1955) 33 min, b&w, 16mm (kinescope)
PRODUCTION: KETC-TV (St. Louis) Public Affairs Department. SPONSOR: St. Louis Parent-Teacher Association. ORIGINAL TELEVISION AIRDATE: unknown (KETC, 1955). ACCESS: One of four episodes available for on-site viewing at the Peabody Awards Collection, University of Georgia Libraries, Athens, Georgia.

A Time for Burning (1966) 58 min., b&w, 16mm
PRODUCTION: Quest Productions. SPONSOR: Lutheran Film Associates. DIRECTORS: William C. Jersey, Barbara Connell. ORIGINAL TELEVISION AIRDATE: Oct. 1967 (dates and times varied), National Educational Television Network. ACCESS: Commercially available on VHS (Vision Video, 1995) and DVD (New Video Group, 2005). NOTE: Academy Award nomination, Best Documentary Feature. Named to the Library of Congress National Film Registry in 2005.

Related Films

Let Us Break Bread Together (How Brotherhood Builds Democracy)
(1954) 26 min., color
PRODUCTION: Film Production Unit, Bureau of Audio-Visual
Instruction, New York City Board of Education. NARRATOR:
Harry I. Rothman. SCRIPT: Frances H. Kohan and Truda T. Weil.
ACCESS: Internet Archive, www.archive.org/details/LetUsBre1954.
NOTE: Covers racial integration of New York City schools.

On Camera, "Private Line," (1958), 25 min., b&w, 16mm (kinescope)
PRODUCTION: KRNT-TV (Des Moines, Iowa) Public Affairs
Department. SPONSOR: Department of Adult Education, Des
Moines Public Schools. ORIGINAL TELEVISION AIRDATE:
Wednesday, Jan. 15, 1958. ACCESS: Available for on-site viewing at
the Peabody Awards Collection, University of Georgia Libraries,
Athens, Georgia.

On Camera, "Private Line," (1958), 25 min., b&w, 16mm
PRODUCTION: KRNT-TV (Des Moines, Iowa) Public Affairs
Department. SPONSOR: Department of Adult Education, Des
Moines Public Schools. ORIGINAL TELEVISION AIRDATE:
Wednesday, Jan. 15, 1958. ACCESS: Available for on-site viewing at
the Peabody Awards Collection, University of Georgia Libraries,
Athens, Georgia.

What about Drinking? (1954) 11 min., b&w, 16mm
PRODUCTION: Centron Productions for Yale University. Discussion Problems in Group Living series. A good, characteristic example
of onscreen discussion. ACCESS: Internet Archive,
www.archive.org/details/WhatAbou1954.

19 "A DECENT AND ORDERLY SOCIETY": RACE RELATIONS IN RIOT-ERA EDUCATIONAL FILMS, 1966–1970

MARSHA ORGERON

After the passage of the National Defense Education Act (NDEA) in 1958, substantial government funds became available for public schools to purchase audiovisual materials and equipment. Coming on the heels of the October 1957 Sputnik launch, the NDEA was inspired by the widespread fear that if communists outperformed the United States in education they might surpass America in other pursuits as well. The NDEA's project of getting "high-tech" materials into the classroom was initially focused on science and mathematics to prepare the next generation of American innovators. However, the Act both coincided with and encouraged the more widespread use of film for teaching an array of educational subjects.

Articles from this era in the industry publication *Educational Screen & Audio-Visual Guide* attest to the acute need for films about topics well beyond the sciences, especially those of the social guidance variety, often categorized as "Guidance," "Human Relations," "Social Studies," or "Social Issues" films. This push to put high-tech materials in the American classroom coincided with the emerging civil rights movement and the continuing impact of school desegregation in the wake of the 1954 *Brown v. Board of Education* decision and the Civil Rights Act of 1964. In the midst of a decade of class- and race-based civil unrest, culminating in a series of riots in the mid- to late 1960s, the nation was confronted with what was widely depicted and perceived as a ghetto crisis.[1] Articulations of concern about the present and future well-being of the nation began to coalesce around American schools, especially of a particular type. As the authors of *Education and the Urban Community* put it, "Call it what you will: the inner-city school, the ghetto school, the slum school; the large urban

---

[1] I use the term "riot" here because it was the predominant word used in the mainstream media and literature of the day, despite the fact that other terms—such as "rebellion," "disturbance," or "insurrection"—also circulated (though less frequently) and signify quite differently.

areas and the schools that are in them are in deep trouble."[2] Many pundits concluded that the American educational system needed to address previously avoided subjects of troubled interracial relations and racial disparities.

Educational films produced in the 1950s that confronted issues of race and discrimination, however obliquely or metaphorically—as we see in *Skipper Learns a Lesson* (1952) and *What About Prejudice?* (1959)—spoke to an implicitly white audience. In these films white kids are taught to change their prejudicial beliefs and behavior to accommodate difference. As William Sloan observed, the nonfiction "integration film" was born in response to the Supreme Court's 1954 decision that led to school desegregation, and this first generation of films was "aimed primarily at preparing the white community for integration."[3] However, the next generation of race-conscious educational films, which are the focus of this essay, uses a different approach. Films of the mid- to late 1960s, such as *Getting Angry* (1966), *Who Cares* (1968), *Joshua* (1968), and *Evan's Corner* (1970), abandon the subject of white youth in need of a lesson about racial tolerance. No longer just encouraging white children to accommodate "difference," these productions are primarily about black youths' reactions to discriminatory or underprivileged environments. An integrationist message still undergirds most of this new generation of films, but they speak to different concerns and constituencies, reflecting widespread anxieties about the kind of explosive behavior associated with black urban areas in this "riot era." The films, then, require consideration in the context of the national preoccupation with riots transpiring in American cities large and small.

These films—which typically revolve around African American youth in New York, Chicago, or Los Angeles—focus not just on various degrees of racially specific anger but also on ways that such resentment might be productively redirected. The young black male protagonists (most often teens or younger) become frustrated, despondent, and angry in response to the daily challenges they face. However, the films under discussion here posit a solution in the form of an idealized, compensatory experience that reminds them of their own and others' humanity to suggest that a positive experience can remedy the anger that would otherwise result in racial disharmony and potentially destructive behavior. In this way, the films can be understood as an attempt to manage racial interactions and perceptions, providing an intriguing glimpse into efforts to represent and to control young audiences during this tumultuous period in American race relations. Within the context of an urban educational crisis, including widespread teacher shortages and strikes, these films also offered frustrated teachers

---

[2] Maurie Hillson, Francesco Crodasco, and Francis Purcell, *Education and the Urban Community: Schools and the Crisis of the Cities* (New York: American Book, 1969), 2.

[3] William Sloan, "The Documentary Film and the Negro: The Evolution of the Integration Film," *Journal of the Society of Cinematologists* 4 (1964–1965): 67.

educational tools for dealing with potentially disruptive behavior in the name of a healthier and less volatile American body politic.

A National Crisis with Educational Ramifications

The films under discussion here—*Who Cares, Joshua,* and *220 Blues*—were made concurrently with an outpouring of literature targeted at educators who taught, as a 1968 book title put it, *On the Outskirts of Hope*. These books focus on the pervasive fear, as the authors of *Community Control and the Urban School* explain, that "resignation and alienation, or a violent opposition to democratic process [read: "rioting"], will become the dominant response of young people in coming decades."[4] Using the term "political socialization" to designate the way that schools needed to "instill in each new generation the political attitudes and behavior patterns that the society deems useful in its adult citizens . . . to preserve stability and consensus," these books suggest a refocusing of the concept of "social guidance" that had been the operating principle behind certain educational films dating back at least to the 1920s.[5]

Reacting specifically to the riots of 1967, President Lyndon B. Johnson tasked the National Advisory Commission on Civil Disorders, better known as the Kerner Commission, with reporting on the problems and solutions to urban blight and unrest. Speaking to the nation on television, Johnson urged Americans to look for "long-range" solutions that would improve "the conditions that breed despair and violence," in order "to achieve a decent and orderly society in America." Seven months after this speech, the commission recommended three areas of response, including working on "new initiatives and experiments that can change the system of failure and frustration that now dominates the ghetto and weakens our society."[6] The idea of a nation filled with *Cities in Crisis*, to use the title of a 1968 educational film, was a serious political and popular preoccupation with ramifications for the American classroom (see fig. 19.1).

Dealing with the "ghetto" or "slum," the prevailing terms in the literature and reporting of the day, was not, according to most commentators, a problem facing just a handful of large northern cities. In *Making Urban Schools Work* (1968), Mario Fantini and Gerald Weinstein predicted that "we are beginning to see that what is happening in large urban areas is really a preview of coming attractions for

---

[4] Helaine Dawson, *On the Outskirts of Hope: Educational Youth from Poverty Areas* (New York: McGraw-Hill, 1968); Mario Fantini, Marilyn Gittell, and Richard Magat, *Community Control and the Urban School* (New York: Praeger, 1970), 217. Brackets mine.

[5] Fantini, Gittell, and Magat, *Community Control*, 216.

[6] *The Kerner Report: The 1968 Report of the National Advisory Commission on Civil Disorders* (Washington, DC: GPO, 1968; reprint, New York: Pantheon, 1988), x, 2.

Figure 19.1. Ad for the Universal Education and Visual Arts release *Cities in Crisis: What's Happening?* (1967) in *Educational Screen and Audio-Visual Guide* (September 1968): 12. Note that young black boys are the human signifiers for the urban crisis and that what seems intended as a disturbing image of the boys could easily be read as a playful one if juxtaposed with positive images.

a major portion of our county . . . even in the non-urban areas."[7] Not only did the problems of the cities threaten to spread to the rest of the population, but these authors repeatedly made the case for the problems of schooling being inseparable "from other problems of the city," often invoking cancer metaphors to describe the way such problems can quickly and dangerously spread to suburban areas.[8]

Schools, then, were both a microcosm of the ghettos and a major staging-ground for intervention. As social worker and educator Helaine Dawson argued in 1968, "Explosions in the various cities cannot be treated singly as peculiar to a particular locality. They are part of the pattern of revolt being fashioned by a dissatisfied minority. Such outbreaks will continue to occur until deeper under-standing, creative planning, and action at the grass-roots level become a way of coping with economic, social, and political problems." As Robert Canot wrote, "The only real hope for the children of the ghetto is education," and classroom films were an ingrained part of American education deemed capable of reaching this alienated demographic.[9]

Educational Screen and Audiovisual Guide was very much tuned in to the educational needs invoked in the literature. In "1968: Year of Diversity and Di-chotomies," Henry Ruark proclaimed that "large cities with their cancerous ghettos [are] living proof themselves of the abysmal failure of 'education-as-is.'" Ruark was an advocate for something he called "individualized *learning*," which I interpret as meaning racially and economically particularized education.[10] We see some evidence of this individualized approach in the numerous films about race relations and the black urban experience in the late 1960s and early 1970s. Roger Gordon's December 1969 *Educational Screen* column acknowledged that "we are uncertain as to the kinds of media that are most effective in given situations in a black inner city classroom." His "Educational Technology" column concluded, "Certain films showing white children in white neighborhoods at a high level of affluence are grossly inadequate in these situations."[11] There was clearly a real desire, perhaps even a sense of desperation, for educational films that would speak to, rather than alienate, a black (and presumably urban) audience. By 1968 a veri-table genre of African American–focused "race" films—by which I mean films explicitly about what it means to be black and, almost always, living in an inner-city environment—were being marketed to American educators. Considered

---

[7] Mario Fantini, *Making Urban Schools Work: Social Realities and the Urban School* (New York: Holt, Rinehart and Winston, 1968), 2.

[8] Roger Woock, ed., *Education and the Urban Crisis* (Scranton, PA: International Textbook, 1970), v.

[9] Dawson, *On the Outskirts*, 5; Robert Canot, "The City's Not for Burning," in Woock, *Education and the Urban Crisis*, 50.

[10] Henry Ruark, "1968: Year of Diversity and Dichotomies," *Educational Screen* (Jan. 1969): 11.

[11] Roger Gordon, "Educational Technology," *Educational Screen* (Dec. 1969): 31.

within the context of calls for "individualized" learning, these films appear to have been primarily targeted at urban classrooms, attempting to fill the representational gap invoked by Gordon in *Educational Screen*. But they may also have been used to speak to those in need of a better "understanding," to use Dawson's term, of the plight of black city-dwellers, perhaps especially for the teachers tasked with steering youth toward the "decent and orderly society" envisioned by the Johnson administration. Documentation about where educational films actually circulated and who saw them is sparse, so we are left to consider the movies themselves.

Managing the Crisis at the Classroom Level

Two classroom films from 1968, *Who Cares* (McGraw-Hill-Lumin Film) and *Joshua* (ACI Productions), illustrate one of the prevailing types of race-focused films of this era. They feature young black males whose anger at their urban entrapment and the white power structure threatens to escalate into uncontainable violence. *Who Cares* complements and is based upon a McGraw-Hill book by the same name, published as part of "The Skyline Series."[12] The film offers us a day in the life of Charles, a preteen African American boy living in one of the urban environments that threatened Johnson's vision of the Great Society. The glimpse we get of Charles's home life suggests that, while far from terrible, it is less than Ozzie-and-Harriet perfect. He is being raised in the city (we are introduced to him kicking a can down a dirty street) by a clearly overworked mother; there is no father present in the film's one brief domestic scene. Charles's mother yells down from their apartment window for her son to hurry and bring the bread he has picked up for breakfast, but Charles seems more interested in kicking the can than in facilitating the morning breakfast ritual. Later in the sequence we watch Charles compete for his mother's attention with a baby whose cries cause her to abandon her interactions with Charles; she is kind, but pressed for time.

Charles also has an older brother who refuses to walk him to school. He makes a joke about Charles having to wear his hand-me-down jacket (an event played up much more in the book, in which Charles is self-conscious about how the jacket is too big for him). On his way to school, Charles pauses at a window display of musical instruments and then drums on the street posts in front of it, suggesting both economic want (having to pretend versus having an actual instrument) as well as untapped creative potential. Subsequent shots emphasize how small and alone Charles is in the cityscape, a little boy in a big world. Three girl schoolmates who encounter Charles in another window-gazing reverie on the street tell him to hurry up or he'll be late to school, to which Charles responds with the titular refrain: "Who cares, who cares anyways."

---

[12] Virginia Brown, Billie Phillips, and Elsa Jaffe, *Who Cares* (New York: McGraw-Hill, 1965).

Charles's next run-in magnifies the tensions he already experienced at home. We see Charles playfully dragging a piece of wood across a metal fence (again, making music) until a boy, who is white, takes the wood from him, to which Charles replies, "Who cares anyway. He can have the whole doggone stick, he can have the whole school." With each utterance, the phrase appears less ingenuous. As this encounter makes clear, Charles's problems are both territorial and economic: he has no clothes of his own, no instrument of his own, and now even his school seems alien. And yet his isolation is also a problem. These feelings are amplified in the next scene on the school playground, where Charles apparently begins to crumble from the stresses he's already encountered. Shots of Charles walking past three jump-roping white girls imply that he is hallucinating: shots of them tauntingly laughing at him are intercut with the reality of their innocuous jump-roping, suggesting a kind of persecution anxiety that manifests itself through a false vision of a world set against him. Charles's legitimate frustrations have now become delusions. Although his experiences may justify his view that the (white?) world is against him, this scene also serves as a reminder of Charles's fragile mental state upon arrival at school. When Charles is caught aimlessly lingering in the schoolyard after the bell rings—his defensive, feigned apathy keeping him outside of the school doors—a white teacher reprimands him and personally escorts him into the school while lecturing Charles about how imperative it is that he finishes his education.

In the classroom, Charles's African American teacher calls him to the front of the class to reject an assignment he's turned in, commenting aloud that "I can't accept this, not when we both know you can do better." Charles's now-conditioned response, "who cares," is revealed to be a defensive posturing that allows him to survive in a world full of obstacles, failures, and humiliations, real or perceived. The teacher's toughness is also important. Instead of letting Charles scrape by, she tries to inspire him to aspire, one of the great challenges articulated by the educational pundits of the era. But this is also the point at which the film takes a significant turn, from escalation to release. The teacher, standing in front of her multiracial class, proclaims that the class has to finish tryouts for the leader of their band. The whole class begins banging away on their instruments. Charles, now fully instrumented, at first yawns, looking disinterested; but then, after some foot and finger tapping, and an emerging smile, he starts playing his bongos. The teacher notices his engagement and brings Charles to the front of the class to lead the band. In this moment on the bandstand, Charles thrives. He moves his arms dramatically about like a conductor and, for the first time in the film, smiles radiantly (see fig. 19.2). At the end of the number the class collectively starts cheering, allowing the teacher to chime in with the moral of the story: "Who cares, Charles? You care, lots of people care." The film closes on an image of Charles victorious, with his teacher's arm around him, still conducting, still smiling. Charles has been recuperated from the alienated margins, drawn into the consensus center.

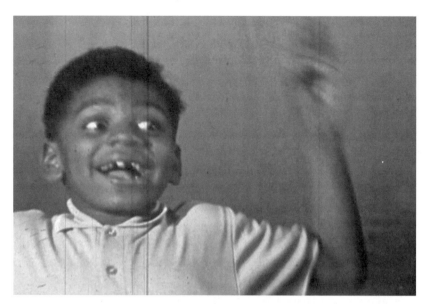

Figure 19.2. Charles gleefully conducts the class in *Who Cares* (1968).

Clearly aimed at an elementary school audience, *Who Cares* explicitly addresses one of the refrains of the educational crisis literature regarding the "burden of self-hatred" that existed in the overcrowded cities of America.[13] As Helaine Dawson opined, "Every person needs a feeling of belonging." Similarly, Wilbert Edgarton contended, "The minority group child as well as the rural and urban poor need a sense of identification and worth."[14] *Who Cares* represents a successful version of this kind of preadolescent intervention and affirmation. Instead of allowing Charles's frustrations to build to the point of explosion (to use the rhetoric of the era), his teacher provides him with a context in which these tensions can be released, effectually negating them. Note that nothing has changed about Charles's environment—he will have to walk the same streets back to the same home at the end of the day. Charles may now have something to smile about, thanks to an affirmative experience in his classroom, but this uplift is only a momentary alleviation of long-term stressors. The film subtly but decisively suggests that Charles's primary problem is not simply his environment, although it is that too, but his paranoid perception of it, which can be altered more easily than the root cause.

Who Cares also appears to have a pedagogical function that extends beyond the student inasmuch as Charles's catharsis is entirely indebted to the teacher's perceptive and sensitive responses to his emotional needs. Although the book

---

[13] Jean Grambs, "The Self-Concept: Basis for Reeducation of Negro Youth," in Woock, *Education and the Urban Crisis*, 102.

[14] Dawson, *On the Outskirts*, 38; Wilbert Edgarton, "Practical Application to Disadvantaged Education," *Educational Screen* (Oct. 1969): 11.

and film are targeted at a young audience, this affirmation of what good, responsive teaching methods look like is worth considering as a secondary function of the film. Administrators and educators, in fact, were having serious discussions about how to instruct teachers to reach children from an array of "marginal socio-economic backgrounds" in not only urban but also rural situations.[15] "Instructional technology" was perceived as one of the key tools for speaking to these constituencies and was part of a larger reevaluation of the "teaching-learning process."[16] Training teachers to raise the self-esteem of their students through positive experiences and productive discussions of such difficult subjects as race was considered a priority in the battle against the "pattern of revolt."

Released the same year as *Who Cares, Joshua* (1968) offers a glimpse of what a person like Charles might be like ten or so years into the future, if he swapped music for athletics, both admittedly stereotypical and limited options. *Joshua* was shot independently in New York City over the course of around four days in Central Park and Harlem by first-time educational film director Bert Salzman, who borrowed film equipment, a cinematographer, and a sound recordist from veteran filmmaker George Stoney.[17] Salzman, who made commercials and industrial films prior to *Joshua*, remembers the tumultuous cultural climate of the 1960s as the impetus for his entrée into educational filmmaking. Citing the assassination of Martin Luther King Jr., the riots, and the Vietnam war as motivational forces, Salzman says he wanted to make a film that was a metaphor for the larger race struggles with which the nation was not-so-successfully grappling. He approached the Anti-Defamation League (ADL) with the story of what would become *Joshua* and was given startup money from the ADL film department; he personally financed the rest. While Salzman was editing the film, Stelios Roccos of ACI, an educational film distributor, saw Salzman's rough cut and bought it outright. After this immediate initial success, Salzman was invited by Roccos to an educational film convention, where he learned how great the demand was for educational films, especially those tackling thorny racial issues.

Salzman's debut film, shot in a verité style, tells the story of a day in the life of recent high-school graduate Joshua. At the beginning of the film, Joshua is shadowboxing in a mirror before he and his mother pack his bags in preparation for his leaving the city on a full athletic scholarship at a Texas college. This domestic frame for the film prepares the audience to consider Joshua as a character in transition, on the precipice of relocation to a new environment far different from the

---

[15] Edgarton, "Practical Application," 10.

[16] Gordon, "Educational Technology," 9.

[17] Interview with Bert Salzman, June 9, 2007. All biographical and circumstantial information about *Joshua* derives from this interview. For more on George Stoney, who made many pioneering documentary and educational films about race in America, see *Wide Angle* 21, no. 2 (1999), a special issue dedicated to his work.

one he now comfortably inhabits. Joshua has a certain bravado to his character that Charles in *Who Cares* utterly lacks: he not only begins the film confidentially shadowboxing but also brags to his friend Henry out the window that "if they want Josh the great on their little old tack team, then they gotta pay for everything. It's what they call a full scholarship, my friend." Also unlike Charles, Joshua does not seem in any way overwhelmed or damaged by his environment; but he is also on the verge of escaping it, for better or for worse. As his mother warns him, he'll need to choose his new friends carefully: "Texas isn't 118th Street, you know."

Joshua leaves his walkup apartment to go to the park for a workout and ends up on a street not unlike the one Charles traverses in *Who Cares*. Fanny, an African American girl about his age, chases after Joshua, giving him a transistor radio as a farewell present. The two horse around in a long, happy, almost delirious play sequence, set to the Box Tops' "Cry Like a Baby," establishing the film's initially jubilant and optimistic tone. A shot of them dissolves into an image of Joshua running full-barrel toward the camera. After a long jog through the park Joshua ends up at the zoo, where he stops for a rest. Here he encounters a young white boy, who is roaring at a sleeping lion in a cage and asks Joshua if he might have better luck waking the lion. Joshua roars; the lion roars back. After telling the kid, and then demonstrating, that he can talk to the animals, Joshua, without any hint of self-consciousness, playfully explains that he learned these things in the jungle. The white kid then asks Joshua the transitional question of the film: "Are you a nigger?" This question is unanswered except through Joshua's lingering, angry gaze at the boy, which dissolves into Joshua's next and differently motivated run through the park.

While running in the park Joshua next encounters an older white boy, about his age, flying a kite. It is pretty clear that Joshua does not accidentally run into him, but rather that he tackles him. After pushing him to the ground Joshua accuses the white boy (whose character has no name in the film or in the credits) of not watching where he is going. The white boy apologizes. Joshua mocks him, threatening to punch him in his "fat face." Here we see Joshua redirecting his anger over the zoo incident in ways that are decidedly antisocial, precisely the kind of behavior that was perceived as dangerous, riot-era anger. After Joshua kicks his kite, calling him "boy" in the process, the white kid, with no apparent ill will intended, calls Joshua "man," which sets off the now visibly upset Joshua who loses control of himself, eventually pinning down the white boy's head. This hostile interaction dramatizes the kind of behavior described in *The Urban R's*: "We may thus expect Negro adolescents . . . to be less restrained than adults in their demands, and to be more vehement in their expectation of immediate rectification of wrong."[18] Here rectification comes in the form of a violent outburst,

---

[18] Robert Dentler, Bernard Mackler, and Mary Ellen Warshauer, *The Urban R's: Race Relations as the Problem in Urban Education* (New York: Praeger, 1967), 219.

perhaps one that Joshua had been preparing for in some way since his shadow-boxing at film's beginning. Though Joshua behaves in an unrestrained way, it is clearly due to the earlier racist affront to his dignity. But this does not, the film suggests, excuse arbitrary retaliation for an unrelated wrong. Indeed, this wrestling scene is followed by a series of shots in which the white kid and Joshua look at each other silently.

In this series of overlapping dissolves, we see thought and thoughtfulness represented as an alternative to the physical confrontation that just transpired (see fig.19.3). When Joshua walks away, the white boy calls him back because Joshua left his radio behind. This act of almost unbelievable generosity is then surpassed when the white kid fixes Joshua's radio, which was broken during the fight. These acts of kindness begin to soften the racial tensions that Joshua brought to this encounter, opening up a dialogue about the kite. As the white kid explains, the kite design was based upon an aerodynamic theory with origins in eighteenth-century science. "I won't bore you with the details," he says. His problem, however, is that he can't run fast enough to fly it. Here we revisit the territory of Charles and his conducting moment, as Joshua takes the kite, runs fast, and flies it. A racially charged fight has been transformed into a collaboration, albeit one initiated by the white boy's conciliatory and, one might argue, patronizing gesture. Although the film stereotypically assigns intellectual versus athletic capacity (the white child, after all, doesn't want to "bore" Joshua with intellectual history), each boy is allowed to showcase his talents. A communal, collaborative experience triumphs over unthinking racism. After a

Figure 19.3. Joshua (Errol Booker) and the kite-flying boy stop to think about their violent encounter in this series of overlapping shots from *Joshua* (1968).

quick, casual farewell, Joshua runs away, and the film ends with a freeze frame on Joshua in mid-stride.

As the one-page ACI instructional flyer for the film suggests, *Joshua* was intended to stimulate discussion about "prejudice and black-white relations" not only for peer high school audiences but also in college and adult settings.[19] The film can be understood as another attempt at intervention in the pattern of escalating anger that riot-era politicians and educators were seeking to defuse, offering—as one review observed—a "basic message that confrontations between blacks and whites can be constructive."[20] As Jean Grambs, discussing the "Basis for Reeducation of Negro Youth," put it: "Hatred breeds aggression. Aggression seeks an outlet."[21] In *Joshua*, the white boy flying the kite is, at first, Joshua's outlet. The film has already established that Joshua is talented and upward bound. However, one ignorant question might still trigger violently antisocial behavior, alerting us precisely to the situation Dawson envisioned when she described the outcome of mistreating poor, black youth: "Their feelings of worthlessness and hopelessness are intensified, and they develop a smoldering hatred of whites."[22]

Joshua is not just a film about appropriate African American behavior in the face of adversity. It is equally about the role that white behavior plays in both creating and reversing racist tensions. Civil interactions are not, according to the film, the responsibility of one racial group; they are universal needs for social order. Joshua is clearly the film's protagonist who experiences both a negative and a positive racial encounter. However, Salzman believes that *Joshua* was shown to both urban and suburban audiences of mixed races and that, like the content of the film itself, it allowed white and black students to articulate their feelings, to confront their racial beliefs, and to resolve differences without fists. Since there are no adult figures intervening in the outcome of this film, and since it was intended to be shown to older teenagers and adults, the stakes here are significantly different: these are peer interactions, unmediated by an authority figure and resolved only through calm consideration of the situation. The social ideal envisioned here is that, in the adult world, anger can be mitigated if it is not met with anger.

Joshua suggests that although one bad encounter can trigger a violent reaction, one good encounter can counteract it. Joshua thus learns a lesson about particularizing his reactions to the white world. The kite-flying boy, who has taken the high road throughout (opining that "it's ridiculous to fight over an accident" from the get-go), sees the productive outcome of his rationality and generosity. He paves the way for integration, allowing Joshua to return to the

---

[19] Flyer for *Joshua*, ACI Films, Inc., A/V Geeks Archive.

[20] "Review of *Joshua*," *Hospital & Community Psychiatry* (July 1971): 228.

[21] Jean Grambs, "The Self-Concept," in Woock, *Education and the Urban Crisis*, 87.

[22] Dawson, *On the Outskirts*, 4.

social order. This is an especially timely lesson for Joshua, given his departure from the city (one reviewer of the film described his Texas destination as "the strange white world," however inaccurately this represents the racial demographic of Texas in the late 1960s).[23] In *Educational Screen* Don Beckwith assessed the film in these terms: "*Joshua* poses a question: can ghetto youth learn to relate to an integrated surrounding? Joshua, on the eve of his 'escape' from the ghetto, experiences, on a small scale, what life will be like on the 'outside.' He begins to realize the need for flexible interaction in human relations."[24] Although I agree with Beckwith's assessment, I think the more important question in both *Joshua* and *Who Cares* would have been: Could films like this help to guide a young, black urban audience away from destructive, antisocial behavior to facilitate Johnson's vision of a "decent and orderly society"? Whether apathetic or violent in nature, both protagonists require, and fortunately encounter, mentorship and kindness (the other behavior being modeled here). When offered, these gestures are salves. Charles's crisis of self-esteem is at least momentarily solved; Joshua's lesson in tolerance serves as a counterpoint to the unthinking, juvenile violence white racism precipitated.

A Different Approach: Fomenting Anger

The two films discussed above offer a progressive but ultimately palliative representation of race relations and African American frustration in particular. However, this was not the only depiction of race relations circulating in the realm of educational film. A notably different take on the subject of race in America, *220 Blues* (1970, King Broadcasting Company), tells the story of Sonny, an African American teenager who appears to be fully and happily integrated in his mixed-race high school and track team (the film's title refers to the 220-dash). All is well until a new black student, Larry, begins to stir things up with comments in class about white racism and the hypocrisies of American democracy, comparing current ghetto conditions to concentration camps. Outside of the classroom, Larry—who is articulate, persuasive, and doggedly persistent—haunts Sonny with his militant preachment about spending too much time with white boys, acting like a "good slave," being a pawn in "whitey's schools," and being a token athlete in what will always remain a dominant white society intent on keeping blacks in their places. At first Sonny dismisses the comments, but Larry's persistence and insights begin to take root. We watch Sonny begin to absorb certain aspects of Larry's discourse and to affect an Afrocentric sartorial style, a far cry from his appearance in the beginning of the film.

[23] "Review of *Joshua*," 227.

[24] Don Beckwith, "Film Evaluations," *Educational Screen* (Jan. 1970): 26.

The film climaxes around a big track meet, at which Larry wants Sonny to demonstrate in an act of solidarity with his "brothers and sisters." Before the meet, Sonny explains to his girlfriend that "if I reject the medal, it will be a symbol of pride and unity." At the meet, Sonny's white track partner, whom he contentedly hangs out with prior to Larry's interruption of the status quo, asks him about the rumor going around school about black athletes planning a demonstration. Bob tells Sonny that such behavior might compromise the scholarship he earned and urges him not to mess up his future. Sonny replies that to demonstrate or not is his decision. The film ends with Sonny successfully running the anchor leg of the relay race, thereby winning the meet for his team. In the grandstand, Larry stands, clearly disappointed by Sonny's victory or expectant of the act of protest to come, as the racially mixed crowd cheers. The film ends in an open-ended fashion with an ambiguous freeze-frame: the white team members stand at the platform to receive their first-place medal, while Sonny hangs back from the group (see fig. 19.4). Will Sonny join the team and receive the award he deserves, or stand with Larry in an act of protest? Or will Sonny act in a fashion resonant of then-recent real-world behavior at the 1968 Olympics, when African Americans Tommie Smith and John Carlos raised their fists at the medal ceremony, signaling black power and solidarity?

220 Blues is extraordinary on a number of levels. First, it does not celebrate integration as an unproblematic solution or ideal. Second, it is not set in a ghetto

Figure 19.4. In the final, ambiguous freeze frame, Sonny (Magere Tualamu) is on the verge of deciding if he will accept the medal he earned in the relay race or stay away from the award platform in an act of racially motivated protest in *220 Blues* (1970).

environment but rather in an apparently middle-class milieu.[25] Further, it gives voice to the ideas behind black separatism and militancy—Larry even refers to "ghetto rebellions" (instead of "riots") at one point—that are absent from other classroom films about race from this period. These ideas are not merely alluded to, but laid out in a series of scenes in which Larry passionately explains his point of view to Sonny and to the film's audience as well. Larry may be aggressive, but he is neither ignorant nor cartoonish about his beliefs, making his perspective difficult to dismiss. His anger may (or may not) seem out of place in this seemingly well-integrated environment, but it is treated as worthy of consideration, which is what Sonny—and perhaps the film's audience, as well—does. Although we see no evidence of racist behavior toward Sonny, Larry has a bigger picture in mind: the history and legacy of racism in America, which threatens the foundation of integrationist politics. In fact, what is most remarkable about Larry is that he is able to spark and stoke feelings of anger and resentment in Sonny that do not appear to have existed prior to his indoctrination, providing a kind of alternate education to what we see in the opening classroom scenes when a white teacher, discussing German and Japanese immigrants, is confronted by Larry for ignoring civil rights issues ("We're not at the Civil Rights movement yet," the teacher ineffectually replies).

This is not to say that Larry is represented as an unproblematically heroic character in the story, as there is no doubt that *220 Blues* figures him as disruptive in terms of Sonny's future plans and ambitions. Whatever choice Sonny makes at film's end (presumably this would be the primary focus of the postscreening discussion), his thoughts about being a black person in an integrated environment have been forever complicated. Larry's ideas have the potential to compromise Sonny's integrated and potentially successful place in the social order. And although Larry talks about black solidarity, we don't see him surrounded by demonstrating African American students in the grandstand in the final scene. He stands alone, an isolated figure attempting to lure Sonny away from the consensus center.

Still, the film offers a rare acknowledgment and articulation of racially specific anger without any conciliatory moment to ensure that the audience understands the way things *should* be. Unlike *Who Cares* or *Joshua*, *220 Blues* presents no transformative experience that quells the frustration and anger that Sonny now feels. Instead, Sonny is awakened to an alternative understanding of his situation in white society but he is also now conflicted about playing the role of

---

[25] In my phone conversation on Jan. 19, 2009, with *220 Blues* screenwriter Ed Leimbacher, he explained that the people he was working with at King Pictures were deliberately pushing the envelope with films that broke from established educational film content and form. He also remembers the film being well received, at least by local (Seattle) teachers.

the "dissatisfied minority," to return to educational pundit Helaine Dawson's terminology. In this way, Larry's function in the film recalls the invasive cancer metaphor that was often invoked to discuss the problems of the ghetto as well as the provocative, militant discourse that was perceived by many as leading to rioting behavior. The existence of a film that encourages the discussion of the legitimacy of black anger and alternatives to integrationist ideology is striking, as is its ambiguous ending. The film also seems directed very specifically at an African American audience who would, like Sonny, find Larry's teachings something to consider when facing choices about how to navigate "the strange white world."

In summation, educational filmmakers in the mid- to late 1960s produced the first body of classroom films that focused directly on racial tension and especially on black male youth with the potential for antisocial behavior. In concert with a wave of literature encouraging educators to tackle racial disadvantage and discrimination head-on, these films allowed for classroom discussions of conflict during an era in which the nation as a whole was anxiously observing escalating disparities and dissatisfaction in urban centers and cities across the country. This type of film seems to have run its course by the end of the 1970s in a fashion that parallels the gradual decline in educational film production and usage as the 1980s approached. It also reflects the decreasing national urgency regarding black militancy and rioting as the decade wore on. Although it is difficult to discern how these various films were received in the classroom by students or teachers who viewed them at the time, they clearly were made with the intention of filling a very real need for broaching crucial subjects that could no longer be ignored in integration-era America.

Filmography

220 Blues (1970) 18 min.; 16mm
PRODUCER: King Screen Productions. DISTRIBUTOR: Phoenix/BFA Films. DIRECTOR: Richard Gilbert. WRITER: Ed Leimbacher. CAST: Magere Tualamu (Sonny), Rickey Ray (Larry), Michael Horton (Bob). ACCESS: A/V Geeks Archive, www.archive.org/details/220_blues.

Joshua (1968) 15 min.; 16mm
Bert Salzman Productions. DIRECTOR/WRITER: Bert Salzman. DISTRIBUTOR: ACI. CAMERA: Bill Godsey. EDITOR: Gary Goch. CAST: Errol Booker (Joshua), Greg Brown (Boy with kite), Gary Allen (young boy), Mira Espinosa (Mother). Alternate title: *Joshua: Black Boy of Harlem.* ACCESS: Academic Film Archive of North America, www.archive.org/details/salzman_joshua.

Skipper Learns a Lesson (1952) 10 min.; 16mm
PRODUCER: A Paul Bunford Production. DISTRIBUTOR:
Encyclopaedia Britannica Films. ACCESS: A/V Geeks Archive,
www.archive.org/details/skipper_learns_a_lesson.

What About Prejudice? (1959) 11 min.; 16mm
PRODUCER: Centron. DISTRIBUTOR: McGraw-Hill. ACCESS:
A/V Geeks Archive, Prelinger Collection, www.archive.org/details/
WhatAbou1959.

Who Cares (1968) 12 min.; 16mm
PRODUCER: Lumin Films. PRODUCTION-DISTRIBUTION:
McGraw-Hill Text-Films. STORY: Virginia Brown, Billie Phillips,
Elsa Jaffe. Correlated with the Skyline Series, Book/C, *Who Cares*
(McGraw-Hill, 1965). ACCESS: A/V Geeks Archive; www.archive.
org/details/who_cares.

Related Films

Dad and Me (1971). King Screen Productions. Distributed by BFA. 11
min. This film depicts a strong and positive relationship between a
young black boy and his father.

Evan's Corner (1970). Stephen Bosustow Productions. Distributed by
Bailey-Film Associates. 23 min. Evan's crowded urban apartment
leaves him no room for himself, so his mother designates a corner for
him to make his own.

Felicia (1965). Stuart Roe for the Anti-Defamation League of B'nai
B'rith. 20 min. This first-person narrated film shows the challenges
Felicia faces in her Watts neighborhood. The film also addresses the
racial and class differences in education.

Getting Angry (1966). Sue and James Stinson Productions. Distributed
by BFA. 10 min. A young African American boy gets a model space
capsule for his birthday and it is accidentally broken on the school
playground. The film shows how anger and blame easily escalate even
when something truly accidental has occurred.

Just One Me (1971). Aims Media Productions. Distributed by ACI. 9
min. In this delirious hippie-spirited film, a young black boy
imagines being lots of different things, ending up wanting only to be
himself.

The Matter with Me (1972). Monroe-Williams Productions. Distributed by Oxford Films. 15 min. A young black boy wanders through a nice white neighborhood only to return to his own blighted community.

A Place of My Own (1968). McGraw-Hill-Lumin Films. 11 min. A cramped apartment is a challenge for young girls growing up in the ghetto.

William: From Georgia to Harlem (1971). Learning Corporation of America. Distributed by Coronet/MCI. 17 min. This film follows William in his migration from the rural south to New York City.

20 EVERYTHING OLD IS NEW AGAIN; OR, WHY I COLLECT EDUCATIONAL FILMS

SKIP ELSHEIMER WITH KIMBERLY PIFER

It is getting harder to walk around my house these days. A recent acquisition of some 700 films from a retired teacher in New York's Hudson Valley has pushed my collection of rescued 16mm films over the 23,000 mark. And more show up almost daily. (As I write this, the postman is leaving a box of eight more.) I collect films for the A/V Geeks Educational Film Archive, founded in 1992.

Some of the films in the A/V Geeks collection come from online auction purchases. But many come from folks like a Hudson Valley teacher, who first found them in a closet and then intervened as someone was about to toss them into a dumpster. These films were never meant to last forever. Educational and industrial films, like dime novels and daily newspapers, were created for a specific audience and time. Their creators, if they thought of lifespan at all, expected these works would soon be discarded in a trash bin.

Over the last fifteen years, what started as a hobby of buying these old, occasionally corny films at state government surplus auctions has morphed into a career of rescuing large collections of them and maintaining the expanding archive that now dominates the eight-bedroom former boarding house I call home. At the least, acquiring and maintaining these films involves constant lugging of rusty, dusty cans of film from one location in my house to another while maneuvering around stacks of other rusty, dusty cans. At the most, it is a true challenge to my wallet and mettle. In 2008, I rented a twenty-five-foot truck and drove thirteen hours to Memphis, Tennessee, to rescue a collection of 3,000 films. The gas alone for this cost more than $700. As I drove back to North Carolina over the Smoky Mountains, creeping along at 30 miles per hour through rain and fog, aggravated big rig truckers laid on their horns and sped past me. This was not the first time I had to commandeer a vehicle beyond my driving skills to carry film or film equipment.

Why do I do what I do? It may seem inexplicable that I go to such lengths to collect prints of films when their original producers saw them as disposable, only revising them every several years to keep up with changes in hairstyles, clothes, and language. The film print itself has a limited lifespan as well; most educational film companies used a cheaper color stock that not so gradually fades to red. Also, most of the film stock I deal with has an acetate base and, over time, begins to deteriorate, to shrink and to stink, releasing a vinegary smell of acetic acid that is faintly evident when venturing into my film storage rooms. For more than a decade, schools and other agencies, strapped for space, have been dumping ("deaccessioning") these films. With the influx of DVDs, movies as computer files, and the Internet, who projects or watches actual films or filmstrips anymore? What is so important about these films that I devote my life to these artifacts deemed obsolete by the institutions that paid for them in the first place?

Simply put, these films still have a lot to teach us. As with all ephemeral media, they provide a snapshot of a specific time, place, or social issue. And, yes, many of them are at times unintentionally hilarious (especially the vintage post–World War II sex, dating, and drug education films), stodgy, and outdated, steeped as they often are in gender and racial stereotypes. But that does not mean that they have nothing to teach contemporary audiences.

The most obvious lesson is the intended one—the reason the film was made to begin with. Even the most poorly produced, lowest-budget educational film has something to reveal about its subject matter. I have joked that these films have taught me good table manners (*Good Table Manners*, 1951), how chocolate is made (*The Great American Chocolate Factory*, 1977), and how to deliver a baby in the backseat of an automobile (*Sudden Birth*, 1966, a police training film).

Further, history does repeat itself. Every film was made to address a perceived problem—from teenage delinquency, venereal disease, and drug addiction to bicycle safety, dental hygiene, and the proper operating procedures of a specific industry—and those problems remain constant topics in educational and industrial films. What changes is how the problems are addressed, which leads us to the less obvious and more interesting meanings to be gleaned from educational films. By looking past the immediate messages and instead examining why these were deemed important and how they were presented, we get a glimpse into the fears and desires of the world the films reflect, as well as the prevailing social issues and educational trends at play when they were made. This is where having a collection of educational films spanning several decades comes in handy. Not only have I been able to examine individual films for these less obvious "outliers," but I have also been able to examine multiple films that address the same topic years apart. This allows us to see change over time. Viewing multiple films on a particular topic made over a span of time provides an overview of the cultural issues educational filmmakers were responding to and how the prevailing attitudes regarding those issues affected the content, tone, and even stylistic treatment of the subject at hand.

Let's examine a handful of films that cover three distinct subject areas: teaching social responsibility, prevention of venereal disease (VD), and teaching science in a religious context. In the first two instances, I'll examine films made over a span of time—in the case of one venereal disease film, as early as 1919—pointing out the ways in which the subjects were handled stylistically and what information was provided. In the last instance, I'll examine films that, while made over a relatively short time frame—roughly one decade—reveal the tenor of the time, and whose influence has carried over in the twenty-first century discourse regarding evolution versus intelligent design.

Social Guidance Goes Bananas

A pair of films made by Coronet, one of the dominant educational film studios of the mid-twentieth century, exemplifies just such a shift in stylistic treatment. *Lunchroom Manners* (1960) and *A Lunchroom Goes Bananas* (1978), cover the same territory. Both introduce the idea of social responsibility within the context of lunchroom etiquette or, more to the point, the lack thereof. One might surmise this was a substantial problem, judging by the sheer volume of films on the topic: *Lunchroom Etiquette* (Sandler, 1969), *Food Doesn't Fly: Lunchroom Manners* (Educational Communications, ca. 1979), *School Lunchroom Manners* (Centron, 1979), a second edition of *Lunchroom Etiquette* (Sandler, 1982), and others. On a more macro level, the films hope to get kids to understand how their behavior affects their ability to relate to and socialize within the larger society of which they are a part, including schoolmates, families, and others they interact with on a daily basis. Beyond this shared goal of behavior modification, however, the two films diverge sharply.

In his 1999 book *Mental Hygiene*, an entertaining and informative examination of social guidance and educational films of the 1940s and 50s, Ken Smith notes that Coronet crafted a "perfect" world, one that was clean, carefully managed, meticulously scripted, and situated firmly in white middle-class America. Coronet dominated the educational film market, in part, because it had its own Hollywoodesque production studio, which can only be described as prolific in its output, cranking out approximately one film every four days, a pace unmatched by its competitors.[1]

The 1960 lunchroom film, creatively titled *Lunchroom Manners*, bears out Coronet's signature style with cookie-cutter precision. In keeping with the prevailing view that depicting children engaging in transgressive behavior might introduce or reinforce the very actions the films aimed to discourage, a nonhuman character acts out the unwanted behavior. A voiceless hand puppet, Mr. Bungle, appears in the proscenium of a Punch and Judy booth staged at the front of an

---

[1] Ken Smith, *Mental Hygiene: Classroom Films 1945–1970* (New York: Blast Books, 1999), 91–93.

Figure 20.1. Mr. Bungle rudely forces his way to the head of the line in *Lunchroom Manners* (Coronet, 1960).

elementary school classroom. He fails to wash his hands before eating, makes a mess in the lunchroom, and disturbs those around him (see fig. 20.1). Mr. Bungle is presented as an outrageous, disagreeable figure. Children may have found him entertaining, but the filmmakers clearly did not want them to relate to Mr. Bungle. Further, there is no discussion between the children and their teacher regarding Mr. Bungle's behavior. In fact, there is no discussion in the film at all. An omniscient narrator details the proper actions the children should take and expresses their inner thoughts, which, without fail, reflect an understanding of the ramifications of Mr. Bungle's "bad" behavior and a decision to act in desirable ways.

Nearly two decades later, Coronet updated *Lunchroom Manners*, and the resulting film could not have been more different. Even the remake's title—*A Lunchroom Goes Bananas*—announces a rejection of the staid style of its predecessor. The only thing that remains the same is the basic message of the film: Behave properly in the cafeteria. *A Lunchroom Goes Bananas* follows what appears to be a kid-run news program doing an investigative piece on a local school whose cafeteria food, in response to the chaos of their "workplace," has decided to go on strike. Anthropomorphized stop-action-animation fruits and vegetables expound on the downsides of cafeteria life and declare that they have had enough. Only when the students agree to improve their wayward behavior do the food items agree to abandon the strike.

In sharp contrast to *Lunchroom Manners*, the kids directly model the bad behavior the filmmakers hope to dissuade. Mr. Bungle is nowhere to be seen, and the omniscient narrator is absent as well. The children in *A Lunchroom Goes Bananas* speak directly to the camera in interviews conducted by the news crew. Not only do they express their opinions about the problem at hand, but they also seem to be more knowledgeable than the adults. The kids have to solve the problem, and the adults are depicted as clueless and ineffectual or, at best, as mere facilitators for the discussion and actions that follow. This represents a departure from how *Lunchroom Manners*—and, in fact, all social guidance films of that earlier period—depicted adults as authority figures and problem solvers. In earlier films, authorities might decide to set aside their say-so to let kids come to the "right" decision, but they are still represented as figures worthy of respect.

So we have two films made by the same company fulfilling the same purpose—and yet they are radically different. What changed in the eighteen years between *Lunchroom Manners* and *A Lunchroom Goes Bananas*? First, Coronet changed. By the 1970s, far more competitors had entered the field of educational filmmaking. Coronet was no longer the undisputed leader, and the company had no choice but to abandon its signature style of tightly scripted homogenization in favor of more modern, even experimental approaches if it hoped to compete.

Of equal importance, the students changed. In the 1950s and early 1960s, showing kids a film in school, especially one aimed at them directly, was a departure. By the 1970s, however, kids were saturated with media options for entertainment as well as education. Shows such as *Sesame Street* (which premiered in 1969) and *The Electric Company* (in 1971) had introduced a level of stimulation unimaginable even ten years earlier. Educational TV both altered the way media addressed youngsters and set a new standard for how to tackle problem topics. Rather than approach children pedantically, these shows treated them as unique and intelligent individuals capable of reasoning through problems, often breaking the fourth wall and addressing them directly.

In addition, educational approaches changed. The model of the teacher as lecturer and students as docile absorbers of knowledge had been replaced with a more engaging classroom dynamic. Teachers were now seen as facilitators of knowledge, regularly engaging students in discussion. Students were encouraged to take a more active role in their learning, a shift reflected in *A Lunchroom Goes Bananas*. We see kids come up with the idea of creating posters to hang in the cafeteria to remind them of behaviors to model or avoid: "Don't Be a Slob," "Taste, Don't Waste," and "Walk, Don't Run."

Also, of course, the filmmakers themselves changed. By the 1970s, production choices were dictated less by Coronet's stylebook and more by the experimental movement, the faster editing pace of contemporary cinema, and individual preferences. Tom Chamberlin, director of *A Lunchroom Goes Bananas,* says that Coronet was "looking for new filmmakers to help them change their image from producers of pedantic classroom films to something a little more hip."[2] Another Coronet director, Larry Pont, recalls that the studio's writers "were influenced by the independent films coming through" in the seventies, "and by the new Japanese work starting to come into the country, particularly the animated stuff. We were strongly influenced by films and TV, particularly by the use of close-ups, quick cuts, and montage."[3]

Lastly, *A Lunchroom Goes Bananas* explicitly acknowledges the world outside the classroom by incorporating the issue of a labor strike and by "covering" it via an enacted investigative news program. By the 1970s, strikes and unionization had become part of the pop culture lexicon. *Norma Rae* (1979), the story of a textile worker who helps to unionize her mill, won Sally Field a Best Actress Academy Award just one year after *A Lunchroom Goes Bananas* hit classrooms. Primetime investigative reporting, exemplified by CBS-TV's *60 Minutes* (which premiered in 1968), had become a familiar news and documentary format. The Vietnam War and Watergate had introduced a level of awareness and cynicism in the general public. So pervasive were these changes that the creators of *A Lunchroom Goes Bananas* could be fairly certain that their middle-school audience possessed a degree of political and social awareness lacking in their *Lunchroom Manners* counterparts. While the earlier Coronet films were informed by current events, in particular the postwar pursuit of a middle-class American Dream and the perceived threat of communism, no direct mention of outside political or social events is ever made. By 1978, that hermetic seal had long since been broken. And while some filmmakers were eager to include these outside influences, the Coronet executives still imposed some restraint. Tom Chamberlin recollected:

> They were quite happy as I remember with the script for *Lunchroom
> Goes Bananas*—with the exception that the rough cut included a food
> fight that they thought should be cut back. It hinged on anarchy, I
> remember them saying. Over all they felt the final movie worked. I
> always thought of it as my most successful "fascist" educational film.
> At the same time I contracted to do *Lunchroom Goes Bananas,* I
> signed a contract to do *Rules Are for Gorillas, Too!,* a remake of
> another early "manners film." When Coronet execs saw the rough cut
> of that film, they nixed it completely, because it advocated anarchy,
> they concluded. It was my last contract with Coronet.[4]

---

[2] E-mail to author from Tom Chamberlin, Apr. 23, 2010.

[3] E-mail to author from Larry Pont, Aug. 19, 2008.

[4] E-mail to author from Tom Chamberlin, Apr. 23, 2010.

Venereal Disease: From Patriotic Threat to Civilian Plague

The two Coronet films provide a snapshot of how schools dealt with a relatively innocuous problem. To see how educational films dealt with an issue of far graver import (targeting, presumably, a slightly older audience), we can look to the extensive catalog of films dealing with venereal disease (VD). We are still fighting the battle against venereal disease. A historical survey of VD films gives a sense of the tension between prevailing societal attitudes about morality and the threat to public health posed by VD. This tension manifests itself most obviously in VD films' representation of abstinence versus prophylaxis. The degree to which any given VD movie covered the use of prophylactics depended on the audience and time period in which it was made.

Of particular interest is how early VD films shone a spotlight on what modern audiences frequently, and mistakenly, perceive as a more innocent time. The first film designed to inform and guide behavior relating to venereal disease was released in 1919 and was directed at American servicemen preparing for duty in World War I.[5] The inevitable exposure of U.S. troops to the temptations of European society created concern in the War Department about the number of soldiers likely to contract VD. Until the development of penicillin in the 1940s, the treatment for VD, in particular syphilis, was lengthy and toxic, producing serious side effects and sidelining infected serviceman for more than a year.

In response to these concerns, the U.S. Commission on Training Camp Activities produced *Fit to Fight* (1919), a full-length motion picture that attempted to demonstrate to soldiers the negative consequences of associating with "loose women." The film tells the story of five draftees and their misadventures with alcohol and prostitutes. In addition to conflating abstinence with the maintenance of one's virility (in contrast to the common view that sexual activity was essential to a soldier's effectiveness), the training film painted getting VD as unpatriotic.[6] Soldiers were implored to think of the cost to the war effort should they become infected. *Fit to Fight,* publicly distributed in a recut called *Fit to Win,* set the tone for venereal disease films for decades to come.

Forty years later, Centron Productions, in conjunction with the Kansas State Board of Health, released *Dance, Little Children*, which takes its name from a rock 'n' roll song and deals with a small town's VD epidemic. The 1960 film, which was aimed at parents and public health officials, discusses sex in a surprisingly frank manner: one teen admits having sex at a baseball game with a girl whose name he does not know, while another teen's motel room tryst,

[5] Allan M. Brandt, *No Magic Bullet: A Social History of Venereal Disease in the United States since 1880* (New York: Oxford University Press, 1987), 68; Eric Schaefer, *Bold! Daring! Shocking! True! A History of Exploitation Films* (Durham, NC: Duke University Press, 1999), 27–30.

[6] Brandt, *No Magic Bullet*, 64, 66.

though not depicted, is strongly implied.[7] Such open acknowledgement of sexual activity in the pre–Sexual Revolution era, especially among teenagers, was rare, a fact that only emphasizes the perceived scope of the problem. The importance of keeping troops healthy necessitated relatively open discussion of VD during wartime, but frank treatment of the subject in schools was unusual.

Dance, Little Children looks at the range of reactions to venereal disease as expressed by the victims' parents. The film's style is that of a documentary. Both the victims and their parents are depicted as real people, not actors, though this distinction is never clearly made. One parent blames sex education for her son's actions, proclaiming, "If my boy hadn't known about such filthy things, he wouldn't have got curious and he wouldn't be sick!" Another parent evinces something akin to pride that his "pantywaist" son "had it in him"; and a third parent disowns his daughter, wondering at the "trash she's been running with." Only one set of parents shows compassion for their child. The filmmakers clearly intend the audience to see this last mother and father as the most reasonable and sympathetic of the bunch. The narrator notes that this girl is "more fortunate than some to have parents who will make the difficult effort to understand."

The teens themselves react to their situation with emotions ranging from shame to indifference. *Dance, Little Children* blames society's obsession with sex and the proliferation of sexual imagery in the media for the teenagers' rampant sexual activity, suggesting that teens are being pushed to grow up too quickly. The film also offers possible psychological explanations for the sexual activity behind the outbreak. The girl with the sympathetic parents tearfully explains that she just wanted her date to like her. Meanwhile, her date's father laments to the family doctor that he doesn't know what more his son wants from him, proclaiming that he has bought the boy "everything in the world he ever asked for." He is utterly mystified by his son's behavior. The doctor replies, "Maybe he wants the thing he seems to have been looking for pretty desperately—somebody who cares."

The film makes it difficult for the viewer to react with a "not in my town, not my children" attitude. Its acknowledgment of the complex psychological motivations behind engaging in sexual activity is unusual for the time in which it was made; it asks the viewer to see the outbreak's victims as real people rather than to adhere to the prevailing opinion that only "bad kids" had sex. Although made more than fifty years ago, the situation and characters still resonate and the reactions of both the parents and teens are no different than one might expect from a similarly themed film today.

---

[7] Although I could find no study guide or advertisement that states the intended audience for *Dance, Little Children*, the filmmakers' focus on the public health threat of VD and their depiction of exaggerated parental reactions to the diagnosis of VD seem to indicate that the intended audience was not necessarily the victims themselves.

Both *Fit to Fight* and *Dance, Little Children* avoid one important component of VD prevention—the use of prophylactics. Both rely on guilt, appeals to morality, and scare tactics to prevent the spread of venereal diseases. Condoms are not even hinted at, let alone discussed in any detail. In 1973, the animated short *VD Attack Plan* addressed the omission of those earlier films. Although other films in the intervening years did address the use of prophylactics, they were almost exclusively aimed at a military audience. *VD Attack Plan*, although used for the military, found a more general audience as well.

The unlikely producer of the film was the Walt Disney Company, known worldwide for its sanitized fairy tale adaptations and live-action family fare. Even the marketing department at the Walt Disney Educational Media Company acknowledged that it was somewhat incredible for their company to address such a vulgar subject as venereal disease. The front page of their promotional brochure announces: "Yes, it's true. Walt Disney Productions has made a significant contribution to the war against VD. *VD Attack Plan*—A fully animated Walt Disney 16mm motion picture."[8] While *VD Attack Plan* includes the points that had become de rigueur for any venereal disease film—the symptoms and effects of syphilis and gonorrhea, the importance of treatment while avoiding phony cures, and, of course, graphic pictures of the ravages of syphilis—Disney also includes condom use, whereas other films of the period mention only abstinence as a form of prevention or do not mention prevention at all.[9] Most film producers knew that school boards would not purchase a film that included such a message, based on the belief that it would encourage sexual activity. Disney addressed this by releasing two versions of the film, the longer of which mentions condoms, the shorter of which does not.[10] The company might have done this so that the film had a wider appeal—the short version for high school students and the longer version for young adults in college or the military—but the fact that they mentioned condoms at all was still groundbreaking. Disney also introduced the surprisingly progressive message that venereal diseases can be spread through same-sex sexual contact, something other VD films would not address for at least another decade.

Although *VD Attack Plan*'s intended audience was teens and young adults, the film pays homage to earlier fit-to-fight VD films aimed at soldiers. It opens with an air raid siren, followed by machine-gun fire spelling out "ATTACK PLAN" on the screen. Next, an animated germ "sergeant" (played by Keenan Wynn, best known

---

[8] Sales brochure for *VD Attack Plan*, A/V Geeks Educational Film Archive. Skip Elsheimer, "VD Attack Plan: A Disney Film about Venereal Disease," *Other Zine* 2 (Spring 2001), www.othercinema.com/otherzine/ozissue2/vd.html.

[9] The film *VD Every 30 Seconds* (1971), for example, addresses prophylaxis by showing a still of "VD: How to Prevent It" brochures.

[10] In addition, the Discussion Leader's Guide for *VD Attack Plan* provides a section on prophylaxis, treatments, and cures, which includes a telephone number for a counseling and referral service operated by and for teens.

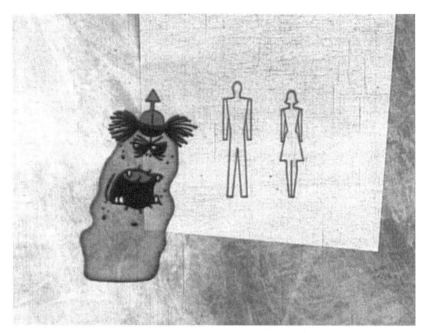

Figure 20.2. The venereal disease sergeant (voiced by Keenan Wynn) lectures his troops in Disney's *VD Attack Plan* (1973).

for his role as Colonel "Bat" Guano in Stanley Kubrick's 1964 film *Dr. Strangelove*) briefs his troops of the Contagion Corps (see fig. 20.2). The troops are phallus-shaped, anthropomorphized syphilis and gonorrhea germs, who wear berets with the initials "S" and "G." Throughout, humor is used to put viewers at ease while still conveying the necessary information. *VD Attack Plan* demonstrates that Disney, despite its trademark sugary view of the world, was not only capable of being ahead of its time on matters such as sexuality but also could be entertaining and sensitive with a topic such as venereal disease. During production, the film's director Les Clark was quoted in an interview about their approach with the film: "We're taking it from the venereal disease germ's point of view of imparting a lot of information without talking down to the youngsters who don't like to be talked down to."[11]

Educational Filmmaking as Religious Propaganda

Whereas the films examined thus far address longstanding issues of health and social guidance and reveal how attitudes toward those subjects have changed over time, the last films I want to look at are of interest because they document the

---

[11] Unpublished Les Clark interview conducted by Chris Finch for John Canemaker's book *Walt Disney's Nine Old Men and the Art of Animation* (Disney Editions, 2001), John Canemaker Papers, Fales Library, New York University.

germination of an idea that has gained considerable traction since the late twentieth century: intelligent design. Starting in 1946 with *God of Creation*, the Moody Institute of Science (MIS) and its founder Irwin A. Moon began producing visually compelling "science" films. These films were based on live science demonstrations that he would perform across the country under the name "Sermons from Science." Moon founded MIS as part of the fundamentalist Moody Bible Institute, his alma mater. Moon was a Christian evangelist who believed that the marvels of nature and science were proof of a divine creator. Topics covered by his films include the life cycle of the grunion fish, bats' use of sonar, the theory of relativity, and the subjective nature of time. Regardless of topic, all MIS films convey the same teleological message: the complexity and wonder of the world could not have happened by accident and, thus, it is proof of God the Creator.

Although the Moody films did not plant the seeds of the intelligent design movement, their wide circulation in schools and churches certainly cultivated those seeds. By 1956, according to Heather Hendershot, MIS films were used by 389 school systems in forty-six states.[12] The Moody Institute took advantage of the widespread increase of audiovisual equipment in American classrooms after World War II. It also was an expression of the nation's Cold War desire to compete with Soviet technology while simultaneously setting the United States apart from the "godless commies" by emphasizing Christian morality. In 1958, Congress passed the National Defense of Education Act (NDEA), the result of the United States' Cold War anxiety regarding the Soviet Union's apparent superiority in the sciences. The NDEA allotted hundreds of thousands of dollars to the acquisition of lab and audiovisual equipment for teaching math and science. Evidence of the impact of the NDEA on MIS film production and distribution can be found in the institute's science film advertisements, which from 1959 on include a variation of the following sentence: "MIS material qualifies for purchase under the provisions of the National Defense Education Act of 1958."[13] Irwin Moon took full advantage of the NDEA, pursuing distribution in the environs of the secular classroom while keeping one foot firmly in the religious territory that was his focus.

The MIS films that made their way into classrooms were truncated versions of the originals, which were intended for church and general audiences as well as military ones. (Beginning in the late 1940s, the U.S. armed services showed the films to personnel as part of its Character Guidance programs.) The revised versions, therefore, lacked the full evangelical sermon that concluded the longer

---

[12] Heather Hendershot, *Shaking the World for Jesus: Media and Conservative Evangelical Culture* (Chicago: University of Chicago Press, 2004), 160.

[13] Marsha Orgeron and Skip Elsheimer, "Something Different in Science Films: The Moody Institute of Science and the Canned Missionary Movement," *The Moving Image* 7, no. 1 (2007): 5.

versions.[14] They nonetheless clearly conveyed Moon's intended message: that the complexity of the world could only be explained by the omniscience of a creator God. This was part of a general acceptance of nondenominational religion in public schools in the 1950s. In 1954, Congress had added the words "under God" to the Pledge of Allegiance, the recitation of which had become a part of American children's school day since the 1940s.

When it came to marketing, however, MIS chose a secular path, its ads making almost no reference to the evangelical tenor of the films. An ad for *Fish Out of Water!* (1954), appearing in the January 1955 issue of *Educational Screen*, sells the film as a simple yet effective documentation and explanation of the life cycle of the grunion. In the movie itself, however, subtle voiceover cues tout the "mysterious wisdom" that guides the grunion in its mating ritual and the "mysterious, unknown way" the fish is generated—positioned, ironically, over a visual of the grunion cells dividing, an entirely explicable process. Such details provide the unmistakably religious message that only a divine plan could account for such miracles. As late as 1973, MIS, despite educational reviews pointing out the religious overtones of the organization's offerings (and some teacher objections to this), still deliberately avoided mention of these religious underpinnings.[15] An ad in *Audiovisual Instruction* from March 1973, for example, refers only obliquely to the "plus factors" found in every Moody educational film.[16]

Setting aside his creationist motive, in many instances Moon is more preoccupied by the need to wow his audience with the technology used to make the films rather than with explaining scientific principles. *The Mystery of Time* (1957), for example, addresses Einstein's theories regarding the inconstancy of space and time while relying heavily on high-speed and time-lapse camera work. At one point, Moon shoots an arrow through a chicken egg, and a close-up of the action is shown in dazzling super-slow motion. Moon follows this with what he calls a "two-day vacation," a time-lapse interlude showing clouds in motion across the sky, traffic in city streets, a football game, and the setting sun. These technological displays, however, exist in a vacuum. Moon spends more time explaining the technology behind the compelling footage than on any of the principles they are supposed to illustrate. All of which belies the true purpose of the films. Viewers may come away feeling as though they have been witness to science at work in the world, but they will possess little more understanding of said science than they had when the lights went down. But for Moon, understanding is beside the

---

[14] James Burkhart Gilbert, *Redeeming Culture: American Religion in an Age of Science* (Chicago: University of Chicago Press, 1997), 17, 121–46. See also Gladwin Hill, "Religion and Science: Both Are Served by Moody Bible Institute Films," *New York Times*, Sept. 11, 1949.

[15] L. C. Larson and Carolyn Guss, "Animals of East Africa," *Educational Screen and Audiovisual Guide* (June 1961): 293–95.

[16] *Audiovisual Instruction* (March 1973): 123.

454 LEARNING WITH THE LIGHTS OFF

point. God's omniscience "explains" the most complex of scientific phenomena and the dazzling camera work is a means for conveying this message. In the end, science proves the existence of God because MIS films say so, but little is presented in the way of evidence for such suppositions beyond the leap of faith required by MIS narratives.[17]

The impact of Moon and the MIS films on the current debate surrounding intelligent design is difficult to ascertain, but given the near-ubiquity of the films in classrooms (and on U.S. military bases) during the 1950s and 60s, as well as their international circulation in multiple languages, it is likely they aided the development of the latter-day Christian intelligent design movement. While Moon insists that the world revealed by science is too wondrous and complex to have come about by accident, he never directly challenges evolution as a theory, preferring a soft-sell approach to creationism. Similarly, intelligent design's proponents are careful not to state that the intelligence in question is "God," but most scientists concur with the federal judge who declared in 2005 that the concept is not science but a thinly veiled religious idea promoted to counter the theory of evolution.[18] Not surprisingly, some MIS films have found a new audience in the Christian homeschooling community. Moody Publishing continues to sell MIS DVDs from its video catalog.

Whether documenting changing values over time or offering insight into the evolution of contemporary discourse, educational films often provide a secondary value that their creators never intended. By capturing the anxieties and desires of the time in which they were made, these films are a gauge of what past mentalities and practices were; they give the lie to the myth of "the good ol' days" and stymie would-be revisionist historians. As our values shift over time, revisiting educational films can give us perspective and remind us that very few cultural trends are truly original or new. Sometimes the values revealed by the films, such as the widespread acceptance of nondenominational religion in public schools, become more telling over time, particularly when viewed in tandem with current events. These are the attributes that most interest me and drive me to continue collecting and rewatching these ephemeral cultural snapshots.

---

[17] Orgeron and Elsheimer, "Something Different," 16–21.

[18] *Kitzmiller v. Dover Area School District,* 400 F. Supp. 2d 707 (M.D. Pa. 2005). The judge agreed with the plaintiffs (parents of students in Dover, Pennsylvania) that the district's attempt to require the teaching of intelligent design as science violated the First Amendment. In 2004, the school board mandated ninth-grade biology teachers read to students a statement declaring: "Intelligent Design is an explanation of the origin of life that differs from Darwin's view." In the United States, the dissemination of the term *intelligent design* is traceable to the Christian conservative organization, the Discovery Institute's Center for Science and Culture, and Phillip E. Johnson's book *Darwin on Trial* (Washington, DC: Regnery, 1991). (A 20th Anniversary Edition appeared in 2010 [Downers Grove, IL: IVP Books].)

Filmography

Unless otherwise indicated, all titles are from the A/V Geeks Archive as 16mm prints and commercial DVD copies (www.avgeeks.com).

Dance, Little Children (ca. 1960), **25 min., 16mm**
PRODUCTON: Centron Films, DISTRIBUTION: Kansas State Board of Health.; U.S. Public Health Service. PRODUCERS: Russell A. Mosser, Arthur H. Wolf. WRITER: Margaret Travis. CINEMATOGRAPHY: Norman Stuewe. EDITOR: Chuck Lacey.

Fish Out of Water! (1954) **10 min.**
PRODUCER: Moody Institute of Science.

Fit to Fight (1918) ca. **60 min., 35mm**
PRODUCER: U.S. War Department, Commission on Training Camp Activities. DIRECTOR-WRITER: Edward H. Griffith. CAST: Raymond McKee (as Billy Hale), Harry Gripp (Chick Carlton), Paul Kelly (Hank Simpson). ACCESS: Not known to survive.

Fit to Win (1919) **6 reels, 35mm**
Edited version of *Fit to Fight,* included new epilogue.
ALTERNATE TITLES: *The Men's Lecture Film;* a companion film, *The End of the Road*, was produced for women audiences. DISTRIBUTOR: Public Health Films; American Social Hygiene Association. ACCESS: Not known to survive.

A Lunchroom Goes Bananas (**Lunchroom Manners, 2nd ed.**) (**1978**) **12 min., 16mm**
PRODUCER: Christianson Productions, for Coronet. CONSULTANTS: James L. Hymes Jr., Mary Sue Kerner. ANIMATION: Jim Blashfield. SCRIPT: Roger Margolis. ACCESS: Coronet Films and Video, VHS (198?), with printed film guide.

Lunchroom Manners (1960) **9 min., 16mm**
PRODUCER: Coronet Instructional Films. EDUCATIONAL COLLABORATOR: Ross L. Allen. ACCESS: Internet Archive, www.archive.org/details/lunchroom_manners.

[The] Mystery of Time (1957) **28 min., 16mm**
PRODUCER: Moody Institute of Science. CAST: Irwin A. Moon. ACCESS: Internet Archive, www.archive.org/details/mystery_of_ time.

VD Attack Plan (1973) 16 min., 16mm
DIRECTOR: Les Clark. WRITER: Bill Bosche. NARRATOR:
Keenan Wynn. ART STYLING: A. Kendall O'Connor. MUSIC:
George Bruns. ANIMATION: Charlie Downs. FILM EDITOR: Jim
Love. CO-ORDINATOR: Virginia Fontanella. ACCESS: Internet
Archive, www.archive.org/details/vd_attack_plan.

Related Films (all 16mm)

Food Doesn't Fly: Lunchroom Manners (1979) 8 min.
PRODUCER: Educational Communications Inc. (ECI).

God of Creation (1946) 29 min.
PRODUCER: Moody Institute of Science. CAST: Irwin A. Moon.
ACCESS: DVD (*God of Creation: A Sermon from Science with Irwin
A. Moon*, 1998) and VHS (Moody Video, 1985) Moody Publishers
(www.moodypublishers.com).

Good Table Manners (1951) 11 min.
PRODUCTION: Coronet Instructional Films.

The Great American Chocolate Factory (1977) 28 min.
SPONSOR: Hershey Foods Corporation. PRODUCTION:
Kennedy-Lee Productions. DISTRIBUTION: Modern Talking
Picture Service. ACCESS: Pennsylvania State University (16mm).

Lunchroom Etiquette (1969) 9 min.

Lunchroom Etiquette, 2nd ed. (1982) 11 min.
PRODUCER: Sandler Institutional Films.

Rules Are for Gorillas, Too! (1983) 11 min.
PRODUCER: Christianson Productions, for Coronet. ACCESS:
Phoenix Learning Group (www.phoenixlearninggroup.com).

School Lunchroom Manners (1979) 10 min.
PRODUCER: Centurion Films/Centron Films.

Sudden Birth (1966) 22 min.
PRODUCER: Bay State Films. SPONSOR: California Peace
Officers Association. ACCESS: Internet Archive, www.archive.org/
details/sudden_birth.

21 CONTINUING ED: EDUCATIONAL FILM COLLECTIONS IN LIBRARIES AND ARCHIVES

ELENA ROSSI-SNOOK

While public libraries, universities, and colleges in America have contrasting institutional profiles, they share a fundamental role in the education of the nation's adult population. Public libraries embody egalitarian access to methods and tools of informal education, while colleges and universities provide training and structure for a professional career. During the first half of the twentieth century, the means of achieving educational goals by these institutions only occasionally included the use of motion pictures. The obstacles and conditions preventing the widespread adoption and collection of educational films, however, would be overcome by World War II and its profound effect on the way Americans thought about both education and nontheatrical film. The extensive employment of the "versatile 16mm film" as an educational instrument for the war effort and the influx of veterans enrolled in college under the GI Bill contributed to a film-conscious, visually inclined postwar America. It also provided the foundation upon which educational film collections within public libraries and higher education institutions were built.[1]

Divesting themselves of the role of repository or commercial distributor, these 16mm educational film collections were accompanied by a range of services and were typically maintained and curated by staff knowledgeable in the educational needs of their community. As a result, educational film collections within schools and libraries represented a wide range of social concerns and cultural interests. Some collections may have been more sophisticated than others, but they were all dedicated to the betterment of society.

Now more than a decade into the twenty-first century, the role of campus and public library educational film collections is fluid, as their traditional function in the classroom or auditorium has shifted. Some collections have transitioned from the audiovisual (A-V) department to the university's archive for

---

Portions of this essay were first published as "Persistence of Vision: Public Library 16mm Film Collections in America," *The Moving Image* 5, no. 1 (2005): 1–27, reprinted here with permission of the University of Minnesota Press.

[1] *Sixty Years of 16mm Film, 1923–1983: A Symposium* (Evanston, IL: Film Council of America, 1954), 90.

academic and historical consideration. In many cases, private archives have acquired collections deaccessioned in favor of cheaper, more portable video formats. Sometimes the role of the institution itself has become undefined, acting as both lender and protector of these special collections. Many public libraries that have guarded their collections from displacement find themselves undertaking the role of preservationist or conservationist. And yet, by having secured copies of productions that are now rare or unavailable elsewhere, they are also fulfilling the role once occupied by 16mm distributors by lending to festivals and programmers. For researchers seeking films representing postwar idealism (*Union Local*, 1951), the Italian stone artisans of the National Cathedral in Washington (*The Stone Carvers*, 1984), or the establishment of cooperative daycare (*Childcare: People's Liberation*, 1970), these films may not be evident in a library catalog. However, they are often still out there, tucked away under the supervision of special collections, university archives, research divisions, or any number of random departments within the institutions that once proudly advertised their availability.

Motion pictures were not entirely absent from American campuses during the medium's seminal period. As early as the 1910s, a number of colleges and universities including Yale, Oklahoma, Michigan, Harvard, and MIT were involved in some form of educational film production. A small number of universities also hosted film libraries. However, the primary objective for these collections was to serve as local, regional, or national distribution center for off-campus groups and organizations and not as audiovisual support for campus classrooms.

Those college courses that did use film were usually operated by extension divisions. Established in those areas of the country dedicated to agriculture, university extension services were created in tandem with the adult education movement at the turn of the century to assist adults and nontraditional students who could not afford or attend traditional on-campus classes, or who wanted to continue their studies after graduation. Before World War II, these courses were more apt to employ visual education methods when doing so was neither common nor popular in higher education. In distance learning programs and remote locations where a lecture or lecturer was difficult to secure or unwelcome, film proved a viable substitute.

By 1941, there were more than thirty extension divisions distributing films, yet relatively few instructors within the institution used this resource.[2] Until the late 1940s, the concept of the university and college lending film library as an extrainstitutional distributor was foremost, with predictions citing that by the

---

[2] L. Paul Saettler, *The Evolution of American Educational Technology*, 2nd ed. (Greenwich, CT: Information Age Publishing, 2004), 111.

close of the first postwar decade five hundred universities and colleges would have film lending libraries that would operate "on a service charge basis for schools in the immediate geographic areas" and "serve organized adult groups."[3]

Several factors contributed to the failure of educational films to permeate campus classrooms. The films being produced were not typically made to follow basic curricula (especially outside of the physical sciences, which tended to attract more film production than other fields of study) and had little merit with instructors. According to Ford Lemler (then director of the University of Michigan Audio-Visual Education Center), "The number of creditable teaching films was relatively small."[4] The problem of the lack of usable films was compounded by a scarcity of projection equipment.

In addition, the "film library" as it was conceived and operated before the war tended to be just that: a repository for films available for distribution. There was not necessarily an audiovisual support team or librarian to oversee the purchase, cataloging, and advertisement of films; to assist professors with film selection and projection; or to act as a liaison with administrators regarding classroom regulations hospitable to film use. Without this presence in the academic community, the film library was often challenging even to locate. It could be a part of the extension division or located within the general library, within the school of education, in a variety of other departments, or maintained by administrative offices.

The use of motion pictures in liberal arts courses was further stymied by the academy's long-standing predilection for lecture, recitation, and the written word. Although film was being used by athletic coaches to train athletes and by medical school programs to train physicians, its application to other areas of instruction was met with resistance or ignorance. As Walter Wittich, director of the University of Wisconsin's Bureau of Audio-Visual Instruction, complained as late as 1954, "the modern college student" was daily engulfed in radio, film, and television, but "the Halls of Ivy" surrounded him with "the traditional, conservative, and often obtuse verbal explanations of comparative philosophies, psychologies, histories, or ideologies."[5] For those professors raised on and trained in oration, the thinking and employment of visual instruction was a radical departure from tradition.

These factors impeded the growth of college film libraries, "both in the numbers of such agencies and in the character and extent of their offerings." The film library, competing against "institutional handicaps," a "deeply ingrained

---

[3] L. C. Larson, "Trends in Audio-Visual Instruction," *Educational Screen* 22, no. 6 (June 1943): 199.

[4] Ford L. Lemler, "The University or College Film Library," in *Film and Education: A Symposium on the Role of the Film in the Field of Education*, ed. Elliott M. Godfrey (New York: Philosophical Library, 1948), 503, 515.

[5] W. A. Wittich, "Colleges and Universities," in *Sixty Years of 16mm Film*, 62.

verbal tradition, inertias, lags, resistances," and its own history of being regarded as an off-campus distributor, did not reach its potential as a full-service audiovisual department until the decade following World War II.[6]

Interest in educational films by public librarians was, as with colleges, rooted in the reconceptualization of public education dating back to the turn of the century. Up until the latter half of the nineteenth century, libraries were, according to Arthur Bostwick's 1910 account, passive "storehouses, first and foremost," designed only to meet the needs of a scholarly clientele.[7] However, in the 1890s, libraries adopted a more expansive code for combating ignorance and "vulgarity." Librarians determined that the spirit of library service should surpass a merely literary function. In accordance, the public library of the 1900s enveloped an ideology of "social obligation" and began providing a large range of services, striving to become "the nation's principal agency of enlightenment."[8] The purpose of the public library, under the newly conceptualized "modern library idea," was to serve the greatest number of people in the most direct possible way and under the most comfortable circumstances.[9] The influx of immigrants to the United States, an increase in the numbers attending high school and college, and the industrial forty-eight-plus-hour workweek were seen as fodder for expanded service, where the library could aid individuals in capitalizing on what little time and resources they had for personal growth.[10] Consequently, public libraries were idealized as educational saviors—the "People's College." Bostwick, a prolific promoter of the "modern library idea," asserted that "the public library, indeed, is the only formal educational influence that is exerted through life . . . the library should take its entire public as its clientele and not simply that part of it which voluntarily seeks it out."[11]

For "modern" librarians attempting to expand services and promote public patronage, the development of educational motion pictures was particularly attractive. While cognizant of the need for a process of securing films for libraries and exhibiting them, supporters of library film service insisted these institutions should incorporate motion pictures into their agenda. Some libraries made a concerted effort to heed this advice; a number of educational film programs sponsored by libraries were screened at the local theaters. The *American Library*

---

[6] Lemler, "University or College Film Library," 503, 515.

[7] Arthur E. Bostwick, *The American Public Library*, 2nd ed. (New York: D. Appleton, 1917), 1 (first published in 1910). Bostwick served as American Library Association president during 1907–08.

[8] Patrick Williams, *The American Public Library and the Problem of Purpose* (Westport, CT: Greenwood Press, 1988), 34.

[9] Bostwick, *American Public Library*, 1.

[10] *World Book Multimedia Encyclopedia*, accessed through online subscription service, Aug. 18, 2003.

[11] Bostwick, *American Public Library*, 14, 25.

Annual noted in 1916 that two libraries had purchased equipment and were projecting films on their premises.[12] These gestures were judged as triumphant progress. At a 1915 conference the ALA president officially announced that, among the activities and services at the public library, "now we are introducing moving picture shows."[13]

Despite technical hindrances—35mm film was costly to rent, difficult to obtain, and required a fireproof projection booth—throughout the 1920s libraries were further encouraged to incorporate motion pictures into their repertoire.[14] In 1923, the 16mm film gauge allowed for cheaper and safer film use, and in 1924, the ALA established a Committee on Relations Between Libraries and Moving Pictures. In 1926, Melvil Dewey, forefather of the modern public library, affirmed, "The public is coming to recognize the library as just as important as the school." While apprehensive about the potential for films to corrupt the public's willingness to read, Dewey conceded that "the motion picture . . . is one of the greatest agencies for education man has yet devised."[15] Encouraged by this endorsement, the small number of libraries that used film as part of their service continued to do so and in 1929, the Kalamazoo (Michigan) Public Library began the unique practice of lending to schools and adult groups their own collection of films that had been deposited by the State Department of Conservation.

However, the widespread adoption of film in libraries was far from realization. At its 1925 conference, the ALA made three recommendations: that a determinate number of urban libraries collect and distribute films to area schools and community organizations; that the libraries dispense information on sources of films; and that an administrative office be established to promote cooperation between public libraries and suppliers of motion pictures. And yet, nearly twenty years later, *Educational Screen* was still prophesying that "public libraries will extend the scope of their free service to include films" and that "a number of libraries will organize a film information service for organized adult groups."[16] By 1940, only Kalamazoo, Michigan, and Beaumont, Texas, had public libraries with film collections—and those were not built on acquisition policy but rather accepted as deposits from government agencies. Even the New York Public Library, a major metropolitan library system, did not even begin programming films until 1940 and was without a dedicated film department until the late

---

[12] Joseph W. Palmer, "'14–'74: Decades of Service," *Film Library Quarterly* 8, no. 1 (1975): 18.

[13] Williams, *American Public Library*, 32.

[14] Willard Morrison, "The 16mm Market and the Audience—A Brief History," in *16mm Distribution*, comp. Judith Trojan and Nadine Covert (New York: Educational Film Library Association, 1977), 11.

[15] Melvil Dewey, "Our Next Half-Century," *Library Journal* 51 (Oct. 1926): 887.

[16] Larson, "Trends in Audio-Visual Instruction," 199.

1950s. According to one overview of the state of the industry before World War II, many libraries' efforts to promote and publicize their film service were "slow to bring results." "People outside of school systems seldom thought of using films as information sources, or, to promote projects and put across ideas."[17]

Much of what slowed film service development in public libraries was the problem of finding and procuring appropriate films. Without the resources to undertake film collection, each production intended for programming or circulation to the public needed to be secured from a distributor. However, nontheatrical distribution was confusing and haphazard, with users generally unsure of how or where to get films. For those persistent librarians who did locate a distributor, because the production companies reevaluated the availability of titles after three to six months in circulation, it was often difficult to obtain certain films without dedicating considerable funds to their purchase. In addition, since the number and frequency of libraries requesting films from distributors was inconsistent, the professional exchanges that earned an income by making prints available were "little interested in meeting the occasional request of the libraries for service." Distributors also complained that librarians were charging an unreported admission price at their screenings and were not always "business-like" in the return of films.[18]

Problems with the nontheatrical market transcended mere inconvenience and were not limited to public libraries. Distribution catalogs supplied only general topics and titles with vague or no synopses and were without production credits. How could one know if *The Feet* would be a stimulating discourse on biology? Would *Meat Packing* be appropriate for a library discussion group? What age group could comprehend *Some Larger Mammals*?[19] Renting a film in advance for preview was financially impossible for most, especially during the Depression, and without an organization to which one could appeal for film reference or an administrative body to assist teachers and educational film programmers in the selection of films, people were left to make selections with little or no guidance.

The films themselves added another dimension to the problem. Many films advertised as educational were inappropriate for instruction: sponsored films too intent on product placement, films with outdated information, Hollywood pictures meant first as theatrical money-makers and secondly as back-door revenue in the nontheatrical market.[20] Prior to World War II, a cycle of discontent

---

[17] Jean Ogden and Jess Ogden, "Bringing Films to Smaller Communities," in *Making Films Work for Your Community* (New York: Educational Film Library Association, 1946), 49.

[18] Orrin G. Cocks, "Libraries and Motion Pictures—An Ignored Educational Agency," *Library Journal* 39 (Sept. 1914): 666.

[19] University of California Extension Division, *Visual Aids to Education: A Catalogue of Educational 16mm and 35mm Motion Picture Films and Glass Slides* (1936–1937 annual), 3.

[20] Wesley F. Pratzner, "What Has Happened to the Documentary Film?" *Public Opinion Quarterly* 11, no. 3 (Autumn 1947): 395.

existed between educational institutions and film producers. Educators feared exposing their audiences to the wrong kind of content; producers knew that investing in the nontheatrical market was risky, yielding small profit margins at best. Too few organizations and institutions were using educational films to merit the kind of capital required for research and production. Hollywood studios, often urged to serve the educational market, were pragmatic about the bottom line. In 1936, Lorraine Noble, a Hollywood writer hired by the American Council on Education to administer its "Educational Film Project," wrote that no "venturesome soul" within the studio system had produced "that vague something known as the educational film" because "under present conditions there is no way by which the actual cost of even a modest film" could be recouped in the school market.[21]

Despite the studies conducted and articles written on the effectiveness of visual educational methods, the resolution of these problems would not come until World War II, when nontheatrical 16mm film became the educational standard. Sixteen-millimeter prints—nonflammable and more portable than the 35mm nitrate prints used in theaters—were the means by which wartime communication was propagated. Rather than wait for the public to enter the movie theater or the soldier to watch and rewatch a demonstration, visually explicit and crucial wartime information was brought to them. Military classrooms, aircraft carriers, battlefield tents, churches, libraries, and civic clubs became important film venues.

The modification of the educational film product to convey democratic ideals and impart timely information stimulated a widespread receptivity that had not existed previously. Studios and producers that once balked at the nontheatrical market were now creating professional educational films for the United States government. From the military experiences of millions of Americans came a new concept of how information could be transferred and behavior modified through informational and training films. In the civilian sector, millions came to understand the war through documentaries. Equipment became familiar. Standards for content were realized. A definition of the *educational film* genre was formulated: "films of 16mm. width which deal with fact rather than fiction and which are intended to reach an audience outside the theatre and to contribute to the process of learning."[22] The days of public ambivalence toward or ignorance of educational films were over.

---

[21] Lorraine Noble, "Modernization, By Way of the Educational Film," *Journal of Educational Sociology* 10, no. 3 (Nov. 1936): 151.

[22] Gerald D. McDonald, *Educational Motion Pictures and Libraries* (Chicago: American Library Association, 1942), 7.

The war also forged routes into mass distribution for the nontheatrical sector. The involvement of the federal government in film production and the desire of film-minded groups and companies to assist in the war effort spurred the creation of a 16mm distribution network. Representatives from the National Association of Visual Education Dealers, the NEA's Division of Audio-Visual Instruction, the Allied Non-Theatrical Film Association, the Visual Equipment Manufacturers Council, and others worked with the federal Office of War Information, the Office of the Coordinator of Inter-American Affairs, and the Department of Agriculture Film Division to make films available to public service centers, which in turn became focal points for distribution to individuals and organizations in their communities. This network "had a profound influence," wrote one of its architects, "in providing a hitherto unknown cohesion in the 16mm distribution industry," and it laid the groundwork for what would become in the postwar years a coordination of obtaining film prints from either commercial distribution agencies or intermediary institutions with film libraries.[23] As a result, nontheatrical distribution grew, "both as a business and as a nonprofit educational or promotional venture." By the early 1950s, the number of organizations loaning such films reached 2,660.[24]

While improvements to educational film and its procurement increased the existence of 16mm film libraries in colleges and universities, there were other potent factors that led to its widespread use, especially in the campus classroom. Between the fall semesters of 1939 and 1943, enrollment of full-time civilian students in regular college programs declined sharply from 1,493,000 to 761,000.[25] The Servicemen's Readjustment Act of 1944, commonly known as the GI Bill of Rights, aimed to prevent a crisis in which millions of returning veterans would have flooded the job market. The bill gave them an incentive to opt for education. By 1947, veterans accounted for 49 percent of college admissions. When the GI Bill ended in 1956, 7.8 million of the nation's 16 million World War II veterans had participated in an education or training program.[26] The influx of a student body trained and entertained with motion pictures during military duty further catalyzed the adoption of film in the college classroom. Instructors, facing classes with rosters of up to eighty students, often used film as a means of capturing and holding attention.

---

[23] Arch A. Mercey, "Social Uses of the Motion Picture," *Annals of the American Academy of Political and Social Science* 250 (Mar. 1947): 100.

[24] Chester A. Lindstrom, "Distribution," in *Sixty Years of 16mm Film*, 37.

[25] Ralph C. M. Flynt, "Postwar College Courses," *Journal of Higher Education* 16, no. 4 (1945): 197–98.

[26] U.S. Department of Veterans Affairs, "Born of Controversy: The GI Bill of Rights," www.va.gov/opa/publications/celebrate/gi-bill.pdf.

Curriculum and teaching methods changed to accommodate the new student body. Colleges and universities in the postwar era were challenged to "provide a greater measure of liberal education . . . an upward extension of the free general education of the secondary school with its inclusive implication."[27] Many higher education institutions began departing from the tradition of specialized schooling to embrace the contemporary standard of liberal arts education. Motion picture use was requested and, in some cases, demanded of professors. Thurman G. Justice's 1946 survey of forty-nine veterans in ten colleges found that the group liked college and excelled in their coursework, but "that the teaching staff was not up to the standards expected; that the lecture material was poorly organized and the lectures ineffectively presented; that colleges, on the whole, seemed to be uninterested in improving their standards and methods of instruction." Justice concluded that "the many suggestions for the use of movies and other visual material indicate that the generous use of such material in military training has had its effect."[28]

Public libraries, more so than colleges, anticipated the role the institution and educational film could fulfill in wartime. From the time the United States entered World War II, public libraries were considered an integral part of the grassroots informational film network. Devoted to informal public education, public libraries were in a prime position to deliver important information to a large population. Authorities considered the use of libraries for the screening and distribution of 16mm films an excellent method for reaching the American public. In 1941, the federal government began employing public libraries to disseminate defense- and war-related documentaries and informational films. In March 1942, librarians representing 122 educational film libraries formed the Educational Film Lending Library Committee to assist agencies, such as the Office of War Information, in depositing their films with libraries. (A year later the committee incorporated as the Educational Film Library Association.[29]) The Office of Civilian Defense and the Coordinator of Inter-American Affairs also soon made available a large number of free educational and training films to any local agencies that could provide them to the general public. Public libraries in several cities—Charlotte, North Carolina; Cleveland, Ohio; Dallas, Texas; Milwaukee, Wisconsin; Gary, Indiana; and Grand Rapids, Michigan—seized this opportunity to enter 16mm film programming, circulation, and collection.

---

[27] Flynt, "Postwar College Courses," 225.

[28] Thurman G. Justice, "What Happens to the Veteran in College?" *Journal of Higher Education* 17, no. 4 (1946): 185–87.

[29] "Educational Film Library Association Organized," *Educational Screen* 22, no. 5 (May 1943): 180–81.

For those libraries unable to commit to instituting a film department or collection, one of the most popular techniques for initiating outreach with these 16mm prints was the film forum program. Emblematic of the public library as a venue for adult education through visual media, the film forum incorporated the screening of an educational film with a group discussion. Often a presentation from an authority on the film's topic preceded the discussion. In the spring of 1941, twenty "strategic" libraries hosted the first nationally organized film forum event—a ten-week series entitled "What We Are Defending," during which adult patrons watched films on the use of America's resources in the defense program followed by discussion on the subject. The American Film Center in New York was responsible for booking and shipping films to the participating libraries.[30] The exercise proved a success and was widely adopted throughout the 1940s. Motion picture programming, once intermittent, became a pronounced aspect of the public library's profile. Criteria for crafting the best program—how long films should be, how and when to lead the discussion, the length of the question and answer period—were established within the budding profession of film librarianship.

Emboldened by the incorporation of public libraries into the national educational film schema, the American Library Association began escalating its advocacy through publications and the creation of significant alliances. A series of reports made by the ALA Audio-Visual Committee throughout 1941 and 1942 declared libraries "the ideal vehicles for arranging public access to films."[31] In 1942, a Joint Committee on Educational Films and Libraries, using a Rockefeller Foundation grant, commissioned Gerald D. McDonald of the New York Public Library to assess the potential of motion picture service in public libraries. His study, published by the ALA as *Educational Motion Pictures and Libraries*, described the necessity of film selection, acquisition, circulation, and care, as well as the establishment of film forums and film cooperatives (the sharing of a collection by a group of libraries). McDonald suggested that public libraries, with their capacity for public service, could become the liaison between producers and distributors and the general public.

The ALA initiated membership in several important educational film organizations, among them the Joint Committee on Film Forums. The ALA was also involved with the Educational Film Library Association from its inception. A wartime member of the National Office of War Information (OWI) 16mm

---

[30] Etta Schneider, "The Literature in Visual Instruction," abstract, *Educational Screen* 19, no. 4 (Apr. 1941): 174.

[31] Clara DiFelice, "Film and Public Libraries: A Survey of the Literature," *Film Library Quarterly* 11, no. 4 (1978): 26. Until 1940, the ALA Audio-Visual Committee was known as the Visual Methods Committee.

Advisory Committee, the ALA became a charter member of the committee's successor, the Film Council of America, "a nonprofit educational corporation organized to promote the production, distribution, and utilization of audio-visual materials primarily on the adult level."[32]

In addition to the issuing of formal reports, professional organizations offered numerous articles and books intended to stimulate and guide public library film service. *Films News*, the journal of the Educational Film Library Association, presented information on a range of services and interests, such as which libraries were programming what, how a film laboratory worked, and reviews of the latest educational films and equipment. *Library Journal* was also active in printing guides for film service. In 1944 it featured "Film—A New Field to Conquer," a guide written by Patricia Blair (Cleveland Public Library Film Bureau), which urged libraries to take their "logical place" in the community by offering 16mm service. Blair identified film as a "powerful ally of the book," saying it should be respected as another medium for "disseminating information and cultural entertainment." Her guide included instructions for acquisition, maintenance, promotion, and programming, as well as a breakdown of the community groups likely to show film library prints.[33] In 1946, the Educational Film Library Association published *Making Films Work for Your Community: A Handbook on How to Use Educational Films in the Community*. The handbook was conceived "for the purpose of answering in some measure the rising tide of requests for assistance in planning film programs at the adult level, which are flooding film libraries today."[34]

A year later, *Library Journal* published two additional resources to assist public library film service: Hoyt R. Galvin's book *Films in Public Libraries* and Karline Brown's essay "What Libraries Are Doing in the Audio-Visual Field." Galvin's proved an essential manual in the establishment of collections and service. Brown's article, the result of a survey conducted by the head of the Films and Recording Center of the Cincinnati Public Library to more fully understand "what other libraries were doing," documented an emerging set of standards for the purchase of films by public libraries.[35] This first generation of film librarians urged colleagues to undertake the collection of 16mm film. "Don't Let Films Scare You," a self-described "light-hearted tale of a public library's start from scratch to build its film library," offered empathetic assistance for those hesitant to adopt this "new" medium.[36]

---

[32] *Sixty Years of 16mm Film*, 4.

[33] Patricia O. Blair, "Film—A New Field to Conquer," *Library Journal* 69 (Oct. 1944): 802, 804.

[34] Ogden and Ogden, *Making Films Work*, 8.

[35] Karline Brown, "What Libraries Are Doing in the Audio-Visual Field," *Library Journal* 72 (1947): 3.

[36] Elizabeth Hill, "Don't Let Films Scare You," *Library Journal* 73 (1948): 1547.

Supporters of 16mm educational film were also pragmatic in their proposals for film collection. Film was a mass medium capable of reaching large numbers, and was therefore arguably cost effective. A single film print had the potential to be viewed by several thousand persons a year for several years, while one copy of a book was limited in the number of readers within the same period of time. Libraries may be committed to the greater good but, as public organizations, they are also held to accountancy. Each library item has a calculable value based on lending statistics. R. Russell Munn, head of the Akron Public Library, explained the math in 1948:

> One two-dollar book will be regarded as paying its way if it is read by fifty people, making the cost per loan 4¢. The average film, on the other hand, will be loaned one hundred or more times, and be seen by 10,000 people. If it cost $50, the cost per person served is 2¢ or half as much as the book.[37]

The cost of the film print decreases to an infinitesimal amount when considering the multigenerational lifespan of healthy celluloid stock.

The problems of educational film production and distribution, which had plagued the nontheatrical market for decades, were also addressed by public library film service. With the withdrawal of federal and military involvement, the postwar nontheatrical educational market was still too small to elicit the funding required of sophisticated commercial production. However, Munn argued, that would change if public libraries became committed purchasers and local distributors of 16mm prints. If two or three hundred libraries throughout the U.S. and Canada undertook this responsibility, they would "constitute a market which would be a great encouragement to the production of documentary and educational films of high quality." The expansion of film collection into those nearly three hundred American public libraries with budgets able to accommodate this enterprise would serve 50 million people.[38] Even if only a portion of that population became borrowers, this would create demand in the public library that would translate into greater and more consistent purchasing by those institutions. Since public libraries needed to provide a constant supply of contemporary information, this would require not just the buying of multiple copies of the same title but also the purchase of more prints of a greater variety of productions. Budgets would be reconfigured to accommodate annual film requisitions. Public libraries, already an influential professional network capable of determining which products were valuable and which were not,

---

[37] R. Russell Munn, "The Film and the Public Library," in Godfrey, *Film and Education*, 369.
[38] Ibid., 370–71.

could become the biggest client of nontheatrical 16mm educational film, determining which types of films should be made. And by disallowing the lending of films to primary, secondary, and higher education schools in their area, public libraries could neutralize the resentment commercial agencies held toward lending libraries.

Spurred by these wartime and postwar opportunities, public libraries increasingly adopted 16mm film. In 1945, only about a dozen large urban libraries were offering film services.[39] But by 1947, the excess of film assistance requests by librarians necessitated the inauguration of a dedicated department within the American Library Association. Established with a $42,000 grant from the Carnegie Corporation and situated at ALA headquarters, the Film Office was an agency for promoting film service in public libraries and assisting librarians on policy, administration, selection, and reference work. In the first two years of the four-year project, under the direction of Patricia Blair, many public libraries received personal assistance in starting film collections. By 1949, approximately seventy more had established collections and services.[40]

To assist economically challenged libraries in establishing film service, the cooperative film circuit was devised. With the flood of inexpensive 16mm projectors being sold off by the armed forces, rural and smaller libraries were able to get equipment, but they needed a low-cost method of securing film prints. The regional film cooperative consisted of a network of several libraries using a large, central collection that dispensed packets of films on a scheduled basis; a member library used its packet for a specific period of time before forwarding it to the next library. In this way, many libraries could benefit from a single collection. The first cooperative circuits were begun in 1948 with two Carnegie Corporation–funded trials at the Cleveland Public Library and the Missouri State Library. The co-op experiment was highly successful, proving, as Patricia Blair later put it, that "the market for films and equipment does not lie in the big cities alone or around college and university cities. It lies as well in every village and hamlet and at every bookmobile stop, however rural."[41] By 1959, there were twenty-five public library film co-ops to service small and medium-sized libraries.

The postwar demand for continuing education, social development, and visual evidence of the world at large had a profound effect on public libraries and the film services they offered. Librarians helped to plan programs for "church

[39] DiFelice, "Film and Public Libraries," 26; Linda Blackaby, Dan Georgakas, and Barbara Margolis, *In Focus: A Guide to Using Films* (New York: New York Zoetrope, 1980), 128.

[40] Blackaby, Georgakas, and Margolis, *Guide to Using Films*, 128.

[41] Patricia Blair Cory, "Public Library Film Services: From Start Till Now," *Film News* 23, no. 3 (1966): 6.

Figure 21.1. Brochure for a 1947 Cleveland Public Library film series.

groups, youth organizations, municipal and state agencies, industrial groups, professional, service and civic clubs, penal institutions, health agencies, Alcoholics Anonymous, Armed Services, museums, PTAs, labor unions, camera clubs, sportsmen's clubs—an endless list of organizations reaching a tremendous variety of people."[42] Some libraries held an annual institute to familiarize programmers with the content, resources, and techniques necessary for successful film programs. The Detroit Public Library offered evenings at which community film programmers could preview prints. Librarians mailed the list of preview screenings with the

[42] Grace T. Stevenson, "Public Libraries," in *Sixty Years of 16mm Film*, 128.

advisement, "If motion picture film is to be used effectively and intelligently as an aid in program planning, it is essential that the planner have firsthand knowledge of the film to be used."[43] Often, the library cosponsored off-site screenings with other community organizations. In some cities, librarians were active in the formation of film societies.

By the 1950s, these aggregate services and programs achieved the predicted effect on the public and the institution. Public library film service flourished throughout the country at mid-century. The Rochester (New York) Public Library, for example, which had shown films in its auditorium since 1938, began its own collection in 1947, as did nearly a dozen other libraries, including the Cincinnati Public Library and the Enoch Pratt Free Library in Baltimore. In 1947, two years after having initiated its film service, the Akron (Ohio) Public Library loaned 7,174 films to more than a quarter million borrowers.[44] In 1948, the ALA Film Office reported forty-five libraries providing motion picture services. That number doubled by 1951, with public libraries screening 55,929 films for nearly three million people.[45] In 1953, the U.S. Office of Education reported 166 public libraries lending films.[46] In March alone, they circulated more than 70,000 films, which were shown to 3.7 million people.[47] In addition to inspiring circulation numbers, libraries were experiencing success with in-house programs. In 1949, for example, the Cleveland Public Library Film Bureau hosted some 1.1 million filmgoers.[48]

As collections proliferated and services matured, policymaking became a concerted objective. Standards for "everything from the mechanical procedures of procuring, processing, and distributing through the far more important community cooperation, programming, and evaluation and appreciation of films" were put forth.[49] Collection policies emphasized the need for nonfiction subjects of general interest and high quality. Counterpointing the "weighted films of special interest groups, and the classroom films on American history," librarians purchased regional productions; films on American music, art, and folk culture; and documentaries on American labor and industry.[50] Any work that was out-of-date, in poor taste, of poor production value, boring, heavy on advertising, or even meant for the classroom was considered "a disservice to the community, to the institution of which it is a part, and to the growth of a mature 16mm film industry."[51] As

---

[43] Detroit Public Library flyer, in the collection of the author.

[44] Munn, "Film and the Public Library," 366.

[45] Cory, "Public Library Film Services," 6.

[46] Blackaby, Georgakas, and Margolis, *Guide to Using Films*, 128.

[47] Stevenson, "Public Libraries," 124.

[48] Virginia M. Beard, "The Saga of a Public Library Film Bureau," *Film News* 11, no. 1 (1950): 8.

[49] Stevenson, "Public Libraries," 126.

[50] Grace T. Stevenson, "75 Years of A.L.A.," *Film News* 11, no. 7 (1951): 21. Also see George Holloway, "Controversy on Film," *Library Journal* 88 (1963): 515.

[51] Stevenson, "Public Libraries," 124–25.

libraries created film collection policies, most participated in an unspoken agreement to disallow what *Film News* called in 1962 "the synthetic entertainment" of the average Hollywood movie. Those libraries that did host feature films typically used productions of a literary nature or of European origin. In 1950, the Cleveland Public Library did not stock 16mm "Hollywood" films but would refer people looking for "entertainment films" to commercial dealers.[52]

By the 1960s, public libraries had reinvented themselves as community A-V centers. Thousands of viewers poured into libraries each month to partake of free screenings while thousands of prints traveled out. Where once a library may have been limited to an individual employee who "also handles films," now entire departments were dedicated to film service. Duties being regularly performed included contacting distributors; selecting films for purchase; reading reviews, news, and borrower evaluations; planning and supervising screenings; doing public relations work; and advising print borrowers.[53]

As a matter of practice, outdated nonfiction films were replaced with more current selections. These deaccessioning and purchasing practices continued for decades, providing a market for dozens of nontheatrical film producers and distribution agencies, including Phoenix Films, Learning Corporation of America, Contemporary Films, Audio Brandon, the nontheatrical division of Films Incorporated, Encyclopaedia Britannica Films, Carousel, Texture, Pyramid, Churchill, McGraw-Hill, Bailey-Film Associates, and Unifilm. On a less industrial scale, some A-V departments, such as the New York Public Library's Donnell Media Center, supported independent filmmakers by buying directly from young, local, and underexposed talents or niche distributors, such as Women Make Movies, New Day Films, Canyon Cinema, and Third World Newsreel.

War-stimulated growth in the area of film collection and service in higher education institutions was also demonstrable in the postwar decades; of sixty-five university and college film libraries surveyed in 1947, thirty-eight had been initiated in the period between 1937 and 1947, with a steep increase in the years following V-J Day.[54] This trend in development continued to gain momentum into the 1950s. In 1951, a special unit of the library at Connors State Agricultural College in Oklahoma was built to combat "limited equipment and inadequate classroom surroundings"; included in the new facility was a special classroom with lightproof shades, acoustical ceilings, soundproof walls, and a storage space for the anticipated purchase of a 16mm collection.[55] At the University of

---

[52] Beard, "Saga of a Public Library Film Bureau," 17.

[53] Choong Han Kim, "A Study of Public Library Film Services" (PhD diss., Rutgers University, 1964), 56.

[54] Lemler, "University or College Film Library," 502.

[55] Lula K. Pratt, "An Integrated Library Audio-Visual Service," *Educational Screen* 30, no. 1 (Jan. 1951): 19.

Connecticut, the use of 16mm sound motion pictures by staff increased from 904 prints in the 1946–47 school year to 3,735 during the 1952–53 school year, with 40 of the 47 departments on campus frequently borrowing films for regular classroom instructional purposes. At the University of Iowa during the 1951–52 school year, campus departments used 13,083 films in classrooms, an increase of 1,823 films over the previous year. At the University of Minnesota, professors in 18 of the 22 schools and colleges of the university regularly used 16mm films in their classes and film bookings doubled from 1,060 in 1951–52 to 2,100 in 1952–53. These figures are a cross-section of higher education audiovisual departments in America during this escalatory period.[56]

By the mid-1950s, increased use of educational film libraries by instructors and groups on campus necessitated structural and administrative changes. Because of pressures to modernize educational services, film libraries began to transition toward a service-oriented, on-campus audiovisual service model (the A-V service model). Where film libraries, especially those managed by extension divisions, traditionally concentrated on regional or local distribution outside of the college or university, now film collections were considered part of classroom support services. Just as the school library offered books and librarians, so too did the A-V service model strive to supply films as well as dedicated staff to work on every aspect of the classroom audiovisual experience. Integrated audiovisual service quickly became the focus of educational film development in colleges and universities. A school's audiovisual center had five functions: (1) distribution of audiovisual materials to school and community groups; (2) teacher training; (3) promotion of film use on campus; (4) production of audiovisual media; and (5) promoting and implementing research in the audiovisual field.[57]

Many colleges and universities adopted the audiovisual service model and name. The naming, or renaming, of the film library to an A-V department signified to users the intentions of the film library in a way that was more evident than in the past: "Educational Materials Services Department," "Audio-Visual Center," "Bureau of Visual Instruction," "Audio-Visual Service Center." This indicated not just the presence of a film library on campus but also the availability of an array of services related to audiovisual methods and mechanics. Finally, those elements that were deemed essential to the progression of film in the classroom had synchronized. The collection and use of 16mm films would progress until the 1980s when more portable and less expensive formats began to dominate.

The beginning of the end of 16mm educational film collections came in the late 1980s. In 1987, the Consortium of University Film Centers asked member

---

[56] Wittich, "Colleges and Universities," 65–68, 72.

[57] Lemler, "University or College Film Library," 520.

libraries and educational film companies to "assess the impact of new technologies upon their operations." The most significant trends reported were the "heavy shift toward ½-inch video and the resulting shift away from 16mm film."[58] Most libraries experienced a decline in the circulation of prints in proportion to the rise of the analog video market. In 1980, the University of California Extension Center for Media and Independent Learning (UC Extension Center), a nontheatrical distributor of films nationwide, reported 90 percent of its revenue came from 16mm rentals; in 1999, 90 percent of its income came from the sales and licensing of videos.[59] By the mid-1990s, libraries and schools were purging their 16mm film collections. The UC Extension Center, an agency with a historic role in educational media that dated back to 1915, closed in 2005. Most commercial nontheatrical producer-distributors no longer exist; those that survived the transition to video did so by disassociating from 16mm film.

While many educational film collections have been disassembled, discarded, and disconnected from their original purpose, some remain intact. Some universities and colleges operate with the same access policies devised sixty years ago: instructors request films for use in their courses, and students study them at in-house screening facilities. As of 2010, the few public libraries still offering 16mm collections—including the New York Public Library; the Miami-Dade Public Library; and, in Maryland, the Prince George's County Memorial Library System and Enoch Pratt Free Library—circulate films to anyone with a library card. Rarely do to they prevent access even to those prints known to be unique master positives.

The position of 16mm collections in their original institutions, however, is precarious. Today the attitude toward 16mm holdings by educational institutions is ambivalent at best. Many, especially those working directly in education or reference services, believe the productions themselves are worthy of study, if not classroom projection; however, the burden of maintaining the collection is often too great. Film prints require substantial physical space and labor. They need to be housed in a climate-controlled environment protected from biological decay resultant from high temperatures, high humidity, mold, insects, and water. They also need to be regularly inspected, cleaned, and tested for acetate decomposition. Equipment for maintenance (splicers, tape, cleaner, reels, inspection machines, and so forth) and projection has become difficult to find and expensive. A reliable 16mm projector can cost well over $1,000. Replacement prints for damaged films can run approximately $500 for one reel—if a negative exists. Finally, the films need to maintain a position in the catalog, to be

---

[58] James Baird, "The Impact of New Technologies on University Film Libraries," *Tech Trends* 33, no. 3 (Apr.–May 1988): 19.

[59] Lissa Gibbs, "Distributor FAQ: University of California Extension," *The Independent* [Cambridge, MA], Oct. 1, 1999, www.independent-magazine.org/99/10/distributor-faq-university-california-extension.

advertised, and promoted, so that prospective users know they exist. As a result of the financial and logistical responsibilities incurred by any substantive 16mm film collection, and with the degradation of funding for learning institutions nationwide, most librarians and A-V managers are being pressured by their institutions' administration to simply discard their 16mm holdings.

The issue of public funding has had the most significant impact on public libraries and their collections. As early as 1974, when motion picture archiving in the United States was largely undeveloped, it was suggested that public libraries act as agencies for "archival" film storage. The concept of librarian as archivist is substantiated when considering that many producers and distributors for the 16mm market discarded their negatives and other various film elements when their companies went out of business, were bought by a huge media conglomerate, or switched to video. This often designates a library's film print as the only duplicating master. However, public library branches are funded with public monies, and the city governments that manage those monies are capricious patrons of the arts and education. Public libraries are often among the first institutions to have their funding cut when the city budget needs balancing. Sixteen-millimeter film collections, unable to produce the circulation statistics that attract continuous funding and yet necessarily requiring what limited resources the library has, are seen as a hindrance to streamlined operational costs. Regardless of how important, unique, or historical these collections are, with the impetus to acquire new formats and the retraction of funds with which to do it, most public libraries have been unable to support their film collections.

Despite the tendency to deaccession film collections to the sanitation department, there are instances of these collections being welcomed into the archival realm as cultural artifacts. For universities that have working archives, and the staff capable of lobbying for further acquisition, the teaching film library has in some cases been transferred as a whole into the archive, as was done at Indiana University.

Another scenario for schools is that the collection continues to be maintained by the library or the A-V center according to conservation standards. Films are kept in a climate-controlled area and monitored for signs of decomposition, and they can only be accessed by staff once transferred to a video format (when the permission of the copyright owner can be obtained). This is a more tenuous course of action as older film titles are infrequently accessed and are therefore susceptible to executive orders to discard. However, by using the prints as telecine masters for migration to DVD or digital files, collection managers are able to maintain and promote the collection. Use can be stimulated through many of the same methods developed in the late 1940s and 50s: programming, catalog advertisement, and outreach to academic departments. This strategy is dependent on funding (and staff enthusiasm), but the argument for maintaining educational titles not in distribution is less difficult to make once a 16mm print is redefined as an "archival master."

A third option, available to both higher educational institutions and public libraries, is the donation or sale of the collection to another party. A niche collector's market for educational film prints has blossomed. As a result, eBay has become an outlet for libraries desperate to unload their holdings. However, the majority of extant educational film collections have been absorbed by federal and private-sector archives. The Library of Congress and the National Archives hold vast collections; the Academic Film Archive of North America and the A/V Geeks Archive, both dedicated exclusively to educational film, have rescued tens of thousands of 16mm prints. When a school or library abandons a collection, archivists now often employ professional networks to place such orphaned films in an archival home. This is cause for both celebration and reflection. A legitimate archive has the resources to allow for the continued health of and access to film documents—catalogers, programmers, conservators, and preservationists working with facilities and budgets tailored to the specifications of celluloid. While this is all very good news for the well-being of individual titles, what is lost is the geographically specific cultural relevance of the collection.

Even if a film collection is received intact—which is rare since they are often deaccessioned in a piecemeal fashion—it is displaced from its parent institution and the population it served. A public library film collection from Albany, New

Figure 21.2. Two 16mm educational film prints deaccessioned from New York State's Upper Hudson Library Federation and Ramapo-Catskill Library System, both of which were acquired by the New York Public Library's Donnell Media Center in the 1990s. (Photograph by Michael Diekmann.)

York, meant to serve the urban center and its rural environs, is not the same as a collection for New York City. Different populations with different interests dictated the acquisition of different films. While there were those titles whose purchase was considered by film librarians to be compulsory, a public librarian ultimately gauged what would be most useful to their community. As a result, one can see patterns of working-class audiences, immigrant communities, or the cultural elite reflected in the assemblage of titles that compose a collection. Even collections accessioned as an unbroken unit, and cataloged and researched as such, lack a degree of contextualization when relocated. Documentaries on the "popcorn lady" of upstate New York, a Polish cafeteria worker, a pastor with a preference for jazz over hymnals, the Loisaida neighborhood, empty lots being converted into playgrounds, Pavarotti's master class at Juilliard—these films lose a component of their relevance if removed from a Manhattan film library and placed in the care of a Midwest archive.

This is not to say that archives are negligent when accessioning unwanted film collections. If not for modern archiving practices and the placement of these materials in a protective zone, "it is entirely possible," as one documentarian wrote presciently nearly four decades ago, "that the twenty-first century will remember entire regions of the nation through nothing but stills and a few unconvincing Hollywood sets."[60] But it is important to consider that educational films have provenance in educational institutions. Their historical purpose in the college classroom or in the library auditorium should not be forgotten.

The legacy of the public library as an outlet for media is now unimpeachable. Few community members are unaware of the library's ability to provide DVDs and Internet service alongside newspapers and periodicals. It is inconceivable that a college course be taught without the aid of audiovisual tools. However, the age of 16mm film collections has passed, leaving in its wake the mass deaccessioning of the collections that took decades to assemble. The institutions' objectives remain the same: to educate and inform. The methods by which they achieve these goals, however, are constantly in flux.

The fate of 16mm educational film collections—too often regarded as archaic compendiums of outdated information—within these institutions is uncertain. Fortunately, and perhaps because of the speed at which our technology is evolving, the current generation of librarians and A-V coordinators is archivally minded. Sixteen-millimeter educational films are being preserved, reformatted, and redistributed because of their cinematic, historical, and, yes, educational value. But stranger and more fortunate still, entire 16mm collections are being referred not to the dumpster but to the increasingly apparent and cooperative network of archives.

---

[60] Seth Feldman, "Expanding: A Nationwide Program for the Study of Film," *Film Library Quarterly* 7, nos. 3–4 (1974): 37.

22 A SELECT GUIDE TO EDUCATIONAL FILM COLLECTIONS

ELENA ROSSI-SNOOK

What follows is an annotated list of institutions with significant educational film holdings. Because many collections have been deaccessioned or changed hands, the annotations also record the history of these changes. This directory is by no means a complete representation of extant collections. Selections are limited to those housing film prints, almost all of which are 16mm. The information comes from institutional websites and consultation with the librarians and staff at these organizations. The guide aims to aid both research and access. Some researchers glean knowledge primarily by examining the descriptive information about works (metadata) available through catalog records, indexes, and published sources. A wider set of users—programmers, curators, collectors, fans, and media producers, as well as students and scholars—want primarily to see the movies, whether in their original film formats, as video copies, or as online versions.

Researchers seeking 16mm educational film titles in libraries do well to search the public online catalog known as WorldCat. A global search engine, WorldCat.org aggregates thousands of library catalogs into one web portal. (There's even a WorldCat app for mobile phones.) An advanced search selecting the format "Visual Material" returns records for various video editions of a film, as well as 16mm holdings. Each record lists participating libraries that hold a copy. Some can be borrowed via interlibrary loan.

However, WorldCat search results need to be analyzed carefully. For example, four films discussed in this book yielded the following results.

- *And So They Live* (1940): Three libraries report having 16mm film prints, although only one (Rutgers University) lists the item in its own catalog. A separate entry for a DVD version reveals that Indiana University created a DVD-R access copy of the film in 2009 (available via interlibrary loan, but not commercially distributed).

- *They Do Come Back* (1940): The only hit, the National Library of Medicine, lists archival 16mm film elements (a print, duplicate negative, and soundtrack negative) and videos (Betacam SP and VHS viewing copy). Note that the National Archives and Records Administration (NARA) catalog is not searched; however, NARA holds the master film materials, video copies, and a free downloadable MP4 version of this item.
- *220 Blues* (1970): Four libraries hold a VHS edition (BFA Educational Media, 198? [*sic*]), while two others list first-edition 16mm prints.
- *The Stone Carvers* (1984): More than 100 libraries report having this work, most with VHS (Direct Cinema, 1985) and a few with DVD editions (Paul Wagner Productions, 2004). No film holdings of this Academy Award–winning film appear. World-Cat (like all catalogs) may give confusing (and confused) metadata, as in this case. The various records identify *The Stone Carvers* as dating from 1984, 1985, 1987, 1988, 1990, the 2000s, or 2004? [*sic*]. Outside of WorldCat, the Library of Congress (catalog.loc.gov) dates its 16mm print of *The Stone Carvers* as "[1987?]," even though the same record notes the film was published in 1984 and deposited for copyright in 1985. Even when information is not erroneous, users often confuse the date of a VHS or DVD release with the original date of a film's release.

As these examples show, WorldCat omits many libraries (and, as a rule, archives), so it should not be considered comprehensive. Further, libraries are often unable to update their catalog records, therefore searches may display records for deaccessioned films or defunct collections.

Reference books compiled for the purpose of locating educational films during the height of film librarianship, though out of print, offer excellent leads on finding titles and distributors. See Table 2 in the editors' introduction to this book for further information about published finding aids.

In reality, the 16mm collections described in these sources have often been broken up. With increasing frequency, 16mm prints are discarded, even when video editions of the same works have not replaced them. In short, many (perhaps most) of the educational films produced in the twentieth century no longer exist. Those that do survive may not be in libraries or archives, making the search for them more challenging still. Yet the twenty-first-century researcher and would-be viewer can still access tens of thousands of such films, albeit with some effort. And while as many as a couple thousand educational films, from multiple nations of origin, have made their way to the Internet, the viewing options there remain extremely limited compared to the universe of possibilities.

Universities and Colleges

Cornell University hosts the Kheel Center for Labor-Management Documentation and Archives, the special collections department of Cornell's Industrial and Labor Relations School. The archive has a 16mm film collection now used mostly for scholarly study, but it does, on occasion, support classroom use as well. When funds are available, films are sent to a lab for digitization.

Dartmouth College initiated its film collection in the late 1940s. The College Library houses 1,700 reels of educational and institutionally oriented material. The films are not cataloged but, until the prints can be made more accessible, librarians can aid researchers with a printed inventory of titles. According to librarian Elizabeth E. Kirk, "Films that no longer reflect current scholarship, but remain valuable to educational film historians, may be donated to institutions with faculty working in this area."

Emory University in Atlanta has a collection of 500 16mm educational films. Faculty can book films for classroom use through a link on Emory's Music and Media Library website: http://web.library.emory.edu/libraries/music-and-media.

Harvard University is an anomaly among the major universities involved with film service. It has a long history of educational film activity but does not follow the Midwestern university model of supporting a centralized audiovisual department with a teaching film library.

Throughout its collection history, films existed separately in different Harvard departments. (The archive seeks to preserve these scattered orphans when searches for them are successful.) In the late 1920s, the university signed a five-year contract with Pathé Exchange, agreeing to prepare a series of films addressing scientific subjects, mainly with the divisions of Anthropology and Geology. The Harvard University Film Foundation, which became the Harvard Film Service in 1934, was chartered in 1928 for the production and collection of educational films. Harvard also hosted a number of significant ethnographic filmmakers whose films have been deposited at the university's Peabody Museum. For a time, students in the Department of Visual and Environmental Studies produced movies (credited to the Carpenter Center for the Visual Arts) that were acquired as educational products by public libraries: *Housemoving* (1968); *The Shout It Out Alphabet Film* (1969); *Sand, or Peter and the Wolf* (1969); and *Moving Pictures—The Art of Jan Lenica* (1975).

Now part of the Fine Arts Library, the archive began as the Film Study Center, but the moniker and mission changed in 1978. The Harvard Film Archive proper opened in 1979, a derivative of the University Film Study Center, which began in the early 1970s for collective use by several New England college film departments. The archive increasingly adopted the role of a central teaching film library.

Many of the nearly 15,000 motion-picture items are of an educational nature. The HFA also acquires collections deaccessioned by other schools and libraries (for example, the Somerville [Massachusetts] High School Collection of some 350 classroom films produced between the 1940s and 80s). Prominent collections include those from individuals (such as curator-educator Amos Vogel, psychologist B. F. Skinner, and documentarian Robert Gardner) and 16mm film distributors (Documentary Educational Resources and Grove Press Film). Prints circulate off-campus to fellow members of the International Federation of Film Archives (FIAF), but the focus of the archive remains campus use. Students, faculty, and researchers may access 35mm and 16mm prints. The archive's theater, which has 16mm/35mm archival-standard film projectors, is available for classes, and serves the public as a cinematheque four days per week. http://hcl.harvard.edu/hfa/access.html.

Indiana University (IU) sits near the apex of contemporary educational film archiving in the United States, below only the Library of Congress. Several archives on campus, such as the Black Film Center Archive and the Kinsey Institute Film Archive, hold significant collections and titles. The Lilly Library houses nearly 4,000 accessible 16mm films in the David S. Bradley Collection. In addition, IU assembled one of the most historically significant university 16mm educational film collections. It began in 1912 within the Bureau of Visual Education, an activity of the Extension Division. The bureau originally circulated lantern slides, models, and exhibits, adding 16mm film when that format became available. In 1940, it became the Audio-Visual Center, which grew into a leading educational film distributor in the 1950s, 60s, and early 70s. Revenue from this loan service subsidized circulation to the eight Indiana University campuses. The university also produced its own 16mm educational films from 1945 to 1985, including the best-selling *Chucky Lou—The Story of a Woodchuck* (1948) and numerous biology films. In the 1980s, the Audio-Visual Center became the Center for Media and Teaching Resources, and in 1993, Instructional Support Services. In 2006, the unit ceased as an independent collection and was transferred to the Indiana University Libraries.

Now titled the Educational and Social Guidance Film Collection, it is treated as an archival collection, hence no longer a candidate for weeding or deaccession. There are approximately 50,000 reels, which include classroom, educational, and training films; films from National Educational Television; local and regional material including promotional films; and Indiana High School Athletic Association productions. In addition, Indiana University acquired 4,000 reels from the University of Illinois in the 1980s. (These films have yet to be integrated into the main collection; currently the titles are accessible only as a paper inventory.)

The IU collection is searchable via a database on campus. On-site viewing is done on a Steenbeck flatbed editor. Although it served the entire United States and its territories until 2006, the university no longer circulates film prints off campus.

The Johns Hopkins University has approximately 300 reels of 16mm film in the Alan Mason Chesney Medical Archives. Most were culled from what had been a larger circulating collection at the School of Medicine's Welch Medical Library. Other titles came from personal collections of faculty. Most are medical and public health films circa 1950–1970, retained for the documentation and study of the institution.

Kent State University deaccessioned its 16mm collection in 2006. Most prints went to the Archive of the History of American Psychology at the University of Akron. Some went to the New York Public Library, which then forwarded duplicate prints to the Prelinger Archives.

New York University began its Film Library in 1940 primarily for the distribution of films off campus. It ceased operations in 1990, at which point the collection was divided among several academic departments, with Cinema Studies (whose Film Study Center took one hundred prints) and Anthropology topping the list. An unspecified number of prints were transferred to the Penn State Libraries audiovisual department in the mid-1990s, although there is no documentation regarding which titles. Rick Prelinger took in other deaccessioned films in exchange for video discs of *Our Secret Century*, ephemeral films he released commercially with the Voyager Company. The NYU Film Study Center and Archive in the Department of Cinema Studies also houses the William K. Everson Collection of 16mm prints (www.nyu.edu/projects/wke) and others donated by documentary filmmaker George Stoney.

Pennsylvania State University maintained 6,000 titles in its collection, with a range of educational films spanning the history of 16mm production. In 2011, however, the university deaccessioned its prints, which went into storage at the Internet Archive's new Physical Archive in Richmond, California.

Pratt Institute. In addition to having a 16mm film teaching library, Pratt acquired part of the Brooklyn Public Library collection. Multi-Media Services (Brooklyn campus library) provides projectors and films to instructors for classroom use. The Pratt collection is searchable through its online catalog. The Brooklyn Public Library collection is not cataloged but titles can be browsed by requesting the two binders of database printouts from Multi-Media Services.

Queens College CUNY. The 16mm collection, which is composed of about 800 films, still exists but is in a state of transition as it migrates from the Media Services department to the Special Collections Archives of the Benjamin S. Rosenthal Library. The typical dichotomy that seems to be at work at many universities and colleges applies here as well: established as a teaching collection under the domain of a media services department, the films are no longer being requested for classroom use, playback equipment is not being collected and maintained, and staff are no longer being trained in their use. However, there is a general acknowledgment of the films' historical value so they are being stored under the authority of the library.

Titles tend to mirror the acquisitions policy for a liberal arts curriculum: feature films, foreign films, experimental films, social documentaries. A title list can be accessed by going to http://qcpages.qc.cuny.edu/Library/ and conducting an Advanced Search. Use "films" for record type and "motion picture" as a phrase.

Access is a major hindrance for any researcher or student wishing to view the collection. Aside from some yet unreclaimed projectors "somewhere on campus," there is no way to view the films. Instructors, especially those affiliated with the Film Studies program, have the option of requesting the use of a lecture hall equipped with a projector and finding a projectionist, but this is not regularly done. The Media Services department, which owned the collection until approximately five years ago, no longer supports this format although there are a few staff members who know how to operate a projector. Film programming on campus is done utilizing DVDs.

Those interested in the film collection should contact the media librarian at the Rosenthal Library.

State University of New York/Nassau Community College began its collection in the mid-1960s. The films were moved from the A-V department to the Media Unit of the library in 1987; this, in turn, was combined with Reference, Circulation, and Acquisitions in 2009. The collection was used heavily through the 1980s. Film prints were made available off-campus through interlibrary loan starting in the 1970s.

Nassau Community College acquired the 16mm educational film collection of SUNY Farmingdale in 1994. It also acquired the New York State Health Films and the New York State Library Film Collection, but these films were then either discarded or sent to the University of Iowa, which archived them. The collection has been weeded and partially deaccessioned. (County regulations require deaccessioned films be thrown out.)

University of Akron owned 1,200 educational film titles. Among these were prints acquired from the Akron-Summit County Public Library. Upon deaccession of the collection in 2009, only a few films were kept, especially those relating to the university's history and those considered rare. The deaccessioned prints were divided among staff members, the university's archive, and the on-campus Archive of the History of American Psychology, with the remainder going to the San Francisco Media Archive. The university library's Media Services makes the retained films available on campus.

The deaccessioning of the Akron collection is a good example of the use of contemporary means of communication and the community of American archivists to keep these collections out of the dumpster. Within the span of a few weeks, the University of Akron library staff contacted the New York Public Library, which referred them to the Prelinger Archives, which in turn referred them to the San Francisco Media Archive.

University of California Extension was one of the major distributors of educational audiovisual material. It began operation in 1915 but closed its distribution unit, the Center for Media and Independent Learning, in 2005. The catalog is still available online, listing 756 titles and contact information for distributors and rights holders (http://ucmedia.berkeley.edu/default.html). After the center closed, some former employees created a commercial distribution company for documentary and educational media, Berkeley Media LLC (www.berkeleymedia.com).

University of California San Diego (UCSD) maintains both its own 16mm film collection and that which was acquired from San Diego County's central media center in the early 1990s. All film materials are under the domain of the Arts Library's Film and Video Collection. For the most part, films are available for scholarship and are not used in the classroom. UCSD conserves all film prints in a cold storage vault; originals are retained even as they are digitized for various access projects.

Some of the San Diego County collection, which includes public library holdings, became part of the university's collection but most are listed only as an online title list: http://libraries.ucsd.edu/locations/arts/resources/featured-collections; "General Title List" includes films about San Diego County. The university's own film collection is cataloged: http://roger.ucsd.edu/search~S3; choose "Films & Videos" and then "Advanced Keyword Search." The Film and Video Collection's curator still purchases 16mm films for this collection.

Access to the film collections is allowed but mediated. Students and nonaffiliated researchers performing legitimate research must contact the library or the Collection's curator to discuss their project and then it is determined whether the print will be screened, viewed on a flatbed, or digitized. Generally, digitization is done when the viewer wishes to study the film multiple times. Instructors can request a film for classroom use but, as with other institutions, the transfer of responsibility from the Media Services department to the library is not clearly defined. Few university staff members know how to run a projector and the library provides only the films. Therefore, if an instructor wishes to use a film from the collections in the classroom, they would have to request the film and loan of the projector from the library and then contact Media Services for a projectionist.

University of Delaware has a collection of 2,500 academic films, available for viewing by university faculty, students, and staff. The Instructional Media Collection Department manages the collection. The films span a wide range of academic subject areas from Anthropology, Biology, and other sciences to Art, Film Studies, History, and the Social Sciences. A viewing carrel is equipped with a 16mm projector for individual use. Faculty may also schedule class showings of 16mm films in the forty-nine-seat Viewing Room. The films are held in cold storage and migrated to video when approval can be obtained by the copyright holder. The Department of Art continues to purchase 16mm prints, integrating its own holdings into the library catalog so they will become more accessible.

The University of Georgia Walter J. Brown Media Archives opened in 1995 and has significant holdings, even apart from its Peabody Awards Collection of 90,000 titles. The 2,000 16mm films that formerly circulated within the university are in two groups. The Center for Teaching and Learning (formerly the Office of Instructional Support & Development) Collection consists of both educational films and prints of theatrical films shown in classes. These no longer circulate but can be searched online (http://media2.isd.uga.edu) and video copies can be requested. The Georgia Center Film Collection is similar in nature, but with greater emphasis on educational, industrial, and sponsored films dating back to the 1930s. The Georgia Center for Continuing Education housed the state's first educational television station, WGTV, which began in 1960 and produced original programming on film and video. The J. Aubrey Smith Collection contains twenty-one films Smith produced in 16mm for the state's Agriculture Extension Service between 1947 and 1960, some sponsored by Rich's department store. Smith also donated his production records. The university Math Club deposited films it collected, as well.

Historically, the educational film collections' primary purpose was to support university instruction and on-campus use, but that has been supplanted by research and stock footage sales. Instructors make requests for access to 16mm films through the Center for Teaching and Learning, which retrieves prints from the archive and makes video or digital copies.

University of Michigan (UM) was involved with both the production and collection of educational films from a relatively early time. The UM film collection began in 1939 as part of the University Extension Division's Visual Education Bureau. The bureau became the Audio-Visual Education Center in 1948 and was responsible for the production and rental of 16mm films both within and outside of the university. The focus of the collection changed in 1978 from statewide distribution to serving the instructional needs of the university. In 1987, the media library became part of the University Library system and was renamed the Film and Video Library. The 16mm rental operation was discontinued in 1992 because of low demand. The collection of 10,000 films is now managed by the Askwith Media Library. The library has an online catalog (http://mirlyn.lib. umich.edu). Searches can be limited to the 16mm format by selecting "Motion Picture" within the format menu.

The library is no longer acquiring 16mm film. The only deaccessioning performed is the regular weeding of multiple copies, although it is foreseen that the collection will eventually undergo heavy weeding with only those films of perceived archival or instructional value being retained.

University of North Carolina Charlotte has the unique situation of holding a 35mm educational film collection. The collection was intended for faculty use only, with subject areas including sociology, chemistry, and history. However, it was phased out of the library's Media Services department by 1999 because of logistical problems with its maintenance. After attempts to donate the collection to campus departments and the State Library (which had already deaccessioned its own collection) the Art History Department took the collection and uses it to teach the history of film.

University of North Texas began its collection in 1950. Its library houses 1,500 titles, the majority of which are cataloged and can be found via http://iii.library. unt.edu. (Click the "Number Search" and choose "Other Call Number" from the drop-down menu; search "MP" to view records of 16mm holdings.) The focus of the collection remains to support teaching and research on campus. Since 1976, the Media Library manages the material. It is available to students, faculty, staff, and community members as well as researchers for on-campus use; faculty may take prints outside of the library but others must view them in-house. The Gerontological Films and Video Collection, established in 1970, rents to organizations off-campus. All others do not circulate off-campus. The films are kept in a climate-controlled environment. The collection is added to when donations of rare titles or titles of regional interest are made.

University of South Carolina (USC) has an Educational Film Collection within the main Thomas Cooper Library (with a database at www.sc.edu/library/ edfilms). Most duplicate titles have been weeded and prints too fragile to circulate were transferred to the library's archival unit. In 2009, USC Libraries created the separate archival film and video unit, the Moving Image Research Collections (MIRC) (www.sc.edu/library/mirc). In addition to the noted Fox Movietone News Collection, MIRC houses unique 16mm educational film resources in its Roman Vishniac Collection of science films; South Carolina's Department of Wildlife films; as well as published films in smaller collections donated by individuals, including films from the Federal Aviation Administration and law enforcement units. Additionally, MIRC holds audiovisual and paper materials from the Columbia-based company Southeastern Educational Film (formerly Southeastern Film Processing Co.), which include mint-condition Super 8mm film loops and other classroom multimedia products.

In 2007, the **University of Southern California** (USC) named its large film collection the Hugh M. Hefner Moving Image Archive (http://cinema.usc.edu/ about/movingimagearchive.cfm). Of its 70,000 works, as many as 15,000 may be classified as 16mm educational films. Among them are a collection of silent-era educational films donated by film preservationist David Shepard and prints transferred from the Los Angeles Public Library. Formerly a longtime distributor of such films, the university holds a collection of catalogs. The archive is part of the School of Cinematic Arts. Elsewhere on campus, USC maintains a Cinematic Arts Library, as well as the David L. Wolper Center for the Study of the Documentary, begun with the personal archive of the prolific film and television producer.

University of Washington's (UW) Educational Media Collection (www.css. washington.edu/emc), which consists mostly of 16mm films, originated in the 1950s. Heavily used on campus, it was also a popular rental collection. The library still receives loan requests from around the United States for some of its 4,000 reels. A contingent of faculty relies on the collection and attempts are being made to digitize requested titles (in cases where permission from rights holders can be obtained). Prints are no longer being projected because of physical fragility. The Educational Media Collection is part of the library's Media Center, which adopted it from the Classroom Support Services Department. The Media Center deaccessions duplicate titles and works that do not appear to be rare (as determined by cross-referencing titles with WorldCat). Deaccessioned films are sent to sister institutions, preferably archives. The UW library's Special Collections also houses some films.

University of Wisconsin (UW) was influential in the seminal years of extension division service. The Madison campus's Bureau of Audio Visual Instruction (BAVI) was initiated in 1914 to lend lantern slides and filmstrips and began lending 16mm films as soon as those became available. The BAVI 16mm collection was a rental library focused on educational films. Prints were lent for a fee to elementary and secondary schools as well as colleges and universities throughout the country (although loans were primarily made within the state). The focus of the collection was off-campus use, but films were available to campus departments for a rental fee. The BAVI also produced its own educational films until 1980.

The film collection was deaccessioned in 1994 and BAVI disbanded in 1996, despite being self-supporting. All 16mm prints went to a private film rental library in Milwaukee, which has since closed. The University of Wisconsin System's other campuses (UW Oshkosh, UW Waukesha, et al.) also hold 16mm and Super 8mm teaching collections.

Washington University in St. Louis has a Film and Media Archive that houses 256 educational films obtained from the St. Louis Public School film library. http://library.wustl.edu/units/spec/filmandmedia.

Yale University has a history of educational film production that dates to the early 1920s, most notably the *Chronicles of America* series (1923–1925), which was distributed by Pathé. However, Yale did not initiate a Film Study Center until the 1960s. The Film Study Center expanded into archival operations in the

2000s and continues to acquire film prints based on recommendations from film studies faculty (www.yale.edu/its/amt/filmstudy). It holds 3,000 titles on 16mm, 300 titles on 35mm, and 50 on 8mm. The role of the collection continues to be for classroom screenings and research on campus only.

Public Libraries

Akron (Ohio) Public Library's head librarian from 1944 to 1967 was one of the great supporters of public library 16mm film service, Robert Russell Munn. His writings document that the Akron Public Library collection was substantial and well curated. Part of the film collection went to the University of Akron, which subsequently deaccessioned most of its holdings.

Boston Public Library On April 23, 2009 the West Tisbury Free Public Library announced its last 16mm film show because its distributor, the Boston Public Library, was no longer making its collection available. Holding one of the last circulating public library film collections, BPL ceased all film operations. The library sold off its 16mm prints at a book sale.

Brooklyn Public Library began their circulating film collection in the 1950s. Most of the collection was deaccessioned in 1998 to Pratt Institute with the exception of forty-two titles (approximately seventy-five prints), which were retained in the library's Brooklyn Collection as visual evidence of the borough's history. Films include Third World Newsreel's *People's Firehouse #1*; a few documentaries made by or about the Brooklyn Public Library; Frank and Caroline Mouris's *Coney*; and *District Leader*, a 1972 documentary on Bernie Bloom, a local party leader in Brooklyn.

Although the library has retained the original film prints for the forty-two remaining titles, they were transferred in 2007 and 2008 to DVD for in-library use only. These DVD copies, unlike the original film prints, are accessible to the public and are cataloged: http://catalog.brooklynpubliclibrary.org/; choose "Advanced Search"; use "film" as the keyword; limit search to "DVD" and "Brooklyn Collection." The Brooklyn Collection's web page can be viewed at www.brooklynpubliclibrary.org/brooklyncollection.

Boulder (Colorado) Public Library collected mostly the 8mm gauge but did acquire a 16mm collection in 1984 through donation. Access can be arranged through special arrangement by contacting the Boulder Public Library.

Dearborn (Michigan) Public Library/Henry Ford Centennial Library began its film collection in 1948 and eventually acquired 3,275 titles. The A-V librarian James Limbacher oversaw the department for twenty-five years and was a contributor to the standards and policies that made film librarianship in America. Dearborn Public Library acquired the Canadian Travel Bureau films in 1952, the Eastman Kodak Rental Library in 1953, and Henry Ford's home movies in 1977.

Circulation ended in 1999 as patrons ceased using the films. Most of the collection was sold to the Prelinger Archives in 1999, with the exception of feature films, which were retained for use in public film series programs. However these too were deaccessioned in 2009, after the film series switched completely to DVD projection.

District of Columbia Public Library/Martin Luther King, Jr. Memorial Library developed a 16mm film collection emphasizing "educational and artistic values for adult audiences." However, by 2010, the library was phasing out its collection. Some prints were donated to the Library of Congress.

Baltimore's **Enoch Pratt Free Library** was one of the first dozen public library film collections, initiated in 1948. Since 1971, the institution has served as the State Library Resource Center and was responsible for statewide 16mm film distribution. The collection is maintained by the Sights & Sounds Department. At its height, the library owned 4,000 titles, of which about half remains. The collection has been weeded of damaged items, duplicates of films with low circulation, dated educational productions, and films accessible on video. The library last acquired 16mm prints in 1992.

Card-holders may borrow films (save for those in a reserve of "archived" titles). Since the mid-1990s, the films most used are those that demonstrate film as art and feature films. Pratt acquired prints from a few county and regional libraries and school systems deaccessioning collections. However, the 16mm collection is diminishing through attrition and weeding and may face deaccessioning.

Maine State Library The 16mm film collection of the Maine State Library functioned as a central distribution library for public libraries and other institutions throughout the state. Films were of an educational and instructional nature. The collection was given to Northeast Historic Film in 2000.

Miami-Dade (Florida) Public Library has nearly 4,000 titles in its 16mm film collection, accessible through the Fine Arts department. Some film programming, mostly for children, continues. Prints circulate to the public and to branch libraries. Local college students are the most frequent borrowers. The library no longer acquires 16mm; however, circulation has shown increase when branch libraries organize film programs. The **Wolfson Florida Archive of the Moving Image** relocated from the public library, where it was created in 1984, to Miami Dade College. The archive collects and screens films documenting Florida history and culture, particularly news footage, documentaries, and home movies (www.mdc.edu/wolfsonarchives).

Mid-Hudson Library System makes available its 16mm holdings to any patron of the seventy member public libraries in New York State's Columbia, Dutchess, Greene, Putnam, and Ulster counties. There are currently 1,400 titles in the collection. MHLS is not practicing any conservation or preservation methods and the future of the collection is uncertain; some films have already been deaccessioned to nearby Vassar College. However, about twenty films a month still circulate to both branches (five use the collection "religiously" for programming) and individuals (one college professor shows their print of *Nanook of the North* every year). The RTI inspection machine—a once-standard piece of equipment for public library film collections but now obsolete—is still used to determine print condition once the film is returned by the borrowing member.

The film catalog and booking request form can be reached through http://avcat.sebridge.org/cgi-bin/welcome_MYDB.pl?MHLS.

The New York Public Library (NYPL), Reserve Film and Video Collection (RFVC) began acquiring prints in 1953, and established a 16mm collection with reference service at the Donnell Library in 1958. Since then, it has been the central circulating film and video collection of the New York Public Library. Its first director, William Sloan, was an active member of both the film library and independent film communities, and was editor of *Film Library Quarterly*.

When the Donnell Library Center closed in 2008, the collection integrated within the New York Public Library for the Performing Arts and took its current name. More than 8,000 16mm prints are archived in a cold storage vault in Princeton, New Jersey. However, the traditional media center services continue: titles are booked for circulation or for in-house screening in the Film Study Room; reference service is available by appointment with the collection's archivist or librarians; films are programmed at the Library for the Performing Arts (located at Lincoln Center) and NYPL branches.

Although purchasing on 16mm has declined substantially, the library continues to acquire rare and exceptional prints from institutions deaccessioning collections. Film prints have been retained from other library systems in the state (Upper Hudson, Ramapo Catskill, Smithtown, Nassau, and independent schools) and elsewhere.

The RFVC is also active in preservation. Works are preserved in their original film gauge; new 16mm prints are made available for on-site screenings. Films preserved include significant independent documentaries, avant-garde works, and children's films. Although the collection has a longstanding policy of not lending for classroom use, instructors are welcome to arrange screenings for their classes in the Film Study Room. In other regards, NYPL is unique among American public libraries, offering access to numerous rare film prints. See www.nypl.org/locations/lpa/reserve-film-and-video-collection.

Northeast Texas Library System (NTLS) began collecting 16mm educational films in 1984 to "help libraries in Texas meet the information, education, programming and entertainment needs of the public and the library by providing access to public performance-authorized media which might be unavailable because of cost, limited distribution or other factors." The collection held 3,000 film prints, which circulated to all public libraries in Texas and the patrons they serve: private citizens, schools, day care centers, nursing homes, community agencies, institutions, and organizations. The NTLS acquired collections from other public libraries and library systems in Texas in addition to the Tarrant County Junior College and the Japan National Tourist Organization.

The state discontinued funding and the collection was deaccessioned in 2000. The 16mm films were donated to the New York Public Library, which retained essential prints and forwarded the rest to the Prelinger Archives.

Prince George's County (Maryland) Memorial Library System/Hyattsville Branch Library began its collection in 1967 and has 1,600 reels of 16mm film. Today it is most used by filmmakers and scholars. A reference service for patrons using 16mm is still provided as is some programming. No new 16mm material is being acquired. Circulation of prints is available to library cardholders. See www.prge.lib.md.us/Hyattsville.

Rochester (New York) Public Library The film collection was deaccessioned in the winter of 2000–2001 to the Visual Studies Workshop (www.vsw.org), a center for media studies located in Rochester. Visual Studies Workshop staff have cataloged the collection and provide access by appointment. Films are projected for researchers in a screening room.

Archives

A/V Geeks LLC maintains a privately held collection of over 23,000 reels of 16mm educational film. The vast majority of the films came from schools and government agencies throwing out used prints. Some came from auctions. Many were donated. The A/V Geeks Educational Film Archive engages in programming and format migration. Founder Skip Elsheimer reports acquisition will continue as long as institutional collections continue to be deaccessioned (www.avgeeks.com).

Academic Film Archive of North America (AFANA) owns about 7,000 16mm prints of educational films. These were acquired through media library and individual filmmaker donations. A champion of the educational film as it was used and collected by public libraries and higher education institutions, AFANA concentrates on the acquisition and promotion of academic films (science and humanities) of quality rather than social guidance films. Founder Geoff Alexander states AFANA's mission is to "acquire, preserve, document, and promote academic film by providing an archive, resource, and forum for continuing scholarly advancement and public exhibition." His archive continues to seek out and acquire 16mm collections, providing online access as funding allows (www.afana.org).

American Archives of the Factual Film (AAFF) was founded in 1974 at Parks Library, Iowa State University, through a significant donation of films and other materials by Ott H. Coelln, longtime editor and publisher of *Business Screen*.

A center for the study of 16mm nontheatrical films, the AAFF collected business, educational, and documentary productions from corporate and other sources. The university closed the collection in 2002 due to budget constraints. In 2007, AAFF's 70,000 reels were acquired by the Library of Congress.

The **Archives of the History of American Psychology** (AHAP) was established at the University of Akron in 1965. In 1976 it initiated the Child Development Film Archives, soon cataloging 3,500 items (more than 800,000 feet of film). The AHAP later acquired parts of the educational film collections of both the University of Akron and Kent State. The mission of the archive is to care for research footage and instructional films. It now owns more than 6,000 films of this nature, complementing an important collection of the papers of 740 psychologists. In 2010, AHAP moved from the library to a renovated campus building of its own. Searchable lists of all A-V holdings, including a film-specific database, are online (www.uakron.edu/ahap) as is a YouTube channel the archive launched in 2009.

Chicago Film Archives (CFA) has a unique relationship to educational film since the city was a center for several long-lived educational film producers and distributors. The archive was incorporated in 2004 to house and care for its first acquisition: 4,500 16mm films from the Chicago Public Library, which deaccessioned the films it collected from the 1950s to 1990. The CFA owns films donated by the Michigan school system, the University of Chicago, the distributor Home Vision, and individuals such as industrial filmmaker Jack Behrend. The archive is engaged in preservation, restoration, public programming, and format migration. It deaccessions only duplicate prints and acquires films based on regional pertinence.

Library of Congress (Motion Picture, Broadcasting, and Recorded Sound Division) holds the largest collection of film and television in the world and the biggest collection of educational films in the United States. The library added substantially to these holdings when it acquired the nearly 60,000 films amassed in the Prelinger Collection of educational, industrial, sponsored, and amateur films in 2002. It also acquired the American Archives of the Factual Film from Iowa State University in 2007. Throughout most of the twentieth century, producers routinely deposited film prints with the library for copyright purposes.

National Archives and Records Administration (NARA) has an enormous collection of films (more than 300,000) created for and produced by the U.S. government, including military, educational, and documentary films produced throughout the twentieth century. The Motion Picture, Sound, and Video unit (in NARA's "Archives II" facility, College Park, Maryland) houses nongovernment educational films acquired as gifts. These include the Ford Motor Company Collection, the *March of Time* Collection (from Time, Inc.), and the Universal Newsreel Library, as well as prints from commercial companies (such as Encyclopaedia Britannica Films) that government agencies acquired.

Northeast Historic Film (NHF), a regional archive for northern New England, acquired the circulating film collection of the Maine State Library in 2000. Of the approximately 600 reels accepted, seventy titles reflecting the mission statement of the archive were pulled for processing and integration into their holdings. The remaining films are kept on-site and are accessible but not cataloged. Arrangements for access should be made in advance by contacting NHF.

Prelinger Archives founder Rick Prelinger began collecting in 1982, accumulating some 60,000 nontheatrical film titles, plus preprint materials collectively totaling perhaps 200,000 cans. Many of these items came from libraries and educational institutions: University of Illinois, New York City Board of Education, Teachers College of Columbia University, New York University, Dearborn (Michigan) Public Library, Anthology Film Archives, and many others. In 2002 the Library of Congress (LOC) acquired the Prelinger Collection, although Prelinger continues to acquire nontheatrical films and currently holds some 2,000 titles. The Internet Archive hosts digital versions of more than 2,000 of these ephemeral films. Prelinger.com lists 3,606 titles from the archive's "active film collection."

The **Texas Archive of the Moving Image** (TAMI) works to locate, preserve, and disseminate historical moving images of Texas. The collection includes industrial, educational, and documentary films. The independent nonprofit organization was founded in 2002. The organization's central project is the TAMI Video Library (www.texasarchive.org), a collection of Texas-related films transferred for online viewing. With the support of the Texas Film Commission, the archive offers free digitization of films depicting the state.

Producers, Distributors, and Licensors

Archive Farms, Inc. is a footage licensing company begun in 2007 by Patrick Montgomery, a documentary filmmaker and collector who founded Archive Films/Archive Photos in 1979. The latter's collection of an estimated 14,000 hours of footage contained many educational films, licensed as archival or stock footage. Archive Films was acquired by a similar company, the Image Bank, in 1997, which was in turn purchased by Getty Images, now the dominant photo and footage licensing business. Archive Farms includes its Educational Film Archive as well as a large Industrial Film Archive and the travelogues of lecturer Burton Holmes.

Encyclopaedia Britannica, Inc. (EBF) no longer sells 16mm prints, but has transferred most productions of Encyclopaedia Britannica Films to video. The company's website (eb.com) offers a limited number of short excerpts for free viewing (with lead-in advertisements) and greater access for subscribers to its content. Its educator's page (info.eb.com) lists 1,185 film titles (dating from 1937 to 1995) for sale on DVD. The 2010 Educational Video Catalog for library sales listed only 150 titles. The original EBF production elements are stored in a former salt mine near Kansas City, Kansas, with no indication that its corporate owner plans to access or preserve them.

NB: The company spelled its name using the ligature "æ"—Encyclopædia Britannica. Though we use the conventional spelling *encyclopaedia* throughout this book, catalog searches for variant spellings can yield dramatically different results. In the case of EB Films, *encyclopedia* returns far fewer records than either the ligature spelling or *encyclopaedia*. (Computer searches treat the latter two identically.)

The **International Film Foundation** (IFF) began in 1945 with filmmaker and educational film advocate Julien Bryan directing the nonprofit organization, which was created "to produce and distribute documentary films that would promote better world understanding." The foundation lists 236 titles, which includes IFF productions and films Bryan made before 1945, including documentaries he made for ERPI Classroom Films, Inc., Encyclopaedia Britannica, the U.S. Office of the Coordinator of Inter-American Affairs (twenty-three films), and the State Department. The IFF retains the original 16mm elements.

The Library of Congress acquired 500 reels of documentary footage that Bryan shot on 35mm nitrate before forming the foundation. Prior to that, all of Bryan's nitrate material shot in Germany and Poland went to the U.S. Holocaust Memorial Museum, while his footage of Japan went to the Showa-kan Museum in Tokyo. A number of 16mm films IFF produced or distributed, including *Boundary Lines* (1948) and *Picture in Your Mind* (1949), were preserved by the New York Public Library.

MacDonald & Associates in Chicago is a commercial film archive and footage licensing service, begun out of the personal collection of historian J. Fred Mac-Donald. One of the largest such collections in the world, it contains extensive nontheatrical film holdings and tens of thousands of other films. Its clients are mostly professional media producers, although researchers can purchase some films in video preview form. Additionally, MacDonald offers online viewing of clips as multimedia illustrations in his historical essays and books, freely available at www.jfredmacdonald.com. LOC acquired the collection in 2010.

Phoenix Films was a major producer-distributor of educational films from its founding in 1973. Phoenix sold "quality educational enrichment films to schools, universities, libraries, and special interest groups." In the 1980s and 1990s, Phoenix purchased 16mm film libraries of other producers and distributors when their parent companies deemed them uneconomical: Bailey Film Associates, Coronet/MTI Films, CBS's BFA Educational Media, Learning Corporation of America, Kratky Film Prague, Pyramid Films, and Stephen Bosustow Productions among them.

Phoenix Films stopped producing and distributing 16mm in 1993, but retains the film elements and prints for remastering in video and digital formats. Now the Phoenix Learning Group, the company claims 6,000 titles.

CONTRIBUTORS

Charles R. Acland is a professor and Concordia University Research Chair in Communication Studies. His books include *Screen Traffic: Movies, Multiplexes, and Global Culture, Swift Viewing: The Popular Life of Subliminal Influence*, and *Useful Cinema*, coedited with Haidee Wasson. Acland is coeditor of the *Canadian Journal of Film Studies*.

Victoria Cain is assistant professor and faculty fellow of museum studies at New York University. She is the coauthor of *Life on Display: Exhibition, Education and Museums*, forthcoming from the University of Chicago Press. She has contributed articles and essays to the *Journal of Visual Culture, Science in Context, American Quarterly*, and *museum+society*. She is completing a book on the history of visual education in the United States.

Skip Elsheimer founded and maintains the A/V Geeks Educational Film Archive of more than 23,000 educational and industrial 16mm films. He curates film programs at such venues at the Museum of the Moving Image, Coolidge Corner Theatre (Brookline, Massachusetts), Anthology Film Archives, Aurora Picture Show (Houston), and Chicago Filmmakers.

Oliver Gaycken is an assistant professor in the Department of English at the University of Maryland, College Park. He is completing a book entitled *Devices of Curiosity: Early Cinema and Popular Science*, which is under contract with Oxford University Press. He is editing a special issue of the *Journal of Visual Culture* with Joshua Malitsky on "Science and Documentary," and his articles appear in *Historical Journal of Film, Radio, and Television; Science in Context*; and *Early Popular Visual Culture*.

Lee Grieveson is Reader in Film Studies and director of the graduate programme in film studies at University College London. He is the author of *Policing Cinema: Movies and Censorship in Early Twentieth Century America*, as well as coeditor, most recently, of *Inventing Film Studies*, with Haidee Wasson, and *Empire and Film* and *Film and the End of Empire*, both with Colin MacCabe.

Alison Griffiths is a professor in the Department of Communication Studies at Baruch College, City University of New York (CUNY), and a member of the doctoral program in theater at the CUNY Graduate Center. She is the author of *Wondrous Difference: Cinema, Anthropology, and Turn-of-the-Century Visual Culture* and *Shivers Down Your Spine: Cinema, Museums, and the Immersive View*. Her most recent book project, *Screens behind Bars: Cinema, Prisons, and the Making of Modern America* examines the earliest uses of cinema in the penitentiary.

Craig Kridel is the E. S. Gambrell Professor of Educational Studies and Curator of the Museum of Education, University of South Carolina, and 2011 Scholar in Residence at the Rockefeller Archive Center. He has most recently edited *The SAGE Encyclopedia of Curriculum Studies* and *Classic Edition Sources: Education* and published with R. V. Bullough Jr. *Stories of the Eight Year Study: Rethinking Schooling in America*.

Katerina Loukopoulou is Henry Moore Foundation Postdoctoral Fellow at the History of Art Department of University College London, where she is working toward publication of her research on the relationship between Henry Moore's sculpture and film. She has published articles in *Film History* and *Film Philosophy*.

Anna McCarthy is associate professor of cinema studies at New York University and coeditor of the journal *Social Text*. She is the author of *The Citizen Machine: Governing by Television in 1950s America* and *Ambient Television: Visual Culture and Public Space*, as well as coeditor, with Nick Couldry, of the anthology *MediaSpace: Place, Scale, and Culture in a Media Age*. Her publications include articles in the *Journal of Visual Culture*, *October*, *GLQ*, the *International Journal of Cultural Studies*, and *montage a/v*.

Devin Orgeron is associate professor of film studies at North Carolina State University. He is the author of *Road Movies* and his articles have appeared in *Cinema Journal*, *The Velvet Light Trap*, *Film Quarterly*, and *The Moving Image*. Devin is coeditor of *The Moving Image*, the journal of the Association of Moving Image Archivists. He is currently writing a book about contemporary American directors and their work in advertising and music videos.

Marsha Orgeron is associate professor and director of film studies at North Carolina State University. She is the author of *Hollywood Ambitions: Celebrity in the Movie Age* and a dozen articles in books and journals such as *Film Quarterly*, *The Moving Image*, *Cinema Journal*, *Quarterly Review of Film & Video*, and the *Historical Journal of Film, Radio & Television*. She is at work on a book about director Sam Fuller's war films, beginning with the 16mm amateur footage he shot of Falkenau concentration camp at the close of World War II, and is coeditor of *The Moving Image*, the journal of the Association of Moving Image Archivists.

Kirsten Ostherr is associate professor of English at Rice University, where she engages in teaching and research on film and media studies, specializing in historical health films and medical imaging technologies. She is the author of *Cinematic Prophylaxis: Globalization and Contagion in the Discourse of World Health* (Duke University Press, 2005), as well as articles on public health, documentary, science fiction, and avant-garde films. Her second book, *Medical Visions: Producing the Patient through Film, Television, and Imaging Technologies*, is forthcoming from Oxford University Press.

Jennifer Peterson is assistant professor in the Film Studies Program at the University of Colorado, Boulder. Her articles have appeared in *Cinema Journal* and *Camera Obscura*, as well as the edited collections *American Cinema's Transitional Era* and *Virtual Voyages: Cinema and Travel*. Her book, *Education in the School of Dreams: Travelogues and Early Nonfiction Film*, will be published by Duke University Press.

Kimberly Pifer is an editor at the 3-C Institute for Social Development in Cary, North Carolina. She received a BA in English from Frostburg State University and a master's degree in professional writing with an emphasis in rhetoric from Old Dominion University.

Miriam Posner is a Mellon Postdoctoral Fellow at Emory University, where she is helping to develop a new digital scholarship program. She received her PhD in Film Studies and American Studies from Yale University. Her dissertation, "Depth Perception: Narrative and the Body in American Medical Filmmaking," examined the ways that physicians have used film to make sense of the human body.

Rick Prelinger, an archivist, writer, and filmmaker, founded Prelinger Archives, whose collection of educational, industrial, and amateur films was acquired by the Library of Congress in 2002. He is the author of *The Field Guide to Sponsored Films*.

Elena Rossi-Snook is the moving image archivist for the Reserve Film and Video Collection of the New York Public Library and visiting assistant professor of film history at Pratt Institute. Her previous publications include the article "Persistence of Vision: Public Library 16mm Film Collections in America" in *The Moving Image*.

Eric Schaefer teaches film and media studies at Emerson College in Boston. He is the author of *"Bold! Daring! Shocking! True!": A History of Exploitation Films, 1919–1959*, and many articles about low-budget films.

Heide Solbrig is an assistant professor of media and culture in the English and Media Studies Department at Bentley College in Waltham, Massachusetts. She produced the documentary *Man and the Middle Class: The Work and Vision of Henry Strauss,* about the eminent postwar industrial filmmaker, and she is writing a book titled *Film and Function: A History of Industrial Motivation Film*. With Elizabeth Heffelfinger, she edited a special issue of the *Journal of Popular Film and Television* on the subject of orphan films.

Dan Streible is associate professor of cinema studies at New York University and the author of *Fight Pictures: A History of Boxing and Early Cinema.* He directs the Orphan Film Project and its biennial symposium.

Gregory A. Waller teaches in the Department of Communication and Culture at Indiana University. His publications include *Main Street Amusements: Film and Commercial Entertainment in a Southern City, 1895–1930*, the sourcebook *Moviegoing in America*, and various articles concerning the history of 16mm distribution, nontheatrical cinema, and itinerant film exhibition during the 1930s and 1940s.

INDEX